# Formal Pragmatics

D1611084

# Formal Pragmatics

*Semantics, Pragmatics, Presupposition, and Focus*

*Nirit Kadmon*

**BLACKWELL** *Publishers*

The right of Nirit Kadmon to be identified as the author of this work has been asserted in accordance with the Copyright, Designs and Patents Act 1988.

First published 2001

2 4 6 8 10 9 7 5 3 1

Blackwell Publishers Inc.
350 Main Street
Malden, Massachusetts 02148
USA

Blackwell Publishers Ltd
108 Cowley Road
Oxford OX4 1JF
UK

*Library of Congress Cataloging-in-Publication Data*

Kadmon, Nirit.
    Formal pragmatics : semantics, pragmatics, presupposition, and focus / Nirit Kadmon.
        p.   cm.
    Includes bibliographical references and index.
    ISBN 0–631–20120–3 (alk. paper)—ISBN 0–631–20121–1 (pbk. : alk. paper)
    1. Pragmatics.   2. Semantics.   3. Presupposition (Logic)   4. Focus (Linguistics)
    I. Title.
    P99 .K3   2000
    306.44—dc21

                                                                    00–025856

*British Library Cataloguing in Publication Data*
A CIP catalogue record for this book is available from the British Library.

Typeset in 10½ on 12½ pt Ehrhardt
by Best-set Typesetter Ltd., Hong Kong
Printed in Great Britain by TJ International, Padstow, Cornwall

This book is printed on acid-free paper.

# Contents

## Part Two  Presupposition

# Acknowledgments

I am extremely grateful to my dear colleagues who read large portions of earlier drafts of this book, and gave me detailed and thoughtful comments and advice. Craige Roberts and Fred Landman each read almost the entire manuscript, and their input was of great help in gradually shaping my conception of the book as a whole as well as in improving my writing on specific topics. Lisa Selkirk read chapters 12 and 13, providing very detailed and helpful comments and advice. Angelika Kratzer read most of part three, and her comments and suggestions were greatly appreciated. Thank you!

I am also grateful to the students in my graduate seminars on presupposition and on focus, spring semesters of 1997, 1998 and 1999, Tel Aviv University: Nurit Assayag, Vita Barabash, Shai Cohen, Yael Golan, Daphna Heller, Galit Sassoon, Alex Terno, Aldo Sevi, Boris Tsvetkov, and Ziva Wijler. In these seminars, we read earlier drafts of this book. The students were great, so it was interesting and fun, and I received very valuable feedback and many good suggestions. Thanks!

Note:  My name is **not** [nírɔt kǽdmə̌n].
My name is, in Hebrew, [nǐrít kǎdmón] (Hebrew consonants and vowels).
The closest you can get to it in English is [nìrít] or [nə̌rít] [kàdmɔ́n].

# Introduction

This book deals with issues, phenomena, and areas of research that are on the border-line of the semantics and pragmatics of natural language. The general approach to linguistics is generative, and the basic approach to the study of meaning and interpretation is model-theoretic. Accordingly, formal analyses will be of central interest. (As already suggested by the title of the book, this interest is by no means limited to "semantics". I am interested in formal analyses of all (aspects of) the phenomena considered here, be they "semantic" or "pragmatic" (or neither, or both).)

In Part One (Dynamic Semantics, Definites, and Indefinites), I introduce the semantic theory developed in Kamp 1981 and Heim 1982, and sample some related work on definite and indefinite NPs. The Kamp–Heim theory, where context of utterance and context-change enter right into the heart of the semantic theory, has been crucial in shaping the view we have today of the semantics-pragmatics interface, and it will be used quite extensively in parts one and two of this book. The material on definite and indefinite NPs involves the pragmatic processes of conversational implicature and accommodation as well as the notion "salience", and illustrates their interaction with semantic interpretation and semantic theory.

In parts two and three, I will be concerned with two areas of research that (seem to) lie on the borderline of semantics and pragmatics, namely presupposition and prosodically marked focus. I will aim to present the state of the art in the research on presupposition and on focus as I see it today, to offer detailed discussion of a number of key issues, and to advance some of my own views and specific proposals.

In Part Two (Presupposition), I will be concerned both with the nature and status of presuppositions and with their behavior in complex sentences (the "projection problem"). Regarding the former, I will address in particular (in chapter 11) the question of whether presuppositions are triggered purely by linguistic convention ("semantically") or as conversational implicatures ("pragmatically"). Regarding "presupposition projection", I will endorse the approach developed by Karttunen, Stalnaker and Heim, where a presupposition must be satisfied by its local context, and I will concentrate quite a bit (see chapters 9 and 10) on the role of accommodation in satisfying presuppositions in various types of examples.

In Part Three (Focus), I will be concerned for a while with the phonological manifestation of focus (section 13.4), and then move on to its interpretation and function.

I believe in associating with focus a model-theoretic entity, be it a structured meaning or a set of alternatives. I will mostly use Rooth's alternative semantics though, largely because I happen to be interested in a number of proposals that have been developed within that framework. Of central interest will be recent attempts to capture the function of focus by means of a single grammatical constraint – stated in terms of the above-mentioned model-theoretic entity – from which the various semantic and pragmatic effects of focusing might be derived (see chapter 17). I am also particularly interested in complex focal structures containing a "contrastive topic", and in the interaction of the "focal presupposition" with other presuppositions (chapters 20 and 21).

This book is not intended to play the role of a general introduction to semantics and/or pragmatics, or to formal technique.[1] I will assume familiarity with formal semantics and with central notions and issues in pragmatics, and my discussion will often directly involve subtle and/or technical aspects of formal theories. At the same time, I will try to make the book as accessible as possible. I prefer simple, informal-sounding language even when I discuss formal matters, and I will try, when space allows me to, to explain specific notions used rather than presuppose them. Some introductory material is also included: chapter 1 (introducing the notion of presupposition and other pertinent matters), section 2.1 (basic introductions to DRT and FCS), chapter 12 (basics of the phonology of prosody, needed for the study of focus).

---

[1] A good introduction to formal semantics which also relates semantics to pragmatic issues is Chierchia and McConnell-Ginet 1990. For a textbook in pragmatics, I refer the reader to Levinson 1983.

# 1

# *Preliminaries*

---

## 1.1 Semantics and Pragmatics

It is not my aim in this book to define or sharpen the distinction between semantics and pragmatics. I am mainly interested in the linguistic phenomena themselves which lie on the borderline. I do think, at the same time, that a certain picture of the semantics-pragmatics interface will emerge from the discussion of phenomena and their analyses throughout the book. I will also include some points of discussion pertaining to the interaction between semantics and pragmatics. Following are a few preliminary remarks.

I do assume a distinction between semantics and pragmatics, despite the fact that it is not clear how this distinction is to be defined exactly (see Levinson 1983, ch. 1, for some discussion). I think there are linguistic phenomena that involve crucial and interesting interactions between different rule systems – rule systems that can be characterized as semantic vs. pragmatic, or conventional vs. conversational, etc. – and I am interested in these phenomena and these interactions.[1]

It may be worth mentioning that I think that some of the "is this semantics or pragmatics" sort of debate that can be found in the literature is terminological. So, it will often happen that I won't care much about whether a particular principle or treatment is **called** semantic or pragmatic. The parts of the "semantics vs. pragmatics" debate that are essential and interesting are those that genuinely deal with questions about what **type** of explanation to use for a given phenomenon and about the interaction and division of labor between different rule systems.

What do I have in mind, then, when I say that I assume a distinction between semantics and pragmatics? I can only give a very rough idea. I take it that semantics covers truth-conditional interpretation. I don't know if it covers things that can't be called truth conditional. At any rate, I think that roughly, semantics only covers "literal meaning." Pragmatics has to do with language use, and with "going beyond the literal meaning."

There is a separate distinction between "what's in the grammar" (linguistic knowledge) and "what's outside the grammar" (principles that may affect language use, but are not specific to language). (What's determined by the grammar is often referred to

---

[1]  See for instance the problem of numeral determiners discussed in 3.1 below.

as "conventional," following Grice.) Not         e is no a priori reason to assume that semantics is in the grammar while pragr         ot. Indeed, I would assume that the two distinctions do not coincide. Let us assume that the grammar contains a semantic component and a pragmatic component. In addition to these, there are certainly factors outside the grammar that affect meaning – probably both factors that affect semantics and factors that affect pragmatics.

Let me give some examples: The rules that compositionally interpret syntactic structures may be considered "semantics in the grammar." The semantic interpretation of conjunction or negation may be an instance of some general logical/cognitive principle that is not special to language, and hence is not in the grammar. The specification of what the expression *as for . . .* , means may be considered "pragmatics in the grammar" (some call it "linguistic pragmatics"). Grice's conversational maxims are instances of general rational principles that govern cooperative behavior – these principles affect "natural language pragmatics" from "outside the grammar." Finally, take Heim's Novelty–Familiarity condition, which says, roughly, that a definite NP must, while an indefinite NP must not, have an antecedent in the discourse. Whether you want to call it semantic or pragmatic, this condition belongs inside the grammar, as it encodes specifically linguistic knowledge about certain types of NP.

## 1.2 Conversational Implicatures

For convenience, let me follow the usage in Chierchia and McConnell-Ginet 1990 and use "A **implies** B" as a neutral term, which just means that A (or the fact that someone has uttered A) gives you some reason to conclude B. So, (1a) implies (1b), (2a) implies (2b), and (3a) implies (3b).

(1)  a.  Sue is walking slowly.
     b.  Sue is walking.
(2)  a.  I went into a house.
     b.  It wasn't the speaker's house.
(3)  a.  Sue's problem is that she hasn't stopped drinking.
     b.  Sue drank.

We talk about different varieties of implication relations, which include entailment, conversational implicature, and presupposition.

(1a) entails (= logically entails) (1b). This is clearly an implication with a semantic reason; (1b) is simply part of the semantic content of (1a).

(2a) doesn't entail (2b). Clearly, (2a) implies (2b) for pragmatic reasons. Following Grice (1967, 1975), we say that (2b) is a **conversational implicature** of (2a). Here is a very very quick review of Grice's idea. According to Grice, principles of rational behavior dictate to the participants in a conversation to cooperate in order to efficiently achieve the goal of their conversation, by following – ceteris paribus – four guidelines which he calls "conversational maxims":

(4)  **Grice's Cooperative Principle**
     The Maxim of Quality – Try to make your contribution true.

② The Maxim of <u>Quantity</u> – Give no more and no less information than required.
③ The Maxim of <u>Relation</u> – Be relevant.
④ The Maxim of <u>Manner</u> – Be clear, unambiguous, brief, orderly.

Grice is interested in the question of how it is that uttering a sentence can imply more than "what is said" (more than the semantic content of the sentence). He proposes that many implications are derived by the hearer on the basis of the conversational maxims. They follow from the combination of the semantic content of the utterance, the conversational maxims, and further background assumptions. Such implications are called by Grice "conversational implicatures." To take just one example, (2b) is taken to be derived by an argument which goes roughly as follows. If it was her own house, the speaker would have known this and it would be relevant information. The speaker is being cooperative; therefore, by Quantity, she would not withhold relevant information. So if it was her own house, she would have said so. But she didn't. Hence, it was not her own house.

Grice's work on conversational implicatures opened up a whole big area of research. Grice gave us the basic notion of a conversational implicature, which may be summed up as in (5) below, and specified some important characteristics of conversational implicatures (among them "defeasibility," to be briefly discussed below).

(5) Principles that are rooted in cooperative behavior of the participants in conversation are responsible for the fact that an utterance may convey more than what is explicitly said.
The extra message derived on the basis of such principles is called a "conversational implicature."

In addition, Grice gave us a preliminary theory of how conversational implicatures are generated, by proposing his famous conversational maxims and sketching the way in which a hearer may calculate an implicature on the basis of those maxims. However, Grice's preliminary theory was only a first shot, with its problems and unanswered questions.

To take just one concrete example, it is not at all clear why it is that when we hear example (2a) above, the following Gricean argument does not seem to go through. If it was not her own house, the speaker would have known this and it would be relevant information. So if it was not her own house, she would have said so. But she didn't. Hence, it was her own house. (Cf. *I broke a leg*, which implicates that it was the speaker's own leg.) More detailed discussion of the shortcomings of Grice's preliminary account is given in Thomason 1990. Note also that implications that are originally based on pragmatic reasoning may become grammaticized or conventionalized to a lesser or greater degree. For instance, the fact that (6a) implies (6b) presumably has a pragmatic, conversational basis; at the same time, (6a) has become a standard formula for making the request, so much so that (7) is grammatical.

(6) a. Can you pass me the salt?
    b. I request that you pass me the salt.
(7) Can you pass me the salt please?

How do we represent the grammaticization of implicatures and how does it bear on the question of how (and when) conversational implicatures are generated?

Since Grice, a considerable body of research on conversational implicatures has been and continues to be developed. It aims to describe the mechanisms that generate conversational implicatures more fully and more explicitly, in a way that will make detailed predictions about which implicatures will arise in which contexts. Unfortunately, this body of research is beyond the scope of this book.

One promising program for developing a formal account of how conversational implicatures are generated is the one presented in Thomason 1990; it is based on the interlocutors' recognizing each other's specific plans (with respect to both non-linguistic goals and the intended organization of the discourse) and accommodating each other in their efforts to carry out these plans.[2] For a recent formal theory of conversational implicatures inspired by Thomason's approach, see Welker 1994. Welker 1994 also includes a useful overview of the literature. As for the relation between conversational implicatures and the grammar, Landman 1998 argues concerning the scalar implicatures of numerals (see chapter 3 below), that although they do arise from Gricean principles, their content has to be calculated by a mechanism that is part of the grammar, a view which seems to fit with the way scalar implicatures of numerals are viewed in e.g. Horn 1992.

I will content myself here with referring the reader to the works just mentioned and to works cited therein. In the remainder of this book, I will basically assume Grice's original characterization and account of conversational implicatures, and will not be concerned with the details of precisely how these implicatures are generated.

It is uncontroversial that conversational implicatures are **defeasible**. What "defeasible" means can be stated more or less as follows. Suppose S will "normally" or "often" imply B. If S sometimes nevertheless fails to imply B, or else this implication can be canceled, we say then that the implication B is defeasible. For example, the implicature in (2b) is defeasible. (8) shows that this implicature can be canceled: while (8) may sound surprising, it is not a contradiction. In (9) and (10), (2a) occurs in a context in which implicature (2b) does not arise.

(8)     I went into a house. It was my house.
(9)     I don't want to tell you whether it was my house or not, but it IS true that I went into a house yesterday.
(10)    I know that we were supposed to stay outside all day, but I went into a house once, because someone cut his hand and I had to (go home and) get some bandages.

Now let me say a few words about why conversational implicatures are defeasible. This is largely due to the fact that they are heavily context-dependent. The Gricean argument that derives (2b) depends on the assumption that the speaker obeys Quantity. But of course, in some contexts the hearers can make that assumption, while in other contexts (such as the one in (9)) they cannot make it. The argument also relies on the hearer's knowledge of what information Quantity would require the speaker to provide. But that, of course, differs from context to context too. In the

---

[2]    See also the end of section 1.7.

context in (10), the house being the speaker's house would not be relevant information, and so Quantity would not require the speaker to provide it. As for why (2a) seems to implicate (2b) even when presented "out of the blue", that is presumably because contexts in which the implicature would arise are relatively common or "normal," and therefore we readily imagine that that is the kind of context in which (2a) is supposed to be considered.

An additional defeasibility-inducing factor is that we usually base our Gricean arguments (partly) on assumptions that seem plausible, rather than assumptions that are known to be true. (We may assume that the maxims are being obeyed and that the speaker is able to recognize her own house even if we can't know these things for sure.) This explains implicature-cancellation (as in (8) above). When we have inferred a conversational implicature, and this implicature gets denied, we readily conclude that one of the assumptions on which we based our Gricean argument was false, and drop the implicature.

Next, let me briefly introduce those Quantity conversational implicatures that are known as **scalar implicatures**. (These were first discussed in detail in Horn 1972.) In examples (11) and (12) below, (b) is considered a "scalar" implicature of (a).

(11)   a.   Kim is competent at linguistics.
      b.   Kim is not more than competent.
(12)   a.   It is a crime to hold left wing views in Colombia.
      b.   It is not a crime to hold other views in Colombia. (Kempson 1982)

The Gricean argument for (11b) goes roughly as follows. If the speaker was in a position to make a stronger, more informative, statement than the one she actually made, for example, that Kim is in fact very good at linguistics, the speaker would have done that, to obey Quantity. If we make the additional assumption that the speaker knows exactly how good Kim is at linguistics, we conclude that the speaker in fact knows that a stronger statement would be false. As usual, the implicature is highly context-dependent – if we fail to make one of the assumptions just noted, it does not arise.

Such implicatures are called "scalar implicatures" following Horn 1972, who discusses their relation to scales such as the following two,

   . . . absolutely wonderful at, very good at, competent at, has some competence . . .

   . . . to hold left-wing views, to hold political views, to hold views . . .

in which you proceed from stronger items to weaker ones. (Each item entails the weaker ones but is not entailed by them.) Horn 1972 suggests that we can formulate a general rule: for any scale of this sort, when we make a statement using a certain item on the scale, we create a scalar implicature that a statement with a stronger item would be false.

Note that when we accept that the "scalar" implications are indeed conversational implicatures, that means that we have taken a stand on the semantics of each item on the scale, namely, that each item is compatible with the stronger items. For example, we have decided that "competent" is literally compatible with "wonderful." We have made the theoretical decision that it is a (Gricean) pragmatic process rather than a semantic relation that makes "competent" imply "not wonderful."

## 1.3 Metalinguistic Negation

Horn 1985 argues convincingly that various operators, and in particular negation, can have – besides their standard use as logical operators – a metalinguistic use, conveying something about the use of the sentence they apply to. For example, in (13), the negation is obviously metalinguistic – it is used to reject the use of the sentence it applies to, because of an objection to the way the word *manage* is pronounced in it; the negation is certainly **not** used to deny the sentence it applies to: (13) is not a contradiction.

(13)   I didn't [mǐ<sup>y</sup>ɔnɨ̆ǰ] to solve the problem – I [mǽnɨ̆ǰd] to solve the problem. (Horn 1985, p. 132)

Metalinguistic negation can be used to reject a sentence on all sorts of grounds (objectionable connotations, pronunciation, word-formation, register, conversational implicatures, etc.). A characteristic intonation contour typically accompanies this use of negation.

Here is an example where metalinguistic negation is used to reject a sentence because of an objection to its conversational implicature:

(14)   She isn't competent at linguistics – She is masterly at the subject!

(from Kempson 1982)

On the assumption that "competent" does not entail "not masterly," (14) is not a contradiction. The negation doesn't deny the sentence it applies to, but rather rejects the use of this sentence on the grounds that "competent" implicates "not masterly."

## 1.4   Contexts and Common Grounds

We use the word *context* to mean a number of different things. I'll try to clarify some uses of this word. Consider the basic notions of **truth** or **verification** (= satisfaction) of a sentence or formula. Truth or verification are always relative to some **facts** or states of affairs. Those we call the "circumstances of evaluation" or the "context of evaluation." (A simple model for extensional logic represents a context of evaluation; a model containing possible worlds and/or times etc. represents a whole collection of contexts of evaluation.)

Besides that, we talk about the "context of utterance." Each utterance occurs in a context. This context includes all sorts of things. It includes previous utterances. It includes the speech situation, including the location, the speaker, addressees, various salient objects, and more. It includes various assumptions that the participants in the conversation make about the world in general and about the subject-matter of the conversation in particular. It includes assumptions that the interlocutors make about the beliefs and intentions of each other. And so on.

The notion of the context of utterance is crucial for the understanding of many phenomena of natural language use and interpretation. Many parameters that are crucial to the very interpretation of utterances (e.g. referents of indexicals, domains of quantification, modal bases, etc.) are contributed by the context of utterance. The felicity of an utterance in terms of relevance and discourse coherence depends on the context of utterance. Conversational implicatures are generated based on the context of utterance. And so on and so forth. As we study various phenomena, we develop formal representations of the context of utterance. More precisely, we develop formal representations of different aspects of the context of utterance. We choose those aspects that are crucial for our current topic of investigation. Sometimes, we also refer to a theoretical construct that represents (the relevant aspects of) the context of utterance as a "context."

Stalnaker 1978 suggests that the central concept needed to characterize the context of utterance is what he calls the **common ground,** or the set of "speaker's presuppositions." This common ground Stalnaker describes as (roughly) the set of propositions whose truth is taken for granted as part of the background of the conversation.

Of course it is not in reality the case that all the participants in the conversation share the same beliefs or know exactly which beliefs they do share, but for purposes of communication we do behave as if there is a certain body of information which is "mutual knowledge," which is shared by the participants in the conversation. And this we call the common ground.

Stalnaker suggests that the essential effect of making an assertion is to extend the common ground. That is, when someone makes an assertion, the content of that assertion is added to the common ground. (Stalnaker adds that this happens provided that the other participants in the conversation do not object.)

Since a common ground is a set of propositions, it can be identified with a set of worlds: the set of worlds in which the propositions of the common ground are true. Stalnaker called this set of worlds the **context set**. The context set contains all the possible worlds which according to the information in our common ground are candidates for being the actual world. (They are the worlds compatible with all we know about the actual world.)

To add a proposition p to the common ground is equivalent to kicking out of the context set all the worlds that are not compatible with p (these worlds are no longer candidates for being the actual world). Thus, as the common ground grows, the context set shrinks.

We have seen then that a set of propositions or a set of possible worlds may be taken to represent a certain (limited, but central) aspect of the context of utterance. Sometimes we refer to the set of propositions or worlds itself as a "context." Other theoretical constructs that represent (certain aspects of) the context of utterance will be discussed below.

Note also that for certain purposes we might want to take into account the differences among the sets of background assumptions made by different participants in the same conversation. Then we may talk about each participant as having her own personal (representation of a) context "in her head." (We assume of course that when successful communication takes place, these individualized "contexts" have a lot in common.)

Finally, let me note that there are important connections between the context of evaluation and the context of utterance. (I think this is especially clear in the light of Stalnaker's view described above.) Sometimes we may think about the actual world as our context of evaluation. Of course, there is a lot that we don't know about the actual world. Which is perfectly consistent with the fact that we can't always tell whether a proposition is true or false. But what we do know about the actual world is part of the context of utterance: it is part of the common ground. So, in as much as we evaluate propositions for being true or false **on the basis of the information available to us,** our context of evaluation and context of utterance converge.

## 1.5  Presuppositions

The notion of presupposition first appears in Frege's work on the nature of reference and referring expressions. His main claims may be summarized as follows.

Frege 1892:   Referring expressions (names, definite descriptions) carry the presupposition that they do in fact refer.
For a sentence to have a truth value, its presupposition must hold.
A presupposition of a sentence is also a presupposition of its negation.

For example, "Kepler died in misery" and "Kepler did not die in misery" both carry the presupposition that the name *Kepler* designates something. If this presupposition doesn't hold, the two sentences have no truth value.[3]

It is standard to say that in the following examples, the (b) sentence is a **presupposition** of the (a) sentence. In each of the (a) sentences, a **presupposition-trigger** can be identified – a lexical item or linguistic construction which is responsible for the presupposition.

| | | | |
|---|---|---|---|
| (15) | a. | Sue stopped drinking. | |
| | b. | Sue drank. | **trigger**: the verb *stop* |
| (16) | a. | Sue's problem is that she hasn't stopped drinking. | |
| | b. | Sue drank. | **trigger**: the verb *stop* |
| (17) | a. | The king of France is bald. | |
| | b. | There is a king of France. | **trigger**: the definite NP |
| (18) | a. | The king of France is not bald. | |
| | b. | There is a king of France. | **trigger**: the definite NP |
| (19) | a. | JOHN drinks too. | |
| | b. | Somebody else besides John drinks. | **trigger**: *too* |
| (20) | a. | Even JOHN drinks. | |
| | b. | John is the least likely to drink. | **trigger**: *even* |
| (21) | a. | It was Fred who ate the beans. | |
| | b. | Somebody ate the beans. | **trigger**: the cleft construction |

What is the basic linguistic intuition on which the notion of presupposition is based? I will follow the line taken in Chierchia and McConnell-Ginet 1990. Like them, I believe that the basic intuition about a presupposition is that it is **taken for granted.** We (speakers of the language) feel, roughly, that it doesn't make sense to utter the sentence unless one already assumes the presupposition. In the words of Chierchia and McConnell-Ginet:

[3] For further historical notes, see Levinson 1983 (ch. 4).

(22)   "The hallmark of a presupposition is that it is taken for granted in the sense that its assumed truth is a precondition for felicitous utterance of the sentence and places a kind of constraint on discourse contexts that admit the sentence for interpretation." (p. 283)

From now on, and throughout the book, I will use "ps" as shorthand for "presupposition."

Traditionally, presuppositions are identified on the basis of the two intuitions pointed out by Frege – that for a sentence to have a truth value, its ps must hold, and that a ps "survives" under negation. I think that a judgment that a certain proposition B must hold for a given sentence S to have a truth value is indeed a very good indication that S presupposes B. That, I think, is directly related to pss being preconditions for felicitous use: a sentence that's faulty, that can't be interpreted properly, can't have a truth value. As for survival under negation – that will be considered in what follows.

The presuppositions of a sentence S survive not only when S is negated, but also when it is questioned, used as a hypothetical assumption, or placed under a possibility modal. For example, sentences (23)–(27) all presuppose that there is a unique king of France, and sentences (28)–(32) all presuppose that Joan used to drink wine for breakfast.

(23)   The king of France is bald.
(24)   The king of France isn't bald.
(25)   Is the king of France bald?
(26)   Perhaps the king of France is bald.
(27)   If the king of France is bald, I will not wear a wig.

(28)   Joan has stopped drinking wine for breakfast.
(29)   Joan hasn't stopped drinking wine for breakfast.
(30)   Has Joan stopped drinking wine for breakfast?
(31)   Perhaps Joan has stopped drinking wine for breakfast.
(32)   If Joan has stopped drinking wine for breakfast, she has probably begun to drink more at lunch.

Survival in this sort of "family of sentences" is often taken to be a crucial test – **the** test, even – for ps status. That is because in general, if a sentence implies something which is **not** presupposed, that implication does not survive in these environments. For example:

(33)   Lee kissed Jenny.
          entails: Lee touched Jenny.
       This entailment doesn't survive in: Lee didn't kiss Jenny.
(34)   It's cold in here.
          possible conversational implicature:
                    I request that you turn on the heater.
       This implicature doesn't survive in: It's not cold in here.

Levinson 1983 takes survival in the "family of sentences" to be a reliable test for ps status. This is directly related to his view of presuppositions as "background" information. Let me discuss these matters.

We can say that utterances divide into background and foreground parts, where what we mean by "foreground" is that the foreground part of the utterance is the main message. Only the foreground part calls for direct responses, such as *Yes, I agree, No, I don't think so, Is that so?, Perhaps*. Levinson 1983 holds that the basic intuition about presuppositions is that a ps is **backgrounded**.

It is certainly true that presuppositions are backgrounded. Since a ps is something which is taken for granted, of course it won't be the main point of the utterance. For example, if you respond to *the king of France is bald* with one of the utterances listed below, you are talking about the baldness, because that's the foreground part of (35). You are not talking about whether there is a king of France, because the ps that there is one is in the background.

(35)    The king of France is bald.
          –   Yes.
          –   Right.
          –   No, I don't think so.
          –   Is that so?
          –   Maybe.

Note that this is exactly the same phenomenon as the fact that presuppositions survive in the "family of sentences." When a sentence is negated, questioned, etc. it is the foreground part that's negated, questioned, etc. So in the negative sentences, the questions, etc., the ps, which is in the background, is unaffected, and it survives.[4]

Now let us examine the status of the information conveyed by the non-restrictive relative clause in (36) below, from Chierchia and McConnell-Ginet 1990.

(36)    Jill, who lost something on the flight from Ithaca to New York, likes to travel by train.

Clearly, the foreground message of (36) is that Jill likes to travel by train. If you respond to (36) with *I don't think so, Perhaps, Well, I wonder*, you will be taken to call into question the main point – Jill's liking trains. You will not be taken to be talking about whether Jill lost something on the flight. Also, compare the two responses in (37). Only the first one is a natural response to (36).

(37)    I don't think so, she doesn't like trains/large vehicles.
          # I don't think so, she didn't lose a thing/she never loses anything.

And now consider the "family of sentences" in (38)–(40) below. Sentences (38)–(40) do not imply that Jill likes to travel by train, but they do all imply that she lost something on the flight.

(38)    Jill, who lost something on the flight from Ithaca to New York, doesn't like to travel by train.

---

[4]    Another test for backgroundedness, from K&P 1979, is *I noticed that S*. The noticing pertains to the foreground message, and not to the background message.

(39)   Does Jill, who lost something on the flight from Ithaca to New York, like to travel by train?

(40)   If Jill, who lost something on the flight from Ithaca to New York, likes to travel by train, she probably flies infrequently.

What have we just learned about the status of the proposition that Jill lost something on the flight from Ithaca to New York in example (36)? We just saw that this proposition passes the traditional test for ps status. Does that mean that it is to be considered a ps of (36)?

Levinson 1983 says that the "family of sentences" test shows that the relative clause in (36) is in the background. Since he thinks that the basic intuition about presuppositions is that they are backgrounded, Levinson concludes from this that the relative clause is presupposed. However, as argued in Chierchia and McConnell-Ginet 1990, this conclusion seems wrong. Chierchia and McConnell-Ginet point out that the proposition that Jill lost something on the flight is **not** taken for granted in (36). Rather, this proposition is new information in (36). Compare with (41), where it **is** taken for granted that Jill lost something on the flight. I think the contrast is clear.

(41)   What Jill lost on the flight from Ithaca to New York was her new flute.

I would definitely agree with Chierchia and McConnell-Ginet that the proposition that Jill lost something on the flight is presupposed in (41) but is not presupposed in (36). Therefore, I conclude that the "family of sentences" test is not a reliable test for ps status.

I do think, and I suppose you will agree with me, that the relative clause is not the foreground message. So let us agree that the "family of sentences" test is a test for foregroundedness – it distinguishes between what's in the foreground and what is not. However, this test does not distinguish between what's not presupposed and what is presupposed: if a proposition is not in the foreground, that doesn't show that it is presupposed.

The reason that I avoided the term "background" in the previous paragraph is that I am not sure whether or not the relative clause in (36) is backgrounded. You might claim that the relative clause is not in the background, but rather "on the side." If so, perhaps "backgrounded" is just another word for being presupposed or for being "taken for granted." In that case, the "family of sentences" test would not be a solid test for either backgroundedness or ps status. On the other hand, we might adopt Levinson's terminology and call the relative clause "backgrounded." In that case, the "family of sentences" test would be a solid test for backgroundedness, but not for ps status: backgroundedness would be a necessary but not a sufficient condition for ps status.

In conclusion, survival in the "family of sentences" is not a foolproof test for ps status. Still, it is a useful test. First of all, if an implied proposition is **not** implied by all the sentences in the "family," then it is definitely **not** a ps. Secondly, it's even fair to say that if a proposition is implied by all the sentences in the "family," that suggests that it may very well be a ps. That is because survival in the "family of sentences" is conspicuously different from the normal behavior of propositions entailed by a clause (i.e. of propositions that are simply part of the truth-conditional content of that clause). If an implied proposition does survive in the sentences of the "family," then we must say something special about that proposition, in order to explain its special behavior. The explanation is not certain to be that our proposition is a ps; for example, the propositions conveyed by non-restrictive relative clauses seem to survive in the same environments for a different reason (because they are parenthetical). But if there is no alternative explanation we can point to, ps status may very well be the right explanation.

Because survival in the "family of sentences" is not a fully reliable test for ps status, our intuitions regarding "being taken for granted" remain an important and indispensable criterion for identifying presuppositions. There is no better proof that a sentence S presupposes a proposition B than our intuition that B is "taken for granted" and is a precondition for felicitous use of S. Directly related to that, we can try out S in contexts where B is already assumed vs. contexts where B is known not to hold, and see in which of these contexts S can be used felicitously.

The view that the hallmark of a ps is that it is taken for granted is the basis of the analysis of the notion of ps proposed in Stalnaker 1974 and Karttunen 1974 (independently). Stalnaker and Karttunen see presuppositions as **requirements on the context**. They take the defining characteristic of the notion of ps to be the following.[5]

(42)   B is a ps of S iff S can be appropriately (= felicitously) uttered only in contexts that contain/entail B.

Stalnaker and Karttunen's insight is incorporated in the most successful treatment of ps and ps projection available today, as will become clear in the chapters to come.

Finally, I must say a few words about the defeasibility of presuppositions. As noted in 1.2 above, conversational implicatures are defeasible. There is some disagreement in the literature concerning the question of whether presuppositions too are defeasible.

Some researchers hold that pss are defeasible, and that this defeasibility is in fact a central characteristic of pss. That is the view taken e.g. in Levinson 1983. The evidence given in the literature for ps defeasibility includes examples of ps cancellations, such as (43), as well as examples that seem to show that pss are context-dependent, such as (44).

(43)   The king of France isn't bald – there is no king of France!
(44)   a.   Sue cried before she finished her thesis.
       b.   Sue died before she finished her thesis.

One can say (43) without contradicting herself. This suggests that the existence ps of definite NPs can be canceled. In (44a), *before* seems to trigger the ps that its complement is true. Certainly, hearing (44a) out of the blue, the intuition that the completion of Sue's thesis is taken for granted is rather prominent. But (44b) definitely does not presuppose the completion of Sue's thesis. So we have here a ps that isn't always present.

---

[5]   Karttunen 1974 defines: Context c *satisfies-the-presuppositions-of* (or *admits*) S iff c entails all of the presuppositions of S. Stalnaker 1974 defines (see p. 203): S presupposes B means that for S to be uttered appropriately, B must be part of the presumed background information.

Other researchers, however, think that certain presuppositions are not defeasible. Chierchia and McConnell-Ginet 1990 offer the view that there is a whole class of presuppositions that are not any more defeasible than entailments are. The class of pss in question is by no means marginal; indeed, it is the class of "hard-core" pss such as the pss of definite NPs, *stop*, *too*, clefts, etc. (In fact, this class includes everything that Karttunen and Peters 1979 (hereafter, K&P) would be willing to call a "presupposition".) On this view, *the king of France* in (43) above does not fail to presuppose that there is a king of France; rather, the negation in this example is metalinguistic, and is used to object to the use of the sentence *the king of France is bald* precisely on the grounds that the definite NP has an existence ps that is not satisfied.

I think that the defeasibility or non-defeasibility of pss is not a simple matter, and I will defer further discussion of it till later (see especially chapter 11).

## 1.6   Presuppositions and Context-Dependent Interpretation

Consider the fact that the very semantic interpretation of utterances often involves parameters that are not explicitly specified in the utterance itself. For example, think about the parameters listed in (45).

(45)   –   Referents of indexicals;
         –   Referent or antecedent for anaphora in the case of definite NPs;
         –   Restrictions on quantification (sometimes referred to as "domain selection");
         –   Modal bases      (for modal statements);
         –   Standards of precision      (for vague predicates);
         –   Reference point in time      (for tense and aspect);
         –   Reference point in space      (for "come" and "go")

Such parameters may be specified explicitly, as in (46)–(49), for instance.

(46)   I, Ebenezer son of Zachariah, hereby declare that. . . .      (indexical)
(47)   Everybody in this room is hungry.      (restriction on quantification)
(48)   Loosely speaking, France is hexagonal.      (standard of precision)
(49)   Aunt Annie is going away from town.      (reference point in space)

But very often an explicit specification of these parameters is incomplete or entirely missing. And yet setting these parameters is crucial to the interpretation (to the truth conditions!) of utterances. So what do we do? I think it's fair to say that we make an educated guess. Of course, we use every clue we can get. Our clues may come from the utterance itself as well as from the context of utterance.

Note that the context may guide us in a variety of different ways. Here are a few. (i) What seems salient and relevant in the speech situation may guide us. For example, in interpreting *Everybody is hungry* as "everybody in this room is hungry." (ii) We may rely on general world knowledge, to tell us what value for a given parameter would be "normal" or "default" for the subject-matter. For example, if the subject-matter is black tulips, it would be normal to pick a standard of precision according to which very dark purple is black enough. (iii) We take into account the value of the parameter in question as it was set in previous utterances – we often assume, in the absence of better clues, that we are supposed to use this parameter as it was set last. For example, in (50), we know where the soldiers and beggars ended up because we assume that the point of reference set in the first sentence (viz. "town") is also the point of reference for the following sentences. And in (51), I probably meant to quantify over the people in our department, just as you had done in the preceding utterance.

(50)  The beggars came to town. Later, the soldiers came. When the soldiers came, the beggars went.

(from Lewis 1979, p. 180)

(51)  You:  Everybody in our department plays chess.
      Me:   But nobody plays bridge.

Now the question arises: are implicit parameters presupposed? Perhaps it makes sense, for instance, to say that in the following examples, the (a) sentence presupposes the (b) sentence. After all, we say that pss are requirements on the context; isn't the context of utterance required to supply the parameter which is not explicitly specified in the utterance itself?[6]

(52)  (a)  I must visit my grandmother.
      (b)  There is a particular modal base which we are supposed to use here. (There is a certain limited set of ('accessible') possible worlds currently under consideration.)
(53)  (a)  The dog is hungry.
      (b)  There is a particular dog which the NP is supposed to refer to.
(54)  (a)  Aunt Annie is coming.
      (b)  There is a particular reference point s.t. movement towards it is 'coming' and movement away from it is 'going.'

I find it difficult to answer this question. I am not sure we have very strong intuitions about whether non-specific statements such as these (b) sentences are "taken for granted," in the sense that they are requirements on the context of utterance.

One thing I do feel certain about is that the value for an implicit parameter is not always set by the context "in advance." The context obtaining immediately before a sentence is uttered need not, and usually does not, contain a "ready" modal base or reference point in space or standard of precision to be used by the coming utterance. It is true that sometimes we take the reference point in space or standard of precision (etc.) set for a preceding utterance and use it again for the current utterance, as noted above. However, as noted above also, that is only one out of a variety of guidelines that help us find the implicit parameter.

As always when a question is hard to answer pre-theoretically, the theory may decide for us. Perhaps we will discover that the best analysis that we can come up with for the treatment of some parameter X is an analysis that stipulates a well-defined requirement on the context obtaining immediately before the utterance. In that case, we would be

---

[6] Roberts 1995 argues in detail for a presuppositional view of implicit parameters and their recovery.

claiming that that stipulated requirement is a ps. Our decision about whether a ps is involved (and which ps is involved) may differ from parameter to parameter.


## 1.7   Accommodation

Lewis 1979 notes that it is not as easy as one might think to say something which is judged unacceptable. For example, says Lewis, "say something that requires a missing presupposition, and straightway that presupposition springs into existence, making what you said acceptable after all." (p. 172) If you say (55) to me, for instance, I will have no trouble accepting it even if it is not already assumed in the context that you have a dog – I will "accommodate" the assumption that you have one.[7]

(55)   My dog is at the door.

Lewis emphasizes the fact that this process truly affects the context of utterance: if you said (55) and nobody objected, then from now on the assumption that you have a dog is truly part of the common ground of our conversation.
   Lewis talks about accommodation not only as a way of avoiding ps-failure, but more generally as a way of adjusting what he calls the "conversational score" in various ways so as to ensure (ceteris paribus and within certain limits) that our fellow-speakers' utterances will come out "true, or otherwise acceptable." (p. 178) This includes adjustments not only of the common ground, but also of reference points for "come" and "go," of standards of precision, of modal bases, and more.
   Usually, we credit our fellow speakers with an intention to say something which is an acceptable utterance: grammatical, interpretable, relevant (in terms of immediate discourse coherence), in agreement with various linguistic conventions, and – even – true (or at least possibly true). As I see it, this tendency of ours affects our assumptions about all of the following: the context of evaluation, the intended semantic interpretation of the utterances we hear, and the context of utterance. Following are some examples.
   Suppose I say (56) to you, and then you open the closet, and in it you see just one thing: a black coat.

(56)   In the closet, you will find a blue coat.

You will probably think that I meant to say something true. You may think to yourself: oh, she didn't identify the color correctly, she meant the black coat. Alternatively, you may conclude that **you** didn't identify the color correctly, and that the coat is actually very dark blue. Note that the latter alternative involves a revision of your own assumptions about the facts (or, in other words, about the context of evaluation).
   The way we disambiguate utterances is partly driven by our wish to accommodate our fellow speakers. For example, suppose I am known to be a poor and unsuccessful

---

[7]   This phenomenon is referred to as "bridging" in the psychological literature. See e.g. Clark 1977 and Clark and Haviland 1977.

model, and I say (57) to you. (57) is structurally ambiguous between (58a) and (58b). But since (58a) is obviously false, you will conclude that I meant (58b).

(57) Successful psychiatrists and models are always rich.
(58) a. [Successful psychiatrists] and models are always rich.
　　　b. Successful [psychiatrists and models] are always rich.

Our wish to credit our fellow speakers with telling the truth also affects the way we guess at implicit parameters that are supposed to go into the semantic interpretation. Here are some examples.

(59) You, me, and other people are in the room.
　　　You:　Nobody in this room is tall.
　　　Me:　But everybody is taller than me.
　　　Obviously, I don't mean 'everybody in this room,' but rather 'everybody in this room except me.' How do you know? Because you assume that I don't mean to say an obvious falsehood.
(60) In the room are you, your brother, me, a stranger, and nobody else.
　　　(a)　You: We are brothers.
　　　I interpret: 'we'=you and your brother. (Otherwise you'd be lying.)
　　　(b)　You: We are four, so we can play bridge.
　　　I interpret: 'we'=all of us in the room. (Otherwise you'd be lying.)
(61) You say: the sidewalk is flat.
　　　I would normally choose to assume a standard of precision loose enough to make your statement true.

Now consider (62). Our wish to credit our fellow speaker with correct use of the linguistic conventions for "come" and "go" will lead us to conclude that the relevant reference point in space in the first sentence is "town," and also that it shifts from "town" to "the shore" in the second sentence.

(62) When the beggars came to town, the rich folk went to the shore. But soon the beggars came after them, so they went home. (Lewis 1979, p. 181)

Returning finally to pss, our wish to see our fellow speakers as saying something interpretable and felicitous will generally drive us to assume (ceteris paribus and within certain limits) that the pss of their utterances hold. Very often, this will involve adding information to our common ground. That is what happens in the example given at the beginning of this section: if I don't know whether you have a dog or not and you say to me *My dog is at the door*, I would normally add to the common ground the assumption that you have a dog. Similarly, if I don't know whether you smoke or not and you say *I haven't managed to quit smoking yet*, I would normally add to the common ground the assumption that you smoke. And so on. Sometimes, we are so willing to accommodate a ps that we would even revise our previous assumptions. If I believe that you don't have a dog, I may revise this assumption when I hear you say *My dog is at the door*, and start to believe that you do have a dog. (Of course our willingness to revise an assumption would depend on how certain we are of that assumption.)

I think that successful "referential" uses of a definite NP with the wrong description (as discussed in Donnellan 1971) may also be considered a type of accommodation. Suppose you open the closet and it contains just two things: a bright pink coat and a black coat. I say (63) to you.

(63)   Look in the pockets of the blue coat.

If you are very sure of your color vision, you may be unwilling to accommodate the ps that there is a blue coat in there. Still, you can accommodate me, by concluding that I meant to refer to the black coat, and looking in the pockets of that coat. Strictly speaking, you will find my utterance somewhat infelicitous, but you will behave as if it was fully felicitous.

I'd like to consider some more examples involving pss. Suppose you don't know anything about the animals I keep or don't keep at home. Suppose we are at my house, and we hear some scratching noises outside. Then I say one of the following.

(55)   My dog is at the door.
(64)   My giraffe is at the door.
(65)   I keep a giraffe here. The giraffe is at the door.
(66)   I keep a dog here. The dog is at the door.

I think you will agree that (64) sounds stranger than either (55) or (65). On the view taken here, the explanation is as follows. (65) is OK because it doesn't presuppose that I have a giraffe. (55) is OK because while it presupposes that I have a dog, this piece of information is very easy for you to accommodate (since it is plausible). (64) is strange because it presupposes that I have a giraffe, a piece of information that you would probably be reluctant to accommodate (since it is rather implausible). On this view, (55) does not directly tell you that I have a dog, but rather "sneaks in" this information, by forcing you to accommodate it. We very often convey information in this indirect manner. Indeed, to say (55) seems more natural than to bother to say the longer utterance in (66). Note that I might choose to say (64) anyway. This creates a special effect, because it is in a sense "unfair" to "sneak in" the implausible and surprising information that I have a giraffe.

Another example: suppose you are on trial for selling crack. Which of the following two questions seems more fair to you?

(67)   Did you sell crack?
(68)   When did you stop selling crack?

On the view taken here, (68) seems unfair because it presupposes that you sold crack. If the hearers didn't have the belief that you sold crack before, they may get tricked into accommodating it now. Certainly, I may choose to say (68) anyway, deliberately "sneaking in" the information that you sold crack; it's just that it would seem unfair.

The principles governing accommodation have been studied by researchers in a number of fields, including traditional grammar, semantics and pragmatics, cognitive psychology and artificial intelligence. It is clear that our tendency to accommodate other speakers is only a tendency – as Lewis puts it, we accommodate "ceteris paribus and within certain limits." In other words, the process of accommodation is constrained. Let me mention here two of the central constraints on accommodation.

1. **Consistency**  When we have firm beliefs about the context of evaluation or context of utterance, we are very reluctant to drop them. Therefore, we are usually unwilling or highly reluctant to accommodate assumptions that are inconsistent with what is already assumed. Further, we are reluctant to accommodate assumptions that seem implausible given what's already assumed, even if those assumptions don't actually contradict what's already assumed. Indeed, assumptions to be accommodated are usually supposed to be uncontroversial and unsurprising (as noted in e.g. Soames 1989 (p. 567) and Heim 1982 (ch. III, section 5.2)). Following are some examples.

Suppose I say (69) to you, and then you open the closet, and in it you see just one thing: a bright pink coat. You will probably **not** choose to revise your own assumption about the color of the coat just in order to be able to see my statement as true . . . So you will conclude that my utterance is false.

(69)   In the closet, you will find a blue coat.

Suppose we are sitting in a room with one door, which is clearly closed. If I say (70), you will not accommodate the assumption that the door is open. Rather, you will conclude that my utterance is infelicitous.

(70)   Close the door.

Suppose, in the real world, today, I suddenly say (71), out of the blue. Obviously, the Earth is not the intended reference point, or I would have said "go" rather than "come." But what's already in the common ground does not make it possible to take the planet Mars as our reference point. So my utterance will seem infelicitous.

(71)   You know what, next year my uncle will come to Mars!

If I say (72) below, you will probably not be willing to accommodate the required ps, viz. that France has a king. Hence, my utterance will seem infelicitous.

(72)   The present king of France is bald.

If I say (64), repeated below, you will probably be reluctant to accommodate the required ps, viz. that I have a giraffe. So you will probably be baffled.

(64)   My giraffe is at the door.

2. **"Bridging"**  (Based on the psychological literature. See Heim 1982, ch. III, section 5.2, and references cited there.) There are constraints on accommodation which require that new material added to the common ground be related to material which is already in it. There has to be some crossreference or "bridge" between the newly added material and something which is already there.

For example, consider (73). (73) sounds perfectly felicitous even without contextual salience or previous mention of an author.[8] So the hearers accommodate the assumption that there is an author that the definite NP is supposed to refer to.

(73)   John read a book about Schubert and wrote to the author.

Note, however, that for the purposes of avoiding ps failure, it would be good enough to accommodate the assumption that some author or other exists and is being referred to. And yet, that is not what the hearers do. What the hearers do instead is accommodate the assumption that there is an author who wrote the book about Schubert that John read, and take the definite NP to refer to that author. This constitutes permissible accommodation, because we have linked the accommodated author to the previously mentioned book.

Accommodation will come up again in various places in this book, and we will have occasion to think again about where it occurs, how it works, and how it is constrained.

Finally, let me add that Thomason 1990 argues that accommodation plays a central role in creating conversational implicatures. Accepting Grice's idea that conversational implicatures are rooted in cooperative behavior, Thomason outlines a program for a new theory of how conversational implicatures are generated, in which the relevant cooperative behavior is that of accommodating one's fellow speakers. According to Thomason, the addressees, who recognize specific plans that the speaker is trying to carry out (concerning both non-linguistic goals and the intended organization of the discourse), seek to accommodate the speaker in his/her efforts to further these plans, and it is this accommodation that produces a conversational implicature. One of Thomason's examples is given in (74).

(74)   Husband to wife: I didn't tell you that I'll need the car this afternoon.
       Implicature:     I'll need the car this afternoon.

The wife is able to recognize that telling her that he'll need the car would be part of the husband's plan to get her to agree to his using the car. She accommodates him in his effort to carry out the plan she has detected, by interpreting his utterance as telling her that he'll need the car (= by getting the implicature that he'll need the car).

---

[8]  If you think that when one mentions a book the author always, automatically, becomes salient, then perhaps (assuming that horses don't always have riders) you will prefer the following example:

(i)   John heard a horse and decided to get some water for the rider.

# Part One

## *Dynamic Semantics, Definites, and Indefinites*

# 2

# Discourse Representation Theory and File Change Semantics

This chapter is concerned with Hans Kamp's Discourse Representation Theory (DRT) and Irene Heim's File Change Semantics (FCS). These two very similar theories were first introduced in Kamp 1981 and Heim 1982. Further basic references are Heim 1983a and Kamp and Reyle 1993.

Section 2.1 is included here for the benefit of those who are not familiar with DRT or FCS. In 2.1.3 and 2.1.4, I give an introduction of each theory in turn. These introductions are independent of each other, and I tried to make them short but complete.

In section 2.2, I give an exposition-in-parallel of DRT and FCS. What I repeat here of the basics of DRT and FCS should be enough to refresh the memory of those readers who are already familiar with these theories (and who have, accordingly, skipped 2.1). The main goals of this section are (i) to clarify why it is that Kamp's and Heim's theories are so similar that they are essentially the same theory, and (ii) to clarify or highlight a few aspects of the theory that are of special interest in the context of this book.

In section 2.3, I give a version of the formal logical language used in DRT, as well as a summary of context change potentials for a few versions of context change semantics.

## 2.1   Introduction to DRT and FCS

### 2.1.1   *Motivation*

The main linguistic motivation for the Kamp–Heim theory comes from three closely related goals: giving a general treatment of indefinite NPs, giving a general treatment of definite NPs (including pronouns in their different uses), and giving a principled way of predicting the range of anaphora possibilities in discourse.

Let me give a very brief sketch of some of the issues involved. (For details, discussion and references, see Heim 1982, ch. I.) In the literature on indefinite NPs, there is tension between regarding indefinites as quantificational and regarding them as referential. On Russell's view, indefinites are existential quantifiers.[1] This analysis provides

---

[1]   See especially Russell 1919, ch. 16.

the right truth conditions for examples like (1) (see (1′)), and handles examples like (2) as well (see (2′)). If *a dog* were a referential expression instead, what would its referent be in (2)?

(1)   A dog came in.
(1′)   $\exists x[dog(x) \wedge x$ came in$]$
(2)   It is not the case that a dog came in.
(2′)   $\neg\exists x[dog(x) \wedge x$ came in$]$

On the other hand, consider the behavior of indefinites as antecedents for anaphora. If *a dog* is an existential quantifier, then the pronoun in (3) is a variable bound by it, as in the formula in (3′).

(3)   A dog came in. It is pretty.      (anaphoric reading)
(3′)   $\exists x[dog(x) \wedge x$ came in $\wedge$ pretty$(x)]$

But how could this kind of analysis extend, for example, to (4)?

(4)   A dog came in. What did it do next?      (anaphoric reading)

Also, why can the scope of *a dog* extend beyond clause boundaries, as in (3), while the scope of other quantifiers can't, as illustrated in (5), where *every dog* can't bind the pronoun?

(5)   Every dog came in. It is pretty.      (anaphora impossible)

It seems that the anaphora would be handled more naturally if *a dog* were considered a referential expression whose referent is picked up by the subsequent pronoun.

   Kamp and Heim take as a major challenge the class of "donkey" examples, which were discussed by ancient and medieval philosophers and raised again in Geach 1962. Donkey sentences are sentences containing an indefinite NP inside an if-clause or a relative clause and a pronoun outside that clause which refers back to the indefinite NP. These examples present a difficult problem over and above the issues already mentioned. Consider for instance examples (6) and (7).

(6)   If a man meets a donkey, he beats it.
(7)   Every man who owns a donkey beats it.

In both examples, the NP *a donkey* can't be referential (obviously, there isn't any particular thing in the world or in the model that the NP can be said to stand for). Is it a quantifier, then? If we want to get the right truth conditions and also account for the anaphora, *a donkey* can't be translated as an existential quantifier, the way *a dog* was translated in (3′) above. It rather appears to function as a universal quantifier in these examples. For example, translating (6) as (6*) is no good, since the variables in x beats y are free, and (6) is more adequately paraphrased as (6**).

(6*)  $\exists x \exists y[man(x) \wedge donkey(y) \wedge x \text{ meets } y] \rightarrow x \text{ beats } y$
(6**)  $\forall x \forall y[(man(x) \wedge donkey(y) \wedge x \text{ meetsy}) \rightarrow x \text{ beats } y]$

If we have to translate (6) as (6**), we have the old problem that the scope of *a dog* extends beyond the clause (cf. (5) again), and moreover, we find that indefinites have to be translated sometimes as existentials and sometimes as universals. Are indefinites ambiguous? Why can they express universality in donkey sentences?

### 2.1.2 Summary of Main Features

As a solution to the above problems, Kamp and Heim propose (independently) a semantic framework with the features given below.

(A) The basic semantic value of a bit of discourse is not its truth conditional content, but rather the role it would play in extending some existing body of information (and determining the truth conditions of the extension).

(B) Definite and indefinite NPs are neither quantificational nor referential. Rather, they function as **variables**. For example, the sentence in (8) is translated as an open formula like the one in (8'). The indefinite NP *a dog* introduces into the formula the variable x. The definite NP *it* is translated as an occurrence of that same variable.

(8)  A dog came in, and it is pretty.
(8')  $dog(x) \wedge x \text{ came in } \wedge pretty(x)$

As noted by Heim, the variables which translate indefinite and definite NPs in the Kamp–Heim system can be regarded as **discourse referents**, in the sense of Karttunen 1976. According to Karttunen, a discourse referent is an entity which, once introduced by an indefinite NP, can serve as an antecedent for anaphora; at the same time, this entity need not correspond with any particular referent in the world or model. In (8), *a dog* is said to introduce a discourse referent and the anaphoric *it* is said to pick up that same discourse referent. In the quantificational example (7) above, *a donkey* is said to introduce a discourse referent, and the anaphoric *it* is said to pick up that same discourse referent.

(C) There is **existential quantification** which takes scope over the entire discourse, and (unselectively) binds all the free variables in it. For example, if an entire discourse contains just the sentence in (8), this discourse will be true iff **there is** a value for x which verifies (8'). (So this discourse will be equivalent to the formula given in (3') above.)

(D) For the treatment of quantification, Kamp and Heim adopt **unselective restricted quantification**, as proposed in Lewis 1975 for sentences with "adverbs of quantification" (such as *usually*, *always*, etc.).

Let me briefly review this analysis. The semantic representation of sentences like the following seven examples consists of three parts – a quantifier, a restriction, and (to use Heim's term) a "nuclear scope." It is assumed that an invisible universal quantifier is associated with plain conditionals like (6).

(9)     A quadratic equation usually has two different solutions.

(Lewis 1975, p. 5)

(10)    $\left\{\begin{array}{l}\text{Usually,}\\\text{Most of the time,}\\\text{Always,}\end{array}\right\}$ if a man meets a donkey, he beats it.

(6)     If a man meets a donkey, he beats it.
(11)    Every dog came in.
(12)    Every farmer has a donkey.
(13)    Most farmers have a donkey.
(7)     Every man who owns a donkey beats it.

In the following sample representations, the round brackets enclose the restriction and the square brackets enclose the nuclear scope.

(9′)    USUALLY (x is a quadratic equation) [x has two different solutions]
(6′)    ∀ (x is a man, y is a donkey, and x meets y) [x beats y]
(11′)   ∀ (x is a dog) [x came in]
(13′)   MOST (x is a farmer) [x has a donkey]

The quantification is restricted to those individuals which satisfy the restriction. For example, (11′) says that all the dogs satisfy the nuclear scope (= came in), and (13′) says that most of the farmers satisfy the nuclear scope (= have a donkey). The quantifiers are unselective, so they bind all the free variables. Hence, (6′) quantifies over pairs of a man and a donkey such that the man meets the donkey (it says that for all such pairs, the man beats the donkey).

(E) The features mentioned above allow Kamp and Heim to adopt the traditional logician's treatment of anaphora – **anaphora as variable-binding** – not only for sentence-internal anaphora, but also for discourse anaphora. (To take just one example, a discourse containing just the two sentences in (3) above is equivalent to the formula in (3′) above.)

### 2.1.3   Kamp's DRT

In DRT, the body of information gathered in a discourse is represented syntactically, by a Discourse Representation Structure (DRS), which is graphically depicted as a box. Statements which the discourse participants assert as facts are entered one after the other into the DRS representing the whole discourse (the "matrix" DRS). But a discourse may also contain subparts with denied or doubtful facts, temporary assumptions, etc. These are represented as separate DRSs embedded in the matrix DRS and possibly embedded within one another, as sketched in (14).

(14)

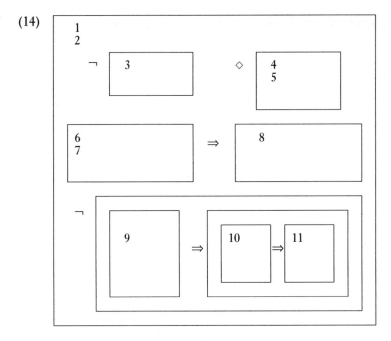

Roughly, 1 and 2 in the matrix DRS are asserted facts, 3 is denied, 4 and 5 are possible, 8 is asserted on the assumptions 6 and 7 (i.e. $6 \land 7 \to 8$), etc. Note how deeply embedded 11 is. There is a hierarchical structure then, of subdiscourses within subdiscourses, which represents the logical structure of the discourse. (This is very much like a mathematical proof with subproofs and temporary assumptions in them.)

There is a set of "construction rules" which map natural language sentences (regarded as syntactic trees) onto their representations within the DRS. The construction rules operate essentially top-down and left-to-right in the syntactic tree.[2] As you go down the tree, each time you hit an operator (e.g. negation) or an NP, there is a relevant construction rule which tells you what to do. The sentences in the discourse are entered into the DRS one by one. For each sentence that is asserted as an independent statement in its own right, you enter its representation (as determined by the construction rules) into the matrix DRS.

Here is what two of Kamp's construction rules do. The construction rule for negation instructs you to create an embedded DRS prefixed by ¬, and to enter the negated sentence into this embedded DRS. The construction rule for indefinite NPs instructs you to do the following:

- Introduce a "new" variable into the top line of the DRS.
  ("new" means a variable which is not yet present in the matrix DRS; "the DRS" means the local DRS in which the NP is represented.)
- Predicate of this variable the descriptive content of the NP.
- Predicate of this variable the rest of the sentence.

---

[2] Given a strict left-to-right procedure, the leftmost NP in the tree will get wide scope. So if the relevant trees are surface structures (rather than LFs, say), the procedure has to be amended to allow other NPs to get wide scope over the leftmost NP. But this need not concern us now.

Given this, we can translate the two-sentence discourse in (15) into a DRS as follows.

(15)
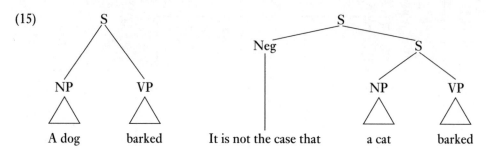

We start with an empty box that is going to contain the entire discourse. We then consider the first sentence. This sentence has to be entered into our empty box (into the matrix DRS), and that gives us the following DRS.

| A dog barked |
| --- |

Going down the tree, we hit the indefinite NP. The rule for indefinites tell us to introduce a new variable (= a variable not yet present in the DRS) into the top line of our DRS, and predicate of it "dog" and "barked." Suppose we pick x. Then, we get the following DRS.

| x |
| --- |
| A dog barked |
|   dog(x) |
| x barked |

The second sentence too has to be entered into the matrix DRS, as follows.

| x |
| --- |
| A dog barked |
|   dog(x) |
| x barked |
| It is not the case that a cat barked |

Going down the tree, we first hit the negation. The rule for negation tells us to do the following.

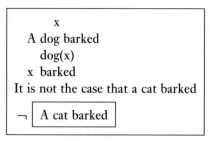

Applying the rule for indefinites again, we finally get the following DRS.

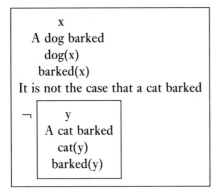

According to the formal theory given in 2.3.1 below, an "official" DRS contains just the formulas that cannot be reduced any further.[3] This means that (the graphic representation of) the "official" DRS of (15) is (16).

(16)

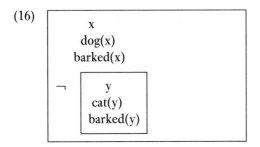

I hope that the above is sufficient illustration of the procedure of translating discourse into DRSs via the construction rules. In what follows, I will take this procedure for granted. I am not concerned with its details. I **am** concerned with the result of this procedure – the DRS representation itself – and with the semantic rules that interpret it.

The set of variables in the top line of a DRS is called the "universe" of that DRS. The rest of the items in the DRS are called "conditions." Take for example (16) above. The embedded DRS has {y} as its universe, and it has two simple conditions: cat(y) and barked(y). The matrix DRS has {x} as its universe, and it has three conditions: the two simple conditions dog(x) and barked(x), and the complex condition

---

[3] In other words, surface English strings and other strings that are not fully reduced are **not** expressions of the version of DRL given in 2.3.1. I will nevertheless often include such strings in my DRS diagrams, in order to help the reader keep track of steps in DRS construction. Note also that in my DRS diagrams, strings like x meets y are freely used to represent atomic formulas like meets(x,y), and material not relevant to the discussion is not fully reduced.

Let us now begin to consider the semantic interpretation of DRSs. In DRT, truth is not defined for sentences. After all, if you consider a sentence on its own, its representation in DRT is nothing more than an open formula. For example, the sentence *A dog barked* is simply represented as follows.

x

dog(x)
barked(x)

But an open formula is not something which is generally true or false on its own. Truth is defined in DRT for an entire discourse. That is, truth is defined for a DRS. The definition goes roughly as follows.

(17)   A DRS is **true** iff there is a value assignment which verifies all the conditions in it.

Note that the truth definition induces existential quantification that takes scope over the entire DRS. As an example, take a discourse consisting of the single sentence *A dog barked*. This discourse is represented as in (18).

(18)

x

dog(x)
barked(x)

DRS (18) is true iff **there is** a value assignment which verifies the conditions dog(x) and barked(x). In other words, DRS (18) is true iff x can be mapped onto an individual in the model which is a dog and barked – so (18) is true iff **there is** such an individual in the model.

The above truth definition allows DRT to explain why indefinite NPs are often associated with existential statements, without analyzing the indefinite NP itself as quantificational. The indefinite NP functions as a variable. This variable may get bound by the existential quantification over the whole discourse, yielding an existential statement. Note that the indefinite NP is not referential, either. Take again DRS (18). Consider a model which contains several dogs who barked. In this model, (18) is true, while the indefinite *a dog* cannot be said to refer to any particular individual.

Kamp's metaphor is that the DRS is a partial picture of the world or the model, and it is true if there is a part of the world/model which is correctly described by it. This is sometimes expressed by saying that a DRS is true if it can be "embedded" into the world/model. For that reason, the assignment functions which match a DRS with a part of the world/model are called "embedding functions." Thus, a DRS is true iff there is an **embedding function** which verifies all the conditions in it.

It is clear what it takes to verify a simple condition. But what does it take to verify the complex condition

¬

y

cat(y)
barked(y)

present in (16)? Every type of condition comes with its own verification clause. The verification clause for a DRS K prefixed with ¬ determines the following.

(19)   An embedding function f verifies ¬ $\boxed{\phantom{}}^{\text{┌K┐}}$ iff it is **not** the case that **there is an** embedding function which extends f and verifies the conditions in DRS K.

(Note that (19) induces existential quantification over the embedded DRS.) Thus, our complex condition from (16) is verified by an embedding function f iff there is no embedding function which extends f and verifies the conditions cat(y) and barked(x). (This means that the whole DRS (16) above is true iff there is an embedding which verifies dog(x) and barked(x) but cannot be extended to an embedding which verifies cat(y) and barked(y).)

   Note: in what follows, I will often use "function f verifies DRS K" as shorthand for "function f verifies all the conditions in DRS K."

   Next, let us consider anaphora. An anaphoric NP is translated into the DRS as an "old" variable – a variable that is already present in the DRS.[4] For example, the two-sentence discourse in (3) is represented as in (20).

(3)    A dog came in. It is pretty.

(20)
```
┌─────────────────┐
│        x        │
│  A dog came in  │
│    dog(x)       │
│   x came in     │
│                 │
│  It is pretty   │
│    pretty(x)    │
└─────────────────┘
```

Given the truth definition above, (20) represents a reading of (3) in which *it* is anaphorically linked to *a dog*: (20) is true iff there is a dog that came in and is pretty. Similarly, the two-sentence discourse in (21) is represented as in (22).

(21)   I have a dog. It doesn't have a bone.

(22)
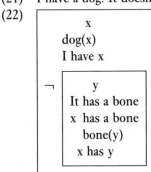

---

DRS (22) is true iff there is an embedding function which verifies the three conditions in it. So, (22) is true iff there is an embedding function which verifies dog(x) and I have x but cannot be extended to an embedding which verifies bone(y) and x has y. So (22) is true iff there is in the model a dog that I have for which it is impossible to find a bone that it has.

And now, let us move on to quantification. As mentioned in 2.1.2 above, DRT treats natural language quantification as restricted and unselective (cf. Lewis 1975). Given an adverb of quantification or a quantificational determiner, the construction rules instruct us to create a complex condition which itself contains a pair of DRSs. For example, the single sentence discourse in (23) and the single sentence discourse in (24) are represented as in (25) and (26), respectively. Note that it is assumed that a plain conditional like (24) implicitly contains the adverb of quantification "always."

(23)   Every man owns a donkey.
(24)   If a man is rich he owns a donkey.
(25)

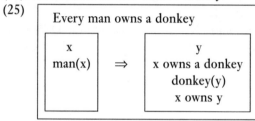

(26)

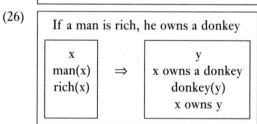

The complex condition represents a tripartite quantificational structure: $\Rightarrow$ represents an unselective universal quantifier, the left-hand (or "antecedent") DRS represents the restriction, and the right-hand (or "consequent") DRS represents the nuclear scope. The verification clause says roughly the following.

(27)   An embedding function f verifies $\begin{array}{c}\ulcorner K_1 \urcorner \\ \boxed{\phantom{x}} \end{array} \Rightarrow \begin{array}{c}\ulcorner K_2 \urcorner \\ \boxed{\phantom{x}}\end{array}$ iff for **every** embedding func-

tion f′ which extends f and verifies the conditions in $K_1$, **there is** an embedding function f″ which extends f′ and verifies the conditions in $K_2$.

(Note that this clause induces universal quantification that takes scope over the entire complex condition and existential quantification that takes scope over the right-hand DRS.) Since there are no variables in the universe of (25), DRS (25) is true iff it is verified by the empty embedding function. Which is the case iff every function which verifies the left-hand DRS in it can be extended to a function which verifies the right-hand DRS in it. The result is that (25) comes out true iff for every man in the model, it is possible to find in the model a donkey that that man owns. Similarly, (26) comes out true iff for every rich man in the model, there is a donkey in the model that that man owns.

Note that (24) is a donkey sentence. In DRT, donkey sentences no longer present a problem: the indefinite NP in the restriction has no quantificational force of its own; it is treated as a variable (plus description), as usual. This variable occurs in the scope of the universal quantification which the semantics associates with the pair of embedded DRSs, and is therefore bound by this quantification.

Note: it is stipulated in DRT that a quantificational NP introduces into the restriction (into the left-hand DRS) a **new** variable. If you want to see why that is necessary, consider what would happen if we choose for the left-hand DRS an old variable, as in (28).

(28)

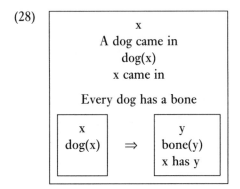

(28) is true iff there is an embedding function f that verifies the conditions in it, including the complex one. f verifies the complex condition iff every extension of f that verifies the antecedent DRS . . . – But we can stop here: the only extension of f that verifies the antecedent DRS is f itself. So we will fail to quantify over all dogs. In contrast, using z instead of x in the embedded DRSs would yield the desired interpretation.

For completeness, I note that the donkey sentences in (6) and (7) are both represented in DRT as illustrated in (29).[5]

(6)    If a man meets a donkey, he beats it.
(7)    Every man who owns a donkey beats it.
(29)

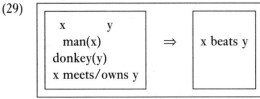

DRS (29) is true iff it is verified by the empty embedding function. So (29) is true iff every embedding function which verifies the antecedent DRS can be extended to a function verifying the consequent DRS. But there are no new variables in the consequent

5   See Kadmon 1987, 1990 for arguments that sentences like (7) should actually receive a somewhat different analysis.

DRS, so the last sentence can be simplified as follows. (29) is true iff every embedding function which verifies the antecedent DRS verifies the consequent DRS. (29) comes out true iff for every pair consisting of a man and a donkey he meets/owns, that man beats that donkey.

Donkey sentences are a good illustration of the utility of discourse referents (i.e. variables which serve as antecedents for anaphora – see 2.1.2 above). Sentence (24) involves no reference at all, in the sense that there is no particular thing in the model which any of the NPs can be said to stand for. The discourse referents x and y allow the speaker to keep track of the things mentioned in the if-clause or relative clause and refer back to them, without presupposing any such reference.

At this point, all the essential ingredients of DRT have been introduced. It is time to get a little more precise.

As you can gather from the discussion above, I am using in this book a formulation of DRT in which the assignment functions (the embedding functions) are **partial** and **expanding**: a function verifying the matrix DRS assigns values only to the variables that occur in its universe; a function verifying a DRS K directly embedded in the matrix DRS is an extension of a function verifying the matrix DRS, an extension assigning values both to variables that occur in the universe of the matrix DRS and to those that occur in the universe of K; and so forth. To define these functions, I use what Kamp calls an **accessibility** relation between DRSs. My definitions, given in 2.3.1 below, determine the following.

(30)   The **accessible universe** $A_K$ of a DRS K is the set of all variables that occur:
    (i)   in the universe of K itself,
    (ii)  in the universes of all the DRSs that graphically contain K, and
    (iii) if K is – or is embedded in – a consequent DRS of a complex condition, also in the universe of the antecedent DRS of that complex condition.

(31)   An **embedding function** for a DRS K in a model $M = \langle D,F \rangle$[6] is a partial function from the set of variables to D which maps all and only the variables in $A_K$ onto members of D.

To illustrate this, we can use the DRSs above. An embedding function for (16) above assigns a value just to x, and an embedding function for the DRS embedded in (16) assigns values to x and y (and to no other variable). An embedding for (25) assigns values to no variable, an embedding for the antecedent DRS in (25) assigns a value to x, and an embedding for the consequent DRS in (25) assigns values to x and y. An embedding for (28) assigns a value to x, an embedding for the antecedent DRS in (28) also assigns a value to x, and an embedding for the consequent DRS in (28) assigns values to x and y. An embedding for (29) assigns values to no variable, an embedding for the antecedent DRS in (29) assigns values to x and y, and an embedding for the consequent DRS in (29) also assigns values to x and y.

And now the semantic clauses mentioned above can be stated more precisely:

(32)   A DRS K is **true** in a model M iff there is an embedding function for K in M which verifies all the conditions in K.

---

[6]   D is "the domain of individuals" = "the universe of discourse"; F is an interpretation function assigning extensions to constants.

(33)   An embedding function f verifies ¬ ⌐K⌐ [ ] iff it is not the case that there is an

embedding function f′ for DRS K which extends f and verifies all the conditions in K.

(34)   An embedding function f verifies ⌐K₁⌐ [ ] ⇒ ⌐K₂⌐ [ ] iff for every embedding func-

tion f′ for K₁ which extends f and verifies all the conditions in K₁, there is an embedding function f″ for K₂ which extends f′ and verifies all the conditions in K₂.

It is useful to note a few facts about how variable-binding works in the formal system that I've just presented. We saw that the truth definition and verification clauses induce quantification that takes scope over single DRSs and pairs of DRSs. Let us take as an example DRS (36) of the discourse in (35).

(35)   A man walked in. He didn't have a hat. Every girl who saw him gave him a flower.

(36)

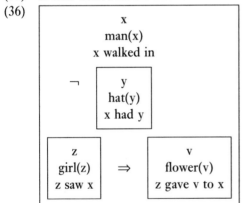

We may think of DRS (36) as if it contained unselective quantifiers over individuals, as in the following diagram. Every DRS has a quantifier attached to it (drawn directly to its left).

(36′)

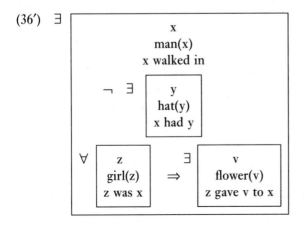

The definition of embedding functions together with the semantic clauses (32)–(34) above determine the following.

(i)  An occurrence of a variable is bound iff the accessible universe of its local DRS contains that variable;

(ii)  A quantifier can only bind variables that occur in the universe of the particular DRS to which it is attached;

(iii)  An occurrence of a variable is bound by the widest-scope quantifier that satisfies (ii) with respect to that variable.

(in other words, an occurrence of a variable is bound by the quantifier attached to the "highest" DRS in whose universe that variable occurs.)

In (36) or (36′) above, all the occurrences of x are bound by the existential quantifier over the matrix DRS, all the occurrences of y are bound by the existential quantifier associated with the DRS prefixed with ¬, all the occurrences of z are bound by the universal quantifier, and all the occurrences of v are bound by the existential quantifier associated with the consequent DRS. In (37) below, the occurrence of y in brown(y) is free. And in (38), all the occurrences of x are bound by the universal quantifier.

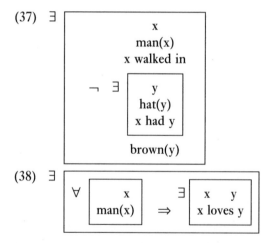

(I assume that the construction rules would never build a DRS like (37) or (38), and yet these are well-formed DRSs according to the syntax of DRL (see 2.3.1 below), and are interpreted as indicated.)

Finally, let me discuss the way in which DRT predicts anaphora possibilities in discourse. To start with a concrete example, consider the contrast in anaphora possibilities between (39) and (40). This contrast is correctly predicted by DRT. Why is anaphora possible in (39)? Because once the pronoun *it* has been translated into a "new" occurrence of the "old" dog-variable, the "old" and "new" occurrences alike fall under the scope of the existential quantifier over the whole discourse, and get bound by it (see DRS (39′)).[7]

---

[7]  If you want to verify that all the occurrences of x in (39′) get bound by the same quantifier, look at the embedding functions that are supposed to assign values to the different occurrences of x. DRS (39′) is true iff there is an embedding f that verifies it. Obviously, f assigns the value to the "old"

(39)    I have a dog. It isn't smart          (anaphora possible)
(40)    I don't have a dog. It is smart.      (anaphora impossible)

(39')                                    (40')

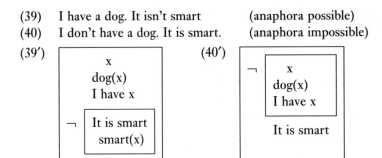

And why is anaphora impossible in (40)? Consider the corresponding DRS in (40'). The second sentence is a new assertion, and that is why it is entered into the matrix DRS. Suppose that in (40') too, we translate the pronoun *it* as an occurrence of x. This would not create an anaphoric interpretation, because the "old" and "new" occurrences of x would not get bound by the same quantifier. The x in the embedded DRS is under the scope of the existential quantifier that has scope just over that embedded DRS, and gets bound by it. But when we translate *it* into x in the matrix DRS, the new occurrence of x would **not** be under the scope of the existential over the embedded DRS, and would not get bound by it.[8]

And now let me describe the DRT treatment of anaphora possibilities in discourse in general terms. Whenever we consider translating an anaphoric NP into an "old" variable, let us call the "old" occurrences of that variable "the antecedent variable" or "the antecedent discourse referent." Now we can summarize the situation as follows. DRT adopts the traditional logician's analysis of anaphora as variable-binding, not only for sentence-internal anaphora, but also for discourse anaphora. Therefore, the following generalization holds.

(41)    **Generalization about anaphora and scope:**
        Anaphora is possible only when the anaphoric element is under the scope of the quantifier that binds the antecedent variable.

occurrences of x. And when does f verify the complex condition? – when it can't be extended to an embedding f′ that verifies the embedded DRS. So the value for the "new" occurrence of x is assigned by f′. But f′ is an extension of f, so f′(x) = f(x). Hence, all the occurrences of x get their value from the same embedding function.

[8]   Again, if you want to verify the binding facts, look at the relevant embedding functions. An embedding f for the matrix verifies the complex condition iff it can't be extended to an embedding f′ that verifies the embedded DRS. So the value for the "old" occurrences of x in the embedded DRS is assigned by f′. Suppose we enter the new condition smart(x) into the matrix DRS. Which embedding would assign the value to the "new" occurrence of x? Well, not f′, since f′ is only supposed to verify the conditions inside the embedded DRS. It is f that is supposed to verify the new condition. However, the universe of the matrix DRS is empty: it doesn't contain x, since the construction rule for indefinite NPs only instructs us to enter the variable corresponding to *a dog* into the universe of the embedded DRS. So an embedding f for the matrix (the empty embedding) would not assign a value to x. So the "new" occurrence of x would not be assigned a value at all – it would remain free. (Note that we couldn't alter the construction rules so that they would introduce x into the matrix DRS as well, since that would yield an entirely wrong result for embedded indefinites. For example, with x in the matrix DRS in (40'), all the occurrences of x would be bound by the existential quantification over the matrix DRS, and the existential over the embedded DRS wouldn't play any role.)

Hence, predictions about anaphora possibilities follow directly from the configuration of quantifiers and their scope in the DRS.

Kamp 1981 stipulates that a pronoun must be translated into a variable which is not only "old" but also **accessible**. A variable is accessible to a given pronoun iff this variable occurs in the accessible universe (see informal definition in (30) above) of the local DRS into which the pronoun is to be entered. This means that the construction of DRS (40′) cannot go on at all, since it doesn't contain any variable that is both "old" and accessible to the pronoun. Now, whenever a pronoun is translated into an accessible variable, it falls under the scope of the quantifier that binds that variable – this follows from the definition of accessibility plus the semantics of DRSs. Hence, Kamp's accessibility constraint on anaphora encodes precisely the generalization given in (41) above.[9] In general, Kamp does not allow a pronoun to be processed at all unless it falls under the scope of a quantifier that binds a potential antecedent variable.

To take some more examples, the contrast in anaphora possibilities between (3) and (5) is also predicted correctly by DRT.

(3)    A dog came in. It is pretty.          (anaphora possible)
(5)    Every dog came in. It is pretty.       (anaphora impossible)

The felicitous anaphora in (3) is represented as in (20) above. The DRS for (5) is in (42) below. In (42), the "old" variable x is not accessible to the pronoun. So the pronoun cannot be processed.

(42)
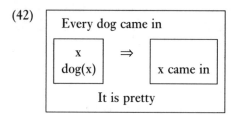

In terms of scope, the x in the antecedent DRS is bound by the universal quantification over the entire complex condition, but the pronoun, back in the matrix DRS, is not under the scope of this quantification. Similarly, DRT correctly predicts that the pronoun in (43) below cannot refer to *a donkey*. (Try to add the second sentence to the matrix DRS in (25) above.)

(43)   Every man owns a donkey. It is grazing.       (anaphora impossible)

## 2.1.4   Heim's FCS

Heim's metaphor is that the body of information gathered in a discourse is much like a collection of file cards. For each indefinite NP, the hearers start a new card; for each

---

[9]   This may not be obvious from the discussion in Kamp 1981, but see the related discussion in Chierchia and Ro010 1984. The same generalization about anaphora and scope is stated clearly by Heim and captured in her system (cf. for example Heim 1983a, p. 181).

definite NP, the hearers update existing cards. Informally, Heim would describe the file assembled in response to the two-sentence discourse in (44) more or less as in (45).

(44)  a.    A dog walked in.
      b.    It saw a cat.

(45)
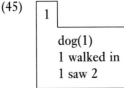
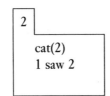

File (45) is said to be true iff the numbers 1,2 can be matched with individuals in the world/model that fit all the descriptions written on the file cards. This means that the card-numbers function as variables, and that the file is true iff there is an assignment function for these variables that verifies all the open formulas written on the file cards.

Heim 1983a states that for her present purposes, a file (as it is informally understood) may be described fully enough by specifying the set of variables (= card-numbers) used in it and the set of assignment functions that verify all the open formulas in it. Heim calls the set of variables in file F "the domain of F," written Dom(F), and she calls the set of assignments that verify everything in the file "the satisfaction set of F," written Sat(F). In her formal theory, then, Heim defines a file F as a set of variables (called Dom(F)) plus a set of assignment functions (called Sat(F)).

In the formal file (= variables + assignments) that corresponds to the informal file described in (45), the set of assignments consists of assignments that assign "truthful" values to variables 1 and 2. Technically, we can use total assignment functions (= assignments that assign values to all the (infinitely many) variables), as in e.g. Heim 1982, or we can use partial assignment functions, that assign values only to 1 and 2, as in e.g. Heim 1983a.[10] If we use total assignment functions, the formal file corresponding to (45) will be the pair consisting of Dom(45) and Sat(45), where

Dom(45) = {1,2}
Sat(45) = the set of total assignment functions g s.t.
          g(1) is a dog, g(2) is a cat, g(1) walked in, and g(1) saw g(2).

If we use partial assignment functions, a file can simply be defined as a set of assignments. The formal file corresponding to (45) would be Sat(45), where

Sat(45) = the set of assignment functions g whose domain is {1,2} s.t.
          g(1) is a dog, g(2) is a cat, g(1) walked in, and g(1) saw g(2).

Dom(45) is recoverable from this set of functions: it is the set of variables to which these functions assign values.

Heim describes each assignment function as a sequence of numbered individuals. For example, the function

[10]   See Landman 1987 for comparison of various versions of the Kamp-Heim theory with total functions and with partial functions.

$$\begin{bmatrix} 1 \rightarrow \text{Blackie} \\ 2 \rightarrow \text{Kitty} \end{bmatrix}$$

is referred to as the sequence ⟨Blackie$_1$, Kitty$_2$⟩. I, however, will continue to talk about assignment functions rather than about sequences. In addition, I will use the standard variables $x_1$, $x_2$, $x_3$, ... etc. instead of 1,2,3 ... etc.

In Heim's framework, the formulas that get semantically interpreted are LFs (logical forms) of natural language sentences. Heim assumes that an LF representation is a syntactic tree in which anaphoric links are unambiguously indicated (by indexing) and scope relations are unambiguously indicated (each operator c-commands its scope). Heim 1983a gives the examples of LFs given in (46a), (47a) and (48a). Each LF represents a possible reading of the sentence in (b) to its right.[11]

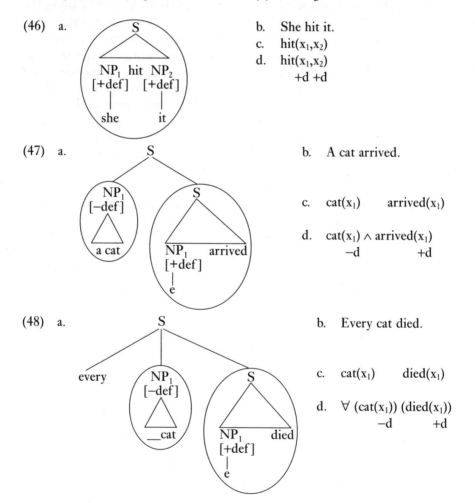

(46)  a.                           b.  She hit it.
                                    c.  hit($x_1$,$x_2$)
                                    d.  hit($x_1$,$x_2$)
                                           +d +d

(47)  a.                           b.  A cat arrived.

                                    c.  cat($x_1$)      arrived($x_1$)

                                    d.  cat($x_1$) ∧ arrived($x_1$)
                                            −d              +d

(48)  a.                           b.  Every cat died.

                                    c.  cat($x_1$)      died($x_1$)

                                    d.  ∀ (cat($x_1$)) (died($x_1$))
                                            −d              +d

As illustrated by the above LFs, Heim 1983a has chosen to make the following assumptions about LF:

---

[11]   The circles are added by me, and are not part of the LF representation.

(i)    Pronouns are merely indexed;

(ii)   All other NPs are lifted out of their sentence and adjoined to S, leaving behind a coindexed trace;

(iii)  Quantificational determiners such as *every* – but **not** indefinite and definite articles – are lifted out of their NP, leaving behind a blank, and adjoined as sister to their NP.

(iv)  All the NPs in LF are marked as either definite or indefinite: definite descriptions, pronouns and traces are [+def], while full indefinite NPs and NPs that have lost their determiner are [−def].

In addition, Heim regards the indexed NPs in the LF representations as variables. More precisely: an indexed NP in argument position (this will always be either a pronoun or a trace) is nothing more than a variable; an indexed NP in non-argument position (such an NP will always contain a predicate) is a complete open atomic formula, where the index is a variable which serves as the argument of the NP-internal predicate. Thus, each of the circled (sub-) trees in (46)–(48) above is an open atomic formula – these (sub-) trees are practically the same as the predicate calculus formulas given in (c) to their right.

Sister atomic formulas with no quantifier as their sister will be interpreted as a conjunction. Therefore, I will talk about an LF such as (47a) as if it were a formula of the form p ∧ q, like the formula in (47d). Two sister atomic formulas preceded by a sister quantifier will be interpreted as a tripartite quantificational structure (quantifier + restriction + nuclear scope). Therefore, I will talk about an LF such as (48a) as if it were a formula of the form ∀(p)(q), like the formula in (48d). In short, the formulas in (d) are convenient abbreviations of the LFs in (a).

In FCS, the basic semantic value of a formula (of an LF representation) is the role it would play in extending an existing body of information, seen as a file. When we process an LF of a sentence asserted as an independent statement in its own right, we update our existing file on account of that LF, and this results in a new file. (The new file represents all the information we had before plus the information conveyed by the processed LF.) Thus, the semantic value of a formula (of an LF representation) is a function from files to files. Such a function is called a **file change potential**. In her specification of file change potentials, Heim uses the following notation.

(49)    Given a file F and a formula (an LF representation) p,
           F + p designates the result of updating F on account of p.

For convenience, I will often use the expression "adding p to file F" to mean "updating file F on account of p." The propositions asserted in the discourse are "added to the file" one by one.

I use in this book a version of DRT with partial assignment functions. Let me use partial assignment functions for FCS as well.[12] This allows me to formally define a file as follows.

---

[12]   For comparison, I have included in 2.3.2 below a version with partial functions and a version with total functions.

(50)   A **file** is a set of assignment functions which all have the same domain.

Given a file F, I define Dom(F) as the domain of the functions in F. I will not use the notation Sat(F), because I have officially identified a file with its satisfaction set.

It is worth emphasizing, as Heim 1983a does repeatedly, that the formal notion of a file as a set of assignments does not cover all the aspects of the informal notion of a file as it is described by Heim (and others). The particular formal notion of a file as a set of assignments is used on the assumption that it is good enough for present purposes (viz. treating definites, indefinites and anaphora).

We may now define some file change potentials. It is assumed that what it takes for an assignment function to verify an atomic formula is defined in the standard way. The file change potential of an atomic formula is defined as follows (cf. Heim 1983a, rule (18), p. 177).

(51)   If p is an atomic formula, then
F + p = {g : the domain of g is the union of the domain of the functions in F with the set of variables that occur in p, and g is an extension of one of the functions in F, and g verifies p}

The clause in (51) tells us that when we add an atomic open formula p to an arbitrary file F, the resulting file, F + p, will be the set of assignment functions that extend the assignments in the old file so as to include any new variables that occur in p, and, in addition to verifying everything the assignments in F verified before, verify p as well. The file change potential of a conjunction is defined as follows (cf. Heim 1983a, rule (16), p. 177).

(52)   If p and q are formulas, then
F + p ∧ q = (F + p) + q

Truth is defined in FCS not for a formula, but rather for a file. The truth definition is given in (53) below (Heim 1983a, p. 171). Note that this definition induces existential quantification over the entire discourse, since it says that a file is true iff **there is** an assignment function in it.

(53)   A file F is **true** iff F ≠ Ø

Let us take an example. Suppose we start with a file that contains no information at all – a file without any file cards. The formal file corresponding to that, call it $F_0$, is the singleton set containing just the empty assignment function.[13] Now the sentence in (54) is asserted. As explained above, the LF of this sentence may be abbreviated as the open formula in (54′).

(54)    A cat arrived.
(54′)   $cat(x_1) \wedge arrived(x_1)$

---

[13]   Note that although $F_0$ is "empty of information," it is not, officially, an "empty file": it is not empty of assignment functions.

If we want to add (54′) to $F_0$, we must apply the file change potential of conjunctions, defined in (52) above. This tells us that we first have to compute $F_0 + cat(x_1)$. To do that, we use the clause for atomic formulas, in (51) above. We get the file in (55).

(55)   $F_0 + cat(x_1) = \{g : \text{the domain of } g \text{ is } \{x_1\}, \text{ and } g \text{ verifies } cat(x_1)\}$

Now clause (52) tell us to add to the file in (55) the formula arrived($x_1$). We compute this (following (51) again) and get the following new file.

(56)   $(F_0 + cat(x_1)) + arrived(x_1) = \{g : \text{the domain of } g \text{ is } \{x_1\}, \text{ and } g \text{ verifies } cat(x_1)$
                            and arrived($x_1$)$\}$

By definition, a file is true iff it is not empty. But this means that the file in (56) is true iff there is an individual in the world/model which is a cat and which arrived. Thus, having processed our sentence, we have ended up with a file corresponding to the information that there is a cat that arrived.

As illustrated by the example just given, the truth definition in (53) allows FCS to explain why indefinite NPs are often associated with existential statements, without analyzing them as quantificational. The indefinite NP is neither quantificational nor referential. It functions as a variable. This variable may get bound by the existential quantification over the file, yielding an existential statement.

Recall the idea that for each indefinite NP, the hearers start a new card, while for each definite NP, the hearers update existing cards. In accordance with this idea, Heim's theory ensures that indefinite NPs function as "new" variables, while definite NPs function as "old" variables. This is done by imposing the condition given in (57) (Heim 1983a, p. 175).

(57)   **The Novelty/Familiarity Condition:**
       Let F be a file, and let p be an atomic formula in the LF representation. The file-incrementation $F + p$ is defined only if for every $NP_i$ that p contains,
           if $NP_i$ is definite, then $x_i \in Dom(F)$, and
           if $NP_i$ is indefinite, then $x_i \notin Dom(F)$.
       Otherwise, $F + p$ is undefined.

To take an example again, consider the two-sentence discourse in (3).

(3)   A dog came in. It is pretty.

Suppose we start with $F_0$. Since $Dom(F_0)$ is empty, the indefinite NP *a dog* may carry any index whatsoever – the corresponding variable will invariably be "new" with respect to $F_0$. Let us imagine that its index is 1. In that case, the LF of the first sentence is the one abbreviated in (58).

(58)   $dog(x_1) \wedge came\text{-}in(x_1)$
           –d            +d

Adding the first sentence to $F_0$, we get the following.

(59)   $F_0 + (58) = \{g :$ the domain of $g$ is $\{x_1\}$, and $g$ verifies $dog(x_1)$ and $came\text{-}in(x_1)\}$

Now we need to add the second sentence to the file in (59). If we imagine that the definite NP *it* carries the index 2, for example, we won't be able to do that. The LF of the second sentence would be the one abbreviated in (60), but such an LF cannot be added to file (59), because $x_2 \notin Dom(59)$. The Novelty/Familiarity Condition determines that the file-incrementation $(59) + (60)$ is undefined.

(60)   $pretty(x_2)$
        $+d$

We have no other choice but to imagine that the definite NP *it* carries the index 1. Then the LF of the second sentence is as in (61), and the Novelty/Familiarity Condition allows us to add it to file (59). The result is as in (62).

(61)   $pretty(x_1)$
        $+d$

(62)   $(59) + (61) = \{g :$ the domain of $g$ is $\{x_1\}$, and $g$ verifies $dog(x_1)$ and $came\text{-}in(x_1)$
        and $pretty(x_1)\}$

The file in (62) is true iff there is an individual in the world/model which is a dog and came in and is pretty. Thus, the pronoun *it* has been interpreted as anaphoric to *a dog*.
   Following is the file change potential of a negative formula.

(63)   If $p$ is a formula, then
        $F + \neg p = \{g \in F :$ it is not the case that there is a $g'$ which extends $g$ s.t. $g' \in$
        $F + p\}$

Let us now process the discourse in (64), represented as in (65).

(64)   A dog came in. It doesn't have a bone.
(65)   a.   $dog(x_1) \wedge came\text{-}in(x_1)$      b.   $\neg (bone(x_2) \wedge x_1 \text{ has } x_2)$
            $-d$          $+d$                              $-d$  $+d$      $+d$

We have already seen that if we add (65a) to $F_0$, we get the file in (59) above. Adding to that (65b), we get the following.

(66)   $(59) + (65b) = \{g :$ the domain of $g$ is $\{x_1\}$, and $g$ verifies $dog(x_1)$ and $came\text{-}in(x_1)$,
        and $g$ cannot be extended to a $g'$ s.t. $g' \in (59) + bone(x_2) \wedge x_1$
        had $x_2\}$

But what is the file $(59) + bone(x_2) \wedge x_1$ had $x_2$? It is as follows.

(67)   $(59) + bone(x_2) \wedge x_1$ had $x_2 = \{g :$ the domain of $g$ is $\{x_1, x_2\}$, and $g$ verifies $dog(x_1)$
        and $came\text{-}in(x_1)$ and $bone(x_2) \wedge x_1$ had $x_2\}$

So the file in (66) above is the same as the file in (68) below.

(68)   (59) + (65b) = {g : the domain of g is {$x_1$}, and g verifies dog($x_1$) and came-in($x_1$), and g cannot be extended to a g′ s.t. the domain of g′ is {$x_1,x_2$}, and g′ also verifies bone($x_2$) ∧ $x_1$ had $x_2$}

We have ended up with a file representing the information that there is in the model a dog that came in for which it is impossible to find a bone that it has.

Let us move on to quantification. As noted in 2.1.2 above, FCS adopts unselective restricted quantification. The file change potential of quantified formulas is defined as in (69).

(69)   If p and q are formulas, then
F + ∀(p)(q) = {g ∈ F : for every g′ which extends g s.t. g′ ∈ F + p, there is a g″ which extends g′ s.t. g″ ∈ (F + p) + q}

For example, consider sentence (23), with the LF abbreviated in (23′).

(23)   Every man owns a donkey.
(23′)   ∀ (man($x_1$)) (donkey($x_2$) ∧ owns($x_1,x_2$))
              −d              −d           +d +d

Suppose we start with $F_0$, and then (23) is asserted. We apply the clause in (69), and get the file in (70).

(70)   $F_0$ + (23′) = {g ∈ $F_0$ : for every g′ which extends g s.t. g′ ∈ $F_0$ + man($x_1$), there is a g″ which extends g′ s.t. g″ ∈ ($F_0$ + man($x_1$)) + donkey($x_2$) ∧ owns($x_1,x_2$)}

To see what this boils down to, we need to compute $F_0$ + man($x_1$), as well as ($F_0$ + man($x_1$)) + donkey($x_2$) ∧ owns($x_1,x_2$). The results of these computations are given in (71) and (72).

(71)   $F_0$ + man($x_1$) = {g : the domain of g is {$x_1$} and g verifies man($x_1$)}
(72)   (71) + donkey($x_2$) ∧ owns($x_1,x_2$) = {g : the domain of g is {$x_1,x_2$} and g verifies man($x_1$), donkey($x_2$) and owns($x_1,x_2$)}

For convenience, we may now rewrite (70) as in (73).

(73)   $F_0$ + (23′) = {g ∧ $F_0$ : for every g′ which extends g s.t. g′ ∈ (71), there is a g″ which extends g′ s.t. g″ ∈ (72)}

What information does our new file (73) = (70) represent? Since the only g in $F_0$ is the empty assignment function, file (73) is true iff it contains that function. But that means that file (73) is true iff for every g s.t. g ∈ (71), there is a g′ which extends g s.t. g′ ∈ (72). Therefore, file (73) is true iff every g with domain {$x_1$} that verifies man($x_1$) can be extended to a g′ with domain {$x_1,x_2$} that verifies man($x_1$), donkey($x_2$) and owns($x_1,x_2$). So we have ended up with a file that represents the information that for every man in the world/model, it is possible to find a donkey that that man owns.

And what if we add a quantified formula to a file that already contains some information? Suppose we want to process the two-sentence discourse in (74).

(74)    a.    A dog came in.    b.    Every dog has a bone.

If we were to process the representation in (75), we would fail to quantify over all men. That is because the existential quantification over the entire discourse which is induced by the truth definition would bind all the occurrences of $x_1$. (I leave it to the reader to verify that; cf. discussion of the same example in 2.1.3 above, DRS (28).)

(75)    a.    $dog(x_1) \wedge came\text{-}in(x_1)$    b.    $\forall (dog(x_1))(bone(x_2) \wedge has(x_1,x_2))$
                    $-d$                $+d$                        $-d$          $-d$          $+d +d$

But the Novelty/Familiarity Condition does not allow us to use the representation in (75), because the NP [__ dog]$_1$ in the LF of (74b), having lost its determiner, is [–def], and cannot be added to a file whose domain already contains the variable $x_1$. Thus, the assumption that that NP in LF which represents the restriction is indefinite plus the Novelty/Familiarity Condition would force us to choose a representation like the one in (76), in which the variable in the restriction is "new."

(76)    a.    $dog(x_1) \wedge came\text{-}in(x_1)$    b.    $\forall (dog(x_3))(bone(x_2) \wedge has(x_3,x_2))$
                    $-d$                $+d$                        $-d$          $-d$          $+d +d$

Processing (76) yields the desired interpretation. Let us add (76) to $F_0$. First, we add (76a) to $F_0$, getting the file in (77).

(77)    $F_0 + (76a) = \{g :$ the domain of g is $\{x_1\}$, and g verifies $dog(x_1)$ and $came\text{-}in(x_1)\}$

Then, we add (76b) to file (77). This yields the file in (78), or, equivalently, the file in (79).

(78)    $(77) + (76b) = \{g \in (77) :$ for every g′ which extends g s.t. the domain of g′ is $\{x_1,x_3\}$ and g′ also verifies $dog(x_3)$, there is a g″ which extends g′ s.t. the domain of g″ is $\{x_1,x_2,x_3\}$ and g″ also verifies $bone(x_2)$ and $owns(x_3,x_2)\}$

(79)    $(77) + (76b) = \{g :$ the domain of g is $\{x_1\}$, and g verifies $dog(x_1)$ and $came\text{-}in(x_1)$, and every g′ with domain $\{x_1,x_3\}$ that extends g and verifies $dog(x_3)$ can be extended to a g″ with domain $\{x_1,x_2,x_3\}$ which verifies $bone(x_2)$ and $owns(x_3,x_2)\}$

Given the truth definition, the resulting file represents the information that there is in the world/model a dog that came in and for every dog in the world/model, it is possible to find a bone that it has.

Following Lewis 1975, bare conditionals are taken to implicitly contain the adverb of quantification "always." Therefore, the file change potential of a conditional is also defined as in (69) above, with the if-clause serving as the restriction and the main clause serving as the nuclear scope:

(80)    If p and q are formulas, then $F + p \rightarrow q$ is also as in (69).

The donkey sentence in (24) may be represented as in (24′). If we add (24′) to $F_0$, we get the file in (81).

(24)    If a man is rich he owns a donkey.
(24′)   $(man(x_1) \wedge rich(x_1)) \rightarrow (donkey(x_2) \wedge owns(x_1,x_2))$
(81)    $F_0 + (24′) = \{g \in F_0 :$ for every $g'$ which extends $g$ s.t. $g' \in F_0 + man(x_1) \wedge$ rich$(x_1)$, there is a $g''$ which extends $g'$ s.t. $g'' \in (F_0 + man(x_1) \wedge$ rich$(x_1)) + donkey(x_2) \wedge owns(x_1,x_2)\}$

File (81) is true iff every g with domain $\{x_1\}$ that verifies man$(x_1)$ and rich$(x_1)$ can be extended to a $g'$ with domain $\{x_1,x_2\}$ that also verifies donkey$(x_2)$ and owns$(x_1,x_2)$. So we have ended up with a file that represents the information that for every rich man in the world/model, it is possible to find a donkey that that man owns.

We see then that in FCS, donkey sentences no longer present a problem. The indefinite NP in the if-clause has no quantificational force of its own; it is treated as a variable (+description), as usual. This variable gets bound by the universal quantification which clause (80) associates with the conditional.

Finally, let me discuss the way in which FCS predicts anaphora possibilities in discourse. When an anaphoric NP bears an index corresponding to an "old" variable, let us call the "old" occurrences of that variable "the antecedent variable" or "the antecedent discourse referent." FCS adopts the traditional logician's analysis of anaphora as variable-binding, not only for sentence-internal anaphora, but also for discourse anaphora. Therefore, the following generalization holds.[14]

(41)    **Generalization about anaphora and scope:**
        Anaphora is possible only when the anaphoric element is under the scope of the quantifier that binds the antecedent variable.

Hence, predictions about anaphora possibilities follow directly from the quantification and scope relations determined by the definitions of truth and file change potentials.

We have already seen three examples of felicitous anaphora – (3), (64) and (24). These examples are repeated below, each followed by its abbreviated LF representation.

(3)     A dog came in. It is pretty.
        LF:   a.   $dog(x_1) \wedge came\text{-}in(x_1)$       b.   $pretty(x_1)$
(64)    A dog came in. It doesn't have a bone.
        LF:   a.   $dog(x_1) \wedge came\text{-}in(x_1)$       b.   $\neg (bone(x_2) \wedge x_1$ has $x_2 )$
(24)    If a man is rich he owns a donkey.
        LF:   $(man(x_1) \wedge rich(x_1)) \rightarrow (donkey(x_2) \wedge owns(x_1,x_2))$

In all three examples, we get an anaphoric interpretation of the pronoun because the occurrence of $x_1$ that corresponds to the pronoun falls under the scope of the quantifier that binds the antecedent occurrences of $x_1$. In the first two examples, all

---

[14]    cf. Heim 1983a, p. 181.

occurrences of $x_1$ are bound by the existential quantification over the entire file – the quantification induced by the truth definition. In the third example, all occurrences of $x_1$ are bound by the universal quantification that clause (80) associates with the conditional.

In contrast, it is not possible to get an anaphoric interpretation of the following examples. (Again, each example is followed by a corresponding abbreviated LF representation.)

(82)  It is not the case that a dog came in. It is pretty.      (anaphora impossible)
      LF:   a.   $\neg\,(dog(x_1) \wedge came\text{-}in(x_1))$      b.   $pretty(x_1)$
                      $-d$                $+d$                           $+d$

(5)   Every dog came in. It is pretty.      (anaphora impossible)
      LF:   a.   $\forall\,(dog(x_1))\,(came\text{-}in(x_1))$      b.   $pretty(x_1)$
                    $-d$              $+d$                              $+d$

(43)  Every man owns a donkey. It is grazing.      (anaphora impossible)
      LF:   a.   $\forall\,(man(x_8))\,(donkey(x_1) \wedge owns(x_8,x_1))$      b.   $pretty(x_1)$
                    $-d$                $-d$              $+d$ $+d$                      $+d$

An anaphoric interpretation is impossible in these examples because the occurrence of $x_1$ that corresponds to the pronoun does not fall under the scope of the quantifier that binds the antecedent occurrences of $x_1$. Consider the first example. Clause (63), which defines the file change potential of a negative formula, induces existential quantification (as in "it is not the case that **there is** a dog that came in"). The occurrences of $x_1$ in (a) are bound by that existential quantification. But the occurrence of $x_1$ in (b) is not under the scope of that quantification. In the last two examples, the universal quantifier takes scope over the restriction and nuclear scope in (a), as determined by clause (69). The occurrences of $x_1$ in (a) are bound by the universal quantifier. But the occurrence of $x_1$ in (b) is not under the scope of that quantifier.

Technically, what happens with such examples is that the Novelty/Familiarity Condition determines that they cannot be fully processed.

Consider, for instance, the first example, (82), and try to add its corresponding LF to an arbitrary file F. We start by adding to file F the formula in (a):

(83)   $F + \neg\,(dog(x_1) \wedge came\text{-}in(x_1))$
              $-d$                $+d$
       $= \{g \in F : g \text{ cannot be extended to a } g' \text{ s.t. } g' \in F + [dog(x_1) \wedge came\text{-}in(x_1)]\}$
       iff $x_1 \notin Dom(F)$;
       undefined otherwise.

Assuming that $x_1 \notin Dom(F)$, we may proceed, but we immediately get stuck: it is now impossible to add to file (83) the formula in (b). If $x_1 \notin Dom(F)$, then $x_1 \notin Dom(83)$. Therefore, the Novelty/Familiarity Condition determines that $(83) + pretty(x_1)$ is undefined. We see then that Heim's theory does not allow a definite NP to be processed at all unless it falls under the scope of a quantifier that binds a potential antecedent variable.[15]

---

[15]   Note that if the theory did allow us to compute $(83) + pretty(x_1)$ – suppose we waived the "familiarity" requirement on the pronoun – an anaphoric interpretation of (82) would still be impossible. To compute (83), we would at any rate have to assume that $x_1 \notin Dom(F)$. So, given that

## 2.2 DRT and FCS

The Kamp–Heim theory is concerned with anaphora in discourse. In particular, it provides an analysis of examples such as the following.

(3)   A dog came in. It is pretty.       (anaphora possible)
(5)   Every dog came in. It is pretty.       (anaphora impossible)
(6)   If a man meets a donkey, he beats it.
(7)   Every man who owns a donkey beats it.

As you know, the usual logician's treatment of anaphora is via variable binding: anaphora is treated as co-variation of occurrences of the same variable. For example, one interpretation of (84) is as in (84′).

(84)    Every candidate thinks she will win.
(84′)   $\forall x[\text{candidate}(x) \rightarrow x \text{ thinks } x \text{ will win}]$

All the occurrences of x here are in the scope of the quantifier, and they are all bound by it. So they are in "co-variation" – all three always have the same value. That is the essence of anaphora. Anaphora is not possible in (5), because (5) would be interpreted as something like (5′a), or, equivalently, (5′b).

(5′)   a.   $\forall z[\text{dog}(z) \rightarrow z \text{ came in}] \wedge x \text{ is pretty}$
       b.   $\forall x[\text{dog}(x) \rightarrow x \text{ came in}] \wedge x \text{ is pretty}$

Translating the pronoun *it* in (5′b) as yet another occurrence of x does not yield an anaphoric (rather than deictic) interpretation of this pronoun, because the last occurrence of x is not in the scope of the quantifier, and does not co-vary with the other occurrences of x.

Keep in mind the reason why in predicate logic occurrences of the same variable bound by the same quantifier are in co-variation: that is of course because of the way the semantic rules for quantified formulas work. Recall how these rules are stated in terms of assignment functions that verify the scope of the quantifier. For example, (84′) is true relative to a (total) assignment g iff for all assignments g′ s.t. g′ agrees with g on all the values except that it may assign a different value to x, g′ verifies the scope. So the three occurrences of x are all assigned a value by the same assignment function, g′.

The Kamp–Heim theory retains the "co-variation" treatment of anaphora. In fact, Kamp and Heim argue (Heim 1982 does so very thoroughly) that discourse anaphora too should be treated as co-variation. Which means that (3) will basically mean something like (3′) and (6) will basically mean something like (6\*\*).

Dom(83) = Dom(F), the assignments in (83) would not assign a value to $x_1$. Hence the assignments in (83) + pretty($x_1$), although they would have to agree with those in (83) on the values of all the variables in Dom(83), would be entirely free in their choice of value for $x_1$ in pretty($x_1$). But that means that this occurrence of $x_1$ would not co-vary with any previous occurrence of $x_1$. So the pronoun would not be interpreted as anaphoric.

(3')    $\exists x[dog(x) \wedge x$ came in $\wedge$ x is pretty]
(6**)   $\forall x \forall y$ [ (man(x) $\wedge$ donkey(y) $\wedge$ x meets y) $\rightarrow$ x beats y]

So, discourse anaphora, just like syntactic anaphora, is treated using value assignments. In Kamp's DRT the assignments used are called "embedding functions," in Heim's theory the assignments used are called "sequences."

Now, Kamp and Heim sought to include in their theory:

(i)    a general treatment of definite NPs,[16]
(ii)   a general treatment of indefinite NPs, and
(iii)  a principled way of predicting anaphora possibilities in discourse.

Regarding (ii), the treatment of indefinites should explain among other things why they seem to yield existential quantification in some examples (like (3) above) and universal quantification in other examples (like (6) above). As for (iii), if the theory is to predict when anaphora is possible and when not (e.g. to account for the contrast between (3) and (5)), then what the theory needs to do – given that anaphora is treated as co-variation – is to determine where there are quantifiers in discourse and how far their scope extends.

A major ingredient of the Kamp–Heim theory is the non-quantificational treatment of definite and indefinite NPs. An indefinite like *a dog* is basically treated as a variable, with descriptions predicated of it:

> *a dog*      is basically treated as:    $dog(x)$
> *A dog came in*   is basically treated as:    $dog(x) \wedge x$ came in.

The indefinite NP has no quantificational force of its own, and it gets bound by what-ever quantifier is around to bind it. That is why it seems to be associated with different quantificational forces in different examples. An anaphoric definite NP, such as the pronoun in (3), is also treated as a variable. It differs from an indefinite NP in that it is treated as an "old" variable. That is what allows it to be anaphoric: it gets translated as an occurrence of the same variable that translates its antecedent NP.

Further, in order to be anaphoric, the definite NP must be translated as a variable-occurrence which **co-varies** with the variable-occurrences that correspond to its antecedent NP. This means that pronoun and antecedent variable-occurrences must be in the scope of, and bound by, the same quantifier. But, what is it that provides a quantifier to bind the antecedent and pronoun in an example such as (3)? This leads us to another major ingredient of the Kamp–Heim theory: there is an existential quantifier which has scope over the whole discourse. If we have a discourse which contains just the following,

   $dog(x) \wedge x$ came in $\wedge$ x is pretty

---

[16]   Kamp 1981 only treats pronouns, but this treatment can be extended to all definites, as in Heim 1982.

then the existential quantifier over the whole discourse binds all the occurrences of x and the discourse as a whole means what we had in (3′) above.

In the Kamp–Heim theory, we have a **dynamic** sort of semantics, in this sense: the basic semantic value of a bit of discourse is not its truth conditional content, but rather the role it would play in extending an existing body of information. This dynamic nature of the theory is crucial in the treatment of indefinites, definites and anaphora sketched above.

Why is that? First of all, we saw that we need a representation of "the discourse as a whole," which is the scope of the existential quantifier mentioned above. But "the discourse as a whole" is not something with a fixed end, but rather something which evolves and expands as the conversation goes on. Secondly, a sentence like *a dog came in* is treated as an open formula, which is not something that will generally be true or false on its own. It is only when this is asserted and gets added to the discourse that it falls within the scope of the existential quantifier over the whole discourse. Only then do we get the effect of an existential statement ("there is a dog that came in"), a statement that will have a truth value. Likewise, *it lay down* doesn't have a truth value on its own. Further, the pronoun *it* has to function as an occurrence of a variable which is "old," which is already there. The sentence *it lay down* only makes sense as an addition to a discourse which contains a variable that can serve as the antecedent.

Let us now recall how a simple discourse is treated in Kamp's DRT and in Heim's FCS, and see how the two theories parallel each other.

(44)  a.  A dog walked in.
  b.  It saw a cat.

In DRT, a discourse containing just the utterances in (44) is represented by the following DRS.

DRS (44):

> x    y
> dog(x)
> x walked in
> cat(y)
> x saw y

DRSs are formulas of a formal logical language, which has a model-theoretic semantics. It is the truth definition for this formal language that induces the existential quantification over the whole discourse. For our specific example (44):

**Truth:**  DRS (44) is true iff **there is** an embedding function which assigns x,y individuals that satisfy the conditions in the DRS.
 e.g. something like this function  $\begin{bmatrix} x \to \text{Blackie} \\ y \to \text{Kitty} \end{bmatrix}$

In FCS: Informally, Heim would describe the file assembled in response to (44) more or less as follows.

File (44):

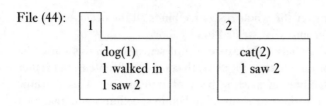

Heim's truth definition for a file says that a file F is true iff its satisfaction set is non-empty:

F is true iff Sat(F) ≠ Ø

That is, iff there is a sequence that satisfies it. So for our example:

> **Truth:** File (44) is true iff **there is** a sequence of individuals corresponding to 1,2 that satisfies the conditions in the cards.
> e.g. something like this sequence ⟨Blackie$_1$, Kitty$_2$⟩
> or, equivalently, this function $\begin{bmatrix} 1 \rightarrow \text{Blackie} \\ 2 \rightarrow \text{Kitty} \end{bmatrix}$

Clearly, so far everything is exactly the same in the two theories.

Note that I assume here that assignment functions are partial. Indeed, I will assume a version of DRT and of FCS with partial assignment functions throughout the following chapters.

Now let us go on to how a particular bit of discourse extends the information already in the discourse.

**"Discourse expansion" in DRT**: Sentence (44b) does not have truth conditions of its own – DRT only specifies what happens when it is added to a DRS. Suppose we already have this DRS:

DRS (44a):

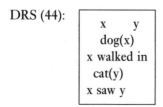

How do we add (44b) to it? The "construction rules" that map English sentences onto their representations in the DRS tell us what to do: The pronoun is a definite NP, so it translates into a variable already in the DRS, viz. x. *A cat* is indefinite, so it translates into a new variable, say y, with the descriptive content predicated of it: cat(y). This gives us DRS (44).

DRS (44):

$$\boxed{\begin{array}{c} x \quad y \\ \text{dog(x)} \\ \text{x walked in} \\ \text{cat(y)} \\ \text{x saw y} \end{array}}$$

I have just described what happens when (44b) is added to a discourse in **syntactic** terms – in terms of the form of the resulting DRS. But we can also talk about the change that occurs here in **semantic** terms. The resulting DRS differs from the old DRS in its truth conditions. It is verified by a different set of embedding functions: DRS (44) is not verified by the set of embeddings with domain $\{x\}$ that verify the conditions dog(x) and x walked in, but rather by the set of embeddings with domain $\{x,y\}$ that verify the above conditions as well as the conditions cat(y) and x saw y. Thus, the semantic effect of adding a bit of discourse into the DRS is to change the set of embedding functions that verify the DRS.

**"Discourse expansion" in FCS**: Had Heim wanted to, she could have given rules that map English onto pictures such as File (44) above, and treated these pictures as formulas of a formal logical language, like Kamp's DRSs. But she hasn't done that. Unlike Kamp, Heim does not use a syntactic[17] level of representation in which there is a representation of "the whole discourse." Instead, in her formal theory, she only has a semantic notion of a file: a file is defined in model-theoretic terms.

Heim 1983a states that for her present purposes it is good enough to regard a file as

|       | its domain            | Dom(F) – i.e. all the card numbers          |
|-------|-----------------------|---------------------------------------------|
| plus  | its satisfaction set   | Sat(F) – the set of sequences that satisfy F. |

That is, in Heim's theory, a file is formally a bunch of variables plus a bunch of value assignments for these variables. Note that when the assignment functions used are partial, there is no need to specify Dom(F) separately – the file can be identified with its satisfaction set. So the use of partial assignments allows us to formally define a file as follows.

(85)   A **file** is a set of assignment functions which all have the same domain.

We may define Dom(F) as the domain of the functions in F.

I have been talking about what happens when (44b) is added to a discourse already containing (44a). We saw that DRT specifies in syntactic terms how to add (44b) to the discourse representation, and from that automatically follows the semantic effect – the change that occurs in the set of verifying embeddings. Now, what Heim does instead is directly specify for each bit of discourse its semantic effect – she directly specifies for each bit of discourse how adding it to a file would change the set of verifying value assignments. In her theory, the semantic value of a bit of discourse is a function from sets of value assignments to sets of value assignments (= from files to files). Such a function is called a **file change potential**.

We see then that while DRT has an intermediate syntactic discourse representation and FCS doesn't, in both these theories what a bit of discourse does, semantically, is change the set of verifying assignments.[18]

---

[17]   By "syntactic" I do **not** mean here "belonging to the syntax of a natural language." I mean "syntactic" in the sense of being a formula rather than a model-theoretic entity.

[18]   For some discussion concerning the **difference** between representing files syntactically (Kamp) and representing them only semantically (Heim), see section 4.3 below.

Now let me briefly go over the formal treatment of definite and indefinite NPs and the file change potential of atomic formulas.

In DRT, definite and indefinite NPs are treated via the "construction rules" that map natural language sentences onto their representations in the DRS. The relevant rules say, roughly, the following.

indefinite NP:                                                              e.g. *a dog* in *A dog walked in.*
    Introduce a new variable (and put it into
    the "universe" = the top line of the DRS);                              x
    predicate of it the descriptive content of the NP;                    dog(x)
    predicate of it the rest of the sentence.                        x walked in

definite NP:                                                               e.g. *it* in *It saw a cat.*
    Pick an old variable;
    predicate of it the descriptive content of the NP (if any);
    predicate of it the rest of the sentence.                        x saw a cat

In FCS, file change potentials are assigned to LFs. Heim assumes that each full (predicate-containing) definite/indefinite NP is a separate atomic formula. For example, the NP *a dog* is represented in LF by the following little tree, which is interpreted just like the open formula dog(x).

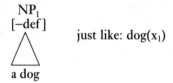

$$\begin{array}{l} \text{NP}_1 \\ [-\text{def}] \end{array} \qquad \text{just like: dog}(x_1)$$

a dog

In Heim's theory, each full definite/indefinite NP has its own file change potential. What is this file change potential? When the NP *a dog* is added to a file (= a set of assignments), how does this change the file? Well, exactly in the same way that adding    x

        dog(x)

to a DRS changes the set of verifying embeddings. The embeddings verifying the DRS we already had – or the assignments in the old file – had to satisfy certain conditions. The embeddings verifying the DRS we have after adding the new formula – or the assignments in the new file – will have to satisfy all the conditions that they had to satisfy before, plus they will have to assign a value to the variable $x$ (= $x_1$), and this value will have to be a dog.

The general rule for how an atomic formula changes the file (Heim 1983a, rule (18), p. 177) says, basically, the following.

(86)    Take an atomic open formula p. When you add it to an arbitrary file F, the resulting file, F + p, will be the set of assignments that extend the assignments in the old file so as to include any new variables that occur in p, and, in addition to verifying everything the sequences in Sat(F) verified before, verify p as well.

Comparing FCS with DRT, we see that LF plays in FCS some of the role that the DRSs play in DRT. LF is where the conditions which are to be satisfied (by the relevant value assignments) are written out as formulas. The difference is that while Kamp's DRSs indicate where these formulas occur within a larger discourse, Heim's LFs do not.

In FCS, the requirement that an indefinite NP must function as a new variable and a definite NP must function as an old one is imposed via the following condition.

(57)   **The Novelty/Familiarity Condition**
Let F be a file, and let p be an atomic formula in the LF representation. The file-incrementation F + p is defined only if for every $NP_i$ that p contains,
if $NP_i$ is definite, then $x_i \in Dom(F)$, and
if $NP_i$ is indefinite, then $x_i \notin Dom(F)$.
Otherwise, F + p is undefined.

For example, the following LF representation, which is an atomic formula, can be added to a file F only if Dom(F) already contains the variables $x_1$ and $x_2$.

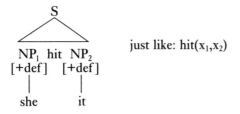

just like: $hit(x_1,x_2)$

And the following NP, which is also an atomic formula, can be added to a file F only if Dom(F) does not contain the variable $x_1$.

NP$_1$
[−def]      just like: $dog(x_1)$

△

a dog

Of course when you hear the NP *a dog* you don't hear what index it has in LF. But in order to be able to add it to the file that you already have in your head, you simply must interpret it as having an index corresponding to a variable which does not yet occur in that file. And the assignments in the resulting file will assign a value to the new variable corresponding to this new index.

We see then that both in Kamp's system and in Heim's, when the NP *a dog* is added to a discourse, it invariably changes the set of value assignments verifying the discourse by extending the set of variables to which the verifying assignments assign values to include one new variable.

Now let us look at some file change potentials of complex formulas.

The file change potential of conjunctions is simply defined as in (87) below. You add the first conjunct to your file, and then to the resulting file you add the second conjunct.

(87)   $F + p \wedge q = (F + p) + q$

To look briefly at negation, take the discourse in (88). The DRS for it is DRS (88).

(88)   a.   I have a dog.
       b.   It didn't see a cat.

DRS (88):

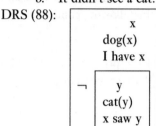

An embedding function g for DRS (88), one which assigns a value to x, verifies DRS (88) iff it verifies all the conditions in it, including the following complex condition.

$$\neg \begin{array}{|l|} \hline y \\ cat(y) \\ x\ saw\ y \\ \hline \end{array}$$

And here is the semantic clause for such a condition:

**Negation in DRT:**
An embedding function g verifies a condition of the form $\neg \Box$

iff it is not the case that there is an embedding function g′ extending g such that g′ verifies the conditions in the negated DRS.

So, an embedding g for DRS (88) verifies the complex condition in it iff that g **cannot** be extended to an assignment g′ which also assigns a value to y and which verifies the conditions cat(y) and x saw y. Hence, the way the negative sentence changes the set of assignment functions that verify the DRS is as follows. You take all the assignments verifying the DRS you had before, and you kick out all the ones that can be extended to an assignment that in addition to verifying the previous conditions will also verify the negated material.

Negative sentences change the file in FCS in exactly the same way, of course. Heim's rule for negative propositions is the following.

**Negation in FCS:**
$F + \neg p = \{g \in F : \text{it is not the case that there is a } g' \text{ extending g s.t. } g' \in F + p\}$

Those gs from the old file that do have such an extension g′ are kicked out, and the new file does not contain them.

Note that the semantic clause for negation induces an existential quantifier, whose scope includes just the negated material ("it is not the case that **there is** a cat that x saw") – this will be relevant later.

Finally, let us look at the file change potentials of quantified sentences. Natural language quantification is treated in the Kamp–Heim theory as unselective, restricted quantification.[19] Take for example the discourse in (89), represented by DRS (89). (For convenience, I marked the three DRSs as $K_0$, $K_1$ and $K_2$.)

(89)  a.  A dog walked in.
      b.  Every man gave it a bone.

DRS (89):

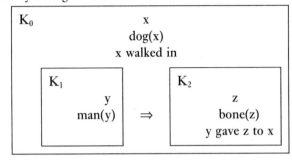

An embedding function g verifies DRS $K_0$ iff it verifies the three conditions in it, including the complex condition $K_1 \Rightarrow K_2$. This complex condition represents a tripartite quantificational structure, which includes an unselective universal quantifier (marked $\Rightarrow$), a restriction (DRS $K_1$) and a nuclear scope (DRS $K_2$). And here is what it takes to verify $K_1 \Rightarrow K_2$.

**Quantification in DRT:**

g verifies $K_1 \Rightarrow K_2$ iff
for every g′ for $K_1$ which extends g and verifies the conditions in $K_1$,
there is a g″ for $K_2$ which extends g′ and verifies the conditions $K_2$.

I leave it to the reader to apply this clause to DRS (89) and to verify that it yields the correct truth conditions for (89).

A few things to note are the following.

First, the clause for quantification introduces two quantifiers: a universal quantifier whose scope includes the restriction and nuclear scope together (in our example, $K_1$ and $K_2$), and an existential quantifier whose scope includes just the nuclear scope (here, DRS $K_2$). ("For **every** man, **there is** a bone that he gave to x.")

Secondly, to get the right results, the variables introduced in the restriction must be new. So, the Kamp–Heim theory stipulates that these variables be new.[20] In our example, the variable introduced in $K_1$ (triggered by the NP *every man*) is not allowed to be x – it must be a variable which does not yet occur in the DRS.

---

[19]  This includes quantification contributed by quantificational determiners such as *every* and *most* or by a (possibly implicit) adverb of quantification.
[20]  For more details, see section 2.1 above.

Thirdly, you may want to consider the way in which the set of verifying embeddings changes when a quantified statement is added to the DRS. We start with $K_0$ looking like this.

$$\boxed{\begin{array}{l} K_0 \qquad\qquad\quad x \\[4pt] \qquad\quad dog(x) \\ \qquad\quad x\text{ walked in} \end{array}}$$

When we add the complex condition $K_1 \Rightarrow K_2$, we take the set of embeddings which verified this initial DRS, and shrink it: we keep in it only the embeddings g of which every extension $g'$ which verifies $K_1$ can be further extended to a $g''$ which verifies $K_2$, and kick out all the other embeddings.

In FCS, quantification works in the same way – here is the clause.

**Quantification in FCS:**

$F + \forall(p)(q) = \{g \in F : \text{for every } g' \text{ which extends g s.t. } g' \in F + p, \text{ there is a } g''$
    which extends $g'$ s.t. $g'' \in (F + p) + q\}$

You may have spotted one superficial difference between DRS and FCS here. In DRT, the clause talks about an assignment verifying (the conditions in) DRS $K_1$ or DRS $K_2$. In FCS, the clause talks about an assignment being a member of $F + p$ or of $(F + p) + q$, which corresponds to talking about an assignment verifying $K_1$ as well as everything we had before in $K_0$, or $K_2$ as well as everything we had before in $K_0$ and $K_1$. But, of course, this superficial difference does not make any real difference, since each assignment for $K_1$ extends an assignment for $K_0$, and each assignment for $K_2$ extends an assignment for $K_1$.

Let us now turn to the way in which the theories of Kamp and Heim predict anaphora possibilities. Compare discourse (39) and discourse (40), and compare their respective DRSs.

(39)  I have a dog. It isn't smart. (anaphora possible)
(40)  I don't have a dog. It is smart. (anaphora impossible)

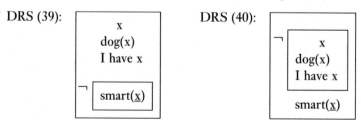

In both examples, the first sentence gives rise to a new variable – the variable x – corresponding to *a dog*. In both examples, the x introduced by the first sentence (that is, the occurrences of x which are not underlined) is intended to function as an antecedent for anaphora. So when we get to the second sentence, we translate the pronoun *it* as yet another occurrence of x (the underlined occurrence). This yields an anaphoric interpretation in the case of (39), but not in the case of (40).

In DRS (39), the antecedent occurrences of x are under the scope of the existential quantifier which has scope over the whole discourse. The new (underlined) occurrence of x is also under the scope of that quantifier, and therefore it will co-vary with the antecedent occurrences of x and anaphora is created. In DRS (40), the antecedent x is under the scope of the existential quantifier which the semantics associates with the negated DRS. The scope of this quantifier covers just the embedded DRS, and extends no further. The new, underlined, occurrence of x is not under the scope of that quantifier, and therefore it won't co-vary with the antecedent occurrences of x, and anaphora is not created.

This illustrates how once the theory has specified where quantifiers occur and how far their scope extends, it automatically predicts the anaphora possibilities, since it has determined where a pronoun would fall within the scope of the quantifier that binds its intended antecedent, and where it wouldn't.

Each of the two theories of Kamp and Heim has a technical way of ensuring that a pronoun will have to fall within the scope of the quantifier that binds its antecedent. In Kamp's theory, there is a syntactic "accessibility" constraint that prohibits translating the pronoun in (40) as x, because the antecedent x is not "accessible" from the position of the pronoun. (DRS (40) is not a legitimate DRS.)[21] And here is what happens in Heim's theory. Consider example (39). Once we have processed the first sentence, we have a file which includes only assignments that verify dog(x) and I have x – the file includes x in its domain. Now we try to add the second sentence. If the pronoun *it* carries the index 1 (corresponding to the variable $x_1 = x$), then the Novelty/Familiarity Condition allows this file incrementation to go through. Therefore, the anaphora is OK. Now consider example (40). The file that we get after processing the first sentence does **not** include assignments that verify dog(x) and I have x, and it does not have x in its domain.[22] But that means that when we hear the second sentence, we can't interpret the pronoun *it* as carrying the index 1: we want to add the second sentence to the file we've obtained so far, and the Novelty/Familiarity Condition determines that with *it* indexed 1 this file-incrementation would be undefined.

I would now like to consider the status of the body of information which is extended by the various bits of discourse, according to the Kamp–Heim theory. Recall the notion of **common ground**, in the sense of Stalnaker 1978 (see section 1.3 above): according to Stalnaker, the central concept needed to characterize the context of utterance is the **common ground**, which is a set of propositions – those propositions whose truth is taken for granted as part of the background of the conversation. Heim 1982 (ch. III, section 4.1) suggests that her files be identified with Stalnaker's common grounds.

On Heim's suggestion then, the file represents (certain limited but central aspects of) the context of utterance. This means that the information contained in a file need not arise only from linguistic text uttered earlier in the conversation. Rather, it may arise also from general world knowledge, from salient facts about the room around us, and so on and so forth. And so Heim's theory, in which each bit of discourse is added to a file, becomes a formal theory of how each bit of discourse adds informa-

---

[21] For details, see section 2.1 above.

[22] On the contrary, because of the negation, when we added the first sentence of (40) to our file, we kicked out all sequences that could be extended to have x in their domain and verify dog(x) and I have x.

tion to the common ground – of how each bit of discourse affects the context of utterance.

Given this, Heim and others often talk about Heim's files as "contexts" and about file change potentials as "context change potentials." I too will adopt this practice below. Keep in mind then that a formally-defined "context" need not represent all the aspects of our intuitive notion of a context of utterance.

Now recall Stalnaker 1978's notion of a **context set**. Since a common ground is a set of propositions, it can be identified with a set of possible worlds: the set of worlds in which the propositions of the common ground are true. Stalnaker called this set of worlds the **context set**.

We see then that we are already familiar with different formal entities that represent the common ground (= the body of information presupposed in a context). For the sake of brevity, I will refer to these as different formal notions of a "context." We have seen above two formal notions of a "context": one of them is a set of possible worlds (Stalnaker), and the other is a formal "file," viz. a set of variables plus a set of value assignments for these variables (Heim). (As explained above, if we use partial assignments, then we can define a formal "file" as a set of assignments.) Of course, other formal notions of a "context" can be defined in addition.

Suppose we want to have an **intensional** version of the Kamp–Heim theory. (For example, because we want to deal with modality.) What would that mean? That instead of just talking about a DRS being verified by an assignment function, we would talk about a DRS being verified by an assignment function in a particular possible world. So the truth definition of DRT would be as follows.

> A DRS is **true** in a world w iff there is an embedding function g that verifies it in w.

To put it differently, we could talk about a DRS as being verified by a pair $\langle w,g \rangle$ of a possible world w and a value assignment g. Therefore, in an intensional version of the theory, a file would be not a set of assignments, but rather **a set of world-assignment pairs**. This then is a third formal notion of a "context": a set of world-assignment pairs.

Definitions of "context change potentials" would of course depend on the relevant formal notion of a "context." In 2.3.2 below, I give several versions of the definitions of context and context change potentials. To take one example here, consider the context change potential of an atomic formula p. In each of (90)–(93) below, the definition in (b) fits the assumptions in (a).

(90)  a.  A context c is a set of worlds. p is a closed atomic formula.
      b.  $c + p = c \cap \{w : p$ is true in $w\}$
(91)  a.  A context is a pair $\langle \text{Dom}(c), \text{Sat}(c) \rangle$, where
              Dom(c) is a set of variables, and
              Sat(c) is a set of total assignment functions.
          p is an atomic formula.
      b.  The context $c + p$ is as follows:
          $\text{Dom}(c + p) = \text{Dom}(c) \cup \{x_n : x_n$ is a variable occurring in $p\}$
          $\text{Sat}(c + p) = \text{Sat}(c) \cap \{g : g$ verifies $p\}$

(92)　a.　A context is a set of partial assignments with the same domain.
　　　　　p is an atomic formula.
　　　b.　$c + p = \{g :$ the domain of g is the union of the domain of the functions in
　　　　　　　c with the set of variables that occur in p, and g is an extension of
　　　　　　　one of the functions in c, and g verifies $p\}$
(93)　a.　A context is a set of world-assignment pairs, where all the assignments have
　　　　　the same domain. p is an atomic formula.
　　　b.　$c + p = \{\langle w,g \rangle :$ the domain of g is the union of the domain of the functions
　　　　　　　in c with the set of variables that occur in p, and g is an extension of
　　　　　　　one of the functions in c, and g verifies p in $w\}$

(It may be useful to note the following. According to both (90) and (91) above, when we add an atomic formula to a (formal) "context," we perform intersection. Hence, according to both (90) and (91) above, when information is added, the (formal) "context" shrinks.)

We have seen then that there are various ways of representing the context of utterance or the common ground: a set of assignments, a set of worlds, a set of world-assignment pairs. These ways are all used side by side in the literature. You choose a representation according to your subject-matter and needs.

If you are interested in discourse anaphora but not in any intensional phenomena, then you can ignore the possible worlds, as I have been doing throughout most of this chapter. If you are interested in treating intensional phenomena, then you need the possible worlds. But if at the same time you don't need to deal with quantification and anaphora in discourse – which are treated via value assignments – then you can forget about assignments and identify the context or common ground with a set of worlds (Stalnaker's context set). Of course, if you want to combine the treatment of anaphora with a treatment of intensional phenomena, then you will need both assignments and worlds, in which case you can represent the context or common ground as a set of world-assignment pairs.

## 2.3　The Formal Theory

### 2.3.1　The Formal Language DRL

Discourse Representation Theory consists of (i) a formal logical language, call it DRL (Discourse Representation Language), which is model-theoretically interpreted, and (ii) a mapping from natural language discourse to DRL. Regarding the mapping, see Kamp 1981; Roberts 1987; Kamp and Reyle 1993. As for DRL, there are various ways of formulating it, and I give my favorite version below. (For comparison of different versions of DRL, see Landman 1987.)

Note that the construction rules that map natural language into DRL ensure that no variable is free in the DRS for the entire discourse. That is, they ensure that a variable occurring in DRS K always occurs in $A_K$. Not being concerned with DRSs containing free variables, I haven't relativized the semantics to assignment functions to free variables.

## DRL

### Syntax

*Vocabulary*
A set of variables: $x_1, x_2, x_3 \ldots$
A set of n-place predicates (for every n): dog, came-in, owns, meets . . .
parentheses (,)      the symbols $\Rightarrow, \langle, \rangle$

*DRSs*
A **DRS (Discourse Representation Structure)** is an ordered pair $\langle U, C \rangle$, where U (the **universe**) is a set of variables and C is a set of **conditions**.

Conditions:

(a)   If $x_1, \ldots, x_n$ are variables and $\alpha^n$ is an n-place predicate, then $\alpha^n(x_1, \ldots, x_n)$ is an atomic condition.
(b)   If K is a DRS, then $\neg \langle K \rangle$ is a complex condition.
(c)   If $K_1, K_2$ are DRSs, then $\langle K_1 \Rightarrow K_2 \rangle$ is a complex condition.

*Note*
All reference to DRSs in the following definitions is to be understood as reference to occurrences of DRSs. I assume, without defining it, an indexing procedure which distinguishes every two occurrences of a DRS, whether they have a super-DRS in common or not. I assume that given an occurrence of a DRS, the index determines uniquely which occurrence of which DRS is its matrix (i.e. the largest DRS which contains it).

Let $K, K', K'', K_1, K_2, \ldots$ be DRSs, $C_{K_n}$ the set of conditions of $K_n$, and $U_{K_n}$ the universe of $K_n$.

*Accessibility*
**Accessibility** is the smallest preorder (reflexive, transitive) on DRSs s.t.

(a)   if $\neg \langle K' \rangle \in C_K$ then K is accessible from K'; and
(b)   if $\langle K_1 \Rightarrow K_2 \rangle \in C_K$ then K is accessible from $K_1$; and
(c)   if $\langle K_1 \Rightarrow K_2 \rangle \in C_K$ then $K_1$ is accessible from $K_2$.

The **accessible universe** of K, $A_K$, is the set of all variables which occur in a universe of a DRS accessible from K.
$$A_K := \{x : \exists K' \text{ accessible from } K \text{ s.t. } x \in U_{K'}\}$$

### Semantics

A **model** M for DRL is an ordered pair $\langle D, F \rangle$, where D is a non-empty set of individuals and F is an interpretation function which assigns to every n-place predicate a set of n-tuples of members of D.

An **embedding function** f for K in a model $M = \langle D, F \rangle$ is a partial function from the set of variables to D which maps all and only the variables in $A_K$ onto members of D.

A DRS K is **true** in a model M iff there is an embedding function for K in M which verifies all the conditions in K relative to M.

In the following verification clauses, I omit the qualification "in M".

(a)   An embedding function f verifies $\alpha^n(x_1, \ldots, x_n)$ iff $\langle f(x_1), \ldots, f(x_2) \rangle \in F(\alpha^n)$.

(b)   An embedding function f verifies $\neg \langle K \rangle$ iff there is no embedding function $f'$ for K which extends f and verifies all the conditions in K.

(c)   An embedding function f verifies $\langle K_1 \Rightarrow K_2 \rangle$ iff for every embedding function $f'$ for $K_1$ which extends f and verifies all the conditions in $K_1$, there is an embedding function $f''$ for $K_2$ which extends $f'$ and verifies all the conditions in $K_2$.

### 2.3.2   Contexts and Context Change Potentials

A VERSION WITH JUST POSSIBLE WORLDS

A **context** is a set of possible worlds.

Context change potentials:

Let c be a context and let p, q be closed formulas.

(1)   If p is an atomic formula, then $c + p = c \cap \{w : p \text{ is true in } w\}$

(2)   $c + \neg p = c - (c + p)$

(3)   $c + p \wedge q = (c + p) + q$

(4)   $c + p \rightarrow q = c - (c + p - ((c + p) + q))$

Note: The above is **not** a version of Heim's File Change Semantics, since it doesn't include a treatment of definites, indefinites and anaphora.

A VERSION WITH TOTAL ASSIGNMENT FUNCTIONS (cf. Heim 1982)

An **assignment function** is a total function from the set of variables to the set of individuals.

A **context** is a pair $\langle \text{Dom}(c), \text{Sat}(c) \rangle$, where
    Dom(c) is a set of variables, and
    Sat(c) is a set of assignment functions.

Context change potentials:

(1)   If p is an atomic formula, then the context $c + p$ is as follows:
    $\text{Dom}(c + p) = \text{Dom}(c) \cup \{x_n : x_n \text{ is a variable occurring in } p\}$
    $\text{Sat}(c + p) = \text{Sat}(c) \cap \{g : g \text{ verifies } p\}$

(2)   If p and q are formulas, then the context $c + p \wedge q$ is as follows:
    $\text{Dom}(c + p \wedge q) = \text{Dom}((c + p) + q)$
    $\text{Sat}(c + p \wedge q) = \text{Sat}((c + p) + q)$

(3)  If p is a formula, then the context $c + \neg p$ is as follows:

Dom$(c + \neg p) =$ Dom$(c)$

Sat$(c + \neg p) = \{g \in$ Sat$(c) :$ there is no $g'$ which agrees with g on all the variables in Dom$(c)$ s.t. $g \in$ Sat$(c + p)\}$

(4)  If p and q are formulas, then the context $c + \forall(p)(q)$ is as follows:

Dom $(c + \forall(p)(q)) =$ Dom$(c)$

Sat $(c + \forall(p)(q)) = \{g \in$ Sat$(c) :$ for every $g'$ which agrees with g on all the variables in Dom$(c)$, if $g' \in$ Sat$(c + p)$, then there is a $g''$ which agrees with $g'$ on all the variables in Dom$(c + p)$ s.t. $g'' \in$ Sat$((c + p) + q)\}$

(5)  If p and q are formulas, then the context $c + p \rightarrow q$ is also as in (4).

## A VERSION WITH PARTIAL ASSIGNMENT FUNCTIONS
### (cf. Heim 1983a)

An **assignment function** is a partial function from the set of variables to the set of individuals.

A **context** is a set of assignment functions which all have the same domain.

(Dom$(c)$ is defined as the domain of the functions in c.)

Context change potentials:

(1)  If p is an atomic formula, then

$c + p = \{g:$ the domain of g is the union of the domain of the functions in c with the set of variables that occur in p, and g is an extension of one of the functions in c, and g verifies p$\}$

(2)  If p and q are formulas, then

$c + p \wedge q = (c + p) + q$

(3)  If p is a formula, then

$c + \neg p = \{g \in c :$ there is no $g'$ which extends g s.t. $g' \in c + p\}$

(4)  If p and q are formulas, then

$c + \forall(p)(q) = \{g \in c :$ for every $g'$ which extends g s.t. $g' \in c + p$, there is a $g''$ which extends g s.t. $g'' \in (c + p) + q\}$

(5)  If p and q are formulas, then $c + p \rightarrow q$ is also as in (4).

## A VERSION WITH PARTIAL ASSIGNMENTS AND POSSIBLE WORLDS

An **assignment function** is a partial function from the set of variables to the set of individuals.

A **context** is a set of world-assignment pairs, where all the assignments have the same domain.

(Dom$(c)$ is defined as the domain of the assignments in c.)

Context change potentials:

(1)  If p is an atomic formula, then

   c + p = {⟨w,g⟩ : the domain of g is the union of the domain of the functions in c
            with the set of variables that occur in p, and g is an extension of one of
            the functions in c, and g verifies p in w}

(2)  If p and q are formulas, then

   c + p ∧ q = (c + p) + q

(3)  If p is a formula, then

   c + ¬p = {⟨w,g⟩ ∈ c : there is no g′ which extends g s.t. ⟨w,g′⟩ ∈ c + p}

(4)  If p and q are formulas, then

   c + ∀(p)(q) = {⟨w,g⟩ ∈ c : for every g′ which extends g s.t. ⟨w,g′⟩ ∈ c + p, there is
              a g″ which extends g′ s.t. ⟨w,g″⟩ ∈ (c + p) + q}

(5)  If p and q are formulas, then c + p → q is also as in (4).


## 2.3.3  Adding Discourse Referents Representing Sets into DRL

For the purposes of chapters 3 and 4, I will want to assume a version of DRL in which
the variables range over sets of individuals, so that they can be used as translations for
both plural and singular non–quantificational NPs. The version that will be assumed in
chapters 3 and 4 is just like the one in 2.3.1 above, except for the following changes.


### Syntax

Instead of the variables $x_1$, $x_2$, $x_3$ . . . , we use the variables $X_1$, $X_2$, $X_3$. . . .

We also add to the vocabulary names for the natural numbers: 1, 2, 3 . . . and the
following symbols: |, |, =, ⊆


### Semantics

The interpretation function F
  (i)   assigns to every n–place predicate $\alpha^n$ a set of n–tuples of subsets of D;
  (ii)  assigns to the added symbols their usual interpretations.

An **embedding function** f for K in a model M = ⟨D,F⟩ is a partial function from the
set of variables to POW(D) which maps all and only the variables in $A_K$ onto subsets
of D.

Note: In the DRS diagrams in the text, x, y, z etc. represent variables which should be
mapped onto singleton sets, i.e. $x_n$ is shorthand for $X_n$ and $|X_n| = 1$. Similarly, in cases
where X and Y are singleton sets, x ∈ Z is shorthand for X ⊆ Z and x = y is shorthand
for X ⊆ Y and Y ⊆ X. In the text, I will not distinguish between an individual and
a singleton set containing that individual (so I will talk as if x, y, z etc. range over
individuals).

# 3

# NPs with Numeral Determiners

This chapter is concerned with the treatment of NPs of the form *n CN* (numeral determiner + common noun phrase), such as *four chairs*, *two telephone lines* and *one trick*. This is a case where semantic interpretation (formulated in DRT) is complemented by conversational implicature.

## 3.1  NPs with Numeral Determiners

If someone utters (1), that often implies that Lisa has exactly three cats. This is often called the "exactly reading" of (1), even though one can argue about whether it is a semantic reading or not.

(1)  Lisa has three cats.

Certainly, NPs with numeral determiners can have an "at least" reading too. For example, suppose I need to borrow four chairs for a meeting I have in my office. Then you can say (2) to me, and I am **not** going to understand that Leif has exactly four chairs.

(2)  Leif has four chairs.

So, the question arises: what does a numeral determiner *n* mean (literally) – "at least n," or "exactly n," or what?

Horn 1972 proposed that the "exactly reading" is not semantic, but created by a scalar implicature.[1] On his analysis, *three* semantically means "at least 3." So (1) is compatible with Lisa having 4 cats, 5 cats, etc. We have the following scale in which each number entails the smaller ones but is not entailed by them:

   . . . . 7, 6, 5, 4, 3, 2, 1

---

[1]  Scalar implicatures are introduced in 1.2 above.

(1) has the scalar implicature in (3). Therefore, we end up concluding that Lisa has exactly three cats.

(3)  Lisa doesn't have more than three cats.

Horn's analysis is supported by the fact that the "no more than n" implication exhibits the familiar characteristics of conversational implicatures. The implication is context dependent – we saw earlier that sentence (2) does not give rise to such an implication in the context where I need to borrow four chairs. And the implication can easily be canceled without creating a contradiction, as in (4).

(4)  Lisa has three cats – in fact, she has five.

At the same time, some will say that there are reasons to think that NPs with numeral determiners do have a semantic "exactly" reading.

For one thing, one tends to feel that in a rather impressive majority of the cases where a numeral determiner is used the hearer gets the "exactly" reading, and it looks like we need to set up a special context to get the "at least" reading. I don't consider this a **very** strong argument. (Note that with *I went into a house* we also need to set up a special context in order to not get the implicature that it wasn't the speaker's house.) And yet I agree that this point does raise some suspicion.

And there is a more serious point. The fact is that in predicative positions, we don't get "at least" readings but only "exactly" readings. For example, (5) cannot mean that there are at least 4 women and one man among the guests, and (6) is definitely false.

(5)  The guests are four women and one man.
(6)  Bill, John and Adam are two boys.

Focusing on *n CN* in argument position, I argued in Kadmon 1985, 1987 that Horn was right about argument positions: the "exactly" reading there is not semantic and arises as a scalar implicature. I argued against an alternative account of *n CN*, and also developed further the treatment of *n CN*, specifying what the "at least" reading of such an NP **is**, and how it differs from the semantics of NPs of the form *[at least n] CN*.[2]

The alternative account that I argued against was suggested to me by Hans Kamp. While Horn treated the "at least" reading as the only semantic reading and gave a pragmatic explanation for the "exactly" reading, Kamp proposed to do the opposite: say that the "exactly" reading is semantic and explain the "at least" reading pragmatically. Kamp suggested that *n CN* and *exactly n CN* will get identical representations – the representation illustrated in (7).

---

[2]  I believe that there are two different possible structures that an NP of the form *at least n CN* can have – *[at least n] CN* vs. *at least [n CN]*. See Kadmon 1987.

(7)  *(Exactly) n CN*

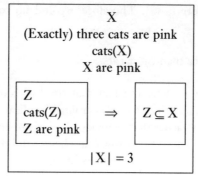

X represents a set. The atomic conditions, cats(X), X are pink, and $|X| = 3$ ("the cardinality of X is 3"), say that X is a set of three pink cats. The complex condition (pair of DRSs) says that any set Z of pink cats is a subset of X, which means that X is the set of all pink cats. (7) is true iff X can be matched with a set in the model which satisfies all these conditions, that is, iff there are exactly three pink cats.[3]

Assuming this treatment of *n CN*, one can try to claim that the "at least" reading is created pragmatically. However, I don't think this will work – I don't see that one could give a plausible and general pragmatic account of the "at least" reading. Here is why.

I think that one would be forced to say that the "at least" reading arises when the DRS is evaluated with respect to a restricted domain of individuals. Take, for example, sentence (8).

(8)  Three cats are pink.

(8) can be true in a situation where the domain of individuals relevant to the conversation (e.g. the animals in the neighborhood) contains more than three pink cats. Assuming the "exactly" DRS (as in (7) above), this would have to be because (8) would then be evaluated with respect to a narrower domain. For example, it could be evaluated with respect to the domain of all the animals in the neighborhood which the speaker knows about, in which case it would claim that there are exactly three pink cats that the speaker knows of in the neighborhood.

This kind of account does not work for all the "at least" readings. First, in some situations, it is impossible to define a domain with respect to which the sentence could be evaluated so as to give it its "at least" reading. Consider (2).

(2)  Leif has four chairs.

How come (2) can be true even if Leif has ten chairs? Perhaps sometimes it could claim something like "Leif has exactly four chairs that he is willing to lend." However, (2) is also perfectly natural in a situation where Leif has ten identical chairs, and he is willing to lend any subset of them. Then the domain narrowing account of the "at least" reading doesn't work, since there is no way of construing (2) as claiming that inside some domain (which is sufficiently narrow), there are exactly four of Leif's chairs.

---

[3]  I assume the version of DRL given in 2.3.3.

Secondly, the domain narrowing approach doesn't work for "at least" readings in negative sentences. Take (9).

(9)  Leif doesn't have four chairs.

On the "at least" reading of (9) ("It is not the case that Leif has at least four chairs"), if Leif has ten chairs, (9) is false. Under the "exactly" semantics plus domain narrowing approach, this reading would have to be analyzed as something like "Leif doesn't have exactly four chairs that he is willing to lend." But then there is a wrong prediction, that the sentence would be true if Leif has more than four chairs to lend.

In addition to not being descriptively adequate, the domain narrowing account is ad hoc, and doesn't seem to apply to anything other than *n CN*. It is not a special case of the familiar process of domain selection – note that domain selection can certainly apply to (10) (this sentence can be about chairs Leif has in his office), whereas the alleged "domain narrowing" can't apply to (10) (this sentence does not have an "at least" reading).

(10)  Leif has exactly four chairs.

Another serious problem with the "exactly" analysis of *n CN* is that it fails to distinguish NPs of the form *n CN* from NPs of the form *exactly n CN*. The fact is that the former have an "at least" reading, while the latter do not (look again at (10)). The "exactly" analysis of *n CN* does not explain this fact.[4]

So much for the arguments against the "exactly" analysis of *n CN*. I hope the reader can see why I found Horn's approach much more convincing.

As for specifying just what the "at least" interpretation of *n CN* is, I argued in the above works for the proposal (suggested to me by Barbara Partee) that *n CN* should be treated exactly in the way Kamp and Heim treat indefinites of the form *a CN*, such as *a cat*. That is, I argued for the treatment illustrated in (11).

(11)  *n CN*  "At least"

$$\begin{array}{|c|} \hline X \\ \text{Three cats are pink} \\ \text{cats}(X) \\ X \text{ are pink} \\ |X| = 3 \\ \hline \end{array}$$

This DRS yields the "at least" truth conditions: The conditions in the DRS say that X is a set of three pink cats. But nothing in the DRS says that it is the set of all pink cats. If X can be matched with a set of three pink cats in the model, (11) is true, regardless of whether there are more pink cats, outside of that set.

Suppose that the sentence *three cats are pink* is uttered, and the proposition it expresses gets added to the common ground. If the context of utterance is such that a scalar implicature is created, then, presumably, the implicature too gets added to the

---

[4]  I don't think the explanation could be a matter of "markedness," since the facts are very clear-cut: *exactly n CN* does not have an "at least" reading.

common ground. I follow Heim 1982 in identifying the body of information to which bits of discourse are added (her file) with the common ground. Accordingly, I see the DRS of the whole discourse as a representation of the common ground. Therefore, I take it that a representation of the implicature will be entered into the DRS. The implicature can be represented by the condition in (12), which says that there are no more pink cats outside the set represented by X.

(12)

$$\boxed{\begin{array}{c} Z \\ \text{cats}(Z) \\ Z \text{ are pink} \end{array}} \Rightarrow \boxed{Z \subseteq X}$$

Note that adopting the treatment of *n CN* illustrated in (11) does **not** mean that *n CN* is treated like *[at least n] CN*. I proposed that *[at least n] CN* should be treated as in (13).

(13)  *[at least n] CN*

$$\boxed{\begin{array}{c} X \\ \text{At least three cats are pink} \\ \text{cats}(X) \\ X \text{ are pink} \\ |X| \geq 3 \end{array}}$$

Given the treatments illustrated in (11) and (13), it is easy to explain why *[at least n] CN* differs from *n CN* in that it doesn't have an "exactly" reading.

The "exactly" reading of *Three cats are pink* is created by adding a scalar implicature to the information represented in DRS (11). We said that the scalar implicature is the claim that there are no more pink cats outside of the set represented by X. Adding this claim to the information represented in DRS (11) entails that there are exactly three pink cats, because the cardinality of the set represented by X is set as equal to 3.

Adding the same claim to the information represented in DRS (13) fails to create an "exactly" reading. The set represented by X in (13) may have more than three members. Therefore, even if there aren't any pink cats outside of that set, there might still be more than three pink cats.

In other words, my analysis might be summed up as follows. Given the existential quantification over the whole discourse, *Three cats are pink* states that there is a set of exactly three cats, while *At least three cats are pink* states that there is a set of at least three pink cats. The two statements are equivalent, of course, but only as long as the scalar implicature has not been added. The scalar implicature (when added), just like the asserted proposition, falls under the scope of the existential quantification over the whole discourse, and adding it to the two statements under consideration creates two logically distinct DRSs.

The treatments illustrated in (11) and (13) also explain why *[at least n] CN* and *n CN* differ from each other in anaphora possibilities.

(14)   Eleven kids walked into the room. They were making an awful lot of noise.
(15)   At least eleven kids walked into the room. They were making an awful lot of noise.

For many speakers, including myself, the following judgments are unshakable: In (14), *they* must refer to a set of eleven kids, while in (15), *they* can refer to the set of all the kids who walked into the room, even if there were more than eleven. Suppose, for example, that twenty kids walked into the room (in which case the first sentence in (14) is true). *They* in (14) can't possibly refer to all twenty kids, but *they* in (15) can.

The treatment of *n CN* as an indefinite has no difficulty explaining these facts. The difference in anaphora possibilities follows from the difference between the representation of *n CN* (with $|X| = n$) and the representation of *at least n CN* (with $|X| \geq n$). The antecedent for anaphora is the variable in the DRS which corresponds to *eleven kids* or *at least eleven kids*, call it X. In the DRS of *Eleven kids walked into the room*, X stands for a set of exactly eleven kids, so a following pronoun must refer to a set of eleven. In the DRS of *At least eleven kids walked into the room*, the set of kids represented by X may have more than eleven members, so a following pronoun may refer to more than eleven kids.

Finally, let me comment on a couple of objections to the proposed treatment of *n CN*.

First, let me respond to the first objection mentioned earlier – to the suspicion raised by the observed prominence of the "exactly" reading. One important reason for the prominence of the "exactly" reading is that it would often contribute more relevant information than the literal "at least" reading. I think that in most situations where one would bother to mention a number at all, exact cardinality would be relevant information. Why would one say *Leif has four chairs* rather than *Leif has some chairs*? More often than not, because the exact cardinality of the set of Leif's chairs is or might be of interest. It is only in contexts where some number is already salient and determines a relevant lower limit on cardinality that exact cardinality would not be relevant. (Such is, for example, the context where someone has expressed a wish to borrow four chairs. Then one only needs to know if Leif has at least four chairs, and it doesn't matter exactly how many chairs he has.) This explains why the "exactly" reading of *n CN* arises very often, and why it is particularly prominent in examples presented out of context (there can't be an already salient number out of context).

Another important reason for the prominence of the "exactly" reading is that very often when we use an indefinite, we refer back to it afterwards using a definite NP. I believe that it follows from the uniqueness property of definite NPs that such anaphora forces an "exactly" reading of the indefinite antecedent.[5] So in fact only indefinites that we don't refer back to can retain their "at least" reading.

So in the end, the fact that the "exactly" interpretation of *n CN* seems more prominent – or more precisely, the fact that it occurs more often – does not seem to me to be so surprising after all, even on the assumption that this interpretation is not part of the semantics of the indefinite NP.

Secondly, let us turn to the other objection mentioned earlier – the fact that in predicative positions *n CN* only has an "exactly" reading. The different effect of *n CN* in predicative positions and in argument positions is easily explained if we adopt the following assumptions. A numeral *n* is invariably adjectival – it is nothing but the predicate that sets the cardinality of a set as equal to n. (In a sense, this means that the bare numeral on its own unambiguously has an "exactly" meaning, as reflected in the DRS conditions of the form $|X| = n$.) Regarding predicative positions, there is nothing more

---

5    See chapter 4 for details.

to say, really: the expression *n CN* functions as a predicate. *Three boys*, for example, denotes the property of being a set of exactly 3 boys. As for argument positions, here *n CN* functions as a full indefinite NP (this can be implemented syntactically by assuming an empty indefinite determiner). For example, *three boys* is an indefinite NP whose descriptive content is the property of being a set of exactly 3 boys.[6]

In DRT terms, the above assumptions mean that *n CN* will introduce a new discourse referent into the DRS only when it occurs in argument position. In predicative position, it will be treated as any other predicate. For example, the DRS for (6) above would be something like (16). (I assume that "are two boys" predicates of a set that it is a set of boys and that its cardinality is 2.) This yields the desired "exactly" reading in predicative positions.[7]

(16)

| Bill, John and Adam are two boys |
|---|
| {b,j,a} are two boys |
| Boys({b,j,a}) |
| \|{b,j,a}\| = 2 |

Another potential objection to the proposed treatment of *n CN* (in argument position) is that examples like (17) below might be taken to provide evidence against the

---

[6] The idea that numerals can be adjectival goes back to Bartch 1973. The idea that the expression *n CN* is either adjectival or a full indefinite NP is due to Partee 1987. Partee suggests the following. A numeral has two possible syntactic categories – it can be an adjective or a determiner – each with its own semantic type. The meanings of the numeral in its two semantic types are interdefinable. An NP with an adjectival numeral has the semantic type $\langle e,t \rangle$, it has an "exactly" meaning, and fits in predicative positions. An NP with a determiner numeral is of type $\langle \langle e,t \rangle,t \rangle$, it has an "at least" meaning, and fits in argument positions. Bittner 1994 takes the further step of suggesting that a numeral is unambiguously a predicate (type $\langle e,t \rangle$). In conjunction with a further predicate (corresponding to my CN), it forms a predicate again. (For example, the predicate denoted by *three boys* is the property of being a set of exactly three boys.) This new predicate may be incorporated into a perfectly normal indefinite-NP-translation of the form $\lambda P[\exists x[Q(x) \wedge P(x)]]$ (type $\langle \langle e,t \rangle,t \rangle$), where x may take as its value a set of individuals (or a plural individual) and Q is the new predicate. Such a translation fits in argument positions, yielding an "at least" reading there. I thank Fred Landman for help with the current paragraph and footnote.

[7] As for examples like (i), represented as in (ii),

(i) We have guests. The guests are three boys.

(ii)

| X |
|---|
| We have guests |
| guests(X) |
| We have X |
| The guests are three boys |
| X are three boys |
| Boys(X) |
| \|X\| = 3 |

the uniqueness property of definite NPs discussed in chapter 4 will ensure an "exactly" reading here too, since it will force X to stand for the maximal collection of guests that "we" have.

proposed "at least" reading, and in favor of assigning *n CN* a semantic "exactly" reading.

(17)   She doesn't have THREE cats – she has SEVEN.

My response to this objection is that I don't think we have in (17) an "exactly" reading of a sentence with logical negation. I think that what we have here is "metalinguistic negation," in the sense of Horn 1985.[8] The speaker does not say that the sentence *she has three cats* is false, but rather rejects this sentence because it commonly gives rise to a scalar implicature, and therefore tends to suggest that "she" has exactly three cats.[9]

## 3.2   About the Notion of "The Pragmatic Wastebasket"

I think that an attempt to treat *n CN* as having an "exactly" semantics and claim that the "at least" reading is created by a pragmatic process of "domain narrowing" is a pretty good example of trying to throw something into "the pragmatic wastebasket."

However, please note that this does not mean that pragmatics **is** a wastebasket. It just means that one may try to use it as such. I think the case of *n CN* is also an example of how one can't get away with using pragmatics as a wastebasket. One can't just say "this is pragmatics" and automatically be content with that. It is quite possible to find convincing arguments against treating something as "pragmatic," in cases where such a treatment would be wrong.

And vice versa, it is quite possible to give solid arguments that a certain phenomenon is due to a particular pragmatic process, when we know enough about that pragmatic process. Then we can recognize this process and find evidence that it is taking place. That is certainly not anything like using pragmatics as a wastebasket. Indeed, it is very important to be able to recognize something as the effect of a pragmatic process, because often it is exactly the interaction of semantic and pragmatic factors that offers the best explanation of a phenomenon.

When Larry Horn said that the "exactly" reading is created pragmatically, he was far from using pragmatics as a wastebasket. He said exactly **how** the reading was created pragmatically, and his was a plausible explanation. Horn used scalar implicature, which is a notion that we can characterize and that we need anyway. And we can see that the "exactly reading" really exhibits characteristics of scalar implicatures.

Recall the treatment of *n CN* illustrated in (11) and the discussion of the difference between *n CN* and *[at least n] CN*. Recall the interaction of semantic and pragmatic factors that is involved here. I think this is a good example of a case where if you have both (i) precise claims about the semantics (I didn't just vaguely say that *n CN* has an

[8]   See section 1.3 above.
[9]   For further discussion concerning the "exactly" reading of *n CN* and the status of the scalar implicature which creates that reading, see Horn 1992, Landman 1998. As noted in 1.2 above, Landman 1998 argues that while the implicature in question does arise from Gricean principles, its content has to be calculated by a mechanism that is part of the grammar, and he proposes such a mechanism. I think this may fit well with the view expressed in Horn 1992, where it is suggested that the scalar implicatures of numerals may contribute to actual semantic content in a way that ordinary scalar implicatures do not.

"at least" semantics, but gave a representation, which has a determined model–theoretic interpretation), and (ii) precise claims about the effect of the pragmatic process under consideration (I said that the scalar implicature was "no more pink cats outside of X"), then you are able to make some actual predictions about when the pragmatic process will have a particular observed effect and when it won't (I predicted that *n CN* will have an "exactly" reading and *[at least n] CN* will not).

Incidentally, what about my response to example (17) above? Was I throwing a counterexample into the pragmatic wastebasket? Well, on the one hand, it is certain that metalinguistic uses of negation do exist. Also, note the focus on *three*. On the other hand, metalinguistic uses of negation are not always as easy to identify with certainty as one might wish. Note that (17) need not carry the particular intonation pattern typical of metalinguistic negation. I leave it to the reader to form their own judgment on this matter.

# 4

# *Semantics and Pragmatics with Definite NPs*

## 4.1 The Existential Presupposition of Definite NPs: Definites as Anaphoric

It is standard to assume that definite descriptions carry an existential presupposition. For example, (1a) presupposes (1b). As argued in Strawson 1950 (contra Russell 1905), speakers' intuitions show that (1b) is a ps rather than an ordinary part of the semantic content of (1a): we feel that (1a) does not really **assert** that there is a king of France, but rather takes it for granted; if there is no king of France, (1a) is not judged to be false, but rather inappropriate.

(1)  a.  The king of France is bald.
    b.  There is a king of France.

What is the source of the existential ps? Strawson returned to the traditional pre-Russellian view: definite descriptions, like names, are referring expressions, and as such presuppose that they do in fact have a referent (cf. Frege 1892); since the referent must fit the description, we get the ps that there is something that fits the description. However, definite descriptions don't always have a referent. For example, the definite description in (2) does not have any particular referent in the world.

(2)  If a man beats a donkey, the donkey kicks him.

The Kamp–Heim system provides an analysis of the existential ps that seems more adequate. In this system, a definite NP translates as an occurrence of an "old" variable.[1] In other words, a definite NP is treated as anaphoric, with an "old" variable ("old" discourse referent) serving as its antecedent. But that means that on the Kamp–Heim theory, there is a well-defined requirement on the context in which a definite NP is uttered: the context (represented as a file or a DRS) must already contain a discourse referent that could serve as the antecedent. (Otherwise, it is impossible to process the

---

[1]  In Kamp 1981, this treatment is proposed for pronouns only, but in Heim 1982, the same treatment is proposed for all definite NPs, including definite descriptions as well as pronouns.

definite NP – the desired context-incrementation is undefined.) In other words, if, following Stalnaker 1974 and Karttunen 1974, we define a ps as a requirement on the context, then the Kamp–Heim theory claims that a definite NP presupposes the existence of a discourse referent that's a potential antecedent. Note that this ps is triggered conventionally: the requirement on the context is taken to be directly imposed by the grammar.

Now, Heim 1982 explicitly claims that all definite NPs are anaphoric (= that a definite NP invariably presupposes the existence of a potential antecedent). How can Heim maintain this claim? Is it true that all definite NPs used felicitously have an antecedent?

Heim's anaphoric treatment of definites is quite compatible with deictic uses of definites. Given that on Heim's approach the file is a representation of the common ground (and not merely of information expressed by preceding utterances), the antecedent discourse referent of a given definite NP need not be triggered by linguistic text. Suppose I point to the (only) door of the room we are in, or look at it, and say (3).

(3)   The door is about to open.

We may assume that because the door of this room is in the immediate utterance situation, and since, furthermore, I raised its salience by attracting your attention to it, the file now contains a discourse referent representing this door. So when I utter (3), the definite NP *the door* can be associated with that discourse referent. In that sense, this NP is anaphoric, even though it does not have a linguistic antecedent.

However, in real life there are also uses of definite NPs where the definite is really "novel," where there is no reason to assume the existence of an "old" discourse referent that could serve as its antecedent. Heim gives the following examples (Heim 1982, p. 371). "As I am walking up a driveway, someone says to me:

(4)   Watch out, the dog will bite you.

There was no previous discourse, there is no dog in sight, and I had no reason to believe that any dog lived here before I heard the utterance." Another example is (5), which (says Heim) does not presuppose contextual salience or previous mention of an author.[2]

(5)   John read a book about Schubert and wrote to the author.

And yet, Heim is able to maintain that definites are always anaphoric even in the face of these examples. Based on Lewis 1979's ideas (see section 1.7), Heim assumes that in the case of "novel" definites, an antecedent discourse referent is accommodated.

The case of "novel" definites illustrates the fact that the pragmatic process of accommodation can be used to handle (apparent) counterexamples to a given semantic theory. This raises the question of whether accommodation is not too powerful as a theoretical tool. If too many cases of anaphora to accommodated antecedents are allowed, this may end up depriving the Kamp–Heim theory of anaphora of much of its content.

---

[2]   If you think that when one mentions a book the author always, automatically, becomes salient, then perhaps (assuming that horses don't always have riders) you will prefer the following example.

  (i)   John heard a horse and decided to get some water for the rider.

I do think that the question about the status of accommodation as a theoretical tool is a serious one, and that each use of accommodation to handle a counterexample ought to be examined carefully. At the same time, I am certain that accommodation is a real phenomenon, and I think it is perfectly legitimate in principle to use it in our theoretical explanations. The reader is invited to go back to section 1.7 above, and review the examples of accommodation given there – I think it can hardly be denied that in many cases accommodation is exactly what really happens in real life. Moreover, the danger of using accommodation too lightly in our theoretical explanations is reduced by the fact that the process of accommodation is known to be constrained in different ways. Indeed, I give in 1.7 many examples of cases where accommodation cannot take place, because it is constrained. The constrained nature of accommodation will (hopefully) guard us against the potential temptation to say "this is accommodation" every time we feel like it and save any crazy hypothesis we feel like saving.

## 4.2  The Uniqueness of Definite NPs

In Kadmon 1987, 1990, I discuss the uniqueness implications associated with definite NPs. I will present part of this material here, because it illustrates interactions between semantics and all sorts of pragmatics: contextually supplied information, scalar implicatures, and accommodation (as a means of satisfying a ps).[3,4] For present purposes, I only wish to discuss simple, unquantified examples; uniqueness under quantification will not be discussed here. A fuller historical survey of views on uniqueness is given in Kadmon 1987 (sections 5.1–5.4), and will not be repeated here.

### 4.2.1  The Uniqueness/Maximality of Definite NPs

According to Russell 1905, definite descriptions carry a uniqueness implication, and that is what distinguishes them from indefinites. For example, (6) implies that there is only one king, while (7) doesn't.

(6)  The king visited me.
(7)  A king visited me.
(8)  The kings visited me.
(9)  a.  Some kings visited me.        b.  Kings visited me.

Now take *the kings*. (8), but not (9a) or (9b), seems to imply that all the kings visited me. If (unlike Russell) we think of the definite NP as referential, we might say that in both (6) and (8), the definite NP refers to the set of all the kings; if the definite is singular, then this set has only one member. Of course there is only one set which contains all and only the kings. So to cover plurals, the claim about uniqueness might be stated as follows. Definite NPs refer to (the unique set which is) the maximal collection of things which fit their descriptive content.

---

[3]  The material in this section is based – with certain alterations, additions and omissions – on sections 1 and 2.1 of Kadmon 1990, "Uniqueness," in *Linguistics and Philosophy* 13.3, pp. 273–324, copyright © 1990 Kluwer Academic Publishers. With kind permission from Kluwer Academic Publishers.
[4]  For an alternative theory of the uniqueness of definite NPs, see Roberts 1993.

Definite NPs used anaphorically in discourse exhibit a similar uniqueness/maximality effect. Evans 1977, 1980 talks about examples like (10) and (11). He calls the pronoun here an "E-type" pronoun. He says that the pronoun refers to a maximal collection determined by the clause containing the antecedent NP.

(10)   John owns some sheep. Harry vaccinates them.
(11)   There is a doctor in London and he is Welsh.

Evans points out a strong tendency to understand (10) as saying that Harry vaccinates all of John's sheep. That is, the pronoun *them* is taken to refer to the maximal collection of sheep owned by John. Similarly, (11) seems to imply that there is only one doctor in London, i.e. *he* is understood to refer to the maximal collection of London doctors. Evans predicts these judgments by interpreting "E-type" pronouns as referring to "the object(s), if any, which verify [the antecedent's clause]." (Evans 1980, p. 340) This analysis extends to anaphoric definite descriptions. For example, *the sheep* in (12) refers to all of John's sheep.

(12)   John owns some sheep. He thought he'd like farming, but he's not so sure now. The sheep are causing him a lot of trouble.

So Evans treats discourse-anaphoric definites in general as referring to the maximal collection determined by the antecedent's clause. I call this collection MAX/S, for short.

### 4.2.2   Opposition to Uniqueness

Strawson 1950 rejects Russell's view of uniqueness, on the grounds that sentence (13) can certainly "have an application" (Russell's phrase) even if there is more than one table.

(13)   The table is covered with books.

Analogous objections have been raised against Evans' treatment of discourse anaphora. Evans himself and others have noted that there are counterexamples to the claim that in all cases of discourse anaphora the anaphoric element refers to MAX/S. For example, the following.

(14)   One day, a man and a boy walked along a road, and the man said to the boy: "Would you like to be king?"

(Evans 1977, p. 516)

(15)   There once was a doctor in London. He was Welsh.

(Heim 1982, p. 31)

(16)   Some friends of mine live in Maine. They play music all night.

(after Sells 1985)

(17)   I have to show this document to some/three colleagues. They are in a meeting, and I am waiting for them. I have to show it to at least two other colleagues, but THEY have already left, and I'll have to catch them tomorrow morning.

It seems that there are no uniqueness implications associated with (14) and (15). (15), for example, can start a story without implying that there was only one doctor in London, i.e. *he* does not have to refer to MAX/S. Similarly, *they* in (16) does not necessarily refer to all of my friends who live in Maine. In (17), reference to MAX/S is explicitly excluded – the first *they* can't be referring to all the colleagues I have to show the document to.[5] Nevertheless, (17) is felicitous, and the speaker doesn't sound like she is contradicting herself. Compare this with (18), which does sound self-contradictory.

(18)   I have to show this document to exactly three colleagues. They are in a meeting, and I am waiting for them. I have to show it to at least two other colleagues, but THEY have already left, and I'll have to catch them tomorrow morning.

In the face of the counterexamples, one can either deny that uniqueness is a systematic phenomenon, or maintain uniqueness and adjust the theory. Examples like (13)–(17) certainly show that a theory where the uniqueness implication is determined strictly and solely by the descriptive material in the definite NP or antecedent's clause cannot be right. However, one can maintain uniqueness and strive to develop a more realistic version of the theory, as many authors have done. We can rely on contextual factors to determine reference to "the unique table in this room," "the unique London doctor that this story is about," etc.

Heim 1982 objects to maintaining uniqueness, because she does not believe in a systematic and general maximality/uniqueness effect. Heim does recognize that there is an intuition that definites are typically unique in some sense, and she attempts to derive that from her theory of definites combined with Gricean conversational principles.

If a definite NP is uttered in a context where there are a number of "old" discourse referents that are equally likely to serve as its antecedent, then the hearer is faced with unresolvable ambiguity, in violation of Grice's maxim of Manner. Heim argues that that is why definites are felt to be unique; since it is assumed that the speaker attempts efficient communication, the use of a definite implies that there is one most likely candidate for its antecedent. This account predicts, for example, that there is a uniqueness implication associated with (19) and that the judgments for (20) are as marked.

(19)   The cat is at the door.                                        (Heim 1982, p. 230)

(20)   John has a cat and a dog. $\left\{ \begin{array}{l} \text{The cat's} \\ \text{?Its} \\ \text{?The pet's} \end{array} \right\}$ name is Felix.

(Heim 1982, pp. 384–5)

For examples with an antecedent NP, such as (20), Heim does not make the same predictions that a more Evansian theory would make. It is true that Heim predicts that the good version of (20) is OK. However, she does not predict a uniqueness effect here

---

[5]   I mean the de re reading of *some/three colleagues*, of course; otherwise the anaphora would not be felicitous.

– she doesn't predict that the NP *the cat* should refer to a unique cat. *The cat* is translated as the same variable (discourse referent) as the one translating *a cat*. So Heim predicts that *a cat* and *the cat* stand for the same cat of John's. But nothing in her system forces these two NPs to stand for the only cat John has, or the only salient one, or even the most likely to be referred to. Evans' uniqueness effect goes beyond Heim's predictions. According to him, there is an implication that John has only one cat (since *the cat* has to refer to MAX/S). Unlike Heim, Evans predicts a contrast between the good version of (20) and (21).

(21)   John has a cat whose name is Felix, and a dog.

If the (restrictive) relative clause is a case of anaphora, it is a case of syntactic (c-command) anaphora, which doesn't display uniqueness effects.[6] Evans predicts that (20) implies that John has only one cat and (21) doesn't, while Heim predicts that (20) and (21) are synonymous.

   The difference in predictions is perhaps even more striking with examples like (22). Here Heim doesn't predict any uniqueness effect, simply because there is no potential ambiguity – the antecedent NP is undoubtedly *a cat*. Heim predicts that (22) is synonymous with (23), in contrast with Evans' prediction that (22) implies that only one cat walked in while (23) doesn't.

(22)   A cat walked in. It sat down.
(23)   A cat who walked in sat down.

   Heim does not see these results as problematic. She discusses Evans' predictions, and concludes that she is inclined to deny any systematic validity to Evans' predictions about referring to MAX/S.
   Heim is aware that Evans' predictions could be made more "realistic" by taking into account the effect of selecting a domain of quantification. Consider her example (24).

(24)   A wine glass broke last night. It had been very expensive.

(Heim 1982, p. 28)

Heim notes that the uniqueness implication would surely have to be restricted to some contextually given place. But, she points out, the glass referred to does not even have to be the only one that broke in the relevant place, since (24) is fine in the following situation. I broke three glasses last night. Two of them had been cheap, and I didn't mind losing them. The third one had been very expensive, and I was upset about losing it. This morning a friend asked me why I was in a bad mood, and I said (24). Heim adds that this may not be an actual counterexample to Evans' theory, since Evans could

---

[6]   I assume here the familiar distinction between *syntactic anaphora*, which is intrasentential, determined at the level of natural language syntax and constrained by properties of syntactic structure, and *discourse anaphora*, which is determined at the level of discourse representation, and may be intersentential. The analysis of uniqueness of Kadmon 1987, 1990 applies only to discourse anaphora, and not to syntactic anaphora.

say that the two cheap glasses were irrelevant since they did not affect the speaker's mood. But given the fact that predicted uniqueness implications and predicted contrasts seem to disappear so easily, she thinks that there isn't strong enough evidence that Evans' predictions hold.

As examples of discourse anaphora are the crucial test cases for Heim's approach, I will concentrate on these examples in what follows.

### 4.2.3 Realistic Uniqueness: Data

I find that careful examination of the data supports the generality of uniqueness and confirms a realistic version of Evans' predictions. I would like to argue for this generalization: definite NPs which are not syntactically (c-command) bound must stand for a set/individual uniquely identified by some property known to the language user.[7]

To see that when the uniqueness requirement is violated the use of definite NPs becomes infelicitous, one must (i) be sure to consider situations where the speaker knows of no property whatsoever which uniquely identifies the set/individual that the definite stands for; and (ii) be aware of factors that sometimes obscure the generality of the uniqueness effect.

**Basic examples:** Consider examples (25) and (26).

(25)  Leif has a chair.
(26)  Leif has four chairs.

Suppose Leif has ten identical chairs and he is willing to lend any subset of them. You know of absolutely no property that would differentiate Leif's chairs from each other. Now, if I need to borrow a chair, you can say (25) to me, and if I need to borrow four chairs, you can say (26) to me. You can use (25) or (26) despite the fact that you are completely unable to uniquely identify any one of Leif's chairs, or any set of four chairs of Leif's. This shows that indefinite NPs don't always stand for a unique individual/set. (Note that the hearer doesn't have to assume that there is a uniquely identifying property, either – I can just simply understand you to say that Leif has at least one/four chair(s).)

In contrast, when you try to use a definite NP to refer back to your indefinite NP, then uniqueness effects show up systematically. Consider (27) and (28), in the same situation as before. I need to borrow a chair/four chairs, and Leif has ten indistinguishable chairs he is willing to lend.

(27)  Leif has a chair. It's not so comfortable, though.
(28)  Leif has four chairs. They are not so comfortable, though.

---

[7]  Some proponents of uniqueness think that the uniquely identifying information must be available to the hearers, while others believe that in some felicitous uses of definites the uniquely identifying information is available only to the speaker. (For details see Kadmon 1987.) I agree with the latter. Therefore, many of the judgments reported below will be from the point of view of the speaker. (Yet hearers too interpret definites as unique, either "directly" or by relying on the speaker.) Relevant data below.

Many speakers cannot use (27) or (28) in such a situation. (For some speakers, this judgment is clearer with (28).) For these speakers, (27)/(28) is only felicitous in situations where they know that they are referring to a chair/a set of four chairs which is uniquely identified by some property they are aware of. From this I conclude that unlike indefinites, definite NPs do have to stand for a unique set/individual.

**Ways of being unique, speakers, hearers:** (27) is felicitous, for example, if Leif has exactly one chair. Then the pronoun *it* refers to the unique chair Leif has. Clearly, a speaker who knows that Leif has exactly one chair can utter (27). And the hearer? Hearers seek to interpret *it* as unique. Hearing (27) out of the blue, one would normally understand that Leif has exactly one chair; this is the paradigm case of a uniqueness implication based on the antecedent's clause.

If Leif has more than one chair, *it* may refer to a chair which is unique in some other way. For example, it could refer to the one chair Leif is willing to lend. If I need to borrow a chair, and you know that there's only one chair Leif would lend, you can say (27), referring to that chair. Given a context of having to borrow a chair, this is also a likely interpretation from the point of view of the hearer.

(28) behaves the same as (27). One can use the pronoun *they* to refer to a set of four chairs if this set is a maximal collection of something. The pronoun can refer to MAX/S (the only four chairs Leif has), or to some other maximal collection (for example, all the chairs Leif is willing to lend).

In some contexts, a definite NP may refer to some specific individual/set the speaker has in mind. For example, in (29).

(29)   Once upon a time, Leif bought a chair. He got it at a tag sale.

One can utter (29) referring to the only pink armchair Leif ever bought, and go on to tell the story of this chair.

Note that in (29), at the time the definite is used, the hearers need not know in what way the chair in the story is unique. This is a typical case where "real" uniquely identifying information only has to be available to the speaker. The hearer is apparently able in the context of a story to rely on the speaker for uniqueness – one interprets *it* as something like "the one chair that the story is about," or "the one chair that the speaker has in mind," or "the one chair that Leif bought at the time the speaker has in mind." Even in a story, hearers do become reluctant to accept a definite, if it seems unlikely that the speaker has a way of uniquely identifying its referent. For example, (30) sounds odd.

(30)   # Once upon a time, Leif bought a chair. In fact, he bought several identical chairs that time. He got the chair at a tag sale.

**Homogeneity:** I said that we should watch out for factors that may obscure the generality of uniqueness effects. Let us look at one such factor. I didn't have a name for it in 1990, but following Barker 1996, I will call it here "homogeneity."

Some speakers are able to use (27) and (28) even in situations where they can't distinguish a unique set of one or four chairs of Leif's. I think uniqueness is obscured here by an extra factor, which operates under limited circumstances. If you feel that you can felicitously use (27) or (28) even if Leif has ten indistinguishable chairs, then I bet you are assuming that all of Leif's chairs are not so comfortable. Try assuming instead that exactly six of Leif's chairs are not so comfortable. (27) and (28) become infelicitous.

We see then that the uniqueness effect disappears (for some speakers) only under special circumstances. The uniqueness effect may disappear in (28) if the predicate "are not so comfortable" would be homogeneously true of all the sets in the model that its antecedent (the variable translating *four chairs*) could be truthfully mapped onto. As is made clear in Barker 1996, the uniqueness effect may also disappear (for some speakers) if this predicate would be homogeneously false of all these sets. Generally, if the predicate predicated of the definite is **not** guaranteed to homogeneously yield the same truth value for all the sets in the model which its antecedent discourse referent could stand for (be mapped onto), then the uniqueness effect shows up again (for all speakers).

Try your judgments from a hearer's point of view – consider B's utterance in (31).

(31)  A:  We need a person who knows a couple of symphonies quite well. Is it true that you are such a person?
        B:  Sure, I know a couple of symphonies well. I can't help humming along with them whenever I hear them on the radio.

As a hearer, what do you think the pronoun *them* refers to? You would probably interpret it as referring to all the symphonies B knows well (and you'd assume that there are only 2 or 3 such symphonies). But suppose you are unwilling to interpret *them* that way, perhaps because it is assumed to be highly likely that B knows twenty symphonies well. Suppose further that it is quite possible that B hums along with exactly seven of the symphonies (s)he knows well. And let us assume, given A's question, that we can rule out the possibility that B is referring to some specific set of 2–3 symphonies (s)he has in mind. What do you feel about B's utterance now? I think B's utterance can't be reconciled with all the assumptions I asked you to make. I think it is plainly infelicitous in a context where all these assumptions are made. When there is no homogeneity, *them* must refer to a maximal collection of symphonies B knows well.

Now consider B's utterance in a context where it is possible that B knows twenty symphonies well, but it is also assumed that a person either hums along with all the symphonies (s)he knows well or with none of them. Now homogeneity holds. I personally don't like B's utterance even in this context. Yet I can see that it might be used in such a context, and I have to agree that it wouldn't sound too bad. And this is a context where *them* does not refer to a maximal collection. So, I take it that for some language users, homogeneity somehow "excuses" a definite from exhibiting the usual uniqueness effect.

We might think about this phenomenon as follows: For all speakers, the pronoun in (28) must, and is assumed to, refer to a unique set. For some speakers, the choice of unique set is allowed to remain undetermined (with *they* referring to some set of four chairs uniquely identified by an unknown property P) in contexts which guarantee homogeneity, because in such contexts, the choice of unique set can't make a difference to the truth value of *they are not so comfortable*.

Or, let me describe this situation along the lines of Chierchia 1992, p. 160. For all speakers, the pronoun *them* in (31) must refer to a unique set. Hence, the context should supply a uniquely identifying property. If the context does not in fact point to any particular property, then we have at our disposal, so to speak, a large number of properties each uniquely identifying a certain set of 2–3 symphonies B knows well. (Never mind what these properties are, obviously they exist.) We can't choose among these properties. So what do we do? Apparently, some speakers are able to just assume that one of the properties will do, doesn't matter which. But of course it won't matter which only in a context that guarantees homogeneity.[8]

**Evans' contrasts:** We are now in a position to evaluate the status of minimal pairs like (24) and (32) (Heim 1982, p. 28).

(24)   A wine glass broke last night. It had been very expensive.

(32)   A wine glass which had been very expensive broke last night.

Evans predicts that (24) should have a uniqueness implication, but (32) shouldn't. Despite Heim's doubts, I believe that this prediction holds. (24) implies that a unique wine glass broke last night. As noted above, Heim has pointed out that the wine glass mentioned in (24) does not have to be the only one that broke (it doesn't have to be MAX/S). However, it **does** have to be unique in **some** way. I must have referred to the only wine glass that broke and was expensive, or the only one that broke and affected my mood, or the glass uniquely identified by some other property I was aware of. Suppose I broke two identical wine glasses, owned by the same person, at the same time. I am completely unable to distinguish between them. In this situation, I cannot felicitously use (24), not even if the number of broken glasses (one or two) is irrelevant, one being enough to make me lose my job. In contrast, I can truthfully and felicitously report my tragedy, in the same situation, using (32). There doesn't have to be any unique glass associated with (32).

### 4.2.4   Cooper's Analysis and Remaining Challenges

I said that, empirically, definites must be unique in some way or another. Cooper 1979 proposed an analysis of pronouns which indeed renders them unique without specifying what the uniquely identifying property has to be. Cooper proposed that in addition to the usual "variable" translation of singular pronouns (of the form $\lambda PP(x)$), pronouns may translate into expressions of the form given in (33).

(33)   $\lambda P \exists x[\forall y[\pi(y) \leftrightarrow y = x] \& P(x)]$
       where $\pi$ is a property-denoting expression containing only free variables and parentheses

---

[8]   Chierchia 1992 talks about another option: we might interpret the piece of discourse as true iff **all** these properties will give a set that verifies the sentence containing the pronoun – this is how Chierchia 1992 gets "universal" ("strong") readings for donkey sentences. Perhaps each of the two options is available for a subset of the speakers.

The value of $\pi$ is to be determined by the context of use. Thus the pronoun is like a Russellian definite description, with the uniquely identifying property determined by the context.

Since the choice of translation is free, a pronoun may receive the variable translation and then refer to some salient individual, possibly one which is not unique in any known way, as noted in Cooper 1979, p. 72. So Cooper didn't predict that all discourse pronouns should be unique. However, if you believe, like me, that the uniqueness of definite NPs is general and systematic, it is easy enough to generalize Cooper's translation to cover definite descriptions, and to obligatorily assign it to all definite NPs which are not syntactically bound.

Cooper has given us, for the first time, an explicit formal analysis of realistic uniqueness, an analysis which is in my opinion correct in letting the uniquely identifying property be fixed by pragmatic factors. However, there are also problems.

First, quite apart from what one has to say about uniqueness, the analysis of anaphora that Cooper assumes is problematic. As discussed in Heim 1982 (pp. 80–1), Cooper's quantificational treatment of pronouns fails to establish a formal link between the pronoun and its antecedent, and is therefore unable to explain why possible interpretations for definites depend on formal properties of the preceding discourse.

Next, there are incorrect predictions about uniqueness. Under Cooper's treatment, if a definite is under the scope of some operator, then the uniqueness implication associated with it must also be under the scope of that operator. As pointed out to me by Fred Landman, this predicts the wrong uniqueness implication for examples like (34).

(34)   A strange man lives here. If he sees a cat, he screams.

Suppose the salient property which would enter the translation of *he* is the one determined by the antecedent's clause. Then, under Cooper's analysis, (34) would be interpreted as something like this: "There is a strange man who lives here. If there is exactly one strange man who lives here and sees a cat, then there is exactly one strange man who lives here and screams." The uniqueness effect here is wrong: one does not understand from (34) anything like "if there is a unique strange man who lives here and he sees a cat, he screams." (34) implies that there is a unique strange man who lives here; that much has the status of a fact in its own right, and is not part of the antecedent of the conditional.

Finally, Cooper doesn't say anything about how the uniquely identifying property is recovered from the context of use, and he is not in a position to show how various pragmatic factors might interact with the analysis of uniqueness.

My work on uniqueness aimed, among other things, to make some progress with respect to the problems just noted. My 1987, 1990 analysis of uniqueness, which is presented in detail in 4.2.5 below, is cast within the Kamp–Heim framework, which has provided us in the meantime with a more adequate analysis of anaphora. (The analysis is formulated in Kamp's version of the theory.) It is now no longer assumed that the existence and uniqueness statements are entered as part of the semantic content of the clause containing the definite NP, and so the problem noted in connection with example (34) above is eliminated. I assume that the file or DRS represents not just information conveyed by preceding utterances, but also pragmatically supplied information. As shown below, this assumption allows us to begin to see in some detail how the property which uniquely identifies a given definite is determined, and how factors like implicature, accommodation, etc. may participate in determining what the definite NP stands for.

### 4.2.5   The Proposed Analysis

The condition given in (35) below is a preliminary version of my analysis of the uniqueness of definite NPs.[9] This preliminary version will suffice for our purposes in this book, since we will not be concerned with uniqueness under quantification. It is stipulated that (35) affects only definites which are not syntactically bound.

(35)   **The Uniqueness Condition (preliminary version)**
A definite NP associated with a variable X which was introduced in the universe of a DRS K is used felicitously only if for every model M,
for all embedding functions f,g for K which verify all the conditions in K relative to M, $f(X) = g(X)$.

The condition in (35) says, roughly, that if a discourse contains a definite NP X, then all the functions which verify this discourse must assign X the same set or individual as a value. In other words, there must be at most one set or individual in the model that X could possibly stand for (be mapped onto). Note that this requirement must be satisfied in all models. This guarantees (i) that the uniqueness of the definite can't depend on accidental properties of the model; and (ii) that although (35) is stated in terms of verifying embeddings, it applies to true and false DRSs alike.

The Uniqueness Condition just states that the definite must be unique, in the sense that there can be only one thing in the model that it could stand for. There is no additional stipulation about uniquely identifying properties. Because the uniqueness requirement can't be satisfied by accidental properties of the model, it follows from it that there must be conditions in the DRS which explicitly state that the definite is unique, i.e. that it is the only thing with some property P. Since there are no further restrictions on what P should be, it can (as far as the uniqueness requirement goes) be any uniquely identifying property present in the DRS.

For a first illustration, consider DRS (A.1).

(A.1)
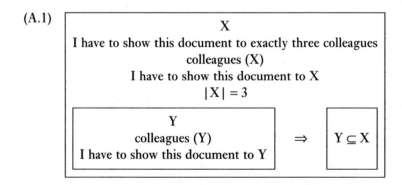

---

[9]   I followed Sells 1985 in stating the principle responsible for uniqueness in terms of embedding functions.

X is the variable of *exactly three colleagues*. (A.1) represents a true piece of discourse iff X can be mapped onto some set in the model which satisfies everything predicated of X in the DRS. The last condition in this DRS, translating the word *exactly*, makes X the set of **all** the colleagues I have to show the document to. (It says that all the sets Y of colleagues I have to show the document to are subsets of X.) If *They are in a meeting* is added to the discourse, the pronoun *they* gets the same variable as its antecedent NP:

(A.2)

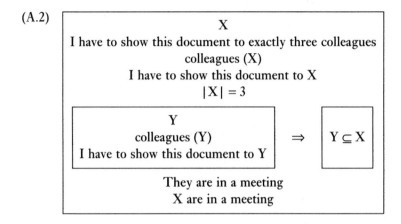

DRS (A.2) satisfies the Uniqueness Condition. The variable of the pronoun is X, and X, as it did all along, represents the set of all the colleagues I have to show the document to. So the pronoun is unique: there can be only one such set in the model.

In the previous example, the uniquely identifying material was directly conveyed by the clause containing the antecedent (and it fixed the referent of the definite as MAX/S). But the part of the DRS which satisfies Uniqueness may also contain material which does not originate in the antecedent's clause. Implicated, accommodated, and contextually supplied material may play a role in satisfying Uniqueness, and hence in determining what maximal collection (= unique set) the definite NP stands for.

The DRS in (B.1) gets the right truth conditions for *I have to show this document to three colleagues*. If this sentence is presented out of the blue, it is likely to have an "exactly three colleagues" reading. As discussed in chapter 3, I believe, following Horn, that this reading is created by a scalar implicature. The implicature transforms the DRS into (B.2).

(B.1)

```
                           X
      I have to show this document to three colleagues
                      colleagues (X)
           I have to show this document to X
                        |X| = 3
```

(B.2)

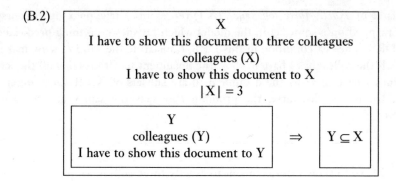

If the discourse continues with *They are in a meeting*, we get (B.3).

(B.3)

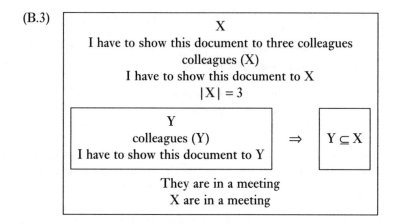

(B.3) satisfies Uniqueness, because the pronoun was assigned the variable X, standing for the unique set of all the colleagues I have to show the document to. Here it was implicated material that fixed the set that the definite NP refers to as MAX/S.

Next example: Suppose I tell you that I need to borrow some furniture. If you then say *Leif has four chairs*, I am likely to assume that you are talking about chairs that I can borrow, and construct a DRS like (C.1). There is also likely to be a scalar implicature that Leif doesn't have more than four chairs that I could borrow. If this implicature is added to the DRS and you continue with *They are not so comfortable*, the result is DRS (C.2).

(C.1)

X
Leif has four chairs
chairs (X)
Leif has X
I can borrow X
$|X| = 4$

(C.2)

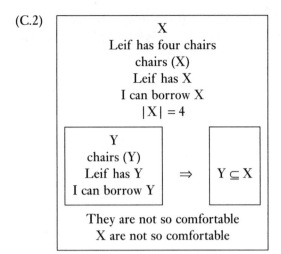

(C.2) satisfies Uniqueness, because *they* got the variable X, which stands for the maximal collection of chairs of Leif's that I can borrow. This time, the set that the definite refers to is based in part on contextually supplied material. That is why it is not MAX/S.

In all the examples above, where the pronoun could felicitously refer back to X, X was unique. Why was it unique? Because the DRS already contained what I call a "uniqueness statement." The "uniqueness statement" is the complex condition in the DRS, the little pair of boxes. A "uniqueness statement" says of some property P that it holds only of the members of X, and not of anything outside of X. The uniqueness statement is then the bit that says about some given property P that this P uniquely identifies the set X.

But what happens if we want a pronoun to refer back to a discourse referent X which is not unique? This would be the case for example if we used the sentence *Leif has four chairs* in a context where a scalar implicature would **not** arise. Well, if a hearer wants a pronoun to refer back to an antecedent X which is not unique in the DRS (s)he has built in her head, what normally happens is that (s)he accommodates a uniqueness statement.

For example, suppose I am looking for a person who has at least four chairs, enough chairs for a meeting we want to hold. Then if you say *Leif has four chairs*, I am not going to conclude that he has exactly four. I am going to simply construct a DRS with a variable, say X, and the conditions chairs(X), Leif has X, and $|X| = 4$. But if you continue by saying *They are not so comfortable*, then I **am** very likely to understand that Leif has exactly four chairs. What happens then is that in order to satisfy the uniqueness requirement on *they*, I accommodate into the DRS a condition like this one:

$$\boxed{\begin{array}{c} Z \\ \hline \text{chairs (Z)} \\ \text{Leif has Z} \end{array}} \Rightarrow \boxed{Z \subseteq X}$$

*They* is associated with X, which, after the accommodation, refers to the unique set containing all of Leif's chairs.

Some clarification may be in order. The fact that Uniqueness can be satisfied by accommodation does not mean that each language user is free to pick any old property and pretend that it uniquely identifies a given definite. That is because, as discussed in 1.7 above, accommodation is a constrained process.

Note, in this connection, that in the last example the uniquely identifying property itself (the property of being chairs of Leif's) is already predicated of X before the accommodation takes place. The only thing that gets accommodated is the "uniqueness statement" – the statement that this property holds of nothing else (nothing outside the set represented by X). I would like to claim that it is fairly easy for a hearer to accommodate such a uniqueness statement in order to satisfy Uniqueness. But the uniqueness statement has to be based on a property which is itself already predicated of the (variable of the) definite. What suitable properties might be present in the DRS depends on the linguistic text and on the nature of pragmatic processes that may contribute additional predicates; generally, the property itself is not accommodated.[10]

Recall the discussion of the dangers of accommodation as a theoretical tool, in 4.1 above. As you see, I felt obliged to argue that my use of accommodation to satisfy Uniqueness was plausible. My argument was that this accommodation is in some sense minimal, and obeys some sort of constraint that forces it to be based on material already present in the discourse representation.

Proceeding to the next example now, consider (17), repeated below. When one encounters the first *they*, one interprets it as "all the colleagues I have to show the document to." (At least, in the absence of contextual information.) The continued text is incompatible with this, and the first *they* is reinterpreted as "all the colleagues I have to show the document to who are in a meeting." The correction that takes place here need not (I think that out of context it definitely does not) create the impression that the speaker is contradicting herself. (17) contrasts with the self-contradictory (18).

(17)   I have to show this document to some/three colleagues. They are in a meeting, and I am waiting for them. I have to show it to at least two other colleagues, but THEY have already left, and I'll have to catch them tomorrow morning.

(18)   I have to show this document to exactly three colleagues. They are in a meeting, and I am waiting for them. I have to show it to at least two other colleagues, but THEY have already left, and I'll have to catch them tomorrow morning.

Analysis: Take the case with *three colleagues*. As mentioned above, (B.3) is the DRS for the first two clauses, plus the scalar implicature which creates the "exactly three" reading.

---

[10]   Perhaps there are some cases where the property itself can be accommodated, but then the choice of accommodated property would be severely restricted.

(B.3)

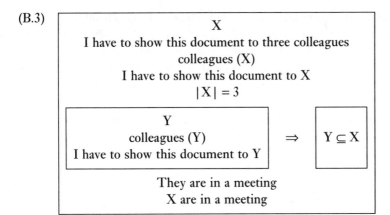

The sentence *I have to show it to at least two other colleagues* contradicts the scalar implicature. Therefore, when this sentence is added, the implicature gets canceled. This leaves the DRS as in (B.4).

(B.4)

```
┌─────────────────────────────────────────────────┐
│                        X                          │
│  I have to show this document to three colleagues │
│                  colleagues (X)                   │
│          I have to show this document to X        │
│                    |X| = 3                        │
│               They are in a meeting               │
│                X are in a meeting                 │
└─────────────────────────────────────────────────┘
```

But now the Uniqueness Condition is violated. Therefore, the hearer must accommodate a condition that makes X a maximal collection. The new condition can be based in part on the information that the members of X are in a meeting, which has been entered into the DRS in the meantime. Such a condition has been accommodated into (B.5). It makes X refer to the set of all the colleagues I have to show the document to who are in a meeting.

(B.5)

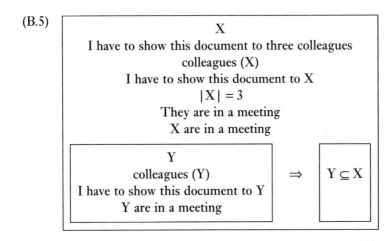

The process just described explains how (17) can be felicitous and non-self-contradictory, is compatible with the intuition that (17) involves correction, and accounts for a natural reading of the first pronoun. A similar process is not possible with (18) (the example with *exactly three colleagues*), and that is why (18) is self-contradictory. The uniqueness statement associated with (18) (the conditional embedded in (A.2) above) is not an implicature, and it cannot be canceled.

The correct prediction concerning (17) relies on the assumption that the Uniqueness Condition has to be satisfied not only by the DRS which obtains immediately after the definite in question is processed, but also by all subsequent revisions and extensions of this DRS. Otherwise, it would have been good enough that *they* satisfied Uniqueness when it was first introduced, and nothing would have had to be accommodated after the cancellation of the implicature which made it unique. That is, examples like (17) show that a definite must remain unique permanently. That is why I have formulated the Uniqueness Condition as a general requirement on DRSs containing a definite. Whenever anything is added to a DRS or changed in it, the result is a new DRS, and this new DRS, like all DRSs, has to satisfy Uniqueness.

I assume, in addition, that the Uniqueness Condition must be satisfied before anything is predicated of the definite in question (not counting its own descriptive content). This is needed in order to get the right predictions about cases involving accommodation. Consider (28) again.

(28)  Leif has four chairs. They are not so comfortable, though.

In a context where the first clause does not trigger a scalar implicature, one would often accommodate the condition that Leif has no more than four chairs. Note, however, that one would **not** accommodate the condition that Leif has no more than four chairs that are not so comfortable. That simply isn't the uniqueness implication which accompanies (28). In other words, the unique set that the definite NP refers to can't be determined on the basis of "are not so comfortable." To predict that, Uniqueness must apply before "are not so comfortable" is predicated of *they*. You can think of it as applying right after the variable of *they* is chosen.

It's the same with definites without linguistic antecedents. Take (36).

(36)  My student asked for reading material on focus.

(36) sounds a bit odd. Why? Because it sounds like I only have one student. That means that in order to make sense of the definite NP, you have accommodated the assumption that I only have one student. You did **not** accommodate the assumption that I only have one student who asked for material on focus. You can't do that, despite the fact that that would be a more plausible assumption. So your accommodation was based just on the definite NP itself, and not on other predicates in the sentence.

Finally, let us return to example (34), repeated below.

(34)  A strange man lives here. If he sees a cat, he screams.

We saw in section 4.2.4 that Cooper's quantificational treatment of pronouns gets the wrong predictions for examples like (34), because it enters the uniqueness statement as part of the antecedent of the conditional. What does my analysis predict for (34)? The DRS is as in (D.1).

(D.1)

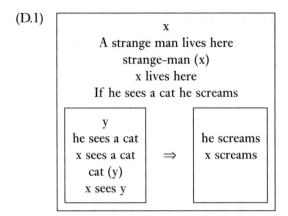

The Uniqueness Condition determines that associating the definite NP *he* with the variable x would be felicitous iff for any model, all the embedding functions verifying the matrix DRS agreed on the value of x. But there is nothing in (D.1) that would guarantee that. So a uniqueness statement must be accommodated into the matrix DRS. Accommodating a uniqueness statement based on what's already predicated of x (on what's predicated of x before anything is predicated of the NP *he*!) will yield the DRS in (D.2).

(D.2)

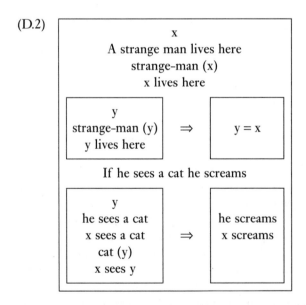

This result is right: the existence and uniqueness of the strange man that lives here have the status of facts in their own right, and are not part of the antecedent of the conditional.

### 4.2.6   Uniqueness is Presupposed

Note that the analysis presented in 4.2.5 claims that the uniqueness of definite NPs is presuppositional in nature. As discussed in 4.1, on Heim's view, a definite NP presupposes an antecedent variable: the use of a definite NP presupposes the existence of a variable which is "old" (present in the DRS and accessible) and which fits the descriptive content of the definite. The effect of the Uniqueness Condition is to add uniqueness to this ps. The current theory claims that the use of a definite NP presupposes the existence of a variable which is not only "old" and fitting the descriptive content, but also unique, in the sense that there is only one set/individual in the model that it could be mapped onto.

For example, look again at the DRS of example (34), given at the end of the last section. In the process of constructing the DRS, the step of moving from

he sees a cat

to

$x_n$ sees a cat (for some variable $x_n$)

can be performed only if the variable $x_n$ is "old," fits the descriptive content of *he* (singular + animate/human + male), and is unique. (Recall that Uniqueness must be checked before anything is predicated of the definite NP.) The strange man variable x is OK for the job in that it is old and fits the descriptive content, of course. But we can't enter the condition x sees a cat into the DRS until we have accommodated a uniqueness statement. Strictly speaking, DRS (D.1) cannot be constructed, because without a uniqueness statement we get stuck at he sees a cat and cannot proceed any further. What we can construct is DRS (D.2), by first accommodating the uniqueness statement and then entering the condition x sees a cat. In short, we can add *he sees a cat* only to a context that already contains the uniqueness statement, which means that *he sees a cat* presupposes that the antecedent of *he* is unique.

If you want to split hairs, perhaps I should note that I never said that you can't **start** processing a definite NP before you make sure that its antecedent is unique. The first step in processing a definite NP is to choose an antecedent variable. Uniqueness is checked after that. So the first step does not presuppose uniqueness. However, I did say that you can't **finish** processing a definite NP – i.e. you can't take your sentence and replace the definite NP with the variable you have chosen – before you make sure that the chosen antecedent is unique. In our example, the final step in processing the pronoun, that of moving from he sees a cat to x sees a cat (=of predicating "sees a cat" of x) does presuppose that x is unique. Perhaps it is fair to say, then, that according to my theory of uniqueness, the act of predicating something of a definite NP presupposes that the definite NP is unique. Predicating "sees a cat" of "he" presupposes that "he" is unique.

Analyzing the uniqueness implications of definite NPs as presuppositional in nature is supported by the intuition that in using a definite NP one is taking it for granted that the NP stands for a unique set/individual. In addition, examples like (34) show that the presuppositional analysis offers the further empirical advantage that when a definite NP occurs under the scope of some operator, the uniqueness implication associated with it is **not** predicted to fall under the scope of that operator. In (34), treating the uniqueness of *he* as presupposed by the antecedent of the conditional (and hence by the entire conditional) ensures that the uniqueness statement must hold independently, and not as part of the antecedent of the conditional.

## 4.3  On the File/DRS as a Representation of the Context of Utterance

**The DRS as the context of utterance:** As noted in 2.2 above, Heim sees her files as representations of the conversational common ground, that is, as representing (a central aspect of) the context of utterance. Therefore, the information contained in a file may arise from linguistic text as well as from non-linguistic contextual factors. It has always seemed natural to me to likewise treat Kamp's DRS as representing the context of utterance. Accordingly, I assume in the work presented in this chapter that in the course of a conversation, the language user develops a DRS which contains not only material which directly represents the text of the conversation, but also additional material supplied by the immediate speech situation, world knowledge, and various pragmatic processes.

I am sometimes surprised to find out that some people do not take it for granted that DRSs represent contexts and may therefore contain "pragmatically supplied" material, but rather question this idea or even object to it.

In this connection, note, first of all, that any adequate theory of how definites are interpreted in real life would have to allow the rule of grammar which interprets definites and/or forces them to be unique to interact with contextually supplied information. The minute we want to actually represent the fact that you can take *The door is open* to mean "the door on which you have just knocked is open," we must in some way represent contextual influence. Perhaps the simplest way we know of doing that is by putting into our semantic representations free variables of which we stipulate that their values are to be supplied by the context of use. That is exactly what Cooper 1979 does when he includes in his interpretation of pronouns a free variable which stands for a uniquely identifying property to be supplied by the context (see 4.2.4 above). I fail to see why anyone should find the strategy of allowing DRSs to contain contextually supplied material any bolder or any more outrageous than the strategy of allowing the value of a variable to be supplied by the context.

Moreover, if we also want to say something about **how** the uniquely identifying property is recovered from the context and about **how** various pragmatic factors might interact with the analysis of uniqueness, then we must also be able to talk about specific bits of pragmatically supplied material and the particular way in which they affect the interpretation of definites. Allowing pragmatically supplied material to be explicitly represented in the DRS is a very convenient way of doing that. As you can see in 4.2.5 above, this strategy has made it possible for me to begin to describe in some detail how factors like implicature, accommodation and contextually supplied information may participate in determining the reference of a definite NP, while, at the same time, stating the uniqueness condition as a general requirement on a single level of representation (on the DRS representing the discourse), without appealing separately to pragmatic processes which interact with uniqueness.

I think that a nice example of what I mean is the treatment of example (17) presented above. We can see what happens when the pronoun gets interpreted as "all the colleagues I have to show the document to" and then reinterpreted as "all the colleagues I have to show the document to who are in a meeting." At the same time, there is no need for any stipulations or specific claims about how implicatures and accommodation interact with the uniqueness condition in such a case. We know independently that there exist scalar implicatures and that implicatures are cancelable, and all we need to do is let this interact with the uniqueness condition. (And with the process of accommodation, which is also independently motivated.) The uniqueness condition itself says absolutely nothing about how the uniquely identifying property might be determined. Because we let pragmatic processes affect the DRS, their influence on what the uniquely identifying property might be follows automatically.

**Semantic vs. syntactic representations of the context:** Recall that Heim's theory does not include a syntactic representation of the context (or of "the whole discourse"). Heim's files, in contrast with Kamp's DRSs, are model-theoretic entities. The work on uniqueness presented above may serve to illustrate why this difference between Heim's FCS and Kamp's DRT may be significant.

I worked in Kamp's framework and could represent an implicature syntactically in the DRS. Therefore, it was also very easy to represent implicature cancellation: all I had to do was to physically erase the implicature from the DRS.[11] But what would we do if we wanted to give the same sort of account in Heim's FCS? A file is just a set of value assignments. When we add an implicature to a file, the set of assignments changes. We get a new file. But in this new file, there is no independent representation of the implicature. How then are we to treat implicature cancellation in this theory? This problem may argue in favor of a level of representation where the propositions assumed in the context are each represented separately.

Note that that would not automatically mean that the context or common ground must be represented syntactically. When we move from a DRS to the corresponding file (=to the set of value assignments that verify the DRS), we lose information. We saw that my treatment of the colleagues example is one place where we might not want to lose that information. To make sure that the information we need is represented, we can either decide that we should indeed use DRSs (i.e. syntactic representations of the context), or else find a way of sufficiently enriching the model-theoretic notion of a file.

## 4.4  Salience and the Geography of the Context of Utterance

Let me recapitulate some of the assumptions we are making: pieces of discourse are added to an existing body of information, called the context or the common ground; the context contains information that was expressed by linguistic text as well as background information and information contributed by pragmatic processes; we use a DRS as a representation of the context.

But there are a lot of questions I haven't addressed. Should a DRS include every proposition stored in our memory? If not, which part of what we know should be represented in the DRS? What's relevant to the current conversation, or "salient" information, or what? Are entailments of propositions that we assume also included in the DRS? Which entailments? Why do conversational implicatures enter the DRS? Do all of them? Should we assume, in addition to the logical structure of discourse that the DRS was devised to represent, some further organization of the DRS, which divides

---

[11]  I assumed that implicatures are marked in the DRS as cancelable.

the information in the DRS into more salient/accessible information and less salient/accessible information?

There is no doubt that various questions about the content and organization of the context of utterance are highly relevant to the study of definite NPs. In particular, some notion of salience (I am using this word as a neutral pre-theoretic term) is obviously crucial to anaphora possibilities, in a way that the original Kamp–Heim theory does not even attempt to deal with. Indeed, there is quite a bit of existing literature on various notions of salience and their role in licensing the use of different kinds of anaphoric expressions. Ariel 1990 presents an extensive study of different types of anaphoric elements (definite descriptions, pronouns, demonstratives, empty NPs . . .) and the differences among them in terms of how easy to access their antecedent is supposed to be. Relevant work within the framework of DRT can be found in Roberts 1993, 1998. (Also see works cited in Ariel 1990 and Roberts 1993, 1998.)

Obviously, there is a whole area of study here, which is beyond the scope of this book. What I will do in this section is just give a few examples that illustrate possible points of interaction between some notion(s) of salience and dynamic semantic theories based on context change, and considerations which might bear on how we view the content and organization of the "context" assumed in such theories. In section 4.5 below, I will present a piece of work that incorporates a particular formal notion of salience into a Kamp–Heim-style notion of context.

Consider the contrast between (37a) and (37b) (due to Barbara Partee, cited in Heim 1982). Also, compare (37b) with (38).

(37)  a.    I dropped ten marbles and found all of them, except for one. It is proba-
            bly under the sofa.
      b.  ?  I dropped ten marbles and found only nine of them. It is probably under
            the sofa.
(38)  I dropped ten marbles and found only nine of them. The missing marble is
      probably under the sofa.

In both (37a) and (37b), the first sentence clearly entails the existence of a missing marble. But in (37a), it is natural to immediately refer to this marble with a pronoun, and in (37b), it is not. Obviously, the contrast comes from the fact that in (37a) there is a linguistic antecedent for the pronoun, while in (37b) there isn't one.

(37b) becomes felicitous if the speaker pauses after the first sentence and looks down at the floor. So, the pronoun can refer to the missing marble even when there is no antecedent NP, provided that the hearers' attention is drawn to the existence of this marble.

(38) sounds natural even when not accompanied by any special gestures. So, a defi-nite description differs from a pronoun – a definite description can more easily be used without a linguistic antecedent. Perhaps it is the description that serves to draw the hearers' attention to the missing marble.

The sort of contrast found in (37) is a central piece of evidence for a theory where formal properties of preceding linguistic text in the discourse play a crucial role in determining possible interpretations for definite NPs (or at least for pronouns). We also see in (37) that the properties of the preceding text which are crucial cannot be reduced to the truth conditions of this text: the first sentence in (37a) and the first sentence in

100 SEMANTICS AND PRAGMATICS WITH DEFINITE NPs

(37b) have the same truth conditions, and nevertheless don't give rise to the same anaphora possibilities. The contrast in (37) motivates the following picture, the picture presented by the Kamp–Heim theory. Definite NPs (or at least pronouns) are anaphoric. In (37a), the NP *one* triggers the introduction into the DRS of a discourse referent, and this discourse referent can serve as the antecedent of the pronoun *it*. In (37b), there is no NP that would be translated as an appropriate antecedent discourse referent.

However, note that what the Kamp–Heim theory assumes is not quite enough for explaining the contrast between (37a) and (37b). Since discourse referents are not triggered only by NPs but also by contextual factors, we have to explain why in (37b) the fact that the first sentence entails the existence of a missing marble is not in itself enough to license the use of the pronoun. Since we are assuming that a salient object in the utterance situation can license anaphora, we will have to refer to some notion of salience in our explanation. It seems that for some reason, the first sentence in (37b) does not make the missing marble salient enough for the pronoun *it* to refer back to it. A gesture (a pause + a look at the floor) may serve to sufficiently raise the salience of the missing marble.

One way of representing the fact that the pronoun is not licensed in (37b) is to claim that the DRS into which we enter the first sentence will not automatically contain a discourse referent standing for the missing marble. This means that we will claim that entailments of the linguistic text do not automatically enter the DRS. When do entailments enter the DRS and when don't they? Here is where we could rely on some notion of salience. We would say that entailed information gets entered into the DRS only if it has actually become salient. And what do we mean by "salient information" here? We presumably mean information which the participants in the conversation have in fact inferred or become aware of. An entailment of the text will enter the DRS only if the language users have in fact inferred it.

And here is another way of representing the fact that the pronoun is not licensed in (37b). Suppose that certain entailments of the linguistic text do automatically enter the DRS. Suppose in particular that the entailment of the first sentence in (37b) that there is a missing marble does automatically enter the DRS. Once we have processed the first sentence in (37b), this entailment will trigger the introduction into the DRS of a discourse referent standing for the missing marble. But, we make a further assumption: pronouns are constrained in use, and may pick as their antecedents only a subset of the discourse referents present in the DRS. Here is where we could rely on some notion of salience. We would say that the discourse referent triggered by the NP *one* in (37a) is salient enough for the pronoun to refer back to it, whereas the discourse referent triggered by the entailment of the first sentence in (37b) that there is a missing marble is not salient enough for the pronoun to refer back to it. Here, it seems that the relevant notion of "salience" has to do with the language users' attention.

The line described in the last paragraph is the line taken in Roberts 1993. Roberts assumes, following work by Grosz and Sidner, that a pronoun processed at a given time t in the discourse may pick up as its antecedent only a discourse referent which is, at t, "attentionally accessible" – that is, only a discourse referent which is included in that portion of the discourse (of the DRS) to which the interlocutors bring their attention at t.[12]

---

[12]   Roberts 1993 notes that the set of "attentionally accessible" discourse referents would be a subset of the set of discourse referents which are "discourse-old" in the sense of Prince 1992 and are included

Let us see what the two approaches just sketched allow us to say about (38) and about its contrast with (37b).

On the first approach (entailments don't automatically enter the DRS), there is no antecedent discourse referent for the NP *the missing marble* in (38) to refer back to – there can't be one any more than there was one in (37b). So, the definite description must refer back to an accommodated discourse referent. It is interesting to note that if that is the case, then the fact that the existence of the missing marble is entailed by the first sentence is not even enough to license the accommodation of a discourse referent for it. An antecedent can be accommodated only for the definite description in (38), and not for the pronoun in (37b).

On Roberts 1993's approach, in all three sentences in (37) and (38), after the first sentence has been processed, there is a discourse referent in the DRS standing for the missing marble. When we interpret the definite NP in the next sentence, is this discourse referent "attentionally accessible"? In (37a), it is, due to the presence of the NP *one*.[13] Therefore, the pronoun can refer back to it. In (37b) and (38), the missing marble discourse referent is not "attentionally accessible." In (38), the definite description simply refers back to this discourse referent, and there is no need for accommodation. In (37b), the definite NP cannot refer back to this discourse referent, because this definite NP is a pronoun, and as such it must have an "attentionally accessible" antecedent.

Let us now turn to the question of how much of what we know is contained in the DRS (i.e. in the context/common ground) that we use for the purposes of a given conversation.

Do we construct in our heads separate DRSs (separate contexts) into which we enter separate conversations? Perhaps we do. In that case, we may take "the context for a given discourse $\alpha$" to be a (small) proper subset of all the propositions that we know or assume. It will presumably contain just those background assumptions that are in some sense salient in connection with the current conversation. Perhaps those assumptions that are relevant to the topic of conversation, and therefore the interlocutors have recalled them or become aware of them. This picture seems to go well with the idea that as a rule, entailments of the linguistic text do not enter the DRS, and that only those entailments which the interlocutors have in fact drawn or become aware of do enter the DRS.

Another approach would go as follows. We identify the context with "everything we know/assume" – there is no boundary separating the two. Abstracting away from changes occurring in our assumptions, this would mean that there will be one big DRS into which we keep entering all pieces of discourse that we wish to add to our context. If we take this approach, it seems natural to assume that certain entailments of the text automatically enter the DRS, whether or not they are "salient" in the sense that the interlocutors are aware of them. And then, as discussed above, we would need some notion or notions of salience – presumably, "salience" which has to do with attention

in that portion of the common ground which Thomason 1990 calls the "conversational record." (Prince's notion of "hearer-old" corresponds with the notion of simply being included in the context/common ground, i.e. with "familiarity" in Heim's sense.)

[13]   I am skipping details here. Roberts explains that at this point in the conversation, the NP *one* is a centered NP (in the sense of e.g. Grosz, Joshi and Weinstein 1983) in the immediately preceding text. See Roberts 1993 and Roberts 1995.

– to distinguish between those discourse referents that can serve as antecedents for definites, or for pronouns, and those that can't.

Certainly, we could develop a combination approach. We could distinguish different DRSs (different contexts) for different conversations, and in addition, within the set of discourse referents in the DRS of a given conversation, we may recognize different degrees of salience. We may for example distinguish at each given point in the conversation those discourse referents which are "attentionally accessible" at that point and those which are not. Alternatively, we may assume a continuum of different degrees of salience (or of ease of getting accessed) of discourse referents, following the line taken in Ariel 1990. Of course, whatever approach we choose, to have a complete picture, we must explicate the relevant notion(s) of salience and decide how to represent them in connection with our context-change based semantic theory.

Finally, let me turn to conversational implicatures. Do conversational implicatures get represented in the DRS? Do all of them? In my work on uniqueness, I assumed that implicatures do enter the DRS. Certainly, I must include in the DRS those implicatures that I actually use. Is this justified? The question may seem particularly interesting if we assume that entailments of the text do not, in general, enter the DRS – why should implicatures and entailments differ in this respect? Of course, one thing which supports my assumption that implicatures enter the DRS is that it seems to work well for my data. As noted in Kadmon 1987, ch. 3, this assumption may also be further motivated as follows.

We said that hearers probably do enter into the DRS those inferences that they in fact draw or become aware of. It is clear that hearers don't in general calculate or become aware of all the logical consequences of what they hear. (Actual) implicatures, on the other hand, are by definition inferences that do get calculated, on the basis of Grice's maxims, in order to find out how the speaker is being cooperative. If they don't get calculated, they don't exist. Thus all implicatures are in fact inferences drawn by the hearer, and all enter the DRS.

Another consideration (due to Fred Landman, p.c.) is the following. However you want to think about the context, once a statement has been accepted into it, information about how and when it was conveyed is lost. Syntactic, morphological and phonological information is already lost when utterances are mapped into DRSs. If you think that the syntactic representation in the DRS is at some stage mapped onto semantic entities ("files" of some sort), for purposes of long term storage in memory, perhaps, then surely some more information gets lost. Now entailments are inseparable from the propositions that entail them. So when you accept a proposition, you can always recover its entailments. Implicatures, on the other hand, are not recoverable from the accepted propositions alone, because they are calculated on the basis of additional factors – the context of utterance, and in the case of Manner implicatures, the very phrasing of the utterance. So if the implicatures are to be preserved, they must be represented in the DRS (and subsequent semantic representations) in their own right.

## 4.5 Referential and Attributive Definites: Formalizing "Salience"

Shimojima 1993 is concerned with Donnellan 1971's well-known distinction between "referential" and "attributive" uses of definite NPs. Shimojima argues that the intuitions which underlie the alleged attributive vs. referential distinction can be accounted for on the basis of an enriched theory of how we keep track of discourse referents, without postulating a difference between attributive definites and referential definites. Shimojima's account involves a certain notion of salience, which is formalized and integrated with the Kamp–Heim theory of definite NPs.

### 4.5.1   Data

Shimojima starts by presenting some data, as follows. Suppose Holmes investigates the murder of Smith. Since we trust Holmes, we enter everything he says into our conversational common ground. Sometimes Holmes indicates that he has changed his mind, and we revise our common ground accordingly. Let us now look at what Holmes says during the investigation. At various points in the course of the investigation, we will stop and evaluate the four statements given in (39) on the basis of the common ground that we have constructed up to that point.

(39)    (i)    Jones is insane.
        (ii)   Bond is insane.
        (iii)  Jones is a Buddhist.
        (iv)   Bond is a Buddhist.

Let us start. Early in the investigation, before he has formed any hypotheses concerning the identity of the murderer, Holmes says (40). Later, Holmes comes to say (41). Holmes then interviews Jones, and reports his sole finding by uttering (42).

(40)    Smith's murderer is insane.        (attributive)
(41)    Jones is Smith's murderer.
(42)    Smith's murderer is a Buddhist.     (referential)

At this point, we stop and evaluate the statements in (39). Based on our current common ground (i.e. based on what Holmes has said so far), the judgments are as follows.

|      |                       |                |
| ---- | --------------------- | -------------- |
| (i)  | Jones is insane.      | TRUE           |
| (ii) | Bond is insane.       | WE DON'T KNOW  |
| (iii)| Jones is a Buddhist.  | TRUE           |
| (iv) | Bond is a Buddhist.   | WE DON'T KNOW  |

Later on in the investigation, Holmes changes his mind, and says (43).

(43)    Bond is Smith's murderer.

At this point, we stop again and evaluate the statements in (39). The judgments based on the current common ground are as follows.

|      |                       |                |
| ---- | --------------------- | -------------- |
| (i)  | Jones is insane.      | WE DON'T KNOW  |
| (ii) | Bond is insane.       | TRUE           |
| (iii)| Jones is a Buddhist.  | TRUE           |
| (iv) | Bond is a Buddhist.   | WE DON'T KNOW  |

Later, Holmes changes his mind again, and says (44).

(44)   Nobody murdered Smith. (It was suicide.)

At this point, the judgements are as follows.

| | | |
|---|---|---|
| (i) | Jones is insane. | WE DON'T KNOW |
| (ii) | Bond is insane. | WE DON'T KNOW |
| (iii) | Jones is a Buddhist. | TRUE |
| (iv) | Bond is a Buddhist. | WE DON'T KNOW |

Finally, Holmes changes his mind once more, and returns to his original hypothesis. He says (41) again.

(41)   Jones is Smith's murderer.

At this point, the judgments are as follows.

| | | |
|---|---|---|
| (i) | Jones is insane. | TRUE |
| (ii) | Bond is insane. | WE DON'T KNOW |
| (iii) | Jones is a Buddhist. | TRUE |
| (iv) | Bond is a Buddhist. | WE DON'T KNOW |

Throughout the evolution of our common ground, we never revised the information that Jones is a Buddhist. Insanity, on the other hand, was first ascribed to Jones, then to Bond, then to nobody, and finally to Jones again. It is precisely this sort of data, notes Shimojima, that the referential vs. attributive distinction is based on. We try to explain the difference by saying that in (42) (*Smith's murderer is a Buddhist*) the definite description *Smith's murderer* was used referentially, whereas in (40) (*Smith's murderer is insane*) it was used attributively.

### 4.5.2   Analysis

Shimojima argues in detail that in order to provide an adequate theory of the data, we need to be able to do the following:

 (i)   Partially identify two discourse referents without merging them completely, so that they may get separated again;
 (ii)   Discard a discourse referent without irrevocably losing the information about it, so that it may still get "reactivated";
(iii)   Having partially identified two discourse referents, distinguish one of them as more "salient" or "dominant" than the other one.

Informally, Shimojima's analysis may be described using Heim's file card metaphor. Suppose we already have three discourse referents, x, y, and z, representing Jones, Bond, and Smith's murderer, respectively. We have the following file.

File 0:

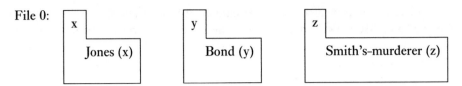

Holmes says (40) (*Smith's murderer is insane*). So, we ascribe insanity to the discourse referent z, and get file 1.

File 1:

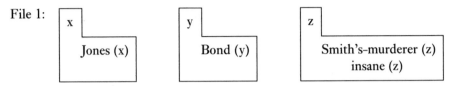

Next, Holmes says (41) (*Jones is Smith's murderer*). What we do in response, suggests Shimojima, is stack the x card on top of the z card:

File 2:

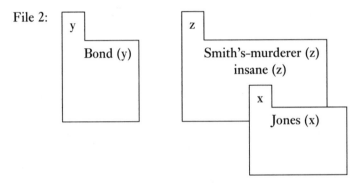

The effect of this move is twofold: the two discourse referents z and x are now partially identified (they represent the same entity), and the discourse referent x is more salient/dominant than z.

Next, Holmes says (42) (*Smith's murderer is a Buddhist*). This sentence is about the entity represented by x and z. So the predicate "Buddhist" must be entered somewhere in the stack consisting of cards x and z. Shimojima suggests that in such a situation, the predicate is predicated of the discourse referent that's the most salient/dominant – it is entered on the card that's on top of the stack. Card x is on top, so the predicate "Buddhist" is entered there. We get the following file.

File 3:

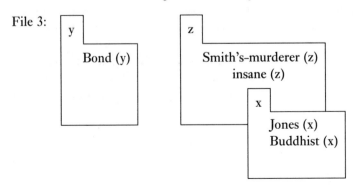

Now we stop and evaluate the statements in (39). Since all three predicates "Jones," "insane" and "Buddhist" are ascribed to the same entity (the one represented by discourse referents z and x), we get that according to file 3, Jones is both insane and a Buddhist. That is the correct prediction – it matches our intuitive judgments at this point in Holmes' investigation.

Next, Holmes says (43) (*Bond is Smith's murderer*). In response, we need to cancel the information that Jones is the murderer, and enter the information that Bond is. So we separate cards z and x, and stack card y on top of card z:

File 4:

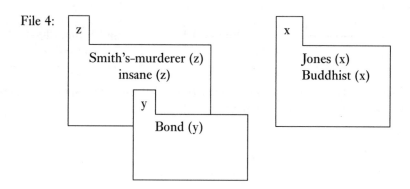

According to file 4, Buddhism is ascribed to Jones, but insanity is ascribed to Bond. That is again the correct prediction.

Next, Holmes says (44) (*Nobody murdered Smith*). We must discard the murderer file card z. Shimojima suggests that instead of throwing it out, we "deactivate" it. Let us represent that by pulling the card from its stack and noting on it that it is not to be mapped onto the model. We get the following file.

File 5:

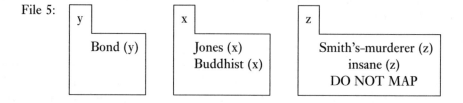

What do we know according to file 5? Since we are to ignore card z, insanity is not ascribed to anyone now. Buddhism continues to be ascribed to Jones, as before. Again, the prediction is right.

Finally, Holmes says (41) (*Jones is Smith's murderer*). In response, we need to cancel the information that there is no murderer, and enter the information that Bond is the murderer. So we reactivate card z, and stack card x on top of it, restoring our file to the following state.

File 6:

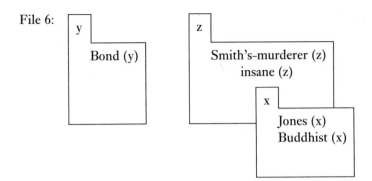

According to file 6, both insanity and Buddhism are again assigned to Jones. This too is the correct prediction.

Note that according to Shimojima's analysis, "identity statements" like (41) and (43) do not add conditions to the file cards, but rather stack together two file cards. Ordinary predicative statements like (40) and (42) do add a condition. As usual in the Kamp–Heim theory, we look for an "old" card fitting the descriptive content of the definite NP. But we don't (necessarily) enter the new condition on that card itself: instead, the new condition must be entered on the topmost card in the same stack.

We see then that the data of subsection 4.5.1 can be handled while retaining a uniform analysis of definite NPs. The intuitions about the alleged referential vs. attributive distinction are taken to be based on our ability to retain two distinct discourse referents even when we have (partially) identified them, and further, on the fact that one of the two discourse referents is always more salient than the other one. (We get a so-called "attributive" use of a given definite NP if when that definite NP is uttered, the most salient discourse referent corresponding to it is the one carrying its descriptive content.)

What is it, exactly, that determines within a stack which file card is on top at each stage in the evolution of the file? Originally, Shimojima suggested that when an "identity statement" is processed, the card corresponding to the subject NP is placed on top of the card corresponding to the object NP, and the rest follows automatically from the order of the utterances in the discourse. But Shimojima himself notes, following Hans Kamp (p.c.), that this does not quite cover the facts.

Suppose Holmes says the following.

(40)  Smith's murderer is insane.     (attributive)
(41)  Jones is Smith's murderer.
(45)  Smith's murderer used a gun.

Shimojima's original suggestion predicts that the definite in (45) must be used "referentially," and can't be used "attributively." That's because when (45) is uttered, the "identity statement" (41) has placed the Jones card on top of the murderer card. However, empirically, a "referential" use of the definite in (45) is felt to be possible too. If Holmes says (45) because he observes gun powder on Jones' hands, then we interpret (45) "referentially." However, if Holmes says (45) because he observes a bullet hole in Smith's body, we can easily interpret (45) "attributively."

The conclusion seems to be that it is not just the phrasing and order of the linguistic text that determines the relative salience/dominance of two partially identified discourse referents. Rather, more "pragmatic" factors are also involved – the non-linguistic situation too may affect the ordering within a stack of file cards.

### 4.5.3   Formulation

It is natural and appealing to use the metaphor of placing a file card "on top of the stack" when we want to talk about some discourse referents as being more salient than others. It is important to remember though that the idea of a card file is only a metaphor. As emphasized in Heim 1983a, Heim has not fully formalized the intuitive notion of a file. Needless to say, she has not formalized the notion of placing a card "on top." One of the nice things about Shimojima's work is that he shows how his notion of "salience," informally described above, may be defined and incorporated into a Kamp–Heim style framework.

The precise formulation of Shimojima's theory depends, of course, on the particular formal notion of context that we choose to use, and can be adjusted to fit one's favorite formal framework. I am not concerned with technical details here. I will sketch below a rough formulation of Shimojima's theory, adapted from the formulation given in his paper, and based on Kamp's DRT.

I think it is fair to say that Shimojima's analysis consists of adding the following five proposals to the usual Kamp–Heim theory.

(i)   The formal notion of context is enriched, by adding to it a **replacer function**. This function maps each variable in the context onto a variable which serves as its **replacer**.

Notation:   $x_i \rightarrow x_j$       "$x_j$ is the replacer of $x_i$"

Explanation: Saying the $x_j$ is the replacer of $x_i$ corresponds to the intuitive idea that the variables $x_j$ and $x_i$ are partially identified, with $x_j$ more salient than $x_i$. ("Card $x_j$ is placed on top of card $x_i$.")

Rough formulation:
A context is defined as a pair:   $c = \langle K, f \rangle$,
where K is a DRS, and f, the **replacer function**, is a (possibly partial) function from $U_K$ to $U_K$.
($U_K$ is the set of variables called the "universe" of DRS K.)

Default: In the absence of any indication to the contrary, the replacer of each variable is that variable itself. (In other words, the default replacer function is the identity function.)

(ii)   The sole effect of an "identity statement" such as (41) or (43) is that it alters the replacer function. According to Shimojima's original suggestion, it contributes the information that the variable corresponding to the subject NP is now the **replacer** of the variable corresponding to the object NP.[14]

(iii)   Ordinary predicative statements like (40) and (42) add conditions to the DRS, as is standard in DRT. However, the processing of a definite NP is slightly altered. We choose an "old" variable that fits the descriptive content, as usual. But instead of replacing the definite NP with the chosen variable, we replace the definite NP with the replacer of that variable. So we enter into the DRS a condition where the predicate is predicated of the replacer of the antecedent variable.

---

[14]   As noted in 4.5.2 above, it seems that in fact we need to allow more "pragmatic" factors to play a role in determining relative salience – and hence in determining which variable becomes the "replacer" and which becomes the "replacee."

(iv)   When we wish to discard a variable, as we do when Holmes utters (44), we do not erase anything from our DRS. Instead, we alter the replacer function: we make this function undefined for the variable in question. So this variable no longer has a replacer.

(v)   Let us distinguish between the information **directly represented** in a context c (independently of the replacer function) and the information **supported** by a context c (via the replacer function).

Rough definitions:
A context $c = \langle K, f \rangle$ **directly represents** that information which is represented in the standard way by DRS K.
Let $f(K)$ be a variant of DRS K, obtained by replacing each variable-occurrence in K with an occurrence of its replacer, and erasing all those conditions of K which contain a variable that has no replacer.
A context $c = \langle K, f \rangle$ **supports** that information which is represented in the standard way by DRS $f(K)$.

It is the information **supported** by a given context c which corresponds with the information which we intuitively take to be part of our common ground. Thus, the theory predicts the judgments of section 4.5.1 on the basis of the information **supported** by our context at each point in Holmes' investigation.

Let us see how these proposals predict the data of subsection 4.5.1. Our initial context, context 0, looks like this:

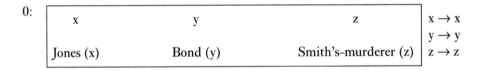

Holmes says (40) (*Smith's murderer is insane*). The antecedent of the definite NP is z, as is standard in DRT. Since the replacer of z is also z, we enter the condition insane(z) into the DRS, and get context 1.

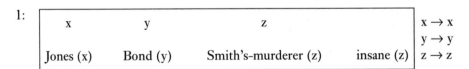

Holmes says (41) (*Jones is Smith's murderer*). This yields context 2.

2:

| x | y | z | | $x \to x$ |
|---|---|---|---|---|
| | | | | $y \to y$ |
| Jones (x) | Bond (y) | Smith's-murderer (z) | insane (z) | $z \to x$ |

Holmes says (42) (*Smith's murderer is a Buddhist*). The antecedent of the definite NP is z. Since the replacer of z is x, we enter the condition Buddhist(x) into the DRS, and get context 3.

3:

| x | y | z | | x → x |
|---|---|---|---|---|
| | | | | y → y |
| Jones(x) Bond(y) | Smith's-murderer(z) insane(z) Buddhisht(x) | | | z → x |

Now let us stop and consider the four statements in (39). In the DRS-variant obtained via the replacer function, all zs are replaced by xs. Therefore, the situation is as follows.

(i)   Jones is insane.          SUPPORTED BY 3
(ii)  Bond is insane.           NOT SUPPORTED BY 3
(iii) Jones is a Buddhist.      SUPPORTED BY 3
(iv)  Bond is a Buddhist.       NOT SUPPORTED BY 3

This makes the correct prediction: at this point in the investigation, we intuitively feel that our common ground contains the information that Jones is both insane and a Buddhist.

Next, Holmes says (43) (*Bond is Smith's murderer*), and that results in context 4.

4:

| x | y | z | | x → x |
|---|---|---|---|---|
| | | | | y → y |
| Jones(x) Bond(y) | Smith's-murderer(z) insane(z) Buddhist(x) | | | z → y |

Let us consider our four statements now. The situation is as follows.

(i)   Jones is insane.          NOT SUPPORTED BY 4
(ii)  Bond is insane.           SUPPORTED BY 4
(iii) Jones is a Buddhist.      SUPPORTED BY 4
(iv)  Bond is a Buddhist.       NOT SUPPORTED BY 4

This makes the correct prediction: the intuition is indeed that at this point, insanity is ascribed to Bond, and Buddhism is ascribed to Jones.

Next, Holmes says (44) (*Nobody murdered Smith*). We must discard the murderer variable z, and we do that by making the replacer function undefined for z. So we get context 5.

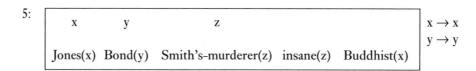

5:

| x | y | z | | x → x |
|---|---|---|---|---|
| | | | | y → y |
| Jones(x) Bond(y) | Smith's-murderer(z) insane(z) Buddhist(x) | | | |

In the DRS-variant obtained via the replacer function, the variable z and the two conditions containing it do not occur. Therefore, the situation is as follows, and again we get the correct prediction.

|      |                     |                     |
|------|---------------------|---------------------|
| (i)  | Jones is insane.    | NOT SUPPORTED BY 5  |
| (ii) | Bond is insane.     | NOT SUPPORTED BY 5  |
| (iii)| Jones is a Buddhist.| SUPPORTED BY 5      |
| (iv) | Bond is a Buddhist. | NOT SUPPORTED BY 5  |

Finally, Holmes says (41) (*Jones is Smith's murderer*). This yields context 6.

6:

| x   y              z                                                    | $x \rightarrow x$ |
|-------------------------------------------------------------------------|-------------------|
|                                                                         | $y \rightarrow y$ |
| Jones(x)  Bond(y)  Smith's-murderer(z)  insane(z)  Buddhist(x)          | $z \rightarrow x$ |

Now the situation is as follows, so again we get the correct prediction.

|      |                     |                     |
|------|---------------------|---------------------|
| (i)  | Jones is insane.    | SUPPORTED BY 6      |
| (ii) | Bond is insane.     | NOT SUPPORTED BY 6  |
| (iii)| Jones is a Buddhist.| SUPPORTED BY 6      |
| (iv) | Bond is a Buddhist. | NOT SUPPORTED BY 6  |

# Part Two

## *Presupposition*

# 5

# *Presupposition Projection: The Basic Analysis*

In this and the following five chapters, I will be concerned with what is called "the projection problem for presuppositions." In my opinion, the most successful and insightful theory of ps projection known today is the theory started by Stalnaker 1974 and Karttunen 1974, and later developed by Irene Heim.

This chapter will be devoted to the basic Stalnaker–Karttunen–Heim analysis. I have chosen to focus here on ps projection in conjunctions and conditionals. In this chapter, I will discuss only examples that exhibit a certain sort of paradigmatic behavior of pss with respect to ps projection; I will deliberately ignore examples that seem to involve ps-cancellation or that exhibit unusual or poorly understood behavior of pss.

## 5.1 Data

Consider the simple, affirmative sentences in (1)–(5).

(1) The king of France is bald.
(2) Joan has stopped drinking wine for breakfast.
(3) JOHN drinks too.
(4) Even JOHN drinks.
(5) It was Fred who ate the beans.

Let us assume that each of these sentences, taken on its own, invariably presupposes its ps: sentence (1) invariably presupposes that there is a unique king of France, sentence (2) invariably presupposes that Joan used to drink wine for breakfast, sentence (5) invariably presupposes that someone ate the beans, etc.[1] Clearly, sentences like (1)–(5) **entail** their pss. For example, (1) not only presupposes that there is a unique king of France, but also entails that.

---

[1]   This assumption may not be quite right. (It seems, in particular, that focusing the trigger tends to weaken or cancel the ps status of the associated ps.) For some relevant discussion, see 11.6 and 21.2 below. Nonetheless, I am now going to make this assumption anyway, as is the usual practice in the literature. (For present purposes, please ignore examples in which the trigger is focused.)

Now, consider what happens if we take one of these sentences and embed it in a more complex sentence. Will the bigger sentence still have the same ps? We often phrase this question in one of the following ways. (i) Will the ps "survive" in the bigger sentence? (ii) Will the bigger sentence "inherit" the ps of the embedded sentence? As is well known, the answer to this question depends on the nature of the linguistic environment in which we embed the sentence.

When we examine ps-carrying expressions embedded under various operators, we see that there are systematic patterns of ps inheritance (of when it is that complex sentences inherit the ps of one of their parts). The "projection problem for presuppositions" is the problem of how to accurately describe these systematic patterns, and how to develop a theory that will account for them.

Karttunen 1973 presents some detailed empirical work on ps projection. He studies different types of operators under which we may embed ps-carrying expressions, and describes some of the basic facts about the projection of pss embedded under such operators. Karttunen divides operators into three groups: "holes," "plugs," and "filters."

"Holes" are operators which "let pss go through": a ps embedded under a "hole" is inherited by the larger sentence containing that "hole." For example, in (6)–(9) below, the underlined items are "holes." The matrix sentence inherits the ps that there is a king of France.

(6)   The king of France is <u>not</u> bald.
(7)   Is the king of France bald<u>?</u>
(8)   It is <u>possible</u> that the king of France is bald.
(9)   Sue <u>knows</u> that the king of France is bald.

"Plugs" do not "let pss go through": a ps embedded under a "plug" is not inherited by the larger sentence containing that "plug." For example, the verb *believe* is a "plug." In (10) below, the clause embedded under *believe* has the ps that Joan used to drink wine for breakfast, but sentence (10) as a whole does not inherit this ps.

(10)   Sue <u>believes</u> that Joan has stopped drinking wine for breakfast.

The "filters" are the connectives – conjunction, disjunction, *if... then....* Sentences (11)–(16) below will serve to illustrate some of the most basic data on ps inheritance in conjunctions and conditionals. These sentences all have sentence (3) (*JOHN drinks too*) embedded in them. Let us assume that sentence (3) presupposes that somebody else drinks besides John.[2] Let us ignore any other ps that (3) might have. Which of sentences (11)–(16) inherit the ps of (3)?

(11)   JOHN drinks too and Mary doesn't like it.
(12)   Bill is not present and JOHN drinks too.
(13)   Bill drinks and JOHN drinks too.
(14)   If JOHN drinks too, then the bottle is empty.
(15)   If the bottle is empty, then JOHN drinks too.
(16)   If Bill drinks, then JOHN drinks too.

---

[2]   This is in fact not quite accurate. The truth seems to be that *too* is anaphoric – see Kripke 1990; Heim 1992. However, that doesn't matter right now.

First of all, sentences (11) and (14), in which (3) occurs as the left-hand clause, inherit the ps. Each of these sentences, taken as a whole, presupposes that somebody other than John drinks.

Secondly, it looks like sentences (12) and (15), where (3) is the right-hand clause, also inherit the ps. It seems that each of these sentences, taken as a whole, presupposes that somebody other than John drinks.

Finally, look at (13) and (16). (3) is again the right-hand clause. Obviously, the special thing about these examples is that the left-hand clause entails the ps of the right-hand clause (if Bill drinks, then someone other than John drinks). Does (13) inherit the ps of (3)? No, it does not. As it happens, (13) **entails** that someone other than John drinks. But it does not take that for granted. (13) can easily be uttered in a context where it is not assumed that somebody else drinks besides John. (13) **tells** you that somebody else drinks. What about (16)? (16) does not inherit the ps of (3) either. (16) certainly doesn't take it for granted that anybody drinks. (In (16), the ps of (3) isn't entailed, either.)

Examples like (11)–(16) show (i) that conjunctions and conditionals behave alike with respect to ps projection, and (ii) that these connectives are "filters," viz. they "let pss go through" only discriminately: sometimes the compound sentences inherit the ps of an embedded clause, and sometimes they don't.

Karttunen 1973 points out that from data such as what we've seen so far, emerges the following generalization. A compound sentence of the form p ∧ q or p → q inherits all the pss of p, and also all the pss of q except those that are entailed by p. Another way of stating the generalization is as follows. In general, the pss of a compound sentence are all the pss of its parts except for those that are "filtered out." The specific rule (or "filtering condition") for a sentence of the form p ∧ q or p → q is the one given in (17).

(17)   Filter out any ps of q which is entailed by p.

Karttunen 1974 points out a complication, which indicates that the generalization about conjunctions and conditionals needs to be refined. The following four examples all illustrate the same thing.

(18)   Geraldine is a Mormon and she has given up wearing her holy underwear!
(19)   There is going to be a depression, and the president of General Motors will lose his job too.
(20)   If Geraldine is a Mormon, she has given up wearing her holy underwear.
(21)   If there is a depression, the president of General Motors will lose his job too.

We are concerned with the ps of the right-hand clause (the ps of "q"):

   ps of q:   Geraldine used to wear holy underwear.
              Someone besides the president of GM will lose their job.

Consider first example (21). Does (21) inherit the ps of q? No, it does not. (21) does not take it for granted that someone besides the president of GM will lose their job. (21) would be fine in a context where it is not assumed that there is going to be a depression, and not assumed that anyone will lose their job at all.

Why is it that (21) doesn't inherit the ps of q? So far, we have only filtered out pss of q that were logically entailed by p. Here we need to filter out the ps that someone besides the president of GM will lose their job, which is **not** logically entailed by the antecedent of (21). (Logically, there can be a depression without anybody losing their job.) What is going on here is quite clear: in context – in a context where it is assumed that during depressions many people lose their jobs – our p does entail the ps of our q. That is why the ps of q is filtered out.

To confirm this idea, try to imagine (21) in a context where it is not assumed that depressions necessarily cause anyone to lose their jobs. Then (21) as a whole does presuppose (= take it for granted) that someone besides the president of GM will lose their job.

Same thing with (18), for example. Does (18) presuppose (take it for granted) that Geraldine used to wear holy underwear? Depends on our contextual assumptions. If we have no assumptions whatsoever about what Mormons wear, then, yes, (18) presupposes that Geraldine used to wear holy underwear. But in a context where it is assumed that Mormons are required to wear holy underwear, (18) as a whole does not presuppose that Geraldine used to wear holy underwear. Why not? Because **in that context** the first conjunct entails the ps of the second conjunct.

Thus, Karttunen 1974 has shown that the entailment relevant to the filtering condition in (17) is "entailment in context." In other words, we should replace (17) with (17′).

(17′)  Filter out any ps of q which is entailed by the context + p.

But wait a minute. We haven't quite finished stating the facts about examples (18)–(21). As pointed out in K&P 1979, even when sentences (18)–(21) do not inherit the ps of q, they do have **some** ps that concerns q: they presuppose that p entails the ps of q. Consider your intuitive judgment about (18) and (20). If they don't presuppose that Geraldine used to wear holy underwear, they do presuppose that if Geraldine is a Mormon, she used to wear holy underwear. Likewise, if (19) and (21) don't presuppose that someone besides the president of GM will lose their job, they do presuppose that if there is a depression, someone besides the president of GM will lose their job. I sum this up in (22).

(22)   If (18)–(21) don't presuppose ps(q), they do presuppose that $p \rightarrow ps(q)$.

In the light of what we've learned from (18)–(21), we might as well re-examine our judgments concerning (12) and (15).

(12)   Bill is not present and JOHN drinks too.
(15)   If the bottle is empty, then JOHN drinks too.

I say above that (12) and (15) seem to inherit ps(q) – that they seem to presuppose that somebody other than John drinks. That is certainly what it looks like when we consider (12) and (15) out of context. However, the fact is that (12) and (15) behave just like (18)–(21). (12) and (15) don't always presuppose ps(q). (12) and (15) are felicitous even in a context c where it is not assumed that ps(q) holds, provided that the context c does guarantee that $p \rightarrow ps(q)$.

Let me illustrate this, using (12). When we hear (12) out of the blue, we judge that it presupposes ps(q) – that is, we judge that it takes it for granted that someone besides John drinks. Out of the blue, we imagine that (12) would be uttered in a context which contains the assumption that ps(q), such as context (A).

> Context (A):   I need a non-drinker to support me in avoiding alcohol. It is known that Bill is a teetotaler. You've just mentioned the (known) fact that Mary drinks.

However, the fact is that (12) need not be uttered in a context where it is already assumed that someone other than John drinks. For example, (12) can be felicitously uttered in context (B).

> Context (B):   I need a non-drinker to support me in avoiding alcohol. The only possible reason for anybody to not be present (in this room) is to drink vodka in the other room.

(12) is felicitous in context (B), because context (B) guarantees that if Bill is not present, then someone other than John drinks. Having looked at context (B), what is it, you think, that (12) does invariably presuppose concerning ps(q)? Well, (12) presupposes that $p \rightarrow ps(q)$.

I think that this more or less covers all the basic facts about ps-projection in conjunctions and conditionals.

## 5.2   The Stalnaker–Karttunen Analysis

I will start with some preliminaries. As noted in section 1.4, both Stalnaker 1974 and Karttunen 1974 see pss as requirements on the context. We can state the Stalnaker–Karttunen definition of what a ps is as in (23).

(23)   B is a ps of S iff S can be felicitously uttered only in contexts that entail B.

Keep in mind that we are not concerned now with how the pss of simple sentences are created – we simply assume them as given. For example, we simply know that the sentence *JOHN drinks too* can be felicitously uttered in a context c only if c entails that someone besides John drinks.

Note that according to definition (23), any tautology is presupposed by any sentence. For example, (24) officially presupposes (25), since any context whatsoever entails (25), and hence (24) can be uttered felicitously only in contexts that entail (25).

(24)   Bill is present.
(25)   If Bill is Japanese then Bill is Japanese.

Of course, if a sentence has only tautologies for "official" presuppositions, then as far as our intuitive judgment is concerned, that sentence has no presuppositions at all.

Finally, let us adopt the following terminology (cf. Karttunen 1974).

(26)   A context c **admits** a sentence S = c satisfies (= entails) ps(S)

By the notation ps(S) I mean "the presupposition of S" (which could be a conjunction of several pss). When a context entails the ps of S we say that it "satisfies" that ps.

Now we get to the main point. Based on their insight regarding what a ps is, Stalnaker 1974 and Karttunen 1974 (each of them independently) also came up with an insightful explanation of ps projection. Their crucial idea is quite simple: **a ps has to be satisfied by its "local" context**.

More explicitly, the general principle of the Stalnaker–Karttunen theory is given in (27).

(27)   A context c admits a sentence S iff each of the constituent sentences of S is admitted by its local context.

The idea is this: when you have a compound sentence, you shouldn't just look at the context in which the compound sentence as a whole is uttered. You have to take into account the separate clauses that are its parts. Each of these clauses has to be admitted by its own local context.

But what **is** the "local context" of each clause? Consider the case of a conjunction. It is very natural, isn't it, to think that the first conjunct is asserted first and added to the context (to the common ground) right away, and the second conjunct is asserted afterwards. In that case, the second conjunct is added to a context (common ground) which already contains the first conjunct. So asserting a conjunction will proceed as sketched in (28).

(28)   Suppose $p \land q$ is uttered in context c.
First, you add p to c. This creates a new context, $c + p$.
Afterwards, you add q to $c + p$.
Hence, c is the local context of p, and $c + p$ is the local context of q.

At this point, our theory of ps projection includes definition (23), principle (27), and the assumptions stated in (28) about what constitutes the local context for each conjunct. The combination of these three things correctly predicts all the facts mentioned above about ps projection in conjunctions, in a very natural way.

What the current theory says about conjunctions may be summarized as in (29).[3] Explanations and illustrations will follow.

(29)   **(i)**   **Concerning:**     ps(p)
**The theory requires just this:** c must satisfy ps(p).
**And so the prediction is:** $p \land q$ inherits ps(p).
**(ii)**   **Concerning:**     ps(q)
**The theory requires just this:** $c + p$ must satisfy ps(q).
**And so the prediction is:** $p \land q$ presupposes $p \rightarrow$ ps(q).

---

[3]   In discussing compound examples, I will carry on referring to clause p, clause q, and contexts c and $c + p$. I take it you will follow me.

The prediction concerning ps(p) is very simple. For example, take (11).

(11)   JOHN drinks too and Mary doesn't like it.

What must hold for (11) to be admitted by c? By (27) and (28), p must be admitted by c, which is its local context. So c must entail that someone besides John drinks. Since c is the context in which (11) as a whole is uttered, we get that (11) must be uttered in a context where it is already assumed that someone besides John drinks. By definition (23), this is exactly the same as saying that (11) presupposes that someone besides John drinks. So, we get the right prediction.

The situation concerning ps(q) is somewhat more complicated, because the requirement imposed by the theory can be satisfied in several different ways.

What does the theory require concerning ps(q)? Since the local context of q is c + p, the theory determines that q must be admitted by c + p. Or, in other words, c + p must satisfy (= entail) ps(q).

First of all, this obviously gives us the correct prediction that if c + p fails to entail ps(q), then c does not admit the conjunction. For example, (12) is not felicitous if c + p fails to entail that someone other than John drinks – (12) is not felicitous if there is no reason to assume that anybody besides John drinks.

(12)   Bill is not present and JOHN drinks too.

Secondly, it is clear that the requirement imposed by the theory can be satisfied "**internally**," so to speak: it can be satisfied by p, without any "help" from the context c. In which case, nothing will be required of c. (To be precise, nothing will be required of c with respect to ps(q).) Such is exactly the case with (13).

(13)   Bill drinks and JOHN drinks too.

In this example, p, all by itself, satisfies ps(q): if Bill drinks, then someone besides John drinks. Therefore, it won't matter in what context (13) is uttered – the ps of q will be satisfied whatever the context is. This correctly predicts our intuitive judgment that (13) does not inherit ps(q), and that (13) as a whole does not, in fact, presuppose anything at all concerning the ps of q.

If it is not the case that p alone entails ps(q), then the theory determines that the initial context c will have to play a role in satisfying ps(q). One case in which ps(q) will be satisfied is if c, all by itself, entails ps(q). This correctly predicts, for example, that (12) will be felicitous in context (A).

> Context (A):   I need a non-drinker to support me in avoiding alcohol. It is known that Bill is a teetotaler. You've just mentioned the (known) fact that Mary drinks.

And there is one more remaining possibility: the theory determines that ps(q) can also be satisfied by the "joined forces" of c and p. This correctly predicts, for example, that (12) will be felicitous in context (B).

Context (B):   I need a non–drinker to support me in avoiding alcohol. The only
possible reason for anybody to not be present (in this room) is to
drink vodka in the other room.

That's it, really. The above paragraphs sum up everything there is to say about
how ps projection works in conjunctions. But let us also ask the following question. What is the "official" general prediction of our theory concerning ps(q)? Is
there something that all conjunctions "officially" presuppose, concerning ps(q)?
The answer is: yes, the theory (that is, (27), (28), and definition (23)) officially
predicts that a conjunction, any conjunction of the form $p \wedge q$, presupposes that
$p \rightarrow ps(q)$.

It is quite easy to see that this is the prediction. What does it mean that c + p must
entail ps(q)? What general requirement does it impose on c? It requires that given the
assumptions in c, p should entail ps(q). But that is just like saying that c should be a
context in which p entails ps(q), that is, c should be a context in which $p \rightarrow ps(q)$. That
is, the theory predicts that $p \wedge q$ will be felicitous only in contexts that entail $p \rightarrow ps(q)$.
By definition (23), that means that the theory predicts that a conjunction $p \wedge q$ (invariably and "officially") presupposes $p \rightarrow ps(q)$.[4]

It remains to verify that the prediction that a conjunction presupposes $p \rightarrow ps(q)$ is
correct. Sure it is. Keep in mind that definition (23) is not supposed to predict judgments on "presupposing in a given context." The notion of "being a ps of S" which is
defined in (23) is the notion of being **invariably** taken for granted by S. Now, let us
first look at (12).

(12)   Bill is not present and JOHN drinks too.

The fact that (12) is felicitous in context (B) shows that (12) does not take it
for granted that someone besides John drinks. So, it is fine that (23) does not predict
that ps(q) is a presupposition of (12). Now, does (12) really presuppose that if Bill
is not present, then someone besides John drinks, as predicted? Yes, it does. It is
exactly because (B) entails this conditional that (12) is felicitous in (B). And what
about context (A)? (A) too entails the conditional, even if it does so trivially. It is

---

[4]   Here is another way of seeing this. If $p \wedge q$ is uttered in a context c, when would c + p satisfy ps(q)
and when wouldn't it? There are exactly four possibilities: either

     (i)   c all by itself entails ps(q);
or   (ii)   p all by itself entails ps(q);
or   (iii)   none of the above holds, but c entails that $p \rightarrow ps(q)$;
or   (iv)   c + p fails to entail ps(q).

c + p will satisfy ps(q) just in case (i) or (ii) or (iii) holds. But that's the same as saying that c + p will
admit q iff (v) holds, since (v) is equivalent to the disjunction (i) or (ii) or (iii).

     (v)   c entails that $p \rightarrow ps(q)$

Hence, we get that the requirement which the theory imposes concerning ps(q) will be satisfied just
in case c entails that $p \rightarrow ps(q)$. That is, the theory predicts that $p \wedge q$ will be felicitous only in contexts that entail $p \rightarrow ps(q)$. By definition (23), that means that the theory predicts that a conjunction
$p \wedge q$ (invariably and "officially") presupposes $p \rightarrow ps(q)$.

impossible to find a context that fails to entail the conditional in which (12) would be felicitous.

What about our early judgment that ps(q) **is** a ps of (12)? I believe that this judgment comes about as follows. We know that c + p must satisfy ps(q). When we hear (12) out of the blue, we tend to imagine that the p wouldn't play any role in satisfying ps(q). (That's because we don't see how Bill's absence could help us conclude anything about his drinking habits.) Hence, we think that c would have to satisfy ps(q) all by itself (as context (A) does). Hence the judgment that (12) presupposes ps(q). Of course, this judgment only concerns what we feel (12) to presuppose **in a context such as we imagine**, where Bill's absence cannot show that he drinks. Therefore, it is quite compatible with the fact that (12) does not presuppose ps(q) in the absolute sense defined by (23).

Now we turn to example (13). Is the official prediction compatible with our intuitive judgment that (13) doesn't presuppose anything concerning ps(q)?

(13)   Bill drinks and JOHN drinks too.

Yes, it is. The predicted ps is that if Bill drinks, then someone besides John drinks. (And no other ps concerning ps(q) is predicted.) But the predicted ps is a tautology, so it will be satisfied trivially by any c. Hence, we get that (13) has no presupposition concerning ps(q) which would impose a real (non-trivial) demand on c. Hence the intuitive judgment that (13) has no ps concerning ps(q) at all.

## 5.3   Things Missing in the Stalnaker–Karttunen Analysis

In this section, I will turn to some desiderata that the Stalnaker–Karttunen theory, insightful as it is, still fails to meet. There are two remaining problems that I am aware of. Let me discuss them in turn.

(i) **Going below the level of the clause:** One problem is that the Stalnaker–Karttunen theory does not go below the level of a complete clause. For that reason, this theory cannot even start to treat the projection of pss whose triggers occur in quantificational contexts. Take for example sentences (30) and (31).[5]

(30)   Every nation cherishes its king.
(31)   A fat man was pushing his bicycle.

What is the ps triggered by the underlined NP – that **who** has a king, or had a bike? And how are we going to derive this ps? Obviously, we would have to go below the level of the clause. We'd have to look at the antecedent NP and the anaphoric NP and see how they are related to each other.

(ii) **The problem of explanatory adequacy:** The second problem is one of explanatory adequacy, and it has to do with the connection between the "content property" and the "heritage property" of the same linguistic item.

I adopt the following terminology, from Heim 1983b.

---

[5]   I mean the anaphoric reading, of course – sentence-internal anaphora.

(32)   Call the "core" meaning of a linguistic item its "**content property**."
       Call that which determines what ps(s) the item triggers its "**ps property**."
       Call that which determines whether/which/how pss of expressions embedded
       under the item are inherited its "**heritage property**."

The Stalnaker–Karttunen theory employs the general principle that a ps of a clause
must be satisfied by its local context. The "heritage properties" of particular connectives interact with this general principle, to give us the predictions about the pss of compound sentences.

Where is it that the "heritage property" is specified in the Stalnaker–Karttunen
theory? What does the "heritage property" consist of? Well, the "heritage property" of
*and*, for example, consists of the specification of local contexts for each conjunct, which
I repeat in (33).

(33)   If $p \wedge q$ is uttered in context c, then c is the local context for p, and $c + p$ is the
       local context for q. ("heritage property" of *and*)

And what is the "content" property of *and*? Stalnaker and Karttunen presumably
assume that it is given by a rule like the one in (34).

(34)   $[\![p \wedge q]\!]^{M,g} = 1$ iff $[\![p]\!]^{M,g} = 1$ and $[\![q]\!]^{M,g} = 1$

Now we get to the problem of explanatory adequacy. We would expect an explanatory theory to give us "heritage properties" that are independently motivated, rather
than arbitrary stipulations. But is the "heritage property" in (33), for example, independently motivated? How? It would be nice if it could be derived from the "content
property" in (34), wouldn't it.

In my opinion, the Stalnaker–Karttunen theory does go a certain way towards the
goal of explanatory adequacy.

First of all, the "heritage properties" that Stalnaker and Karttunen suggest don't
seem so arbitrary – they can be motivated independently of the ps projection facts.
Stalnaker and Karttunen both assume that there are independent facts and principles
that determine for each clause in a compound sentence what its local context is. They
assume, correctly, that (33) makes very good sense: it seems obvious that when you utter
a conjunction you first assert the first conjunct and then assert the second conjunct –
I think that's a pretty good explanation of why (33) is the case. Similarly, the proposal
in (35) for the "heritage property" of *if . . . then . . .* (see Karttunen 1974) does not seem
arbitrary at all.

(35)   If $p \rightarrow q$ is uttered in context c, then c is the local context for p, and $c + p$ is the
       local context for q. ("heritage property" of *if . . . then . . .*)

The motivation for (35) may not be quite as obvious and simple as the motivation
for (33). Yet, if you think about it, (35) too makes very good sense. While p is not
asserted, it **is** added to c temporarily – as a temporary assumption – so its local
context is c. As for q, as emphasized in Stalnaker's work, q is asserted (only) under
the assumption that p – so certainly the local context of q includes p (despite the

fact that p is not permanently added to the common ground). So, the local context of q is $c + p$.[6]

Secondly, Stalnaker 1974 says explicitly that he sees the specification of local contexts (the "heritage property" of the connective) as following from (i) the semantics ("content property") of the connective, and (ii) general assumptions about how the common ground is incremented (which Stalnaker calls "pragmatic").

At the same time, Stalnaker does **not** propose a theory of how the "heritage property" is derived (which he openly admits). Certainly, Stalnaker and Karttunen don't actually derive the "heritage property" of an item from its "content property," or explicitly define the relation between the two. It is because of this that the Stalnaker–Karttunen theory is not as explanatory as one might wish.[7]

## 5.4   Some Remarks on Karttunen and Peters 1979

In their famous paper K&P 1979, Karttunen and Peters do a number of different things (in particular, they give an analysis of the ps of *even*, and they discuss some ps-like conversational implicatures). But what their paper is most famous for is its system for treating ps projection. For a number of years, K&P 1979 was generally regarded as **the** "classic" paper on the general approach of Stalnaker, Karttunen and K&P to ps projection, and people would often consider and contrast just two theories of ps projection: that of K&P 1979 and that of Gazdar 1979a,b. Nevertheless, K&P's system of treating ps projection does not constitute an integral part of the presentation of the basic analysis of ps projection given in this chapter. In this section, I will digress from my presentation and add a very short discussion of K&P 1979's treatment of ps projection.

**K&P's treatment of ps projection:** Let me briefly review some central features of K&P's treatment of ps projection. K&P do not make any new proposals concerning what the heritage properties of the connectives are, but rather take over Karttunen's findings. (And they say so in their paper.) K&P adopt Karttunen's conception that a ps is a requirement on the context, so they take it that the context in which a sentence (be it simple or complex) is uttered would have to entail the ps of that sentence.

K&P's contribution to the problem of ps projection is that they treat ps projection **compositionally**. K&P give a formal Montague-style system in which they compositionally derive the pss of sentences, starting from the single morphemes at the bottom and going up the tree.

---

[6]   I do want to note that the motivation for the "heritage property" of *or*, given in (i) (following Karttunen 1974, fn. 5) may not be as clear as that for the "heritage properties" of *and* and *if . . . then*. . . .

    (i)   If $p \vee q$ is uttered in context c, then $c + \neg q$ is the local context for p, and $c + \neg p$ is the local context for q. ("heritage property" of *or*)

Are we supposed to add to the initial context c the **negation** of a disjunct? Why? When?

[7]   The problem of explanatory adequacy was originally raised in Gazdar 1979a, where it was directed against K&P 1979. However, to the extent described in the text, this problem is also a problem for the Stalnaker–Karttunen theory. (It is explicitly mentioned as such in Beaver 1993a.)

In order to do that, K&P have to assume that the lexicon provides the properties of each morpheme that are relevant to building up the pss of larger expressions. K&P assume, specifically, that the lexicon specifies three properties per morpheme: its "content property," its "ps property," and its "heritage property." The three properties have to be specified separately – they are independent of each other.

K&P do not include any formal representation of context in their system. Therefore, they must state the heritage properties of various items without making reference to context. They do that by simply specifying exactly what the inherited ps is supposed to be. Take for example the case of conjunction. Recall that what the Stalnaker–Karttunen theory says about the local contexts in conjunctions predicts that a conjunction inherits ps(p) and also presupposes p → ps(q). What K&P do is simply stipulate the desired prediction, as a rule of the grammar: their rule for conjunctions is as in (36).

(36)   $ps (p \land q) = (ps(p) \land (p \to ps(q)))$

**Critique:** Certainly, the fact that K&P gave a compositional treatment of ps projection was in itself important at the time, showing as it did that it was possible to treat a phenomenon that was commonly considered "pragmatic" formally and compositionally. At the same time, more central to my present concerns are the following questions: what new insights does K&P's analysis offer into the workings of ps projection, and to what extent does it improve the empirical coverage? So let us consider these questions.

I don't see that K&P's analysis offers new insights into the principles that govern ps projection. In fact, I think that the fact that the K&P theory leaves out all reference to local contexts renders it less explanatory than Karttunen's original analysis. Karttunen's analysis goes some way towards explaining **why** a conjunction should presuppose ps(p) $\land$ (p → ps(q)), by showing how this ps is derived from some plausible assumptions about the local contexts of the two conjuncts. The K&P theory is as a matter of fact based on Karttunen's insight, but it does not formalize **that insight**; K&P's formal theory doesn't in any way contain any hint as to why the ps of a conjunction should be ps(p) $\land$ (p → ps(q)) and not some other, completely different, ps.

As for empirical coverage, there is one important area where K&P's formalism does achieve more than Karttunen's original analysis. Recall sentences (30) and (31).

(30)   Every nation cherishes its king.
(31)   A fat man was pushing his bicycle.

As mentioned in section 5.3, the Stalnaker–Karttunen theory can't treat the pss of such sentences, because it doesn't go below the level of the clause. In contrast, K&P's theory does go below the level of the clause. In fact, K&P predict that (30) presupposes (37).

(37)   Every nation has a king.

This prediction is taken to be correct, both in K&P 1979 and in subsequent research (see e.g. Heim 1983b). Intuitively, (30) is commonly (though perhaps not always) judged to be taking (37) for granted.[8] This is a nice prediction which nobody was able to make previously.

Unfortunately, as K&P point out in a footnote, their system gets incorrect predictions for examples like (31). K&P predict that (31) presupposes (38).

(38)   A fat man had a bicycle.

(38) is too weak: it isn't a good enough ps that **some** fat man or other had a bike. What we want, speaking somewhat vaguely, is for the fat man in (31) and the fat man in (38) to be the same one . . .

The wrong prediction about (31) is a serious problem, not only because (31) is a fairly basic sort of example, but also because the problem is not accidental, but rather reflects an inherent weakness of K&P's system. Because of the way K&P separately derive the "content property" and the "ps property" of an expression, there is no obvious way for them to define scope and binding relations between the semantic interpretation ("content") and the presupposition. (This is discussed in e.g. Heim 1983b and Beaver 1993a.)

Given the balance of things, and given, furthermore, that Heim 1983b has provided in the meantime an improved treatment of ps projection below the level of the clause, I have decided not to include a more detailed discussion of K&P's system of ps projection in this book. In previous sections, we have looked at the original Stalnaker–Karttunen analysis; let us now go on from there.

## 5.5   Heim's Analysis (Part 1): "Content" and "Heritage" Combined

As noted in 5.3, the Stalnaker–Karttunen theory was lacking in explanatory adequacy because it failed to derive the "heritage property" of an item from its "content property," or explicitly define the relation between the two. Heim 1983b offers a formally explicit theory where the "content" and "heritage" properties are not only linked to one another, but reduced to one and the same thing: the context change potential.

The basics of context change semantics are already familiar to the reader of this book: a formal notion of "context" is defined (e.g. a set of worlds, a set of assignments, or a set of world-assignment pairs), and the semantics recursively defines for every expression not its truth conditions, but rather its context change potential (ccp), which is a function from contexts to contexts. From now on, + will be used to represent context-incrementation (= application of a ccp to a context):

(39)   notation:   c + S will now mean
                         "the result of applying the ccp of S to c."

Recall that on the Stalnaker–Karttunen approach, a ps is defined as a requirement on the context of utterance – it may be defined as in (23).

---

[8]   For further discussion of the data, see chapter 10 below.

(23)   B is a ps of S iff S can be felicitously uttered only in contexts that entail B.
(The Stalnaker–Karttunen definition of ps)

Heim incorporates the idea that a ps is a requirement on the context into context change semantics, by specifying ccps in such a way that a context-incrementation $c + S$ will be defined only for contexts c that entail ps(S). Thus, ccps become **partial** functions from the set of contexts to the set of contexts. The two most basic principles of Heim's theory of ps projection may therefore be stated as follows.

(I)   The semantics recursively defines for each expression a ccp (context change potential), which is a partial function from the set of contexts to the set of contexts.

(II)   B is a ps of S iff $c + S$ is defined only for contexts c that entail B.

The rest of the job is done by the definitions of ccps for various expressions.

For our present purposes, let us regard simple, affirmative sentences such as the following as closed atomic formulas.

(1)   The king of France is bald.
(2)   Joan has stopped drinking wine for breakfast.
(3)   JOHN drinks too.
(4)   Even JOHN drinks.
(5)   It was Fred who ate the beans.

It is generally assumed in context change semantics that what it takes for an atomic formula to be true/verified in a given possible world is defined in the standard way. So we may assume that for each closed atomic formula S, the set of worlds in which it is true (= the proposition expressed by S) is given. Let us also assume that the pss of closed atomic formulas are given: we are not interested at the moment in how these pss are triggered, so we will regard them as primitives. So, we assume that for each closed atomic formula S, ps(S) is given. Finally, let us define a context as a set of possible worlds. By "context c entails proposition p" we will mean that $c \subseteq p$.

Given the assumptions stated in the last paragraph, the ccp of a closed atomic formula S will be defined as follows.

(40)   For any closed atomic formula S,
$$c + s = \begin{cases} c \cap \{w : S \text{ is true in } w\} & \text{if } c \text{ entails ps(S);} \\ \text{undefined} & \text{otherwise.} \end{cases}$$

Consider for example sentence (1). According to (40), (1) can only be added to contexts that entail that there is a (unique) king of France. (40) also determines that when $c +$ (1) is defined, it is computed by intersecting c with the set of worlds in which the king of France is bald. The result is a new context, containing only worlds where the king of France is bald (= a context in which the king of France is bald).

To see how Heim's basic analysis of ps projection works, we will now consider the ccps of some connectives. Let S,A,B be formulas.

We start with negation. Heim defines the ccp of negation as in (41). This ccp captures both the "content property" of negation and its "heritage property."

(41)  $c + \neg S = c - (c + S)$

To illustrate how this ccp works, let us suppose that we add (6) to context c. According to (41), the result is as in (42).

(6)  The king of France is not bald.

(42)  $c + (6) = c - (c + (1))$

That is, when we apply the ccp of (6) to c, we have to subtract from c the result of applying the ccp of (1) to c. That is, we have to subtract from c the intersection of c and the proposition expressed by (1). That is, we have to subtract from c all the worlds of c in which (1) is true. That's kicking out the worlds where the king of France is bald. So (6) affects the context such that it retains only worlds where the king of France is not bald. This is as it should be, so (41) gives us the correct "content property" for (6).

As for the "heritage property," we want to predict that, as noted in section 1.5, pss survive under negation. In other words, we want to predict that negation is a "hole." This too is correctly predicted by (41). (41) says that in order to compute $c + \neg S$, we must compute $c + S$ (so that we can then subtract it from c). Therefore, $c + \neg S$ is defined only if c entails ps(S). According to the definition of ps given in (II) above, that means that ps(S) is a ps of $\neg S$. So (41) correctly predicts that $\neg S$ inherits the ps of S.

In the familiar Karttunen terminology: (41) predicts that negation is a "hole"' because it determines that in a sentence of the form $\neg S$, the local context of S is the initial context c.

Heim defines the ccps of conjunctions and conditionals as in (43) and (44). Again, each ccp captures both the "content property" and the "heritage property" of the connective in question.

(43)  $c + A$ and $B = (c + A) + B$
(44)  $c + $ If $A, B = c - (c + A - ((c + A) + B))$

(43) formulates the familiar idea that when you add a conjunction to your context, you first add the first conjunct, and then you add the second conjunct to the resulting context. Therefore, (43) gives us the familiar Stalnaker–Karttunen effect. Officially, it works as follows. To compute $c + A$ and B, we must compute both $c + A$ and $(c + A) + B$. Hence, $c + A$ and B is defined only if both $c + A$ and $(c + A) + B$ are defined. Hence, $c + A$ and B is defined only if c entails ps(A) and $c + A$ entails ps(B). As discussed in section 5.2 above, this correctly predicts the facts of ps projection in conjunctions.

Certainly, (43) also gives us the right "content property." When we apply a conjunction A and B to context c, we first increment c with A. This kicks out the worlds inconsistent with A, and we are left just with worlds of c where A is true. Then, we increment the result with B. This kicks out the worlds inconsistent with B, and we are left just with worlds of c where A is true and B is true. Which is as it should be.

Now consider the ccp of conditionals in (44). Let us start with the "content property." To take an example, consider (45).

(45)   If there is light in the window, then Sue is at home.

What should the effect be of adding (45) to a context c? The resulting context should contain only worlds in which (45) is true. The worlds in c where there is no light in the window will remain as they are, since (45) is (trivially) true in them all. And what about the worlds in c where there is light in the window? Out of those, we will want to keep only the worlds in which Sue is at home (since (45) is true in them), and kick out the worlds in which Sue is not at home (since (45) is false in them). In short, we want to ensure that when we add a conditional to a context c, we kick out of c all those worlds in which the antecedent is true but the consequent is false. That is exactly what (45) does. Here is how. The context $(c + A) + B$ is the same thing that we have to compute in (43): it is the set of worlds of c where both A and B are true. This set we subtract from the context $c + A$, which is the set of worlds of c where A is true. The result of this subtraction is the set of worlds of c in which A is true but B is not. This set is of course exactly the worlds that we wanted to kick out. So indeed, we kick them out: we subtract this set of worlds from c.

How about the "heritage property" of *if . . . then . . .* ? (44) captures that, too. The two context-incrementations that have to be computed in (44) are exactly the same as those that have to be computed in (43). Hence, even though the ccps are in other respects different, we correctly predict the same behavior with respect to ps projection.

In the familiar Karttunen terminology: (44) gets the right predictions about ps projection in conditionals, because it determines that in a sentence of the form if A, B, the local context of A is the initial context c, and the local context of B is $c + A$.

To sum up what we have seen in this section: under Heim's theory, the semantic value of a compound sentence (viz. its ccp) expresses simultaneously both the "content property" and the "heritage property" of the connective in question. This theory is obviously more elegant and more explanatory than a theory where the "heritage" and "content" properties of an item are specified separately.

I will add a few remarks concerning the explanatory achievement of Heim's theory. When Gazdar 1979a raised the problem of explanatory adequacy for the K&P 1979 theory, one point in his criticism was the following. Because of the separation of "content" and "heritage" properties, the K&P system leaves open the possibility that there would be another connective which is truth-conditionally (i.e. content-wise) just like *if . . . then . . .* , but is different from *if . . . then . . .* with respect to ps projection. This is bad because (presumably) we don't find such a connective in natural language. That is, K&P provide no explanation for the fact that a given "content property" is matched with the particular "heritage property" that it is in fact matched with, and not with some other, different one.

Heim argues in her 1983b paper that her own theory does not share this drawback. Heim 1983b says that the ccps that she proposes are just what one is forced to come up with if one wants to account for the truth-conditional (informational) content, and these ccps automatically yield the correct "heritage" effect. However, as noted in Soames 1989, that is not the case.[9] For example, suppose we define the ccp of conjunctions as in (46a) or in (46b). This will give us the same "content" as (43), but it will determine a different "heritage" property. Hence, we don't have a full answer to the

---

[9]   Heim acknowledges this in her later work.

question of why it is that *and* has the "heritage" property that it has and not a different one.[10]

(46)   a.   c + A and B = (c + B) + A                          hypothetical ccps
        b.   c + A and B = (c + A) ∩ (c + B)                   (from Soames 1989)

To sum up, while the need to get the "content" right certainly puts severe restrictions on what the ccp might be, it does not narrow down the possibilities so much that it actually determines what "heritage" property we are going to predict.

I will continue to present Heim's theory of ps projection in chapters 9 and 10 below. In chapter 10, we will see how Heim's theory handles the second problem noted in section 5.3 above, viz. the problem of analyzing ps projection below the level of the complete clause.

---

[10]   One might hypothesize that it is a matter of actual progress in time that determines that the first conjunct is processed first. Note that this is not so obviously right, if you think, like Karttunen 1974, fn. 5, that the ccp of disjunction is the "symmetric" ccp given in fn. 6 above.

# 6

# *Presupposition Projection: Filtering vs. Cancellation*

---

The Stalnaker–Karttunen–Heim theory of ps projection has a well-known rival: the approach to ps projection of Gazdar 1979a,b and Soames 1979. In this chapter, I will discuss this rival, and consider Soames 1982's idea of a synthesis between the two approaches. I will call the Gazdar–Soames approach the "cancellation" approach, and the Stalnaker–Karttunen–Heim approach the "filtering" approach.[1]

Before discussing the cancellation approach, I would like to stress an important feature of the filtering approach, and make clear what I mean by the word "filtering."

On the filtering approach (= the Stalnaker–Karttunen–Heim approach), a ps is not "defeasible"; it absolutely must be satisfied. Recall that a ps of sentence S is defined as something that is entailed by **all** the contexts in which sentence S can be felicitously uttered. Recall how things work in a compound sentence that fails to inherit a ps of one of its constituent clauses. Take for example (1) or (2).

(1)  Somebody has solved the problem and it is Lauri who solved it.
(2)  If the problem has been solved, then it is Lauri who solved it.
      ps(q):   somebody has solved the problem.

On the filtering approach, ps(q) is not "defeasible." The reason that the matrix sentence does not inherit ps(q) is that this ps is satisfied internally – it is satisfied by the p.

I use the term "filtering" precisely and solely to refer to the phenomenon that I've just mentioned: the phenomenon of a ps that fails to be inherited by a bigger sentence because it (the ps) is satisfied locally. By the term "filtering mechanism" I refer to those principles of the grammar that cover this phenomenon.

So far, I have been carefully avoiding all sorts of examples that complicate matters or that look like counterexamples to the filtering approach. In this and the following chapters, I will no longer avoid the more problematic examples. We shall see what we can make of them.

---

[1]  I don't think "filtering" is such a great name, but this word has been associated with Karttunen's work for a long time.

## 6.1   The Cancellation Approach to ps Projection

I will now quickly introduce the cancellation approach. This will be only a summary, as I am not concerned with details of formulation. The readers interested in more detail and more discussion are referred to Soames 1979, Gazdar 1979a,b, and Soames 1982.

In contrast with the filtering approach, the cancellation approach treats pss as "defeasible." They are defeasible in the sense defined by (I) and (II) below. My summary of the cancellation approach is given in (I)–(IV).

(I)   What a trigger triggers is a **potential presupposition**. This potential ps may or may not become an actual ps of the sentence containing the trigger.

(II)   A potential ps may get canceled, and then it does not become actual. The **cancellation mechanism** is this: a ps is canceled whenever

   a.   that ps is inconsistent with assumptions already in the context; or
   b.   that ps is inconsistent with one of the conversational implicatures of the **matrix** sentence containing the trigger.

(III)   No filtering mechanism is recognized.[2] Instead, Gazdar 1979a,b and Soames 1979 claim that **all** the pss of the embedded clauses are potential pss of the matrix sentence. This predicts that each and every one of these pss will become an actual ps of the matrix sentence, unless it is canceled by the cancellation mechanism in (II).

(IV)   There is a stipulation to the effect that a ps is something which is "known" or "taken for granted," unless it is canceled.[3]

For an illustration of how this system works, look again at (1) and (2).

(1)   Somebody has solved the problem and it is Lauri who solved it.
(2)   If the problem has been solved, then it is Lauri who solved it.

The **matrix** sentence has a **potential** ps that someone has solved the problem, which is triggered by the cleft construction. However, this ps does not become an actual ps of the matrix sentence. In (1) and (2), there is a clause (the first clause) which addresses precisely the question of whether someone has solved the problem or not. This creates a conversational implicature that the speaker is not regarding the truth value of *somebody has solved the problem* as something that's taken for granted in the conversation. This implicature is inconsistent with presupposing that someone has solved the problem, so the potential ps is canceled.

In what way might the system just introduced be superior to the filtering approach? The main empirical motivation for the cancellation mechanism comes from examples of the sort illustrated by (3)–(5).

---

[2]   At least, there is no filtering in Gazdar 1979a,b and Soames 1979. By 1982, Soames has changed his mind.
[3]   Gazdar and Soames each have their own way of stipulating this. They must stipulate it, because in their system a ps is not defined in any way as something taken for granted in the context.

(3)  It is possible that John has children and it is possible that his children are away.
(4)  If I realize later that I haven't told the truth, I will confess it to everyone.
(5)  If John hasn't just stopped smoking, he has just started smoking.

In these examples, the filtering mechanism fails to "filter out" a ps that in fact is not inherited by the matrix sentence. Such examples have made Gazdar and Soames both convinced that the filtering approach is not good enough, empirically, and that a cancellation mechanism is needed.

First, let us see why the filtering approach has a problem with these examples.

Regarding (3), *possible* is a "hole" – witness the fact that *it's possible that John's children are away* inherits the ps that John has children. Hence, the second conjunct, q, presupposes that John has children. Now, ps(q) is **not** satisfied internally in (3) – the first conjunct, p, does not entail it. Therefore, the filtering approach predicts an intuition that (3) presupposes ps(q), or at least $p \rightarrow ps(q)$. This is a wrong prediction.

Regarding (4), assuming that *realize* triggers a factive ps, the antecedent, p, presupposes that "I" haven't told the truth. The filtering approach predicts that ps(p) is inherited by (4) as a whole. This is a wrong prediction.

Example (5) is a conditional with conflicting pss:

ps(p):  John smoked in the "immediate" past.
ps(q):  John did not smoke in the "immediate" past.

Again, the filtering approach predicts that ps(p) should survive. But this is a wrong prediction.

And now, let us see how the cancellation approach accounts for these examples.

(3)  It is possible that John has children and it is possible that his children are away.

The cancellation approach accounts for the fact that (3) does not presuppose that John has children as follows. That John has children is a potential ps of (3), triggered by the definite NP *his children*. In general, *possibly S* conversationally implicates that the truth value of S is not known. Hence (3) conversationally implicates that it is not known whether John has children or not. This is inconsistent with presupposing that John has children, so this ps is canceled.

(4)  If I realize later that I haven't told the truth, I will confess it to everyone.

The cancellation approach accounts for the fact that (4) does not presuppose that "I" haven't told the truth as follows. That "I" haven't told the truth is a potential ps of (4), triggered by the factive verb *realize*. Conditionals always conversationally implicate that their antecedent is **not** presupposed. This is inconsistent with the speaker of (4) presupposing that (s)he hasn't told the truth, because if the speaker had known that she hadn't told the truth, she would have also known that she'd already realized that. Therefore, the ps is canceled.

(5)   If John hasn't just stopped smoking, he has just started smoking.

The cancellation approach accounts for the fact that (5) does not presuppose that John smoked in the "immediate" past as follows. That John smoked in the "immediate" past is a potential ps of (5), triggered by *stopped*. The speaker conversationally implicates that for all (s)he knows, the antecedent and the consequent each might be true. This is inconsistent with presupposing that John smoked in the "immediate" past, because if the speaker presupposes that, she already knows that the consequent is false. Therefore, the ps is canceled.

Another kind of example which is a problem for the filtering approach but can be handled by the cancellation approach is cases of cancellation by context, such as (6). It seems that B's utterance does not presuppose that A has a dog. The filtering approach does not account for this, if we assume that negation is a "hole." On the cancellation approach, that A has a dog is a potential ps of B's utterance. Since it conflicts with the earlier assertion A, this ps is canceled.

(6)   A:   I don't have a dog.
      B:   So at least you don't have to walk your dog.

In addition to the empirical motivation for the cancellation approach, Gazdar 1979a,b claims that unlike K&P 1979's theory, his own theory is explanatory. Gazdar explains that that is because his cancellation mechanism consists of general principles regarding the way utterances affect the context. The general principles Gazdar refers to may be summarized as follows.

(i)   Information that arises from utterances in the conversation is added to the context (common ground) **only if it does not contradict anything that's already in the context.**

(ii)   Each utterance affects the context as follows: First, its content is added to the context (unless it contradicts the context); Then, each of its conversational implicatures is added to the context (ditto); Then, each of its potential presuppositions is added to the context (ditto).

Gazdar points out that on his theory, the patterns of ps inheritance follow from the above general principles: the reason that a ps can be canceled by a conversational implicature is that pss are added last, after the implicatures. When you get to the ps, the implicature is already in the context. If the potential ps is in conflict with the implicature, principle (i) determines that it is not added to the context, and so it does not become an actual ps.

Gazdar contrasts his way of deriving the inheritance patterns with K&P's theory: K&P 1979 posit special "heritage properties" of individual lexical items, while on Gazdar's theory, there is no need to do that. Note, however, that Gazdar could not direct the same criticism against Heim 1983b, because on Heim's theory, there aren't any separate heritage properties. Therefore, while Gazdar's theory may be more explanatory than K&P's, I see no reason to consider it more explanatory than Heim's.

## 6.2  Critique of the Cancellation Approach

In this section, I will discuss some problems with the cancellation approach. I will start with two conceptual problems, and then turn to empirical problems.

**Why should implicatures cancel pss and not vice versa?** The cancellation approach stipulates that conversational implicatures cancel pss. Obviously, Soames and Gazdar stipulated this because they believed that it was motivated empirically. Indeed, for their approach to work, they **had** to make this stipulation. However, this stipulation bothers me. Why should implicatures cancel pss and not vice versa? To put it in terms of principle (ii), why would it be that the implicatures are added to the context before the pss are? If anything, it seems that it would make more sense to assume the opposite – that the pss are added to the context before the implicatures are. Here is why.

Conversational implicatures, everybody agrees, are not "conventional," are not determined purely by the grammar. Rather, they are based on Grice's maxims, which are instances of general principles of cooperative behavior. Conversational implicatures are very heavily context-dependent. It is not just that they are "defeated" when inconsistent with something already in the context; they are also heavily dependent on what's **relevant** in the context, and will generally arise only in some contexts and not in others. Conversational implicatures are not entailed by the sentences that implicate them.

Presuppositions, at least the "hard core" cases of ps, make a rather different impression. They don't seem nearly as easily "defeated" as conversational implicatures are, or as context-dependent. It is usually assumed that presuppositions of a simple, affirmative sentence are not only presupposed but also **entailed** by the sentence. (Recall also Chierchia and McConnell-Ginet 1990's claim that there is a whole class of pss that are no more defeasible than entailments are.) It also seems that presuppositions are tied to the meaning of their triggers. Because of all this, pss are commonly taken to be "conventional," to be determined by the grammar alone. Indeed, K&P 1979 classify presuppositions as "conventional implicatures."

Given this difference, it seems more natural to expect that pss would be added to the context before implicatures are, and not as Gazdar would have it. It seems rather implausible that there is a general principle (of grammar? of what?) determining that implicatures, which are not determined by the grammar, are prior to pss, which are determined by the grammar, and can cancel them.[4]

**On the notion of a "cancelable ps"**: Another thing that bothers me quite a bit concerning the cancellation approach is the very notion of a "cancelable ps."

I agree with Chierchia and McConnell-Ginet 1990 that the basic intuition about a ps is that it is "taken for granted," in the sense that a ps of a sentence is a **precondition for felicitous use** of that sentence. In other words, a ps is not merely something that "is taken for granted," but something that "**must** be taken for granted," it is truly a requirement that a trigger imposes on the context.

Now, why is it that a ps must be taken for granted? I can't believe that it is merely because there happens to exist a rule of the grammar that arbitrarily stipulates that pss are taken for granted. I think there must be a deeper reason. I think there must be something about the trigger that makes the ps truly indispensable. I think that an adequate

---

[4]  This point is also made in Landman 1986.

theory of how pss are triggered would have to derive, on the basis of the semantics of the trigger plus additional (non-arbitrary) principles, not just the content of the ps, but also its being an indispensable precondition for the (felicitous) use of the trigger – a precondition that it would simply be impossible to do without.

The manner in which the existence ps of definite NPs is triggered, briefly discussed in 4.1 above, may serve to illustrate the idea of a ps being indispensable. Recall that on the Kamp–Heim theory, a definite NP is analyzed as anaphoric to an "old" discourse referent. That is, in order to process a definite NP, you must associate it with an appropriate antecedent discourse referent that's already present in the context. It is a direct consequence of this analysis that a definite NP presupposes the existence of an appropriate antecedent discourse referent for it. A separate stipulation to that effect is not needed. The existence of an antecedent discourse referent is simply indispensable – the definite NP cannot be processed without it.

What bothers me about the notion of a "cancelable" ps is that I cannot reconcile it with the conception of ps as something that's indispensable. How can you "cancel" something that you can't do without? I don't understand what this could possibly mean. Since I can't feel that I really understand the notion of ps **unless** I think of pss as indispensable, I think that the cancellation theory is wrong, in that it doesn't reflect correctly what a ps really is.

Let me now turn to empirical problems with the cancellation approach. Note, first, that Soames and Gazdar don't say anything about ps projection below the level of an entire clause. That's already an empirical drawback. Secondly, there are some serious counterexamples to the cancellation approach.

**Counterexample no. 1:** Soames 1982 offers just one kind of counterexample to the cancellation approach. This kind of counterexample is illustrated in (7). (The two sentences in (7) illustrate the same thing.) The problem is that the cancellation mechanism fails to cancel ps(q).

(7)    a.    If someone at the conference solved the problem, it was Julius who solved it.
       b.    If John has twins, Mary will not like his children.

Consider ps(q) – in (7a), that someone solved the problem, in (7b), that John has children. The conditional as a whole does not inherit ps(q). These are classical examples where p satisfies ps(q), and that's why ps(q) is not inherited. So the filtering approach deals with them easily. In contrast, the cancellation mechanism cannot handle these examples.

It might be useful to look first at a similar example that cancellation **can** deal with. Recall how the "cancellationists" treat example (2).

(2)    If the problem has been solved, then it is Lauri who solved it.

Due to the cleft construction, (2) has a potential ps that someone has solved the problem. A conditional always implicates that the truth value of the antecedent is not taken for granted. So, there is an implicature here that it is not taken for granted that someone has solved the problem. This is inconsistent with presupposing that someone has solved the problem. So the implicature associated with p cancels the potential ps triggered by q.

Now go back to (7a). To cancel ps(q), the cancellation theorists would want to rely on a conversational implicature. What would the relevant implicature be? The implicature associated with p again? Well, no, this won't work. The implicature associated with p is that it is not taken for granted that someone at the conference solved the problem. But this implicature does not help us cancel ps(q), because it is not in conflict with presupposing that **someone** solved the problem (maybe someone outside the conference solved the problem). So the cancellationists incorrectly predict that the ps triggered by q becomes an actual ps of (7a).

I entirely agree with Soames 1982 that this single kind of example is enough to show that the cancellation mechanism is not enough, and that a filtering mechanism is needed. After all, we are dealing here with some of the most basic data on ps projection in compound sentences. Certainly any theory of ps projection ought to be able to deal with the classical examples where ps(q) is not inherited.

It is quite obvious that in examples like (7a) and (7b), the fact that ps(q) is not inherited by the matrix sentence is due to its relation to p. The filtering approach deals with this fine: it says that in these cases, ps(q) is satisfied internally, by p. And where does the cancellation approach go wrong? Well, the cancellationists will have to use the p for deriving a canceling implicature. But that can only work for a subset of the "internal satisfaction" examples. In fact, it only works for the special case where p is a necessary condition for ps(q).

**Counterexample no. 2:** Let us go on to example (8), attributed by Heim 1983b to Peters (p.c.).

(8)  If John has children, Mary will not like his twins.
     ps(q):  John has twins
     Observed ps of (8):  $p \rightarrow ps(q)$
     The cancellation mechanism, incorrectly, simply cancels ps(q).

Out of the blue, example (8) sounds a bit odd. Why? Because it sounds like the speaker is taking it for granted that if someone has children, (s)he has twins. That is, we observe that (8) presupposes that if John has children, he has twins. This ps is correctly predicted by the filtering approach.

In contrast, the cancellation mechanism predicts, incorrectly, that (8) doesn't have any ps that involves ps(q). (8) conversationally implicates that it is not taken for granted that John has children. This is inconsistent with presupposing that John has twins. Hence, on the cancellation approach, the ps is canceled by the implicature.

Note that the reason that ps(q) is canceled in (8) is that p is a necessary condition for it. The cancellation mechanism gets rid of ps(q) **whenever** p is a necessary condition for ps(q).

Adding up what we've learned from the two kinds of counterexample just considered, it turns out that the cancellation approach got the wrong generalization: the correct generalization is, roughly, that ps(q) "disappears" whenever p is a **sufficient** condition for it (when p entails it); the cancellation approach encodes instead the incorrect generalization that ps(q) "disappears" whenever p is a **necessary** condition for it. In short:

(9) In conjunctions and conditionals:
Filtering gets rid of ps(q)
iff p is a sufficient condition for ps(q). RIGHT
Cancellation gets rid of ps(q)
iff p is a necessary condition for ps(q). WRONG

**Counterexample no. 3:** Example (10), from Landman 1986, is a different sort of counterexample to the cancellation approach. In this example, a ps fails to get canceled by a conversational implicature that's already in the context. It rather looks like it is the implicature that gets canceled, instead.

(10) a. Assume: A state can either have a president or a king, but not both.
b. If there is a president of Bessarabia, he lives in the palace. The king did not come out of the palace yesterday to make his speech.

Landman 1986 says that (10b) presupposes that there is a king (of Bessarabia). I agree with him. (10b) may sound odd, but it does, at any rate, presuppose that there is a king. The ps that there is a king is definitely not canceled.

But on the cancellation approach, this ps **should** be canceled. The conditional conversationally implicates that there may very well be a president of Bessarabia. We add this to the context. Of course, this implicature is inconsistent with presupposing that there is a king of Bessarabia. So the cancellation approach predicts that when we get to the second sentence, its potential ps that there is a king of Bessarabia should be canceled.

I think (10) nicely refutes the idea that implicatures are stronger than pss in that they cancel pss and not vice versa. When we hear (10), we can't fail to feel that the NP *the king* presupposes that there is a king of Bessarabia. We certainly don't cancel this ps. What we start wondering about, in fact, is the conversational implicature. Having learned from the second sentence that the speaker already assumes that Bessarabia has a king and not a president, we find it hard to understand why the speaker uttered the conditional. But that means that we have, in fact, canceled the implicated assumption that there may well be a president of Bessarabia. It is because we've canceled this implicature that it is unclear why the speaker used the conditional.

In conclusion, it seems to me that the evidence against an analysis that consists of a cancellation mechanism without a filtering mechanism is overwhelming.

## 6.3 On the Filtering + Cancellation Synthesis

I think it is clear that we haven't got a real alternative to the filtering approach. So, I think we must definitely stick with our filtering mechanism. The question remains, then, what to do with the various examples that are not covered by the filtering theory.

First of all, let me say a few words about what I consider to be the problem examples. To the best of my knowledge, all the real problem examples are such that the filtering mechanism predicts a ps that doesn't exist in reality. Examples of this type include (3)–(4), repeated below, as well as further examples that will be discussed in the following chapters.

(3)   It is possible that John has children and it is possible that his children are away.
(4)   If I realize later that I haven't told the truth, I will confess it to everyone.
(5)   If John hasn't just stopped smoking, he has just started smoking.

I agree with Soames 1982 that the alleged counterexamples where filtering fails to predict a ps that does exist can be dismissed. (For details, see Soames 1982, appendix A7.)

Now, what to do about the problem examples. Soames 1982 suggested a synthesis: he suggested to combine a filtering mechanism with a cancellation mechanism. How would one do that? Well, either you filter first and cancel afterwards, or you cancel first and filter afterwards.

Soames 1982 argues that we cancel first and filter afterwards. His only argument for choosing this order is examples like the ones in (11).

(11)   a.   John has children and his sons are bald.
       b.   Maybe John has children and his sons are bald.
       c.   If J has children and his sons are bald, then baldness is probably hereditary.
            (     p     &     q     )
            ps(q):   John has sons
(12)   $p \rightarrow ps(q)$ = if John has children, he has sons.

The filtering approach predicts that the conjunction (11a) presupposes (12), and also that (11b) and (11c) inherit this ps. Soames claims that the conjunction does **not** presuppose (12), and that this is "most evident" for (11a) and (11c). Soames says that the speaker only commits herself to the **possibility** that "if John has children he has sons," but not to the actual truth of this conditional. Hence, Soames believes that filtering alone yields the wrong prediction.

Soames argues that the fact that the sentences in (11) don't presuppose (12) shows that ps(q) must be canceled before filtering. That is because the sentences in (11) don't have an implicature that can cancel (12) after the filtering mechanism has created it. Each sentence implicates that the conjunction is not assumed to be false, and hence that (12) is not assumed to be false. But this implicature leaves open the possibility that (12) is assumed to be true. Therefore, the implicature is not in conflict with (12), and so it can't cancel (12). Soames concludes that the cancellation mechanism must apply first. Then it would cancel ps(q): each sentence in (11) implicates that it is not taken for granted that John has children, which is inconsistent with presupposing that John has children.

To sum up, based on his judgment that the sentences in (11) do not presuppose (12), Soames 1982 believes (i) that such sentences are a counterexample to a theory that uses filtering alone; and (ii) that they provide an argument for applying cancellation before filtering.

I disagree with Soames' judgment concerning the sentences in (11). I think that these sentences do presuppose (12). Recall that we have already looked at an example very much like the ones in (11), in section 6.2 – example (8), repeated below. (8) is just like

(11) in that p is a necessary but not sufficient condition for ps(q). Since conditionals and conjunctions behave alike with respect to ps projection, (8) should not be any different from (11a).

(8)   If John has children, Mary will not like his twins.
       ps(q):   John has twins
       Observed ps of (8):   p → ps(q)

This example is cited in Heim 1983b, who attributes it to Peters (p.c.). Peters' and Heim's judgment is that (8) presupposes p → ps(q), as predicted by the filtering approach, and I agree with them. My judgments on (11a–c) are not different from my judgment on (8).

   It might be a useful exercise to try examples like (8) and (11a–c) in a context that does not entail that if John has children, he has sons/twins. Consider (13)–(16).

(13)   I don't in any way assume about anybody that their having children would entail that they have twins. All I'm saying is that if John has children then Mary will not like his twins.

(14)   I don't in any way assume about anybody that their having children would entail that they have sons. All I'm saying is that John has children and his sons are bald.

(15)   I don't in any way assume about anybody that their having children would entail that they have sons. All I'm saying is that maybe John has children and his sons are bald.

(16)   I don't in any way assume about anybody that their having children would entail that they have sons. All I'm saying is that if John has children and his sons are bald, then baldness is probably hereditary.

I think (13)–(16) all sound definitely strange. I think the first sentence clashes with the ps triggered by *his sons/twins*. This becomes even clearer if you contrast them with examples like the following, which sound OK.

(13′)   I don't in any way assume about anybody that their having children would entail that they have twins. All I'm saying is that if John has children then in case he has twins, Mary will not like his twins.

(15′)   I don't in any way assume about anybody that their having children would entail that they have sons. All I'm saying is that maybe John has children, and if so, maybe he has sons and his sons are bald.

(16′)   I don't in any way assume about anybody that their having children would entail that they have sons. All I'm saying is that if John has children and they happen to be sons and his sons are bald, then he'll have trouble marrying them all off.

   A supporter of Soames' judgment might argue that if, for example, you utter (8), and I raise an eyebrow at you, then you could defend yourself by responding with (13′). However, I don't think this argument works. I think such a response would be a lousy defense. I'd tell you that if you meant (13′) you should have said (13′). And if the supporter of Soames' judgments thinks (13′) is a reasonable response, then that supporter must be treating (8) as if the expression *in case he has twins* is implicit in it, in which case the ps of *his twins* is satisfied locally.

Back to our main theme, let us see what (11a–c) really show about the ordering of cancellation and filtering. We know that if (11a–c) **don't** presuppose (12), they **support** the "cancel first filter after" hypothesis. The funny thing is that if they **do** presuppose (12), they **refute** the "cancel first filter after" hypothesis. If examples (11a–c) and (8) presuppose p → ps(q), then they show that it cannot be right to "cancel first and filter after." In these examples, cancellation cancels too much. If we start with cancellation, it will irrevocably get rid of ps(q) altogether. Filtering can't restore ps(q) in order to then derive p → ps(q).

Based on the judgment that (8) and (11a–c) do presuppose p → ps(q), we can draw the following conclusions.

(i)     Filtering (alone) has no problem with this particular sort of example.
(ii)    A "cancel first filter after" synthesis cannot be right.
(iii)   The possibility remains open that a "filter first cancel after" strategy might work
        – after all, (11) was Soames' only argument against it.

Having discussed the synthesis idea, what are we left with? I think that as far as the empirical facts go, we are left with a possibility of using cancellation as some sort of addition to Heim's theory. When we come across a ps that our filtering mechanism fails to get rid of, it seems that we can still consider canceling it. However, I am not sure we would **want** to do that. Since Landman's example (10) indicates, contra Gazdar and Soames, that we can't assume that cancellation of a ps by implicature is the general case, we could only claim that cancellation by implicature operates in special cases. But this is not general and seems ad hoc. (What special cases? Why do they allow cancellation?) Also, as I argue above, invoking cancellation seems like a dubious move, because it is not clear how the idea of ps cancellation could be reconciled with the conception of ps as something that must be taken for granted because it is indispensable.

# 7

# Presupposition Projection: Interlude

---

In chapter 5, I introduced the basics of the Stalnaker–Karttunen–Heim "filtering" analysis of ps projection. Let me repeat here the core ideas:

1. (Stalnaker–Karttunen)
   **Pss are requirements on the context:** B is a ps of S iff S can be uttered felicitously only in contexts that entail B.
   As emphasized at the beginning of chapter 6, we are talking here about an absolute requirement that must be satisfied: pss are not taken to be "defeasible."

2. (Stalnaker–Karttunen)
   **A ps has to be satisfied by its local context.** The "heritage properties" of linguistic items consist of specifications of local contexts.
   For example, the "heritage property" of *and* may be expressed as follows: if a conjunction p ∧ q is uttered in context c, then c is the local context of p and c + p is the local context of q. Given this, the theory says that ps(p) must be satisfied by c, and ps(q) must be satisfied by c + p. Which predicts that the conjunction inherits ps(p) and also presupposes p → ps(q).

3. (Heim)
   **Context change potentials (ccps): "heritage" and "content" combined.** The semantic value of each expression is its ccp, which is a partial function from the set of contexts to the set of contexts. The ccp of a complex expression encodes at one and the same time both (i) its truth-conditional content (since the ccp tells you how the expression changes the truth conditions of the context to which it is added), and (ii) which pss it "inherits" from its parts (since the ccp tells you what the local contexts are for the various parts).

I think that the Stalnaker–Karttunen–Heim "filtering" analysis is successful and insightful. We saw above that it correctly predicts paradigmatic data such as that presented in section 5.1. It also formulates a coherent and intuitively valid conception of the notion of ps, and very elegantly reduces "heritage" and "content" to a single property.

However, the basic filtering analysis presented in sections 5.2 and 5.5 (and summarized immediately above) is not enough. There are many types of examples that require accounts that go beyond basic filtering.

For one thing, I haven't yet presented the analysis of ps projection below the level of a complete clause. In chapter 10, I will discuss Heim's account of this, and Beaver's.

And, of course, there are all the (real or apparent) counterexamples to the filtering analysis which we still need to account for. These include, among others, examples like (1)–(3) (repeated here from chapter 6), as well as the well-known examples where negation seems to behave as a "plug," such as (4) below.

(1)   It is possible that John has children and it is possible that his children are away.
(2)   If I realize later that I haven't told the truth, I will confess it to everyone.
(3)   If John hasn't just stopped smoking, he has just started smoking.
(4)   The king of France isn't bald – there is no king of France!

Since the filtering theory seems like a good theory, and, moreover, we don't seem to have a viable alternative (see section 6.2), it seems to me that we must hold on to filtering. The question remains, then, what to do when we do come across a ps that our filtering mechanism fails to get rid of.

In chapter 6, I reached the conclusion that, as far as the empirical facts go, we might invoke cancellation of pss in some special cases, in order to get rid of a ps that fails to get "filtered out." However, I also argued that this did not seem like a very desirable option, because of the difficulty of reconciling the idea of ps cancellation with the conception of ps as something that must be taken for granted because it is indispensable.

In chapters 8–11, we are going to look at a variety of examples that filtering alone does not account for. Rather than resort to cancellation in order to deal with such examples, we will consider a number of different factors that may account for various problem examples. Before I start, let me give you an idea of what's to come by listing the factors I have in mind. (i)–(iii) will be discussed in chapter 8, (iv) in chapters 9 and 10, and (v) in chapter 11. (vi) will only show up again in chapter 21.

**Some factors that may explain (apparent or real) "disappearance" of presuppositions that are not "filtered out":**

 (i)   ambiguities (one lexical item with two different ccps)
 (ii)   shifts in contextual assumptions
(iii)   metalinguistic operators
(iv)   accommodation
 (v)   context-dependence of "conversationally triggered" pss
(vi)   interactions between pss of different triggers

As is evident from this list, my arguing above against the Gazdar–Soames cancellation mechanism does not mean that I object to the idea that "pragmatic" factors play an important role in explaining the behavior of pss. On the contrary, I am convinced that Gazdar and Soames were right in thinking that pragmatic factors (including "pragmatics-outside-the-grammar") are crucial here. In particular, I believe that the use of metalinguistic operators and the process of accommodation are very central here, and that they give us the correct account of many cases of (apparent) "ps disappearance."

# 8

# *Presupposition Projection: Negation, Shifts in Contextual Assumptions, and Metalinguistic Operators*

So far, we have only been talking about negation as being a "hole" – we were concerned with the fact that pss survive under it, as in example (2).

(1)   The king of France is bald.
(2)   The king of France isn't bald.

However, what about examples where a ps whose trigger is under negation seems to "disappear"? For instance, examples like (3)–(5).

(3)   (from Chierchia and McConnell-Ginet 1990, p. 314)

    A, *noticing the open door*:    Was it you who opened the door to the porch? I closed it at lunchtime.

    B:   Well, it wasn't me who opened it, because I've been gone all afternoon, and it wasn't Joan who opened it, because she was with me, and it wasn't any of the kids who opened it, because they're on a field trip, and I strongly suspect that nobody opened it – there was a lot of wind this afternoon, you know.

(4)   The king of France isn't bald – there is no king of France!
(5)   A:   I don't have a dog.
    B:   So at least you don't have to walk your dog.

## 8.1   Shifts in Contextual Assumptions

First of all, let us consider examples like (3). Do they constitute counterexamples to the filtering theory? Each of the cleft sentences in (3), taken in isolation, presupposes that somebody opened the door to the porch. Now, does B's utterance presuppose that? Do the cleft sentences as they occur in B's utterance presuppose that? Given the sentence *I strongly suspect that nobody opened it*, one might get the impression that the presupposition "disappears."

    However, I don't think the ps "disappears" at all. It seems quite obvious to me that we have here a case of **giving up a contextual assumption** in mid-utterance. The cleft sentences in B's utterance do presuppose that somebody opened the door to the porch. To start with, speaker B accepts A's assumption that somebody opened the door to the porch. So B can utter the cleft sentences felicitously – their ps is satisfied. The sentence *I strongly suspect that nobody opened it* is inconsistent with the context that admitted the cleft sentences earlier. At this point, speaker B revises the context: she gives up her assumption that someone opened the door to the porch. After all, it is very clear that contexts don't always get incremented monotonically – that sometimes we change the context by dropping an assumption that was made earlier. We see, then, that examples like (3) are not counterexamples to the filtering theory.

This point is made in Chierchia and McConnell-Ginet 1990, and also in Beaver 1993a, section 4.4. Note that it is typical (though, in my opinion, not necessary) that the speaker of an example like (3) actually believes the assumption which satisfies the ps to be false, but nevertheless accepts it temporarily, for the sake of discussion. Beaver sees the temporary adoption of this assumption as a kind of accommodation (he calls it "temporary global accommodation"). Beaver notes that we can expect the shift in contextual assumptions involved here to be highly marked – speakers don't arbitrarily change contextual assumptions without warning.

Beaver 1993a suggests that the same phenomenon might be at work in examples like (6) and (7): the speaker of (6) is temporarily taking the perspective of somebody who thinks that the speaker is lying, the speaker of (7) is temporarily taking the perspective of someone who believes that whatever is being done is allowed. The sentence carries the factive ps of *realized* or *aware* as usual, and the speaker is uttering the sentence in a (temporary) context in which this ps is satisfied.

(6)   If I realize later that I haven't told the truth, I will confess it to everyone.
(7)   I was not aware that you are allowed to do that! *(Said e.g. by a teacher to a child who is smoking behind the bicycle sheds.)*

To sum up, we cannot always talk about a "fixed" ever growing common ground which keeps getting monotonically incremented as the discourse proceeds. In many situations, it is crucial to see that there is more than one ever growing common ground per conversation, and that sometimes speakers "shift common grounds" during the conversation. These shifts in contextual assumptions allow us to account for a class of apparent counterexamples to the filtering theory: in examples like the ones discussed in this section, the ps does **not** "disappear"; rather, it is appropriately satisfied by the context in which the sentence is uttered (a context that may be inconsistent with other contexts assumed at other points in the same conversation).

## 8.2   Lexical "Hole" vs. "Plug" Ambiguities?

Yet, there are also examples where a ps does seem to disappear, even though filtering fails to get rid of it. For example, the existential ps of the definite NP *the king of France* or *your dog* really does seem to "disappear" in (4) and (5) above. Let us focus on (4).

(2)   The king of France isn't bald.
(4)   The king of France isn't bald – there is no king of France!

Sentence (4) does not presuppose that there is a king of France. It is definitely **not** taken for granted in (4) that there is a king of France. Nor does sentence (2) as it occurs in (4) presuppose that there is a king of France: while the second part of (4) is inconsistent with the assumption that there is a king of France, our intuitive judgment is that this part does not create a contradiction or involve giving up a contextual assumption. It seems, intuitively, that the speaker of (4) never makes the assumption that there is a king of France, not even temporarily. Evidently, we have in (4) a case where a ps fails to survive under negation.

On the view of Russell 1905, (2) and (4) illustrate a scope ambiguity.[1] But of course, on Russell's view, the "existential ps" is not considered a ps at all. Russell provides no explanation for the intuition that (2) takes it for granted that there is a king of France. So, Russell's analysis of (2) and (4) is not good enough. (Not even if we were willing to treat definites as quantificational.)

The question remains, then, why it is that while pss often do survive under negation, they do not survive under negation in examples such as (4). K&P 1979 propose that the reason is that **negation is lexically ambiguous**. According to K&P 1979, there are two kinds of negation:

(i) Ordinary negation: negates content and retains the ps (= is a "hole")

(ii) Negation that applies to "the total meaning of its target sentence," ignoring the distinction between content and ps (K&P 1979, p. 47): negates content and ps: $\neg(p \wedge ps(p))$; lets no ps through (= is a "plug")

When the negation in (2) is of the second kind, (2) entails that either there is no king of France, or there is one but he isn't bald. Which is consistent with the second part of (4).

The analysis of negation as lexically ambiguous between a "hole" interpretation and a "plug" interpretation seems ad hoc. In addition, it fails to explain the fact that pss usually do survive under negation – they seem to "disappear" only under threat of contradiction. To account for this fact, we would need yet another ad hoc stipulation, to the effect that the "hole" interpretation is preferred.

I would also like to say a few words about the nature of a "plug" interpretation of negation, or, indeed, of any other operator.

To get a "plug" interpretation of an operator, we insert the ps (the presupposed proposition) under the scope of the operator, alongside the proposition containing the ps trigger. (As is transparent in the expression $\neg(p \wedge ps(p))$.) Indeed, if we want a "plug" interpretation, we **must** do that. We must, in fact, insert the ps so that it would precede the proposition containing the trigger, under the scope of the "plug."

The reason for that is our conception of ps as something that must be taken for granted because it is indispensable. Take a proposition p and its presupposition, ps(p). Suppose p is sitting under the scope of a "plug" operator. Since our conception of ps is incompatible with the idea of ps cancellation (see 6.2 above), we can't say that the

---

[1]   For Russell, the definite is an existential quantifier, which can have wide or narrow scope relative to the negation. Sentence (2) is ambiguous between (2a) and (2b).

(2a)   $\exists x\, [\text{King-of-France}(x) \wedge \forall y[\text{King-of-France}(y) \rightarrow y = x] \wedge \neg\, \text{Bald}(x)]$

(2b)   $\neg\, \exists x\, [\text{King-of-France}(x) \wedge \forall y[\text{King-of-France}(y) \rightarrow y = x] \wedge \text{Bald}(x)]$

"plug" somehow cancels ps(p) – we must assume, instead, that ps(p) is satisfied somehow. But we want to make sure that ps(p) will not "project upward" beyond the scope of the "plug." Therefore, we must say that ps(p) is satisfied by the local context of p, under the scope of the "plug."

More concretely, let us consider possible ccps for negation. The ccp in (i) makes negation a "hole" (see section 5.5). If we want to formulate a ccp that will make negation a "plug," we can do that as in (ii).

(i)   $c + \neg p = c - (c + p)$    "hole" (Heim 1983b)
(ii)   $c + \neg p = c - (c + ps(p) + p)$    "plug"

The ccp in (ii) yields the desired interpretation for sentence (2) as it occurs in (4): "either France doesn't have a king, or France has a king and he isn't bald." This is achieved by subtracting from the initial context c not simply c incremented with p, as in (i), but rather c incremented with ps(p) and p. Which is a way of inserting ps(p) under the scope of negation, into the local context of p. Indeed, (2) with "plug" negation is treated exactly as if it was (2′).

(2′)   It is not the case that France has a king and he is bald.

It is not possible (as far as I can see) to make negation a "plug" in any other way, viz. without inserting ps(p) under the scope of negation into the local context of p.

Now one might be tempted to respond as follows. Kadmon is wrong, since the ccp in (iii) below will give us the desired "plug" negation, without inserting ps(p) into the local context of p. If p is a set of worlds, then it should be perfectly possible to directly subtract p from c. (After all, set subtraction is well defined even if p contains worlds that are not in c.) And since (iii) doesn't instruct you to increment c with p, it does not require that c satisfy ps(p). Hence, (iii) predicts that the ps of p will not be inherited.

(iii)   $c + \neg p = c - p$

However, this reasoning is wrong. Suppose that there is indeed a set of worlds associated with p (despite the fact that the basic semantic value of p is not a set of worlds but a ccp). Call this set $W_p$. So, $c - p$ means "subtract $W_p$ from c." Now there are two options: we can make either assumption (a) or assumption (b) below.

(a)   $c - p$ is defined just in case $c + p$ is defined;
(b)   In computing $c + \neg p$, we are allowed to freely subtract $W_p$ from c, regardless of whether $c + p$ is defined or not.

The option that would seem to fit best with the rest of Heim's theory is option (a). It would make sense to claim that (roughly) if c fails to satisfy ps(p), then you can't do anything with p in context c, period. So, in cases of ps failure, just as $c + p$ is undefined, so is $c - p$. But, if we take option (a), the ccp in (iii) would not give us a "plug" interpretation at all, because $c + \neg p$ would be undefined if c fails to satisfy ps(p). Option (b) seems to me to be less in the spirit of the theory as a whole and more ad hoc, but suppose we take it anyway. Then it becomes crucial to know what $W_p$ is supposed to be. For concreteness, take example (2), on the "plug" interpretation. What is the set of worlds $W_{(1)}$ associated with sentence (1) (*The king of France is bald*)? Well, presumably, it is the set of worlds where France has a king and he is bald. (Certainly, it can't contain worlds where France has no king, because we don't want to subtract such worlds from c when we increment c with sentence (2).) But this means that we are back where we started: we see that, via the definition of $W_p$, we have put in the ps ("France has a king") again. In short, (iii) doesn't alter the fact that to get the "plug" effect, we must, in effect, insert ps(p) in the local context of p, under the scope of the negation.

## 8.3   Presupposition and Metalinguistic Operators

In 8.2, I have only been talking about negation as logical negation (possibly ambiguous between a "hole" interpretation and a "plug" interpretation). However, recall that negation need not be interpreted as logical negation: it is often used, instead, as metalinguistic negation, in the sense of Horn 1985 (see section 1.3). This allows us to give a more satisfactory account of the non-uniform behavior of pss under negation.

We can say that the negation in (4) is **metalinguistic negation**, and that that is why the existential ps does not survive.[2] The negation in (4) is not logical – it is not used for claiming that the proposition that the king of France is bald is false. Rather, the negation in (4) is used to reject the utterance *the king of France is bald* – to claim that this utterance is in some way inappropriate. Indeed, the speaker of (4) is saying that the utterance *the king of France is bald* is inappropriate exactly because its ps is not satisfied.

The metalinguistic negation account of (4) is well motivated. As Horn 1985 shows very clearly, it is certainly true that in natural language, operators can be used metalinguistically. As noted in Horn (1985; mid p. 135), it would be economical to assume that that is what explains why pss don't always survive under negation. If the "disappearance" of ps under negation can always be attributed to metalinguistic negation, then that may eliminate the need to posit a lexical ambiguity of logical negation. Note also that (4) would normally carry the intonation pattern typical of metalinguistic uses of negation.

One way of stating the difference between logical negation and (the relevant instance of) metalinguistic negation would be as follows. There are two possibilities:

   (i)   adding ¬p to the context;
   (ii)  refraining from adding p to the context.

Suppose that when we have "ordinary," logical, negation, we add ¬p to the context, and ¬ is a "hole." Perhaps some uses of (metalinguistic) negation express something more like (ii): the speaker refuses to add p to the context, or expresses the opinion that it would be impossible to do so. When we refrain from adding p to the context, the context need not satisfy the ps of p.

---

[2]   When K&P 1979 talk about their second kind of negation, they sound, in some respects (but not others), as if they were talking about what Horn was later to call metalinguistic negation.

Now, can the "disappearance" of ps under negation **always** be attributed to met-alinguistic negation? For example, what about (5)? It is certainly not assumed by B that the existential ps of *your dog* is satisfied; evidently, this ps fails to survive under the negation in B's utterance. Can we say that this negation is metalinguistic? I don't know. What do you think?

(5)  A:  I don't have a dog.
     B:  So at least you don't have to walk your dog.

Other operators besides negation have metalinguistic uses, and this may account for further examples where a ps seems to disappear. For example, conditionals like the ones in (8) and (9).

(8)  If Nixon knows that the war is over, the war is over. (Wilson 1975)
(9)  If the queen did not open parliament today, there is a queen. (Landman 1986)

We need to explain why the factive ps of *know* and the existential ps of *the queen* are not inherited in (8) and (9). As discussed in Landman 1986, conditionals like (8) and (9) have a special sort of use. Being tautologies, they can't be used to convey new infor-mation. Rather, they make old information explicit. In particular, the point of these conditionals is to make explicit the ps of the antecedent clause. For example, the point of (9) is to remind the hearers of (or highlight) the fact that the antecedent clause pre-supposes the existence of a queen, by making this presupposition explicit. Given this special use of the conditionals under consideration, it seems natural (to me, as well as to Fred Landman, p.c., 1993) to say that these conditionals are in fact used metalin-guistically. (The metalinguistic message is something like: "Don't forget that if one can use the antecedent clause felicitously, that means that one already presupposes that there is a queen".)

# 9

# *Presupposition Projection and Accommodation*

In this chapter, I will be concerned with the process of accommodation and its role in determining our intuitive judgments about ps "inheritance."

In the case of a ps trigger under a metalinguistic operator, the filtering mechanism does not apply, and the ps in question does not have to be satisfied at all. In contrast, we assume that in all the cases to be discussed in this chapter, filtering applies as usual. Accommodation crucially interacts with filtering, and it is this interaction which is responsible for many of our intuitive judgments about ps.

## 9.1 "Linguistic" vs. "Cognitive" Presupposition

The importance of accommodation in determining our judgments on ps "inheritance" is already evident when we look at the paradigmatic data treated by Karttunen (section 5.1 above). Take for example conjunctions like (1)–(3).

(1)  Geraldine is a Mormon and she has given up wearing her holy underwear!
(2)  We need more napkins and JOHN will have a beer too.
(3)  Bill drinks and JOHN drinks too.

What the Karttunen–Stalnaker–Heim theory says about the ps of the second conjunct can be stated, equivalently, as in (4) or (5).

(4)  $p \wedge q$ can be felicitously uttered only in a context c s.t. $c + p$ entails ps(q).
(5)  $p \wedge q$ presupposes $p \rightarrow ps(q)$.

(5) is the "official" prediction of the theory. But, of course, the intuitive judgment on what a given conjunction presupposes doesn't always match this "official" prediction. Intuitively, we may easily accept that example (1) presupposes $p \rightarrow ps(q)$, but we would judge that (2) presupposes ps(q) and that (3) presupposes nothing.

As discussed in section 5.2 above, it is easy to explain our judgments on (1)–(3) based on the idea that $c + p$ must satisfy ps(q). Take example (2). When we don't actually have the relevant information about the context in which (2) is uttered, we tend to imagine that p wouldn't play any role in satisfying ps(q). Therefore, we conclude that it is the c that would have to satisfy ps(q). In other words, we accommodate the assumption ps(q) into c (or at least we imagine that if we were to accept (2), we would have to accommodate ps(q) into c). In the case of (1), we tend to imagine that p **would** play a role in satisfying ps(q), and we tend to accommodate p → ps(q) into c. In the case of (3), p all by itself satisfies ps(q), so nothing needs to be accommodated into c.

We see then that the intuitively felt ps is in fact that assumption which we would accommodate when we don't have the relevant information about the context of utterance. This is noted in Beaver 1993b, section 4.3. (Beaver also gives a formal representation of this process of accommodation, as filtering on epistemic alternatives.) Beaver 1993b calls the "official" ps predicted by the filtering mechanism the "**linguistic ps.**" ("Linguistic," because it can be determined by the linguistic form of the sentence.) He calls the assumption that hearers actually seem to accommodate when faced with the sentence (i.e. the ps which we intuitively judge the sentence to have) the "**cognitive ps.**" Let us adopt these terms.

## 9.2   Local Accommodation as Responsible for ps "Disappearance"

Now we continue our survey of factors that may explain the "disappearance" of pss that are not "filtered out." I would say that **the** major factor that is responsible for such disappearance is what Heim 1983b has dubbed "local" accommodation. Local accommodation naturally accounts for all the classical examples of "ps disappearance" raised by Gazdar and Soames, and more.

### 9.2.1   Heim's Analysis (Part 2): negation with global and local accommodation

In chapter 8, we discussed the phenomenon of ps "disappearance" under negation and a couple of possible explanations for it. Heim 1983b offers her own account of the behavior of pss under negation. Her account is based on the distinction between "global" and "local" accommodation.

Think for a moment about accommodation in relation to context change potentials. Suppose I utter (6), out of the blue.

(6)   My dog is at the door.

If you didn't know that I had a dog, then you are faced with the problem that you have just heard (6) in a context c that does not admit it. So you can't apply the ccp of this sentence to your context. c + (6) is undefined. Of course, you don't stop there baffled, but rather accommodate the assumption that I have a dog. And then you can process my utterance. In other words, you amend c to c + Nirit has a dog, and add sentence (6) to that amended context:

c + Nirit has a dog   +   Nirit's dog is at the door.

Now let me present Heim 1983b's account of ps under negation. We assume that the ccp of negation is as Heim proposed, i.e. as in (i).

(i)  $c + \neg S = c - (c + S)$      'hole' (Heim)

Suppose you hear $(8) = \neg(7)$ in a context where it is **not** assumed that France has a king, nor that France doesn't have a king.

(7)   The king of France is bald.
(8)   The king of France isn't bald.

The ccp of (8) instructs you to perform the context incrementation $c + (7)$. But you can't do that, because $c + (7)$ is undefined. What do you do? You can accommodate $ps(7)$, viz. the assumption that France has a king. But now you have a choice – you can proceed in two different ways.

One, you can perform "global" accommodation, as described in (9).

(9)   You amend your initial context c to $c + ps(7) = c +$ France has a king.
      Instead of computing $c + \neg(7)$, you compute $c + ps(7) + \neg(7)$.
      This will give you $c + ps(7) - (c + ps(7) + (7))$.

Taking this option, you end up with a new context that contains only those worlds of c where France has a king, and that king is not bald.

Using the accommodation described in (9) is like pretending that the initial context in which (8) was uttered was the amended context. Heim notes that this kind of accommodation can be called "global" accommodation in both of the following two senses.

> "global" accommodation, sense #1: Whenever you are supposed to use the initial context c, you use the amended context instead.
> "global" accommodation, sense #2: The accommodated assumption stays in the context for good.

Clearly, the accommodation in (9) is "global" in sense #1. It is also "global" in sense #2, because the accommodated assumption stays in the context after we have finished processing the whole sentence: we end up with a new context in which it is assumed that there is a king of France. That's what I mean by "the accommodated assumption stays in the context for good." (Of course, the accommodated assumption stays in the context for good **unless** it is explicitly given up. But giving up assumptions is a possibility that Heim's theory doesn't deal with.)

Your second option is to perform "local" accommodation, as described in (10).

(10)   Amend c to $c + ps(7)$ only for the purpose of computing $c + (7)$.
       So instead of computing $c + \neg(7)$ like this:
       $c + \neg(7) = c - (c + (7))$,
       you compute it like this:
       $c + \neg(7) = c - (c + ps(7) + (7))$.

Taking this option, you end up with a new context that contains those worlds of c in which either there is no king of France, or there is one but he isn't bald.

It is easy to see why the accommodation described in (10) is called "local" accommodation. Note that it is not "global" accommodation in either of the above two senses.

Regarding sense #1: you don't pretend "globally" that the context entails that France has a king, but rather amend the context that way only at the point where you can't do without this amendment. Regarding sense #2: the accommodated assumption does **not** stay in the context for good. We end up with a context where it is not assumed that there is a king of France. The ps of (7) was only assumed temporarily.

Local accommodation gives us the effect of "the second kind of negation" (= "plug" negation) of K&P 1979: (8) contributes the information that either there is no king of France or there is one but he isn't bald. Indeed, I think it is fair to say that the effect of local accommodation is that we interpret (8) as if it was (8') – as if the underlined bit in (8') was implicit in (8).

(8')  It is not true that [France has a king and the king of France is bald].

And here is a representation of global and local accommodation for sentence (8) using DRSs:[1]

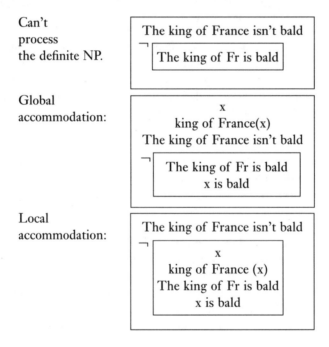

| Can't process the definite NP. | The king of France isn't bald<br>¬ ⌐ The king of Fr is bald ⌐ |

| Global accommodation: | x<br>king of France(x)<br>The king of France isn't bald<br>¬ ⌐ The king of Fr is bald / x is bald ⌐ |

| Local accommodation: | The king of France isn't bald<br>¬ ⌐ x / king of France (x) / The king of Fr is bald / x is bald ⌐ |

Heim proposes that there is a general principle that determines that global accommodation is ceteris paribus preferred to local accommodation. That means that we always perform global accommodation, unless we are forced (for example, by threat of contradiction) to perform local accommodation.

When we hear (8) in a context where it isn't known if there is a king of France or not, we can use global accommodation. Since global accommodation is the preferred option, that is what we do. The effect is that we behave just as if (8) was uttered in a context that satisfies the ps. This is exactly analogous to the way we treat a sentence like *my dog is at the door*.

---

[1]  I'm ignoring uniqueness here.

But when we hear (8) in the context of (11), we have no choice but to perform local accommodation, otherwise we'd get a contradiction.

(11)   The king of France isn't bald – there is no king of France!

The effect is that we manage to process (11) in a context that does **not** satisfy the ps, and also to go on assuming that the ps does not hold, afterwards.

Note that if we just proceed according to the ccp of negation, (8) is predicted to inherit the ps of (7). But in (11), we do something extra: we satisfy the ps of (7) by local accommodation, with the effect that the ps isn't inherited.

I think we might apply the terminology of Beaver 1993b to such cases too. The "linguistic" ps of (8) is ps(7). When Beaver defines the "cognitive" ps as what the hearers actually accommodate when faced with the sentence, he means that which is globally accommodated. The globally accommodated assumption coincides with what the hearers intuitively judge the sentence to presuppose. In examples like (11), local accommodation eliminates the need for global accommodation, and hence determines that there is no "cognitive" ps.

How does Heim's account of ps "disappearance" under negation compare with K&P 1979's "two kinds of negation" account?

In a way, these two accounts are very similar: they get exactly the same result (ps inheritance is blocked), and by exactly same means (viz. by inserting the ps (the presupposed proposition) into the local context of the proposition containing the ps trigger, under the scope of the negation). Note that if we formulate a ccp for "plug" negation as in (ii) (see section 8.2), then on both accounts, the crucial point is that instead of computing $c + p$, we compute $c + ps(p) + p$.

(ii)   $c + \neg p = c - (c + ps(p) + p)$      'plug'

The two accounts differ on what they attribute the insertion of $ps(p)$ to: the one account attributes it to a lexical property of "plug" negation, the other attributes it to the process of accommodation. The two accounts also differ regarding the fact that ps "disappearance" under negation only occurs under threat of contradiction: the "two kinds of negation" account doesn't explain this fact, whereas Heim suggests that this is due to a general preference for "global" over "local" accommodation.

Given these differences, there is reason to think that Heim's account is preferable to the "two kinds of negation" account. If it can be shown that local accommodation is a general phenomenon that operates under other operators besides negation, and that the preference for global accommodation can be explained (or, at least, is systematic), then Heim's account is certainly better than the "two kinds of negation" account. Instead of stipulating an idiosyncratic property of negation, including not only a lexical ambiguity but also a stipulation to the effect that the "ordinary" negation is preferred, we would now have general principles of accommodation.

A possible advantage of Heim's account over the "metalinguistic negation" account (see section 8.3) is that her account naturally covers not only examples like (11) but also examples like (12) (where it is not so clear that we could maintain that the negation is metalinguistic): Given A's utterance in (12), we can't "globally" assume that speaker A has a dog, so when we get to B's utterance in (12), we perform local accommodation, as indicated in (12′).

(12)  A:  I don't have a dog.
      B:  So at least you don't have to walk your dog.
(12′) A:  I don't have a dog.
      B:  So at least you don't [have a dog and have to walk your dog].

At the same time, since it is quite clear that metalinguistic operators exist, it could very well be the case that both metalinguistic operators and local accommodation are factors that are responsible for ps "disappearance."

### 9.2.2  ps "Disappearance" and Local Accommodation: a compound sentence with conflicting pss, and further cases

Heim's treatment of ps "disappearance" under negation extends to ps "disappearance" under other operators. As I said above, I think that local accommodation is a major factor responsible for ps disappearance and naturally accounts for all the Gazdar–Soames classical examples of ps disappearance and more.

To take an example, let us look at (13), which is one of the classical examples of ps "disappearance": a conditional whose antecedent and consequent have conflicting pss. I assume that the ccp of conditionals is as in (15).

(13)  If John hasn't just stopped smoking, he has just started smoking.

$$\underbrace{\hspace{4cm}}_{p} \quad \underbrace{\hspace{4cm}}_{q}$$

(14)  ps(p):  John smoked in the "immediate" past.
      ps(q):  John did not smoke in the "immediate" past.
(15)  $c + p \rightarrow q = c - (c + p - ((c + p) + q))$

The intuitive judgment is that (13) is felicitous, and it has no presupposition regarding John's smoking habits. And what does the filtering mechanism predict? For a context c to admit (13), both $c + p$ and $(c + p) + q$ must be defined. That means that c must entail ps(p) and $c + p$ must entail ps(q). However, $ps(q) = \neg ps(p)$. So c must entail ps(p) and $c + p$ must entail $\neg ps(p)$. That would be possible only if $c + p$ is false, i.e. empty.[2] Which yields the prediction that it should be impossible to add (13) to any context consistent with p. Or in other words, that it should be possible to add (13) only to a context c that entails $\neg p$. Or, in other words again, that (13) presupposes $\neg p$ (= John has just stopped smoking). (Which also means that (13), trivially, presupposes itself.)

Obviously, the prediction based on the filtering mechanism alone is wrong. (13) is perfectly all right in a context that does not entail (13) itself, nor $\neg p$ (= John has just stopped smoking). It would be pointless to utter (13) in a context that does entail $\neg p$, and we don't. For the same reason, it would be absurd to globally accommodate $\neg p$, and we don't.

---

[2]  The reason is this: Suppose c entails ps(p). Then c contains only worlds in which ps(p) is true. $c + p$ is the intersection of c and p, so if it is non-empty, in all of its worlds ps(p) is true. To entail $\neg ps(p)$, $c + p$ must be a subset of the set of worlds in which $\neg ps(p)$ is true (= the set of worlds in which ps(p) is false). So if $c + p$ is non-empty, $c + p$ does not entail $\neg ps(p)$. $c + p$ will be able to entail $\neg ps(p)$ only if it is empty.

But adding to filtering the option of local accommodation allows us to make the correct prediction.

Let r = John has just stopped smoking.

$p = \neg r$

$ps(p) = ps(r) =$ John smoked in the "immediate" past

The ccp in (15) tells us that

$$c + (13) = c - (c + \neg r - ((c + \neg r) + q)).$$

Given the ccp of negative statements, we get that

$$c + (13) = c - (c - (c + r) - ((c - (c + r)) + q)).$$

Suppose we hear (13) in a context c which entails neither ps(p) nor ps(q). We are able to process sentence (13) in context c, without globally accommodating any assumptions, because we can compute c + (13) using local accommodation (underlined), as follows.

$$c + (13) = c - (c - (c + \underline{ps(r)} + r) - ((c - (c + \underline{ps(r)} + r)) + \underline{ps(q)} + q))$$

$$\underbrace{\phantom{xxxxxxxxx}}_{\text{I}} \quad \underbrace{\phantom{xxxxxxxxxxxxxxxxxx}}_{\text{II}}$$

$$\underbrace{\phantom{xxxxxxxxxxxxxxxxxxxxxxxxxxxxxxxxxx}}_{\text{III}}$$

**I**

$c - (c + ps(r) + r)$ is the set of worlds of c minus those where John smoked in the "immediate" past, and has just stopped smoking. Call it I. The set I is the set of worlds of c where either John didn't smoke in the "immediate" past, or else he did smoke in the "immediate" past and still smokes.

**II**

Now look at the expression marked with a double line. First, to our set I, we need to add ps(q) = John didn't smoke in the "immediate" past. This leaves us with those worlds of c where John didn't smoke in the "immediate" past. Next, we add q. We get that the expression marked with a double line denotes the set of worlds in which John didn't smoke in the "immediate" past but he has just started smoking. Call it II.

**III**

Next, we must subtract II from I. We get the set of worlds where either John didn't smoke in the "immediate" past and still doesn't, or else John smoked in the "immediate" past and still smokes. Call it III.

Finally,

we must subtract III from c. We end up with a new context consisting of all and only those worlds of the initial context c in which either John didn't smoke in the "immediate" past and he has just started smoking, or else John smoked in the "immediate" past and has just stopped smoking.

According to this account, we interpret (13) as if it was (13′) – as if the under-lined bits in (13′) were implicit in (13). This seems to me to be a plausible analysis of (13).

(13′)   If John hasn't [smoked in the "immediate" past and just stopped smoking], then he has [not smoked in the "immediate" past] and just started smoking.

Similarly, other examples from the literature can be explained by local accommoda-tion. Here are a few examples, with indication of a possible form of local accommoda-tion that would explain the "ps disappearance." (Several of the examples given in the literature are disjunctions. I am not discussing disjunctions in this book, but I will just mention a couple of examples.)

(16)    If I realize later that I haven't told the truth, I will confess it to everyone.
(16′)   If I haven't told the truth and I realize later that I haven't told the truth, I will confess it to everyone.
(17)    It is possible that John has children and it is possible that his children are away.
(17′)   It is possible that John has children and it is possible that he has children and his children are away.
(18)    If Mary's boss doesn't have children, then it wasn't his child who won the fellowship.
(18′)   If Mary's boss doesn't have children, then it is not the case that he has a child and it was his child who won the fellowship.
(19)    Either Bill met the king of Slobovia or he met the president of Slobovia.
                    (Soames 1982 shows, contra Karttunen 1974, that (19) is a problem.)
(19′)   Either Slobovia has a king and Bill met the king of Slobovia or Slobovia has a president and he met the president of Slobovia.
(20)    Either there's no bathroom in this house or it's in a funny place.
                    (from Roberts 1989, attributed to Partee, p.c.)
(20′)   Either there's no bathroom in this house or there is one but it's in a funny place.

## 9.3   Modal Subordination: ps Satisfaction in Intensional Contexts

In this section, I would like to look at the phenomenon of "modal subordination," which is described and analyzed in Roberts 1989, 1996a.

### 9.3.1   Preliminaries: quantification over possible worlds

Following Roberts 1989, let us refer to a clause or formula which is independently asserted as a statement in its own right – one which is claimed to be true in the actual world – as being **factual**.[3] A clause or formula which is not an independent assertion – one that expresses an irrealis proposition – is said to be **non-factual**.

Let us consider the following clause, call it p, as it occurs in examples (21)–(26).

---

[3]   For convenience, I say "the actual world" when I mean "the world of evaluation for the entire sen-tence/discourse" (even though in fact conversations are not always about the actual world).

p = John is driving right now

(21)  John is driving right now.
(22)  If John has rented a car, he is driving right now.
(23)  John might be driving right now.
(24)  In view of the fact that/Since John has rented a car, he might be driving right now.
(25)  John would be driving right now.
(26)  If John has rented a car, he would be driving right now.

In (21), p is factual. So (21) conveys the information in (21′). In terms of context-change semantics, when (21) is asserted in a context c, p is added to c permanently. We consider all the worlds in c (= all the candidates for being the actual world before (21) is asserted), and kick out the ones where p is false. So in all the worlds of the resulting context, c + (21), (= in all the candidates for being the actual world after (21) is asserted), p is true. So we might say that (21) conveys the information in (21″).

(21′)  p is true in the actual world w*.
(21″)  For every world w s.t. w is a candidate for being the actual world, p is true in w.

In (22)–(26), p is non-factual, and is not added permanently to our evolving context. And yet here too, p is claimed to be true in some world or worlds. Which worlds? The topics of modality and conditionals are beyond the scope of this book, and I can't attempt any sort of serious discussion here. But let me quickly sketch a certain picture of what examples (22)–(26) mean, which I think might be useful, especially in the context of Roberts' work on modal subordination.

Consider example (22). Let us assume, as in fact we have been doing so far, that a simple one-case indicative conditional like (22) basically expresses material implication, as reflected in the familiar ccp in (27).

(27)  $c + $ if $A, B = c - (c + A - ((c + A) + B))$

Under this assumption, the information conveyed by (22) can be specified as in (22′). In terms of context change semantics, when we add (22) to c, we consider all the worlds of c in which John has rented a car, and of those we keep in our context only the worlds where John is driving. Thus, the information conveyed by (22) can be specified as in (22″a), or, equivalently, as in (22″b).

(22′)  *John has rented a car* → p is true in the actual world w*.
(22″)  a.  For every world w s.t. w is a candidate for being the actual world, *John has rented a car* → p is true in w.
      b.  For every world w s.t. w is a candidate for being the actual world and *John has rented a car* is true in w, p is true in w.

Focusing on (22″b), we see that the "if"-clause serves to restrict the quantification over possible worlds. p is claimed to be true not in all the candidates for being the actual world, but only in those candidates where John has rented a car.

Next, consider example (23). Here, p is under the scope of a possibility operator. Therefore, (23) claims that there exists a world in which p is true. As is well known, the quantification induced by modal/intensional operators is restricted. It is standard to assume that the modal operator quantifies over a subset of the set of possible worlds, which we call "the accessible worlds" or "the worlds corresponding to the modal base." Let us refer to this set of worlds as ModBase(w). (Read: "the worlds accessible from w" or "the modal base set of worlds for world of evaluation w".) We have, then, that (23) conveys the information in (23′). Or, assuming context change semantics, the information conveyed by (23) may be specified as in (23″).

(23′)   There is a world $w' \in$ ModBase(w*) s.t. p is true in $w'$.
(23″)   For every world w that is a candidate for being the actual world, there is a world $w' \in$ ModBase(w) s.t. p is true in $w'$.

We take the modal base to be a crucial parameter in the interpretation of modal/intensional statements. Of course, modal bases are seldom given explicitly. Rather, the hearer chooses a plausible modal base, based on clues from the utterance itself and from the context of utterance (see section 1.6 above). In fact, we may say that modal bases, as well as other implicit parameters, are "accommodated," in the sense of Lewis 1979 (see section 1.7, and cf. Roberts 1995, 1996a).

Now, consider example (24). Clearly, the "in view of"/"since"-clause restricts the quantification over possible worlds. One way of expressing that is by saying that the "in view of"/"since"-clause gives us partial information about the modal base. (This clause specifies one member of the "modal base set of propositions" – the set of propositions whose intersection is the "modal base set of worlds".) So, we can specify the information conveyed by (24) as in (24′), or as in (24″).

(24′)   There is a world $w' \in$ ModBase(w*) s.t. p is true in $w'$.
       restriction:   ModBase(w*) contains only worlds in which John has rented a car.
(24″)   For every world w that is a candidate for being the actual world, there is a world $w' \in$ ModBase(w) s.t. p is true in $w'$.
       restriction:   for any world w, ModBase(w) contains only worlds in which John has rented a car.

(Certainly, the "in view of"/"since" clause also tells us something else – it imposes a factive ps: it tells us that in all the worlds that are candidates for being the actual world before (24) is asserted, John has rented a car.)

Example (25) is just like example (23), except that the modal operator is that of necessity. (25) conveys the information in (25′) or (25″).

(25′)   For all worlds $w' \in$ ModBase(w*), p is true in $w'$.
(25″)   For every world w s.t. w is a candidate for being the actual world, for all worlds $w' \in$ ModBase(w), p is true in $w'$.

Finally, consider (26). (26) looks a lot like (22), and may even appear at times to be synonymous with (22). But in fact, there is good reason to treat it differently. Empirically, (26) differs from (22): unlike (22), (26) is consistent with the possibility that (in the actual world) John has rented a car but is not driving it. This fact is straight-forwardly explained if we assume that the word *would* stands for a necessity operator, just as it did in example (25).

Assuming that *would* in (26) is a necessity operator, (26) is just like (25), except that the "if"-clause restricts the quantification over possible worlds. One way of expressing that is by saying that the "if"-clause gives us partial information about the modal base. (It specifies one member of the "modal base set of propositions".) So, we can specify the information conveyed by (26) as in (26'), or as in (26").

(26')  For all worlds $w' \in$ ModBase($w^*$), p is true in $w'$.
        restriction:  ModBase($w^*$) contains only worlds in which John has rented
                      a car.
(26")  For every world w s.t. w is a candidate for being the actual world, for all worlds
        $w' \in$ ModBase(w), p is true in $w'$.
        restriction:  for any world w, ModBase(w) contains only worlds in which
                      John has rented a car.

(This time, there is no factive ps. Therefore, there may still be candidates for being the actual world in which John has not rented a car.)

Think about possible modal bases for (26). Suppose we choose a preferential sort of modal base – we interpret the sentence as if the clause *in view of John's preferences* were implicit in it. Then sentence (26) tells us that in all the worlds in which John has rented a car and his wishes come true, he is driving. Note that that is perfectly consistent with the possibility that John has rented a car but is not driving it after all, due to a flat tire, say. (He **would** be driving it, if he could . . .) Of course, we may happen to take the sort of epistemic modal base which identifies ModBase(w) with the initial context c (= the set of worlds that are candidates for being the actual world immediately before (26) is asserted). Note that in that case, (26) would end up conveying exactly the same information as (22).

## 9.3.2  Preliminaries: satisfaction of ps

In the examples below, the italicized expression triggers a ps, which is (presumably) inherited by the (b) sentence as a whole. In all of the examples in group (I), the ps of the (b) sentence is obviously satisfied by the (a) sentence. Why is that? – That's very easy to explain. Suppose the example as a whole is uttered in a context c. In (a), the clause *John has a car* or *Sue smokes/smoked* occurs as factual. Therefore, when (a) is added to c, a discourse referent standing for John's car, or else the information that Sue smokes/smoked, enters the context permanently. Which means that the context c + (a) satisfies the ps of (b).

GROUP I:  THE ps IS DIRECTLY SATISFIED

(28)  a.  John has a car.
      b.  *It* is in the garage.
(29)  a.  John has a car.
      b.  *It* **ought** to be in the garage.
(30)  a.  John has a car.
      b.  He **wants** to sell *it*.

(31)  a.  Sue smoked.
      b.  She *quit* last year.
(32)  a.  Sue smokes.
      b.  She **should** *quit* at once.
(33)  a.  Sue smokes.
      b.  She **wants** to *quit* at once.

Now consider the examples in group (II) below. Think of the (a) and (b) sentences in each example as spoken in succession by the same person.

GROUP II:   THE ps IS NOT SATISFIED

(34)  a.   John doesn't have a car.
      b. # *It* is in the garage.

(35)  a.   John doesn't have a car.
      b. # *It* **ought** to be in the garage.

(36)  a.   John doesn't have a car.
      b. # He **wants** to sell *it*.

(37)  a.   **Possibly**, John has a car.
      b. # *It* is in the garage.

(38)  a.   **Possibly**, John has a car.
      b. # He **wants** to sell *it*.

(39)  a.   **If** John has a car,
           he doesn't use it much.
      b. # Let's drive *it* around the park.

(40)  a.   **If** John is practical,
           he's rented a car.
      b. # *It* is in the garage.

(41)  a.   Sue has **never** smoked.
      b. # She *quit* last year.

(42)  a.   Sue doesn't smoke.
      b. # She **should** *quit* at once.

(43)  a.   Sue doesn't smoke.
      b. # She **wants** to *quit* at once.

(44)  a.   **Maybe** Sue has smoked.
      b. # She *quit* last year.

(45)  a.   **Maybe** Sue smokes.
      b. # She **wants** to *quit* at once.

(46)  a.   **If** Sue smoked,
           she didn't smoke much.
      b. # She *quit* last year.

(47)  a.   **If** Sue was a drinker,
           she also used to smoke.
      b. # She *quit* smoking last year.

The (a) + (b) sequence sounds odd. Why? – Presumably, because the ps of the (b) sentence is not satisfied. But why isn't the ps satisfied? We can easily explain that, if we make the following assumption.

(48)   The scope of operators is sentence-bound.

If the scope of the operator (in boldface) in the (a) sentence is sentence-bound, then the clause *John has a car* or *Sue smokes/smoked* is under the scope of that operator, whereas the (b) sentence is not under the scope of that operator. Hence, we have the following: sentence (a) is factual, the clause *John has a car* or *Sue smokes/smoked* is non-factual, sentence (b) is factual. Since (a) and (b) are two independent factual statements, context-incrementation must proceed as follows: (c + (a)) + (b). However, because the clause *John has a car* or *Sue smokes/smoked* is non-factual, that clause does not get permanently added to our evolving context, and the context c + (a) does not satisfy the ps of the (b) sentence.

(Note: In examples (34)–(40), anaphora is impossible because of the scope constraint on anaphora (see chapter 2): the pronoun *it* is not under the scope of the quantifier that binds the intended antecedent variable (the variable triggered by *a car*). As becomes clear when you consider the parallel examples in (41)–(47), the scope constraint on anaphora is in fact a special case of the more general constraint on ps-satisfaction imposed by the Stalnaker–Karttunen–Heim theory of ps projection. The general constraint is that a ps must be satisfied by its local context. Since the configuration of operators and their scope determines what the local contexts are, all presuppositional phenomena, including anaphora, crucially interact with scope relations.)

### 9.3.3   The Problem

The phenomenon studied in Roberts 1989, 1996a is illustrated by the examples in group (III).

GROUP III:   HOW IS THE ps SATISFIED?

(49)   a.   John **doesn't** have a car.
      b.   *It* **would** be in the garage.

(Roberts 1996a)

(50)   a.   It is **possible** that John has children
      b.   and it is **possible** that *his children* are away.

(Gazdar)

(51)   a.   A thief **might** break into the house.
      b.   *He* **would** take the silver.

(Roberts 1989, due to Landman, p.c.)

(52)   a.   **Maybe** Sue used to smoke.
      b.   But she **would** have *quit* before her nephew came to live with her.

(53)   a.   **If** Sue succumbs and starts smoking, I'll be upset.
      b.   Certainly she **must** *quit* before her nephew comes to live with her.

(54)   a.   **If** John is practical, he has rented a car.
      b.   He **would** be driving *it* right now.

(55)   a.   You **must** smoke, it's great fun.
      b.   You **can** *quit* when you're older.

(56)   a.   You **should** buy a lottery ticket and put it in a safe place.
      b.   *It* **might** be worth a million dollars (if you were lucky).

(Roberts 1996a)

(57)   a.   Maxine **should** become a carpenter.
      b.   Her friends **would** *discover* she could build things, and she'd be very popular on weekends.

(Roberts 1996a)

(58)   a.   Sue **intends** to start smoking,
      b.   but she **must** *quit* before her nephew comes to live with her.

(59)   a.   Mary is **considering** getting her PhD in linguistics.
      b.   She **wouldn't** *regret* attending graduate school.

(Roberts 1996a)

(60)   a.   John **wants** to catch a fish.
      b.   He **intends** to eat *it* for supper.

(Roberts 1996a)

(61)   a.   Alice **fears** there is a squirrel in her kitchen cabinets.
      b.   She **hopes** to trap *it* alive and turn *it* loose outside.

(Roberts 1996a)

(62)   a.   Jan **expects** to get a puppy soon.
      b.   She **intends** to keep *it* in her back yard.

(Roberts 1996a)

The examples in group (III) seem to be similar in their structure to the examples of group (II): embedded in the (a) sentence, under the scope of some operator, there is a clause which (potentially) satisfies the ps triggered in the (b) sentence. However, unlike the examples of group (II), the examples in group (III) sound fine. Why is that? How is the ps of the (b) sentence satisfied? After all, the crucial ps-satisfying clause in the (a) sentence is non-factual and does not get permanently added to the context, exactly as in group (II).

One might try to account for the felicity of examples from group (III) by dropping the assumption that scope is sentence-bound (cf. Groenendijk and Stokhof 1990; Dekker 1993). For example, suppose that the scope of "if . . . then . . ." in (54), repeated below, need not end at the end of the (a) sentence. In that case, we could claim that the (b) sentence is part of the consequent of the conditional – that (54) is interpreted as indicated in (54′). In which case the ps of *it* is satisfied locally, within the consequent of the conditional.

(54)　a.　**If** John is practical, he has rented a car.
　　　　b.　He **would** be driving *it* right now.
(54′)　**If** John is practical, he has rented a car and would be driving *it* right now.

However, as discussed in Roberts 1989, 1996a, this approach can work only for a small subset of the problematic examples. Consider example (51), repeated below.

(51)　a.　A thief **might** break into the house.
　　　　b.　*He* **would** take the silver.

If we try and insert the (b) sentence under the scope of the possibility operator occurring in the (a) sentence, we will get the wrong truth conditions. (44) would be interpreted as saying this: "that a thief will break in and he would take the silver is a possibility." Which is consistent with the possibility of a thief breaking in who would not take the silver. But that is wrong. In reality, (51) is not consistent with the possibility of a thief breaking in who would not take the silver. In reality, (51) is interpreted roughly as follows: "it is possible that a thief will break in, and if that happens, the thief will (definitely/necessarily) take the silver." In other words, we have in (51) two modal operators whose scopes are independent of each other.

We have the following unexplained phenomenon, then. There are many examples with the logical form schematically described in (63) (adapted from Roberts 1996a, section 1), that are intuitively judged to be felicitous. Given the usual Stalnaker–Karttunen–Heim assumptions about the satisfaction of ps, it is impossible for the ps of the (b) sentence to be satisfied directly by the clause embedded in the (a) sentence. Therefore, it is not at all clear how the ps of (b) gets satisfied.

(63)　Sentence (a): operator [$_S$ . . . element satisfying ps triggered by $\alpha$ . . .]
　　　　Sentence (b): operator$_{intensional}$ [$_S$ . . . ps-trigger $\alpha$ . . .]
　　　　(There is no element satisfying the ps triggered by $\alpha$ in sentence (b).)

### 9.3.4　Entailment-based Account?

Roberts 1996a notes that for some of the problematic examples, analyses have been proposed on which ps satisfaction is guaranteed by a combination of (i) a general assumption concerning the sort of modal base required for the intensional operator involved, plus (ii) an entailment of the (a) sentence. (See Lakoff 1972; Karttunen 1974; McCawley 1981; Heim 1992.) For example, consider (62), repeated below. Let us assume that (62b) conveys the information in (64).

(62) a. Jan **expects** to get a puppy soon.
   b. She **intends** to keep *it* in her back yard.

(64) For every world w s.t. w is a candidate for being the actual world, for all worlds w′ ∈ {w″ : w″ is compatible with the intentions Jan has in w}, *Jan will keep it in her back yard* is true in w′.

Since our intentions are generally contingent on our expectations, it is natural to assume that we have the general restriction in (65).

(65) For any world w,
   {w″ : w″ is compatible with the intentions Jan has in w} ⊆
   {w″ : w″ realizes the expectations Jan has in w}

Now, sentence (62a) entails that in all the worlds that realize Jan's intentions, she will get a puppy soon. Therefore, given the assumption in (65), we get that (64) only requires the clause *Jan will keep it in her back yard* to be true in worlds in which Jan will get a puppy soon. In terms of context-incrementation, when we compute the result of adding (62b) to a context which already contains (62a), we will have to add *Jan will keep it in her back yard* only to contexts in which Jan will get a puppy soon – contexts which satisfy its ps.[4] So adding (62b) to a context which already contains (62a) will be defined. Hence the correct prediction that (62) is felicitous.

 Roberts does not deny that there are examples in which ps satisfaction is indeed guaranteed in the manner just illustrated. She points out, however, that there are also many felicitous examples with the structure given in (63) to which such an entailment-based account cannot apply. To give just one example, take (49), repeated below: clearly, (49a) does not entail about any worlds that John has a car in them, and does not guarantee that the modal base for (49b) will include only worlds in which John has a car.

(49) a. John **doesn't** have a car.
   b. *It* **would** be in the garage.

In contrast, Roberts' own analysis, to be presented in 9.3.5 below, can cover the full range of examples under consideration.

---

[4] We may assume here that the ccp of (62b) is as in (i) (cf. Heim 1992).

  (i) c + *Jan intends to keep it in her back yard*
    = the set of all the worlds w in c s.t. {w″: w″ is compatible with the intentions Jan has in w}
     + *Jan will keep it in her back yard* = {w″: w″ is compatible with the intentions Jan has in w}

(Note that if c + *Jan will keep it in her back yard* = c, that means that *Jan will keep it in her back yard* is true in all the worlds in context c.)

## 9.3.5 Roberts' Analysis: local accommodation of restrictions

According to Roberts 1989, 1996a, the ps of the (b) sentence in our problematic examples is satisfied by an accommodated restriction on the quantification over possible worlds – an accommodated restriction which is suggested by the material in the (a) sentence.

Take for instance example (49), repeated below once more. The proposition "John has a car" is made very salient by (49a). Therefore, when we get to (49b), we readily accommodate it as a restriction on the quantification over possible worlds. We interpret (49b) as if the underlined bit in (49b′) was implicit in it.

(49)    a.   John doesn't have a car.
        b.   *It* **would** be in the garage.
(49b′)   <u>If John had a car,</u> it would be in the garage.

The clause *it be in the garage* is interpreted as semantically subordinate to the proposition "John has a car": it is only claimed to hold given the hypothetical assumption that John has a car, it is only claimed to hold in worlds where John has a car. So, the clause *it be in the garage* is only ever supposed to be added to a (hypothetical) context in which John has a car. Therefore, its ps is satisfied by its local context.

Roberts 1989 dubbed the phenomenon illustrated by the examples in group (III) "modal subordination." It should now be easy to see why: according to her analysis, the clause under the scope of the modal/intensional operator, the one containing the ps-trigger, is interpreted (via accommodation) as semantically subordinate to a particular irrealis proposition that was considered in previous discourse.

Roberts 1989, 1996a regards the accommodated restriction as partial information about the modal base of the modal/intensional operator involved. She says that when we hear (49b), we accommodate the information that "John has a car" is a member of the "modal base set of propositions" for the necessity operator **would**. Given this, the information conveyed by (49b) may be described as in (66).

(66)    For every world w s.t. w is a candidate for being the actual world, for all worlds
        w′ ∈ ModBase(w), *it be in the garage* is true in w′.
            restriction:   for any world w, ModBase(w) contains only worlds in which
                           John has a car.

It is clear that given the accommodated restriction on ModBase(w), the proposition "it is in the garage" is indeed only claimed to be true in worlds in which John has a car. If you explicitly write out the ccp of (49b) and apply it to an arbitrary context c, you will see that given the accommodated restriction on ModBase(w), in the course of computing c + (49b), *it be in the garage* will have to be added only to contexts in which John has a car – contexts which satisfy its ps.[5] So the context-incrementation c + (49b) will be defined. Hence the correct prediction that (49) is felicitous.

---

[5]   The ccp of (49b) may be stated as in (i).

    (i)   c + *necessarily (it be in the garage)*
          = the set of all the worlds w in c s.t. ModBase(w) + *it be in the garage* = ModBase(w)

(Note that if c + *it be in the garage* = c, that means that *it be in the garage* is true in all the worlds in context c.)

The rest of the examples in group (III) are analyzed in the same manner. For instance, we interpret (50), (51) and (61) as indicated in (50′), (51′) and (61′). The underlined clause is accommodated, providing partial information about the modal base for the intensional operator in (b).[6]

(50′)   a.   It is possible that John has children
         b.   and if John does have children, it is possible that his children are away.
(51′)   a.   A thief might break into the house.
         b.   If a thief breaks into the house, he would take the silver.
(61′)   a.   Alice fears there is a squirrel in her kitchen cabinets.
         b.   Assuming there is a squirrel in her kitchen cabinets, she hopes to trap it alive and turn it loose outside.

Roberts notes that the kind of accommodation involved in modal subordination is local accommodation, since the accommodated proposition is not added to our evolving context permanently.

Of course, the usual objection may be raised that accommodation is too powerful as a theoretical tool. Isn't it too easy, when we notice that the examples in group (III) are (apparent) counterexamples to "filtering," to attribute their felicity to accommodation? Won't this allow too many examples? After all, there are other examples with the same structure (the structure in (63)) which are not felicitous. (There are a few, for example, in group II.) What's to keep accommodation from licensing the bad examples? Moreover, given Heim's conjecture that local accommodation is generally dispreferred, why is local accommodation performed so readily in group (III)?

I have already had occasion to note that accommodation is a constrained process (see sections 1.7, 4.1) – various factors may disfavor this process, or disallow it entirely. That is what explains why modal subordination is not always possible. Indeed, Roberts 1996a discusses a number of cases where modal subordination is impossible, and indicates in some detail the factors that combine to disfavor accommodation in these examples. Let me mention just two examples here.

Why can't (42b) be interpreted as indicated in (42b′)?

(42)    a.   Sue doesn't smoke.
         b.   # She should quit at once.
(42b′)   If Sue smokes, she should quit at once.

We may make the general assumption that deontic modals require a modal base which reflects the subject's circumstances in all relevant respects (cf. Thomason 1981). But given (42a), that means that should must be interpreted relative to a modal base where Sue doesn't smoke. Therefore, it is impossible to accommodate into the modal base of should the information that Sue does smoke. After all, the most basic constraint on accommodation is that it must not result in an inconsistent context.

---

[6]  Comparing (50′) with (17′) in 9.2.2 above (It is possible that John has children and it is possible that he has children and his children are away), we see that certain examples of "ps disappearance" can be alternatively treated either as modal subordination or as involving another form of local accommodation. Possibly, this will in some cases allow for different interpretations that can be detected empirically.

And why can't (67b) be interpreted as in (67b′) or as in (67b″)?

(67)    a.   Because public transportation is unreliable, John **should** buy a car to commute to work.

        b. # He **would** have enjoyed *it* in the bad weather last winter.

(Roberts 1996a)

(67b′)   <u>If John buys a car,</u> he would have enjoyed it in the bad weather last winter.

(67b″)   <u>If John had bought a car,</u> he would have enjoyed it in the bad weather last winter.

We may assume that deontic modals are future-oriented. Hence, (67a) is about what John should do in the future. But that precludes both of the indicated interpretations. In (67b′), where the accommodated bit is about a future purchase of a car, as suggested by (67a), the problem is that (67b) is about the past, so its ps can't be satisfied by the future purchase of a car. As for (67b″), since it considers the (counterfactual) possibility that John bought a car in the past, it is irrelevant to John's present obligations, and hence irrelevant to (67a).

We have talked about constraints that may block accommodation, but it is no less important to note the other side of the coin: a number of different factors may combine to favor and encourage a certain act of accommodation, as stressed in Roberts' work.

Roberts 1996a argues that the accommodation postulated by her theory is very well motivated. It is **not** the case that the accommodated restriction of Roberts' analysis is nothing more than a desperate repair-strategy aimed to avoid ps-failure. The modal base is an indispensable parameter in the interpretation of the (b) sentence. Since it is not explicitly given by the sentence, the hearer must recover what it is – as is perfectly normal with modal bases. So the search for the modal base is going on independently of the need to satisfy the ps. The non-factual proposition explicitly mentioned in the first clause then seems like an obvious and suitable candidate for one of the propositions of the modal base. Moreover, using it as part of the modal base would establish a link of relevance between sentence (a) and sentence (b). This explains why the examples in group (III) sound so smooth and natural.

Now, in some examples with the structure under consideration (the structure in (63)), there is no modal subordination; instead, global accommodation is performed. For example, in the case of (68), most speakers prefer the interpretation in (68′) (global accommodation) to the interpretation in (68″) (local accommodation resulting in modal subordination).

(68)    a.   Since he saved his money last summer, John **could** buy a car.

        b.   He **should** sell *it*, if he needs money now.

(Roberts 1996a)

(68′)   Since he saved his money last summer, John could buy a car.
       <u>Hence, he bought a car.</u>
       He should sell it, if he needs money now.

(68″)   Since he saved his money last summer, John could buy a car.
       If <u>he did buy a car and</u> he needs money now, he should sell it.

But if local accommodation is dispreferred, why don't we find global accommodation in all or most examples of the structure under consideration?

Well, because the accommodated clause is non-factual in the (a) sentence, the (a) sentence sometimes entails that it is false, as in (49), and often implicates that it is not known to be true, as in (50). This makes global accommodation of the clause in question impossible or implausible. When, at the same time, local accommodation is both plausible and well-motivated, local accommodation is performed.

(49) a. John **doesn't** have a car.
     b. *It* **would** be in the garage.
(50) a. It is **possible** that John has children
     b. and it is **possible** that *his children* are away.

Moreover, Roberts 1996a suggests that there is no inherent preference for global accommodation per se. She explains the impression that global accommodation tends to be preferred to local as follows.

Roberts suggests that hypothetical contexts in general are constrained to be as similar as possible to the assumptions about the actual world. Roberts sees this constraint as part of a general strategy aimed at efficient maintenance of the common ground. We want our interlocutors to share our assumptions about the context. But often, our assumptions about a hypothetical context that we talk about are not spelled out. (As when that hypothetical context is an implicit modal base.) Obviously, the default assumption that hypothetical contexts are maximally similar to the actual world helps our interlocutors to recover the intended hypothetical context correctly.

Regarding accommodation, Roberts notes that as far as the direct need for accommodation is concerned (the need to recover an implicit modal base, the need to ensure ps satisfaction, etc.), all that's needed is local accommodation. Viewed this way, local accommodation is seen as more basic than global accommodation, and the question to ask is this: why is there a tendency for the local accommodation to "project upward," so to speak, and become global? The answer, says Roberts, can be found in the constraint discussed in the last paragraph. Given the general strategy of keeping the assumptions used "locally" as similar as possible to the assumptions about the actual world, the proposition that needs to be accommodated locally is also accommodated globally, as long as there is no inconsistency or other problem to prevent that.

## 9.3.6 *Appendix: restrictions accommodated in further examples*

Roberts 1989, 1996a argues that her analysis of modal subordination can also cover examples like the ones in groups (IV) and (V).

GROUP IV: ps-TRIGGER UNDER ADVERB OF QUANTIFICATION

(69) a. **Usually** Fred buys a muffin on the way and eats it at the office.
     b. *It*'s **always** oat bran.
(70) a. Fred **always** buys a muffin on the way and eats it at the office.
     b. *It*'s **usually** oat bran.

GROUP V:   ps-TRIGGER NOT UNDER THE SCOPE OF ANY EXPLICIT OPERATOR

(71)   a.   **Every** frog that saw an insect ate it.
     b.   *It* disappeared forever.
(72)   a.   **Most** chess sets come with a spare pawn.
     b.   *It* is taped to the top of the box.
(73)   a.   **Usually** Fred buys a muffin on the way and eats it at the office.
     b.   He buys [a cup of coffee]$_F$, *too*.

The (b) sentences in group (IV) contain an adverb of quantification. We can analyze the (b) sentences in group (V) as containing an implicit universal adverb of quantification. Therefore, we can analyze all the examples of groups (IV) and (V) as involving an accommodated restriction on the quantification induced by the adverb, as illustrated by (69′) and (71′). As usual, the accommodated restriction is based on material which is explicit in the (a) sentence.

(69′)   a.   Fred usually buys a muffin on the way and eats it at the office.
      b.   <u>When Fred buys a muffin on the way and eats it at the office</u>, it is always oat bran.
(71′)   a.   Every frog that saw an insect ate it.
      b.   <u>When a frog saw an insect and ate it</u>, it (always) disappeared forever.

To add another type of example, I think that (74) can fairly easily be interpreted as indicated in (74′).

(74)   a.   **If** John bought a sports car today, he is dying to show it to us.
     b.   He is driving *it* here right now, in fact.
(74′)   a.   If John bought a sports car today, he is dying to show it to us.
      b.   In fact, <u>if he bought a sports car today</u>, he is driving it here right now.

In the examples of the present subsection too, the (b) sentence is semantically subordinate to an accommodated proposition. Is this subordination properly called "modal"? Well, that depends on whether we analyze adverbs of quantification and simple indicative conditionals as implicitly modalized. But even if we don't, we do have quantification here: over n-tuples of individuals in the case of the adverbs (see, e.g., 2.1.2), over possible worlds in the case of the conditional (see 9.3.1, discussion of example (22)). The accommodation restricts this quantification.

If you think that the subordination in (74) is not as natural as in the other examples, that might be precisely because there is no modal operator in (74). Perhaps local accommodation is better motivated when there is a modal operator that forces us to look for a modal base, as discussed above. Indeed, (75), with its explicit modal, seems to allow subordination more easily than (74) does.

(75)   a.   **If** John bought a sports car today, he is dying to show it to us.
     b.   He **would** be driving *it* here right now, in fact.

## 9.4   On the Status of Accommodation, Local and Global

In this chapter, we have encountered two opposing views concerning local accommodation. Is local accommodation basic and normal (as suggested in Roberts 1996a), or exceptional and dispreferred (as suggested in Heim 1983b)?

Beaver 1993b agrees with Heim 1983b. He offers the following view. Global and local accommodation are quite different in their status. Global accommodation should be seen as "a natural part of the orderly communication process in which conversational participants gradually determine their common ground." (Beaver 1993b, p. 67)[7] Local accommodation of ps is quite different: to perform local accommodation is to downright alter the meaning of what the speaker has actually said, acting as if the speaker said, or meant to say, something different. This is a marked and complicated process, which occurs only if the hearer has good reason to believe that the speaker can't have meant what (s)he actually said. This way of looking at local accommodation would explain the (alleged) facts that local accommodation is performed only under threat of contradiction, and that global accommodation is always preferred to local. On this view, it seems unlikely that examples which sound very natural and seem easy to process involve local accommodation.

It may be tempting to adopt Beaver's view. However, I think things are rather more complicated than Beaver allows for. I would like to side with Roberts 1996a and argue that there is no inherent preference for global accommodation relative to local accommodation.

Let us examine more carefully the circumstances under which local accommodation is performed.

Certainly, it is a prominent fact that local accommodation is often performed when it would be **impossible** to perform global accommodation. In some cases, the reason that global accommodation could not be performed is that it would be inconsistent with the existing context, as in the following examples.

(76)   I don't have a cello.
     # If I sell it, I'll be able to pay for the car.

(77)   YOU:   I don't have a dog.
     ME:   So at least you don't have to walk your dog.
     [Global accom impossible. Local accom OK, though sounds a bit like a joke.]

(49)   a.   John doesn't have a car.
     b.   *It* **would** be in the garage.
     [Global accom impossible. Local accom resulting in modal subordination OK.]

In other cases, global accommodation is ruled out because of something inherent to the example itself. That is what happens in the classical Gazdar–Soames examples of ps "disappearance," where global accommodation would necessarily lead to Quantity violation. For instance, in the following examples.

---

[7]   Beaver suggests that his formalization of global accommodation as filtering on epistemic alternatives "perhaps" gives it less of a feeling of a repair strategy, and makes it seem more like part of the orderly process of communication. (Beaver 1993b, p. 55)

(18)   If Mary's boss doesn't have children, then it wasn't his child who won the fellowship.

(20)   Either there's no bathroom in this house or it's in a funny place.
       [In (18), (20), if $p \rightarrow ps(q)$ or just $ps(q)$ were to be accommodated into the initial context c, c would entail that p is false.]

(13)   If John hasn't just stopped smoking, he has just started smoking.

(19)   Either Bill met the king of Slobovia or he met the president of Slobovia.
       [In the case of (13), (19), the example "linguistically" presupposes ¬p and hence "linguistically" presupposes itself; cf. 9.2.2.]

(16)   If I realize later that I haven't told the truth, I will confess it to everyone.
       [In (16), if $ps(p)$ ("I haven't told the truth") is in the initial context c, then c entails that p is false, since the speaker can't realize "later" something which she already knows.]

However, I believe that local accommodation is also performed in many cases where global accommodation would **not** be impossible. For example, I think it is perfectly possible to make sense of (78) either by globally accommodating the assumption that John bought a car or by locally accommodating it as part of the modal base for *should* (= by modal subordination).

(78)   a.   If John bought a sports car today, he is dying to show it to us.
       b.   He should be driving it here right now, in fact.

But let us leave aside modal subordination and look at something more basic: the ps of the antecedent of a one-case indicative conditional.

I believe that in the following examples, which were suggested to me by Lenore Shoham (p.c.), local accommodation is quite natural, despite the fact that global accommodation would be possible too.

(79)   If Sue stopped smoking yesterday, she will get a prize from the health bureau.

(80)   If Sue stopped smoking yesterday, then she did something good for her health yesterday.

(81)   If Sue stopped smoking yesterday, for example, that would explain why she is nervous/chewing candy all the time today.

$ps(p)$ = Sue smoked (in the "immediate" past of some reference time yesterday)

When heard out of the blue, examples (79)–(81) may or may not create the impression that it is presupposed that Sue smoked. In other words, each example may, but need not, "cognitively" presuppose $ps(p)$. I believe the hearer is in fact quite likely to judge that the example does not presuppose that Sue smoked. (Especially so, I think, in the case of (81).) I believe there is a fairly clear contrast between (79)–(81) and examples (82)–(84) below: while (82)–(84) suggest very strongly that it is presupposed that Sue smoked, that is not the case with (79)–(81). What these judgments suggest is that out of the blue, examples (79)–(81) naturally allow for either global accommodation or local accommodation.

(82)   If Sue stopped smoking yesterday, you will no longer be able to bum cigarettes off her.

(83)  If Sue stopped smoking yesterday, we can throw out the ashtrays.

(84)  If Sue stopped smoking yesterday, I'm going to stop smoking too.

And it should be useful to also consider the judgments on (79)–(81) in context. Take (79), for instance. (79) would be natural in a context where it is known that the health bureau is handing out prizes for healthy acts, and we wonder if and how Sue, who wants a prize badly, might have secured a prize from the health bureau. Suppose you hear (79) in such a context, and you don't know anything about Sue's smoking habits. I think that in this situation, it is possible that you would choose to globally accommodate the assumption that Sue smoked, but you may very well choose **not** to accommodate this assumption. It is, I believe, very natural in such a context to perform local accommodation instead, and interpret (79) as indicated in (79′).

(79′)  If Sue <u>used to smoke and</u> stopped smoking yesterday, she will get a prize from the health bureau.

We see, then, that local accommodation is not performed only under threat of contradiction or Quantity violation. Even in cases where global accommodation would be possible, the hearer may prefer to perform local accommodation instead, presumably because the hearer judges that it is no less likely (or even more likely) that the "linguistic" ps is **not** "globally" assumed than that it **is** "globally" assumed.

Note that there is nothing about (79)–(81) that should lead to the conclusion that the speaker can't have meant what (s)he actually said. That means that Beaver's view predicts that local accommodation would not be performed here, contrary to fact. Further, it is not at all clear, intuitively, that when you interpret (79) as in (79′) you are taking the speaker to have meant something different from what she actually said. In addition, the reading in (79′) is perfectly natural, and there is no intuition that the utterance is particularly hard to process. (Similarly for (80) and (81).)

There is of course a way to retain Beaver's view of local accommodation despite all this: we could deny that the interpretation given in (79′) is the result of local accommodation. (And similarly for other examples that seem to refute Beaver's view.) However, this possibility is not without its disadvantages. We would be forced to claim that "Sue smoked" is **asserted** as an integral part of the processing of *Sue stopped smoking*. (See discussion of "plug" interpretations in section 8.2 above.) Why would it be asserted? Presumably, because of the semantics (including presuppositional properties) of *stop* and/or of *if . . . then. . . .* But then we would have to claim that there is a semantic ambiguity: "Sue smoked" is asserted in some cases (e.g. when (79) is interpreted as in (79′)), but not in others (i.e. not when the ps that Sue smoked is judged to be inherited).

Now, I think Beaver's characterization of local accommodation is correct for **some** examples, where local accommodation is indeed marked and amounts to deciding that the speaker meant something other than what she actually said. That is because for certain examples, I personally do have an intuition that the ps gets satisfied not quite smoothly, and that the speaker is being somewhat jocular or sloppy. For example, I feel that way about (77) and (85).

(77)  YOU:   I don't have a dog.
      ME:    So at least you don't have to walk your dog.

(85)  Either she doesn't have a car, or it's hidden behind the kiosk.

In fact, I even think that the intuition that something special is going on with such examples in itself supports the idea that local accommodation exists. (Besides the support provided by the very difficulty of accounting for the examples (in a non ad hoc manner) otherwise.)

However, I think it is quite reasonable to believe that cases of local accommodation do not all feel the same. We know that there are examples where a ps "disappears" for no obvious reason which sound perfectly natural and smooth, including, for instance, (79)–(81) above. I think it is natural and economical to assume that here too ps "disappearance" is due to local accommodation, albeit local accommodation that is more readily and effortlessly performed. I think it makes sense to assume that if a given act of local accommodation is nothing more than the only available strategy for repairing ps failure, it would feel forced and marked, whereas if it is well-motivated beyond the need for repair, it would feel natural and unmarked. (Cf. Roberts' discussion of the naturalness of modal subordination, alluded to in 9.3.5 above.)

Let us take stock. The data on ps projection are generally quite variable and diverse. It seems that pss sometimes get "inherited" and other times "disappear" even when the structure of the example is kept constant. Take for instance the case of a ps of the antecedent of a conditional. It has always been considered a clear and basic goal of the filtering theory to predict "inheritance" in such a case. And yet we saw in this section that a ps of an antecedent can "disappear" after all. And not only under threat of contradiction, either. In addition, some cases of ps "disappearance" seem special and marked, while others seem natural and smooth. The variability of the data can be explained if we assume, first of all, that accommodation – or more precisely, the phenomenon of accommodating (inserting) something into the context that has not been explicitly mentioned – exists, and, secondly, that accommodation (be it local or global) comes in degrees of naturalness.

Moreover, we know why it is that accommodation comes in degrees of naturalness. We know that for each act of accommodation that one might consider performing, be it local or global, there may be lots of different factors that either favor or disfavor it. An act of accommodation may serve many purposes at once (ps-satisfaction, specification of implicit parameters, etc.), or few, or none; it may add to discourse coherence or not; it may add information which is consistent or inconsistent with the context, information which is more plausible or less plausible; it may insert material that is more salient or less salient, more obviously "bridged" (linked to other things in the context) or less obviously "bridged"; etc. (See 1.7, 4.1, 9.3.5 above.) Such considerations combined together determine for each potential act of accommodation the extent to which it would be feasible and desirable. Given this, it should come as no surprise that accommodation comes in degrees of naturalness, forming a whole continuum of acts of accommodation, ranging from impossible to very easy.

Recall Roberts' idea that while global accommodation is not inherently preferred, it is favored by practical principles for the maintenance of the common ground (see 9.3.5 above). This idea fits well into the picture sketched here. The suggested pull towards global accommodation is just one of many factors that determine the relative desirability of alternative acts of accommodation. It explains why there appears to be some tendency to prefer global accommodation, while being consistent with the large variety of examples where local accommodation is a natural option.

# 10

## *More on ps Projection and Accommodation: ps Projection Below the Level of the Clause*

### 10.1  Introduction

It is time to consider ps projection below the level of the complete clause. Consider examples (1)–(4) below, from Heim 1983b. If we assume the standard Kamp–Heim framework plus the usual filtering analysis of ps projection (without accommodation), we get the prediction that these examples all carry a "universal" ps – that they presuppose (1')–(4'), respectively. (This is pointed out in Heim 1983b. Details below.)

(1)   A fat man was pushing his bicycle.
(2)   No nation cherishes its king.
(3)   Everyone who serves his king will be rewarded.
(4)   Every nation cherishes its king.

(1')   Every fat man had a bicycle.                    (universal ps)
(2')   Every nation has a king.                        (universal ps)
(3')   Everyone has a king.                            (universal ps)
(4')   Every nation has a king.                        (universal ps)

But this prediction is rather problematic. Intuitively, the prediction seems reasonable enough for example (4), but it seems wrong for examples (1) and (2), and doubtful for example (3).

At the same time, it is not that easy to say what examples (1)–(4) do presuppose, intuitively. Let us look at the original ps triggered by the definite NP: presumably, the ps is that "he"/"it" has/had a bike/king. Assuming the usual Kamp–Heim framework, this ps is about a discourse referent introduced in the very same sentence. In each example, the first NP (being indefinite or quantificational) introduces into the context a new discourse referent standing for a person or a nation, and the ps is **about that discourse referent**. Presumably, if we want to correctly predict the ps of the entire example, we will need to look at the details of what the ps about the new discourse referent consists of and the ways in which this ps might get satisfied.

Heim 1983b proposes an account of examples (1)–(4) which is based on accommodation. According to Heim's account, in the course of processing the example, it is possible to accommodate **concerning the newly-introduced discourse referent** the information that it has/had a bike/king. This makes it unnecessary to "globally" accommodate the universal proposition indicated in $(1')–(4')$ into the context which obtains immediately before the example is processed. Therefore, the examples need not "cognitively" presuppose the "linguistic" universal ps which is predicted by a pure filtering account.

Beaver 1993b proposes an alternative account of the same examples. According to Beaver's account, the definite NP does not exactly presuppose that the newly-introduced discourse referent has/had a bike/king. Instead, the definite NP presupposes that some fat man had a bike or that some nation/person has a king, and asserts that the newly-introduced discourse referent does. Beaver's account does not predict that there should be any "linguistic" universal ps associated with examples (1)–(4).

This chapter will be devoted to examples like (1)–(4) and their analysis. I think the data are not clear-cut and not simple, and I will try to give a more complete picture of the data. I will give a presentation of Heim's and Beaver's accounts of the examples under consideration. (The presentation of Heim's account will complete the exposition of Heim 1983b's theory of ps projection given in this book.) I will discuss Heim's and Beaver's accounts in some detail, and examine their goals and predictions. Finally, I will suggest that the examples under consideration support the view of local and global accommodation presented in section 9.4 above.

Each of the two accounts to be considered here aims to cover without additional stipulations examples of (at least) all four types illustrated by (1)–(4) above. Therefore, to evaluate the overall success of each account, we must look at the predictions that it yields for all four types of example. Nevertheless, I have chosen to separate in this chapter my discussion of existential statements of the kind illustrated by (1) from my discussion of quantified statements like the ones illustrated in (2)–(4). I think this will allow for a clearer presentation and discussion, given the complexity of the subject-matter. Of course, I still think that we need to look at both the existential and the quantified statements involved before we reach our final conclusions about the right way to treat the complete range of examples under consideration.

Note that since we are now dealing with quantification and anaphora in discourse, we can no longer simply regard a context as a set of possible worlds. For our present purposes, let us define a **context** as a set of ordered pairs $\langle w,g \rangle$, each consisting of a possible world w and a partial assignment function g, where all the assignments g have the same domain. Context change potentials will be defined accordingly (see section 2.3.2). A context c **entails** a formula $\phi$ iff $c + \phi = c$. (And it follows that a context c entails an atomic formula $\phi$ iff for every $\langle w,g \rangle$ in c, g verifies $\phi$ in w.)

## 10.2 Existential Statements

### 10.2.1 Some Unproblematic Existential Statements

Perhaps it would be useful to look first at some existential statements that do not give rise to the problem described in section 10.1 – for instance, examples (5)–(7) below. In contrast with example (1) above, in (5)–(7), the original ps triggered in the VP is not about the discourse referent introduced by the subject NP. It is a ps about the world, not about the man/professor that's being discussed.

(5)   A fat man was praising the king of Slobovia.
(6)   Some professor regrets the fact that the earth is round.
(7)   A CONSERVATIVE professor supported the measure, too.

We assume Heim 1983b's theory of ps and ps projection (see section 5.5), including the standard Kamp–Heim framework and the usual filtering analysis of ps projection. This theory predicts that examples (5)–(7) should "linguistically" presuppose (5″)–(7″), respectively.

(5″)   If there is a fat man,                                                    (conditional ps)
         there is a king of Slobovia.
(6″)   If there is some professor,                                               (conditional ps)
         then the earth is round.
(7″)   If there is a conservative professor,                                     (conditional ps)
         then some non-conservative professor supported the measure.

To see why, consider (5). Given the Kamp–Heim theory, (5) is represented as a conjunction of two open formulas, as in (8), where x is a new variable introduced by the indefinite *a fat man*.

(8)    DRT:

| x |
| --- |
| fat man(x) |
| x was praising the king of Slobovia |

       FCS:      fat man(x)    and    x was praising the king of Slobovia
                     A                            B

Try to add this conjunction to an arbitrary context c. Formula B must be added to c + A, so c + A must entail ps(B). In other words, c + A must entail that there is a king of Slobovia. How could c + A entail that? c + A contains the information in c plus the information that a fat man exists plus the information that the newly introduced discourse referent x is a fat man. Since x was not present in c, there couldn't have been any information about it in c. Therefore, the entailment couldn't possibly be derived on the basis of any further information beyond the information in c plus the information that a fat man exists. Therefore, c + A entails that there is a king of Slobovia iff c entails (5″) above. What we see then is that (5) can be added to a context c only if c entails (5″). Therefore, (5) is predicted to "linguistically" presuppose (5″).

Regarding the conditionals in (5″)–(7″), it seems unlikely that the antecedent actually has something to do with the consequent. Therefore, an accommodating hearer would normally assume that the initial c entails the conditional for the trivial reason that c entails its consequent. In other words, the hearer of (5)/(6)/(7) would normally perform global accommodation of the consequent into the context which obtains immediately before the example is processed. This predicts, correctly, that (5)–(7) should "cognitively" presuppose (5‴)–(7‴) below.

(5‴)   There is a king of Slobovia.                                     (ps inherited as is)
(6‴)   The earth is round.                                              (ps inherited as is)
(7‴)   Some non-conservative professor supported the measure.    (ps inherited as is)

### 10.2.2  Our Problem in Existential Statements

The problem starts when we turn to examples like (1) and (9)–(12), in which the original ps triggered in the VP is about the discourse referent introduced by the subject NP.

(1)   A fat man was pushing his bicycle.
(9)   Some nation cherishes its king.
(10)  A student stopped smoking.
(11)  A Slobovian museum is selling its Picasso. (Fred Landman, p.c.)
(12)  A pious Mormon is mending her holy underwear.

It is a little difficult to give a pre-theoretical description of the presupposition which is intuitively associated with such examples. Regarding (1), for example, the intuition is that it is presupposed, roughly, that the fat man the sentence is about had a bike. But our intuition is explicated rather nicely under Heim's theory, since, as already indicated above, the Kamp–Heim framework allows us to regard the original ps triggered in the VP as a ps about the discourse referent introduced by the subject NP.

Consider (1). (1) is represented as a conjunction of two open formulas, as in (13).

(13)  DRT:

> x
> fat man(x)
> x was pushing x's bicycle

FCS:     fat man(x)   and   x was pushing x's bicycle
           A                        B

In A, x is a new variable introduced by the indefinite *a fat man*. In B, the pronoun *his* has been translated into the old variable x, and the NP *his bicycle* has been translated into x's bicycle. The NP *his bicycle* being definite, it triggers the presupposition that there exists something fitting the description x's bicycle. Hence, formula B presupposes that x had a bicycle.[1]

Now, what does the example as a whole presuppose? It turns out that Heim's filtering theory of ps projection predicts that examples (1) and (9)–(12) should "linguistically" presuppose the following.

(1')   Every fat man had a bicycle.                                    (universal ps)
(9')   Every nation has a king.                                       (universal ps)
(10')  Every student used to smoke.                                   (universal ps)
(11')  Every Slobovian museum has a Picasso.                          (universal ps)
(12')  Every pious Mormon has holy underwear.                         (universal ps)

---

[1]  If you want a bit more detail: Actually, at the point where *his bicycle* has been translated as x's bicycle, the processing of *his bicycle* has not yet been completed. The NP *his bicycle* is a definite NP, and it needs an antecedent variable, call it z. This antecedent variable z must fit the descriptive content, which is at this point represented as: x's bicycle. Hence, formula B presupposes that there is an old discourse referent z standing for a bicycle of x's.

To see why, consider (1). Try to add (1) to an arbitrary context c. c + A must entail ps(B). In other words, c + fat man(x) must entail that x had a bicycle.[2] Since x was not present in c, there couldn't have been any information about it in c. Therefore, for c + fat man(x) to entail that x had a bike, c would have to entail that every fat man had a bike. (This is pointed out in Heim 1983b.) What we see then is that (1) can be added to a context c only if c entails (1'). Therefore, (1) is predicted to "linguistically" presuppose (1').

If the hearer is going to accommodate something into the context which obtains immediately before (1) is processed, she would have to accommodate (1') – there is no alternative. This accommodation would turn the "linguistic" ps in (1') into a "cognitive" one. But does (1) have such a ps? No, it seems perfectly clear that (1) does **not** presuppose that every fat man had a bike. More generally: it seems that empirically, existential examples like the ones in (1) and (9)–(12) do not have a universal ps. Indeed, that much seems to be uncontroversial in the literature. Hence, there is a problem with the prediction made by a pure filtering account.

### 10.2.3  Intuitions

What, empirically, do existential statements like (1) and (9)–(12) presuppose, if anything?

(1)    A fat man was pushing his bicycle.
(9)    Some nation cherishes its king.
(10)   A student stopped smoking.
(11)   A Slobovian museum is selling its Picasso.
(12)   A pious Mormon is mending her holy underwear.

My own judgment tends to be that these statements don't presuppose anything. I feel certain that these examples do not have the "universal" ps of 10.2.2 above. Do these examples presuppose concerning any individual that it has a bike/ has a king/ used to smoke, etc.? I think not. For example, I think it is perfectly felicitous to utter (1) in a context where it is not known of any individual that (s)he had a bike. In sum, it seems to me, intuitively, that existential statements like (1) and (9)–(12) do not inherit the ps of the definite NP in any form.

However, I have two reservations to note.

First, as pointed out to me by Fred Landman (p.c.), it seems that if the indefinite subject NP is interpreted as "specific" and is taken to refer to a particular individual (cf. "a certain fat man that we know"), the sentence as a whole may have a ps concerning that particular individual. Indeed, sentence (1) seems then to inherit the ps that the fat man we're talking about had a bike. Still, if I don't interpret the indefinite subject

---

[2]    In a bit more detail: B gets further reduced to the formula x was pushing z ∧ x's bicycle(z), where x must be an old variable standing for a fat man, and z must be an old variable standing for x's bike. Consider adding this formula to the context c + fat man(x). This context obviously provides an appropriate antecedent variable x, due to fat man(x). But it is up to the context c to entail the existence of a bike of x's, and thereby license the introduction of an appropriate antecedent variable z into the context before our formula is processed.

as "specific" and I interpret the example as a mere existential statement, I judge that the example as a whole does not have a ps.

Secondly, I believe that the existential examples under consideration are likely to suggest that some sort of a general default assumption is presupposed. This point is due to Craige Roberts (p.c.), who has made a similar comment concerning example (2). In my opinion, her comment holds for examples like (1) and (9)–(12) as well. For example, I think (1) is likely to suggest that some default assumption about the ownership of bicycles is being presupposed, an assumption which makes it seem plausible that "our fat man" had a bike. Perhaps (1) is only really/perfectly felicitous in a context containing such an assumption.

It seems to me that the default assumption behind (1) could be the generic assumption that fat men in general have bicycles (not entailing that all fat men really do have a bicycle, nor that there really is some fat man who actually has a bicycle). It seems to me that another default assumption that would also make (1) seem perfectly felicitous would be the assumption that some fat men have bicycles, or simply that it is fairly plausible for fat men to have bicycles.

In the light of what I just said, it should come as no surprise if it is not entirely easy to judge whether our examples "cognitively" presuppose any of the following.

| | | |
|---|---|---|
| (1′) | Every fat man had a bicycle. | (universal ps) |
| (9′) | Every nation has a king. | (universal ps) |
| (10′) | Every student used to smoke. | (universal ps) |
| (11′) | Every Slobovian museum has a Picasso. | (universal ps) |
| (12′) | Every pious Mormon has holy underwear. | (universal ps) |
| | | |
| (1‴) | Some fat man had a bicycle. | (existential ps) |
| (9‴) | Some nation has a king. | (existential ps) |
| (10‴) | Some student used to smoke. | (existential ps) |
| (11‴) | Some Slobovian museum has a Picasso. | (existential ps) |
| (12‴) | Some pious Mormon has holy underwear. | (existential ps) |

(1″)   If there is a fat man,                                (conditional existential ps)
       there is a fat man who had a bicycle.

(9″)   If there is a nation,                                 (conditional existential ps)
       there is a nation that has a king.

(10″)  If there is a student,                                (conditional existential ps)
       there is a student who used to smoke.

(11″)  If there is a Slobovian museum,                       (conditional existential ps)
       there is a Slobovian museum that has a Picasso.

(12″)  If there is a pious Mormon,                           (conditional existential ps)
       there is a pious Mormon who has holy underwear.

We saw that Heim's theory (without accommodation) predicts the "universal" pss given in the first group. There are also some theories in the literature (K&P 1979; Cooper 1983; van der Sandt 1989) that predict the existential pss in (1‴) and (9‴)–(12‴), while Beaver 1993b predicts the pss given in (1″) and (9″)–(12″). Can any of these pss be detected empirically? My intuition is that our examples do not really have any of these pss. However, as noted above, the intuition tends to be that for our examples to seem perfectly felicitous, some default assumption has to be made in the context. And the hypothetical ps in each of the three groups does come close to some default assumption that would make the example seem perfectly felicitous.

To sum up, as far as I can tell, our examples do not "cognitively" presuppose any particular information – neither a universal statement, nor an existential statement or a conditional existential statement of the types indicated above. I think the examples do sound rather better if we are making, or are willing to make, some default assumption or another that would render it plausible that the original ps associated with the VP holds of the discourse referent introduced by the subject NP.

### 10.2.4 Heim's Analysis (Part 3): existential statements

Heim 1983b argues that we can get the right prediction for examples like (1) by allowing filtering to interact with accommodation.

Heim's theory predicts that sentence (1), repeated below with its FCS representation, "linguistically" presupposes (1'), just as we saw in 10.2.1.

(1)    A fat man was pushing his bicycle.

      fat man(x)    and    x was pushing x's bicycle
       A                         B

(1')   Every fat man had a bicycle.

However, (1) can be computed with the accommodation indicated in (14).

(14)   DRT:

|  | x |
|---|---|
| Formula A: | fat man(x) |
| Accommodate ps(B): | x had a bicycle |
| B can now be processed: | x was pushing x's bicycle |

      FCS:    $((c + A) + ps(B)) + B$

Employing this strategy, we manage to process sentence (1) even in a context that does not entail that every fat man had a bike. Indeed, if we employ this strategy, we can process (1) in any context. Which means that (1) has no "cognitive" ps, as desired.

Note that the new context that we end up with does not entail that every fat man had a bike either. We end up with a new context that entails that x is a fat man, had a bike, and was pushing his bike. Given the existential quantification induced by the truth definition for a DRS or a context, we get that if (1) is an independent statement asserted in its own right (in which case it would occur in the matrix DRS), (1) ends up meaning "there is a fat man who had a bike and was pushing it."

It is interesting to note that the intuition that (1) presupposes some sort of a general default statement which makes it plausible that "our fat man" had a bike can also be explained on the basis of Heim's analysis. Given that accommodated assumptions are in general constrained to be consistent with what is known and preferably to also be plausible and unsurprising, hearers are unwilling to perform the accommodation indicated in (14) if they consider the assumption that x had a bike implausible. So a context is required for (1) where it **is** plausible that x had a bike.

Is the accommodation indicated in (14) local or global? Heim 1983b, who posits a general preference for global accommodation, would **like** to say that this accommodation is global, because the interpretation based on this accommodation is a very natural one. (Heim talks about this accommodation as being performed with the ease typical of global accommodation.) Heim 1983b suggests that the accommodation under consideration could indeed be regarded as global. Recall that we noted, in 9.2.1 above, two senses of "globality":

> **"global" accommodation, sense #1:** Whenever you are supposed to use the initial context c, you use instead c as amended by adding the ps to it.
> **"global" accommodation, sense #2:** The accommodated assumption stays in the context for good.

Heim suggests that we take sense #2 as the definition of "globality." The accommodation we performed in the case of (1) is not global in the first sense. However, it is global in the second sense: the information that x had a bike remains in the context (we end up with a new context where it is still assumed that x had a bike). That, on Heim 1983b's view, explains why the reading obtained by this accommodation is so natural and why hearers don't feel any particular pressure to accommodate instead the general assumption that fat men have bikes.

Fred Landman (p.c.) notes that there is a problem with Heim's argument that this instance of accommodation is global, if we consider non-assertions. Take for instance example (15).

(15)   Was a fat man pushing his bicycle (on the tow-path)?

(15) does not presuppose that every fat man had a bike. Hence, it too would presumably involve the kind of accommodation indicated in (14). But here the accommodated information does **not** remain in the context after (15) is processed, so how can the accommodation be regarded as global?

Well, it should be clear from the discussion in section 9.4 that I do not believe that global accommodation is inherently preferred. So I think that even if the accommodation in (14) is to be considered local, Heim's account of the ps disappearance in (1) can still hold.

But, there is one remaining problem. As noted in 10.2.3, my intuition is that (1) has no "cognitive" ps at all. My informants generally confirm this judgment. If this intuition is reliable, then (1) **never** presupposes its predicted "linguistic" ps. It seems that Heim herself assumes that it never does. But Heim does not explain why that should be the case. Assuming that the accommodation in (14) is global doesn't help, since, after all, accommodating the universal ps into the initial context would be global accommodation as well (in fact, it would be global in both senses). Why should the accommodation indicated in (14) be always preferred to globally accommodating the universal statement into the initial context?

This problem may motivate Beaver's view that it would be better not to predict a "linguistic" universal ps to start with. On the other hand, it is hard to prove that existential examples like (1) really never have a "cognitive" universal ps. Maybe sometimes they do have a "cognitive" universal ps, after all. Perhaps the reason that it is impossible (or next to impossible) to globally accommodate the universal statement in the case of (1) is simply that we are all quite sure that not all fat men have bicycles. In that case, we might be more likely to judge that there is a universal ps if we choose a different example. How about (12), for instance? Do you judge that the speaker of (12) is taking it for granted that all pious Mormons have holy underwear? Are you likely or willing to accommodate this universal assumption into the common ground?

(12)   A pious Mormon is mending her holy underwear.

All in all, Heim's theory, including accommodation, seems to work quite well. Let us sum up. We have in (1) an open formula – x was pushing x's bicycle – in which the x must be an old variable. This open formula can be added to a given context only if that context entails that that same discourse referent x had a bike. Because in example (1) the discourse referent x is a new one (being triggered by the indefinite *a fat man*), obviously nothing could have been predicated directly of it in the preceding context. Hence, the ps would have to be satisfied in one of the following two ways.

   (i)   We add (1) to a context in which the universal statement that every fat man had a bike is assumed. (This statement may happen to be assumed in a given context; perhaps under appropriate circumstances, hearers might even choose to accommodate it into their common ground.)
   (ii)  We accommodate the information that x had a bike in the manner indicated in (14) above.

Since in the real world fat men don't always have bicycles, (ii) seems to be a natural option to take if (1) is presented out of the blue; hence the judgment that (1) has no "cognitive" presupposition.

### 10.2.5   Beaver: Existential Statements Without Accommodation Which is Local in Sense #1?

Beaver 1993b is interested in dealing with the presuppositional properties of quantified and existential statements like (1)–(4) without invoking local accommodation – not even the kind of accommodation that Heim uses for example (1) (global in sense #2 but local in sense #1). He offers an interesting and elegant modification of Heim's filtering theory, which avoids predicting a "cognitive" universal ps for examples like (1)–(4) by not predicting a "linguistic" universal ps to start with. In this subsection, I will continue to focus on existential statements only.

Beaver essentially takes over the theory of ps projection of Heim 1983b. This includes the basic principle that a ps must be satisfied by the local context, as well as the context change potentials posited by Heim for the quantifiers and connectives. Beaver's theory is stated in the form of a logic which he calls "Kinematic Predicate Logic," with a dynamic semantics (based on the ideas of Groenendijk and Stokhof 1990, and also Dekker 1992). I will not give Beaver's complete logic or discuss its details, because I think Beaver's modification of Heim's theory is independent of his particular formulation, and can be presented and discussed without it. Nevertheless, I will start by giving Beaver's formulation of the representation and semantics of ps. I do that (i) in order to give the reader an idea of what Beaver's formulation looks like, and (ii) because it is easy to give a precise and general statement of the theory in Beaver's own formulation.

Beaver represents a ps in the logic, as a formula in its own right, headed by the operator $\partial$. On Beaver's theory, the VP of our example (1), *was pushing his bicycle*, is translated as a conjunction of two formulas, as indicated in (17).

(1)　　A fat man was pushing his bicycle.
(16)　subject NP:　fat man(x)　　　(Continue to call this formula A.)
(17)　VP:　　　　$\partial$ x had a bicycle $\wedge$ x was pushing x's bicycle

It is the formula in (17) that gets added to the local context of the VP, the context reached when *a fat man* has been processed. Let us continue to call that context c + A. The ccp of a formula headed by $\partial$ is given in (18).

(18)　　$c + \partial p = \begin{cases} c+p \text{ iff for every } \langle w,g \rangle \in c, \ \exists f \text{ s.t. } \langle w,f \rangle \in c+p \\ \text{undefined otherwise} \end{cases}$

(18) determines that while processing the VP, one must (i) check that c + $\partial$ x had a bike is defined, and (ii) if it is, add x had a bike to c + A. Only after that will x was pushing x's bicycle be added to the context too. As will be clarified in detail below, what is checked in step (i) is that c + A contains the purely factual information that there is a fat man who had a bike, while the information added to c + A in step (ii) is the information that the discourse referent x had a bike. So much for Beaver's formulation.

I would say that Beaver's modification of Heim's theory of ps consists of the following two changes.

(i)　For Heim, a ps is not asserted; for Beaver, a ps is (also) asserted.
(ii)　For Heim, c satisfies a ps $\alpha$ iff
　　　　　for every $\langle w,g \rangle \in c$, $\exists g' \supseteq g$ s.t. $\langle w,g' \rangle \in c + \alpha$;
　　　for Beaver, c satisfies a ps $\alpha$ iff
　　　　　for every $\langle w,g \rangle \in c$, $\exists f$ s.t. $\langle w,f \rangle \in c + \alpha$.

Beaver's crucial move, as far as eliminating the "linguistic" universal ps is concerned, is the one given in (ii). So let me first discuss this move.

Consider example (1) and its representation (à la Heim), repeated below.

(1)　　A fat man was pushing his bicycle.
　　　fat man(x) $\wedge$ x was pushing x's bicycle
　　　　　A　　　　　　　　　　B

The ps of formula B is itself an open formula: ps(B) = x had a bicycle. ps(B) must be satisfied by the local context of B, c + A. According to Heim 1983b, c + A satisfies ps(B) iff for every $\langle w,g \rangle$ in c + A, g(x) had a bike in w. We might state Heim's assumption more generally as in (19).

(19)   c satisfies a ps $\alpha$ iff for every $\langle w,g \rangle \in c$, $\exists g' \supseteq g$ s.t. $\langle w,g' \rangle \in c + \alpha$.

Assumption (19) guarantees that Heim's theory will predict a universal "linguistic" ps for (1): it follows from (19) that – as I just noted – c + A is required to satisfy the condition that for every $\langle w,g \rangle$ in c + A, g(x) had a bike in w.[3] As discussed in 10.2.2 above, since x is necessarily a new variable in A, c + A satisfies this condition just in case c entails that every fat man had a bike.

Now, Beaver does not want to predict a "linguistic" universal ps. Therefore, Beaver modifies Heim's theory by replacing (19) with (20). (That is what's expressed in Beaver's formulation as the definedness condition on the ccp of $\partial p$.)

(20)   c satisfies a ps $\alpha$ iff for every $\langle w,g \rangle \in c$, $\exists f$ s.t. $\langle w,f \rangle \in c + \alpha$.

This means that for Beaver, c + A is no longer required to satisfy the condition that for every $\langle w,g \rangle$ in c + A, g(x) had a bike in w. Instead, what (20) requires of c + A is that for every world of c + A, there should be at least one possible value of x in the model that will verify in that world everything predicated of x in c + A as well as in ps(B). Since x is necessarily a new variable in A, this means that what (20) requires of c + A is that for every world of c + A, there should be at least one possible value of x in the model which is a fat man (the predicate in A) and had a bike (the predicate in ps(B)) in that world. In short, Beaver's theory determines that c + A satisfies ps(B) iff in every world of c + A, there is a fat man with a bike. This will hold only if in every world of c which contains a fat man, there is a fat man with a bike. In other words, if c entails that if there is a fat man, there is a fat man with a bike. This then is the "linguistic" ps predicted by Beaver: if there is a fat man, there is a fat man who had a bike. A universal ps is not predicted anymore.

Beaver explains the nature of the move from (19) to (20): while on Heim's theory, what's presupposed is both factual information and information about discourse referents, on his own theory, what's presupposed is factual information only. To see this, consider again the ps just discussed: ps(B) = x had a bike.

Suppose c + A satisfies the condition derived from (19), viz. that for every $\langle w,g \rangle$ in c + A, g(x) had a bike in w. That means that whatever assignment g you care to choose – provided that it is one of the assignments of c + A (i.e. one of the gs paired with some world w in c + A) – this g is guaranteed to give x a value that had a bike (in the world(s) with which g is paired). In other words, however you care to pick the value for x – provided that it's a truthful value given the information in c + A – this value is guaranteed to have had a bike. Which means that in context c + A, the **discourse referent** x is known to have had a bike. So, for ps(B) to be satisfied, it must be known in the local context of B about the discourse referent x that it had a bike. We see then that for Heim, what's presupposed by formula B is a piece of information about a discourse referent. That was exactly why Heim predicted a universal ps: since the discourse referent is new

---

[3]   If you want more detail: According to (19), c + fat man(x) satisfies ps(B) iff for every $\langle w,g \rangle$ in c + fat man(x), there is a g' extending g s.t. $\langle w,g' \rangle$ is in (c + fat man(x)) + ps(B). The ps of B – x had a bicycle – can be further reduced to the formula bicycle(z) $\wedge$ x had z. Hence, for every $\langle w,g \rangle$ in c + fat man(x), there must be a g' extending g s.t. $\langle w,g' \rangle$ is in (c + fat man(x)) + bicycle(z) $\wedge$ x had z. Since g' $\supseteq$ g, g'(x) = g(x), and so g(x) must be a fat man who had a bike.

in A, any information known about it must follow from information about fat men in general.

Beaver, in contrast, requires c + A to satisfy the weaker condition, derived from (20), that in every world of c + A, there is a fat man who had a bike. According to this, ps(B) is satisfied iff the context c + A contains the information that there is a fat man who had a bike. For ps(B) to be satisfied, c + A is not required to contain any particular piece of information about the discourse referent x. (It is, of course, known in c + A that the discourse referent x is a fat man, but the ps of B does not require c + A to contain any further information about this discourse referent.) In particular, for ps(B) to be satisfied, it need not be known in c + A about the discourse referent x that it had a bike: c + A is allowed to contain assignments that assign x as a value a fat man that didn't have a bike. We see then that for Beaver, what's presupposed by formula B is a purely factual piece of information, in the sense that this information is a property of worlds (and not of world-assignment pairs) – what's presupposed by formula B is a piece of information that does not concern "the individual that the speaker has in mind," but just the facts as they are. There are no novel discourse referents that we must already know things about, and no universal ps is predicted.

I now move on to the other change that Beaver introduces into the theory, viz. treating a ps as (also) asserted. First, note that I am using the term "assert" here in a broad sense: "to assert $\alpha$ in context c" simply means "to add $\alpha$ to the context c"; since c may be a local "temporary" context, $\alpha$ need not be factual (in the sense of being an independent assertion in its own right). Now, think once more about ps(B) = x had a bicycle.

If you **assert** x had a bicycle in some context c, that adds to c some information about the discourse referent x: in the resulting context c + x had a bicycle there are only world-assignment pairs $\langle w,g \rangle$ where g(x) had a bike in w; that is, it is known in c + x had a bicycle that the discourse referent x had a bike. In that sense, x had a bicycle carries some information about discourse referents.

As noted above, on Heim's theory, a context satisfies the ps x had a bicycle just in case the information about discourse referents carried by x had a bike is already in that context. That is, a context that satisfies the ps x had a bike is just like a context where x had a bike has already been asserted. In contrast, we saw that on Beaver's theory, a context that satisfies the ps x had a bike does **not** have to contain the information about discourse referents carried by x had a bike. That is, a context that satisfies the ps x had a bike is **not** just like a context where x had a bike has already been asserted. So, what about the information about discourse referents carried by x had a bike? Here is where the idea that a ps is (also) asserted comes in. On Beaver's theory, when you encounter a formula $\phi$ which has a ps, it is not enough to simply check that ps($\phi$) is satisfied by the local context, and if so, to go ahead and add $\phi$ to this context. Rather, Beaver stipulates, as part of how a statement with a ps is processed in his theory, that once you have checked that the local context satisfies (à la Beaver) ps($\phi$), what you do next is assert ps($\phi$) – that is, add ps($\phi$) to the context. (This is expressed in Beaver's formulation by formulas of the form $\partial p$ and their ccp, which instructs you to add p to the context.) Only then can you go on and add $\phi$ itself. This ensures that on Beaver's theory too, $\phi$ is added to a context which already contains all the information carried by ps($\phi$), including the information about discourse referents.

To see how this works, consider again our example (1). Take the point where we already have the context c + A (= c + fat man(x)), and are now faced with B (= x was pushing x's bicycle). On Heim's theory, if c + A satisfies ps(B), it contains only world-assignment pairs $\langle w,g \rangle$ such that g(x) is a fat man in w and g(x) had a bike in w. On Beaver's theory, if c + A satisfies ps(B), it contains only worlds where there is a fat man who had a bike. At the same time, it may well contain world-assignment pairs $\langle w,g \rangle$ such that g(x) is a fat man in w but g(x) didn't have a bike in w. Once we find that c + A does satisfy (à la Beaver) the ps of B, what we do next is assert ps(B) = x had a bike in c + A – that is, we add x had a bike to c + A. This step can't add to the context any purely factual information (= it can't kick out any worlds), since all the purely factual information carried by ps(B) is already in c + A, but it does add the information that the discourse referent x had a bike: asserting x had a bike kicks out of the context all the pairs $\langle w,g \rangle$ such that g(x) didn't have a bike in w. This leaves us with just the kind of context that satisfies ps(B) à la Heim: a context containing only pairs $\langle w,g \rangle$ such that g(x) is a fat man in w and g(x) had a bike in w. To this context, on Beaver's theory as well as on Heim's, we add B. (Adding B kicks out all the pairs $\langle w,g \rangle$ such that g(x) wasn't pushing the bike of g(x) in w.)

But, one might wonder, is it actually crucial to ensure that all the information carried by ps($\phi$) gets asserted (added to the context)? Couldn't Beaver simply allow $\phi$ to be added to any context which satisfies ps($\phi$), even if that context doesn't contain the information about discourse referents carried by ps($\phi$)? Well, it seems that ps($\phi$) must indeed get asserted at some point – I will now show why. I will talk about (1) again, to be concrete.

To assert B in context c + A is to kick out assignments g which don't verify B because g(x), a fat man with a bike, wasn't pushing his bike. But what about the assignments g in c + A such that g(x) is a fat man who didn't have a bike? After all, on Beaver's theory, a context c + A satisfying ps(B) may well contain such assignments. For example, suppose that the model is as described in (21), and the initial context c is the context given in (22).

(21)   There are three individuals in the model: j, b, m.
       (Hence, there are three assignments for x:
           $g_j(x) = j$   $g_b(x) = b$   $g_m(x) = m$
       In the two possible worlds $w_1$ and $w_2$, the facts are as stated below.
       $w_1$   j is a fat man, j had a bike, j was not pushing his bike.
               b is a fat man, b had no bike.
               m is not a fat man.
       $w_2$   j is a fat man, j had a bike, j was not pushing his bike.
               b is not a fat man.
               m is not a fat man.

(22)   $\{\langle w_1,g_j \rangle, \langle w_1,g_b \rangle, \langle w_1,g_m \rangle, \langle w_2,g_j \rangle, \langle w_2,g_b \rangle, \langle w_2,g_m \rangle\}$

In that case, c + A is the context given in (24).

(23)   (22) + A = $\{\langle w_1,g_j \rangle, \langle w_1,g_b \rangle, \langle w_2,g_j \rangle\}$

Context (23) satisfies (à la Beaver) ps(B). Suppose we don't assert ps(B), but directly assert B. What is the effect of adding B? Well, adding B will obviously kick out the pairs

$\langle w_1,g_j \rangle$, $\langle w_2,g_j \rangle$, because the value of x wasn't pushing his bike. And what about $\langle w_1,g_b \rangle$?

The theory will have to either determine that $\langle w_1,g_b \rangle$ is kicked out too, or that it stays in. Imagine first that the theory determines that $\langle w_1,g_b \rangle$ stays in. In that case, the context (22) + (1) comes out true (non-empty). So, it is predicted that (1) is compatible with (22), just because (22) has a world where some fat man had no bike. But this is a wrong prediction. Intuitively, (1) can't be true just because some fat man had no bike, and is incompatible with (22). Taking the other alternative, we get the right prediction: if the theory determines instead that when B is asserted, $\langle w_1,g_b \rangle$ is kicked out, then the context (22) + (1) comes out false (empty), as desired. But to say that asserting B kicks out $\langle w_1,g_b \rangle$ – or, more generally, to say that asserting B kicks out all the assignments g in c + A such that g(x) is a fat man who didn't have a bike – is to say that B asserts, among other things, its own ps. We see then, that we are forced to take Beaver's position: it is not enough to say that ps(B) has to be satisfied (à la Beaver), and we must also say that ps(B) is asserted.

To sum up, on Beaver's theory the situation is as follows. The VP of (1), *was pushing his bike*, does not truly **presuppose** the information that "the individual that the speaker has in mind" had a bike: the context to which the subject NP has already been added (c + fat man(x)) need not contain this information. The VP only presupposes that some fat man had a bike. At the same time, this VP **asserts** that "the individual that the speaker has in mind" had a bike. Hence, on Beaver's theory, the so-called ps of the VP, which can be represented by the formula x had a bike (or the formula $\partial$ x had a bike), can actively add new information. (It can't add new information about the facts as they are, but it **can** add new information about discourse referents.)

Beaver's theory does not predict a universal ps for example (1) as a whole, and that seems fine. Now let us examine the prediction that Beaver's theory does make.

Beaver 1993b does not discuss (or even mention) the pss that his theory predicts for the existential and quantificational examples considered. However, it is not difficult to see what the prediction is. It has already been noted above that Beaver's theory determines that (1) "linguistically" presupposes (1″). (See discussion directly below (20).) Similarly, (9)–(12) are predicted to "linguistically" presuppose (9″)–(12″).

(1)     A fat man was pushing his bicycle.
(9)     Some nation cherishes its king.
(10)    A student stopped smoking.
(11)    A Slobovian museum is selling its Picasso.
(12)    A pious Mormon is mending her holy underwear.

(1″)    If there is a fat man,                                      (conditional existential ps)
        there is a fat man who had a bicycle.
(9″)    If there is a nation,                                       (conditional existential ps)
        there is a nation that has a king.
(10″)   If there is a student,                                      (conditional existential ps)
        there is a student who used to smoke.
(11″)   If there is a Slobovian museum,                             (conditional existential ps)
        there is a Slobovian museum that has a Picasso.
(12″)   If there is a pious Mormon,                                 (conditional existential ps)
        there is a pious Mormon who has holy underwear.

And what is the "cognitive" ps that Beaver predicts? Well, if the sentence is uttered in a context that does not entail the "linguistic" ps, then that exact ps would have to be accommodated into the context at some point or another before the VP is processed. That is because on Beaver's theory, the requirement on the local context of the VP is that it entail a certain piece of factual information, rather than information about a discourse referent. In the case of (11), for example, the VP can be processed only if its local context entails that some Slobovian museum had a Picasso. The accommodation would have to be performed either before or after the subject NP is processed. In the case of (11), we would have the two hypothetical options given in (24) (accommodation underlined, ps asserted à la Beaver italicized).

(24)  a.   $c + (11'') + (11) =$
           $c + (11'') + $ Slobovian museum(x) + *x has a Picasso* + x is selling its Picasso
      b.   $c + (11) =$
           $c + $ Slobovian museum(x) $+ (11'') + $ *x has a Picasso* + x is selling its Picasso

Option (24a) would turn the conditional "linguistic" ps into a "cognitive" one. If no relevant information is actually assumed in the context – as is quite likely when (11) is presented out of the blue – this option should result in an intuition that (11) presupposes (11''). If it happens to be already assumed in the context that the antecedent of the conditional is true, this option should result in an intuition that (11) presupposes the consequent of the conditional. Similarly for the other examples. Hence, the accommodation in (24a) should result in an intuition that each of our examples presupposes either the corresponding conditional above or the corresponding existential statement below.

(1''')    Some fat man had a bicycle.                    (existential ps)
(9''')    Some nation has a king.                        (existential ps)
(10''')   Some student used to smoke.                    (existential ps)
(11''')   Some Slobovian museum has a Picasso.           (existential ps)
(12''')   Some pious Mormon has holy underwear.          (existential ps)

Option (24b), on the other hand, would determine that there is no "cognitive" ps at all.

Note, incidentally, that on Beaver's theory the interpretation of (11) is always "there is a Slobovian museum that has a Picasso and is selling it." On Heim's theory, this interpretation was the result of accommodating x has a Picasso after processing the subject NP, and was never accompanied by a ps. On Beaver's theory, this interpretation may or may not be accompanied by the ps in (11'') (or the one in (11''')), depending on whether the accommodation is as in (24a) or as in (24b).

As discussed in 10.2.3 above, I think the empirical fact is that our existential examples do not have a "cognitive" ps. More precisely, I think that if they do presuppose anything, they do not presuppose any particular piece of information, but rather some default assumption or another that would render accommodation plausible.

Therefore, I think that for existential statements, the results of Beaver's theory are not that different from those of Heim's theory. Both theories determine a "linguistic" ps that does not seem to show up empirically. Certainly, I do **not** feel that Beaver's existential pss match my intuitions any better than Heim's universal pss do. Both theories allow us to derive an interpretation which is an existential statement without any ps, and on both theories that interpretation is based on accommodating something into our evolving context at the same point: at the point right after the subject NP is processed and right before the VP is processed. If we make the natural assumption that the accommodation just mentioned should be more readily executed given some default assumption that would render it plausible, that would explain why both Heim's universal pss and Beaver's existential pss don't seem that far off, even if they don't constitute actual pss.

If anything, I think that Heim's theory seems better. First, Heim's theory seems simpler and conceptually more natural. Secondly, it is easier to explain why Heim's universal ps doesn't show up than why Beaver's existential ps doesn't show up: the universal ps is more likely than the existential ps to clash with our background information, explaining why the "linguistic" ps does not get globally accommodated into the initial context. Finally, note that while Beaver's main motivation for his theory was to avoid relying on accommodation performed after the subject NP is processed, it turns out that on his theory too the most natural, ps-less interpretation of the example is derived on the basis of just such an act of accommodation.

## 10.3 Quantified Statements

The predictions of a pure filtering analysis of ps projection concerning quantified examples are exactly parallel to the predictions concerning existential statements. I will briefly go over these predictions in 10.3.1 and 10.3.2 below.

### 10.3.1 Some Unproblematic Quantified Statements

Here are a few quantified statements, with their corresponding tripartite representations. Note that in (26) and (27), the (a) sentence is a "multi-case" conditional; following Kamp and Heim, I assume that the (a) and (b) sentences are equivalent and receive the same representation.

(25)   No nation admires the king of Slobovia.
       NO (nation(x)) (x admires the king of Slobovia)
(26)   a.   If a man admires the king of Slobovia, he is stupid.
       b.   Every man who admires the king of Slobovia is stupid.
            $\forall$ (man(x) $\wedge$ x admires the king of Slobovia) (stupid(x))
(27)   a.   If a man is stupid, he admires the king of Slobovia.
       b.   Every stupid man admires the king of Slobovia.
            $\forall$ (man(x) $\wedge$ stupid(x)) (x admires the king of Slobovia)

As the reader can verify for herself, given the ccps in (28) and (29), Heim 1983b's theory of ps and ps projection predicts that examples (25)–(27) should "linguistically" presuppose (25″)–(27″), respectively.

(28)   c + no (p) (q) = {⟨w,g⟩ $\in$ c : for no g′ which extends g s.t. ⟨w,g′⟩ $\in$ c + p, is there a g″ which extends g′ s.t. ⟨w,g″⟩ $\in$ (c + p) + q}

(29)    $c + \forall$ (p) (q) = {$\langle w,g \rangle \in c$ : for every $g'$ which extends $g$ s.t. $\langle w,g' \rangle \in c + p$,
there is a $g''$ which extends $g'$ s.t. $\langle w,g'' \rangle \in (c + p) + q$}

(25″)   If there is a nation,                                                    (conditional ps)
         there is a king of Slobovia.
(26″)   If there is a man,                                                       (conditional ps)
         there is a king of Slobovia.
(27″)   If there is a stupid man,                                               (conditional ps)
         there is a king of Slobovia.

Since in each case it seems unlikely that the antecedent actually has something to do with the consequent, we get the correct prediction that (25)–(27) should all "cognitively" presuppose that there is a king of Slobovia.

### 10.3.2   Our Problem in Quantified Statements

Again, the interesting examples are those in which the original ps is about a discourse referent previously introduced in the same sentence. For instance, the following examples.

(2)     No nation cherishes its king.
(30)    No student stopped smoking.
(31)    No Slobovian museum is selling its Picasso.
(32)    No pious Mormon is mending her holy underwear.

(3)     Everyone who serves his king will be rewarded.
(33)    Every student who stopped smoking will be rewarded.
(34)    If a Slobovian museum sells its Picasso, the profits go to charity.
(35)    Every pious Mormon who mends her holy underwear will be rewarded.

(4)     Every nation cherishes its king.
(36)    Every student stopped smoking.
(37)    Every Slobovian museum is selling its Picasso.
(38)    If a Mormon is pious, she mends her holy underwear.

Heim's filtering theory of ps projection predicts that these examples "linguistically" presuppose the following.

(2′)  = (3′)  = (4′)              Every nation/person has a king.       (universal ps)
(30′) = (33′) = (36′) = (10′)   Every student used to smoke.          (universal ps)
(31′) = (34′) = (37′) = (11′)   Every Slobovian museum has a Picasso.
                                                                        (universal ps)
(32′) = (35′) = (38′) = (12′)   Every pious Mormon has holy underwear.
                                                                        (universal ps)

The reasoning leading to these predictions is parallel to the reasoning concerning the existential example (1), in 10.2.2 above. To take just one quantificational example, consider (4), and its representation in (39).

(39)   DRT:

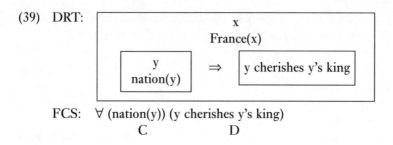

FCS:   $\forall$ (nation(y)) (y cherishes y's king)

              C               D

The ccp of quantificational statements determines that the context-incrementation $c + (4)$ is defined only if $c + C$ entails ps(D). ps(D) = y has a king. So (4) can be added to a context c only if $c + $ nation(y) entails that y has a king. But $c + $ nation(y) would entail that y has a king just in case c entails that every nation has a king. As in (1), the reason is that our variable is, and must be, new. Recall that the Kamp–Heim theory stipulates that a quantificational NP introduces a **new** variable.[4] So in (39), the variable y that *every nation* introduces into the restriction is new. Given that y is a new variable, there couldn't have been any information about it in c. Therefore, for $c + $ nation(y) to entail that y has a king, c would have to entail that every nation has a king. We get the prediction, then, that (4) "linguistically" presupposes that every nation has a king.

As long as the hearer is going to accommodate something into the context which obtains immediately before the example is processed, the accommodation should turn the "linguistic" universal ps into a "cognitive" one. But do our quantified examples really have a universal ps? As a matter of fact, it seems that not all of them do. So, again, there is a problem with the predictions made by a pure filtering account.

### 10.3.3   *Intuitions*

What, empirically, do our quantified examples of 10.3.2 presuppose, if anything?

With regard to examples like (4) and (36)–(38), it seems quite clear that they do indeed have a universal ps, as predicted by filtering – that they presuppose that every individual satisfying the restriction satisfies the ps triggered in the nuclear scope.

(4)   Every nation cherishes its king.
(36)   Every student stopped smoking.
(37)   Every Slobovian museum is selling its Picasso.
(38)   If a Mormon is pious, she mends her holy underwear.

For example, it seems that (4) presupposes that every nation has a king. Some support for our intuition that this is a ps rather than a mere entailment comes from the fact that it survives in (40).

[4]   Concerning the reason for this stipulation (cf. 2.1.3 above), just think what we would get if we chose x for the nation variable in the pair of DRSs. We would fail to quantify over all nations, because functions extending the embedding function g for the matrix DRS will give x the same value it got from g, so x will stay France; all we'd be saying would be that if France is a nation, it cherishes its king, which is not what (4) says.

(40)    If every nation cherishes its king, then all kings are lucky.

Note also that given our knowledge that Israeli museums don't all of them have Picassos, (41) sounds rather strange.

(41)    Every Israeli museum is selling its Picasso.

Further support for the universal ps comes from exchanges like the following, which seems very odd. (This point is due to Craige Roberts, p.c.)

(42)    A:    Not every nation has a king.
        B:    But every nation cherishes its king.

That examples like (4) and (36)–(38) have the universal "cognitive" ps is a piece of data which is assumed in K&P 1979 and Heim 1983b, and is, I think, basically agreed on in the literature.

    And yet, I would like to point out that the universal ps sometimes disappears. Several of my informants are perfectly happy to accept (4) in a context that entails nothing whatsoever about nations having kings, interpreting (4) as indicated in (43).

(43)    "Every nation that has a king cherishes its king."

Fred Landman (p.c.) supports the possible disappearance of the universal ps with example (44). (44) seems perfectly felicitous despite the fact that we know that not every mother has a daughter. Evidently, we interpret it as in (45).

(44)    Every mother tells her daughter to watch out for that kind of man.
(45)    "Every mother that has a daughter tells her daughter to watch out for that kind of man."

    As far as I can tell, whether or not examples like (4) presuppose a universal statement, they do not presuppose any kind of existential statement. I think that (4) may implicate that some nation has a king, but it does not entail or presuppose that.

    Let us move on to another group of examples. What, if anything, do examples like (2) and (30)–(32) presuppose?

(2)     No nation cherishes its king.
(30)    No student stopped smoking.
(31)    No Slobovian museum is selling its Picasso.
(32)    No pious Mormon is mending her holy underwear.

Cooper 1983 claims that (2) presupposes that every nation has a king, and Beaver 1993b disagrees with this claim. I agree with Beaver. My intuition is that examples like the ones in (2) and (30)–(32) do not have a universal ps. In that respect, my judgments on these examples are not any different from my judgments on the existential examples considered in 10.2.3. In fact, I tend to judge that, like their existential counterparts, (2) and (30)–(32) do not have a "cognitive" ps at all.

Of course, examples like the ones in (2) and (30)–(32) as well as the existential example of 10.2.3 will automatically be OK in a context entailing the relevant universal statement, but that doesn't mean that they "cognitively" presuppose that statement. The example does not **require** the context to entail the universal statement.

Perhaps examples like (2) and (30)–(32) do presuppose some sort of a general default assumption, as Craige Roberts (p.c.) has pointed out to me. In this respect, too, these examples pattern like the existential examples. For example, (2) seems to presuppose some default information about kings: perhaps we are making the generic assumption that nations in general have kings, perhaps we assume that some nations have kings, perhaps we simply assume that it is fairly plausible for a nation to have a king.

Lerner and Zimmermann 1981 claim that (2) presupposes that **some** nation has a king. Again as in the case of the existential examples, I think it is not entirely easy to judge whether examples like (2) and (30)–(32) have either the universal ps discussed above or the existential ps just mentioned, because these hypothetical pss are not very far from certain default assumptions that could help the example seem perfectly felicitous. Note also that even if (2) is felt to presuppose that some nation has a king, this judgment can be naturally explained as due to Gricean reasoning (why would it be relevant to say (2), if no nations have kings anyway?), and need not be attributed to "projection" of the existential ps of *its king*. At any rate, my judgment is that (2) does not presuppose the existential statement. I think that (2) can be uttered perfectly felicitously in a context that does not entail that some nation has a king.

The last remaining group of examples is the ones like (3) and (33)–(35). What, if anything, do examples like these presuppose?

(3)    Everyone who serves his king will be rewarded.
(33)   Every student who stopped smoking will be rewarded.
(34)   If a Slobovian museum sells its Picasso, the profits go to charity.
(35)   Every pious Mormon who mends her holy underwear will be rewarded.

The judgments on such examples seem to vary and oscillate quite a bit. For instance, sometimes (3) is judged to presuppose that everybody has a king, and sometimes (3) is judged to presuppose nothing about anybody having a king. K&P 1979 think that such examples do not "cognitively" presuppose anything. Heim 1983b thinks that sometimes they have a "cognitive" universal ps, but sometimes they don't. Intuitively, I tend to agree with Heim, and I think that (46) below is a bit odd. However, most of my informants have a clear and persistent judgment that such examples do not have a universal ps, and that the exchange in (46) is OK.

(46)   A:   Not every person has a king.
       B:   But every person who serves his king will be rewarded.

My intuitive impression is that (3) **can** "cognitively" presuppose that everybody has a king, even though – under the right circumstances – it is also possible for (3) to "cognitively" presuppose nothing. The intuition about the universal ps is a bit elusive, but let me try to pin it down. Consider examples (47) and (48).

**Context for examples (47) and (48):**
I am lecturing to an audience of 50 persons, of whom 9 are taking my course for credit. It is a known fact that the persons taking the course for credit must hand in a squib in order to pass the course.

(47)   Everybody who hands in his/her squib by Monday will get comments.
(48)   Everybody who hands in a squib by Monday will get comments.

Suppose, first, that I utter (48) in the given context. This may imply that I undertake to write comments on a person's squib even if that person is not taking my course for credit. In other words, by "everybody," I may well mean "everybody in this audience." Now, does (48) in any way imply that "everybody" is writing a squib? No, absolutely not.

Now suppose I utter (47) in the given context. Does (47) sound as if I am assuming that "everybody" is writing squibs? I think it does. My intuition is that it is presupposed in (47) that "everybody" is writing squibs; it's just that it is not clear what "everybody" means. The thing is, judgments are subtle here because of contextual restrictions on the quantification: the audience may select a domain of quantification narrow enough to ensure that "everybody" is indeed writing squibs. Therefore, let us try to make the domain of quantification explicit. I believe that my utterance (47) can be interpreted as in (47′), and it can also be interpreted as in (47″) or even as in (47‴). Let us assume that what "everybody" means is fully explicit in (47′), (47″) and (47‴).

(47′)   "Everybody in this audience who hands in his/her squib by Monday will get comments."
(47″)   "Everybody taking this course for credit who hands in his/her squib by Monday will get comments."
(47‴)   "Everybody writing a squib who hands in his/her squib by Monday will get comments."

Suppose you are in the audience, and you are just sitting in on my course. Suppose you interpret my utterance (47) as in (47′). Make sure you keep this interpretation in mind. (This interpretation may be encouraged by imagining that I said first "Now listen carefully, you guys, all of you" and then said (47).) I think you may very well feel a little startled by my utterance; you may feel like saying "Hey, wait a minute, we are not all supposed to be writing squibs, are we?". This judgment has been confirmed by members of actual audiences to whom I presented the example. In short, I think that if my utterance (47) is interpreted as in (47′), I sound as if I am incorrectly assuming that all 50 persons in the audience "have a squib" (a squib they are writing, or at least a squib they are supposed to write).

Of course, you don't have to interpret my utterance (47) as in (47′). You can interpret it as in (47″) or in (47‴) instead. In that case, I would **not** sound as if I was making an obviously false assumption. (Certainly not if I meant (47‴).) In fact, your natural choice may very well be to interpret my utterance as in (47′) or (47‴), in order to accommodate me rather than attribute to my utterance a ps that fails to hold. Note, however, that if my utterance is interpreted as in (47″), it still has a universal ps, one that seems to hold in the context given: it presupposes that everybody taking the course for credit "has a squib" (a squib (s)he is writing, or at least a squib (s)he is supposed to write). If (47) is interpreted as in (47‴), it is intuitively felt to presuppose nothing, and no wonder: the ps of the definite NP is satisfied locally by the added restriction on the quantification.

In sum, I think that examples like the ones in (3) have a universal "cognitive" ps, unless there is an implicit restriction on the quantification which locally satisfies the original ps which is triggered by the definite NP or the verb *stop* (etc.). Indeed, we might say that the universal ps is always there, but becomes trivial with the right implicit restriction. For example, if we imagine that there is independent contextual motivation for restricting the quantification in (3) to persons with kings, we get that the predicted universal ps becomes "every person that has a king has a king" – a trivial ps.

As far as I can tell, whether or not examples like (3) presuppose a universal statement, they do not presuppose any kind of existential statement. I think that (3) may implicate that some person has a king, but it does not entail or presuppose that.

### 10.3.4   Heim's Analysis (Part 4): quantified statements

We saw that Heim's filtering mechanism, all by itself, predicts a universal ps for all our quantified examples. Regarding examples like (4), Heim 1983b is satisfied with this prediction. (She also notes that for such examples, K&P 1979 make the same prediction.)

(4)   Every nation cherishes its king.

Regarding examples like (3), Heim 1983b shows that once filtering is allowed to interact with accommodation, her theory will predict that despite the "linguistic" universal ps, it is quite possible for (3) to have no "cognitive" ps. Consider the tripartite representation of (3), given in (49).

(3)   Everyone who serves his king will be rewarded.
(49)   $\forall$ (y serves y's king) (y will be rewarded)
　　　　　　　E　　　　　　　　　　F

Formula E presupposes that y has a king. It is possible to amend the initial context c to c + y has a king just for the purpose of performing the context incrementation c + E – that is, c + (3) can be computed with local accommodation as follows.

$$c + (3) =$$
$$\{\langle w,g \rangle \in c : \forall g', g' \supseteq g \,\&\, \langle w,g' \rangle \in (c + ps(E)) + E, \exists g'', g'' \supseteq g' \,\&\, \langle w,g'' \rangle \in ((c + ps(E)) + E) + F\}$$

| | | |
|---|---|---|
| here | local | local |
| c | accom | accom |
| stays | | |
| as is | where:   ps(E) = y has a king | |

When you employ this strategy, you manage to add the sentence to an initial context c that doesn't satisfy ps(E). Hence, the effect is that (3) does not have any "cognitive" ps about kings. You end up with a new context that doesn't contain any accommodated assumptions, and what the sentence ends up meaning is the following.

(50)   "Everybody who has a king and serves him will be rewarded."

Thus, Heim offers a way of reconciling the judgments that (3) has a universal ps with the judgments that it doesn't: she predicts that (3) has a "linguistic" universal ps, but argues that the hearers may perform local accommodation, and then the sentence has no "cognitive" ps.

I would like to note that the local accommodation under consideration restricts the quantification in (3) to persons who have kings. This fits with my impression of the data as reported in 10.3.3 above: indeed, (3) has a universal "cognitive" ps, unless there is an implicit restriction on the quantification which locally satisfies the original ps triggered by the definite NP.

Heim 1983b does not discuss this matter, but in fact her view that global accommodation is generally preferred to local would predict that (3) should normally be judged to have a "cognitive" universal ps, and would lose that ps only under threat of contradiction (or Quantity violation, or some such problem). This prediction does not hold, since in fact the disappearance of the universal ps of (3) is very natural and common. In my opinion, that is yet another indication that Roberts 1996a is right, and there is no inherent preference for global accommodation. (See section 9.4.) Local accommodation is often easily available even when global accommodation is an option too. Indeed, in the case of (3), the local accommodation in question is very well motivated, and should therefore be readily performed. Entering the additional restriction on the quantification is not a desperate repair strategy whose only purpose is to avoid ps failure. Rather – as is well known – the addition of implicit restrictions on quantification (sometimes called "domain selection") is a normal and common process that takes place almost always, whether or not there is a ps around that needs to be satisfied.

Finally, regarding examples like (2), Heim 1983b briefly notes that while her theory predicts the "linguistic" universal presupposition, when local accommodation is brought into play, this may result in a weaker "cognitive" ps, or none.

(2)   No nation cherishes its king.

Let us examine Heim's results in a bit more detail. First, let us go back to examples like (4).

(4)   Every nation cherishes its king.

Heim thinks that the predicted "linguistic" universal ps is fine. However, there is a further question, which Heim 1983b does not address: what about local accommodation? Wouldn't the option of performing local accommodation be available in the case of (4), as elsewhere, and wouldn't that predict that the universal ps may "disappear" here too?

I repeat the tripartite representation of (4) in (51) below. Since the ps trigger occurs in the nuclear scope, it looks like there are two different ways of performing local accommodation that would satisfy the ps: the information that y has a king can be accommodated either into the nuclear scope of (4), or into the restriction of (4).

(51)  DRT:

$$\boxed{\quad \boxed{\begin{array}{c} y \\ \text{nation}(y) \end{array}} \quad \Rightarrow \quad \boxed{\;y \text{ cherishes } y\text{'s king}\;}\quad}$$

FCS:   $\forall\ \underset{\text{C}}{(\text{nation}(y))}\ \underset{\text{D}}{(y \text{ cherishes } y\text{'s king})}$

Accommodation into the nuclear scope would be represented in DRT by simply entering into the nuclear scope DRS (=right-hand DRS) in (51) the condition y has a king. In FCS terms, accommodation into the nuclear scope means computing c + (4) as follows.

$$c + (4) =$$
$$\{\langle w,g\rangle \in c : \forall g',\, g' \supseteq g\ \&\ \langle w,g'\rangle \in c + C,\, \exists g'',\, g'' \supseteq g'\ \&\ \langle w,g''\rangle \in \underset{\underset{\text{accom}}{\text{local}}}{((c + C) + ps(D)) + D}\}$$

This accommodation would yield the interpretation "every nation has a king and cherishes its king," with (4) not having any ("cognitive") ps about kings.

Accommodation into the restriction would be represented in DRT by entering y has a king into the restriction DRS (=left-hand DRS) in (51). In FCS terms, it means computing c + (4) as follows.

$$c + (4) =$$
$$\{\langle w,g\rangle \in c : \forall g',\, g' \supseteq g\ \&\ \langle w,g'\rangle \in \underset{\underset{\text{accom}}{\text{local}}}{(c + C) + ps(D)},\, \exists g'',\, g'' \supseteq g'\ \&\ \langle w,g''\rangle \in \underset{\underset{\text{accom}}{\text{local}}}{((c + C) + ps(D)) + D}\}$$

This accommodation would yield the interpretation "every nation that has a king cherishes its king," again with (4) not having any ("cognitive") ps about kings.

We see then that if the two forms of local accommodation just indicated are possible for (4), then it is predicted that the universal ps of (4) would sometimes "disappear," and that then (4) would be interpreted either as in (52a) or as in (52b). Would that be the right prediction?

(52)  a.  "Every nation has a king and cherishes him."     (no ps)
      b.  "Every nation that has a king cherishes him."     (no ps)

The large majority of my informants feel that (52b) is a possible interpretation of (4), while (52a) is not. This suggests that local accommodation into the restriction is possible, while local accommodation into the nuclear scope is not. I think there is good reason to think that such is indeed the case.

Consider local accommodation into the restriction, which would yield the interpretation in (52b). My informants accept this interpretation, and we saw some evidence in 10.3.3 that it does indeed exist. Moreover, we have already seen some reason to expect that such accommodation would be readily performed, viz. the fact that it is an instance of the common process of adding implicit restrictions on quantification (= "domain selection"). It is quite possible for contextual information to restrict the quantification in (4) to nations with kings, completely independently of the need to satisfy the ps. In such an event, it should be very easy to get the interpretation in (52b), as indeed it is. Note that after the contextual restriction of the domain to nations (and tribes and states and clubs) that have kings, the predicted universal ps becomes "every nation that has a king has a king," so we might say that the universal ps is still there, but has become trivial.

Now consider local accommodation into the nuclear scope. I think it is quite clear indeed that the interpretation in (52a) is not available. Under such an interpretation, (4) would not presuppose that every nation has a king, but rather assert it. Surely, it is impossible to interpret (4) that way. Note also that (53) below does not have the interpretation "if every nation has a king and cherishes him, then all kings are lucky."

(53)    If every nation cherishes its king, then all kings are lucky.

Therefore, we need a way of blocking accommodation into the nuclear scope.

Note first that local accommodation into the nuclear scope is not independently motivated. It is much more common to add implicit restrictions on quantification than to implicitly alter the nuclear scope. So local accommodation into the nuclear scope would be a mere repair strategy whose sole motivation is to satisfy the ps. Hence, such accommodation should be difficult to perform.

Secondly, there might be something to the idea that global accommodation is ceteris paribus preferred to local. It might be the case that when local accommodation is nothing more than a repair strategy, global accommodation is indeed highly preferred relative to it. If so, I think there is some reason to expect that local accommodation into the nuclear scope should never be performed. Here is why. We saw that local accommodation into the nuclear scope of (4) is not independently motivated beyond the need to satisfy the ps. So the hearer should prefer to perform global accommodation, if possible. Therefore, local accommodation into the nuclear scope should occur only in case global accommodation contradicts what seems right or plausible to the hearer. What assumption would global accommodation contradict? Well, the assumption that **not** all nations have kings. However, local accommodation into the nuclear scope would not eliminate this contradiction. Global accommodation puts into the initial context the proposition that all nations have kings. Local accommodation into the nuclear scope would have the effect of making (4) assert that same proposition. So we get a contradiction either way. Hence, there is no reason to prefer the local accommodation into the nuclear scope, and global accommodation is preferred to it. (This leaves open the possibility that under the right circumstances, local accomodation into the restriction is preferred to both.)

Fred Landman (p.c.) notes that the reasoning just presented would not work for non-assertions. For example, why not accommodate "every nation has a king" into the nuclear scope in (54), resulting in the interpretation in (55)? I leave it to the reader to decide if (54) can actually be interpreted this way or not.

(54)  Does every nation cherish its king?
(55)  "Is it true that every nation has a king and cherishes him?"

We can now return to the exchange in (42) and see exactly why it sounds so strange.

(42)  A:  Not every nation has a king.
     B:  But every nation cherishes its king.

(42B) has a linguistic universal ps that contradicts (42A). Therefore, global accommodation is impossible. Local accommodation into the nuclear scope is impossible for the reasons just discussed. Local accommodation into the restriction is also impossible, because the context in which (42B) is uttered clearly suggests that the conversation is about nations with and without kings, and hence that the quantification in (42B) is not supposed to be restricted to just nations with kings. So ps failure is unavoidable.

Now, let us examine Heim's results concerning examples like (2). I assume that (2) is represented as in (56) below, and that the relevant ccp is as in (28), repeated below.

(2)  No nation cherishes its king.
(56)  no (nation(y)) (y cherishes y's king)
        C          D
(28)  $c + no (p) (q) = \{\langle w,g\rangle \in c : $ for no $g'$ which extends $g$ s.t. $\langle w,g'\rangle \in c + p$, is there a $g''$ which extends $g'$ s.t. $\langle w,g''\rangle \in (c + p) + q\}$

Heim is certainly right when she notes that allowing local accommodation to interact with filtering correctly predicts that example (2) need not have a "cognitive" universal ps. Accommodation into the restriction would be as follows, yielding the interpretation in (57).[5]

$c + (2) =$
$\{\langle w,g\rangle \in c : \forall g', g' \supseteq g \ \& \ \langle w,g'\rangle \in (c + C) + ps(D), \nexists g'', \langle w,g''\rangle \in ((c + C) + ps(D)) + D\}$
                           local                       local
                          accom                 accom

(57)  "No nation that has a king cherishes him."  (no ps)

However, this prediction seems too weak. Don't we also need to predict that (2) **never** has a "cognitive" universal ps? After all, the intuition, as reported in 10.3.3, seems to be that (2) has no "cognitive" ps at all.

Thus, in the case of (2), we run into the same problem that we ran into with regard to the existential example (1): Heim's theory does not explain why the "linguistic" universal ps doesn't ever show up as "cognitive." Even worse, Heim's theory does not explain why (1) and (2) contrast in that respect with (4) and (3). Why is it that examples like (4) and (3) can retain their universal ps, but examples like (1) and (2) cannot?

---

[5]  Accommodation into the nuclear scope, if possible, would yield the equivalent interpretation "no nation is s.t. it has a king and cherishes him."

What is it that blocks global accommodation of the universal ps into the initial context in the case of (1) and (2), without blocking it in the case of (4) and (3)?

(1)   A fat man was pushing his bicycle.
(2)   No nation cherishes its king.
(3)   Everyone who serves his king will be rewarded.
(4)   Every nation cherishes its king.

The problem seems like a serious one. At least initially, and with the examples presented out of context, the intuitive contrast between (4) and (2) seems quite clear: (4) presupposes that every nation has a king, and (2) does not. But the two examples are so similar in how their ccp is computed, that the theory cannot but make the same prediction for both, and it is hard to see where the difference might lie.

Well then, perhaps we should discard the ccp in (28), and replace it with a ccp for no (p) (q) that will turn the operator no (p) into a "plug" for ps. We would have to use a ccp as in (58).

(58)   $c + no$ (p) (q) = {$\langle w,g\rangle \in c$ : for no $g'$ which extends g s.t. $\langle w,g'\rangle \in c + p$, is there a $g''$ which extends $g'$ s.t. $\langle w,g''\rangle \in ((c + p) + ps(q)) + q$}

In other words, we would have to claim that at some point – in fact, "locally" – ps(q) gets added to the context.[6] This is of course just like using (28) plus local accommodation in that ps(q) is entered "locally" and that's what's going to keep (2) from presupposing that every nation has a king. But there is also a crucial difference. While entering ps(q) by local accommodation is optional, the insertion of ps(q) as dictated by (58) is obligatory. Therefore, (58) guarantees that (2) will never presuppose that every nation has a king.

However, positing (58) seems like a rather ad hoc solution. In fact, it destroys a major advantage of Heim's local-accommodation-based account of ps "disappearance." What was nice about Heim's account, we always thought, was precisely the fact that it eliminated the need for positing "plug" interpretations. And here we go and posit a "plug" interpretation again.

Note that if the contrast between (1),(2) and (3),(4) is real, then Beaver's approach of not predicting the "linguistic" universal ps for any of our existential and quantified examples is not going to solve all our problems either. It would work well for (1) and (2), but not for (3) and (4).

At this point, one might want to go back and re-examine the data; after all, the kind of judgment involved tends to be quite tricky. The contrast between (1),(2) and (3),(4) seems real, but perhaps it is not as sharp as all that. One could, perhaps, maintain the view that all four examples actually behave more or less alike. After all, it is hard to prove that (1) and (2) **never** have a "cognitive" universal ps (regarding (1), see 10.2.4 above). One might claim that all four examples easily have interpretations without any "cognitive" ps, and can also potentially have a "cognitive" universal ps. One might claim that there is a continuum of how easy it is to judge that the universal statement is presupposed: very easy with (4), harder with (3), even harder though not impossible with

---

[6]   As noted in section 8.2, I don't think there are any other ways of creating "plug" interpretations. See discussion there.

(1) and (2). Finally, one might hypothesize that the universal ps comes to mind more easily in the case of (4) and (3) simply because these examples themselves take the form of universal statements.

In sum, we saw in this chapter that Heim 1983b makes a series of correct predictions concerning the presuppositional properties of existential and quantified statements, using local and global accommodation. (In all examples under consideration, a "linguistic" universal ps is predicted, which indeed shows up empirically in examples like (4) and (3). Due to accommodation, the universal ps need not become "cognitive," as indeed reflected in the empirical facts.) That's in addition to explaining the behavior of negation as a "plug" under threat of contradiction (section 9.2.1). So Heim's overall theory seems quite general and successful. At the same time, Heim's theory seems to face a serious problem with examples like (1) and (2), since it doesn't explain the impression that the universal ps never shows up empirically in these examples.

### 10.3.5  Beaver: quantified statements without local accommodation?

In 10.2.5 above, I presented Beaver's modification of Heim's theory of ps projection. We saw that for existential examples like (1), Beaver's theory does not predict a "linguistic" universal ps, and predicts instead a "linguistic" conditional existential ps. The same is true for our quantified examples. Take for instance example (3). Let us assume that (3) is represented as in (59). I repeat the relevant ccp in (29).

$$(59) \quad \forall \quad \underbrace{(\text{person}(y) \wedge y \text{ serves y's king})}_{\displaystyle \underbrace{\phantom{xxxxxxxxxxxxxxxxxxx}}_{G} \begin{array}{c} G' \qquad\qquad\quad G'' \end{array}} \quad \underbrace{(y \text{ will be rewarded})}_{H}$$

(29)  $c + \forall(p)(q) = \{\langle w,g \rangle \in c :$ for every $g'$ which extends $g$ s.t. $\langle w,g' \rangle \in c + p$, there is a $g''$ which extends $g'$ s.t. $\langle w,g'' \rangle \in (c + p) + q\}$

Note that $c + G = (c + G') + G''$. Formula $G''$ has a ps: $ps(G'') = y$ has a king. $ps(G'')$ has to be satisfied by the context $c + G'$, and on Beaver's theory that means that $c + G'$ must satisfy the condition that for every $\langle w,g \rangle \in c + G'$, $\exists f$ s.t. $\langle w,f \rangle \in (c + G') + y$ has a king. So $c + G'$ must entail that there is some person who has a king. Hence $c$ must entail that if there is a person, there is a person who has a king. We see, then, that Beaver's theory predicts no universal ps, and that it predicts the "linguistic" ps in (3'') below. Similarly, the "linguistic" pss predicted for (2) and (4) are the ones in (2'') and (4'').

(2'')  If there is a nation,                                        (conditional existential ps)
       there is a nation that has a king.
(3'')  If there is a person,                                        (conditional existential ps)
       there is a person who has a king.
(4'')  If there is a nation,                                        (conditional existential ps)
       there is a nation that has a king.

And what is the "cognitive" ps that Beaver predicts? Consider (3). In a context that does not entail the "linguistic" ps, that exact ps would have to be accommodated at some point before formula G″ is processed. That is because on Beaver's theory, the requirement on the local context of G″ is that it entail a certain piece of factual information, rather than information about a discourse referent. G″ can be processed only if its local context entails that some person has a king. We would have the two hypothetical options given in (60) (accommodation underlined, ps asserted à la Beaver italicized).

(60)  a.  $c + (3″) + (3) = \{\langle w,g \rangle \in c + (3″) :$ for every g′ which extends g s.t. $\langle w,g′ \rangle \in$ $(c + (3″) + G′) + y$ *has a king* $+ G″$, there is a g″ which extends g′ s.t. $\langle w,g″ \rangle \in ((c + (3″) + G′) + y$ *has a king* $+ G″)$ $+ H\}$

   b.  $c + (3) = \{\langle w,g \rangle \in c :$ for every g′ which extends g s.t. $\langle w,g′ \rangle \in (c + G′) + (3″)$ $+ y$ *has a king* $+ G″$, there is a g″ which extends g′ s.t. $\langle w,g″ \rangle \in ((c$ $+ G′) + (3″) + y$ *has a king* $+ G″) + H\}$

Option (60a) – i.e. global accommodation – would turn the conditional "linguistic" ps into a "cognitive" one. If it happens to be already assumed in the context that the antecedent of the conditional is true, this option would result in an intuition that (3) presupposes (3‴) below.

(3‴)  There is a person who has a king.              (existential ps)

On the other hand, option (60b) – i.e. local accommodation into the restriction – would determine that there is no "cognitive" ps at all. As far as I can see, the interpretation based on (60b) would be as in (61). But that's equivalent to (62), and hence to (63). This seems unnecessarily complicated, perhaps, but it is an OK result empirically.

(61)  For every person y s.t. [(if there is a person,) some person has a king] and y has a king and y serves his king, y will be rewarded.
(62)  If it is true that [(if there is a person,) some person has a king], then every person who has a king and serves him will be rewarded.
(63)  Every person who has a king and serves him will be rewarded.

Note that on Beaver's theory the interpretation of (3) is always "every person who has a king and serves him will be rewarded." On Heim's theory, this interpretation was the result of locally accommodating y has a king into the restriction, and was never accompanied by a ps. On Beaver's theory, this interpretation may or may not be accompanied by the ps in (3″) (or the one in (3‴)), depending on whether the accommodation is global, as in (60a), or local, as in (60b).

Similar results hold for examples (2) and (4). Global accommodation would result in (2) and (4) either inheriting the "linguistic" ps as is, or having the "cognitive" existential ps in (2‴) = (4‴).

(2‴) = (4‴) There is a nation that has a king.              (existential ps)

Local accommodation – be it into the restriction or into the nuclear scope – would determine that there is no "cognitive" ps at all. The interpretation of (2) and (4) would depend on whether the ps (about the discourse referent) gets asserted as part of the restriction or as part of the nuclear scope (Beaver doesn't say which it is). The interpretation would be either "no/every nation that has a king cherishes him" or "no/every nation has a king and cherishes him." (With or without an accompanying existential ps, depending on the type of accommodation used.)

As discussed in 10.3.3, I believe that the ps-less interpretations are possible and natural, and I think – though I admit that this judgment is somewhat tricky – that Beaver's conditional existential or existential pss do not show up empirically.

Let us take stock. As discussed in 10.2.5, Beaver's results about existential statements like (1) are not that different from Heim's. The same holds for (2). For (1) and (2), both theories predict a "linguistic" ps that seems to never show up empirically. Both theories allow the ps to disappear due to accommodation. As for examples like (3) and (4), Beaver predicts an existential ps that does not seem to show up empirically, while Heim predicts a universal ps that does seem to show up empirically (more clearly so in the case of (4)). This suggests that Heim's predictions are superior to Beaver's. How would Beaver explain the fact that a universal ps does show up empirically? (Beaver 1983b does not discuss examples like (4).)

(One might try to argue that the alleged "cognitive" universal ps of (4) and (3) is nothing more than a possible default assumption that would render local accommodation plausible. However, that would fail to explain why the intuition that the universal statement is presupposed persists even when that statement is assumed to be false, as in example (42).)

(42)  A:  Not every nation has a king.
      B:  But every nation cherishes its king.

## 10.4  Conclusion

I conclude that Beaver's predictions seem to be inferior to Heim's. I also see no reason to revise what I said in 10.2.5 above: I think that Heim's theory is simpler and conceptually more natural, and I think that Beaver's goal of doing without local (or local in sense #1) accommodation has not been reached, since on his theory too, the perfectly natural (and often the most natural) ps-less interpretations would have to be based on such accommodation.

In general, I think that the examples of this chapter provide further support for the view of accommodation presented in section 9.4. Local accommodation (as well as accommodation which is local in sense #1 only) is not inherently dispreferred, and can be readily executed when well motivated beyond the need to repair ps failure. Given this assumption, most of the facts regarding our existential and quantified examples can be dealt with in a simple and natural manner. We easily derive the natural ps-less interpretations. Also, we are able to distinguish between the available and unavailable interpretations of examples like (4), based on the idea that local accommodation into a restriction can be quite natural (since it is "domain selection"), whereas local accommodation into a nuclear scope is unnatural (since it is not independently motivated).

# 11

# *Presupposition Triggering and the Behavior of Presuppositions*

In the preceding chapters, I said very little about how pss are triggered. I would like to address this issue now. There is a debate in the literature: some hold that pss (or at least some "hard-core" pss) are grammatical properties of their triggers, whereas others hold that pss (or at least some of them) are based on conversational principles. I think that it is in fact very difficult to find solid empirical support for any of the different views on ps triggering. In this chapter, I will examine a number of relevant arguments, and argue that they are inconclusive. Some researchers try to draw a line between two sets of pss which are taken to behave differently, and suggest that they differ in their mode of triggering. I will show that the behavior of pss of all types – from the most easily disappearing pss that are clearly conversational implicatures up to the most stable and robust looking pss in existence – is more uniform than has often been assumed in the literature, defying such attempts.

## 11.1   Conventional Triggering vs. Conversational Triggering

To facilitate discussion, let me first present some terminology that I will be using. First of all, I follow Chierchia and McConnell-Ginet 1990 in making a distinction between

   (i)   **conventionally triggered implications** – implications determined by the grammar (plus a logic) alone; and
   (ii)  **conversationally triggered implications** – implications which require further non-linguistic premises.

(Conventionally triggered implications include entailments and Grice's conventional implicatures; conversationally triggered implications include Grice's conversational implicatures (both generalized and particularized).)

Let me give a couple of examples. Take the fact that sentence (1) implies that Sue is no more than competent at linguistics. This is a classic example of an implication which is triggered conversationally – we have here a scalar implicature, based on conversational principles, which are not part of the grammar.

(1)    Sue is competent at linguistics.

Consider, in contrast, the Kamp–Heim view on how the existential ps of definite NPs is triggered. According to the Kamp–Heim theory of definite NPs, the triggering of this ps is conventional – it is due to a grammatical property of definite NPs: a definite is translated as an old discourse referent; if there is no appropriate antecedent in the context, the definite cannot be processed.

Another point of terminology concerns the term *presupposition* itself. K&P 1979 treat conventional triggering as a defining characteristic of pss. But that is a terminological decision that they made. We can choose between the following two options.

  (i)    We decide to call everything that is intuitively felt to be "taken for granted" by the sentence/utterance a "ps" of that sentence/utterance. In other words, we call everything which is felt to be a requirement on the context a ps.
  (ii)   We decide to define as a "ps" only that which is both "taken for granted" and "conventional."

K&P 1979 chose the second option, and their choice may have been fairly influential.[1] Yet I prefer the terminology indicated in (i); this terminology is in accordance with Stalnaker's original usage, and is also adopted in Chierchia and McConnell-Ginet 1990. Stalnaker 1974 (see especially pp. 203–6) says the following. Characterizing pss as requirements on the context is a description of the facts (i.e. of our intuitions about the phenomenon that we call "ps"). How these facts should be explained (i.e. **why** the ps is there = how it is triggered) is a different question. Perhaps in some cases the ps facts have a semantic explanation, but probably, in other cases the explanation is Gricean. The terminology I will adopt, then, is the one on which whatever is intuitively "taken for granted" is a ps.

  In this chapter, I will be concerned with the question of how pss are triggered – are some or all of them triggered conventionally? are some or all of them triggered conversationally? The reason that we take this to be a contentful question is that we assume that the mode of triggering will matter. We expect that the behavior of various implications will reflect their particular mode of triggering. In particular, we expect that implications triggered conversationally – but not implications triggered conventionally – are going to be what we often call "defeasible."

  I think the term "defeasible" is misleading. "Defeasible" could mean various things. For example, on the Gazdar–Soames theory of ps projection, saying that a ps is "defeasible" means that a ps can be canceled. Being cancelable is, I think, a strange and unexplained property to attribute to pss (see chapter 6), and is not really the sort of "defeasibility" found with conversational implicatures. There is no correlation between being cancelable and being conversationally triggered; indeed, on the Gazdar–Soames theory, a ps is both conventionally triggered and cancelable. I think that when we talk

---

[1]    K&P 1979 take pss to be a non-truth-conditional aspect of meaning and so (as they are part of the meaning and yet not truth-conditional) to fall under Grice's conventional implicatures. I agree with Levinson 1983 that assimilating pss to conventional implicatures is a terminological decision: I think it is precisely choosing to limit the term ps to things "conventional."

about "defeasibility" in the context of conversational implicatures, a more suitable term is "context-dependence."

What characterizes conversational implicatures, then, is that they are context-dependent. For example, take (2) and (3) below. B's utterance gives rise to a scalar implicature (that B doesn't have more than two dogs) in (2) but not in (3), because of the difference in what would count as relevant information in the given context.

(2)  A:  And what animals do you have?
     B:  I have two dogs.
(3)  A:  One dog won't be enough. We need somebody who could show up with two.
     B:  I have two dogs.

Cancellation-after-the-fact of conversational implicatures can also be described in terms of context-dependence. For example, I would describe what happens in (4) below as follows. When one hears the first sentence, out of the blue, one tends to imagine that in the (unknown) context of utterance, precise numbers of objects are relevant information. Hence, the hearer tends to get a scalar implicature. Hearing the second sentence, one says to oneself: "Oops, I was wrong, the precise number couldn't have been all that relevant, or the speaker would have said 'three dogs' right away; I wasn't meant to get a scalar implicature."

(4)  I have two dogs. In fact, I have three.

In short, some major motivation for distinguishing between the two modes of triggering would be differences in context-dependence. The clear context-dependence of conversational implicatures is nicely explained, since they are based on principles which involve considerations of relevance in context. If we find implications that are not context-dependent, that would be naturally explained by saying that they are strictly determined by a convention of the grammar.

Let us now turn to the different views about pss triggering.

It is common among filtering theorists to assume, explicitly or implicitly, that pss are triggered conventionally. Certainly, filtering theorists assume that at least some hard-core pss are triggered conventionally – for example the existential ps of definites, and the pss of *stop* and of *too*. In fact, the filtering theory of ps projection as it is usually formulated applies only to conventionally triggered pss. Recall that on the Stalnaker–Karttunen–Heim theory, a ps is defined as follows.

(5)  B is a ps of S iff S can be felicitously uttered only in contexts that entail B.

This definition does not apply to pss that are context-dependent, since it says that **all** the contexts in which a sentence can be felicitously uttered must satisfy (= entail) its ps. Hence, filtering as it stands does not apply to conversationally triggered pss.

At the same time, there are many researchers who argue that various pss are conversationally triggered. For example, Boër and Lycan 1976 argue for conversational triggering of a number of pss (e.g. existential pss of definite NPs, factive pss, the ps of *manage*). Kempson 1975 and Wilson 1975 argue that factive pss are conversationally triggered, and later on Levinson 1983 and Chierchia and McConnell-Ginet 1990 too argue for this view. The different researchers differ on whether they take all pss to be triggered conversationally, or just a subset of them. Chierchia and McConnell-Ginet 1990 claim that some pss (e.g. the factive pss) are conversationally triggered, while other pss are conventionally triggered. I think it is fair to say that Boër and Lycan 1976 as well as Levinson 1983 would argue that all pss are in fact conversational implicatures.[2]

It seems clear to me that the major motivation behind the view that pss are conventionally triggered is an impression that, empirically, pss are not context-dependent, and that in that respect they differ essentially from conversational implicatures.

Now, it can't be an entirely straightforward and indisputable fact that, empirically, pss are not context-dependent. After all, the filtering theorists have run into a lot of cases of ps "disappearance," and have had to find ways of dealing with them, as discussed in the preceding chapters. In my opinion, the impression that, empirically, pss are not context-dependent is based on two facts. One, the fact that a typical hard-core ps is entailed by the simple affirmative clause containing the trigger. For example, the fact that (6) entails (7).

(6)   Sue stopped smoking.
(7)   Sue smoked.

Two, there is a feeling that a typical hard-core ps doesn't "disappear" as easily as a typical conversational implicature – it seems that while it is easy to find contexts where an implicature won't arise, one has to look harder to find contexts where a "hard-core" ps will "disappear."

The motivation for the conversationalist's view comes from the opposite impression: the impression that pss **are** context-dependent. This can be divided into two parts. First of all, even if we concentrate just on hard-core pss and the familiar facts about them, one might prefer to see as more significant the fact that these pss do "disappear" sometimes. This fact is explained automatically and without recourse to local accommodation only by the conversationalist's approach. Secondly, one might try to find empirical evidence showing that pss, or some pss, are in fact more context-dependent than is often assumed. If, for example, some pss are clearly context-dependent in a way that the typical hard-core pss are not, that would lend much plausibility to the view that some pss are conversationally triggered while others are conventionally triggered.

Before I start to examine arguments in support of one or the other of the views of ps triggering, let me concentrate on some familiar data on hard-core pss, and sketch a preliminary comparison of a conventionalist's account of triggering and a conversationalist's account of triggering. Consider sentences (6) and (8) and their ps in (7).

(6)   Sue stopped smoking.
(8)   Sue didn't stop smoking.
(7)   Sue smoked.

**A conventionalist's account:** We take pss to be conventional and not context-dependent. This automatically explains the fact that (6) **entails** (7): a ps is simply some-

[2]   Boër and Lycan and Levinson argue that some alleged pss are nothing but entailments, and they only invoke conversational principles in the rest of the cases. But I think that means just what I said in the text: they would argue that all real pss (rather than mere entailments) are conversationally triggered.

thing which is always there, it can't fail to be implied. And why does the negative sentence (8) also presuppose (7)? This fact is explained by saying that negation is a "hole" to ps, and therefore the ps of (6) is automatically "inherited" by (8).

There is also a problem: in (9) below, (8) does not seem to presuppose (7); but if negation is a "hole" and pss are not "defeasible," how come the ps "disappeared"?

(9)   Sue didn't stop smoking – she never used to smoke!

However, there are a number of ways in which this problem can be overcome. For example, by saying that in (9) we have "metalinguistic negation," or by invoking local accommodation.

**A conversationalist's account:** On the conversational triggering account, (7) would be a conversational implicature of (6) and of (8). Or rather, we would have to say more than that: we would have to say that (6) and (8) **conversationally implicate that (7) is taken for granted**. (After all, we need to explain the fact that (7) is felt to be presupposed = taken for granted.) I think that it is perfectly plausible that, indeed, (6) and (8) often conversationally implicate that (7) is taken for granted. The Gricean argument would be, roughly, this: if it is not already taken for granted that Sue smoked, why would it be relevant to discuss the issue of whether she stopped or not?

Of course, the conversational triggering account wouldn't have any problem with (9) above: this would simply be an instance of the well-known phenomenon of a conversational implicature getting canceled. No need to invoke local accommodation or any special explanation.

And what about the fact that (6) **entails** (7)? Well, we are used to thinking that this should be explained by the theory of ps, but perhaps it need not be so explained. I think it makes perfectly good sense to say that (6) – but not (8) – happens to entail (7), due to the semantics of *stop*. One might hold that the implication that both (6) and (8) **take it for granted** that (7) holds is independent, and is based on conversational principles.

Concerning the fact that not only the affirmative (6) but also the negative (8) presupposes (7), I have already suggested a Gricean explanation that would work for both (6) and (8): since both (6) and (8) seem to be about whether Sue stopped smoking or not, both may appear to require the prior assumption that Sue smoked in order to seem relevant. Let me note also that in my opinion, ps inheritance under negation can perfectly well be explained just as it is explained on the conventionalist's view: I think there is nothing to prevent us from relying on the idea that negation is a "hole" to ps, regardless of the mode of triggering of the ps. Here I agree with Chierchia and McConnell-Ginet 1990, who hold that ps projection is independent of the mode of triggering. For more on this, see section 11.3 below.

In conclusion, I don't see that either of the two accounts just sketched is a priori more plausible than the other.

## 11.2   Some Fairly Clear Examples of Conversationally-Triggered pss

There are certain pss that are so clearly context-dependent, that it is hard to deny that they are in fact conversational implicatures. Two cases of the sort I am interested in are (i) certain pss of reports on speech–acts, and (ii) certain pss of subjunctive conditionals. Both of these cases are discussed, and attributed to Gricean principles, in Boër and Lycan 1976 as well as in K&P 1979. Another case is the "factive ps" of *before*, noted in Levinson 1983.

Consider some examples.

(10)   Sue promised John an official invitation.
(10′)  John wanted an official invitation.

(11)   If Shakespeare were the author of Macbeth, there would be proof in the Globe Theater's records for the year 1605.
(11′)  Shakespeare is not the author of Macbeth.

(12)   Sue cried before she finished her thesis.
(12′)  Sue finished her thesis.

(10) may imply (10′), (11) may imply (11′), and (12) may imply (12′). I think that all these implications are fairly prominent out of the blue. On the terminology I have adopted, these implications are, in fact, pss. That is because the intuition is not merely that it is implied that proposition (10′) or (11′) or (12′) is true, but rather that it is implied that the proposition in question is being **taken for granted**. (Note also that these implications survive in the "family of sentences": like other pss, they tend to also be implied by the corresponding denials, questions, etc. I will return to this issue in section 11.3 below.)

The pss just noted are all quite clearly context-dependent. While the typical hard-core ps is entailed by the simple affirmative clause containing the trigger, the pss discussed here clearly are not. The pss discussed here will arise in some contexts but not others. To briefly go through the three cases: that (10) does not entail (10′) is illustrated by the fact that (13) and (14) are not contradictions;

(13)   Sue promised John an official invitation. That was a nice gesture, perhaps, but it didn't really do him much good, since he never wanted an official invitation.
(14)   Sue promised John an official invitation. All she really meant was to annoy him, though; she knew very well that he didn't want to be invited.

(11) does not entail (11′), since (11) would be felicitous in a situation where we don't know if Shakespeare wrote Macbeth or not, and are trying, without prejudice, to think of possible evidence that would decide this question; as for example (12), it becomes perfectly clear that *before* does not entail the truth of the before-clause, if you consider sentence (15).

(15)   Sue died before she finished her thesis.

The extent to which pss (10′), (11′) and (12′) are context-dependent strongly suggests that they are conversational implicatures. And, indeed, it seems possible to construct suitable Gricean arguments that will account for them.

Take, for example, (11′). (11′) can be derived by a Gricean argument based on the fact that (11) cannot be used in a context where it is taken for granted that Shakespeare did write Macbeth, which seems to be a solid fact. K&P's way of expressing this fact is by proposing that a subjunctive conditional $p \rightarrow q$ presupposes (conventionally) that

¬p is an epistemic possibility. Given that the speaker is able to use (11), if we make the additional assumption that she has the information about the authorship of Macbeth, it follows that she must be assuming that Shakespeare did **not** write Macbeth – i.e. she must be assuming (11'). Of course, in contexts where the speaker is not assumed to have the information about the authorship of Macbeth, this Gricean reasoning won't apply, and that is why in the context given above (we are honestly looking for evidence to settle the authorship question), there is no intuition that the speaker is taking (11') for granted.

K&P 1979 suggest that (10') is derived by a Gricean argument that goes something like this.

(16)    A "preparatory condition" (à la Searle 1965) for performing the speech act of promising John an official invitation is for John to want one. Normally, since speakers cooperate and follow certain norms of trust, it can be assumed that when one performs a speech act, its preparatory conditions hold. Hence one would normally assume that if Sue promised John something, he wanted it. Therefore, if the speaker of (10) had known that that was not the case, (s)he would have given us this relevant information rather than mislead us. So we get the implicature (10'), that John wanted an official invitation.

This argument is actually not good enough. As K&P admit, it doesn't explain the intuition that (10') is not just implied, but is implied to be taken for granted. In my opinion, the implicature that (10') is taken for granted comes from the hearer's attempt to imagine why (10) might be a relevant thing to say. The hearer easily imagines that the piece of contextual information that makes (10) relevant is that John wants an invitation, and that (10) is a speculation on John's chances of getting his wish fulfilled.

I believe that the implication of (12) that (12') is taken for granted is also due to the hearer's guess about why it is that (12) is a relevant thing to say. (12) would be relevant, for example, in a context where the question under consideration is "when did Sue cry," but only provided that Sue's finishing her thesis is an event that occurred and can help with the timing of Sue's crying. (12) would also be relevant in a context where we are interested in the amount of pain that Sue's finishing her thesis gave her, on the assumption that that is an event that occurred. It is harder to imagine a context where (12) is relevant despite the fact that Sue did not finish her thesis. Hence, the hearer tends to imagine that (12') is being taken for granted.

Of course, trying to imagine some contextual assumptions which would render the current utterance relevant is a classical trigger of implicatures. For example, take the classical case of B's utterance in (17).

(17)    A:    I am out of petrol.
        B:    There is a garage around the corner.
(18)    The garage has petrol to sell.
(19)    Garages (generally) have petrol to sell.

B's utterance implicates (18) – or perhaps it rather implicates (19). This implicature is based on the hearer's attempt to imagine what it is that makes B's utterance relevant. Now, this implicature too is a ps: it is my judgment that B's utterance doesn't merely imply (18) or (19), but it rather implies that B takes it for granted that (18) or (19) holds. I believe, more generally, that many conversational implicatures based on the hearer's wish to find out why an utterance is giving relevant information in its context are in fact pss.

I think that it is by no means surprising that conversationally triggered pss vary a lot in how easily "defeasible" they appear to be. Surely, for some utterances it would be easy to imagine all sorts of contexts where they would be relevant, and for other utterances it would be harder. The more easily and prominently contexts in which the ps holds come to mind, the less "defeasible" that ps appears to be.

I also think that this line of thought can be taken a step further: it could be that in some cases it would be so difficult to imagine a context where the ps is not assumed but the utterance is still relevant, that the ps would make the impression of being "non-defeasible." In other words, if there is a continuum of conversationally triggered pss that are harder and harder to "defeat," there is no reason why there shouldn't be, at one end of this continuum, some pss that are so hard to "defeat" that we are tempted to regard them as conventionally triggered. This means that if we take the view that all pss are conversational implicatures, it might still be possible to explain the impression that the typical hard-core pss are not context-dependent.

## 11.3   ps Triggering and ps Projection

It is worth checking if by observing the projection behavior of various kinds of pss and implicatures it might be possible to find some support for one or another of the views on ps triggering.

K&P 1979 argue that the ps of subjunctive conditionals differs in its projection behavior from those pss that they regard as "real" pss (= conventionally triggered pss). I think this could potentially be interesting, since I think that, in principle, showing dissimilarity in behavior is a pretty good argument for differing analyses. To find a clear difference in projection behavior here could support the idea that the two classes of pss are triggered differently. However, I think that K&P's argument is not valid.

K&P claim that the implication (20′) of (20) doesn't survive under negation or under a modal, and that that shows that (20′) is not a ps.

(20)   If it were raining outside, the drumming on the roof would drown out our voices.
(20′)  It is not raining outside.
(21)   It is not the case that if it were raining outside, the drumming on the roof would drown out our voices.
(22)   It is unlikely that if it were raining outside, the drumming on the roof would drown out our voices.

I think K&P are wrong about the facts. If (20) is spoken and heard, then the participants in the conversation can be sure that their voices are not being drowned out by rain. Therefore, it so happens that if (20) is spoken and heard, it actually **entails** (20′), by modus tollens. Now I grant that there is a clear contrast between (20) and (21)–(22). But the contrast is that the former entails (20′) while the latter do not, a contrast which doesn't bear on the inheritance of (20′) **as a ps**. Besides being entailed by (20), (20′) is also presupposed by (20), i.e. taken for granted by it. I think that as a ps, (20′) does survive in (21) and (22): (21) and (22) are quite as likely to imply that (20′) is taken for granted as (20) is.

The fact of the matter seems to be that all pss exhibit the same projection behavior. There is even considerable similarity between the projection behavior of pss and of non-presuppositional implicatures.

Levinson 1983, pp. 223–4, argues that the familiar projection behavior of pss is paralleled by the projection behavior of conversational implicatures. Levinson gives one example: the conversational implicature (24) of (23). He says that the implicature (24) survives in (25), just like a ps, and is "filtered out" in (26), again just like a ps.

(23)   John has some of the tools.
(24)   (Speaker knows that) John has not got all of the tools.
(25)   It's possible that John has some of the tools.
(26)   John has some of the tools, if not all of them.

I think Levinson is right about (25), and that, generally, conversational implicatures survive in the "family of sentences." (Examples will be given below.) I don't think, on the other hand, that Levinson's example (26) really shows that implicatures get "filtered out." When we say that a ps gets "filtered out" we mean that it gets satisfied by the local context. But there is no ps to be satisfied by the context when it comes to an implicature like (24). It doesn't make sense to talk about non-presuppositional implicatures as being "filtered out."[3]

But let us concentrate on conversational implicatures which are pss. I find that the projection behavior of pss that are clearly conversationally triggered exactly parallels the familiar projection behavior of hard-core pss.

Let us consider again examples like the ones discussed in section 11.2 above. (10) implicates (10″), (27) implicates (27″), (12) implicates (12″), and B's utterance in (28) implicates (28″). These implicatures are context-dependent, so they do not always arise; yet out of the blue, they are quite likely to arise.

(10)   Sue promised John an official invitation.
(10″)  It is being taken for granted that John wanted an official invitation.

(27)   If it were raining outside, it would be possible to hear the rain through that window over there.
(27″)  It is being taken for granted that it is not raining outside.

(12)   Sue cried before she finished her thesis.
(12″)  It is being taken for granted that Sue finished her thesis.

(28)   A:   I have to pay my water bill.
        B:   There is a post office around the corner.
(28″)  It is being taken for granted that water bills can be paid at post offices.

---

[3]   It is true of course that (26) doesn't implicate (24) – that's presumably because the if-clause implicates that for all the speaker knows, it is possible that John has all the tools. Note that (24) doesn't survive in (i), either. These are cases of implicature cancellation which have nothing to do with "filtering."

   (i)   If John has some of the tools, he has all of them.

Do these implicatures survive in the "family of sentences"? Yes, I believe they do. I think that the sentences below have the same implicature as the corresponding simple affirmative. (29)–(32) still imply (10″), (33)–(35) still imply (27″), (36)–(38) still imply (12″), B's utterance in (39)–(40) still implies (28″). As before, the implications do not always arise; after all, they are conversational implicatures. But, also as before, they are quite likely to arise out of the blue.

(29)  Sue didn't promise John an official invitation.
(30)  Maybe Sue promised John an official invitation.
(31)  Did Sue promise John an official invitation?
(32)  If Sue promised John an official invitation, then Bill will be upset.

(33)  It is not the case that if it were raining outside, it would be possible to hear the rain through that window over there.
(34)  Perhaps if it were raining outside, it would be possible to hear the rain through that window over there.
(35)  Is it true that if it were raining outside, it would be possible to hear the rain through that window over there?

(36)  It is not true that Sue cried before she finished her thesis.
(37)  It is quite likely that Sue cried before she finished her thesis.
(38)  Did Sue cry before she finished her thesis?

(39)  A:  I have to pay my water bill.
      B:  There isn't a post office anywhere around here.
(40)  A:  I have to pay my water bill.
      B:  Is there a post office around here?
(41)  A:  I have to pay my water bill.
      B:  If there is a post office nearby, I'll be going there anyway.

In addition, the implicatures under consideration seem to behave just like ordinary hard-core pss in that they get satisfied by the local context. For example, (42) as a whole and (43) as a whole do not imply (10″), and (44) as a whole does not imply (27″). In these sentences, the conversationally triggered ps is satisfied internally.

(42)  John really wanted to be invited, and Sue promised him an official invitation.
(43)  If John really wanted to be invited, then Sue promised him an official invitation.
(44)  It is not raining outside, but if it were raining outside, the rain would not be disturbing us.

What do we learn from the uniform projection behavior? For one thing, we learn that one can't base an argument for dividing pss into conversationally triggered vs. conventionally triggered on dissimilarity in projection behavior. But can we also draw some more positive conclusion?

One might think that the uniform projection behavior actually argues in favor of a uniform analysis of ps triggering. Presumably, in favor of treating all pss as conversationally triggered. The idea would be that if some pss are treated as conversationally triggered while others are treated as conventionally triggered, then the uniform projection behavior remains unexplained. However, I don't think this argument is valid. Do we have any good reason to assume that the mode of triggering of pss is crucial in determining their projection behavior? I don't think so. It could very well be the case that the similarity in projection behavior is due to general principles that are independent of the mode of triggering.

Indeed, the filtering theory of ps projection makes no reference to the mode of triggering. To cite Chierchia and McConnell-Ginet 1990 (p. 313):

> While there can be two sources for pss, we would expect that their projection properties are the same, since the ccp of nonatomic sentences is independent of how the pss of atomic sentences are triggered.

Of course the definition of ps which is assumed by the filtering theory as it is usually formulated (as in (5) above or (45) below) does not allow for context-dependence of pss. However, this definition can be revised. Once we have a definition of ps that allows for context-dependence, the filtering theory will be able to apply to conversationally triggered pss exactly as it applies to conventionally triggered pss.

Chierchia and McConnell-Ginet 1990 suggest that definition (45) could be replaced by the definition in (46),

(45)   S presupposes B iff
       S can be felicitously uttered in a context c
       only if c entails B.
(46)   S presupposes B relative to a set of premises $P$ iff
       S can be felicitously uttered in a context c in which premises $P$ hold
       only if c entails B.

where the set $P$ includes premises about human actions, and in particular Gricean conversational principles, and possibly also more specific premises. Definition (46) covers the fact that a conversationally triggered ps may arise in some contexts and fail to arise in other contexts. $P$ is a characterization of those contexts in which the ps will arise. For example, take sentence (47) below and its ps (47′). The conversational implicature that (47′) is taken for granted arises in some contexts and not others. The contexts in which it does arise are, roughly, those contexts in which (48) holds. Which is reflected by the fact that definition (46) allows us to not simply define (47′) as a ps of (47), but rather define (47′) as a ps of (47) relative to the premise given in (48).

(47)   I promise you an official invitation.
(47′)  You want an official invitation.
(48)   People perform speech-acts only if they take it for granted that their preparatory conditions hold.

Note that given the definition in (46), a ps is in some sense "non-defeasible," and in another sense "defeasible." Given a context where the set of premises $P$ holds, the ps is an absolute requirement on the context, and must be satisfied. At the same time, a ps need not be satisfied in all contexts, and the minute you reach the conclusion that in the real context of utterance the relevant set of premises does not hold, you no longer expect the ps to hold. The minute you decide that (48) actually doesn't hold, you no longer take (47) to presuppose (47′). As Chierchia and McConnell-Ginet put it: pss like

(47') are "defeasible" because the premises relative to which they are presupposed are retractable.

It is also worth noting that it could be the local context that determines that the relevant set of premises holds, and hence that the ps in question is felt to be present. For example, suppose that our common ground includes Grice's maxim of Relevance. That in itself is not enough to determine that (49) will presuppose (28').

(49)   There is a post office around the corner.
(28')   Water bills can be paid at post offices.

But B's utterance in (28), as well as the consequent clause in (50) (where the conditional is metalinguistic) do presuppose (28').

(28)   A:   I have to pay my water bill.
         B:   There is a post office around the corner.
(50)   If you want to pay your water bill, there is a post office around the corner.

We see here that a proposition present in the local context of (49) – the proposition that the addressee wants to pay her water bill – combines with the maxim of Relevance to form a set of premises relative to which (28') is presupposed.

I suspect that some might find the idea that the filtering theory of ps projection applies to conversationally triggered pss surprising, for the following reason. The filtering theory determines the "inheritance" of pss in a compositional sort of way, which seems just what you'd expect given the assumption that pss are conventional properties of their triggers. However, that might not be what you'd expect for conversational implicatures. We are used to thinking about Gricean arguments as applying to a whole sentence as a unit, and so we probably expected that a separate Gricean argument would apply to each complex sentence. Is it possible that the implicatures of complex sentences depend in a systematic way on the implicatures of the parts?

My response to this includes three points. One, you can't get away from the facts, and the facts seem to be that conversationally triggered pss systematically involve local contexts. After all, some pss are as clearly conversationally triggered as any conversational implicature is, and their projection behavior is just like that of hard-core pss. This then may be our lesson: even phenomena that are (partly) based on extralinguistic factors may be linked to separate clauses within a complex sentence, and their behavior may systematically depend on the parts and structure of the complex sentence.

Secondly, if you want to ask **why** it is that the conversationally triggered pss of complex sentences should systematically involve local contexts, that question is independent of simply applying the filtering projection theory in order to predict the right pss. After all, when we applied filtering to conventionally triggered pss, that didn't explain why they systematically involved local contexts, either. We never used the mode of triggering in order to explain why the local contexts were crucial.

Thirdly, on further reflection, it does not seem so strange that conversationally triggered pss should depend on their local context. After all, each clause is uttered in its local context – isn't it natural to assume that it is required to be relevant in that local context? Recall also that as illustrated with examples (28) and (50) above, the local context can play a crucial role in determining whether an implicature will arise or not. It is quite natural that likewise, the local context can play a crucial role in satisfying an implicated ps, once it has arisen.

## 11.4   ps Triggering and the "ps Property"

The main argument put forth by Levinson 1983 in favor of assimilating pss to conversational implicatures is that it eliminates the need to posit a "ps property" as an additional part of the lexical entry for each trigger, besides the usual semantics of the trigger. Levinson says that it is ad hoc and unexplanatory to stipulate separately in the lexicon for each trigger what ps it triggers. It would be better if the ps triggered by an item could be predicted on the basis of its semantics. Levinson believes that this goal would be easier to achieve if pss are derived with the help of conversational principles. I think this is a point that should be seriously considered. Certainly, we do want, if possible, to have a theory where an item's "ps property" can be derived from its "content property." At the same time, I think that given what we know today, Levinson's argument turns out not to be very strong.

After all, we have already seen Heim reduce the "content property" and "heritage property" of operators into one and the same property (the ccp) – perhaps the "content property" and "ps property" of ps-triggers can also be collapsed into one? In fact, on Heim's theory, the "content property" and "ps property" of definiteness have already been collapsed into one, in the form of the rule that a definite NP translates as an old discourse referent. It would be interesting to see if the same can be done with a lot of triggers, including various individual lexical items like *stop* and *even*, cleft constructions, etc.

Note also that in some way or another, any analysis will have to derive the ps of each given trigger. The conversationalist will certainly not posit independent "ps properties" in the lexicon, but (s)he would have to show that all pss can in fact be derived based on conversational principles. Levinson admits that that is not so easy to do, and suggests that the task might be accomplished if rich enough logical forms are posited for the ps triggers, logical forms on the basis of which suitable Gricean arguments can be constructed. (Levinson 1983, p. 222, gives as an example the treatment of the pss of cleft constructions proposed in Atlas and Levinson 1981.) The question is, is that going to be more elegant and less ad hoc than trying to collapse the "content property" and "ps property" of various triggers into one conventionally-given property. I think we won't know until we've compared the two approaches for a variety of examples.

It may even be the case that the question of how, specifically, each particular ps might be derived from the semantics of its trigger (with or without the help of conversational principles) will eventually lead us in the direction of the theory that some pss are triggered conversationally while others are triggered conventionally: when the easiest and most elegant way of deriving the ps of a certain trigger is to posit a semantics for it that incorporates both "content" and ps-triggering, we might as well have that ps triggered conventionally; when the easiest and most elegant way of deriving the ps of a certain trigger is to give a Gricean argument, we might as well have that ps triggered conversationally.

## 11.5   Factive pss

As noted above, Chierchia and McConnell-Ginet 1990 argue that factive pss are conversationally triggered, while other pss (e.g. those of definite NPs, *too*, *stop*) are conventionally triggered. Chierchia and McConnell-Ginet 1990 maintain that the hard-core pss which they take to be conventionally triggered are no more "defeasible" than entailments are. (The cases where such hard-core pss "disappear" are attributed to shifts in contextual assumptions, metalinguistic operators, etc.) They argue that factive pss are "defeasible" (that is, context-dependent) in a way that the hard-core pss are not.

The factive pss of e.g. *know*, *regret* and *discover* are entailed by the basic affirmative clause. For example, (51)–(53) entail (51′)–(53′), respectively.

(51)   Jim discovered that Bill is a spy.
(51′)   Bill is a spy.
(52)   John regrets getting a PhD in linguistics.
(52′)   John got a PhD in linguistics.
(53)   Sue knows that Kim is a spy.
(53′)   Kim is a spy.

Generally, factive pss, like other pss, survive in the "family of sentences." For example, the presuppositions (51′), (52′), and (53′) survive in sentences (54), (55)–(56), and (57), respectively.

(54)   If Jim discovers that Bill is a spy, there will be trouble.
(55)   Does John regret getting a PhD in linguistics?
(56)   John doesn't regret getting a PhD in linguistics.
(57)   Sue doesn't know that Kim is a spy.

Note that the facts we have seen so far suggest that factive pss are a fairly paradigmatic type of ps, resembling in their behavior the typical hard-core pss.

Now, Chierchia and McConnell-Ginet point out that in some cases, the factive ps does not survive. For example, (58) doesn't presuppose that Kim is a spy, and (59) doesn't presuppose that Bill is a spy.

(58)   I don't know that Kim is a spy.
(59)   If I discover that Bill is a spy, there will be trouble.

Also, the ps of sentence (60) below is context-dependent: if (60) is uttered in response to the news that John just dropped out of graduate school, it doesn't presuppose that John got a PhD in linguistics.

(60)   At least John won't have to regret that he got a PhD in linguistics.

Chierchia and McConnell-Ginet argue that the absence of a factive ps in these instances suggests that a factive ps is not determined by an intrinsic (i.e. conventional) property of the factive verb, but is a conversational implicature. (They also attempt to provide some relevant Gricean arguments, that will explain how the factive ps is created in some cases and why it is absent in other cases.) In addition, Chierchia and McConnell-Ginet suggest that examples like (58)–(60) show that there is a difference in "defeasibility" between factive pss and other pss. They claim that factive pss are "defeasible" in a way that the typical hard-core pss are not, which would be explained if while the former are conversationally triggered, the latter are conventionally triggered.

I think that Chierchia and McConnell-Ginet's argumentation here is problematic. First of all, I would like to dispute the claim that factive pss are "defeasible" in a way that other pss are not. As I tried to make clear in section 9.4 above, I don't believe that ps "disappearance" is such a marked occurrence as it is often taken to be. I think pss often "disappear" in the right context, even when there is no threat of contradiction or of Quantity violation. I find that factive pss behave in this respect just like the most hard-core pss you might think of, such as the pss of definites and of *stop*. For example, the following two sentences are both judged to presuppose the relevant ps in some contexts, and to fail to presuppose it in other contexts.

(54)   If Jim discovers that Bill is a spy, there will be trouble
(61)   If Sue stopped smoking, she'll get the health prize. (Shoham, p.c.)

As noted in 9.4, (61) is fine in a context where nothing is known about Sue's smoking habits, and then (61) does not presuppose that Sue smoked. Likewise, (54) is fine in a context where it is not known at all what sort of game Bill is playing and Jim has been sent to look into the matter. In this sort of context, (54) does not presuppose that Bill is a spy. And even the existential ps of definite NPs may "disappear" under similar circumstances, as illustrated by (62), which can easily be used in a context where it is not assumed that Bill has (or had) a fortune.

(62)   If Bill lost his entire fortune at cards, for example, that would explain why he looks so upset.

So, I don't think the "disappearance" of the factive ps in (58)–(60) is such an unusual occurrence as Chierchia and McConnell-Ginet take it to be, and I don't think it so clearly distinguishes factive pss from other, more hard-core pss.

Secondly, we must not forget that we have at our disposal various means of dealing with ps "disappearance": local accommodation, shifts in contextual assumptions, etc. If we are ready to say that it is local accommodation that accounts for the "disappearance" of all sorts of pss in many examples, including (61), I don't see any reason why we shouldn't be equally ready to say that it is local accommodation that is responsible for the "disappearance" of factive pss, in examples like (54), as well as in examples like (58)–(60). The only thing which is special about the case of factive pss would be that in the case of factives, the use of first person happens to provide a very good reason why the initial context in which the example is uttered would not be able to satisfy the ps, and so the use of first person invariably forces the hearer to perform local rather than global accommodation.

To sum up, I don't think factive pss are more "defeasible" (that is, context-dependent) than other, "hard-core" pss are. Therefore, I think that the case of factive pss does not provide a valid argument in favor of the theory that some pss are conventionally triggered while others are conversationally triggered.

## 11.6   ps "Disappearance" in Simple Affirmative Examples

As noted above, the motivation behind the view that all pss are conversationally triggered is the impression that pss are, in general, context-dependent, since they do often "disappear." The "defeasibility" of pss is indeed a popular argument in favor of assimilating pss to conversational implicatures. (See, e.g., Levinson 1983.) I think that this argument as it is usually presented in the literature is not convincing: the apparent "defeasibility" of pss does not in itself show that pss are not conventionally triggered, because it can be explained by local accommodation, shifts in contextual assumptions, metalinguistic operators, etc. As a matter of empirical observation, pss appear to be quite similar to conversational implicatures in that they often "disappear," but it is, after all, possible that the reason for this superficial similarity is not that pss are conversational implicatures, but rather that conventional triggering + local accommodation on the one hand and conversational triggering on the other hand yield similar effects of ps "disappearance."

Despite what I just said, it has occurred to me that there might be a more serious argument in favor of conversational triggering of pss lurking in the so-called "defeasibility" facts. That is because – surprising as it may seem – I believe that even the most hard-core pss sometimes "disappear" even from simple affirmative examples.

Consider again (6) and its ps (7). Let us check a little more carefully the predictions of the conventionalist's account and of the conversationalist's account.

(6)   Sue stopped smoking.
(7)   Sue smoked.

The theory on which pss are conventional and not "defeasible" predicts not just that (6) **entails** (7), but also that (6) invariably **presupposes** (7), i.e. that (6) should be judged to invariably take (7) for granted. In contrast, the theory on which pss are conversational implicatures does not predict that (6) invariably presupposes (7): the conversational implicature that (7) is taken for granted is expected to arise in some contexts and fail to arise in other contexts. I think the predictions just mentioned are often implicitly taken to support conventional triggering. That is because, since (6) entails (7), it is commonly assumed that in fact (6) invariably presupposes (7). However, I would like to dispute this assumption. I would like to argue that while (6) entails (7), it can fail to presuppose (7).

Suppose our linguistics department wins a health prize if ten members of the department perform healthy acts during the school year. Suppose you have been very curious to know if we get the prize, because you knew of nine healthy acts already, and only one was missing. Suppose the list of healthy acts for the year has just been posted on the bulletin board. Suppose further that you had no previous knowledge concerning Sue's smoking habits. I think that, having glanced at the list, you are entitled to exclaim: "Hey, listen, we get the prize! Sue stopped smoking!". This scenario suggests to me that, to say the least, it is very hard to support, empirically, the claim that (6) invariably presupposes (7). Indeed, I think that it shows that intuitively, (6) may fail to presuppose (7). I don't see that the situation with (6) differs in any way from the situation we find with Shoham's example, (61).

(61)   If Sue stopped smoking, she will get the health prize.

Just as (61) shows that a ps may "disappear" in an antecedent of a conditional, the scenario I just gave for (6) shows that a ps may also "disappear" in the simple affirmative clause containing the trigger.

To take another hard-core ps trigger, consider (63), and its ps (64).

(63)   Lord Humphrey lost his entire fortune at cards last night.
(64)   Lord Humphrey had a fortune.

Suppose you and I are investigating a mysterious series of personal disasters that have been plaguing the members of the Drones Club in recent weeks. Our common ground does not include much information about Lord Humphrey, and none about his financial affairs. I think that having just overheard a member of the club utter (63), you are entitled to phone me right away and utter it yourself. "Hey, listen," you'd say, "there's a new disaster! Lord Humphrey lost his entire fortune at cards last night!" I think that in this way you can felicitously utter (63) without taking it for granted that Lord Humphrey had a fortune. This suggests that the ps of definite NPs too is capable of "disappearing" in simple affirmative examples.

Perhaps the "disappearance" of pss of simple affirmative examples can be used to argue against conventional triggering and in favor of conversational triggering, even for hard-core pss. If the ps of *stop* and of definites is conventionally triggered, then we would expect it to be an absolute requirement on the context, which must invariably be satisfied. How could the ps of (6) or (63) "disappear," then? Because the example is just the simple affirmative clause containing the trigger, the "disappearance" of the ps can't be due to metalinguistic operators or to the ps being satisfied by local accommodation. Therefore, given conventional triggering, it is hard to explain that "disappearance." On the other hand, conversational triggering provides a natural explanation: if the implication that (7) or (64) is taken for granted is a conversational implicature, then of course it is context-dependent, and would sometimes fail to arise.

But then again, perhaps we should re-examine the assumption that local accommodation can't occur in simple affirmative examples. Consider again the case where our existing context does not satisfy the ps that Sue used to smoke, and someone nevertheless felicitously asserts (6). Let us represent asserting (6) as in (65), which is supposed to mean something like (66) or (67).

(65)   ASSERT: Sue stopped smoking
(66)   I hereby assert that Sue stopped smoking.
(67)   Let us add to our existing context (common ground) 'Sue stopped smoking.'

Let us try to maintain the idea that the ps of *stop* is conventionally triggered and so the sentence *Sue stopped smoking* invariably presupposes that Sue used to smoke. To avoid ps failure, we would presumably have to rely on accommodation. But we do have two options, don't we? One option is to pretend that it is already known that Sue used to smoke, and then process the assertion in (65). This would of course be global accommodation, and would create the "cognitive" ps that Sue used to smoke. Another option is to amend the assertion, as indicated in (68). (If you like, to accommodate the ps under the scope of the ASSERT operator.)

(68)   ASSERT: <u>Sue used to smoke and</u> Sue stopped smoking

The second option might be called local accommodation, and it would explain the intuition that (6) may fail to have a "cognitive" ps. When we take this option, we do not feel obliged to assume the ps "ahead of time"; instead, we interpret the speaker as implicitly asserting that ps.

   In sum, as far as I can tell, even the "disappearance" of pss from simple affirmative examples could be explained both on the assumption that their triggering is conversational and on the assumption that their triggering is conventional.


## 11.7   Conclusion

In this chapter, we examined several aspects of the behavior of pss, and tried to see what we could infer regarding the way pss are triggered. We have looked at pss ranging from the most robust-looking to the most easily "disappearing" – as sketched in (69) – identifying a ps as such by the intuition that it is taken for granted, being a precondition for felicitous utterance.

(69)   "hard-core" pss:   <u>structural triggers:</u> definite NPs, clefts
                           <u>lexical triggers:</u> *stop*, *too*
                           Entailed by simple affirmative examples.

       factive pss:        <u>lexical triggers:</u> *know, regret, discover, forget*
                           Entailed by simple affirmative examples.

       "unentailed" pss    <u>structural triggers:</u> subjunctive conditionals
       with triggers:          (ps under consideration: negation of antecedent)
                           <u>lexical triggers:</u> *promise, before*
                           Not entailed by simple affirmative examples.

       heavily context-    No particular trigger.
       dependent pss:      e.g.,   (28)   A:   I have to pay my water bill.
                                          B:   There is a post office around the corner.
                                          (ps: Water bills can be paid at post offices.)
                           Not entailed by simple affirmative examples.

   I have tried to show that the behavior of pss is more uniform than has often been assumed in the literature. In particular, I suggested that the following facts hold for our entire range of pss, including all four categories mentioned in (69).

(i)   Each ps shows up equally well in the entire "family of sentences." (affirmative example, negation, question, under possibility operators, in antecedents of conditionals)

(ii)   Each ps may be satisfied internally (by its local context).
(iii)  Each ps may always "disappear," even from simple affirmative examples.
       (Even when entailed, it may fail to be taken for granted.)

The basically uniform behavior of pss defies attempts to draw a line between two sets of pss whose different behavior could be attributed to different modes of triggering. Perhaps you thought that factive pss are not always present in the "family of sentences," suggesting that while "hard-core" pss are triggered conventionally, factive pss are triggered conversationally? Well, "hard-core" pss are not always present there either. (See 11.5.) Perhaps you thought that "unentailed" pss do not show up in the "family of sentences," suggesting that while "entailed" pss are triggered conventionally, "unentailed" pss are triggered conversationally? Well, they do show up there. (See 11.3.) Perhaps you thought that "entailed" pss are always present in the affirmative examples, suggesting that while "unentailed" pss are triggered conversationally, "entailed" pss are triggered conventionally? Well, they are not always present there. (See 11.6.)

Pss do differ from each other, of course, in that some appear more robust than others. Some pss are confidently judged to be present in a wide variety of contexts of utterance, and also out of the blue. Other pss are not as often judged to be present, and it is easy to think of contexts in which they "disappear." There are even pss that only show up in very special contexts (see last category mentioned in (69)). But how robust a ps seems to be is a matter of degree. There is a whole continuum of pss of various degrees of robustness, a continuum on which no point of qualitative difference in robustness can be found. All pss are context-dependent (even in simple affirmative examples); the difference lies in how common or easy to think of the contexts are – the contexts in which the ps is present, and those in which the ps is absent.

Some pss – those of the last category mentioned in (68) – are just exactly classical examples of relevance-based conversational implicatures, and are heavily context-dependent. Indeed, it had to be pointed out that they are in fact pss. Further, since they are not triggered by any particular construction or lexical item, there isn't any element whose grammatical properties could "conventionally" induce the ps. These pss, then, are undeniably triggered conversationally.

Regarding all other pss – the first three categories in (68) – it seems to me that both a "conversational" and a "conventional" analysis of their triggering are in principle feasible. I have examined a number of considerations that might settle the "conventional vs. conversational" matter, and found them inconclusive. I don't think the mode of triggering affects projection behavior (presence in the "family of sentences" and satisfaction by local contexts). (See 11.3.) I think that even if we take some pss to be triggered purely conventionally, it remains possible to explain their "disappearance," even in simple affirmative examples, relying on local accommodation. (See 11.6.) I think that even if we decide that all pss are triggered conversationally, that is not incompatible with the fact that some pss seem rather firmly attached to their triggers. (See end of 11.2.)

In my opinion, it is quite reasonable to analyze some pss as triggered conventionally and others as triggered conversationally. In principle, I see no reason why the two modes of triggering should not create two sets of pss whose behavior is quite similar. Note, in particular, that either mode of triggering should lead to context-dependence: if a ps is triggered conversationally, it will arise only in some contexts and not in others, for obvious reasons; if a ps is triggered conventionally, it will disappear only in some contexts and not in others – after all, local accommodation is a constrained pragmatic process that will be able to take place only under appropriate circumstances.

I think that what is needed is comparison of the two approaches to triggering for a variety of specific cases, looking into the details of how triggering would work for each specific case. When we consider deriving a specific ps "conventionally," we should find out if we are able to come up with a grammatical property of the trigger that will directly create that ps. Preferably, a property which will not be a separate ad hoc addition to the "content property" of the trigger. When we consider deriving a specific ps "conversationally," we should find out if we are able to come up with an appropriate Gricean argument. Note that the Gricean argument must surely be based in a large part on the meaning of the trigger, so the grammatical properties of the trigger would play a crucial role at any event. Note also that to seriously evaluate the process by which the desired implicature is to be derived (based on the meaning of the trigger plus conversational principles), one should preferably rely on a more fully developed theory of conversational implicature than the one originally sketched by Grice.

I think that for each specific case, we should aim to choose the easiest and most elegant account of triggering that we can find. It is quite possible that in some cases, it would be easy to show that the semantics of the trigger directly creates the ps, and hard to find relevant conversational considerations. Then we treat those cases "conventionally." It is quite possible that in some cases, it would be hard to attribute the ps to grammatical properties of the trigger alone, and easy to find relevant conversational considerations. Then we treat those cases "conversationally." (I admit that I would not be too surprised if the first generally turn out to be cases of relatively robust-looking pss while the latter generally turn out to be cases of pss that disappear relatively easily.)

# Part Three

*Focus*

# 12

# *Some Basics of the Phonology of Prosody*[1]

---

Note: In the terminology of prosody, the same word often takes on widely diverging meanings when used in different theoretical traditions. I will introduce a particular set of technical terms as used in a particular view of prosody, and I will try to use this terminology consistently.

## 12.1  Stress

We say that in the word *shampoo*, the second syllable bears heavier stress than the first one. But what **is** stress? Phoneticians agree that perceived stress involves a number of different acoustic correlates, including intensity (loudness), syllable duration, intonational (pitch) prominence, and more. Nowadays, generative phonologists, following Liberman 1975 and Liberman and Prince 1977, generally agree that stress is a rhythmic phenomenon.[2]

   When we hear a regular sequence of similar sounds, such as musical notes or syllables occurring at regular time intervals, we have a strong tendency to perceive an internal organization of these sounds within the sequence. Even when the sequence consists of the very same sound o repeated over and over again at regular intervals,

o o o o o o o o o . . .

we tend to perceive every other sound, or every third sound, as more "accented" or "stressed" than the others, and so the sequence is heard as organized into pairs or triples. This kind of organization, involving alternation between "stronger" and "weaker" sounds (or "beats" or "pulses"), we call "rhythm." Rhythm can be completely abstract,

[1]  I am grateful to Mary Beckman for allowing me to use her "Notes on Intonation" and "Notes on Stress," which have been extremely helpful in writing this chapter. (My exposition in 12.1 and 12.2 is at times very closely based on hers.)

[2]  A good overview and critique of the extensive debate in the literature concerning the nature of stress is given in Ladd 1980, ch. I and II. The idea that linguistic stress may be a rhythmic phenomenon was already suggested in Householder 1957. In Liberman 1975, this idea was developed in detail for the first time. A good recent reference on stress is Hayes 1995.

like the rhythm our perception imposes on a regular sequence of identical sounds. Usually, in music and speech alike, rhythm has acoustic correlates. For example, suppose we have a sequence of sounds that are almost identical, except that some of them are slightly longer in duration than the others, or somewhat louder. Then it is those longer/louder sounds that are heard as "stressed," and this guides us in dividing our sequence into pairs, triples or other rhythmic groups. Thus, if O is a slightly longer or louder sound than o, then (1) is heard as a 3/4 (waltz) rhythm, and (2) as a 2/4 rhythm.

(1)  O  o  o  O  o  o  O  o  o...
(2)  O  o  O  o  O  o  O  o...

One way of representing rhythmic structure, called the **metrical grid** (proposed for linguistic rhythm in Liberman 1975), is illustrated in (3)–(5).

```
      x           x           x
      x    x  x x    x  x x    x  x
(3)   um pa pa um pa pa um pa pa      3/4
```

```
      x    x    x    x
      x  x  x  x  x  x  x  x
(4)   la la la la la la la la      2/4
```

```
      x           x           x
      x    x    x    x    x    x
      x  x  x  x  x  x  x  x  x  x  x  x
(5)   ta fa te fe ta fa te fe ta fa te fe      4/4
```

The higher the column of xs over a syllable, the heavier the relative stress of that syllable is. Thus, (3) and (4) correspond to (1) and (2), respectively. (5) describes a 4/4 rhythm: we can think of it as a sequence of quadruples of syllables, in each of which the first syllable, [ta], bears the heaviest relative stress, the third, [te], bears a lesser stress, and the rest ([fa], [fe]) are unstressed.

Part of the phonology of a language, then, is going to pertain to its rhythm. In each language, there are certain phonetic differences between syllables which we analyze as reflecting differences in "stress" at an abstract phonological representation of rhythm.

In English, there is a basic stress distinction which is acoustically reflected primarily in the segmental content of the syllable. In the syllables that are rhythmically the weakest, the vowel must be "reduced" (i.e. it must be a schwa or a very short lax vowel of indeterminate quality). We distinguish between these syllables, which are said to be "unstressed," and all the other syllables, which are "stressed" (and pronounced with a "full" vowel).

In addition, we find in English that in each word, one of the syllables is felt to be rhythmically stronger than all the other ones. (So if there are two or more stressed syllables in the word, they are not equally strong.) The rhythmically strongest syllable in the word is said to bear the "primary stress" of the word. Primary stress is acoustically manifested in greater duration and loudness than the syllable would otherwise have. Also, the location of the primary stress within a word is often marked by the presence of an intonational event.[3]

---

[3]  See section 12.3 below.

For the purposes of this book, let me assume, following Prince 1983 and Selkirk 1984, that linguistic stress patterns are represented (exclusively) by means of the metrical grid. The rhythmic distinctions mentioned above can be represented on the grid in the manner illustrated by the following examples. An unstressed syllable has a column of only one x, while a stressed one has a column of at least two. Primary word stress is represented by a column of (at least) three xs.

```
(6)   primary stress:                  x            ← 3rd syll – heaviest stress
      full vowel stress:   x           x            ← 1st and 3rd syll stressed
      syllable:            x    x   x   x           ← 2nd, 4th syll unstressed
                           eks  plə neɪ šn             (with reduced vowel)
                           ex   pla na  tion

(7)   primary stress:      x
      full vowel stress:   x    x
      syllable:            x  x x   x
                           le ǰɪ sleɪ čǝr
                           le gi sla ture

(8)   primary stress:            x
      full vowel stress:         x
      syllable:            x     x                  ← 1st syll unstressed (with
                           ɪks   pleɪn                  reduced vowel)
                           ex    plain

(9)   primary stress:            x
      full vowel stress:   x     x                  ← both syll stressed (with
      syllable:            x     x                      full vowels)
                           šæm  pu
                           sham poo
```

Regarding stress patterns in English, I assume further that there are rhythmic patterns above the level of a single word – in compounds, phrases, sentences – which are also reflected in timing, loudness and intonation, and which are also represented phonologically by means of the metrical grid. A few example patterns are given in (10) and (11).

```
(10)  a.  x                        b.               x
          x          x                 x            x
          x          x                 x            x
          x    x     x x               x    x     x x
          lighthouse keeper            lightweight boxer
(11)                                                x
                      x                             x
            x         x    x                        x
            x         x    x                        x
       x    x x x   x x   x    x     x   x
       The mayor of Paris won their support.
```

And what is it that determines stress patterns? I will not be concerned with the phonological rules that determine (sometimes in combination with idiosyncratic lexical specifications) stress patterns within words, and will simply treat these patterns as given. As for stress patterns above the level of a single word, I will assume that they are partly determined by morphological and syntactic structure, and partly by the pragmatically-driven placement of intonational events. But any further discussion of stress patterns above the level of a single word is deferred to sections 12.3 and 12.4 below.


## 12.2  Intonation

Acoustically, linguistic intonational patterns consist of changes in the pitch of our voice, as produced at the vocal folds. So contours of the fundamental frequency (= $F_0$) of our voice serve as the phonetic representation of intonation.

Here I will digress a little. *To satisfy my own curiosity, I have gathered together a few facts regarding pitch: Physically, what we perceive as sound is microscopic variations of the air pressure. These can be caused by a vibrating object, such as a door we've knocked on, or a piano string. A sound has "pitch" if these variations are regular, periodic (that is, if they occur at identical time intervals), and the pitch is measured by the frequency of the variations. For example, if a string vibrates periodically at a rate of 440 times per second, the resulting sound has a frequency of 440 Hz, which means that it is the A of the middle octave of the piano (the one marked a'). The sound generated by our vocal folds has pitch, because the vocal folds vibrate in a way that possesses the necessary periodicity.*

*The difference between normal speech and singing is as follows. During speech, the rate at which the vocal folds vibrate changes continuously: the rate obviously remains constant for periods of time that are long enough for periodicity (and hence pitch) to be detected, and yet it changes rapidly, in such a way that the pitch of our voice keeps gliding up and down. In singing, the rate at which the vocal folds vibrate changes much less often, and it mostly changes abruptly: we keep the pitch constant for the whole length of a sung musical note, and then another note, and so on, (usually) switching from one note to the next without going through the pitches in between. And, of course, the pitches reached in singing are fixed: we use an inventory of specific frequencies with specific, musically relevant, intervals between them.*

*In nature, vibrations (of objects, of the air) are always complex. For example, take a vibrating string. There is a major movement of the whole length of the string, whose largest amplitude is in the middle of the string. But, at the same time, there is a similar but smaller-scale movement in each half of the string, whose largest amplitude is in the middle of the half, and whose frequency is double the frequency of the major movement. Similarly, each quarter of the string vibrates too, and so on. The smaller the "sub-vibration," the larger its frequency. But this means that when a string vibrates – or when our vocal folds vibrate – the resulting sound is not a single tone, but rather a whole bundle or "spectrum" of tones, of different frequencies. These tones are called "partials." The lowest partial (the partial with the lowest frequency, the one caused by the biggest-scale vibration) is called the "fundamental," and the other partials are called the "overtones."*

*It is the fundamental which we perceive as **the** tone heard. (This is true even in cases where some of the overtones are actually louder than the fundamental.) That is why when we talk about intonation or melody, we refer to the frequency of the fundamental (to $F_0$).*

*The partials are generated with descending loudness – the higher the quieter – where the fundamental is the loudest. But if the generated spectrum passes through a resonator, this will change the relative loudness of the partials. A resonator – such as the body of air in our vocal tract, for example – transmits certain frequencies more efficiently than it does others. The frequencies that go through the easiest are called the "resonance frequencies" of the resonator. A tone with a frequency identical or close to one of the resonance frequencies will go through the resonator easily and come out amplified, whereas other tones will come out damped. The resonance frequencies of the human vocal tract are usually referred to as the "formant frequencies." Of the spectrum generated by the vocal folds, the partials matching the formant frequencies come out louder. When we change the shape of the vocal tract (by moving the tongue, rounding the lips, lowering the larynx, and so on), this changes the formant frequencies. It is the formant frequencies that (by determining which of the overtones are amplified) determine what we perceive as vowel quality and the timbre of the voice.*

Having completed my digression, I return to intonation patterns in natural language. While an $F_0$ contour is continuous, it is possible to identify in it distinct intonational "events," such as a peak of high pitch, or a sharp fall in pitch. This allows for a phonological analysis of intonation contours as a sequence of distinct tonal entities. Following Liberman 1975, it is generally agreed that these tonal entities have an independent identity from the text (are represented autosegmentally), and are lined up with texts by linguistic rules.

The tonal entities comprising the phonological representation of an intonation contour are distributed over an utterance rather sparsely (compared with the distribution of tones in lexical tone languages), and may be quite restricted in distribution (i.e. in where in the utterance they may occur). In English, there are stress-related tonal entities, that must line up with metrically strong syllables, and peripheral tonal entities, that are not stress-related and occur only at edges of prosodic phrases (see Liberman 1975).

Regarding prosodic phrases: It is standard to assume that an utterance may be comprised of one or more prosodic phrases called the "intonation phrase." Intonation phrase boundaries can generally be, and sometimes are, marked by a (nonhesitation) pause. They are often marked by lengthening of the last syllable in the phrase. I will also assume, following Beckman and Pierrehumbert 1986, a further relevant unit of prosodic phrasing in English, called the "intermediate phrase." An intonation phrase consists of a sequence of one or more intermediate phrases. Even when not marked by rhythm (pauses, lengthening), prosodic phrases can be identified on the basis of intonational characteristics (e.g. the presence of peripheral tones).

Finally, it is important to note that the choice and placement of tonal events may be semantically/pragmatically interpreted. For peripheral tones, an example is the sharp final rise signaling a question. In English, placement of stress-related tonal entities is interpreted (see 13.4), and so is the choice of these entities (e.g. a low tone often indicates previous mention in the discourse).

Pierrehumbert 1980 offers a very elegant theory of English intonation, which combines a phonological component, characterizing the tonal entities that a well-formed intonation contour in English may be comprised of, and a (quantitative) phonetic component, which maps the abstract phonological representations into $F_0$ contours. In the remainder of this book, I will assume the theory of intonation summarized below, based on Pierrehumbert 1980, as modified in Beckman and Pierrehumbert 1986.

English intonational contours are phonologically analyzed into sequences of relatively high and relatively low tones (written H and L). The theory distinguishes three kinds of tonal entities: "pitch accents," "phrase accents" and "boundary tones."

A "pitch accent" is a tone or tone sequence that aligns with one particular syllable within a phrase. (A syllable aligned with a pitch accent is said to be "accented".) In English, the alignment of pitch accents with the text depends on the stress pattern of that text. For one thing, a pitch accent is always aligned with a stressed syllable.[4] There are six pitch accents in English, the ones listed in (12).

(12)   Simple pitch accents:      H*      L*

        Bitonal pitch accents:     H*+L   H+L*   L*+H   L+H*

The asterisk marks a tone which has to occur at (be associated with) some particular stressed syllable. In bitonal accents, the unstarred tone precedes or follows the associated (starred) tone at some distance without belonging to any particular syllable. There is at least one pitch accent per intermediate phrase.

A "boundary tone" is a tone which occurs at the edge of the intonation phrase. English has two boundary tones, shown in (13).

(13)   Boundary tones:      H%      L%

There is one boundary tone at the very end of each intonation phrase. (Also, there may be a leading boundary tone at the beginning of the intonation phrase, if it occurs after a pause. I will usually ignore leading boundary tones.)

A "phrase accent" is a tone which is affiliated with the intermediate phrase. English has two phrase accents, which are notationally recognized by being separate and unmarked, as in (14).

(14)   Phrase accents:      H      L

There is one phrase accent per intermediate phrase. Roughly, it occurs some time after the last pitch accent in the phrase (with a tendency to occur at the end of the word carrying that accent), and fills up the space up to the boundary of the phrase.

The above mentioned pitch accents, phrase accents and boundary tones are taken to be the entire inventory of phonological "building blocks" for English intonation contours. A well-formed intonation contour for an English intonation phrase is any sequence of such building blocks put together in accordance with the principles mentioned above: each intonation phrase ends with (and possibly begins with) exactly one boundary tone; each intonation phrase is divided into one or more intermediate phrases; each intermediate phrase contains one or more pitch accents, followed by exactly one phrase accent. Thus, with our ten "building blocks," we can transcribe any intonation contour in English.

Let us look at some examples (most of them taken from Pierrehumbert 1980). First, we look at examples with a single intonation phrase, consisting of a single intermediate phrase. So in each example there is a single boundary tone at the very end, preceded by a single phrase accent. In (15), a few different tunes are given for the phrase *Anna*. Each contains one pitch accent, which is associated with the only stressed syllable, viz. the first one.

---

[4]   Further details concerning the alignment of pitch accents with texts of varying stress patterns will be discussed in section 12.4.

(15)  a.  Anna
          H* L L%

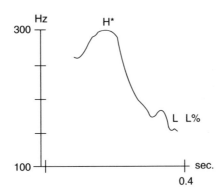

A peak of high pitch on the first syllable, followed by a drop to the bottom of the speaker's range. Such intonation would typically be used when *Anna* is an (exhaustive) answer to a question. For example, as in:

A:  Who are you going to marry?
B:  Anna.

(Call a L L% ending a 'declarative terminal fall'.)

  b.  Anna
      H* L H%

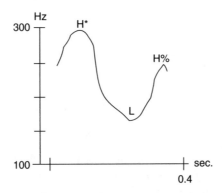

Like the tune in (a), except that the pitch rises again after the low phrase accent. Such a tune would be used when *Anna* is an **incomplete** answer to a question, indicating that the list may be continued. For example, in this piece of discourse:

A:  Who shall we invite?
B:  Anna, . . .
C:  Ginny, . . .
B:  Do we want to invite Sarah, too? . . .     etc.

(The L H% ending is called a 'continuation rise'.)

c.   Anna
     L* H H%

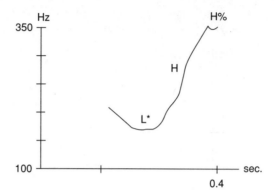

A contour very low on the first syllable, and rising up to the end. This is a
typical tune when *Anna* is used as a question ('Is it Anna?'). (This contour
is referred to as 'question intonation'.)

d.   A          nna
     L* + H   L H%

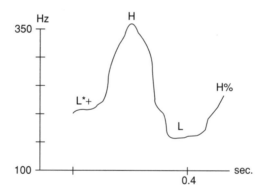

This contour starts at a rather low pitch level, which is maintained for a little
while, and then rises – which corresponds to the L* + H pitch accent. After
that, the contour goes down again, and a continuation rise is pronounced
(corresponding to the L H% ending, as in (b) above). Such a contour would
occur, for example, in the following discourse, if speaker B is not sure that
Anna counts as interesting, and so she is not sure that she is really answering A's question.

A:   What interesting people came to the party?
B:   Anna.

(This contour may be called the 'uncertainty contour,' following Ward and
Hirschberg 1985, who analyze its pragmatic function in detail.)

(16) is one more example with the "uncertainty contour," with more syllables in it (so it's easier to see/hear in detail how the tune is aligned with the text). (From Ward and Hirschberg 1985)

(16)   A:   Does Alan have any redeeming features?
     B:   He's a good badminton player.
              L* + H       L H%

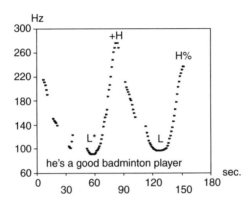

        The use of this tune indicates that B is not sure that being a good badminton player is a true redeeming feature.

In (17), a few different tunes are given for the phrase *Another orange*, each containing two pitch accents. (Note that the pitch accents are associated with the two stressed syllables.)

(17)   a.   Another o range
           H*    H* L  L%

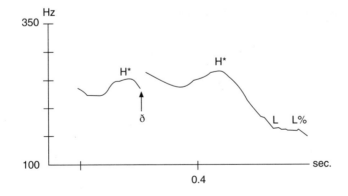

        This is probably the most common intonation pattern for neutral declarative sentences in American English, sometimes called the 'hat pattern.' (This utterance can serve as an answer to 'What's this?'.)

b.  A  nother  o  range
   H% L*    H* L  L%

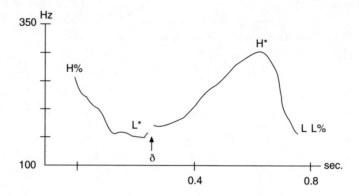

Declarative. Conveys surprise, or implies that the speaker is repeating something she really should not have to repeat.

c.  Another  o  range
    H*    L* H H%

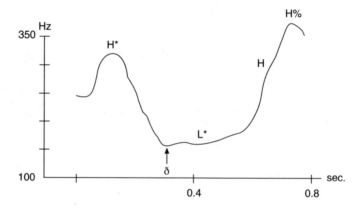

Question pattern. ('Is it another orange?')

d.  Another  o  range
    L*    L* H H%

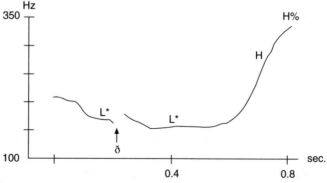

Question pattern. (Sounds more surprised, I think.)

Finally, prosodic phrasing is illustrated in (18) and (19). Each of the utterances in (18) is made up of two intonation phrases. The utterances in (19) have just one intonation phrase again, but in (19b) the intonation phrase is made up of two intermediate phrases.

(18)  a.  Anna      came with Manny
          H* L H%             H* L L%

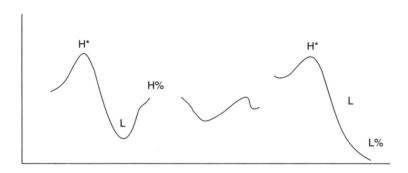

Two intonation phrases.
Addresses the question: 'What about Anna? who did she come with?'

  b.  Anna      came with Manny
      H* L L%             H*  L H%

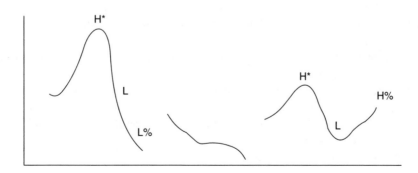

Two intonation phrases.
Addresses the question: 'What about Manny? who came with him?'

(19)  a.  "I" means insert
        H*          H* L L%

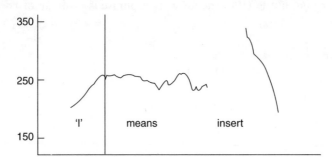

One intonation phrase, containing one intermediate phrase.

b.  "I"      means insert
     H* L            H* L L%

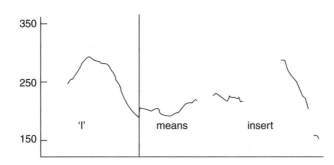

One intonation phrase, containing two intermediate phrases.

The syllable carrying the last pitch accent in an intermediate phrase is always the prosodically most prominent syllable in that phrase. Thus, the last pitch accent is special. It is called the "nuclear accent." Clearly, it is the juxtaposition of this last pitch accent with the L or H phrase accent following it that is largely responsible for its per-ceived prosodic strength, since this juxtaposition creates very distinctive rising or falling patterns. For example, a H* pitch accent followed by a L phrase accent yields a sharply falling pattern which makes this H* accent stand out more than would an otherwise identical prenuclear H* accent.[5]

Pierrehumbert 1980 includes a substantive phonetic component interpreting the phonological representations presented above. Phonetic details are not of particular concern in this book, yet it is important to note that besides the sequence of phono-logical tonal entities and their alignment with the text, there is a number of other factors that influence the shape of the actual $F_0$ contour.

One of these factors is the **pitch range**, the overall range of $F_0$ values within which we define what it means for a H tone to be "relatively high" and a L tone to be "rela-

---

[5]  Some post-nuclear syllables may carry an "echo accent," which is "a miniature replica of the nuclear accent" (Pierrehumbert 1980, section 5.2), and which doesn't count as a real pitch accent. Cf. also Bolinger 1986, pp. 126–7.

tively low." The pitch range is reset at the beginning of each new intermediate phrase. (The bottom of the pitch range is called the **baseline**, and that's where the lowest L tones are realized. The baseline declines slightly through the utterance. The $F_0$ values of both L and H tones are scaled with reference to the baseline.) Pitch range is partly determined by the shape and size of a speaker's larynx: men have lower pitch ranges than women and children do, because of their longer, more massive vocal folds. One's pitch range expands when one speaks emphatically or speaks up to be heard above noise. In addition, we use variations in our pitch range to mark certain aspects of the organization of the discourse (see Pierrehumbert and Hirschberg 1990).

Pierrehumbert supplies quantitative phonetic **interpolation** rules that determine the shape of the $F_0$ contour in between tones. The interpolation is mostly monotonic, but there is one exception: between two H tones there is a dipping in the contour (see for example (17a) above).

Some phonetic phenomena that further affect $F_0$ values in English are the following.

(i) **phrase accent spreading**: As noted above, the phrase accent usually fills up the space from sometime after the last pitch accent up to the boundary tone.

(ii) **Downstep**: After any bitonal pitch accent, the overall pitch range of the intonation contour is reduced.

(iii) **Upstep**: After a H phrase accent, everything is higher than it normally would be.

Downstep affects the $F_0$ value of H tones quite noticeably (much beyond the scaling of H tones to the declining baseline). This effect is illustrated in (20): because the pitch range is reduced, the second H tone is lower than the first one.

(20) Another orange
   H* + L  H*  L L%

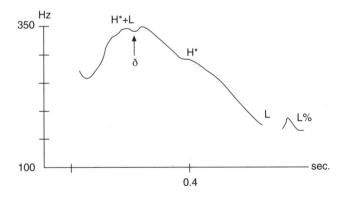

(One use of this contour is to convey judiciousness.)

Upstep creates a second rise at the end of the "question intonation" L* H H%. This can be seen clearly in (21), where there is a fairly long stretch filled up by the H phrase accent.

(21)   Does Manitowoc have a library?
          L*          H          H%

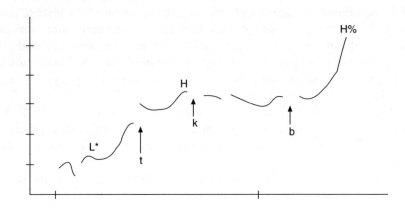

Also, Upstep determines that when a H phrase accent is followed by a L boundary tone, this creates a sort of plateau or a partial fall, instead of a considerable fall in pitch. This is illustrated in (22). In fact, in (22), we can see the effects of both Downstep and Upstep: the second H is lower than the first one (Downstep), and the pitch doesn't go down much at the end (Upstep).

(22)   A        nna
          H* + L   H   L%

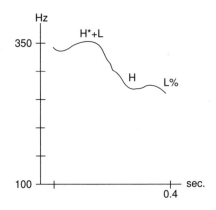

      This pattern could be used for calling out to Anna.
      ('vocative contour')

      Another factor that influences actual $F_0$ values is the **prominence** of a given pitch accent.[6] Pierrehumbert defines prominence as the combined effect of (i) the relative metrical strength of the syllable bearing the pitch accent, and (ii) the amount of empha–

---

[6]   Here "prominence" is used as a technical term. Note that I generally **don't** use the word in this technical sense.

sis that the speaker wishes to give to the word or phrase containing the pitch accent. For H tones, greater prominence means higher $F_0$, and for L tones, it tends to mean lower $F_0$. (If a syllable $\alpha$ is more stressed than another syllable $\beta$, the prominence of $\alpha$ will be at least as great as that of $\beta$. Other than that, there is great variability in prominence, depending on emphasis.) To take a few examples, consider first (15a) (declarative form of *Anna*): the more emphasis the speaker puts on this utterance, the higher the prominence of the H* pitch accent, which means that its $F_0$ value is higher. Now consider (17a) (the 'hat pattern') and (17d) (a question pattern) above. In each of these examples, the second pitch accent is more prominent than the first one: we see that in (17a), the second H* is higher than the first, and in (17d), the second L* is lower than the first. (This higher prominence is attributed by Pierrehumbert to stronger stress.)

In what follows, I will use and discuss phonological representations of intonation, leaving aside the phonetics. The tonal transcriptions used should give a fairly good idea of the actual intonation contour (especially if you keep in mind the effect of Upstep).

## 12.3 On the Separate Existence of Stress Patterns

Intonation can guide us in our perception of stress patterns. Let us take a few examples. How do speakers know that the primary stress of *explanation* is on the third syllable and that the primary stress of *legislature* is on the first syllable? If we consider the citation forms of these words, given in (23), it is obvious that the location of the pitch accent can serve as a clue to the location of the primary stress within the word.

(23)   explanation                     legislature
       H* L  L%                        H* L  L%

Next, consider the phrase *a lightweight boxer* uttered in a context where the question "What sort of an athlete is he?" has been raised. Speakers would intuitively say that the main (strongest) stress of the phrase is on the first syllable of *boxer*. How do we know that? Well, in the context described, it is natural to utter the phrase as in (24a), or maybe as in (24b) or (24c).

(24)   a.   A lightweight boxer
              H*          H* L  L%
       b.   A lightweight boxer
              L*          L* H  H%
       c.   A lightweight boxer
              H* + L     H* L  L%

That is, the phrase has the nuclear accent (=the last pitch accent) on the syllable that is felt to carry the main stress. Hence, the location of the nuclear accent can serve as a clue to the location of the main stress in the phrase.[7] Finally, consider (25). If we judge

---

[7]   Recall, in this connection, that the nuclear accent is particularly prominent in the intonation contour, due to the distinctive falling or rising patterns created by its juxtaposition with the following phrase accent.

that *lightweight* here is less stressed than it was in (24), surely we are influenced by the absence of a pitch accent.

(25)  A:  He is a lightweight what?      B:  A lightweight boxer.
                                              H* L L%

Indeed, there is much experimental evidence showing that the location of intonational events is an important and often the main clue to what speakers intuitively describe as "stress." This state of affairs may lead to the view that – except perhaps for the distinction between stressed and unstressed syllables – stress patterns do not have a (phonological) existence independent of intonation patterns. Such a view is advocated in e.g. Bolinger 1958, 1981. On such a view, what is called the "primary stress" of the word would be considered nothing more than the potential location for a pitch accent; prosodic prominence would always mean the presence of a pitch accent, with special prominence to the nuclear accent; and there would be no separate category of being prominent rhythmically or "stress-wise."

Given this, it may be worth emphasizing that the view adopted in this book is that stress patterns do have a (phonological) existence independent of intonation patterns, as abstract rhythmic patterns. For arguments in favor of this view, I refer the reader to Ladd 1980, ch. II, and Selkirk 1984, sections 4.3.2, 5.3.

Perceived rhythmic prominence is not always reflected in the presence of intonational events. For example, in (26)–(27), the primary stress of *explanation*, *legislature*, *housekeeper* or *keeper* is not marked by the presence of a pitch accent, but speakers still feel that they can hear where it is.

(26)  I don't WANT an explanation.
(27)  I don't CARE for legislature.
(28)  A:  What is she?
      B:  A LIGHThouse keeper.
(29)  A:  What kind of a housekeeper is she?
      B:  A LIGHT housekeeper.

Similarly, although there is no intonational reflection of this, in (30), *boxer* seems to be more stressed than *lightweight*, whereas in (31), *lighthouse* seems to be more stressed than *keeper*.

(30)  I don't WANT to see the lightweight boxer.
(31)  I don't WANT to see the lighthouse keeper.

Such intuitions are standardly taken to be evidence for the phonological existence of the metrical patterns in question.[8]

---

[8]  Admittedly, the evidence from intuitions is not conclusive. After all, the perceived patterns may be illusions based on speakers' knowledge of potential locations for pitch accents, as claimed in Bolinger's work. (See, e.g., Bolinger 1986, p. 73.) However, there is also some experimental evidence that the perceived rhythmic prominences are acoustically manifested in timing (pauses, syllable duration) and loudness. In an experiment reported in Bolinger and Gerstman 1957, it was found that there

Returning now to accented syllables, on the view adopted here, they are taken to be syllables where intonational prominence and metrical prominence meet, so to speak. It is assumed, for example, that the primary stress and the H* pitch accent on the third syllable of the citation form of *explanation* are two phonological phenomena that occur on the same syllable. Regarding the nucleus, it is assumed that the syllable carrying the nuclear accent is also, simultaneously but separately, the most heavily stressed syllable in the phrase.

## 12.4  Intonation and Stress

As has already become clear above, there are important links between the intonation contours and rhythmic patterns of English utterances. Besides the fact that the units of prosodic phrasing relevant to intonation are also relevant to rhythm (pauses, lengthening), there are certain correlations between stress patterns and the location of pitch accents. I assume that the following correlations hold.

(i)   Only stressed syllables can be accented;
(ii)  Any accented syllable is always metrically stronger than any
      unaccented syllable in the same intermediate phrase.
(iii) The nuclear accent is metrically stronger than any other pitch accent.

(i) is a clear empirical fact: it can be directly observed that syllables with reduced vowels cannot be accented. For example, note the impossibility of (32b), and note that if a syllable which is normally unstressed is to carry a pitch accent, it becomes stressed (see, for example, (34f) below).

(32)  a.          x                 OK
            x    x                   'normal': e.g. an impatient answer
            x    x
            Shampoo                  Two p.a.s. Both on stressed syllables.
            L* H*  L  L%

      b.          x                 IMPOSSIBLE
                  x                 ('normal' stress pattern of the word)
            x    x
            Ca  noe                 Two p.a.s. The first on an unstressed syllable.
            L* H*  L  L%

As for (ii) and (iii), what is observed easily and directly is that the accented syllables are felt to be more prosodically prominent than any of the unaccented ones (e.g. examine

was a substantially longer pause between *light* and *house* in utterances of (29B) than in utterances of (28B). (Of course, this is what makes it possible for a hearer to tell whether a recording heard out of context is a rendition of (29B) or of (28B).) As discussed in Ladd 1980 (ch. II), on the view of stress taken here, we may take this difference in timing to be a clue to the stress pattern: it is a phonetic/phonological reflection of the fact that in (28B), *kee* is more stressed than *house*, whereas in (29B), *house* is more stressed than *kee*. (The longer pause in (29B) is a way of providing the space needed for two stresses on two adjacent syllables.).

the relative prosodic prominence of the various primary word stresses in (33) below), and that the last pitch accent is the most prosodically prominent. It is a theoretical interpretation of this observation that the intonational prominence of an accented syllable always correlates with metrical prominence of that syllable.[9] Note that it follows from (ii) and (iii) that the nuclear accent (= the last pitch accent) and the maximal metrical prominence in the intermediate phrase always coincide. Some illustration of (ii) and (iii) can be found in (34)–(35) below. Regarding (iii), note the contrast between (34c) and (35c): as a short answer exhibiting the 'normal' stress pattern of the word, *California* can contain two pitch accents, which is compatible with (iii), while *Abernathy* cannot contain two pitch accents, that being incompatible with (iii).

(33)  (Single intermediate and intonation phrase, all pitch accents marked)

    a.   Legumes are a good source of vitamins.
           pa            pa  pa      pa

    b.   Legumes are a good source of vitamins.
           pa            pa        pa

    c.   Legumes are a good source of vitamins.
           pa            pa    pa

    d.   Legumes are a good source of vitamins.
           pa                    pa

    e.   Legumes are a good source of vitamins.
           pa

    f.   Legumes are a good source of vitamins.
                     pa

    g.   Legumes are a good source of vitamins.
                              pa

(34)  a.        x           OK
           x   x        'normal': citation form, or short answer
           x x x  x
           Ca li fornia     The p.a. is on the primary-stressed syllable.
             H*L L%

    b.        x           IMPOSSIBLE
           x   x        ('normal' stress pattern of the word)
           x x x  x
           Ca li fornia     The p.a. is on the first syllable, while the
           H*   L  L%    third syllable is metrically stronger.

    c.        x           OK
           x   x        'normal': e.g. an impatient short answer
           x x x  x
           Ca li fornia     Two p.a.s. The last one is more stressed.
           L*   H*L L%

    d.   x             IMPOSSIBLE
           x   x        (not the 'normal' stress pattern of the word)
           x   x
           x x x  x
           Ca li fornia     Two p.a.s. The last one is less stressed.
           L*   H*L L%

---

[9]  Some relevant discussion is in section 12.3 above.

e.    x                OK

```
        x   x              As in: You say [kæ]lifornia, not [ka]lifornia
        x   x              (not the 'normal' stress pattern of the word)
        x x x  x
        Ca li fornia       The p.a. is on the first syllable, which is
        H*    L  L%        also the strongest metrically.
   f.     x                    OK
        x x                As in: It's spelled ca[lɪ]fornia, not ca[la]fornia
        x x x              (not the 'normal' stress pattern of the word)
        x x x  x
        Ca li fornia       The p.a. is on the second syllable, which is also
            H*L  L%        stressed (with unreduced vowel) and the
                           strongest metrically
(35) a.  x                 OK
        x     x            'normal': citation form, or short answer.
        x  x  x  x
        Abernathy          The p.a. is on the primary-stressed syllable.
        H*    L  L%
   b.   x                  IMPOSSIBLE
        x     x            ('normal' stress pattern of the word)
        x  x  x  x
        Abernathy          The p.a. is on the third syllable, while the
              H*  L  L%    first syllable is metrically stronger.
   c.   x                  IMPOSSIBLE
        x     x            ('normal' stress pattern of the word)
        x  x  x  x
        Abernathy          Two p.a.s. The last one is less stressed.
        L*  H*  L  L%
        (or
        H*)
```

Obviously, if there are correlations between intonation and stress, the grammar must be organized in such a way that these correlations can be derived. I will assume the following theory, proposed in Selkirk 1984.

(A)    We start with surface structure – i.e. texts with their morphological and syntactic structure, and devoid of intonation contours or metrical grids.

(B)    Sentences are divided into prosodic phrases, and tonal entities are added: peripheral tones are assigned to prosodic phrases (see section 12.2), and a process called **pitch accent assignment** assigns pitch accents not to a specific syllable, but rather to a constituent. (Selkirk argues that the relevant constituents are single words or word-parts.) We may assume, for example, that the pitch accent in (33e) is assigned to *legumes*. Of course, there is much freedom in choice and placement of pitch accents.

(C)    The resulting level of representation, called "surface structure cum intonation," is the one that will be interpreted semantically and pragmatically on the one hand, and aligned with a metrical grid on the other. Stress rules, i.e. the rules that build up and shape the metrical grid, will now apply cyclically.

(D)   Some of the stress rules apply independently of pitch accents; for example, the rules determining the ("normal") stress pattern of a word. The stress patterns determined by such rules can affect the realization of the pitch accent in the constituent to which it was assigned: a rule of **pitch accent association** is posited, which associates the pitch accent with the metrically strongest syllable in the constituent. For example, if a pitch accent is assigned to *legumes*, then it is associated with the first syllable, the one bearing the primary stress.

(E)   A stress rule called the **Pitch Accent Prominence Rule** is posited, which guarantees (by adding entries on top of grid columns) that any accented syllable is going to be metrically stronger than any unaccented syllable in the same intermediate phrase. It also guarantees that the accented syllables will possess a certain "absolute" degree of stress – according to Selkirk, a grid column of at least four levels. This rule overrides all other grid-building rules.

Selkirk's theory just sketched provides for a simple account of a number of central facts. The pitch accent prominence rule (PAR, for short) directly encodes correlations (ii) and (i) noted above, and captures the fact that in these ways, the stress pattern of an utterance heavily depends on pitch accent placement. This kind of theory is also consistent with the intuition that in most of the examples above, the pitch accents serve to give emphasis not to a particular syllable, but rather to the whole word. The only examples above where that is not the case are (34e–f), and here we may take the pitch accent to be assigned to a constituent smaller than a word. Further, Selkirk's theory also has the advantage of providing as an input to the semantics and pragmatics a level of representation which contains just the aspects of prosody that seem relevant: choice of tonal entities and pitch accent assignment are clearly relevant to the (pragmatic) meaning of the utterance, whereas the complete stress pattern of the utterance doesn't seem to be. Finally, Selkirk's theory also captures the fact that pitch accent placement partly depends on stress patterns: it accounts for the observation that whenever a single pitch accent is felt to be assigned to a whole word, it must be associated with the primary stress of that word.

(Perhaps at this point I should note the following. It seems that in cases like (34c) above, the two pitch accents together serve to emphasize the word as a whole. Hence we might want to say that both are assigned to the word as a whole (cf. Selkirk 1984, ch. 5, fn. 38). If so, the theory would have to say something about how they are to be associated.)

It is commonly assumed, following Chomsky and Halle 1968, Liberman 1975, Liberman and Prince 1977 and others, that English utterances exhibit rule-governed rhythmic organization above the level of a single word which is dependent on morphological and syntactic structure.[10] Specifically, we may assume (as in Selkirk 1984, ch. 4) that the following two rules, which apply cyclically, specify the position of the heaviest stress within a syntactic phrase, and the position of the heaviest stress within a compound.

(i)   The **Nuclear Stress Rule**:
      Given a syntactic phrase, the strongest primary word stress in the rightmost immediate constituent of the phrase is promoted to become the strongest stress in the entire phrase.

---

[10]   This is a standard assumption, although it is denied in e.g. Bolinger 1958, 1972, 1981.

(ii)  The **Compound Stress Rule**:
Given a compound, the strongest primary word stress in the leftmost immediate constituent of the compound is promoted to become the strongest stress in the entire compound.

These rules, just like the rules that govern stress-patterns within words, are not sensitive to the presence of pitch accents. However, again just like the word-internal rules (see (34e–f) above), their effect can be overridden by the Pitch Accent Prominence Rule (PAR).

Let us restrict our attention to the Nuclear Stress Rule (NSR, for short). Its effect may be illustrated by the following derivations.

(36)  a.  p.a. assignment (to words) + primary word stress + p.a. association:

```
  x                         x    x          x              x
  x                         x    x          x              x
  x    x    x          x   x x x    x x     x    x    x    x
  I know that        [s [NP the mayor of Paris ] [VP won their support ] ]
  H*        L                                                   L%
```

b.  NSR in the NP and VP:

```
                                 x                          x
  x                         x    x          x              x
  x                         x    x          x              x
  x    x    x          x   x x x    x x     x    x    x    x
  I know that        [s [NP the mayor of Paris ] [VP won their support ] ]
  H*        L                                                   L%
```

c.  NSR in the embedded S:

```
                                                            x
                                 x                          x
  x                         x    x          x              x
  x                         x    x          x              x
  x    x    x          x   x x x    x x     x    x    x    x
  I know that        [s [NP the mayor of Paris ] [VP won their support ] ]
  H*        L                                                   L%
```

d.  The NSR in the higher cycles leaves the heaviest stress in the entire sentence on the very last syllable, just as it is in (c).

e.  However, the PAR overrides this, and puts the heaviest stress in the sentence on *know*. The stress patterns created by the NSR remain intact only within the embedded (and pitch-accent-less) S:

```
  x
  x                                                          x
  x                                   x                      x
  x                              x    x          x           x
  x                              x    x          x           x
  x    x    x          x   x x x    x x     x    x    x    x
  I know that        [s [NP the mayor of Paris ] [VP won their support ] ]
  H*        L                                                   L%
```

(37)  a.   p.a. assignment (to words) + primary word stress + p.a. association:

```
              x           x            x
              x           x            x
          x  x x x      x x          x  x
[s [NP The mayor of Paris ]   [VP won it ] ]
        H*          H*              H* L  L%
```

b.   NSR in the NP and VP:

```
                          x
              x           x            x
              x           x            x
          x  x x x      x x          x  x
[s [NP The mayor of Paris ]   [VP won it ] ]
        H*          H*              H* L  L%
```

c.   NSR in the S:

```
                                       x
                          x            x
              x           x            x
              x           x            x
          x  x x x      x x          x  x
[s [NP The mayor of Paris ]   [VP won it ] ]
        H*          H*              H* L  L%
```

d.   The PAR has no additional effect, since the representation in (c) already meets its requirements.

Note that on the theory presented, it is the NSR which is responsible for the intonation–stress correlation number (iii) above, namely, the fact that the last pitch accent is always the strongest metrically. (Except that since nothing has been said about cases of two pitch accents per word, we haven't covered correlation (iii) within words.) This effect of the NSR is illustrated by the last example above, example (37).

(38)  a.   Final result of NSR applications (which is exactly as in (37)):

```
                                       x
                          x            x
              x           x            x
              x           x            x
          x  x x x      x x          x  x
[s [NP The mayor of Paris ]   [VP won it ] ]
                  H*                    L  L%
```

b.   The PAR overrides the above placement of the strongest stress in the sentence:

```
                          x
                          x            x
                          x            x
              x           x            x
              x           x            x
          x  x x x      x x          x  x
[s [NP The mayor of Paris ]   [VP won it ] ]
                  H*                    L  L%
```

To sum up: We see that pitch accent placement (which itself obviously serves semantic/pragmatic purposes) plays an important role in determining stress patterns (via the PAR). At the same time, intonation-independent rules like the syntax-dependent NSR determine default stress-patterns on the phrasal (or compound) level, patterns which show up wherever the stress pattern is not completely determined by pitch accent placement.

# 13

# *Focus and Focus Identification*

## 13.1 The Notion of "Focus" to be Discussed in this Book

Grammatical means of marking the way information is organized in discourse have been studied for a long time, notably by the Prague school (see e.g. Sgall et al. 1986 and references cited there). Involved are notions like "psychological subject" and "psychological predicate," "theme" and "rheme," "topic" and "comment," "given" and "new," as well as "(information) focus" – in fact, more than one notion of "focus." A survey of the vast literature in this area is far beyond the scope of this book. I will concentrate on a particular notion of prosodically marked focus, the one that was studied in some detail in Jackendoff 1972.[1] I think a certain consensus has emerged concerning this notion of focus, and much research has been concerned with it in recent years.

It is not difficult to quickly illustrate the notion of focus that I am talking about. Consider the following examples. Capitals mark the word of greatest prosodic prominence in the sentence (where the nuclear pitch accent and heaviest stress coincide).[2] Assume that each sentence is pronounced as a single intonation phrase, with a declarative terminal fall.

(1)  I introduced BILL to Sue.
(2)  I introduced Bill to SUE.

(3)  I only introduced BILL to Sue.
(4)  I only introduced Bill to SUE.

---

[1]  Jackendoff's own starting point for the study of focus was the discussion in Chomsky 1971. I believe that the notion of focus discussed by Chomsky and Jackendoff may be identified with the notion of focus (or "point of information focus") discussed in Halliday 1967.

It seems to me that Jackendoff's notion of focus **cannot** be identified with Bolinger's "information focus." For example, Bolinger 1972 (p. 634) says that in (i) "elucidate" is the point of information focus, while the focus of (i) (in the sense of this book) is clearly broader.

(i)  I can't finish in an hour – there are simply too many topics to ELUCIDATE.

[2]  I am temporarily ignoring pre-nuclear pitch accents now, but see 13.4.

Examples (1) and (2) differ in the discourse contexts in which they can be used. For example, of the following question–answer pairs, the ones on the left are felicitous, while the ones on the right are not.

| | | | | | |
|---|---|---|---|---|---|
| (5) | A: | Who did you introduce to Sue? | (5′) | A: | Who did you introduce to Sue? |
| | B: | I introduced BILL to Sue. | | B: | I introduced Bill to SUE. |
| (6) | A: | Who did you introduce Bill to? | (6′) | A: | Who did you introduce Bill to? |
| | B: | I introduced Bill to SUE. | | B: | I introduced BILL to Sue. |
| (7) | A: | What did you do at the party? | (7′) | A: | What did you do at the party? |
| | B: | I introduced Bill to SUE. | | B: | I introduced BILL to Sue. |

Examples (3) and (4) differ not just in the discourse contexts in which they can be used, but also in their truth conditions: if I introduced Bill to Sue and Jane and performed no other introductions, then (4) is false and (3) is true.

We observe, then, that there is a correlation between certain prosodic patterns and certain pragmatic and semantic effects. "Focus" is a theoretical notion which is used in order to account for this correlation. We say that there is a certain part of the sentence which we call "focus." This part of the sentence is marked by (contains) a peak of prosodic prominence, and is involved in the relevant pragmatic and semantic effects. Roughly, the focus part of the sentence is "the answer to the question." Thus, the focus of (1) is *Bill*, while the focus of (2) may be *Sue*, as in dialog (6), and it may also be the whole VP, as in dialog (7). In (3) and (4), if *Bill* is the focus we get the interpretation "only Bill," and if *Sue* is the focus, we get the interpretation "only Sue."

I think it is fair to say that much research on focus in generative linguistics deals with that same notion of focus that Jackendoff 1972 discussed and that I have just illustrated. This includes a considerable body of formal, model-theoretic work on focus, developed since the early- or mid- eighties until today. Some of this body of work will be presented and discussed in the following chapters.[3]

I think we know more or less what phenomena we would like to account for using the notion of focus I am talking about: it is generally agreed that all – or most – of the phenomena listed in section 13.2 below are pragmatic and semantic effects of focus. Moreover, there is even some general agreement concerning some basics of the analysis.

There are at least three basic ideas that are taken over from Jackendoff 1972 by subsequent research. First, we assume that being focused is a property of syntactic constituents.[4] We call a focused syntactic constituent "a focus." Focus is marked as a feature (usually written as a subscript F) on syntactic constituents. For example, the above mentioned choices of focus for sentence (2) are represented as follows.

---

[3]   I will not, alas, be able to cover that part of this body of work which combines focus-induced interpretations with dynamic semantics. This is an important area of research, which would indeed fit nicely as a continuation of or sequel to this book. However, space will not permit. For treatments of focus-sensitive quantification in a dynamic framework, see Krifka 1992; Rooth 1995. For a dynamic treatment of examples with *only* (separating ps from assertion and covering anaphors), see Krifka 1993.

[4]   This assumption is already present in Halliday 1967; Chomsky 1971.

(8)  a.  I introduced Bill to [Sue]$_F$.      b.  I [introduced Bill to Sue]$_F$.
         (NP focus, as answer to (6A))          (VP focus, as answer to (7A))

The idea is that the feature F is interpreted both phonologically and semantically/pragmatically. More than one constituent may be marked as focus, as in (9), for example.

(9)  A:  Who did you introduce to who?
     B:  I introduced [Bill]$_F$ to [Sue]$_F$.

A second widely accepted idea might, I think, be described as follows. Very roughly, the focus part of the sentence denotes one particular value picked out of a set of alternative values, which "fits into" an open/incomplete statement corresponding to the rest of the sentence. For example, we might say that the focusing in (1) above indicates that "Bill" is one particular individual picked out of a set of individuals, which "fits into" the following open/incomplete statement.

(10)  I introduced __ to Sue.

The third idea is that focus triggers a presupposition. A first guess might be that focus triggers an existential presupposition. For example, it might look like (1) above presupposes that there is some individual who I introduced to Sue. However, this seems wrong if we consider the following dialog.

(11)  A:  Who did you introduce to Sue?
      B:  I introduced NOBODY to Sue.

B's response explicitly denies the alleged existential ps, while it seems to have the same focal structure as (1). Jackendoff suggests instead that focus triggers the ps that the set of truthful values corresponding to the focus position is coherent, or well-defined, or amenable to discussion, or under discussion. For example, he would say that the focus in (1) triggers the ps that the set of individuals that I introduced to Sue is (or could be) under discussion. Different variations on what it is that focus presupposes have been developed in subsequent research.

It might be useful to alert the reader already at this point to the fact that while I have just described a certain notion of focus that many researchers seem to agree on and study, this notion of focus is not yet clearly and uniformly defined. While the correlation between prosody and pragmatic and semantic effects that we are interested in is easy enough to illustrate, it is not at all easy to define in general terms.

As I said above, there is some agreement on a range of pragmatic and semantic phenomena that are regarded as effects of focusing. And yet, it is quite possible that some phenomena that have been regarded in the literature as effects of focusing should not be so regarded, or do not involve the same notion of "focus." It is not easy to tell. There is no general agreement in the literature about what it is that defines "focus," and it is difficult to point to a single basic (pre-theoretic) intuition that lies behind this notion. Is focus consistently the "new information" in the sentence, and if so, in what sense, exactly? Does focus consistently involve "contrast," and if so, in what sense, exactly?

Some researchers think, in fact, that we must distinguish different kinds of "foci," each playing a different role.[5]

The phonological manifestation of focus is not entirely straightforward either. Prosody often gives us only partial information about what part of the sentence is its focus; it is well known, for one thing, that prosody often doesn't disambiguate between "narrow" and "broad" focus. For example, while the position of the peak of prosodic prominence in sentence (2) tells us that *Sue* is part of the focus, it allows for "narrower" focus on *Sue* vs. "broader" focus on the VP, as illustrated above. Much of the difficulty of identifying foci on the basis of prosody lies in the fact that peaks of prosodic prominence do not just serve to mark focus, but rather play other roles (more on that in 13.4 below).

## 13.2   Some Phenomena: Pragmatic and Semantic Effects of Focus

### 13.2.1   Discourse Congruence

It has long been noted that the position of prosodic prominence in an utterance restricts the discourse contexts in which the utterance can be used felicitously.

Question-answer pairs are the kind of dialog most often referred to in this connection. An early reference is Paul 1880. In a felicitous (coherent, natural, appropriate) question-answer pair, the position of prosodic prominence in the answer correlates with the questioned position in the question. For example, of the pairs in (12), the ones on the left are felicitous, while the ones on the right are not.

(12)   A:   What does Carl like?          A:   Who likes herring?
       B:   Carl likes HERRING.          B:   Carl likes HERRING.
       A:   Who likes herring?           A:   What does Carl like?
       B:   CARL likes herring.          B:   CARL likes herring.

Paul 1880 calls the part which answers the question (and which contains the peak of prosodic prominence) the "psychological predicate," and that is the part we now call "focus."

Many researchers use question-answer congruence as the major (if not the only) test for identifying the focus of a given utterance. I myself will regularly identify the focus on the basis of this test. (See also section 13.3 below.)

Also mentioned often are the cases of explicit, "binary" contrast. Felicitous examples of explicit binary contrast are given in (13), on the left. Again, the pairs on the right are not felicitous.

(13)   A:   Carl likes spinach.          A:   Miriam likes herring.
       B:   No, Carl likes HERRING.      B:   No, Carl likes HERRING.
       A:   Miriam likes herring.        A:   Carl likes spinach.
       B:   No, CARL likes herring.      B:   No, CARL likes herring.

---

[5]   See e.g. Rochemont 1986; Erteschik-Shir 1986, 1998; Kiss 1998; Vallduví and Vilkuna 1998.

Of course the effect of focus on discourse congruence is not limited to cases of contrast and question-answering that are as simple and explicit as the examples given above. For example, take the pieces of discourse given in (14). Again, the ones on the left are felicitous, while the ones on the right are not. (This example is from Rooth 1985.)

(14)  A:  There isn't much Carl likes          A:  Why are you buying herring?
          to eat. It will be a problem              Nobody really likes it.
          to have him over for dinner.
      B:  Carl likes HERRING. And I           B:  Carl likes HERRING. I'm
          like herring too. So it'll              buying it for him.
          be OK.

      A:  Why are you buying herring?          A:  There isn't much Carl likes
          Nobody really likes it.                  to eat. It will be a problem
                                                   to have him over for dinner.
      B:  CARL likes herring. I'm            B:  CARL likes herring. And I
          buying it for him.                      like herring too. So it'll
                                                  be OK.

## 13.2.2  The Focal Presupposition

As noted in 13.1, it is generally agreed that focus triggers a presupposition. Following Jackendoff 1972 (p. 276), let us call this ps the "focal ps." But what **is** the focal ps?

Sometimes, the intuition seems to be that the ps triggered by the focus is an existential presupposition. For example, (15) below may be judged to presuppose that someone likes Bill.

(15)  MARY likes Bill.

This ps seems to survive under "holes" (= in "the family of sentences"). For example, (16) and (17) too seem to presuppose that someone likes Bill.

(16)  It is possible that MARY likes Bill.
(17)  If MARY likes Bill, then Larry will be jealous.

However, as noted in Jackendoff 1972, focus is not always accompanied by an existential ps. For example, (18) below, which seems to have the same focal structure as (15), does not have an existential ps: this example is perfectly felicitous even though it explicitly denies the claim that someone likes Bill.

(18)  NOBODY likes Bill.

(Jackendoff 1972, p. 246)

To sharpen the intuition that focus does not generally trigger an existential ps, it is useful to compare ordinary sentences with prosodically marked focus with their cleft counterparts.[6]

---

[6]  This is pointed out in, e.g., Rooth 1996.

It seems clear that cleft constructions do consistently trigger an existential ps. For example, (19) presupposes that someone likes Bill.

(19)   It is MARY who likes Bill.

This judgment is supported by the fact that the following examples are not felicitous. (If (21) and (22) are acceptable at all, that is only if the speaker is taken to be revising her assumptions in mid-utterance, adopting, for the purposes of the second sentence, the assumption that someone does like Bill.)

(20)   # It is NOBODY who likes Bill.
(21)   ??Nobody likes Bill. Unless it is MARY who likes him.
(22)   ??I don't know if anybody likes Bill. Perhaps it is MARY who likes him.

Similarly, example (23) seems contradictory.

(23)   #I doubt that anyone won the departmental lottery this week, because it's unlikely
       that it's MARY who won it, and I know that nobody else did.
                                                                      (due to Rooth 1994, 1996)

There is no parallel support for the idea that ordinary focus too has an existential ps. (15) contrasts with (19) in that the following examples are fine, suggesting that (15) does not have an existential ps.

(24)   NOBODY likes Bill.
(25)   Nobody likes Bill. Unless MARY likes him.
(26)   I don't know if anybody likes Bill. Perhaps MARY likes him.

Similarly, example (27) seems perfectly felicitous.

(27)   I doubt that anyone won the departmental lottery this week, because it's unlikely
       that MARY won it, and I know that nobody else did.
                                                                      (due to Rooth 1994, 1996)

And yet the focus in (18) does seem to trigger **some** ps. According to Jackendoff 1972, the focal ps of both (15) and (18) is, roughly, as in (28).

(28)   The set of individuals who like Bill is
               'a coherent set in the present discourse'
       or      'well-defined in the present discourse'
       or      'amenable to discussion'
       or      'under discussion.'

More generally, according to Jackendoff, focus triggers the ps that the set of values that truthfully "fit into" the focus position is coherent, or well-defined, or amenable to discussion, or under discussion.

At this point, the following question arises: is there a difference between (i) the intuition that focus yields a "focal ps" à la Jackendoff and (ii) the intuition concerning the effect of focus on discourse congruence? Perhaps these two "effects" are the same thing, actually. If (15) presupposes that the set of individuals who like Bill is under discussion, that means that (15) is felicitous only in certain contexts (those in which this set is under discussion). But isn't that exactly the effect on discourse congruence illustrated in 13.2.1 above? We say that (15) is good as a response to, e.g., *Who likes Bill?* or *SUE likes Bill*, but not to, e.g., *Who does Mary like?* or *Mary likes LARRY*. This seems to be the same as saying that (15) is good in contexts where the set of individuals who like Bill is under discussion, and not, e.g., in contexts where the set of individuals that Mary likes is under discussion.

### 13.2.3 Focusing Adverbs

Jackendoff 1972 (p. 247) attributes to Fischer 1968 the observation that the interpretation of words such as *even* and *only* is sensitive to choice of focus.

In the case of *only*, there is a clear truth-conditional effect. If I introduced Bill to Sue and Jane and performed no other introductions, then (29) is true and (30) is false. If I introduced Bill and Tom to Sue and performed no other introductions, then (29) is false and (30) (with narrow focus on *SUE*) is true.

(29)  I only introduced BILL to Sue.
(30)  I only introduced Bill to SUE.

With other adverbs, the choice of focus affects the presupposition, rather than the truth conditions. For example, the sentences in (31) presuppose that I introduced someone other than Bill to Sue, whereas the sentences in (32) presuppose that I introduced Bill to someone other than Sue.

(31)  a.  I also introduced BILL to Sue.
      b.  I introduced BILL to Sue, too.
      c.  I even introduced BILL to Sue.

(32)  a.  I also introduced Bill to SUE.
      b.  I introduced Bill to SUE, too.
      c.  I even introduced Bill to SUE.

*Even* induces an additional presupposition, which also depends on the choice of focus: (31c) presupposes that my introducing Bill to Sue was less likely than my introducing other people to Sue, while (32c) presupposes that my introducing Bill to Sue was less likely than my introducing Bill to other people.

Jackendoff 1972 talks about the meaning of the focusing adverb as "associated with the focus." Rooth 1985 adopts the term "association with focus" and applies it generally to all semantic effects of focus – that is, to all cases where some operator is focus-sensitive in the sense that different choices of focus (in an argument of that operator) result in different truth conditions or different presuppositions.

### 13.2.4   Modals, Adverbs of Quantification, Generics: focus-sensitive quantification

Halliday 1967 notes that choice of focus affects the interpretation of statements with modals. His example is a sign in the London underground saying "Dogs must be carried." This sign is ambiguous, and may be disambiguated by focusing:

(33)   Dogs must be CARRIED.
(34)   DOGS must be carried.

(33) tells you that if you have a dog with you, you must carry it (presumably, the intended interpretation of the sign), whereas (34) tells you that you must have a dog that you carry with you (cf. "Shoes must be worn"). Here, again, different choices of focus yield different truth conditions.

Rooth 1985 observes a similar effect with adverbs of quantification, such as *always* and *usually*. Rooth gives the following examples.

(35)   In Saint Petersburg, OFFICERS always escorted ballerinas.
(36)   In Saint Petersburg, officers always escorted BALLERINAS.

(37)   MARY always takes John to the movies.
(38)   Mary always takes JOHN to the movies.

If a non-officer ever escorted a ballerina, (35) is false but (36) may still be true. If an officer ever escorted a non-ballerina, (36) is false but (35) may be true. Similarly, Sue taking John to the movies will falsify (37) but not (38), while Mary taking Bill to the movies will falsify (37) but not (38).

Note also the following example (from Sgall et al. 1986), illustrating that generic sentences exhibit a similar effect.

(39)   One SMOKES in the hallway.
(40)   One smokes in the HALLWAY.

As noted in Partee 1991, these examples all involve restricted quantification. For instance, (33), (38) and (40) would be analyzed roughly as follows (restriction in round brackets, nuclear scope in square brackets).

(33′)   In all (deontically accessible world w s.t. there is a dog x here in w), [x is CARRIED in w].
(38′)   All (events/situations of Mary taking someone to the movies) are [events/situations of Mary taking JOHN to the movies].
(40′)   Generic Operator (x smokes) [x is in the HALLWAY].

Partee 1991 offers the following conjecture: as a default option, unfocused material corresponds to the restriction, while focus corresponds to the nuclear scope.

Partee suggests, moreover, that this sort of focus-sensitive quantification is what is going on in many known semantic effects of focus. That includes, for instance, the case of focusing adverbs. To take an example, note that (29) from 13.2.3 above is interpreted roughly as in (29'); the unfocused material serves to restrict the quantification, while the focus occurs only in the nuclear scope.[7]

(29')   Of all (properties of having introduced x to Sue), the only property I have is [the property of having introduced BILL to Sue].

Of the various cases of focus-sensitive quantification, association of *only* with focus will be my main example. Other cases, alas, will have to be touched upon only briefly, if at all. For work on the focus effect with adverbs of quantification, see e.g. Rooth 1985, 1995; Krifka 1992 (see also Krifka 1995 on generic examples); von Fintel 1994. I will briefly return to this effect in section 21.1.

### 13.2.5   *Reasons*

Dretske 1972 points out the truth conditional effect of focus exhibited by the following examples.

(41)   The reason Clyde MARRIED Bertha was to qualify for the inheritance.
(42)   The reason Clyde married BERTHA was to qualify for the inheritance.
(Dretske 1972, pp. 417–18)
(43)   If Clyde hadn't MARRIED Bertha, he would not have been eligible for the inheritance.
(44)   If Clyde hadn't married BERTHA, he would not have been eligible for the inheritance.
(45)   If Clyde doesn't MARRY Bertha, he won't be eligible for the inheritance.
(46)   If Clyde doesn't marry BERTHA, he won't be eligible for the inheritance.
(Dretske 1972, pp. 432–3)

Let us evaluate these examples assuming the scenario in (47) below. Following the marriage, it seems clear that (41) is true, whereas (42) is false (Clyde married BERTHA to avoid altering his lifestyle). Of the subjunctive conditionals, (43) seems true (or at least likely to be true), whereas (44) seems false (or at least likely to be false). Similarly with the indicative conditionals – before the marriage, (45) seems true, whereas (46) seems false.

(47)   Clyde is a dedicated bachelor who does not want to live permanently with a woman. Yet Clyde finds out that he will inherit a lot of money if he is married by the age of 30. Clyde solves this dilemma by marrying his friend Bertha, a dedicated archeologist who is out of the country almost all the time.

Here are some more examples exhibiting a similar effect.

(48)   Why did Clyde MARRY Bertha?
(49)   Why did Clyde marry BERTHA?

---

[7]   Cf. the "domain selection" analysis (Boër 1979; Rooth 1985) introduced in chapter 16.

(50)  John's HITTING Mary caused the uproar.
(51)  John's hitting MARY caused the uproar.

(52)  Clyde gave ME the tickets by mistake.
(53)  Clyde gave me THE TICKETS by mistake.                 (Dretske 1972, p. 413)

(54)  It's odd that Clyde MARRIED Bertha.
(55)  It's odd that Clyde married BERTHA.

I think it is fair to say that all of Dretske's examples have to do with reasons. To take one of the less obvious cases, note that (54) and (55) can be paraphrased as follows.

(54′)  The reason that what Clyde did was odd was that he got married.
(55′)  The reason that what Clyde did was odd was that his bride was Bertha.

Dretske 1977 conjectures, in fact, that all examples where focus affects truth conditions have a causal component in their semantics.
   I will briefly discuss (52)–(53) in sections 17.2 and 17.3, and will briefly return to the conditional examples in section 21.1.

### 13.2.6   Negation

Jackendoff 1972 says that negation too "associates with focus." The intuition behind this is that "often negation does not seem to apply to an entire sentence, but only to part of it" (Jackendoff 1972, p. 254). Consider for example (56) and (57). It seems that in (56), the speaker denies that Maxwell's victim was the judge, but without denying that Maxwell killed someone with a silver hammer, whereas in (57), the speaker denies that the hammer in question was silver, but without denying that Maxwell killed the judge with a hammer.

(56)  Maxwell didn't kill the JUDGE with a silver hammer.
(57)  Maxwell didn't kill the judge with a SILVER hammer.

This is not a truth–conditional effect. It rather seems to do with discourse congruence or the "focal ps": (56) presupposes concern with who the individuals are that Maxwell killed with a silver hammer, whereas (57) presupposes concern with the kind of hammer that Maxwell used in killing the judge. (Cf. Horn 1989; Vallduví 1990.)
   The same effect shows up with a variety of other propositional operators. For example:

(58)  Maxwell probably killed the JUDGE with a silver hammer.
(59)  Maxwell probably killed the judge with a SILVER hammer.

                                                              (cf. Rooth 1996)

(60)  Did Maxwell kill the JUDGE with a silver hammer?
(61)  Did Maxwell kill the judge with a SILVER hammer?

                                                              (cf. Kuno 1980)

### 13.2.7 Superlatives

Jackendoff 1972 attributes to Bowers 1969 the observation that choice of focus affects the interpretation of sentences with superlatives, such as (62)–(63). In (62), it is understood that Bill is one of the three men alluded to (cf. #*Of the three men, John hates MARY the most*), while in (63), it is understood that John is one of the three men alluded to (cf. #*Of the three men, MARY hates Bill the most*).

(62)   Of the three men, John hates BILL the most.
(63)   Of the three men, JOHN hates Bill the most.

### 13.2.8   Bare Remnant Ellipsis and VP Anaphora

Consider (64) and (65). There are a lot of constructions of this sort. The second clause contains either ellipsis or an anaphoric element in place of a part of the sentence which includes the verb and possibly some of its arguments, and it is interpreted on the basis of the first clause.

(64)   John eats apples more than Mary.   ('more than Mary eats apples')
(65)   John embarrasses Mary by criticizing her in public more often than he does it to Sue.   ('more often than John embarrasses Sue by criticizing her in public')

Focus can play a disambiguating role in the interpretation of such constructions, as seen in the following examples. On the optionality of this effect, see section 17.2. For an analysis, see section 17.3.

(66)   John hates BILL more than MARY.      ('more than John hates Mary')
(67)   JOHN hates Bill more than MARY.      ('more than Mary hates Bill')
(68)   Kim likes LEE well enough, but not ROBIN.      ('Kim doesn't like Robin')
(69)   KIM likes Lee well enough, but not ROBIN.      ('Robin doesn't like Lee')
(70)   KIM managed to impress Lee, but that wouldn't have happened with Robin. ('Robin wouldn't have managed to impress Lee')
(71)   Kim managed to impress LEE, but that wouldn't have happened with Robin.      ('Kim wouldn't have managed to impress Robin')
(72)   KIM visited Lee before ROBIN.      ('before Robin visited Lee')
(73)   Kim visited LEE before ROBIN.      ('before Kim visited Robin')
(74)   MOM wants her to choose ME, and DAD – SUE.
('Dad wants her to choose Sue')
(75)   MOM wants HER to choose me, and DAD – SUE.
('Dad wants Sue to choose me')

### 13.2.9   Scalar Implicatures

Rooth 1992 points out that the choice of focus plays a role in determining scalar implicatures. His example (p. 82) is the following. Suppose Mats, Steve and Paul take a calculus quiz, which is graded on the spot. George asks Mats how the quiz went. If Mats' reply is (76), this tends to yield a scalar implicature that Mats did no better than passing. If Mats' reply is (77), this tends to yield a scalar implicature that Steve and Paul didn't pass.

(76)   Well, I [passed]$_F$.
(77)   Well, [I]$_F$ passed.

Rooth notes (but doesn't discuss) the fact that the effect may involve not just a peak of prosodic prominence, but also a particular pitch contour. I think the effect may be present without the special contour – for example, imagine the following examples pronounced with an ordinary declarative terminal fall.

(78)   MOST conductors are competent pianists.
(79)   Most conductors are COMPETENT pianists.

(78) tends to suggest that not all conductors are competent pianists, whereas (79) tends to suggest that it is not the case that most conductors are excellent pianists. (I think that in each example, the two implicatures just described may actually be present at the same time, with the focus drawing special attention to one of them; cf. 17.2 below.) For an analysis of this effect, see section 17.3.

### 13.2.10   Sentence-Internal Contrasting Phrases

Chomsky 1971 discusses the example in (80). He states that "contrastive intonation" is necessary in such "parallel constructions." Example (81) is from Rooth 1992 (p. 80). It is to be thought of as the beginning of a joke.

(80)   John is neither EAGER to please, nor EASY to please, nor CERTAIN to please.
(81)   An AMERICAN farmer was talking to a CANADIAN farmer . . .

It seems that the prosodic peaks in such examples do not restrict the discourse contexts in which the example can occur in the way discussed in 13.2.1 above. Rather, they seem to play a different pragmatic role, viz. to indicate contrast between two (or more) phrases within the sentence. The contrast seems symmetric; e.g. the emphasis on *American* is motivated by the contrast with *Canadian*, and vice versa – the emphasis on *Canadian* is motivated by the contrast with *American*. The emphasized words in such examples are commonly taken to be foci; perhaps foci of a particular type (cf. Rochemont 1986, ch. 2). But see 18.1.2 below.

## 13.3   Focus and Question–Answer Pairs

I believe that the intuition that focus is the answer to the question being addressed is a basic and crucial one. I tend to think that it is in fact the most basic and crucial intuition about focus. Hence, like many researchers before me, I believe in using question–answer pairs as a central means of identifying foci and investigating the empirical behavior of focus. (I am also sympathetic to making the "answer to the question" intuition the basis of a formal analysis of focus, as in Roberts 1996b; see chapter 17.)

Consider the generalization that the focus in the answer correlates with the questioned position in the question. It is based on contrasts like the following.

(82)  A:  Who did you introduce to Sue?
      B:  I introduced Bill to Sue.          FELICITOUS
              H* L L%
(83)  A:  Who did you introduce to Sue?
      B:  I introduced Bill to Sue.          INFELICITOUS
                      H* L   L%

Obviously, by "answer" we mean an utterance that explicitly expresses an answer to the question, excluding other felicitous responses. So the replies in (84) and (85), for instance, are not relevant to the above generalization. ((85B) may well implicate an answer to (85A) or even contextually entail one, but it does not explicitly express one.)

(84)  A:  Who hit you?
      B:  I don't know.
(85)  A:  Was Smith officially invited?
      B:  Jones was officially invited.

What I would like to do here is bring up a further point, viz. the following. By "answer" we actually mean what might be called a **truly direct answer**. The intuitions here are more subtle, but let me try to clarify what I mean.

Consider (87)–(90) as replies to (86). All these replies explicitly express an answer to (86). And yet, there is an intuitive difference, I think, between (87) and the rest: (87) is a truly direct answer, in a way that (88)–(90) are not.

(86)  Was Smith officially invited?
(87)  He was officially invited.
          H*    L        L%
(88)  Everybody was officially invited.
          H*    L                L%
(89)  He was officially invited three months in advance.
                          L*              H* L L%
(90)  He was officially invited . . .
          L*+H L     H%

(87) seems to be the only reply that does nothing more and nothing less than directly answer question (86). (88) and (89) clearly provide more information than was requested; I think they each seem to be concerned with a somewhat broader topic/question than the one raised in (86). (90) turns the discussion to the variety of manners of invitation, suggesting that one other than "officially" is of greater interest.

In sum, the utterance-pairs that display our generalization are pairs of a question and a truly direct answer to it. It is the focus of a truly direct answer – but not of other replies – that must correspond to the questioned position in the question. So, the intuitions about what constitutes a truly direct answer to a given question might be subtle, but they are crucial to the identification of focus and to studying its empirical behavior.

Most of the time, when we identify foci or study them, we don't talk about the notion of a truly direct answer. Why is that? Well, most of the time, we automatically pick responses that are clearly intended as truly direct answers. Also, we often deliberately pick examples where the focus is easy to identify on the basis of prosodic clues (in particular, we often use non-sentence-final narrow foci, as in (82)).

Take for instance the case of (82) and (83) above. It is very clear, intuitively, that (82B) is a truly direct answer to (82A). Also, the prosody strongly suggests that *Bill* is the focus. So we can safely conclude that the focus is on *Bill*, and don't even give it a second thought. We also note that "the focus in the answer corresponds to the questioned position in the question," and don't give that a second thought. The prosody of (83B) strongly suggests that *Bill* is not the focus. So we note that "in the answer to (83A), the focus cannot fail to correspond to the questioned position." Without thinking about it, we are talking here about a truly direct answer. Note that (83B) expresses the very same proposition as (82B), and is clearly intended as a truly direct answer as well.

Note also that we needn't really worry about whether (83B) is a truly direct answer or not, since (83B) is an entirely infelicitous response, and hence certainly not a possible truly direct answer. Compare with (88), which is a felicitous response to (86): to maintain the generalization that focus must correspond to the questioned position, we must make sure that while (88) does answer (86), it is not a truly direct answer to it.

It is worth keeping in mind that in many examples identifying the focus may be a matter of debate, and it is worth keeping in mind that such a debate may often involve the question of whether a given answer is a truly direct one or not. I think that ignoring speakers' intuitions about what constitutes a truly direct answer can easily lead us astray in our efforts to identify foci and study their behavior. I will have occasion to resort to such intuitions in what follows (see especially chapter 20).

Certainly, there will be cases where speakers can't intuitively tell if a reply is a truly direct answer or not. Just as there are cases where truth value judgments or grammaticality judgments are unclear. As is the usual practice, we will rely on the clear(er) cases as our evidence, and let the resulting theory decide the status of the unclear cases.

## 13.4 Focus and Pitch Accents

Note: In what follows, capitals continue to mark the word of greatest prosodic prominence in the sentence (where the nuclear pitch accent and heaviest stress coincide). Also, pitch accents are sometimes marked with *pa*, instead of specifying which particular pitch accent this is; in that case (just as when Hs and Ls are used), **all** the pitch accents in the relevant intermediate phrase are marked. Whenever intonation is not marked, assume, as a default, that the sentence under consideration is pronounced as a single intonation phrase containing a single intermediate phrase.

### 13.4.1 Focus is Marked by the Presence of Pitch Accents in it

We assume that a "focus" is a syntactic (or morphological) constituent which is marked in surface structure with the feature F, and that foci are reflected both in semantic and pragmatic effects and in prosodic patterns.

Following Selkirk 1984 (section 5.3.2), let us assume that the kind of prosodic prominence which serves to mark focused constituents in English is the pitch accent. We assume that pitch accent placement is constrained in such a way that the positions of pitch accents in a given sentence can help us identify the focused constituent(s) in that sentence.[8]

As a start, we may note that roughly, there are pitch accents inside but not outside the focus. That is, the following empirical generalizations seem to hold.[9]

(91)  Every pitch accent occurs within a focus.
(92)  Every focus contains at least one pitch accent.

These two generalizations together already cover a certain array of facts. For example, they permit the grammatical configurations in (93)–(96) and rule out the impossible configurations in (97)–(100).

(93)    She [kissed]$_F$ Ronnie                    OK
              H*      L      L%
(94)    She kissed [Ronnie]$_F$                    OK
                    H* L L%
(95)    She [kissed Ronnie]$_F$                    OK
              H*          H* L L%
        or
        H* + L H* L L%

---

[8]  Other aspects of the prosody (prosodic phrasing, choice of tones) also provide information regarding the focal structure, but I will leave that aside for the moment.

[9]  These generalization are empirical claims made by the theory of Selkirk 1984 (see her section 5.3.2). Lisa Selkirk (p.c.) argues that (91) is in fact open to question, since configurations like (i) seem possible. (The choice of L* as the pitch accent on *introduced* indicates previous mention in the discourse.)

(i)      I introduced [Bill]$_F$ to Sue.
              L*      H*      L   L%

I am not sure I am convinced by (i). I agree that (iii) is a felicitous answer to (ii). However, I am not sure that the focus in (iii) is on Bill.

(ii)   Who did you introduce to Sue?
(iii)  I introduced Bill to Sue.
              L*   H* L  L%

The intuition is clear, I think, that (iii) has the air of the speaker being forced to spell out something all over again (probably indicating to the person asking (ii) that they were already supposed to possess the requested information). Selkirk would take the L* to be focus-external, as in (i), and would presumably ascribe the intuition just mentioned to the choice of L* indicating previous mention. I would be inclined to include the L* in the focus. I would say that (iii) is not a truly direct answer to (ii), and has the focus on the entire VP or S. The placement of L* indicates the broad focus, and the broad focus in turn is what indicates to the hearer that the speaker is repeating the information all over again. The choice of L* corresponds to the mention of *introduced* in the question. I will continue to assume that generalization (91) holds.

(96)    [Amanda]_F kissed [Ronnie]_F            OK
        H*              H* L L%
        or
        H* + L          H* L L%
        or
        H* L            H* L L%
(97)    She [kissed]_F Ronnie                   IMPOSSIBLE
            H*       H* L L%
(98)    She kissed [Ronnie]_F                   IMPOSSIBLE
            H*       H* L L%
(99)    [Amanda]_F kissed [Ronnie]_F            IMPOSSIBLE
                        H* L  L%
(100)   She [kissed]_F Ronnie                   IMPOSSIBLE
                    H*  L  L%

All the good focus-plus-pitch-accents configurations in (93)–(96) meet the requirements of (91) and (92). (97) and (98) fail because there is a pitch accent outside the focus, (99) fails because there is a focus without a pitch accent, and (100) fails for both reasons.

But how do we know that the facts are as stated? Before I continue, it is worth clarifying how such facts are established. What we do is try out the sentence with the indicated intonation in a context where the focus is independently expected to be as marked, and see if the result is felicitous. Often, we use for that purpose dialogs consisting of a question and a truly direct answer to it (see section 13.3), in which we are able to identify the focus – independently of prosody – as "the answer to the question." For instance, the facts in (93)–(100) are based on the following data.

(101)   A:  What did she do to Ronnie?
        B:  She kissed Ronnie.                  FELICITOUS
                H*    L    L%
(102)   A:  Who did she kiss?
        B:  She kissed Ronnie.                  FELICITOUS
                    H* L L%
(103)   A:  What did she do at the party?
        B:  She kissed Ronnie.                  FELICITOUS
                H*      H* L L%
(104)   A:  I heard that a person kissed another person,
            but I don't know who the two persons were.
            Who kissed who?
        B:  Amanda kissed Ronnie                FELICITOUS
                H*              H* L L%
            or
                H* + L          H* L L%
            or
                H* L            H* L L%
(105)   A:  What did she do to Ronnie?
        B:  She kissed Ronnie.                  INFELICITOUS
                H*      H* L L%

(106)  A:  Who did she kiss?
      B:  She kissed Ronnie.               INFELICITOUS
             H*    H* L L%

(107)  A:  I heard that a person kissed another person,
           but I don't know who the two persons were.
           Who kissed who?
      B:  Amanda kissed Ronnie         INFELICITOUS
                H* L L%

(108)  A:  What did she do to Ronnie?
      B:  She kissed Ronnie.               INFELICITOUS
             H* L L%

In what follows, I will most often just state the facts as I take them to be, leaving it to the reader to construct actual examples that verify these facts.

Returning to our two generalizations, it seems reasonable to incorporate (91) ("no pitch accents outside the foci") into the theory more or less as it is. But when it comes to where pitch accents are placed inside a focus, things seem to get rather more complicated. Generalization (92) ("at least one pitch accent per focus") is not sufficient; for example, (92) does not rule out the configurations in (109)–(111) below, which seem – at least in simple, minimal contexts – to be impossible. (It seems that in these examples, the indicated intonation is compatible only with a narrower focus – focus on *met*, *mayor* or *red*.) Evidently, we need a stronger statement than (92).

(109)  She [met Ronnie]$_F$          SEEMS IMPOSSIBLE
        H* L   L%

(110)  The [mayor of Chicago]$_F$ won it   SEEMS IMPOSSIBLE
         H*   L           L%

(111)  It was an ex-convict [with a red shirt]$_F$   SEEMS IMPOSSIBLE
                  H*  L L%

## 13.4.2  The Right-End Hypothesis

When configurations like (109)–(111) above are compared with configurations like (112)–(117) below,

(112)  She [met Ronnie]$_F$          OK
        H* H* L L%

(113)  She [met Ronnie]$_F$          OK
        H* L L%

(114)  The [mayor of Chicago]$_F$ won it   OK
         H*        H* L   L%

(115)  The [mayor of Chicago]$_F$ won it   OK
              H*  L   L%

(116)  It was an ex-convict [with a red shirt]$_F$   OK
                  H*  H* L L%

(117)  It was an ex-convict [with a red shirt]$_F$   OK
                   H* L L%

a generalization about pitch accent placement within foci suggests itself, which may be, very roughly, stated as in (118).

(118)   **The right-end hypothesis about pitch accent placement within foci**:
A focused constituent must contain a pitch accent on the primary stress of a word at its right end.

One form of this hypothesis is put forward in Halliday 1967 (p. 207), and another in Jackendoff 1972.

The right-end hypothesis offers an explanation for the impression that ambiguities between "broader" vs. "narrower" foci are restricted (roughly) to examples with a pitch accent at the right end of a large constituent. For instance, it explains why while (119)–(121) are ambiguous between "narrow" focus on the word with the pitch accent and "broad" focus on (any of) the larger constituent(s) enclosed in brackets, the focus in (122)–(126) seems to be unambiguously "narrow" (with the bracketed constituent(s) unable to be focused).

(119)   I [took him to a bookstore]          focus ambiguous
                      H* L L%

(120)   The [mayor of Chicago] won it     focus ambiguous
                        H*     L   L%

(121)   He was [warned [to look out for [an ex-convict [with a [red shirt]]]]]
                                                                          H* L L%

(122)   I [took him to a bookstore]          narrow focus only
                  H* L            L%

(123)   The [mayor of Chicago] won it     narrow focus only
                  H*   L                L%

(124)   He was [warned [to look out for [an ex-convict [with a [red shirt]]]]]
                                                              H* L       L%

(125)   He was [warned [to look out for [an ex-convict [with a [red shirt]]]]]
                                                  H*  L                     L%

(126)   He was [warned [to look out for [an ex-convict [with a [red shirt]]]]]
                          H*  L                                             L%

However, it is not at all clear that some viable form of the hypothesis under consideration could be found and maintained.

Obviously, it would be wrong to claim that the focused constituent must contain a pitch accent in its rightmost word (cf., for example, *Amanda [HIT me]*$_F$, which is OK). It has been proposed (in Jackendoff 1972) that the focused constituent must contain a pitch accent on the syllable to which the Nuclear Stress Rule (see section 12.4) assigns the strongest stress within that constituent. However, as argued extensively in the literature, this NSR-based approach is refuted by a large variety of examples, such as the following.[10]

---

[10]   For more data refuting the NSR-based approach see Schmerling 1976; Ladd 1980; Selkirk 1984; Gussenhoven 1984 (as well as many of the examples occurring below). Bolinger 1972 shows that a revised approach based on Bresnan 1971 would not work either.

| | |
|---|---|
| (127) I want to SAY something. | S or VP focus possible[11] |
| (128) John doesn't READ books. | VP focus possible |
| (129) I've got CHILDREN to feed. | S or VP focus possible |
| (130) My MOTHER's coming. | S focus possible |

It has also been proposed (in Halliday 1967) that the focus must contain a pitch accent on its last "accentable" word. But, as pointed out in Ladd 1980 (pp. 84–5), this presupposes that the notion of "accentable" is well-defined, with a dichotomy between accentable and non-accentable words, whereas in truth, it is not at all clear that such a dichotomy could be defined. Are "content words" accentable while "function words" are not? Are nouns accentable while verbs are not? It seems that such attempts won't work. For instance, the following examples show that *(my) shop*, *speak* and *(the) publisher* couldn't be classified as either accentable or non-accentable.

| | |
|---|---|
| (131) Some burglars broke into my SHOP last night. | S focus possible |
| (132) Some BURGLARS broke into my shop last night. | S focus possible |
| | (Bolinger 1972, p. 639) |
| (133) How many languages do you SPEAK? | broad focus possible |
| | (Ladd 1980, p. 82) |
| (134) How many LANGUAGES do you speak? | broad focus possible |
| (135) She sent her sketches to the PUBLISHER. | VP focus possible |
| (136) She sent her SKETCHES to the publisher. | VP focus possible |
| | (Selkirk 1984, her (5.12)) |

In short, it seems clear that pitch accent placement within foci is not determined by some right-end rule which is based purely on syntax and/or the lexicon. Indeed, there is reason to suspect that pitch accent placement within foci is not governed by a right-end rule at all.

### 13.4.3  Focus Identification and the Role(s) of Pitch Accents

And yet, the fact remains that pitch accent placement does often help us to decide how "narrow" or "broad" the focus is. I believe that the correct explanation for this must be based on the role(s) that pitch accents play as devices for **marking subconstituents within the focus**. To my mind, that is the most important insight embodied in the theories of pitch accent placement within foci given in Ladd 1980 and Selkirk 1984, 1996.

Consider each of the following examples. Can the example have the entire sentence as its focus? (Can it answer "What's up?"?) Assume throughout that *is coming* is interpreted as "is about to visit me".

---

[11]  As in:

(i)   A:  What's up?
      B:  [s I want to SAY something ]F.
(ii)  I didn't say that you were wrong, I only said that [s I want to SAY something ]F.
(iii) A:  What do you want to do?
      B:  I want to [vP SAY something]F.

| (137) | a. | My mother is singing |
|---|---|---|
| S focus | | H*         H* L L% |
| easy | b. | My mother is singing |
| | | H% L*          H* L L% |
| | c. | My mother is singing |
| | | H* + L    H* L L% |

| (138) | a. | My mother is coming |
|---|---|---|
| S focus | | H*          H* L L% |
| bad | b. | My mother is coming |
| or | | H% L*          H* L L% |
| unusual | c. | My mother is coming |
| | | H* + L    H* L L% |

| (139) | a. | My mother is singing |
|---|---|---|
| S focus | | H*    L         L% |
| possible | b. | My mother is singing |
| in | | L*    L         L% |
| context | | |

| (140) | a. | My mother is coming |
|---|---|---|
| S focus | | H*    L         L% |
| easy | b. | My mother is coming |
| | | L*    L         L% |

| (141) | My mother is singing |
|---|---|
| in context | H* L L% |

| (142) | My mother is coming |
|---|---|
| in context | H* L L% |

Look first at (137) and (140). Here, S focus is clearly very natural. For (138), S focus is not natural at all; the sentences in (138) are certainly not the expected response to "What's up?" or to "Why are you cleaning the house?". For (139), (141) and (142), S focus is possible, but only if the context is set up in the right way (sample contexts are given below). If you think about this sort of data, it very quickly becomes clear that the location of pitch accents tells us something about the informational status of sub-constituents within the focus.

In (137)–(142), the pitch accents seem to mark, separately, the subject NP and/or the verb (or VP). In fact, it seems that the presence or absence of a pitch accent tells us whether the sub-constituent refers to something (relatively) expected or unexpected. Here is some illustration of this. (141) is a natural response to "what's happening?" only when reference to the mother is likely in the context, as in (143) below.[12] In contrast, (137) is a natural response to "what's happening?" "out of the blue," or in a context where reference to my mother is (relatively) unexpected, as in (144).

(143) A: My parents are here, and a lot of other guests.
      B: What's happening?
      A: My mother is singing.
                    H* L L%
(144) A: We have a lot of people in the living room.
      B: What's happening?
      A: My mother is singing.
         H% L*          H* L L%

[12] The observation that whether or not an example can have broad focus may depend on the context goes back to Schmerling 1976. Schmerling notes that (i) **can** have broad focus on the entire predicate NP, if spoken in the context of a hospital or medical convention. (At a high society cocktail party, (ii) would have to be used instead.)

(i) This is the doctor I was TELLING you about.
(ii) This is the DOCTOR I was telling you about.

(139) is a natural response to "what's happening?" only in a suitable context, for example, in (145). In contrast, (140) is a natural "out of the blue" piece of news, as in (146).

(145)  BACKGROUND:  We're at the school of music. It is part of your general knowledge that my mother is a well-known singer. People seem to be moving towards the auditorium.

you:  What's happening?
me:  My mother is singing.
      H\* L     L%

(146)  A:  Hi, what's up?
B:  My mother is coming.
      H\* L     L%

Apparently, "is coming" does not need to be highlighted by a pitch accent; presumably because given the mention (and accenting) of "my mother", the action is "rather highly predictable" (Bolinger 1986, p. 105).

Consider also examples (147) and (148), as "out of the blue" responses to "what did John do this weekend?".

(147)  He read a book about Schubert and wrote to the author.
    pa         pa    pa    pa

(148)  He read a book about Schubert and wrote to the author.
    pa         pa    pa

The two examples are interpreted differently: "the author" in (147) is the author of the previously-mentioned book, whereas "the author" in (148) is Schubert.[13] So it seems that the presence or absence of a pitch accent in the NP *the author* tells us whether the referent of this NP has just been mentioned (and is therefore very salient) or not.

I am not able to supply any kind of a definition of what it is exactly that pitch accents mark. I can only say that they mark a constituent as "highlighted," or "unexpected", or "not immediately salient," or something of that sort.[14] And yet I think that taking the "highlighting" role of pitch accents as given can be quite a good basis for a theory of prosody-based focus identification.

I would like to suggest that the "highlighting" or "marking as unexpected" (or whatever) role of pitch accents is **the** most important factor in prosody-based focus identification, and should be given an even more central place in the theory than it occupies in the theories of Ladd 1980 and Selkirk 1984, 1996 (to be discussed in 13.4.4), simultaneously allowing less of a role to syntactic/morphological/rhythmic factors.[15]

Let us assume that a pitch accent inside a focus may serve to mark a sub-part of that focus as "highlighted," or "unexpected," or "not immediately salient," or whatever. I think that such an assumption can go a long way towards explaining how pitch accent placement helps us identify the focus. More than that, I also think that the explanation

---

[13]  This contrast is due to Lisa Selkirk (class lectures, the mid 80s, UMass/Amherst).

[14]  But see Schwarzschild 1999 for a model-theoretically-defined notion of "givenness" and its relation to marking by pitch accents. This interesting new paper diverges quite radically from the general approach taken here – it actually offers a theory where focus as such does not receive a semantic/pragmatic interpretation – and I will not be able to discuss it within the bounds of this book.

[15]  Schwarzschild 1999 too argues for giving less of a role to syntactic factors regarding pitch accent placement and interpretation.

does not even require us to posit any rule which directly relates pitch accent placement to focus.

Let me try to explain what I have in mind. Let us not make any assumptions at all about the phonological interpretation of the feature F. Let us make the following preliminary assumption concerning the semantic/pragmatic interpretation of F: the material outside the focused constituent(s) must correspond to the question which is currently being addressed in the context of utterance; as such, this material is invariably "expected" in that context. Pitch accent placement can help us identify the focus in the following manner.

Given an utterance, a hearer may consider any constituent in it to see if it is a possible focus. Suppose you consider the possibility that a certain constituent X is the focus. You check the pitch accents inside X. If the pitch accents seem to mark those words or phrases in X that are "unexpected in the context" (or whatever), but none of the words or phrases in X that are "expected in the context" (or whatever), then X is a possible focus. For example, in the context in (144), it is neither expected that speaker A would talk about her mother nor that A would talk about singing. So the configuration

[ My mother is singing ]$_F$
  H% L*      H*L L%

is fine in that context. In the context in (145), talk of singing is quite expected, so the configuration

[ My mother is singing ]$_F$
     H*   L      L%

is fine in that context. Visiting is quite an expected thing to be reported (of mothers) in general, so the configuration

[ My mother is coming ]$_F$
     H*   L      L%

is fine in many contexts (and therefore "out of the blue"). If, on the other hand, the pitch accents **don't** seem to mark exactly those parts of X that are "unexpected," then X is **not** a possible focus. For example, in the context in (144), talk about the mother is not expected, so the configuration

[ My mother is singing ]$_F$
        H* L L%

is not possible in that context. And on the assumption that "is coming" can't be "unexpected" in our sentence at all (as long as it simply reports a visit), the configuration

[ My mother is coming ]$_F$
  H% L*      H* L L%

would be completely ruled out, as desired.

Now note that examples (139) and (140) can have a "narrow" NP focus (they can answer "who is singing?" and "who is coming?", respectively). The hearer can ascertain that this is possible based on the same sort of consideration as above: if the VP is not part of the focus, then it is highly "expected," by virtue of being part of the question addressed by the utterance; relative to that, the NP – the answer to the question – is "unexpected"; hence, the pitch accent is appropriate.

Note also that out of the blue, the focus of (139) might, at first sight, seem to be unambiguously narrow. That is probably because it is relatively hard to imagine a context of utterance like (145), where, simultaneously, the question "who is singing?" is **not** being addressed, and yet reference to singing **is** relatively expected. I think it may well be that examples whose focus is genuinely unambiguously "narrow" are extreme cases of such a situation – cases where it is altogether impossible to construct a context of utterance that would allow a "broad" focus.[16]

Finally, note that generalization (91) ("no pitch accents outside the focus") follows automatically from the assumption that any part of the utterance which corresponds to the question currently being addressed in the context is "expected" in that context, since "expected" parts cannot contain pitch accents.

To sum up, I would say that things work roughly as follows. Pitch accents mark sub-constituents within the utterance as (relatively) "highlighted" or "unexpected" or "non-salient" or whatever. This means that any pitch accent placement is fine in the right context: it is fine as long as all and only the sub-constituents marked by a pitch accent are "unexpected" (or whatever it is) in the context. If it is hard to find a context in which a given pitch accent placement would be good, this pitch accent placement would sound strange "out of the blue." If it is absolutely impossible to find such a context, the pitch accent placement would be ruled out altogether.

And what does all this have to do with focus identification? As far as sub-constituents inside the focus go, there is nothing to add: they must be either "expected" and unaccented, or else "unexpected" and accented. As for sub-constituents outside the focus, it follows from our assumptions about the interpretation of focus that they must be "expected" and hence unaccented. What helps us identify the focus is that we know we must look for a focus-plus-pitch-accents configuration that obeys these constraints.

Of course, the picture I have just sketched leaves open important issues. First of all, there are details to be filled in, concerning both the definition and the interpretation of "being marked by a pitch accent." Secondly, it has been proposed by many researchers that the distribution of pitch accents to words or phrases is at least partly governed by structural principles (based on syntax or morphology or stress), often principles that refer directly to the notion of a focused (F-marked) constituent; the question arises whether such structural principles might not indeed be at work, in addition to the contextual factors discussed in this section. A number of specific hypotheses about marking by pitch accents will be considered in the next subsection.

---

[16] Besides, I suspect that various examples that have been assumed in the literature to only allow "narrow" focus do in fact allow a "broader" focus as well, in the right context.

### 13.4.4 Specific Hypotheses about Marking by Pitch Accents

#### 13.4.4.1 Ladd: accentability and "deaccenting"
Ladd 1980 (p. 85) proposes the following principle.

(149) **Ladd's Focus Rule:**
   A pitch accent must go on the most accentable syllable of the focus.

Ladd accepts the assumption that it is word-stress that determines accentability within a word. Other than that, Ladd states that there is a variety of poorly understood factors that determine relative accentability among words. These factors Ladd divides into two groups:

   (A)   Factors that determine a basic hierarchy of accentability
         These factors include: (i) syntactic and semantic considerations that make certain positions within a constituent more accentable than others (for example, Ladd says that such considerations determine, roughly, that within a compound the left-hand side is more accentable); and (ii) a "poorly understood hierarchy of parts of speech," whereby nouns are more accentable than other content words and content words are more accentable than function words.
   (B)   Factors that cause "deaccenting"
         "Deaccenting," according to Ladd, is a lowering of the accentability of a given word or constituent, relative to the basic hierarchy of accentability. Ladd suggests that deaccenting can happen for "quite a variety of reasons," including definiteness, the fact that the reference of proper names is usually fixed in the context, the fact that certain things are already under discussion in the context, etc. Ladd's generalization is that an item is deaccented if (for some reason or another) its full interpretation relates it to the context of utterance.

Ladd denies then that the NSR or some other structural principle is an absolute constraint on pitch accent placement. He believes instead that there is a fairly large and heterogeneous variety of factors that affect the placement of pitch accents. (I believe that Ladd is right about both of these things, for reasons that I hope will become clear below.)

Regarding the factors that are supposed to govern relative accentability, note, first of all, that many of the factors Ladd has in mind seem to affect the extent to which the word is – or is likely to be – "old" or "salient" or "expected" or "unimportant" (or whatever) in the context of utterance. This concerns factors of both of the two presumed groups. Regarding group (A), why is it, for example, that content words are more accentable than function words? isn't that precisely because they tend to be more "unexpected" or "important" in the context? Regarding group (B), what "deaccenting" seems to signal is precisely that an item is "expected" or "known" or "salient" or whatever in the context of utterance.

Ladd does not attempt to decide whether a pitch accent means "new" or "unexpected" or "highlighted" or something else. I believe that this is as it should be. Allowing flexibility in the interpretation of pitch accent placement is very much in the spirit of Bolinger's work, over many years, on the role(s) of prosodic prominences. (See e.g. Bolinger 1986.) As Ladd 1990 puts it (p. 815), "Bolinger's work has made it clear beyond any doubt that accent placement is capable of expressing countless subtleties."

Certainly, pitch accents regularly signal that the referent of a given constituent is "new" or "unexpected" or "non-salient" in the context, as illustrated in 13.4.3 above. But pitch accents may also signal something else – for instance, that the speaker attaches special importance to a given constituent or wishes to highlight it. To give just one example, Bolinger (1986, p. 90) notes that the final word *fish* in (150) is certainly not "new" or "unexpected," and suggests that repeating and accenting this word "serves a kind of pointing function," akin to "holding one's hands up in mock horror at contemplating the object."

(150)   Raw fish is good for you, but after all, who likes raw FISH?

In addition to factors that involve the interpretation of the presence or absence of pitch accents in context, Ladd 1980 allows for the possibility that more arbitrary principles that have to do with linguistic structure and/or the lexicon also affect pitch accent placement. I believe that this too is as it should be. Ladd takes such factors to play a major role in determining the basic accentability hierarchy. For example: the principle that (in English) nouns are more accentable than words of other syntactic categories; the principle that makes the left-hand side of a compound more accentable than the right.

Allowing structural grammatical principles some role in pitch accent placement would complicate somewhat the picture sketched in 13.4.3 above. However, it gives us one way of explaining the impression that certain dominant patterns and strong tendencies in pitch accent placement are observed which are hard to explain just in terms of the meanings conveyed by pitch accent placement.

Take, for instance, the impression that the nuclear accent tends to be placed towards the right end, which originally gave rise to the NSR-based approach. We may look for explanations that have to do with the interpretation of pitch accent placement, as Bolinger would (and has). For instance, one plausible explanation is that placing an item in a right-end position is in itself a way of highlighting it (cf. Giora 1983). But we could also hypothesize that the NSR, or some other rule sensitive to syntactic structure, does determine default patterns of accent placement that show up whenever they are not overruled by other considerations.

As argued in Ladd 1990, one very good reason to believe that there exist arbitrary grammatical principles that influence pitch accent placement is that patterns of pitch accent placement show cross-linguistic variation. One of Ladd's examples is the following. In a discussion of a strange old man and the things that are unusual about him, in English one would have to say (151), while in Italian, one would say (152); indeed, (153) is "an attested sentence spoken by a very fluent Italian speaker of English" (p. 811).

(151)   It's the SHOES he wears.
(152)   Sono le  scarpe che  PORTA.
        are   the shoes that wears
(153)   It's the shoes he WEARS.

Here is another example: (154) in English can easily have a maximally broad focus (on the entire matrix clause). In contrast, the parallel Hebrew example in (155) must have a narrow focus on *lihiyot* ("to-be"). (In Hebrew, one might say something like (156) to convey the idea of (154).)

(154) I'm awfully glad there are guys who want to be dentists.     (Ladd 1980)

pa                                     pa

(155) ani nora   smexa še-yeš  ka'ele še-rocim  lihiyot rof'ei–šinayim.

pa                                     pa

      I   awfully glad   that-exist such  that-want  to-be  dentists

(156) ani nora   smexa še-yeš   ka'ele še-bexol-ofen rocim lihiyot rof'ei–šinayim.

pa                            pa

      I   awfully glad   that-exist such   that-anyway    want   to-be   dentists

Similarly, an English preposition can bear the sole pitch accent of a broad VP or S focus, as in (157) and (158), whereas no such thing is possible in Hebrew.

(157) The buttermilk's the best part OF it.                 (Selkirk 1984, her 5.31))

(158) *Roseanne, having failed to comply with her sister's list of dos and don'ts while babysitting her child:* Well, you got your kid alive, and THAT wasn't even ON your list.

(From the TV show "Roseanne," noted by Ziva Wijler)

In sum, for reasons indicated in this and the preceding subsection, I believe that Ladd is right in allowing both the marking of words by pitch accents as "highlighted"/"unexpected" and more arbitrary structural principles to play a role in the theories of pitch accent placement and prosody-based focus identification. I also believe that Ladd is right in not positing any very general or very dominant structural constraint on pitch accent placement, since I have not been convinced by proposals that do ascribe to structural factors a dominant role – see 13.4.2 regarding the NSR, and see the discussion of Selkirk's theory in 13.4.4.2 below.

There are also some features of Ladd's theory that are problematic or questionable.

As noted in Selkirk 1984 (section 5.2.1) and also in Bolinger 1986 (p. 100), a serious shortcoming of Ladd's approach (which it shares with the NSR-based approach) is that it only concerns the obligatory presence and placement of a single pitch accent within the focus. The problem is that it therefore fails to say anything about whether the focus will contain more than one pitch accent, where additional pitch accents might fall, and what their function might be. (Also, Ladd's account fails to rule out pitch accents outside the focus.)

Ladd's Focus Rule says that pitch accent placement (partly) depends on the feature F. It is not clear to me what the empirical advantage is of this claim. As indicated in 13.4.3 above, I think it is possible to explain how pitch accent placement helps us identify the focus without positing a rule which directly relates pitch accent placement to focus.

Finally, Ladd's view is that "deaccenting" needs to be distinguished from a basic hierarchy of relative accentability. It is not clear to me what the empirical advantage is of this position, either. Here is why.

It is not clear to me what the intention is behind the "deaccenting" vs. basic hierarchy distinction. Perhaps the idea is that the factors of group (A) determine structural-grammatical rules that determine default patterns while the ones in group (B) represent considerations of the interpretation of pitch accent placement that may overrule them. Alternatively, the idea might be that we should separate from each other the (possibly conflicting) considerations that favor placing a pitch accent and considerations that disfavor placing a pitch accent – cf. the distinction between "accenting" and "deaccenting" made in Bolinger 1986.[17]

Either way, as far as I can tell, there is no need for one's theory to stipulate that there are two groups of factors that differ in their status. In what sense is one group of factors more basic than another? What empirical advantage do we gain by saying that certain items are "in principle" of high accentability but get "demoted" to low accentability? I think it is simpler to say that a variety of factors which have to do both with relative "importance" or "expectation" in context and with more arbitrary or structural considerations jointly determine the relative accentability of different items in the same utterance, and finally the speaker's decision on which to accent and which not to accent.

### 13.4.4.2 Selkirk: accenting and argument structure

I would now like to take a look at the theory of pitch accent placement and interpretation developed in Selkirk 1984, 1996. That pitch accent placement is largely dependent on what's "new" in the context is one of the main features of Selkirk's theory. In addition, this theory makes the claim that pitch accent placement and interpretation is partly dependent on (syntactic) argument structure.[18]

In (159) below, I have formulated a version of Selkirk's theory. I have replaced Selkirk's F feature with my own "pa-marked" feature.[19] That is because I wish to avoid confusion: "pa-marked" (transparently) means no more and no less than "is being marked by the presence of an actual pitch accent," and may hold of a non-focus; the F feature, in contrast, will be confined to foci, in the sense of this book. The version in (159) combines the way pa-marking "projection" is defined in Selkirk 1984 with the interpretation principles of Selkirk 1996.

(159)   **A version of Selkirk's theory of marking by pitch accents**
  (A)   All pitch accents are assigned to a word or word-part.
  (B)   (i)   A constituent to which a pitch accent is assigned is (invariably) pa-marked.
        (ii)  A constituent may be pa-marked if it contains at least one pa-marked sub-constituent *which is either its head or an argument of its head.*
        Other constituents may not be pa-marked.

---

[17]  The first option would seem to involve a more essential distinction, but then some principles that Ladd includes in group (A) seem to me to involve expectation in context (i.e. interpretation of pitch accent placement). As for the second option, it would reflect the feeling that one may have special reasons to highlight an item vs. special reasons to "play down" an item (cf. Bolinger 1986, ch. 7), but I think that these are two sides of the same coin.

[18]  Another theory which makes the same claim is that of Gussenhoven 1984, 1991.

[19]  I assume that pa-marked is a feature of syntactic constituents at the level of "surface structure cum intonation" (see 12.4), and that (A) and (B) are well-formedness conditions on that level.

(C)   (i)   A maximal (= non-embedded, "highest") pa-marked constituent is defined as a **focus** (in the sense of this book), to be interpreted by the semantic/pragmatic theory of focus.

(ii)   An embedded pa-marked constituent is interpreted as "new" in the discourse, while a constituent which is not pa-marked is interpreted as "given".

(A) encodes the claim that the placement of a pitch accent depends on stress patterns only within a word, but not in larger constituents. Recall that in Selkirk's framework presented in 12.4 above, a pitch accent is first assigned to a constituent, and later associated with the main stress of that constituent. Given (A), the stress-dependent rule of pitch accent association will only ever apply within a single word.

Turning to (B), let us ignore for the moment the italicized part. (B-i) says that a word with which a pitch accent is associated is pa-marked. The recursive clause (B-ii) allows the pa-marked feature to "project upward," so that a single pitch accent may simultaneously serve to mark an embedded constituent and a larger constituent containing it. (B) determines that (160), for instance, is compatible with the two representations in (161) and (162).

(160)   He introduced his mother to us.
                H*       L  L%
(161)   He [introduced [his [mother]$_{pa-marked}$]$_{pa-marked}$ to us ]$_{pa-marked}$
                                         pa
(162)   He [introduced [his [mother]$_{pa-marked}$]$_{pa-marked}$ to us]
                                         pa

Such representations are interpreted by the clauses in (C). (C-i) predicts, correctly, that (160) can both have a VP focus (answering "what did he do?") and an NP focus (answering "who did he introduce to us?"). In (161), the maximal pa-marked constituent is the VP, so the VP is the focus of the sentence. In (162), the maximal pa-marked constituent is the NP *his mother*, so this NP is the focus. You see then that the focus is itself pa-marked, and it may "inherit" this marking from a sub-constituent (where it is an actual pitch accent which ultimately licenses the pa-marked feature on all these nested constituents).

Selkirk 1984 has put forth the suggestion that the particular pitch accent placement inside the focus indicates the informational status of sub-parts of the focus, along the lines already described in subsection 13.4.3. It is this suggestion that is represented by (C-ii). Consider for instance the examples in (163), from Selkirk 1984 (section 5.2.1).

(163)   a.   She sent the book to Mary.        VP focus possible
                       pa        pa
         b.   She sent the book to Mary.        VP focus possible
                                 pa

Selkirk notes that the two versions can answer "What did she do next?", i.e. they can both have VP focus. This is correctly predicted by her theory, which declares the following two representations to be well-formed.

(164)  a.  She [ sent [the [book]$_{pa-marked}$]$_{pa-marked}$ [to [Mary]$_{pa-marked}$]$_{pa-marked}$ ]$_{pa-marked}$
                        pa                    pa

      b.  She [ sent [the book] [to [Mary]$_{pa-marked}$]$_{pa-marked}$ ]$_{pa-marked}$
                                       pa

Selkirk also notes that while (163a) is a natural "out of the blue" response to "What did she do next?", (163b) can answer such a question only when reference to a certain book is expected – e.g. in a context where Jane's job is illustrating books, and we've been talking about her current book. This too is explained on the basis of the representations in (164). In (163a), represented as in (164a), both direct object and indirect object are pa-marked; hence, by (C-ii), they are both interpreted as "new." In (163b), represented as (164b), the direct object is not pa-marked, so, by (C-ii), it is interpreted as "given" – that is, as referring to something "expected" or "previously mentioned."

Originally, in Selkirk 1984, there was no distinction between the highest F-marked (my "pa-marked") constituent and other F-marked/pa-marked constituents. Each F-marked constituent was considered a "focus," so that there were embedded as well as non-embedded foci. The distinction is introduced in Selkirk 1996, motivated by the difference in interpretation between foci (in the sense of this book) and other F-marked/pa-marked constituents. As discussed in Rooth 1985 (pp. 23–4), there is quite a difference. If you consider embedded F-marked/pa-marked NPs like the ones in (164a), their function is, roughly, to mark the referent of the NP as "new" (or – more accurately, in my opinion – "non-salient" or "unexpected") in the context. Which has nothing to do with the role of that NP in the sentence as a whole. The role of maximal F-marked/pa-marked constituents, on the other hand, has everything to do with their role in the sentence as a whole: the maximal F-marked/pa-marked constituent is interpreted as that part of the sentence which answers the question addressed by the sentence. In short, maximal F-marked/pa-marked constituents are foci, in the sense of this book, while embedded ones are not.

Let us move on. The italicized part of (B-ii) brings in the structural notion of (syntactic) argument structure. The claim is that a constituent can be marked by a pitch accent by "inheritance" only if it "inherits" this marking from a head or argument sub-constituent. This claim is based on the observation that a lone pitch accent on a modifier or adjunct does not seem to allow for a broad focus on a larger constituent. For instance, of the following pitch-accents-and-focus configurations, the ones in (168) and (171) seem to be impossible.

(165)  [A red ant]$_F$ bit me.               OK
       H* H*  L  L%

(166)  [A red ant]$_F$ bit me.               OK
       H*  L  L%

(167)  A [red]$_F$ ant bit me.               OK
       H*     L  L%

(168)  [A red ant]$_F$ bit me.               SEEMS IMPOSSIBLE
       H*     L  L%

(169)  He [painted the shed yesterday]$_F$.   (Halliday 1967)   OK
              H*  L  L%

(170)  He painted the shed [yesterday]ₐF      OK
          H* L L%
(171)  He [painted the shed yesterday]ₐF     SEEMS IMPOSSIBLE
          H* L L%

These facts are correctly predicted by clause (B–ii) (with the italicized part). There are no well-formed representations of (168) and (171) in which the relevant NP or VP is pa-marked, since neither the head nor an argument of the head of that NP or VP contains any pitch accents.

However, it is not quite right that arguments and heads are the only sub-constituents whose pa-marking may be "inherited" by a larger constituent. As Selkirk is well aware, there are a lot of counterexamples to this claim. Some are given in (172)–(181). In each example, the bracketed constituent must clearly be able to be pa-marked, for two reasons: (i) the bracketed constituent can itself be the focus, and (ii) this constituent would have to be able to "pass up" its pa-marking to some larger constituent, which can also be the focus. But that is incompatible with (B–ii), because neither the head of the bracketed constituent nor an internal argument of its head is pa-marked.[20]

(172)  [My GERANIUM plant] is almost dead.                     (Bolinger 1972)
(173)  There were [CRAWLING things] all around.                (Bolinger 1972)
(174)  I'm doing it for [JOHN's sake].                         (Bolinger 1972)
(175)  I'm afraid old Fred has [a MEDICAL problem].      (Bolinger 1986, p. 94)
(176)  She's just finished [a WONDERFUL series of sketches].
(177)  I'm cleaning because [my MOTHER's coming].
(178)  Today is special because [my MOTHER is singing].
(179)  Here's [the page that you LOST].
          pa

(180)  Here's [a page that you LOST].               As usual,
          pa                            all pitch accents are shown.

(181)  You should have [said so YESTERDAY].
          pa

A note on the data would be in order. I am not claiming that in all of the above examples broad focus (on the bracketed constituent or on a larger one) is possible "out of the blue." I certainly agree that (176) and (178), for instance, would have narrow focus out of the blue. And yet broader focus is possible in the right context. As illustrated in 13.4.3 above, the bracketed clause in (178) may well be focused in a context in which singing is expected of my mother. Similarly, broad focus may be available for (176) in a conversation about Jane the illustrator, and so on.

In response to the counterexamples, Selkirk 1984 amends her theory by adding the clause in (182).[21]

[20]  If we assume the subject NP originates inside the VP, then (177) and (178) can be accounted for, as suggested in Selkirk 1996, by adding to (B–ii) the further provision that pa-marking of a constituent licenses the pa-marking of its trace.
[21]  Selkirk 1984, section 5.2.3. I continue to use my formulation of Selkirk's theory.

(182)   (B)   (iii)   A **redundant** constituent may be pa-marked.
where "redundant" basically means: it contributes nothing to the interpretation of the sentence containing it.

The amended theory allows a constituent to carry the pa-marked feature even if it does not contain any pitch accents, so long as it is a "redundant" constituent. This correctly predicts, for example, that in (172) and (173), the entire bracketed NP can be focused: since the unaccented head noun is "redundant," it's allowed to be pa-marked; it is this pa-marking of the head noun that gets "passed up" to the mother NP.

This move of Selkirk's seems untenable to me. First, I think (182) is a rather ad hoc and surprising addition to the theory. It is quite odd I think that while pa-marking is normally correlated with "new" or "unexpected" information, exceptional (pitch-accent-less) pa-marking is suddenly correlated with none other than just those constituents that cannot possibly be "new" or "unexpected."

Secondly, as far as I can see, Selkirk's amended theory predicts, incorrectly, that there can be a focus that contains no pitch accents at all. For example, (183) would be incorrectly predicted to be felicitous, just because *plant* is "redundant."

(183)   A:   I didn't hear you. What did you give to who?
B:   I gave [my geranium plant]$_F$ to [Sue]$_F$.
pa

Finally, I think that (182) does not cover all the counterexamples. Yes, I see that it can cover (172) and (173). But, how about examples like (178), (180), (181)? I think that in these examples, the unaccented head of the indicated constituent cannot be considered "redundant."

Indeed, the empirical generalization about examples (172)–(181) seems to simply be that the unaccented head of the indicated constituent is "old" or "expected" or "predictable" or whatever – in other words, that it has precisely that characteristic which is typical of unaccented constituents within a focus. This I think adds force to my first point above. Further, it fits well with the view that (i) the unaccented heads in question are **not** pa-marked, and (ii) the absence of the pa-marked feature on these heads **does** get interpreted (signaling that they are "old" or "expected").

In sum, the idea that heads and arguments but not modifiers and adjuncts can "pass up" their pa-marking seems questionable to me.

An argument vs. non-argument or argument vs. head distinction has also been claimed to play a role. First, a revision of (C-ii) was proposed: it was stipulated in Selkirk 1984 that the presence/absence of pa-marking on non-arguments does not get interpreted. This was based on examples like (184) and (185).

(184)   A:   Has John read Slaughterhouse-Five?
B:   No, John doesn't read books.                                      (Ladd 1980)
pa
(185)   John bought a red tie.                                      (Selkirk 1984, her (5.48))
pa                    pa

In (184), the pa-marked *read* is evidently "given," while in (185), the non-pa-marked *bought* and *red* can, it seems, be "new" (as when a surprising piece of news is reported out of the blue). The proposed revision of (C-ii) can cover these cases. Note, however, that (186) is an example parallel to (184) (the pa-marked *compliments* being quite as "given" as *read* was), which the proposed revision leaves unexplained. Does the presence/absence of pa-marking on arguments not get interpreted either?[22]

(186)   A:   Why don't you go and give her a compliment?
        B:   Sorry, I can't. I don't give compliments. It's a strict policy.
                                     pa

Then, the "projection" of pa-marking got revised instead: the modification in (187) was proposed in Rochemont 1986, and later adopted in Selkirk 1996.

(187)   (B)   (i)   A constituent to which a pitch accent is assigned is (invariably) pa-marked.
              (ii)   A constituent may be pa-marked if its *head* is pa-marked.
              (iii)   A *head* may be pa-marked if it has an *internal argument* which is pa-marked.
             Other constituents may not be pa-marked.

The idea is to account for the observation that unaccented heads can be "new" (the verbs in (185) above and (163b) below can, it seems, be "new"), while holding on to the view that unaccented arguments cannot. The verb in (185) is allowed to be pa-marked despite the fact that it contains no pitch accent, as in (188). No such license is granted to arguments, so *the book* in (163b) must be "given."

(188)   [ [John]_pa-marked [ [bought]_pa-marked [a red [tie]_pa-marked]_pa-marked ]_pa-marked ]_pa-marked
        pa                                  pa
(163)   b.   She sent the book to Mary.      VP focus possible
                    pa

I am not convinced that the head vs. argument distinction should enter pa-marking "projection." I find it somewhat counterintuitive that an actual pitch accent should serve to mark a constituent which doesn't contain it. I think, at any rate, that (187) is not empirically adequate. Note that (187) actually forces any verb contained in a focused VP to be interpreted as "new," since the pa-marked feature would have to be projected up to the VP via that verb. But that means that the ability of *read* in (184) to be interpreted as "old" remains unexplained. Further, I would question the very observation which prompted the modification in (187), since it is not clear to me that unaccented words can really be interpreted as "new."

I am not at all sure that (185), for instance, is really felicitous with S focus when *red* is "new" or "unexpected." Suppose there was no talk of shopping or colors at all, and I report the events of the day "out of the blue." Would I pronounce (185) as marked? I think not. I think the most natural pronunciation is with four pitch accents, one on each content word. If shopping is frequent or expected, then I may drop the pitch accent

---

[22] Schwarzschild 1999 suggests that the **presence** of pa-marking does not get interpreted as "new" at all, and that it is just the **absence** of pa-marking that does get interpreted as "given" (regardless of argument structure).

on *bought*, but I would not drop the pitch accent on *red*. Our sentence is much more likely I think to be pronounced with just the two pitch accents indicated if we replace red with *new*, for the obvious reason that "red" is likely not to be "expected," while "new" probably is "expected" (in the context of shopping).

More generally, I think that it is not as easy to have large foci with very few pitch accents in them as is sometimes assumed in the literature; more pitch accents per focus than we used to think may actually be necessary. To take one more example, I think that contrary to what is sometimes assumed in the literature, for (189) to have a broad focus, a number of pitch accents must be spread throughout the utterance. (Cf. Bolinger 1986, p. 100.)

(189)    He was warned to look out for an ex-convict with a red SHIRT.

This strongly suggests that when pitch accents are absent, their absence **does** get interpreted (indicating a low degree of novelty or importance): when that interpretation is uncalled for, the pitch-accent-impoverished example seems infelicitous.[23]

Concluding 13.4.4.2, the idea that pitch accent placement and interpretation directly depend on (syntactic) argument structure seems questionable to me.

### 13.4.5   The Emerging Picture

What picture are we left with at this point? Regarding pitch accent placement, I am inclined to assume the following.

 (i)    Pitch accents are assigned (in the sense of Selkirk 1984) to words (or other small items), and these words (or items) carry the syntactic feature pa-marked. Inside the item, the pitch accent is associated with the most heavily stressed syllable.
 (ii)   As a general rule, pitch accent placement is not phonologically/syntactically predictable.
 (iii)  As a general rule, pitch accent placement gets semantically/pragmatically interpreted.
 (iv)   pa-marked items are interpreted as more "highlighted" than items that are not pa-marked.[24] The interpretation of pitch accent placement is not that strict: an item may be "highlighted"/not "highlighted" for a variety of different reasons. A central reason is being "new"/"given" or "unexpected"/"expected," but there are other reasons too.

Regarding assumption (i), Selkirk's position that pitch accents are only assigned to a word or word-part seems plausible, since only within words is it really clear, empiri-

---

[23]   Regarding the number of pitch accents in large foci, I might add that another relevant factor is phonetic neutralization of pitch accents. It might not always be easy or even possible to hear if a given word carries a pitch accent or not. We know that pitch accents can have greater or lesser "prominence" in Pierrehumbert's sense (see end of section 12.2). If the "prominence" is particularly great, the pitch accent sounds emphatic (which often helps to bias narrow focus). If the "prominence" is particularly low, we may fail to hear that there is a pitch accent there altogether, especially in an utterance that provides little space for each pitch accent. For example, a series of H tones may get neutralized into a sort of high plateau, if the H tones are not very high and there is not enough space to realize the dippings in pitch in between.

[24]   Also, the item carrying the nuclear accent is more "highlighted" than other accented items.

cally, that pitch accent placement depends on rhythmic structure (in English). And yet I have a reservation. If you feel that the "right-end" effect is quite robust and are not satisfied with other explanations for that, you might want to insist that sometimes (though not always) it happens that a pitch accent does get assigned to a larger constituent and then falls on the syllable to which the NSR assigns the heaviest stress. I think it would be hard to either refute or find clear support for such a hypothesis.

Regarding (ii), I do not believe, at this point, that there is (in English) any absolute or very general constraint on pitch accent placement based on syntactic, morphological or rhythmic structure. Excepting, of course, the dependence on stress within a word. At the same time, our theory does need to allow factors other than the relative "novelty" or "importance" (or whatever) of items to also sometimes affect pitch accent placement.

I think that relative "novelty" or "importance" is an important factor which tends to outweigh others. But suppose we have a string of equally "new" or "important" items. It is quite possible, indeed almost certain, that placement of pitch accents within that string is not entirely random, but is influenced by various factors, which may include all or some of the following:

- language-specific structural principles (see discussion of Ladd's view in 13.4.4.1 above);
- the wish to add force to the utterance as a whole by placing pitch accents at its extreme ends (see Bolinger 1986, ch. 6), or, alternatively, a phonological principle that calls for greater prosodic prominence near the edge of prosodic phrases (see Selkirk 1996);
- the effect of speed and phonetic material on how easy it would be to produce and perceive a pitch accent (cf. Bolinger 1986, pp. 51–3).

The position expressed in (iii) is that as a general rule, the presence or absence of pa-marking on a constituent gets interpreted. Can this position be maintained in the face of examples like (184)–(186), repeated below?

(184)   A:   Has John read Slaughterhouse-Five?
         B:   No, John doesn't read books.                                      (Ladd 1980)
                              pa
(186)   A:   Why don't you go and give her a compliment?
         B:   Sorry, I can't. I don't give compliments. It's a strict policy.
                              pa
(185)   John bought a red tie.                                      (Selkirk 1984, her (5.48))
         pa                    pa

(184) and (186) contain accented items that seem "given," and (185) contains unaccented items that seem "new." Well, once we adopt the position in (iv) – that while pa-marking means "highlighted" it does not necessarily mean "new" – we can say that the pitch accent on *read* or *compliments* gets interpreted as "highlighting" these words, without marking them as "new." Similarly, *bought* and *red* in (185) could be said to be "played down" (relative to *John* and *tie*) without being marked as "given." Further, as already argued in 13.4.4.2 above, I would dispute the claim that (185) can really have an S focus with just the two pitch accents marked, and I believe, in general, that more

pitch accents per broad focus are necessary than has often been assumed in the literature, precisely because the absence of pitch accents does get interpreted.

I haven't yet said anything about focus. Where does the notion of focus (in the sense of this book) fit into our picture?

I propose that prosody-based focus identification is basically achieved along the lines suggested in 13.4.3: the hearer must search for a pitch-accents-and-focus configuration such that the interpretation of pa-marking is appropriate in the context of utterance (and whatever further constraints on pitch accent placement there might be are also met). Apart from that, I think that two alternatives are open to us: either we define focus as the maximal pa-marked constituent, as in Selkirk 1996, or else we do not assume any structural rule linking focus to pa-marking at all, as suggested in 13.4.3 above.

A theory incorporating the first alternative may be expressed as follows. Note that the formulation in (190) does not assume an F feature at all.[25]

(190)　**Theory One (Focus as a maximal pa-marked constituent)**

> Add a rule which allows the feature pa-marked to "project upward":
> > (v)　A constituent may be pa-marked if it contains at least one pa-marked subconstituent.
>
> Define:　A **focus** is a maximal pa-marked constituent.
>
> The grammar specifies that focus is interpreted (very roughly) as follows:
>
> > The focus is "the answer to the question currently addressed in the context," while the rest of the sentence corresponds to "the question currently addressed."
>
> No further rules of grammar are necessary. Prosody helps us identify the focus as follows:
>
> > Given that any maximal pa-marked constituent is defined as a focus, it is impossible for a constituent to be pa-marked without being contained in a focus. So we know that constituents outside the focus must not be pa-marked. We also know that each constituent – big or small – inside the focus should be pa-marked iff it makes sense in the context to highlight it (relative to other items) rather than play it down, and not pa-marked iff it makes sense in the context to play it down rather than highlight it – except for the influence of other factors, in the event that the reasons for highlighting/playing down are not definitive. When we hear an utterance and try to identify its focus, we look for a pitch-accents-and-focus configuration compatible with all of the above.

Note that one consequence of Theory One is that constituents larger than a word (or other small item) will get interpreted by the grammar as "highlighted." Consider for instance example (191), on its most prominent reading, viz. with focus on the entire sentence.

---

[25]　Notationally, "pa-marked" in (190) could of course be replaced with "F" throughout. I did not do that because I confine the F notation to foci, in the sense of this book. If you accept Theory One, then you may take me to use "F" in this book as nothing more than an alternative notation for the pa-marked feature of the maximal pa-marked constituent.

(191)   Here's the DOCTOR I was telling you about.

Clearly, *doctor* is "new"/"highlighted," while the relative clause is not. Since focus is defined as the maximal pa-marked constituent, pa-marking in (191) must have projected up from *doctor* to the entire predicate NP, to the VP, to the entire sentence. The theory determines therefore that these larger constituents are interpreted as "new"/"highlighted." This is not incompatible with my intuition: I think it makes sense to say that even though the relative clause is "given"/"expected" relative to *doctor*, the whole NP containing it is "new"/"unexpected," and so are the VP and the S (we didn't know that we were going to run into that doctor).

A theory incorporating the second alternative mentioned above may be expressed as follows.

(192)   **Theory Two (Focus not directly marked as such by pitch accents)**

Add the feature F:
   At surface structure, a constituent may carry the syntactic feature F.

Define:   A **focus** is an F-marked constituent.

The grammar specifies that focus is interpreted (very roughly) as follows:

   The focus is "the answer to the question currently addressed in the context," while the rest of the sentence corresponds to "the question currently addressed."

No further rules of grammar are necessary. Prosody helps us identify the focus as follows:

   Given the interpretation of pa-marking in (iii) above and the interpretation of focus specified here, items outside the focus are always too "old" or "expected" or "relatively unimportant" to be pa-marked. So we know that items outside the focus must not be pa-marked. We also know that an item inside the focus should be pa-marked iff it makes sense in the context to highlight it (relative to other items) rather than play it down, and not pa-marked iff it makes sense in the context to play it down rather than highlight it – except for the influence of other factors, in the event that the reasons for highlighting/playing down are not definitive. When we hear an utterance and try to identify its focus, we look for a pitch-accents-and-focus configuration compatible with all of the above.

Note that I have not included in Theory Two a rule that allows the feature pa-marked to project upward. Given that on this theory focus is not linked by any grammatical rule to pa-marking, I think that allowing projection of pa-marking is not necessary. Here is why.

Consider (191) once more, assuming again that the whole sentence is focused.

(191)   Here's the DOCTOR I was telling you about.

If pa-marking were allowed to project upward, the predicate NP, the VP, the entire S could be pa-marked – but only optionally, since pa-marking projection is not needed here in order to ensure S focus. Now that means these larger constituents could optionally be represented by the grammar as "new"/"highlighted." As already noted above, my intuition is that it does make sense to say that these larger constituents are "new"/"highlighted" too. But are they **marked by the pitch accent on** *doctor* as "new"/"highlighted"? I do not see that anything forces us to assume that they are; why shouldn't a constituent actually represent "new" information without being so marked? Also, it seems unreasonable to me that the grammar should mark anything via a syntactic feature that is both optional and completely abstract; how would the hearer ever know whether the NP, VP, S is pa-marked or not?

## 13.5   Focus, Prosodic Phrasing, and Peripheral Tones

This section is no more than a footnote. I mainly wanted to emphasize here that prosodic phrasing and choice of peripheral tones also provide information regarding focal structure. How it is exactly that they fulfil this role is a fascinating topic, that will not be addressed in this book.

   (193) and (194) illustrate a typical pattern, identified and studied in Jackendoff 1972, where the answer to the question being addressed is pronounced with a falling melody (ending an intonation or intermediate phrase), whereas what is often referred to as a "contrastive topic" is pronounced with a rising melody (ending an intonation phrase).

(193)   A:   I know who Bill kissed, but what about Larry? Who did Larry kiss?
       B:        Larry        kissed        Nina.
         (L+)H* L H%        (L+)H* L L%
(194)   A:   I know who kissed Mary, but what about Nina? Who kissed Nina?
       B:        Larry        kissed        Nina.
     (L+)H* L (L%)        (L+)H* L H%

I will discuss the semantic/pragmatic interpretation of such examples in some detail in chapter 20. I will take it for granted there that the falling and rising melodies in question enable us to identify certain focal elements, although I will have nothing to say about **how** they enable us to identify these focal elements. I will not be making any assumptions about the semantic/pragmatic interpretation that the grammar might associate with these melodies or with their parts. (Nor will I assume that these melodies mark the focal elements in question unambiguously.) All that will be left for future research.

   Let me also mention that Selkirk 1999 (section 3.3) suggests, within optimality theory, that there is a constraint in English that calls for aligning the right edge of a focus with the right edge of an intermediate phrase. To see what this suggestion is based on, consider the following scenario. I report to you a short entry that I have just read in Mary's journal: she loaned her rollerblades to Robin. All the content words are "new," so the pitch accent placement in (195)–(196) is appropriate. At the same time, I am surprised that Mary loaned her precious *rollerblades*, of all things. This, says Selkirk, allows me to simultaneously focus *rollerblades*. Now there is a contrast between (195) and (196): with the intention to focus *rollerblades*, I can utter (195), but not (196). The proposed constraint accounts for this contrast.

(195)  She  loaned  her  <u>rollerblades</u>  to Robin.
　　　　H*　　　H* L　　　　H* L L%
(196)  She loaned her  <u>rollerblades</u>  to Robin.
　　　　H*　　　H*　　　　　H* L L%

I think I agree that in the scenario described, (195) is OK but (196) is not. However, I would question the assumption that in that scenario *rollerblades* is a focus, in the sense of this book. I think *rollerblades* would receive special prosodic prominence and sound emphatic. But I would prefer to say that *rollerblades* is not a focus, for the following reasons: (i) *rollerblades* does not seem to be the answer to a question being addressed; (ii) this position would allow us to retain the generalization that no pitch accents can occur outside a focus (see (91) above); (iii) I think that intuitively, the whole S or VP is focused (answering, say, "what happened on July 24th?," or "what else did she do?"), and I would be reluctant to posit an additional, embedded focus.

# 14

# *Focus: Focus–Induced Interpretations*

---

## 14.1 Focus-Induced Interpretations

Consider sentences (1) and (2). To capture the truth conditions of these sentences, we usually map them both onto one and the same model theoretic entity – typically, the one specified in (3).

(1)  John introduced [Bill]$_F$ to Sue.
(2)  John introduced Bill to [Sue]$_F$.
(3)  the proposition that John introduced Bill to Sue
     = the set of worlds in which John introduced Bill to Sue

But if we want to treat focus and explain its pragmatic and semantic effects (see section 13.2), we obviously need to distinguish between (1) and (2).

Therefore, current formal theories of the semantics/pragmatics of focus associate with each sentence a model-theoretic entity which directly reflects its focal structure. I will call this entity a **focus-induced interpretation**. Each of (1) and (2) above will have its own distinct focus-induced interpretation, either instead of or in addition to the familiar semantic interpretation in (3).

The first proposals concerning the formal semantic/pragmatic treatment of focusing can be found in Jackendoff 1972. Jackendoff uses a level of representation in which the focus (= F-marked constituent) is replaced by a variable; for example, (4) and (5) correspond to our sentences (1) and (2). Jackendoff calls this representation "Presupp$_s$," but I prefer to call it the "ps skeleton," following Rooth 1985.

(4)  ps skeleton of (1):   John introduced x to Sue.
(5)  ps skeleton of (2):   John introduced Bill to y.

Jackendoff suggests that focus induces the ps that the set of values which verify the ps skeleton is under discussion or amenable to discussion. For example (D is the domain of individuals in the model):

(6)  focal ps of (1) à la Jackendoff:
     $\{d \in D : $ John introduced d to Sue$\}$ is under/amenable to discussion.

(7)  focal ps of (2) à la Jackendoff:
$\{d \in D : \text{John introduced Bill to } d\}$ is under/amenable to discussion.

The sentence is taken to assert that the denotation of the focus is a member of this set. For example:

(8)  assertion of (1) à la Jackendoff:
Bill $\in \{d \in D : \text{John introduced } d \text{ to Sue}\}$
(9)  assertion of (2) à la Jackendoff:
Sue $\in \{d \in D : \text{John introduced Bill to } d\}$

In 13.1, I tried to describe the idea behind Jackendoff's formulation in terms as neutral as possible: roughly, the focus denotes one particular value picked out of a set of alternative values, which "fits into" an open/incomplete statement corresponding to the rest of the sentence. Jackendoff's suggestions fit quite well with the intuition – which I take to be a very basic one – that the focus is "the answer to the question currently being addressed": after all, to look for the individuals which verify the ps skeletons in (4) and (5) is to look for the correct answers to the questions in (10) and (11) below, respectively. In each case, the focus provides one correct answer. This in turn explains why (1) can answer (10) but not (11) while (2) can answer (11) but not (10).

(10)  Who did John introduce to Sue?
(11)  Who did John introduce Bill to?

Jackendoff further suggests that there is an interpretation rule which applies to a focus-sensitive adverb such as *only* or *even* and "associates its interpretation with the focus," although he doesn't attempt to formulate such a rule.

In the 1980s, two main formal, model-theoretic theories of focus were developed, which have come to be known as the **structured meaning** and the **alternative semantics**[1] theories of focus. I think it is fair to say that both theories reflect Jackendoff's insights, each in its own way. Each of the two theories specifies in detail what the focus-induced interpretations are that are taken to be employed by the grammer, how these interpretations are derived, and how they interact with the semantics of questions, focusing adverbs, etc. to produce the different pragmatic and semantic effects of focus.

In the following two sections, I will present as simply as I can the basics of these two theories. Note that I will be confining myself here to focus-induced interpretations of complete clauses.

You will note that at least as far as the basics go, the two theories are not that different from each other. I will not include a comparison between the two. For discussion of possible empirical differences, see von Stechow 1989; Krifka 1992; see also section 15.4. In the following chapters, the discussion will be formulated in terms of alternative semantics (although I think that much of it could be formulated in terms of structured meanings equally well), largely because I happen to be interested in a number of proposals that have been developed within that framework.

---

[1]  Pronounce *alternative semantics* as a compound, with main stress on *alternative*.

## 14.2  Structured Meanings

The structured meaning theory of focus was developed in von Stechow 1981; Cresswell and von Stechow 1982; Jacobs 1983; von Stechow 1989. On this theory, the focus-induced interpretation of a sentence is an ordered sequence whose members are (i) the property obtained by $\lambda$-abstracting on the focus/foci, and (ii) the ordinary semantic interpretation(s) of the focus/foci. This sequence is called a "structured meaning." For example ($[\![\ ]\!]$ means "the semantic value of"):

(12)  the structured meaning of (1):  $\langle[\![\lambda x[\text{introduce}(j,x,s)]]\!], \text{Bill}\rangle$
      i.e. $\langle$the property of having been introduced by John to Sue, the individual Bill$\rangle$

(13)  the structured meaning of (2):  $\langle[\![\lambda y[\text{introduce}(j,b,y)]]\!], \text{Sue}\rangle$
      i.e. $\langle$the property of being somebody that John introduced Bill to, the individual Sue$\rangle$

(14)  John introduced [Bill]$_F$ to [Sue]$_F$.

(15)  the structured meaning of (14):  $\langle[\![\lambda x,y[\text{introduce}(j,x,y)]]\!], \text{Bill,Sue}\rangle$
      i.e. $\langle$the relation that holds between x and y iff John introduced x to y, the individuals Bill,Sue$\rangle$

Obviously, the truth-conditional content of a sentence can easily be recovered from its structured meaning, by applying the property denoted by the $\lambda$-abstract to the semantic interpretation(s) of the focus/foci.

The structured meaning is used as a basis for explaining the various effects of focusing. Let me illustrate this with two of the most extensively studied effects: question-answer congruence, and the truth-conditional effect observed with the focusing adverb *only*.

According to one theory of questions (Egli 1974; Hausser 1976; Tichy 1978; Scha 1983), a wh-question denotes a property obtained by $\lambda$-abstracting on the wh-phrase(s). On the theory of Groenendijk and Stokhof 1982, the derivation of a question-denotation involves just such an abstract. Given one of these theories, a simple constraint on question-answer pairs can be stated: the property in the structured meaning of the answer must be identical to the property denoted by the question (or its underlying $\lambda$-abstract). This forces the focus position(s) in the answer to match the questioned position(s) in the question, as desired.

Let us assume, for the sake of simplicity, that *only* in auxiliary position is a sentential adverb. Based on Horn 1969's semantics of *only*, we may formulate the following semantic rule for sentential *only* (cf. Rooth 1996, p. 276).

(16)  Let $\langle Q^n, \alpha_1, \ldots, \alpha_n\rangle$ be the structured meaning of sentence S.
      The sentence onlyS asserts that for all sequences $\langle\beta_1, \ldots, \beta_n\rangle$, if $Q^n(\beta_1, \ldots, \beta_n)$ is true, then $\langle\beta_1, \ldots, \beta_n\rangle = \langle\alpha_1, \ldots, \alpha_n\rangle$.
      The sentence onlyS presupposes that $Q^n(\alpha_1, \ldots, \alpha_n)$ is true.

Rule (16) predicts that sentences (17), (18), (19) assert (17′), (18′) and (19′), or – more informally – (17″), (18″), and (19″), yielding the desired effect of focus on the truth conditions of these sentences.

(17)    John only introduced [Bill]$_F$ to Sue.
(18)    John only introduced Bill to [Sue]$_F$.
(19)    John only introduced [Bill]$_F$ to [Sue]$_F$.

(17′)   For any d ∈ D, if $[\![\lambda x[introduce(j,x,s)]]\!](d)$ is true, then d = Bill
(18′)   For any d ∈ D, if $[\![\lambda y[introduce(j,b,y)]]\!](d)$ is true, then d = Sue
(19′)   For any $d_1,d_2$ ∈ D, if $[\![\lambda x,y[introduce(j,x,y)]]\!](d_1,d_2)$ is true, then $d_1$ = Bill and $d_2$
        = Sue.

(17″)   'Nobody other than Bill was introduced by John to Sue'
(18″)   'Nobody other than Sue was someone that John introduced Bill to'
(19″)   'None other than ⟨Bill, Sue⟩ were s.t. John introduced the first to the second'

    Note that this theory has no trouble covering examples with multiple foci, as
illustrated above with (14) and (19).[2]


## 14.3    Alternative Semantics

The alternative semantics theory of focus was proposed in Rooth 1985. On this theory,
each sentence receives two distinct model-theoretic interpretations: an ordinary semantic value (to be marked $[\![\ ]\!]^o$), and a separate focus-induced interpretation (to be marked
$[\![\ ]\!]^f$), called the "p-set" (Rooth 1985) or the "focus semantic value" (Rooth 1992, 1996).
    The focus-induced interpretation – the focus semantic value – is the set of all propo-
sitions obtainable by replacing the/each focus with an alternative of the same type. For
example, the focus semantic value of (1) can be described as follows.[3]

(20)    $[\![(1)]\!]^f$ = {the proposition that John introduced d to Sue : d ∈ D}

To make this example more concrete, suppose that the only individuals are John, Bill,
Sue and Mary. Then the focus semantic value of (1) is as in (21).

(21)    {$[\![$John introduced John to Sue$]\!]^o$,
        $[\![$John introduced Bill to Sue$]\!]^o$,
        $[\![$John introduced Sue to Sue$]\!]^o$,
        $[\![$John introduced Mary to Sue$]\!]^o$}

Similarly, the focus semantic values of (2) and (14) are as follows.

(22)    $[\![(2)]\!]^f$ = {the proposition that John introduced Bill to d : d ∈ D}
(23)    $[\![(14)]\!]^f$ = {the propositions that John introduced $d_1$ to $d_2$ : $d_1,d_2$ ∈ D}

    Let me briefly show how this is used in accounting for question-answer congruence
and for the semantic effect observed with *only*.

---

[2]   This refers to multiple foci which all have the same status. For discussion of examples containing
two foci which differ from each other in their status, see chapter 20.
[3]   Rooth's informal description of the same set would be as in (i). (Cf. Rooth 1992, 1995.) This is
deliberately a bit sloppy, for ease of exposition; actually, a proposition, being a model-theoretic entity,
doesn't have a form.

(i)   $[\![(1)]\!]^f$ = the set of propositions of the form "John introduced x to Sue"

According to Hamblin 1973, a question denotes the set of propositions that constitute all the (partial) answers to that question – true and false answers alike. Given this, a simple constraint forcing question-answer congruence can be stated as follows: the focus semantic value of the answer (a set of alternative propositions) must be identical to the denotation of the question (also a set of alternative propositions).

We continue to assume that *only* in auxiliary position is a sentential adverb. Based on Horn 1969's semantics of *only*, we may formulate the following semantic rule for sentential *only* (cf. Rooth 1996, p. 277).

(24)   The sentence onlyS asserts that for all propositions $p \in [\![S]\!]^f$, if p is true, then p $= [\![S]\!]^o$.
       The sentence onlyS presupposes that $[\![S]\!]^o$ is true.

Rule (24) predicts that sentences (17), (18), (19) assert (17*), (18*) and (19*), or – more informally – (17**), (18**), and (19**), yielding the desired effect of focus on the truth conditions of these sentences.

(17)   John only introduced [Bill]$_F$ to Sue.
(18)   John only introduced Bill to [Sue]$_F$.
(19)   John only introduced [Bill]$_F$ to [Sue]$_F$.

(17*)   For every proposition p s.t. p = the proposition that John introduced d to Sue (for some $d \in D$): if p is true, then p = the proposition that John introduced Bill to Sue.

(18*)   For every proposition p s.t. p = the proposition that John introduced Bill to d (for some $d \in D$): if p is true, then p = the proposition that John introduced Bill to Sue.

(19*)   For every proposition p s.t. p = the proposition that John introduced $d_1$ to $d_2$ (for some $d_1, d_2 \in D$): if p is true, then p = the proposition that John introduced Bill to Sue.

(17**)   'No proposition that John introduced d to Sue is true, other than the proposition that John introduced Bill to Sue'
(18**)   'No proposition that John introduced Bill to d is true, other than the proposition that John introduced Bill to Sue'
(19**)   'No proposition that John introduced $d_1$ to $d_2$ is true, other than the proposition that John introduced Bill to Sue'

Note that this theory too has no trouble covering examples with multiple foci, as illustrated above with (14) and (19).[4]

## 14.4   Deriving Focus-Induced Interpretations

Of course I haven't said anything yet about where the focus-induced interpretations come from. Certainly, the theory – be it a structured meanings theory or an alternative semantics theory – will have to derive these somehow. Assuming that English sentences

---

[4]   Cf. footnote 2 above.

are translated into a logical language and that that logical language gets model-theoretically interpreted, the theory will have to specify either translation rules into the logical language or semantic rules of the logic that would guarantee that an appropriate focus-induced interpretation be assigned to each English sentence.

There are various proposals in the literature regarding the way focus-induced interpretations are derived. I prefer to assume that focus-induced interpretations are derived in the simplest way one can think of – i.e. something like the following. You take the usual logical translation of the sentence. To get the focus semantic value of the sentence, you replace the translation of the focused constituent with a variable of the appropriate type, and take the set of propositions obtained by all value assignments to that variable. To get the structured meaning, you λ-abstract on the focus, and take the sequence consisting of the denotation of that λ-abstract and the denotation of the focus. The definitions of focus-induced interpretations given in 14.5.4 and 14.5.5 below are formulated along these lines. Any further discussion relating to this choice of mine is deferred to chapter 18.

## 14.5    Formalization

### 14.5.1    Some Assumptions and Some Desiderata

We assume that at that level of representation of natural language (or at least English) syntax which gets semantically interpreted, focused constituents are marked with the feature F. We also assume that at that level, scope relations are encoded in some way or another.

For concreteness, let us assume that the relevant syntacic level is LF (as assumed in e.g. Rooth 1985; Kratzer 1991). I will assume that at LF, scope relations are encoded in the position of NPs: some NPs may have been raised from their base positions and adjoined to S, thus acquiring wide scope.

Following Rooth 1985, I assume that foci are interpreted in situ – that is, I do **not** assume a syntactic rule that raises the focus and adjoins it to S at LF. (For some relevant discussion, see chapter 19 below.)

I assume that LFs are translated into formulas of a model-theoretically interpreted logical language. I will not be concerned with the translation procedure. I will simply try to use logical translations that seem plausible for the sentences under consideration.

If we want to treat focus, there are a couple of features that our logical language must have.

First, the logic must clearly be intensional. To see this, suppose we have an extensional logic. Take a model with exactly four individuals, John, Bill, Sue and Mary, and just the following 1-place predicate extensions.

> bold → {Bill,Sue}
> beautiful → {Bill,Sue}
> virile → {Bill,John}
> cunning → {Bill,John,Mary}

The dialog in (25) below is predicted to be felicitous, while in reality it is not.

(25)   A:   Who is bold?
       B:   [Sue]$_F$ is beautiful.

In terms of structured meanings, if (25A) is interpreted as $[\![\lambda x[bold(x)]]\!]$ and the focus-induced interpretation of (25B) is the structured meaning $\langle[\![\lambda x[beautiful(x)]]\!],\ Sue\rangle$, then we have the same predicate-denotation in each, viz. the set {Bill,Sue}. In terms of alternative semantics, $[\![(25A)]\!]^\circ = \{[\![bold(x)]\!]^g\ :\ g(x) \in D\}$ and $[\![(25B)]\!]^f = \{[\![beautiful(x)]\!]^g : g(x) \in D\}$, so we get that $[\![(25A)]\!]^\circ = [\![(25B)]\!]^f = \{1,0\}$.

    Similarly, consider (26) below, in the same model. Intuitively, (26) is false, since Sue is both bold and beautiful. However, because of the extensionality it is predicted to be true.

(26)   Sue is only [bold]$_F$.

The structured meaning interpretation would be the following,

   Sentence (26) asserts that for any $\mathbf{P} \in POW(D)$,
   if $[\![\lambda X[X(s)]]\!](\mathbf{P}) = 1$, then $\mathbf{P} = [\![bold]\!]$.

which is true, since the truth value $[\![\lambda X[X(s)]]\!](\mathbf{P})$ is 1 for no predicate-extension other than $\mathbf{P} = (Bill,Sue\} = [\![bold]\!]$. The alternative semantics interpretation would be the following,

   Sentence (26) asserts that for any member $t \in [\![Sue\ is\ [bold]_F]\!]^f = \{[\![X(s)]\!]^g : g(X) \in POW(D)\}$, if $t = 1$, then $t = [\![Sue\ is\ [bold]_F]\!]^\circ = [\![bold(s)]\!]^\circ$.

which boils down to $[\![bold(s)]\!]^\circ = 1$, and is therefore true as well.

    Secondly, our intensional logic should allow focus-induced interpretations to inter-act with variable binding operators. We need to be able to compute the focus semantic value of an expression containing free variables, keeping track of the value assignments for those free variables.[5] For instance, suppose we want to interpret (27), and suppose that we arrive at a logical translation more or less as in (28).

(27)   Someone only loves [Sue]$_F$.
(28)   $\exists x\ [only\ [love(x,s_F)]]$

    To be able to interpret *only* here, we need the focus semantic value of the open formula love(x,s$_F$); it should be, roughly, the set of propositions stating that x loves d (for some $d \in D$), where the value of x is fixed (since x is bound from outside). So we need to somehow relativize the focus semantic value to a value assignment for x.

    There are various intensional logics that satisfy these conditions, of course, and a number of logics have been used in the literature on focus. (Rooth 1985 uses the system of UG (Montague 1970), von Stechow 1989 uses an intensional $\lambda$-categorial language, in the sense of Cresswell 1973.)

---

[5]   This point was articulated by Fred Landman (p.c.), in connection with Rooth 1985's decision to choose a UG-style intensional logic (discussed in Rooth 1985, pp. 46–9).

I will use as my basic logic the language L below, largely based on the language L given in Kratzer 1991. Kratzer's language is an intensional $\lambda$-categorial language as used in Cresswell 1973, but given a more Montagovian appearance. We have the type assignments familiar from extensional logic. Names are treated extensionally (the possible denotations of type e are individuals), but other types are intensional, since the possible denotations of type t – the type of complete formulas – are not truth values, but rather propositions = sets of possible worlds.

## 14.5.2  The Language L

### THE LANGUAGE L

#### Syntax

*Types*
(1)  e is a type.
(2)  t is a type.
(3)  if $\sigma$ and $\tau$ are types, then $\langle \sigma, \tau \rangle$ is a type.

*Vocabulary*
constants of type e:      j, b, s, m . . .
constants of type $\langle e,t \rangle$:      dog, cat, bold, beautiful, walk, smile . . .
constants of type $\langle e, \langle e,t \rangle \rangle$:      love, invite . . .
constants of type $\langle e, \langle e, \langle e,t \rangle \rangle \rangle$:      introduce . . .
constants of type $\langle \langle e,t \rangle, \langle \langle e,t \rangle, t \rangle \rangle$:      a/some, every, two, no . . .
constants of type $\langle \langle \langle e,t \rangle, t \rangle, \langle e,t \rangle \rangle$:      LOVE, INVITE . . .
Variables:      For every type $\tau$, natural number n, $v_{n,\tau}$ is a variable of type $\tau$.

*Syntactic rules*
For any types $\tau$, $\sigma$,

(1)  Every constant or variable of type $\tau$ is an expression of type $\tau$.
(2)  If $\alpha$ is an expression of type $\langle \sigma, \tau \rangle$ and $\beta$ is an expression of type $\sigma$, then $(\alpha(\beta))$ is an expression of type $\tau$.
(3)  If $\phi$, $\psi$ are expressions of type t, so are the following.
$$\neg \phi \qquad (\phi \wedge \psi) \qquad (\phi \vee \psi) \qquad (\phi \rightarrow \psi)$$
(4)  If $\alpha, \beta$ are expressions of type e, then the following is an expression of type t.
$$(\alpha = \beta)$$
(5)  If $\phi$ is an expression of type t and u is a variable of any type, then the following are expressions of type t.
$$\exists u[\phi] \qquad \forall u[\phi]$$
(6)  if $\phi$ is an expression of type t and u is a variable of type $\sigma$, then the following is an expression of type $\langle \sigma, \tau \rangle$.
$$\lambda u[\phi]$$
(7)  if $\phi$ is an expression of type t, so are the following.
$$\Box[\phi] \qquad \Diamond[\phi]$$

## Semantics

*Model*

A **model** M for L is an ordered quadruple $\langle D_M, W_M, <_M, F_M \rangle$, where $D_M$ is a non-empty set of individuals, $W_M$ is a non-empty set of possible worlds, $<_M$ is an accessibility relation on $W_M$, and $F_M$ is an interpretation function which assigns to each constant of type $\tau$, for any type $\tau$, a denotation in $D_{\tau,M}$.

*Semantic domains*

$D_{\tau,M}$ (the set of possible denotations of type $\tau$ in model M) is defined for any type $\tau$ and any model M as follows.

(1)  $D_{e,M} = D_M$
(2)  $D_{t,M} = POW(W_M)$
     (= the power set of $W_M$)
(3)  For any types $\sigma, \tau$, $D_{\langle \sigma, \tau \rangle, M} = D_{\tau,M}{}^{D_{\sigma,M}}$
     (= the set of functions from $D_{\sigma,M}$ to $D_{\tau,M}$)

*Assignment functions*

For any model M, an **assignment function** g for M is a function that assigns to each variable of type $\tau$ a member of $D_{\tau,M}$, for any type $\tau$.

*Semantic values (in a model) relative to an assignment function*

The notation $[\![\ ]\!]^{M,g}$ indicates a semantic value in model M relative to assignment function g for M.

For any model M and assignment function g for M,

**basic expressions:**

For any constant $\alpha$, $[\![\alpha]\!]^{M,g} = F_M(\alpha)$
For any variable $\alpha$, $[\![\alpha]\!]^{M,g} = g(\alpha)$

**complex expressions:**

(1)  For any types $\sigma, \tau$, if $\alpha$ is of type $\langle \sigma, \tau \rangle$ and $\beta$ is of type $\sigma$, then
     $[\![(\alpha(\beta))]\!]^{M,g} = [\![\alpha]\!]^{M,g}([\![\beta]\!]^{M,g})$.
(2)  If $\phi, \psi$ are of type t, then the following hold.
     $[\![\neg\phi]\!]^{M,g} = W_M - [\![\phi]\!]^{M,g}$
     $[\![(\phi \wedge \psi)]\!]^{M,g} = [\![\phi]\!]^{M,g} \cap [\![\psi]\!]^{M,g}$
     $[\![(\phi \vee \psi)]\!]^{M,g} = [\![\phi]\!]^{M,g} \cup [\![\psi]\!]^{M,g}$
     $[\![(\phi \rightarrow \psi)]\!]^{M,g} = [\![\neg\phi]\!]^{M,g} \cup [\![\psi]\!]^{M,g}$
(3)  If $\alpha, \beta$ are of type e, then for all $w \in W_M$,
     $w \in [\![(\alpha = \beta)]\!]^{M,g}$    iff    $[\![\alpha]\!]^{M,g} = [\![\beta]\!]^{M,g}$.
(4)  If $\exists u[\phi]$ is of type t, then for all $w \in W_M$,
     $w \in [\![\exists u[\phi]]\!]^{M,g}$    iff
         for some $g'$ for M identical to g except that it may assign a different value to
         u, $w \in [\![\phi]\!]^{M,g'}$
(5)  If $\forall u[\phi]$ is of type t, then for all $w \in W_M$,
     $w \in [\![\forall u[\phi]]\!]^{M,g}$    iff
         for every $g'$ for M identical to g except that it may assign a different value to
         u, $w \in [\![\phi]\!]^{M,g'}$

(6)   If $\alpha$ is of type $\tau$ and u is a variable of type $\sigma$, then
$[\![\lambda u[\alpha]]\!]^{M,g}$ = that function $f \in D_{\langle\sigma,\tau\rangle,M}$ s.t. for any $h \in D_{\sigma,M}$,
$f(h) = [\![\alpha]\!]^{M,g[u\to h]}$,
      where $g[u \to h]$ is a function identical to g except (perhaps) that it assigns
      to u the value h.
(7)   If $\Box[\phi]$ is of type t, then for all $w \in W_M$,
      $w \in [\![\Box[\phi]]\!]^{M,g}$      iff      for every $w' \in W_M$ s.t. $w < w'$, $w' \in [\![\phi]\!]^{M,g}$
(8)   If $\Diamond[\phi]$ is of type t, then for all $w \in W_M$,
      $w \in [\![\Diamond[\phi]]\!]^{M,g}$      iff      for some $w' \in W_M$ s.t. $w < w'$, $w' \in [\![\phi]\!]^{M,g}$

*Semantic values (in a model)*
For any model M and any expression $\alpha$,

$$[\![\alpha]\!]^M = \begin{cases} [\![\alpha]\!]^{M,g} \text{ (g arbitrary assignment for M)} \\ \qquad \text{iff   for any g, g' for M, } [\![\alpha]\!]^{M,g} = [\![\alpha]\!]^{M,g'} \\ \text{undefined otherwise} \end{cases}$$

## Notes

When using L in the text, specifications of the tie to the model (superscripts and subscripts M, etc.) will usually be suppressed.

Variables $v_{1,e}$, $v_{2,e}$, $v_{3,e}$ will be abbreviated as x,y,z, respectively;
$v_{1,\langle e,t\rangle}$, $v_{2,\langle e,t\rangle}$, $v_{3,\langle e,t\rangle}$ will be abbreviated as X,Y,Z, respectively.

For convenience, let us assume that whenever j,b,s,m are used, $F(j)$ = John, $F(b)$ = Bill, $F(s)$ = Sue, $F(m)$ = Mary.

### 14.5.3   Focus Interpretation – a Start

I assume that English sentences are translated into fairly ordinary logical formulas. The ordinary semantic values assigned by the semantic rules in 14.5.2 above (marked $[\![\ ]\!]$, with superscipts for a model and possibly for an assignment function) constitute the ordinary semantic values of the corresponding English expressions (marked $[\![\ ]\!]^o$). I assume that there are special, additional, semantic rules of the logic, which assign to each formula a focus-induced interpretation.
    To treat focus, we want to allow the feature F to be inherited by the logical translation. So we add to the language L the syntactic rule in (29) and the semantic rule in (30).

(29)   If $\alpha$ is an expression of type $\tau$, so is the following.
                $[\alpha]_F$
(30)   For any expression $\alpha$, $[\![[\alpha]_F]\!]^{M,g} = [\![\alpha]\!]^{M,g}$.

    Take for instance sentences (1), (2), (14). Obviously, they would be translated into the logical formulas in (1'), (2'), (14'). Given a model M for L, (1'), (2') and (14') all have the same ordinary semantic value, viz. the one in (31). That is, the set of worlds in (32).

(1)     John introduced [BILL]$_F$ to Sue.
(2)     John introduced Bill to [Sue]$_F$.
(14)    John introduced [Bill]$_F$ to [Sue]$_F$.

(1′)    introduce($b_F$)(s)(j)        abbreviated as:   introduce(j,$b_F$,s)
(2′)    introduce(b)($s_F$)(j)        abbreviated as:   introduce(j,b,$s_F$)
(14′)   introduce($b_F$)($s_F$)(j)     abbreviated as:   introduce(j,$b_F$,$s_F$)

(31)    $F_M$(introduce)(Bill)(Sue)(John)
(32)    $\{w \in W_M : \text{John introduced Bill to Sue in w}\}$

### 14.5.4  *Alternative Semantics*

An alternative semantics theory will stipulate that each formula of the logic receive, in addition to its ordinary semantic value, a focus semantic value. To mark the latter, I will use the notation $[\![\ ]\!]^f$ for formulas of the logic as well as for English sentences.

I will assume a definition of focus semantic values based on substitution into focus position(s), following Kratzer 1991 and Roberts 1996b.[6] For present purposes, an informal version of the definition may be stated as follows (see Roberts 1996b, section 2.1).

(33)    $[\![\phi]\!]^{f-M,g}$, the **focus semantic value** of a formula $\phi$ relative to an arbitrary model M and an arbitrary assignment function g, is the set of all ordinary semantic values obtained by replacing the F-marked subformulas in $\phi$ with variables, and then interpreting the result relative to every assignment $g'$ which is identical to g except perhaps for the values of those variables.

A formal definition corresponding to (33) may be formulated as in (34) (cf. Kratzer 1991, sections 4.1–4.3).

(34)    (i)     Add to the syntax:
                For every type $\tau$, natural number n, $v_{F-n,\tau}$ is a focus-variable of type $\tau$.
                (Variables $v_{F-1,e}$, $v_{F-2,e}$, $v_{F-3,e}$ abbreviated as $x_F$,$y_F$,$z_F$, respectively.)
                        Note: Focus-variables are variables, and as such are assigned values by the assignment functions.
        (ii)    For any formula $\phi$, $/\phi/$ is the result of replacing each F-marked subformula in $\phi$ with a distinct focus-variable matching that subformula in type.
        (iii)   $[\![\phi]\!]^{f-M,g} = \{[\![/\phi/]\!]^{M,g'} : g'$ is identical to g except that it may assign different values to the focus-variables in $/\phi/\}$

We may assume that the same definition of semantic values in a model (i.e. **not** relative to an assignment function) given above for ordinary semantic values applies to focus semantic values as well. That is, we have the following.

(35)    For any model M and any expression $\alpha$,

$$[\![\alpha]\!]^{f-M} = \begin{cases} [\![\alpha]\!]^{f-M,g} \text{ (g arbitrary assignment for M)} \\ \qquad \text{iff} \quad \text{for any g, } g' \text{ for M, } [\![\alpha]\!]^{f-M,g} = [\![\alpha]\!]^{f-M,g'} \\ \text{undefined otherwise} \end{cases}$$

---

[6]   Cf. 14.4 above.

Assuming the definitions just given, the focus semantic values of (1′), (2′), (14′) above are as in (36)–(38), which boil down to (39)–(41). Note that each member of the focus semantic value is itself a set of possible worlds. (I have omitted the superscript M, and will usually do so below.)

(36)  $[\![(1')]\!]^{f\text{-}g} = \{[\![introduce(j,x_F,s)]\!]^{g'} : g'$ is identical to g except that it may assign a different value to $x_F\}$

(37)  $[\![(2')]\!]^{f\text{-}g} = \{[\![introduce(j,b,y_F)]\!]^{g'} : g'$ is identical to g except that it may assign a different value to $y_F\}$

(38)  $[\![(14')]\!]^{f\text{-}g} = \{[\![introduce(j,x_F,y_F)]\!]^{g'} : g'$ is identical to g except that it may assign a different value to $x_F,y_F\}$

(39)  $[\![(1')]\!]^{f} \quad = \{[\![introduce(j,x,s)]\!]^{g} : g$ is an assignment function$\}$

(40)  $[\![(2')]\!]^{f} \quad = \{[\![introduce(j,b,y)]\!]^{g} : g$ is an assignment function$\}$

(41)  $[\![(14')]\!]^{f} = \{[\![introduce(j,x,y)]\!]^{g} : g$ is an assignment function$\}$

This can be used to explain question-answer congruence if we assume, following Hamblin 1973, that questions (10), (11), (42) denote precisely the sets in (39), (40), (41), respectively.

(10)  Who did John introduce to Sue?

(11)  Who did John introduce Bill to?

(42)  Who did John introduce to who?

And what about "association of *only* with focus"? One thing we could do is add *only* to the language L syncategorematically and interpret it as in (44) (assertion only). (Cf. von Stechow 1989.)

(43)  If $\phi$ is an expression of type t, so is the following.

only[$\phi$]

(44)  If only[$\phi$] is of type t, then for all models M, $w \in W_M$,

$w \in [\![only[\phi]]\!]^{M,g}$ iff for all $p \in [\![\phi]\!]^{f\text{-}M,g}$, if $w \in p$ then $p = [\![\phi]\!]^{M,g}$.

Assuming the focus semantic values in (39)–(41), we get that (17)–(19) are interpreted as in (45)–(47).

(17)  I only introduced [Bill]$_F$ to Sue.

(18)  I only introduced Bill to [Sue]$_F$.

(19)  I only introduced [Bill]$_F$ to [Sue]$_F$.

(45)  $[\![(17)]\!]^{o} = \{w \in W :$ for all $p \in \{[\![introduce(j,x,s)]\!]^{g} : g$ assignment$\}$, if $w \in p$ then $p = [\![introduce(j,b,s)]\!]\}$

(46)  $[\![(18)]\!]^{o} = \{w \in W :$ for all $p \in \{[\![introduce(j,b,y)]\!]^{g} : g$ assignment$\}$, if $w \in p$ then $p = [\![introduce(j,b,s)]\!]\}$

(47)  $[\![(19)]\!]^{o} = \{w \in W :$ for all $p \in \{[\![introduce(j,x,y)]\!]^{g} : g$ assignment$\}$, if $w \in p$ then $p = [\![introduce(j,b,s)]\!]\}$

Finally, let us return to sentence (27). As noted in 14.5.1 above, assuming that (27) receives the translation in (28), we need the focus semantic value of the open formula love(x,s$_F$).

(27)   Someone only loves [Sue]$_F$.
(28)   ∃x [only [love(x,s$_F$)]]

And indeed, the definition in (34) above assigns to this open formula the required focus semantic value. The focus semantic value, relative to an arbitrary assignment function g, is as follows.

(48)   $[\![love(x,s_F)]\!]^{f\text{-}g}$ = {$[\![love(x,x_F)]\!]^{g'}$ : g′ is identical to g except that it may assign a different value to x$_F$}

Given (48), the semantics given in 14.5.2 above, and the treatment of *only* specified in (43), (44), it follows that the ordinary semantic value of (28) (assertion only), for any assignment g, is as in (49). And that boils down to (50).

(49)   $[\![(28)]\!]^{o\text{-}g}$= {w ∈ W : for some g′ identical to g except that it may assign a different value to x, w ∈ $[\![only[love(x,s_F)]]\!]^{g'}$}
        = {w ∈ W : for some g′ identical to g except that it may assign a different value to x, for all p ∈ {$[\![love(x,x_F)]\!]^{g''}$ : g″ is identical to g′ except that it may assign a different value to x$_F$}, if w ∈ p then p = $[\![love(x,s_F)]\!]^{g'}$}
(50)   $[\![(27)]\!]^{o}$   = {w ∈ W : for some g, w ∈ $[\![only[love(x,s_F)]]\!]^{g}$}
        = {w ∈ W : for some g, for all p ∈ {$[\![love(x,y)]\!]^{g'}$ : g′ is identical to g except that it may assign a different value to y}, if w ∈ p then p = $[\![love(x,s)]\!]^{g}$}

### 14.5.5   Structured Meanings

For present purposes, let me informally describe a semantic rule assigning structured meanings to formulas of the logic as follows.

(51)   A **structured meaning** of a formula $\phi$ containing n F-marked subformulas, relative to an arbitrary model M and an arbitrary assignment function g, is an ordered sequence $\langle Q^n, \alpha_1, \ldots, \alpha_n \rangle$, where
        $Q^n$ is the ordinary semantic value relative to M,g of the $\lambda$-expression obtained by successively $\lambda$-abstracting on all the F-marked subformulas (using a new variable each time, so as not to bind any preexisting variables in the process), and
        $\alpha_1, \ldots, \alpha_n$ are the ordinary semantic values relative to M,g of the F-marked subformulas, ordered s.t. successive applications of $Q^n$ to $\alpha_1$ through $\alpha_n$ in that order would yield $[\![\phi]\!]^{M,g}$.

The structured meanings can either serve as **the** sole model-theoretic interpretation of the corresponding English sentence or be seen as an additional (focus-induced) interpretation alongside the ordinary semantic value. It doesn't matter which, since all the information contained in the ordinary semantic value is obviously retained in the structured meaning.

    We may assume that structured meanings in a model (i.e. **not** relative to an assignment function) are defined in the obvious way.

    The structured meanings assigned to (1′), (2′), (14′) are as in (52), (53), (54), respectively.

(52)  ⟨[[λx[introduce(j,x,s)]]], Bill⟩
(53)  ⟨[[λy[introduce(j,b,y)]]], Sue⟩
(54)  ⟨[[λx[λy[introduce(j,x,y)]]]], Bill, Sue⟩
      or:
      ⟨[[λy[λx[introduce(j,x,y)]]]], Sue, Bill⟩

This can be used to explain question-answer congruence if we assume, following Egli 1974; Hausser 1976, that questions (10), (11), (42) denote precisely the first members of (52), (53), (54), respectively.

(10)  Who did John introduce to Sue?
(11)  Who did John introduce Bill to?
(42)  Who did John introduce to who?

As for "association of *only* with focus," we could continue to assume that *only* is added to the language L syncategorematically as before (see (43) above), and interpret it as in (55) (assertion only).

(55)  If only[$\phi$] is of type t, and ⟨$Q^n$, $\alpha_1$, . . . ,$\alpha_n$⟩ is the/a structured meaning of $\phi$ relative to M,g, then for all w ∈ W,
      w ∈ [[only[$\phi$]]]$^{M,g}$    iff    for all sequences ⟨$\beta_1$, . . . ,$\beta_n$⟩, if  w ∈ $Q^n$($\beta_1$, . . . ,$\beta_n$) then ⟨$\beta_1$, . . . ,$\beta_n$⟩ = ⟨$\alpha_1$, . . . ,$\alpha_n$⟩.

Assuming the structured meanings in (52)–(54), we get that the ordinary semantic values associated with (17)–(19) are as in (56)–(58).

(17)  I only introduced [Bill]$_F$ to Sue.
(18)  I only introduced Bill to [Sue]$_F$.
(19)  I only introduced [Bill]$_F$ to [Sue]$_F$.

(56)  [[(17)]]$^o$ = {w ∈ W : for all d ∈ D, if w ∈ [[λx[introduce(j,x,s)]]](d) then d = Bill}
(57)  [[(18)]]$^o$ = {w ∈ W : for all d ∈ D, if w ∈ [[λy[introduce(j,b,y)]]](d) then d = Sue}
(58)  [[(19)]]$^o$ = {w ∈ W : for all $d_1$,$d_2$ ∈ D, if w ∈ [[λx[λy[introduce(j,x,y)]]]]($d_1$,$d_2$) then $d_1$ = Bill and $d_2$ = Sue}

Finally, we return again to sentence (27), translated as in (28).

(27)  Someone only loves [Sue]$_F$.
(28)  ∃x [only [love(x,$s_F$)]]

Given rule (51) above, we get that the structured meaning of love(x,$s_F$) relative to an arbitrary assignment function g, is as follows.

(59)  ⟨[[λy[love(x,y)]]]$^g$, Sue⟩

Given (59), the semantics given in 14.5.2 above, and the treatment of *only* specified in (43), (55), it follows that the ordinary semantic value of (28) (assertion only), for any assignment g, is as in (60). And that boils down to (61).

(60)   $[\![(28)]\!]^{o-g}=$ {w ∈ W : for some g′ identical to g except that it may assign a different value to x, w ∈ $[\![$only[love(x,s$_F$)]$]\!]^{g'}$}

= {w ∈ W : for some g′ identical to g except that it may assign a different value to x, for all d ∈ D, if w ∈ $[\![\lambda y[love(x,y)]]\!]^{g'}$(d) then d = Sue}

(61)   $[\![(27)]\!]^{o}$ = {w ∈ W : for some g, w ∈ $[\![$only[love(x,s$_F$)]$]\!]^{g}$}

= {w ∈ W : for some g, for all d ∈ D, if w ∈ $[\![\lambda y[love(x,y)]]\!]^{g}$(d) then d
= Sue}

## 14.6   What is Needed Next?

In the present chapter, a partial answer was given to the following very basic question:
semantically/pragmatically speaking, what is focus? The partial answer given was this:
choice of focused constituents is reflected in focus-induced interpretations; focus-
induced interpretations can be modeled either as structured meanings or as Rooth's
focus semantic values.

Another (related but distinct) question is this: how are the various effects of focusing created? The basic idea, already indicated in the present chapter, is that the hypothesized focus-induced interpretations play a role in creating those effects. However, we
would like to know a lot more about exactly when and exactly how this happens.

We said in this chapter that the focus-induced interpretation is closely related to a
question-denotation. Certainly this should help to explain question-answer congruence:
there could now be rule(s) or principle(s) that utilize this close relation. But what would
these principles be, exactly? Can we derive them from a general theory of how information is organized in discourse, say? And how do the relevant principles apply in other
and more complex cases of discourse congruence (see 13.2.1 above)?

We said in this chapter that focus-induced interpretations enter the interpretation
of focusing adverbs. But why do they, and when, and how? For the sake of exposition,
we assumed above that the very semantic rule that interprets *only* directly refers to the
focus-induced interpretation of the argument of *only*. But is that the theory we want?
Are there indeed semantic rules that directly access focus-induced interpretations? Are
the semantic effects of focusing constrained in any way? how? Are these effects obligatory or optional? And so on and so forth.

In chapters 16 and 17 below, I will be concerned first merely with how focusing
effects are created, and then with the search for a more complete characterization of
what focus is. Of course, the two questions, while distinct, are very closely related
indeed.

# 15

# *Problems with Focus-Induced Interpretations*

Certainly, the above formulation of the basic logic, the semantics of *only* and the focus-induced interpretations is not without its problems. In this chapter, I will present some of the known problems. My main goals are: (i) to clear up the stage for the following chapters by indicating what problems will be left aside; (ii) to separate out the problems so that it might be easier to see/ask/determine which of these problems (if any) directly concern the definition of focus-induced interpretations; (iii) to highlight Schwarzchild's problem (section 15.3).

## 15.1   The Usual (Limited) Success with Intensionality

Suppose that the facts in the real world are as in (1). As noted in 14.5.1 above, we still judge as follows: (2) is infelicitous. (3) is false, since Sue is both bold and beautiful (in other words, (3) entails (4)).

(1)   the bold individuals = the beautiful individuals = {Bill, Sue}
(2)   A:   Who is bold?
      B:   [Sue]$_F$ is beautiful.
(3)   Sue is only [bold]$_F$.
(4)   Sue is not beautiful.

It seems that given the formalization of chapter 14, we are able to predict these intuitions. Our intensional model allows us to distinguish between [[bold]] and [[beautiful]]: they can be two different functions from individuals to propositions (= to sets of worlds). (Two functions which happen to agree on the following: the real world is included in the values assigned to Bill and to Sue, but not in the value assigned to any other individual.)

   But, as discussed in Rooth 1985, pp. 85–6 (fn. 13), there is more to worry about. Here's an easy problem: what if we evaluate (2) and (3) in a model where [[bold]] and [[beautiful]] are **not** distinct? For instance, a model as in (5).

(5)    $w = \{w_1, w_2\}$   $D = \{Sue, Bill\}$

$$[\![bold]\!] \;\; = \;\; [\![beautiful]\!] \;\; = \;\; \begin{bmatrix} Sue \rightarrow \{w_1, w_2\} \\ Bill \rightarrow \{w_1\} \end{bmatrix}$$

Given the assumptions we have been making about questions and *only*, in this model, (2) would come out felicitous, and (3) would **not** come out false just because Sue is both bold and beautiful.

Well, this is not really a problem, if we take models as in (5) to represent a situation where the predicates *bold* and *beautiful* are in fact synonymous. Compare with (6) and (7) below, assuming that *unmarried man* and *bachelor* are synonymous. It seems that intuitively (6) is felicitous (it is certainly better than (2)), and it seems that we would **not** judge (7) false just because John is both an unmarried man and a bachelor (in other words, we would **not** judge that (7) entails (8)).

(6)    A:    Who is an unmarried man?
       B:    [John]$_F$ is a bachelor.
(7)    John is only [a bachelor]$_F$.
(8)    John is not an unmarried man.

To account for the intuitions about (2) and (3), we could assume that English speakers, who know *bold* and *beautiful* not to be synonymous, invariably presuppose a model in which they have distinct semantic values.

Of course we do run into more serious trouble when we get to logically/mathematically defined properties. For instance, take the properties "be the square of 3" and "be the square of −3". Presumably, these properties have the same intension. In terms of the logic assumed here,

$$[\![\text{the square of 3}]\!] \;\; = \;\; [\![\text{the square of } -3]\!] \;\; = \;\; \text{that function that assigns to 9 the}$$
value W and assigns to all other
numbers the value ∅.

Arguably, though, they are two distinct properties. Indeed, intuitively, (9) is non-trivial, (10) is infelicitous, and (11) is false.

(9)    Nine is both the square of 3 and the square of −3.
(10)   A:    What is the square of 3?
       B:    [Nine]$_F$ is the square of −3.
(11)   Nine is only the square of [three]$_F$.

However, as noted by Rooth, this is by no means a problem specific to the theory of focus. It is well known that standard possible world semantics is not "intensional enough" for all needs – as evident, in particular, in the study of propositional attitudes. So it seems reasonable to leave this problem aside for the moment, merely noting that

Rooth's theory of focus is yet another realm where a "more intensional" logic would be needed.

## 15.2   Things That *Only* Should Not Exclude

Our current treatment of *only* makes statements with *only* exclude too many things. Assuming (12), we predict that (13) entails (14), (7) entails (15), (16) entails (17), and (18) entails (19).

(12)   If only[$\phi$] is of type t, then for all w ∈ W,
       w ∈ $[\![$only[$\phi$]$]\!]^{M,g}$    iff    for all p ∈ $[\![\phi]\!]^{f-M,g}$, if w ∈ p then p = $[\![\phi]\!]^{M,g}$.

(13)   John only [swims]$_F$.
(14)   John does not have a brother.
(7)   John is only [a bachelor]$_F$.
(15)   John is not a man.
(16)   Paula only painted [a still life]$_F$.
(17)   Paula did not paint apples.

(adapted from Kratzer 1989)

(18)   Peter only saw [the secretary of state]$_F$.
(19)   Peter did not see the special envoy to the Middle East.

(adapted from Bonomi and Casalegno 1993, section 4.3)

But these predictions are wrong. In context, (13) can easily mean that of all exercise activities, John only swims, in which case (13) would not exclude John's having a brother. (7) definitely does not exclude John's being a man. Paula's still life may well have contained apples, in which case (16) would not exclude her having painted apples. (18) can easily mean that the secretary of state was the highest official Peter got to see, in which case it would exclude his having seen the president, but not his having seen the special envoy to the Middle East.

For the case of (13), the solution seems obvious: in context, the quantification induced by *only* will, of course, be implicitly restricted by the familiar process of "domain selection." So *only* will only exclude things that are relevant in the context.[1] When we describe John's exercising, his having a brother is not relevant.

But can "domain selection" cover all of the above cases? That is questionable, because it is not clear that the things that *only* should not exclude are necessarily (intuitively) irrelevant. Is being a man irrelevant when talking about John's being a bachelor? One might argue that it is in fact relevant, in that it is a necessary condition for being a bachelor. Painting apples can hardly be considered irrelevant to painting a still life with apples in it. And it is not clear that having seen the special envoy must be irrelevant when (18) is understood not to exclude it.

(7) presupposes that John is a bachelor, which entails that John is a man. So the case of (7) shows that *only* should not exclude things **entailed** by what's being presupposed. Schwarzschild 1994 ensures that entailed things not be excluded, by making a slight

---

[1]   This fact was noted and utilized in Rooth 1985. See chapter 16.

change to the semantics of *only*, which may be expressed by replacing our (12) with (12′).

(12′)   If only[$\phi$] is of type t, then for all w ∈ W,
     w ∈ ⟦only[$\phi$]⟧$^{M,g}$     iff      for all p ∈ ⟦$\phi$⟧$^{f-M,g}$, if w ∈ p then ⟦$\phi$⟧$^{M,g}$ ⊆ p.

(7) would now be taken to claim that John has no other properties besides being a bachelor **and properties entailed by that**. However, such a move does not cover the cases illustrated above with (16) and (18). Painting a still life does not entail painting apples.

     The "lumping" relation of Kratzer 1989 will provide a way of covering more of the facts. Kratzer 1989 argues that the crucial point about the case of (16) is this: if in the actual world Paula painted a still life with apples in it, then, in the actual world, her painting those apples was not a distinct fact from her painting that still life. Intuitively, the fact that she painted that still life encompasses the fact that she painted those apples. Kratzer captures this intuition by defining a "lumping" relation between propositions. In the actual world, the proposition that Paula painted a still life is said to **lump** the proposition that she painted apples.[2] If we formulate the semantics of *only* as indicated in (20) (filling in the definition of lumping and the relevant details of the semantic system, of course), we will get the right prediction both for (7) and for (16).

(20)   If only[$\phi$] is of type t, then for all w ∈ W,
     w ∈ ⟦only[$\phi$]⟧     iff      for all p ∈ ⟦$\phi$⟧$^f$, if w ∈ p then ⟦$\phi$⟧ lumps p in w.

     This is still not good enough for (18), though. Intuitively, seeing the secretary of state does not "lump" – that is, does not include as an integral part of it – seeing the special envoy to the Middle East. Bonomi and Casalegno 1993, section 4.3, suggest that on the reading we are interested in ("Peter did not get as high as the president"), (18) is interpreted with reference to a scale of facts (ordered by how rewarding they are to Peter, or how impressive, or whatever):

(21)   saw the special envoy ≤ saw the secretary of state ≤ saw the president.

If we interpret (18) using the rule in (22), we will get the desired reading. Assuming that ≤ is determined by the context to be as in (21), (18) will not entail (19).

(22)   If only[$\phi$] is of type t, then for all w ∈ W,
     w ∈ ⟦only[$\phi$]⟧     iff      for all p ∈ ⟦$\phi$⟧$^f$, if w ∈ p then ⟦$\phi$⟧ ≤ p,
     where the ordering ≤ is to be supplied by the context.

     The exposition above presupposes that the matter of things that *only* should not exclude is a problem that the semantic analysis of *only* should handle. However, it might make more sense to hypothesize instead that entailed or lumped propositions are excluded from the domain of quantification for *only* due to a general constraint

---

[2]   For details, I must refer the reader to Kratzer's paper.

(a constraint on "domain selection," if you like), one that excludes entailed or lumped entities from domains of quantification in general. (Cf. Carlson 1977, p. 346ff; Kratzer 1989, p. 609; Schwarzschild 1997, p. 10.) (For cases like (13), and perhaps also for scalar readings as in (18), we would stick to the idea that the unwanted propositions are excluded from the domain of quantification for *only* because of being irrelevant.)

Under the alternative semantics theory of focus (but not the structured meaning theory), the following approach is also open to us, in principle. We could try to exclude entailed or lumped propositions from the domain of quantification for *only* via the definition of focus-induced interpretations. That is, a focus semantic value would be defined in such a way that it would never include both a proposition p and some other proposition q which is entailed or lumped by p.

In the following chapters, I will leave the problem of things that *only* should not exclude aside.

## 15.3   Schwarzschild's General Problem with Defining Sets of Alternatives in Terms of Full Semantic Domains

Here is a feature common to Rooth's alternative semantics theory of focus and to theories of the semantics of questions which take a question to denote the set of possible answers: given a sentence/question, the theory associates with it a set of alternative propositions, by substitution of all possible semantic values for a given position in that sentence/question. Schwarzschild 1994 (section 1.3.2) points out an unsolved problem faced by any theory which uses full sets of possible semantic values in this way.

To illustrate the problem, consider sentence (23), and its focus semantic value in (24).

(23)   Sue is [bold]$_F$.
(24)   $[\![(23)]\!]^f = \{[\![X(s)]\!]^g : g \text{ assignment function}\}$

Surely, the idea is that $[\![(23)]\!]^f$ should contain propositions like "Sue is beautiful," "Sue is cunning," "Sue is honest," "Sue is charismatic." The problem is that in fact, $[\![(23)]\!]^f$ turns out to also contain, for example, the proposition "Mary is beautiful." After all, the function $[\![\lambda x[\text{beautiful}(m)]]\!]$ is also a member of $D_{\langle e,t \rangle}$, and is therefore a possible semantic value for the variable X. But this is a disastrous result. It predicts, for instance, that (3) could be judged false just because Mary is beautiful (or in other words, that (3) entails (25)).

(3)   Sue is only [bold]$_F$.
(25)   Mary is not beautiful.

(Note, in this connection, that while a terrible pedant might insist that (13) does entail (14), and somebody who is a little crazy might even insist that (7) entails (15), it would never occur to anyone to insist that (3) entails (25).)

(13)  John only swims.
(14)  John does not have a brother.

(7)  John is only [a bachelor]$_F$.
(15)  John is not a man.

This suggests that the status of "Mary is beautiful" in relation to (3) is different from the status of the things that *only* should not exclude that were discussed in 15.2.)

As noted by Fred Landman (p.c.), Schwarzschild's problem is quite general and quite nasty. Obviously, by the same reasoning, $[\![(23)]\!]^f$ contains not only "Mary is beautiful" but also any other proposition whatsoever. Indeed, the substitution-of-all-possible-semantic-values method of deriving sets of alternative propositions works fine only for sentences (or questions) whose foci (or wh-phrases) are of type e. Given a focus (or wh-phrase) of any other type, it invariably derives the same set of alternative propositions: the set of all propositions. This of course completely undermines the very idea of using the sets of alternatives derived by this method as the desired focus-induced interpretations or question-denotations.[3]

It seems that with respect to Schwarzschild's problem, the structured meaning theory of focus fares rather better. The structured meaning theory does manage to assign to distinct sentences distinct focus-induced interpretations, regardless of the semantic type of the focus. For instance, take the structured meaning of (23), given in (26); it does not involve assigning alternative values to X, and it contains just two, specific, well-defined, functions.

(26)  $\langle [\![\lambda X[X(s)]]\!], [\![bold]\!] \rangle$

I would like to note, however, that given our current assumptions about *only*, Schwarzschild's problem is re-created when we get to sentence (3). Given the structured meaning theory, (3) is interpreted as in (27).

(27)  $[\![(3)]\!]^\circ = \{w \in W : \text{for all } P \in D_{\langle e,t \rangle}, \text{ if } w \in [\![\lambda X[X(s)]]\!](P), \text{ then } P = [\![bold]\!]\}$

Since $[\![\lambda x[beautiful(m)]]\!]$ is a member of $D_{\langle e,t \rangle}$, we get, here too, the familiar incorrect prediction that (3) entails (25). Evidently, Schwarzschild's problem is a general problem with quantification over the full semantic domains of types other than e.

It seems, then, that the solution to Schwarzschild's problem should not be a change specific to the theory of focus-induced interpretations, but rather a general change to our semantic theory.

It seems, in fact, that what we want is a more restrictive definition of semantic domains for natural language. Take for instance the set of possible denotations for one-place predicates. Given the type theory of chapter 14, this set is $D_{\langle e,t \rangle}$, defined as the full set of functions from D to $D_t$. So it includes $[\![\lambda x[beautiful(m)]]\!]$ and lots of other functions that result in the same kind of problem. However, it seems that these troublesome functions are not (linguistically, common-sensically) true properties of indi-

---

[3] Excluding constant functions like $[\![\lambda x[beautiful(m)]]\!]$ from the sets of alternatives used will not solve our problem, which can easily be varied by constructing similar problem cases with other kinds of functions.

viduals. So it seems natural not to include them as possible denotations of natural language predicates. We should include as possible denotations of linguistic one-place predicates only what are (linguistically, common-sensically) true properties of individuals.

But how do we do that? That is by no means immediately obvious. Fred Landman (p.c.) suggests that the difficulty lies in the fact that a type theory such as the one assumed here is not fine-grained enough to express the intuitive difference between inappropriate denotations and linguistically sensible ones. Landman suggests that Schwarzschild's problem could be solved in a natural way if we use a more fine-grained semantic framework. For instance, suppose we use a system based on event-types (Link 1987; Krifka 1989; Bonomi and Casalegno 1993; Landman 1999). In that case it would be possible, suggests Landman, to restrict possible one-place predicate denotations, for instance, to event-types which have at least one argument role defined on them which is a "real subject role" (agent, experiencer, etc.) and not a logically constructed one.

## 15.4 Conclusions re Choice of Focus-Induced Interpretation?

Focus semantic values and structured meanings are two different proposals regarding the nature of focus-induced interpretations. Is one of them better than the other? Are we able at this point to reach any conclusions that would bear on making a choice between them?

Rooth 1996 suggests that his focus semantic values proposal constitutes a somewhat stronger (more restrictive) – and hence somewhat more explanatory – theory of focus-induced interpretations. Rooth says (p. 278) that "it seems only a slight exaggeration to say that [the structured meanings theory] gives access to all the information which could possibly be relevant, namely the semantics of the focused phrase and the semantics of the rest of the sentence." He notes that this information makes it possible, for instance, to define the verb-meaning in (28) (illustrated in (29)), which is a "quite implausible" operator.

(28) 'tolfed $\phi$' means: 'told the focus of $\phi$ that $\phi$'
(29) I tolfed [that [he]$_F$ resembles her] = I told him that he resembles her
     I tolfed [that he resembles [her]$_F$] = I told her that he resembles her
     I tolfed [that [he]$_F$ resembles [her]$_F$] = I told them that he resembles her

It is not possible to define the same meaning given alternative semantics, because that theory does not assume any model-theoretic entity which is recognizable as "the focus of $\phi$": the focus semantic value of $\phi$ – the only semantic entity that reflects the choice of focus in $\phi$ – is just a set of propositions. So alternative semantics explains why we don't find this sort of verb-meaning in natural language.

I personally don't find this argument very strong. First of all, as Rooth himself has repeatedly stressed, to make the theory of focus explanatory, we need to go beyond just positing focus-induced interpretations. (This will be discussed in detail in the coming chapters.) So we had better judge the explanatory power of the entire theory of focus (and focus effects) and not just the focus-induced interpretation alone. Secondly, there can be all sorts of constraints that limit plausible meanings of natural language expressions, some of them not necessarily linguistic (but rather cognitive).

Also, Schwarzschild's problem discussed in the previous section seems to suggest, if anything, that the extra information contained in the structured meaning (as compared with Rooth's focus semantic value) is actually needed. The definition of focus semantic values based on substitution-of-all-possible-semantic-values fails to yield distinct focus-induced interpretations (for focus-types other than e), as discussed in 15.3 above. In contrast, the definition of structured meanings does succeed in doing that much.

In the following chapters, I will use alternative semantics. That is largely because I happen to be interested in a number of proposals that have been developed within that framework. Despite Schwarzschild's problem, I will be using the theory as formulated in chapter 14, including the substitution-of-all-possible-semantic-values method of defining focus semantic values.

# 16

# *Association with Focus: The "Domain Selection"/"Free Parameter" Analysis*

We now return to the question – alluded to in 14.6 above – of how, exactly, the various effects of focusing are created. Semantic effects of focusing and how they come about are the main concern of Rooth 1985. Rooth includes here truth-conditional effects as well as effects on ps (as in the case of *even* – see 13.2.3), and he refers to all such effects as cases of "association with focus."

Recall that in chapter 14, the following semantic rule for *only* was used, which makes direct reference to the focus-induced interpretation of the argument of *only*.

(1)  If only[$\phi$] is of type t, then for all w ∈ W,
      w ∈ $[\![$only[$\phi$]$]\!]^{M,g}$      iff      for all p ∈ $[\![ \phi ]\!]^{f\text{-}M,g}$, if w ∈ p then p = $[\![ \phi ]\!]^{M,g}$.

We could presumably construct a descriptively adequate theory of "association with focus" by continuing to postulate various semantic rules that have direct access to focus-induced interpretations as needed, until we cover all the semantic effects of focusing. However, such a theory would not be very explanatory, since it would be both ad hoc and weak. Certainly, a theory which would constrain semantic effects of focusing (excluding, for instance, strange verb-meanings such as the "tolfed" of 15.4 above) and/or derive focusing effects from more general principles would be preferable. This chapter will focus on one significant step towards a more explanatory theory.

Rooth 1985 proposes and argues for what he calls a "domain selection theory of association with focus." The basic idea underlying this analysis is also proposed in Boër 1979. The same sort of analysis is referred to in Rooth 1992 as the "free parameter" hypothesis about association with focus.

Let us consider first Dretske 1972's examples (2) and (3) below (repeated from 13.2.5). Recall the Clyde and Bertha story: Clyde is a dedicated bachelor who does not want to live permanently with a woman. Yet Clyde finds out that he will inherit a lot of money if he is married by the age of 30. Clyde solves this dilemma by marrying his friend Bertha, a dedicated archeologist who is out of the country almost all the time.

Given this story, (2) seems true (or at least likely to be true), whereas (3) seems false (or at least likely to be false).

(2)   If Clyde hadn't MARRIED Bertha, he would not have been eligible for the inheritance.
(3)   If Clyde hadn't married BERTHA, he would not have been eligible for the inheritance.

Boër 1979 proposes the following account. Let us assume Lewis 1973's analysis of counterfactuals: very roughly, a counterfactual conditional claims that in all those possible worlds **that are the most similar to the world of evaluation** in which the antecedent is true, the consequent is also true. But similarity between worlds can be measured differently in different contexts. So the hearer must recover the intended similarity measure. Based on the Clyde and Bertha story, the hearer can immediately figure out that worlds in which the antecedent is true are of two relevant sorts: those in which Clyde remains single, and those in which he marries someone else. It is "contrastive stress," says Boër, that helps the hearer decide which of the two sorts is to be considered: "contrastive stress" on *married* suggests the first sort of worlds, while "contrastive stress" on *Bertha* suggests the latter sort.

Next, let us consider association of *only* with focus. Leaving focus aside for a moment, it is pointed out in Rooth 1985 that the quantification induced by *only* – like any other quantification – is often implicitly restricted by the familiar process of "domain selection." Look at (4)–(6): (4) can easily mean "of all my brothers, only John came," (5) can easily mean "of all exercise activities, John only swims," (6) can easily mean "of reasons not to accompany Mother to the concert, the only one that holds is that John asked me out."

(4)   Only John came.
(5)   John only swims.
(6)   The only thing is, John asked me out.

Now Rooth 1985 points out that if we take domain selection into account, we need not assume that the semantics of *only* ever has direct access to foci or to focus semantic values. Instead, we can let the choice of focus affect the pragmatic process of selecting a relevant domain of quantification.

According to the theory proposed by Rooth, then, the semantic rule for sentential *only* is **not** as in (1). Instead, we may posit the rule given in (7), where C is a contextually determined set of relevant propositions.

(7)   If only[$\phi$] is of type t, then for all $w \in W$,
$w \in [\![\text{only}[\phi]]\!]^{M,g}$      iff      for all $p \in C$, if $w \in p$ then  $p = [\![\phi]\!]^{M,g}$.

Example (6), for instance, would now mean that of all relevant propositions, the only true one is that John asked me out. Note that in (6), the entire argument of *only* is (probably) focused. In such a case, focusing does not narrow down the domain of quantification; we use contextual information alone to narrow it down. When only part of the argument of *only* is focused, however, the focal structure will help us narrow down the domain of quantification.

Consider, for instance, examples (8)–(10).

(8)   John only introduced [Bill]$_F$ to Sue.
(9)   John only introduced Bill to [Sue]$_F$.
(10)  John only introduced [Bill]$_F$ to [Sue]$_F$.

Given rule (7), these three examples are all semantically interpreted as specified in (11).[1]

(11)  a.   the asserted proposition is:
           $\{w : \text{for all } p \in C, \text{ if } w \in p \text{ then } p = [\![introduce(j,b,s)]\!]\}$
      b.   i.e.: 'No relevant proposition is true other than the proposition that John introduced Bill to Sue.'

The focal structure now plays a role in determining the set $C$ of relevant propositions. Rooth 1985 states that the relevant domain of quantification is simply identified with the focus semantic value of the argument of *only*. Rooth 1992 revises this and states that the relevant domain of quantification is restricted to be a subset of the focus semantic value of the argument of *only*, since there can obviously be further contextual restrictions on the domain of quantification.

If the quantification in (8)–(10) is restricted only by the focal structure, and there are no further contextual restrictions, we get the following.

(12)  For (8), $C = [\![introduce(j,b_F,s)]\!]^f = \{[\![introduce(j,x,s)]\!]^g : g \text{ assignment}\}$;
      For (9), $C = [\![introduce(j,b,s_F)]\!]^f = \{[\![introduce(j,b,y)]\!]^g : g \text{ assignment}\}$;
      For (10), $C = [\![introduce(j,b_F,s_F)]\!]^f = \{[\![introduce(j,x,y)]\!]^g : g \text{ assignment}\}$.

This yields the desired truth conditions for (8)–(10), when considered out of context. As acknowledged in Rooth 1992, in context, $C$ may be restricted further. For instance, the values of x and y may be restricted to "kids from John's class."

Dretske's account of (2)–(3) and Rooth's account of (8)–(10) should be enough to illustrate the general idea of the "domain selection"/"free parameter" analysis. The general idea can be stated as follows: semantic effects of focusing are created when the focal structure plays a role in fixing implicit restrictions on quantification.[2] In (2)–(3), focus helped fix the similarity measure, and thereby helped determine how the quantification over possible worlds was to be restricted. In (8)–(10), focus helped determine how the quantification induced by *only* was to be restricted.

The "domain selection"/"free parameter" analysis of association with focus seems like a step in the right direction. It offers some insight into the reason that focusing exhibits semantic effects, it avoids the use of ad hoc semantic rules, it suggests that we

---

[1]   I continue to assume, for simplicity, that auxiliary *only* is a sentential adverb.
[2]   An almost equivalent way of putting this is to say that semantic effects of focusing are created when the focal structure plays a role in fixing the value of some implicit semantic parameter (cf. 1.6). (I think that in practice it would always be a parameter which is/determines a restriction on quantification.)

might be able to constrain focusing effects by limiting them to fixing an implicit restriction on quantification.[3]

(The examples of Rooth 1992 (see section 17.3 below) suggest, however, that focus effects are probably **not** constrained just to cases of fixing an implicit restriction. As stressed in Rooth 1992, p. 106, there exist focusing effects that seem to require a somewhat different account.)

---

[3]   Or the value of an implicit semantic parameter.

# 17

# *Focus: The More Complete Analysis*

## 17.1  Introduction

What is the complete answer to the following question: what **is** focus? In other words, what should the complete semantic/pragmatic theory of focus consist of? Rooth 1985 provides one part of the theory by formally defining focus-induced interpretations (his "p-sets" = focus semantic values). He also informally suggests a second part of the theory, viz. the following: it is conveyed by the choice of focus that the members of the focus semantic value are alternatives under consideration (Rooth 1985, p. 63).

Perhaps the above is basically all there is to say about the semantics/pragmatics of focus. (Although not a complete **formal** theory.) That would be a rather general and simple theory of what focus is. Or perhaps the theory of focus needs to be revised in some way(s). At any rate, it should ideally remain simple and general.

The other question we seek to answer is: how are the various effects of focusing created? "Ideally," says Rooth 1985 (p. 62), "one would like to derive association with focus as a kind of theorem." The idea is that effects of focusing should ideally follow from a combination of two things: (i) the complete semantic/pragmatic theory of focus, and (ii) independently needed theories in other domains.

For instance, take the association of *only* with focus. The fact that the domain of the quantification induced by *only* must be a subset of the focus semantic value of the argument of *only* should ideally follow from the theory of focus combined with the general theory of domain selection. Indeed, at a rough, informal level, we seem to be quite close to this ideal already: assume that the focus semantic value of the argument of *only* is a set of alternatives that are under consideration, and therefore salient in the context; assume that domains of quantification are restricted by sets that are salient in the context; it follows that the focus semantic value will restrict the quantification. Similarly, discourse congruence effects should ideally follow from the theory of focus combined with the general theory of how information is organized in discourse. And so on.

Obviously, the answers to our two questions are very closely related: a good theory of focus would include precisely what's necessary to yield, in combination with theories in other domains, an explanatory theory of focusing effects.

## 17.2 The Optionality of Focus Effects

An important empirical observation, which the analyses of focus and focusing effects will have to account for, is that focusing effects are **optional**, in the following sense.

(1)   A construction/phenomenon that typically exhibits a particular focusing effect (if combined with a focal structure that supports that effect) need not **always** exhibit that effect (even when combined with a focal structure that would support that effect).

Let us look at a few examples of this optionality. Here is an example from Dretske 1972. (2) below suggests that the part of Clyde's action that was wrong was that the recipient of the ticket was "me" rather than some other person. The expression *by mistake* typically "associates with the focus" in this manner (if combined with a focus narrow enough to support this effect).

(2)   Clyde gave [me]$_F$ the tickets by mistake.

(Dretske 1972, p. 428)

However, this effect does not **always** show up (even when there is a narrow enough focus to support the effect). Dretske 1972 notes that in the context given in (3), (2) does **not** exhibit the typical "association of *by mistake* with focus." In this context, (2) is perfectly compatible with the understanding that Clyde's mistake was that he handed over the tickets rather than some other object.

(3)   <u>Context:</u>   Clyde gave me the tickets by mistake – he should have given me the passport. You think it was George to whom Clyde gave the tickets by mistake (you think Clyde should have given the passport to George instead of the tickets). I correct you and say (2).

It is noted in Rooth 1992 that "association of *only* with focus" is optional too. We know that *only* typically exhibits a semantic "association with focus" effect (if its argument contains a narrow enough focus). For instance, (4) is typically interpreted as suggested by (5).

(4)   They only [eat]$_F$ rice.
(5)   . . . They don't [sell]$_F$ rice or [process]$_F$ rice.

And yet, *only* does not **always** associate with the focus contained in its argument. For instance, example (6) below can easily be interpreted as suggested by (7), and John's utterance in (8) below can easily be true even if John happens to have introduced Lee to Sue (which was not related to his mother's wishes).

(6)   People who [grow]$_F$ rice generally only [eat]$_F$ rice.

(Rooth 1992, p. 109)

(7)   . . . They don't eat [meat]$_F$, or [bread]$_F$.
(8)   Father:   Is it true that of all the things Mother asked you to do at her ball you only managed to introduce Steve to Sue?
       John:     Not exactly . . . [grin] I only introduced [Bill]$_F$ to Sue.

I offer the following case: In (9) below, the focal structure seems to disambiguate the elliptical clause, suggesting that the intended reading is the one indicated in (10a). But the disambiguation effect is not always present. For instance, in the piece of discourse given in (11), (9) would have the reading indicated in (10b), focal structure notwithstanding.

(9)    Sue likes [me]$_F$ more than [Kim]$_F$.
(10)   a.    'more than Sue likes Kim'
       b.    'more than Kim likes me'
(11)   A:    Did you say that Sue likes your work more than Pim does?
       B:    No, you got it all wrong. I said that Sue likes [me]$_F$ more than [Kim]$_F$.

And, one more case: A scalar implicature of a given example is typically based (in part) on its focal structure – e.g. (12) tends to implicate (14) while (13) tends to implicate (15).

(12)   [Most]$_F$ conductors are competent pianists.
(13)   Most conductors are [competent]$_F$ pianists.
(14)   Not all conductors are competent pianists.
(15)   It is not the case that most conductors are excellent pianists.

However, as noted in 13.2.9, I think that each of (12) and (13) can simultaneously have both of the scalar implicatures in (14) and (15). This means that not all the scalar implicatures associated with these examples are based (in part) on the focal structure.

The optionality of focusing effects plays an important role in the view of focus and focusing effects offered in Rooth 1992, to be discussed immediately below.

## 17.3   The Focus Interpretation Principle (Rooth 1992)

Retaining the Rooth 1985 conception of focus semantic values, Rooth 1992 aims to make progress on the second part of the theory of focus, viz. the part that characterizes the use of focus semantic values. Instead of the idea that focusing indicates that the members of the focus semantic value are alternatives under consideration, Rooth 1992 proposes a principle called the **Focus Interpretation Principle** (FIP, for short), which may be stated as follows.[1]

(16)   **Rooth's Focus Interpretation Principle**
       A constituent may be focused
          iff
       it is contained in a clause S of which the following holds:
       somewhere in the environment there is an (independently) salient set of propositions – call it $\Gamma$ – s.t.

---

[1]   I believe this is a faithful enough statement of Rooth's idea, although he never states his FIP quite this way. I have taken into account the FIP as given in Rooth 1992, p. 86, as well as Rooth's discussion and examples, and the revision proposed on p. 90.

> (i)   $\Gamma \subseteq [\![S]\!]^f$, and
> (ii)  $[\![S]\!]^o \in \Gamma$, and
> (iii) there is some proposition p s.t. $p \neq [\![S]\!]^o$ and $p \in \Gamma$.

I should note that, unlike Rooth, I continue, for simplicity's sake, to only be concerned with focus semantic values of complete clauses. (I will also continue to assume that *only* is a sentential adverb.) To see how the FIP works, I think it is easiest to start with an example.

**Example (I): association of *only* with focus**   Consider examples (17) and (18), translated as in (17′) and (18′), which are both interpreted as in (19) (assertion only, value of C contextually supplied).

(17)   John only [introduced Bill to Sue]$_F$.
(18)   John only introduced [Bill]$_F$ to Sue.
(17′)  only [ [introduce(b)(s)]$_F$ (j) ]
(18′)  only [ introduce(b$_F$)(s)(j) ]
(19)   {w : for all p ∈ C, if w ∈ p then p = $[\![$introduce(b)(s)(j)$]\!]$}

In (17) and (18), the focus is actually contained in two different clauses. Let us look at the smaller, embedded clause – the one which serves as the argument of *only*. Does this clause satisfy the requirement in the FIP? We need to look for some salient set $\Gamma$ which is present somewhere in the environment. The set C, the domain of quantification for *only*, is a natural candidate. Now, does C satisfy conditions (i)–(iii)? That depends on the choice of focus (i.e. on whether we are looking at (17) or at (18)) and on the value of C (as determined by various contextual clues).

Let us take example (17), and let us suppose that the context fixes the value of C as the set in (20) (the set of good deeds that John could have performed at his mother's ball, say).

(20)   {'John introduced Bill to Sue,'
        'John politely chatted with Aunt Betty,'
        'John danced with the neighbor's daughters,'
        'John helped supervise the evening's program' . . .}

C satisfies condition (i), since it is a subset of the focus semantic value, given in (21), of the relevant embedded clause.

(21)   $[\![$[introduce(b)(s)]$_F$ (j)$]\!]^f$ = {$[\![X(j)]\!]^g$ : g assignment}

C also satisfies condition (ii), since the proposition "John introduced Bill to Sue" is the ordinary semantic value of our clause. C also satisfies condition (iii), since it contains as members other propositions, distinct from "John introduced Bill to Sue." It is therefore predicted that if C is set to (20), the VP focus in (17) is felicitous. This is a correct prediction: empirically, example (17) is compatible with the domain of quantification suggested in (20).

Now let us consider example (18). Suppose first that the domain of quantification C is again fixed as the set in (20). In that case, C cannot serve to satisfy the requirement in the FIP. C does not even satisfy condition (i), since it is not a subset of the focus semantic value, given in (22), of the relevant embedded clause (or that of the matrix clause, either).

(22)   $[\![\text{introduce}(b_F)(s)(j)]\!]^f = \{[\![\text{introduce}(x)(s)(j)]\!]^g : g \text{ assignment}\}$

But what if the domain of quantification C is fixed as the set in (23)?

(23)   {'John introduced Bill to Sue,'
        'John introduced Kim to Sue,'
        'John introduced Lee to Sue,'
        'John introduced Jo to Sue'}

In that case, C can serve to satisfy the requirement in the FIP once more. The set in (23) **is** a subset of the focus semantic value, given in (22), of our embedded clause; further, it contains as members the ordinary semantic value of that clause, as well as other propositions distinct from it. This yields the correct prediction that if C is set to (23), the focus in (18) is felicitous.

Finally, consider example (18) as it occurs in the following context.

(8)   Father:   Is it true that of all the things Mother asked you to do at her ball you only managed to introduce Steve to Sue?
      John:     Not exactly . . . [grin] I only introduced [Bill]$_F$ to Sue.

Here, the domain of quantification of *only* is obviously something like (20). But that means that the FIP cannot be satisfied in the manner described in the last paragraph. Yet the FIP **is** satisfied, in the manner described below.

The ordinary semantic value of (18) – the proposition "John only introduced Bill to Sue" (with C set to something like (20)) – is obviously contrasted in this context with the proposition "John only introduced Steve to Sue" (with C set to something like (20)), which is explicitly referred to in the previous utterance. (This is an instance of what I referred to in 13.2.1 above as an "explicit binary contrast.") Note that the contrast is present independently of the focus – a printed form of example (8) minus the F-marking would still be understood as drawing this contrast.[2]

The explicit binary contrast in (8) immediately makes salient a "comparison class" within which the two propositions are contrasted. It is possible that no other comparison class comes to mind except simply the set containing just these two propositions. It is also possible that a larger comparison class comes to mind – perhaps the set that contains the proposition that John only introduced d to Sue (with C set to something like (20)), for every individual d who is an eligible young man that was present at the ball. (Assuming, of course, that Steve and Bill are included among the relevant young

---

[2]   When the contrast is being drawn, the question of who the "correct" individual is is not yet settled, so at that point the members of C are not fully identified: we don't know if C contains "John introduced Steve to Sue" or "John introduced Bill to Sue" (or both). Note that this is quite normal. In real life, C can easily be identified as "the set of things Mother asked John to do at her ball" without full knowledge of what those things actually are.

men.) At any rate, it is the comparison class within which the explicit binary contrast is being drawn that serves as the set $\Gamma$ required by the FIP.

Look at the matrix clause this time (i.e. the whole of example (18)). Its focus semantic value is as in (24).

(24)   $[\![only[introduce(b_F)(s)(j)]]\!]^f = \{[\![only[introduce(x)(s)(j)]]\!]^g : g \text{ assignment}\}$

The comparison class within which the contrast is being drawn satisfies the requirement in the FIP: it is a subset of the focus semantic value, given in (24), of the relevant clause, it contains the ordinary semantic value of that clause, and it contains at least one other proposition. This yields the correct prediction that in the context given in (8), the focal structure of example (18) is felicitous.

We see then that the choice of focus in (18) need not always be licensed by the selection of the domain of quantification for *only*. Instead, it can be licensed by some other semantic/pragmatic phenomenon, such as the explicit binary contrast present in (8).

Finally, note that in the association with focus cases too, the set $\Gamma$ which serves to satisfy the FIP (i.e. the domain of quantification C for *only*) can be regarded as a comparison class. After all, members of the domain of quantification C are being compared and contrasted with each other: one member of the domain (i.e. the ordinary semantic value of the argument of *only*) is presupposed to be true, while all the other members are claimed to be false.

**Discussion**   Let me now state in more general terms some of the things that were already illustrated by examples (17) and (18), and add some further points of discussion concerning the nature and role of the FIP.

The FIP is a constraint on the use of focus. Technically, it determines that a choice of focus is felicitous only if the following holds.

(25)   The focus is contained in a clause S s.t.
$[\![S]\!]^o$ and at least one other proposition are both members in some salient set $\Gamma$ which is a subset of $[\![S]\!]^f$.

To put the matter in diagrammatic form, the FIP requires the following (where S is a clause containing the focus).

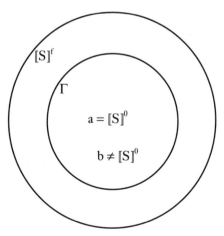

Intuitively, the FIP may be said to determine that $[\![S]\!]^\circ$ must be compared/contrasted with at least one other proposition, within a comparison class $\Gamma$ which is a subset of $[\![S]\!]^f$.

Of course, it is no coincidence that Rooth 1992 prefers not to make any reference to the notion "contrast" in his FIP. How to define a "comparison" or a "contrast" is not a simple matter. I would not want to commit myself to the view that "comparison" or "contrast" can be **defined** in terms of membership of two distinct elements in the same set. Yet I do think it is helpful to intuitively think of the FIP as requiring a comparison or contrast. Or at least as requiring the preconditions for comparison/contrast, i.e. the circumstances in which a comparison/contrast can be drawn. It seems to me that it **is** a **precondition** for felicitously comparing/contrasting two elements x and y with each other that these x and y be distinct elements in the same (salient) set.

It should be clear at this point that it is via the set $\Gamma$ that the FIP succeeds in regulating the interaction between focus semantic values and semantic/pragmatic phenomena. The FIP determines that a choice of focus is felicitous only if some set $\Gamma$ with the properties specified in the FIP is present in the environment. But what that means is that for each given focus there must be, somewhere "around," a semantic or pragmatic construct/phenomenon that makes reference to a set $\Gamma$ that might serve to satisfy the FIP. Moreover, the semantic/pragmatic phenomenon in question will indeed serve to satisfy the FIP only if the value of $\Gamma$ is set to a subset of the focus semantic value of the clause containing the focus – hence the focusing effect.

Here we stumble upon something that may be a little confusing: is it the value of $\Gamma$ that determines the choice of focus, or is it the choice of focus that determines the value of $\Gamma$? The answer is that it works both ways – as is usual whenever implicit parameters interact with other factors.

Take for instance examples (26) and (27), and consider the interaction between the implicit domain of quantification for "every" and the truth value of my utterance. Does the domain of quantification determine the truth value, or vice versa?

(26)  context:   I am in a room with some other people.
      Nirit:     Everybody in this room is taller than me.
(27)  context:   I am obviously feeling very lively and alert.
      Nirit:     Everybody in this room is terribly sleepy.

Well, it works both ways. If a certain domain of quantification is in fact selected, that determines the truth value. For instance, if the domain of quantification is fixed as "everybody in this room," then my utterance is false (since I am not sleepy / taller than myself). On the other hand, the process of domain selection may well be (partly) dependent on the truth value that my utterance is expected to have. An accommodating hearer would pick the domain "everybody in the room except Nirit" in order to make it possible for my utterance to be true.

The same goes for, e.g., domain selection and the choice of focus. As illustrated above, when we fix the domain of quantification for *only*, that determines whether the FIP is satisfied or not. On the other hand, the process of domain selection is (partly) dependent on the expectation that the choice of focus be felicitous. That is why it is fair to say that the choice of focus affects the interpretation of *only*. And more generally, that the choice of focus affects the value of some set $\Gamma$ in its environment.

It is therefore (I think) fair to say that, intuitively, the theory of Rooth 1992 predicts that the choice of focus would typically constrain the comparison class within which some comparison/contrast is being drawn between the ordinary semantic value of the relevant clause and some other proposition. Given the hearer's accommodating wish to render the choice of focus felicitous, the choice of focus constrains the comparison class by forcing it to be a subset of the focus semantic value of the relevant clause.

Pivotal support for Rooth's FIP comes from the optionality of focusing effects, discussed in 17.2 above. It should be clear at this point that the FIP predicts this optionality, and why it does. The FIP does not say anything about the nature of the semantic/pragmatic phenomenon that would give rise to the crucial set $\Gamma$. Nor does it say anything about which clause, out of all the clauses containing the focus, should serve to satisfy the FIP. In the environment of a given focus there may be more than one salient phenomenon that could in principle serve to satisfy the FIP (in combination with a choice of some clause or another). But one phenomenon is enough. Once one particular phenomenon does in fact serve to satisfy the FIP, the other salient phenomena need not interact with the choice of focus at all. This was illustrated by the case of example (18) in context (8). Once the explicit binary contrast is used to satisfy the FIP, the selection of domain of quantification for *only* does not interact with the choice of focus at all.

Regarding the choice of clause containing the focus, it is worth keeping in mind that this choice may be crucial in determining the actual focusing effect. This point was already made in Dretske 1972. In (28), I marked the two clauses found in Dretske's example from 17.2 above. The two possible interpretations that were noted in 17.2 are repeated in (29).

(28)  [S₁ [S₂ Clyde gave [me]_F the tickets] by mistake]
(29)  a.  Clyde's mistake was that Clyde gave the tickets to me rather than to some other person.
          (*by mistake* associated with the focus on *me*. This interpretation is prominent out of the blue.)
      b.  Clyde's mistake was that he handed over the tickets rather than some other object.
          (No association with focus. This interpretation is possible when (28) is contrasted with *Clyde gave George the tickets by mistake*.)

Dretske suggests that in the case of (29a), *me* functions as the focus of the embedded clause, whereas in the explicit binary contrast that allows for (29b), *me* functions as the focus of the entire matrix clause.

In terms of Rooth's theory, we would say that the focus on *me* may satisfy the FIP either via S₂ or via S₁. In the former case, the FIP determines that $[\![S_2]\!]^o$ must be compared/contrasted with a proposition "of the form" "Clyde gave d the tickets"; the only phenomenon "around" which would make such a contrast salient is the distinction between the mistaken action and the correct action, so we must infer that the mistake concerned the identity of the recipient. In the latter case, the FIP determines that $[\![S_1]\!]^o$ must be compared/contrasted with a proposition "of the form" "Clyde gave d the tickets by mistake"; this requirement is immediately satisfied by the contrasting proposition explicitly mentioned in the discourse, regardless of where Clyde's mistake lies.

Rooth 1992 refers to the clause used in satisfying the FIP as "the level at which the focus is interpreted." Nowadays, Rooth calls it "the scope of the focus."

Of course, the FIP is proposed as a general principle, based on a variety of examples that exhibit a variety of focus effects. So we had better go through a couple more examples, and satisfy ourselves that the FIP works for them too.

**Example (II): Question–Answer Congruence**    Consider examples (30) and (31) below. Let us assume Hamblin's theory of questions (where a question denotes the entire set of possible answers to it). Specifically, we may assume that the question *Who smiled?* denotes the set in (32).

(30)   A:   Who smiled?        (31)   A:   Who smiled?
       B:   [Bill]$_F$ smiled.              B:   Bill [smiled]$_F$.
(32)   ⟦who smiled?⟧$^o$ = {⟦person(x) $\wedge$ smiled(x)⟧$^g$ : g assignment}

The focusing in (30B) is felicitous because it satisfies the FIP as follows. The denotation of the preceding question is salient, and serves as the crucial set $\Gamma$. The question-denotation is a subset of ⟦[Bill]$_F$ smiled⟧$^f$, given in (33).

(33)   ⟦[Bill]$_F$ smiled⟧$^f$ = {⟦smiled(x)⟧$^g$ : g assignment}

Further, the question-denotation obviously contains ⟦[Bill]$_F$ smiled⟧$^o$ as a member. Finally, if it makes any sense to ask the question in the first place, then its denotation must contain at least one other possible answer, i.e. at least one proposition distinct from ⟦[Bill]$_F$ smiled⟧$^o$. (Intuitively, the answer offered by B is compared/contrasted with alternative answers, within the comparison class consisting of all possible answers, which is in turn a subset of the focus semantic value of B's utterance.)

The focusing in (31B) is infelicitous, because it does not satisfy the FIP. The focus semantic value of (31B) is as in (34).

(34)   ⟦Bill [smiled]$_F$⟧$^f$ = {⟦X(b)⟧$^g$ : g assignment}

But there isn't any salient set in the environment which could serve as the necessary comparison class $\Gamma$. The only salient set around is the denotation in (32), which is **not** a subset of the focus semantic value in (34).

**Example (III): scalar implicatures**    As noted in 13.2.9 above, (12) tends to have the scalar implicature in (14), whereas (13) tends to have the scalar implicature in (15); at the same time, both examples can have both implicatures.

(12)   [Most]$_F$ conductors are competent pianists.
(13)   Most conductors are [competent]$_F$ pianists.
(14)   Not all conductors are competent pianists.
(15)   It is not the case that most conductors are excellent pianists.

A scalar implicature involves a salient scale of propositions – the implicature is that all the propositions on the scale that are stronger than the proposition being explicitly asserted are false. I assume that completely independently of focusing, scales corresponding to various items in the sentence may become salient, provided that they are of some interest in the context (cf. Hirschberg 1985). Thus, both (12) and (13) may well make salient both of the following scales.

(35)   'all conductors are competent pianists,'
       'almost all conductors are competent pianists,'
       'most conductors are competent pianists,'
       'half of the conductors are competent pianists,'
       'a few conductors are competent pianists'
(36)   'most conductors are pianists of wonderful outstanding genius,'
       'most conductors are excellent pianists,'
       'most conductors are competent pianists,'
       'most conductors are more or less adequate pianists'

Consider (12). Suppose that scale (35) is indeed salient. The set of propositions on this scale can serve as the comparison class $\Gamma$ needed to satisfy the FIP: it's a subset of the focus semantic value of (12), it contains the ordinary semantic value of (12) as a member, and it contains other, distinct propositions as members. (Intuitively, there is a contrast here between the asserted proposition, which is claimed to be true, and at least one other, stronger proposition, which is implicated to be false.)

When (12) is presented out of the blue, a hearer must search for a set that would satisfy the FIP. This makes (35) salient (forcing the accommodating hearer to assume that (35) is in fact of some interest), and gives rise to implicature (14). That is why the focal structure creates a bias towards implicature (14).

Certainly, (12) can be felicitous even if it does not implicate (14), and even if scale (35) is not salient, provided that something else will serve to satisfy the FIP. For instance, the explicit binary contrast in (37) is sufficient to make it felicitous. Bias towards (14) is found when there is no "something else" around that will satisfy the FIP.

(37)   I am not claiming that [all]$_F$ conductors are competent pianists. I don't have ade-
       quate information to support that (even though I actually think it may be true).
       What I am saying is that [most]$_F$ conductors are competent pianists.

The reasoning regarding (13) and its prominent implicature (15), based on scale (36), is analogous.

**Example (IV): binary contrast and bare remnant ellipsis**   Consider examples (38) and (39).

(38)   Sue likes Lee, but it's not the case that Sue likes Kim.
(39)   Sue likes Lee, but it's not the case that Kim likes Lee.

In each example, the two propositions expressed by the two affirmative clauses are obvi-
ously being contrasted with one another (one is claimed to be true, the other claimed to be false). This immediately makes salient a comparison class within which the con-
trast is being drawn. It is possible that no other comparison class will come to mind except simply the set containing just these two propositions. (For (38), the set in (40); for (39), the set in (41).) It is also possible that a larger comparison class will come to

mind. For instance, the set relevant to (38) might be as in (42). (Assuming, of course, that Lee and Kim are among the neighbor's kids.)

(40)   {'Sue likes Lee,' 'Sue likes Kim'}
(41)   {'Sue likes Lee,' 'Kim likes Lee'}
(42)   {the proposition that Sue likes d : d is one of the neighbor's kids}

Now consider possible focal structures for (38) and (39). The focal structures in (43) seem much more likely than the focal structures in (44).

(43)   a.   Sue likes [Lee]$_F$, but it's not the case that Sue likes [Kim]$_F$.
       b.   [Sue]$_F$ likes Lee, but it's not the case that [Kim]$_F$ likes Lee.
(44)   a.   [Sue]$_F$ likes Lee, but it's not the case that Sue likes [Kim]$_F$.
       b.   Sue likes [Lee]$_F$, but it's not the case that [Kim]$_F$ likes Lee.

Why is that? The explanation is not hard to find: the focal structures in (43) are fully licensed by the contrast which is being drawn between the two affirmative clauses, whereas the focal structures in (44) are not.

Let me illustrate this with example (38). (I omit the explanation for (39), which is precisely analogous.) A plausible comparison class for the contrast being drawn in (38) is something like (40) or (42) above. If the focal structure is as in (43a), such a set would simultaneously serve to satisfy the FIP for both affirmative clauses. The two affirmative clauses in (43a) have the same focus semantic value – the one in (45).

(45)   {$[\![like(s,x)]\!]^g$ : g assignment function}

For each clause, our comparison class is a subset of its focus semantic value, it contains its ordinary semantic value as a member, and it contains at least one other proposition as a member. So the FIP is satisfied. If the focal structure is as in (44a), on the other hand, our plausible comparison class can only serve to license the focus of the second clause. The comparison class fails to license the focus of the first clause, because it is not a subset of its focus semantic value, given in (46).

(46)   {$[\![like(x,l)]\!]^g$ : g assignment function}

In the absence of any other salient set in the environment that might serve to satisfy the FIP here, the focus of the first clause would be rendered infelicitous, ruling out (44a) as a whole. That is why, out of the blue, (44a) seems infelicitous.

Vice versa (recall that these things work both ways): the focal structure in (43a) assists the hearer in finding a relevant comparison class, whereas the focal structure in (44a) does not. (43a) presents the two clauses as being of the same type, since the shared focus semantic value highlights the fact that they are both of the form "Sue likes x." In other words, the focusing in (43a) immediately suggests what sort of comparison class we are dealing with here. (44a), on the other hand, presents the two clauses as being of two different types, since the choice of foci highlights the fact that the first clause is of the form "x likes Lee" and the second clause is of the form "Sue likes x." So (44a) does not assist (and probably hinders) the hearer in her quest for a relevant comparison class.

Next, consider (47)–(49) below. The sentence in (47) is ambiguous. But the examples in (48) and (49) are not ambiguous: (48) means the same as (38), and (49) means the same as (39). Why is that?

(47)  Sue likes Lee, but not Kim.
(48)  Sue likes [Lee]$_F$, but not [Kim]$_F$.  ('Sue doesn't like Kim')
(49)  [Sue]$_F$ likes Lee, but not [Kim]$_F$.  ('Kim doesn't like Lee')

Obviously, *but not Kim* in (47) is perfectly capable of getting interpreted as either "but Sue doesn't like Kim" or "but Kim doesn't like Lee." The focal structure directs the hearer to one rather than the other of the two potential interpretations. Given the discussion above, it is not hard to see why. The hearer of (48) must find a comparison class within which the contrast is being drawn. The focus semantic value of the first clause – the set in (45) above – is an obvious candidate. But this construal of the contrast is compatible only with the first of the two potential interpretations. Similarly, the choice of focus in the first clause of (49) suggests that the relevant comparison class is the set in (46), and that is compatible only with the second interpretation.

## 17.4  Some Related Issues

### 17.4.1  The FIP and the Focal ps

What is the status of the constraint on focusing imposed by the FIP? Should this constraint be regarded as a ps?

I have already had occasion to note, in 1.6 above, that I don't have a very clear intuition regarding the presuppositional status of the need to fix the value of implicit semantic parameters. For example, take the need to fix the domain of quantification of *only*. Does example (18) **presuppose** that the domain of quantification for *only* has been fixed?

(18)  John only introduced [Bill]$_F$ to Sue.

I am not sure. In a sense it is being taken for granted here that there is some specific domain of quantification that is supposed to be used. On the other hand, it is not intuitively clear that that is a precondition that must be satisfied "in advance" by the context in which (18) is uttered.

In a way, things are even less clear with the requirement imposed by the FIP. After all, it is not immediately clear, intuitively, that this precise requirement even exists. Rooth had to survey a variety of examples and look at them carefully in order to even come up with this particular requirement. Now suppose it **is** the correct requirement: suppose that indeed, a focus must always have a matching comparison class – it must always indicate (via the focus semantic value) a superset of some comparison class within which the ordinary semantic value is compared/contrasted with some other proposition(s). Intuitively, are you able to tell whether the existence of a matching comparison class is "taken for granted" in the sense that it is as a precondition imposed on the context of utterance? I personally don't have a clear intuition about that.

Rooth 1992 decides to "temporarily identify the constraints introduced by focus interpretation as presuppositions." (p. 91) This means that Rooth's FIP can be regarded as providing a definition of the old notion of "focal ps." Instead of just saying that focusing presupposes that the focus-induced interpretation is "under discussion" or "amenable to discussion," along the lines of Jackendoff 1972, we would now be saying that focusing presupposes that the focus-induced interpretation delimits a comparison class within which the ordinary semantic interpretation is being compared/contrasted with some other proposition(s).

Rooth 1992 takes a step towards formulating the FIP as imposing a ps, by introducing a "focusing operator," marked ~, which is stipulated to be ps-inducing. I am not going to use this operator, but since it occurs regularly in Rooth's current writings, let me just introduce it briefly.

Wherever there is a focus, Rooth adds a corresponding "focusing operator," marked ~, which comes with a variable-argument, marked $\Gamma_n$ (where n is a natural number). The ~ operator takes scope over some clause or another.[3] For instance, we can think of example (28) as having the two possible LFs indicated in (50) and (51).

(28)   $[_{S_1} [_{S_2}$ Clyde gave $[me]_F$ the tickets] by mistake]
(50)   $[_{S_1} [_{S_2}$ Clyde gave $[me]_F$ the tickets] by mistake] ~ $\Gamma_1$
(51)   $[_{S_1} [_{S_2}$ Clyde gave $[me]_F$ the tickets] ~ $\Gamma_8$ by mistake]

The choice of "the level at which the focus is interpreted" (= the "scope" of the focus), which was left open by the formulation of the FIP above, is now marked by the position of the ~ operator: In (50) the focus gets interpreted at the level of $S_1$, and in (51) the focus gets interpreted at the level of $S_2$. (Of course that does not alter the fact that the choice of "scope" is free, since we do freely choose which focus-containing clause to adjoin the ~ to at LF.) The variable-argument attached to ~ stands for a set of propositions. The ~ operator has two arguments then: a clause and a variable standing for a set of propositions.

Rooth states the semantics of ~ more or less as in (52). S stands for a clause/formula and $\Gamma_n$ (n natural number) stands for a variable ranging over sets of propositions.

(52)   S ~ $\Gamma_n$   presupposes that the value of $\Gamma_n$ is a subset of $[\![S]\!]^f$ which contains as members $[\![S]\!]^o$ and at least one other proposition.

The addition of ~ $\Gamma_n$ to a clause S contributes nothing at all to the proposition asserted by S (i.e. to $[\![S]\!]^o$). Its only contribution is to determine that clause S presupposes precisely that which is required by the FIP. And what does it mean that S ~ $\Gamma_n$ presupposes something about the value of $\Gamma_n$? Well, the idea is that the $\Gamma_n$ is required to be **anaphoric**, i.e. that it must have an **antecedent**, which is present elsewhere in the representation of the sentence or discourse. It is the antecedent which would have to play the role of the comparison class $\Gamma$ and satisfy the familiar conditions imposed by the FIP.

---

[3]   The ~ operator could be introduced either at LF or in the logic. Rooth usually uses a ~ operator which adjoins to some clause at LF. (Actually, Rooth allows the ~ operator to adjoin to a constituent of any kind, but I will continue to talk about full clauses only, as I have been doing so far.)

A simple example is that of the question–answer paradigm. Suppose that example (30) above is represented at LF as something like (53).

(53) [$_{\text{Discourse}}$ [$_{S_i}$ Who smiled?] [$_{S_j}$ [Bill]$_F$ smiled]~ $\Gamma_k$]

What the clause in (52) is taken to say is that for $S_j \sim \Gamma_k$ to be felicitous, there must be in the discourse an appropriate antecedent for $\Gamma_k$ which satisfies the familiar FIP conditions. Assuming that anaphora is represented at LF by coindexing, it is easy to see that if $k = i$, this requirement is satisfied. $S_i$ is the antecedent of $\Gamma_k$, so the value of $\Gamma_k$ is $[\![S_i]\!]^o$. Now are the FIP conditions satisfied? Yes, they are: as already discussed in 17.3 above, $[\![S_i]\!]^o$ is indeed a subset of $[\![S_j]\!]^f$ which contains as members $[\![S_j]\!]^o$ plus at least one other proposition.

## 17.4.2 The "Strong Hypothesis" Regarding Focus Effects

It has been noted above that the FIP is supported by the optionality of focus effects. That's because the FIP does not force any specific phenomenon to interact with the focus. At the same time, the FIP is perfectly compatible with there being some other rules of the grammar, in various domains, that do force certain phenomena to interact with focus in specific ways. Such rules could yield **some** focus effects that are **obligatory**.

Rooth 1992 suggests that it would be nicely restrictive if we could maintain that there are **no** rules of the sort just mentioned, and **no** obligatory focus effects. The idea is that there wouldn't be any morpheme- or construction-specific rules (e.g. rules for the lexical semantics of *only*, the organization of questions and answers in discourse, the computation of certain scalar implicatures, the interpretation of bare remnant ellipsis, etc.) which directly refer to the notion of focus. For instance, the semantic rule in (54) would be ruled out, and nothing in the grammar would be able to **force** *only* to associate with the focus.

(54) If only[$\phi$] is of type t, then for all $w \in W$,
$w \in [\![\text{only}[\phi]]\!]^{M,g}$     iff     for all $p \in [\![\phi]\!]^{f-M,g}$, if $w \in p$ then $p = [\![\phi]\!]^{M,g}$.

This position can be referred to as the "strong hypothesis" regarding focus effects.

Rooth 1992 also adds that if one so desired, one could introduce some obligatory focus effects, causing only partial weakening of the "strong hypothesis". This could be achieved by allowing the ~ operator to be introduced at LF not only by free adjunction, but also by morpheme- or construction-specific rules. For example, if obligatory association of *only* with focus were desired after all, it could be forced as follows. Suppose that the domain of quantification of *only* is explicitly marked at LF as a free variable $C_n$. Then there could be a rule which requires a coindexed $\sim\Gamma_n$ to be adjoined to the argument of *only*. For instance, example (18) would obligatorily receive a representation along the lines of (55), in which there is a $\sim\Gamma$ adjoined to $S_2$, such that $\Gamma$ and $C$ are coindexed.

(18) John only introduced [Bill]$_F$ to Sue.
(55) [$_{S_1}$ only($C_i$) [$_{S_2}$ John introduced [Bill]$_F$ to Sue] ~ $\Gamma_i$]

Such a move would weaken the overall theory somewhat, but it would still allow us to maintain that there are no **semantic or pragmatic** morpheme- or construction-specific rules which make direct reference to focus.

## 17.5  Minimize Focused Material

We saw that the FIP requires foci to be contained in a clause S whose ordinary semantic value $[\![S]\!]^\circ$ is contrasted/compared with some distinct member(s) of $[\![S]\!]^f$. This successfully predicts, for instance, that (56b) can be licensed by explicit binary contrast with (56a) (as illustrated by the felicity of utterances like (57)). That's because $[\![(56a)]\!]^\circ$ is both distinct from $[\![(56b)]\!]^\circ$ and a member of $[\![(56b)]\!]^f$.

(56)  a.  Steve kissed Sue
      b.  [John]$_F$ kissed Sue.          GOOD + PREDICTED
(57)  Steve kissed Sue, but it is not the case that [John]$_F$ kissed Sue.

Similarly, it is successfully predicted that (58b) can felicitously be contrasted with (58a) (note the felicity of (59)).

(58)  a.  Steve kissed Sue
      b.  [John]$_F$ kissed [Mary]$_F$.     GOOD + PREDICTED
(59)  Steve kissed Sue, but it is not the case that [John]$_F$ kissed [Mary]$_F$.

It is also successfully predicted that (60b) **cannot** be licensed by explicit binary contrast with (60a) (note the infelicity of (61)). That's because $[\![(60a)]\!]^\circ$ is not a member of $[\![(60b)]\!]^f$.

(60)  a.  Steve kissed Sue.
      b.  John kissed [Sue]$_F$.          BAD + PREDICTED
(61)  #Steve kissed Sue, but it is not the case that John kissed [Sue]$_F$.

And yet, it seems that the FIP is not good enough: Schwarzschild 1994 points out that there are certain infelicitous contrasts that it fails to rule out. For example, the FIP fails to predict the fact that (62b) **cannot** felicitously be contrasted with (62a) (note the infelicity of (63)). That's because $[\![(62a)]\!]^\circ$ is both distinct from $[\![(62b)]\!]^\circ$ and a member of $[\![(62b)]\!]^f$.

(62)  a.  Steve kissed Sue.
      b.  [John]$_F$ kissed [Sue]$_F$.       BAD + PREDICTION FAILURE
(63)  #Steve kissed Sue, but it is not the case that [John]$_F$ kissed [Sue]$_F$.

In an analogous manner, the FIP fails to predict that (64b) **cannot** (directly) answer (64a).

(64)  a.  Who kissed Sue?
      b.  [John]$_F$ kissed [Sue]$_F$.       BAD + PREDICTION FAILURE

Another problematic example which Schwarzschild brings up in this connection is (65).

(65)  Whaddya mean [Mary]<sub>F</sub> appointed John?
    a.  [John]$_F$ appointed John.
    b.  John [appointed John]$_F$.

The fact is that while (65a) can felicitously be contrasted with the underlined clause, (65b) cannot be so contrasted. However, the FIP fails to predict that. That's because the proposition expressed by the underlined clause is both distinct from $[\![(65b)]\!]^o$ and a member of $[\![(65b)]\!]^f$ (since the VP meaning can be replaced by $[\![$was appointed by Mary$]\!]^o$).

Schwarzschild 1994 suggests that an additional constraint is necessary – roughly, the constraint in (66).[4]

(66)  **Minimize Focused Material**
    If you wish to contrast (the proposition expressed by) a clause S with some proposition p, then out of all the possible focal structures for S which allow this contrast (under the FIP), you must choose a focal structure where as little material as possible falls within the focused constituent(s).

It has been pointed out to me by Ziva Wijler (p.c.) that given the ideas discussed in chapter 13 above (in particular, in 13.4.3 and 13.4.5), it seems that it should be possible to dispense with the "Minimize Focused Material" principle, without losing empirical coverage. As discussed in chapter 13, I believe that we should do well to assume that pitch accents are assigned to words (or other small items) and are generally interpreted as "highlighting" the word (or item) in question – all that, independently of the phenomenon of "focus," in the sense of this book. But it seems that this assumption in itself already accounts for the infelicitous contrasts above, independently of the theory of focus: (62b) cannot be felicitously contrasted with (62a), because in the context of (62a), "highlighting" *Sue* is uncalled for; the same explanation applies to (64); (65b) cannot be felicitously contrasted with the underlined clause, because in the context of that clause, "highlighting" *John* in his role as appointee is uncalled for, whereas "highlighting" *John* in his role as the appointing agent is called for and missing.

At any rate, in what follows, I will leave the idea that focused material should be minimized aside.

## 17.6  Focus as a Discourse-Regulating Device: Introduction

It is an old and widely held view of focus that sees focus as a device whose essential role is to help regulate the flow of information in discourse. Surprisingly, perhaps, most model-theoretic work on focus does **not** attempt a formal representation of such a view. More than that: the FIP of Rooth 1992 – the first attempt to provide a model-theoretic characterization of the use of focus – may be said, in fact, to express an **opposing** view.

---

[4]   In Schwarzschild 1999, a similar constraint plays an important role in the proposed theory of pitch accent placement and interpretation.

We saw that Rooth's FIP requires foci to be involved in some contrast or comparison. However, the FIP says nothing at all about what kind of contrast/comparison that should be. Therefore, all sorts of semantic and pragmatic phenomena involving contrast/comparison can serve to satisfy the FIP. The result is that focus may, but need not, play an essentially discourse-regulating role. If the phenomenon satisfying the FIP happens to be an explicit binary contrast with a preceding utterance, or question-answering, then the raison d'être of that focus is (obviously) its involvement in discourse congruence. A focus licensed by "association with focus," on the other hand, has little to do with discourse congruence; the essential function of a focus licensed by *only* is to help fix the domain of quantification of *only*, which is not a function specifically geared to regulating the flow of discourse.

I will now turn to recent work by Roger Schwarzschild and Craige Roberts, which insists, more in line with the traditional view, that focus invariably plays an essentially discourse-regulating role. Schwarzschild 1994, 1997 and Roberts 1996b independently develop theories where Rooth's FIP is replaced with an alternative constraint on the use of focus, which is explicitly formulated in terms of the relationship to preceding utterances or "moves" in the same discourse. Thus, the role of focus is uniformly and invariably tied to discourse congruence.

How, under such a view, might the large variety of focus effects – and in particular the semantic ones – be accounted for? It has been proposed in Taglicht 1984 and in Vallduví 1990 that semantic effects of focusing may be derived as indirect consequences of the essentially discourse-regulating function of focus. That is also the position adopted by Schwarzschild and Roberts. Schwarzschild and Roberts concentrate on the association of *only* with focus. They both claim that foci which are associated with *only* affect discourse congruence in the usual manner, just like any other foci. They each develop their own detailed theory of how the association of these foci with *only* might be derived from their involvement in discourse congruence.

I end this section with a note: In their accounts of the association of *only* with focus, both Schwarzschild and Roberts make use of both parts of the content of *onlyS*: the "asserted part," viz. "of the domain of quantification for *only*, no proposition other than $[\![S]\!]^0$ is true," and the "presupposed part," viz. "$[\![S]\!]^0$ is true." In the remainder of this chapter, I will therefore assume, for convenience, that both of these parts are included in the truth conditional content of *onlyS*. In the informal descriptions of propositions below, I will use the locution "only $\alpha$ has this property," intending it to mean the following: "$\alpha$ has this property **and** none other than $\alpha$ has this property."

## 17.7   The Obligatoriness of Focus Effects

In this section, further empirical observations will be presented, which constitute a problem for Rooth 1992's theory of focus, and motivate a treatment of focus as a discourse-regulating device. Schwarzschild's and Roberts' theories of focus will be presented in 17.8 and 17.10.

We saw in 17.2 above that various effects of focusing are optional. For instance, the association of *only* with focus in (18) below is optional. We saw that in the right context, the focus may serve some other role, and not affect the domain of quantification for *only* at all.

(18)   John only introduced [Bill]$_F$ to Sue.

It is now time to note that at the same time, there are obligatory effects of focusing as well.

First of all, the familiar effects which focusing has on discourse congruence are, quite generally, entirely obligatory. For instance, the focusing indicated in (67) renders (67) felicitous, and the focusing indicated in (68) renders (68) infelicitous – there are no two ways about that.

(67)   A:   John introduced Steve to Sue.
     B:   Oh no, John introduced [Bill]$_F$ to Sue.    FELICITOUS
(68)   A:   John introduced Steve to Sue.
     B:   Oh no, John introduced Bill to [Sue]$_F$.    INFELICITOUS

Secondly, there seems to be good reason to believe that **every** focus affects the congruence of discourse in the familiar way – in other words, that focus, any focus, obligatorily plays a discourse-regulating function. Let me elaborate on this point a bit.

It is often assumed in the literature that a focus which is associated with a focusing adverb, i.e. determines the domain of quantification for it, does not play any other role besides that. That must be the reason, for instance, that Rooth 1992 holds that the effect of associated foci on the focus semantic value of the sentence containing the adverb should be "neutralized" (cf. Rooth 1992, pp. 94–5) – according to Rooth, if *only* in (18) above associates with the focus, then that focus does not affect $[\![(18)]\!]^f$ at all: $[\![(18)]\!]^f = \{[\![(18)]\!]^o\}$. This means that the focus of (18) will not be able to play a role, for instance, in explicit binary contrast between (18) and some other sentence. Roberts and Schwarz-schild both reject this approach, and hold instead that associated foci affect discourse congruence in the usual manner, like any other foci. Here is some motivation for their view.

Consider first the following examples, which are merely illustrations of the familiar discourse-regulating role of focus: (70a) can be felicitously contrasted with (69a) (note the congruence of dialog (67) above), whereas (70b) and (70c) cannot (see (68) above). Similarly, (70a) can (directly) answer (69b), while (70b) and (70c) cannot.

(69)   a.   John introduced Steve to Sue.
     b.   Who did John introduce to Sue?
(70)   a.   John introduced [Bill]$_F$ to Sue.
     b.   John introduced Bill to [Sue]$_F$.
     c.   John introduced [Bill]$_F$ to [Sue]$_F$.

Now Schwarzschild 1994, 1997 argues that the examples in (71) below simultane-ously exhibit very much the same discourse congruence effects as above **as well as** asso-ciation of *only* with focus.

(71)   a.   John only introduced [Bill]$_F$ to Sue.
     b.   John only introduced Bill to [Sue]$_F$.
     c.   John only introduced [Bill]$_F$ to [Sue]$_F$.

The fact is that (71a) can be contrasted with (69a) or (directly) answer (69b), whereas (71b) or (71c) cannot. (Note (72) and (73) below). This, says Schwarzschild, "seems suspiciously like what we saw above [with (70)]".

(72)  A:  Who did John introduce to Sue?
       B:  John only introduced [Bill]$_F$ to Sue.     FELICITOUS
(73)  A:  Who did John introduce to Sue?
       B:  John only introduced Bill to [Sue]$_F$.     INFELICITOUS

At the same time, *only* in the examples in (71) is perfectly capable of associating with the focus. For instance, for (71a), we get the reading "John introduced only Bill to Sue." Data of this sort strongly suggest that associated foci do play a discourse-regulating role at the same time.

This further suggests that foci **invariably** play a discourse-regulating role, whether they are "not associated" or "associated." Indeed, says Schwarzschild (1997, introduction), it would have been surprising if it **weren't** so: that would have meant that language has an elaborate syntactic-phonological system concerned with regulating the flow of discourse which may suddenly shut down when a focus occurs under the scope of a focusing adverb.

Last but not least, here is another form of obligatoriness in focusing effects: **in context**, cases of "association with focus" too seem to become obligatory. As emphasized in Schwarzschild's work, the fact seems to be that in felicitous dialogs like the ones constructed on the basis of (69) + (71), *only* **must** associate with the focus. For instance, in dialog (72) above, (72B) definitely means "John introduced only Bill to Sue"; in the context of (72A), no other reading seems available.

Some might want to explain the seeming obligatory character of such cases of association by appeal to relevance in context, or other "non-grammatical" factors. However, Schwarzschild 1997 brings up examples where such a move would seem particularly difficult. Consider (74)–(75).

(74)    Eva only gave xerox copies to the [graduate students]$_F$.
(75)    a.    No, [Petr]$_F$ only gave xerox copies to the graduate students.

                                                       (Partee 1991)
    b.    No, it was [originals]$_F$ that she only gave to the graduate students.

                                               (Schwarzschild 1997)
    c.    No, she only gave [originals]$_F$ to the graduate students.

                                               (Schwarzschild 1997)

If (74) is followed by (75a), *only* still "associates" (so to speak) with *graduate students*: we get the reading "Petr gave copies only to the graduate students." This shows (among other things) that such a reading is perfectly relevant and plausible in the context of (74). If (74) is followed by (75b), we still get the same sort of reading, i.e. association of *only* with *graduate students*: "she gave originals only to the graduate students." However, if (74) is followed by (75c), this sort of reading is no longer available. Instead, (75c) must be interpreted with *only* associating with the focus: "she gave to the graduate students only originals." (For that reason, (75c) sounds less relevant or cohesive with (74) – "to the point of anomaly," says Schwarzschild – compared with (75a) and (75b).)

We must conclude that in the context of (74), association of *only* with focus in (75c) is obligatory, despite the fact that considerations of relevance as well as discourse congruence seem to favor another reading.

The data reviewed in this section are a problem for the theory of Rooth 1992 (which allows too much optionality), and give rise to the following two questions.

(i)  The first question carries promise: if all foci are uniformly recognized as essentially discourse-regulating devices, might it not be possible to derive "association with focus" as a consequence of this discourse-regulating role? And mightn't the obligatoriness of "association with focus" be explained in this manner?

(ii)  The second question is a problem: supposing that all foci are invariably involved in discourse congruence, how would our theory be able to allow dialogs such as (72), in which an utterance containing *only* follows an utterance that does not contain *only*? We have been assuming that for a given utterance B to be congruent with a preceding utterance A, A must denote a subset or member of the focus semantic value of B; that, however, does not seem to be the case here – how come?

## 17.8  Focus as a Discourse-Regulating Device: The Contrast Constraint (Schwarzschild 1994, 1997)

Schwarzschild 1994 bases his characterization of the function of focus on explicit binary contrast as well as question-answering. Schwarzschild argues that each given utterance is invariably supposed to be **contrasted with a preceding utterance**, be that preceding utterance (or "contrast target") a statement or a question. The position of focus determines whether the intended contrast is felicitous or not.

Schwarzschild 1994 proposes a general constraint on felicitously contrasting a given utterance B with some other utterance ("contrast target") A. Assuming Hamblin's theory of questions (a question denotes the set of possible answers), a version of Schwarzschild's constraint might be stated more or less as follows.[5]

(76)  **Constraint on Contrast in Discourse**
An utterance B is felicitously contrasted with another utterance A
only if
$[\![A]\!]^o \neq [\![B]\!]^o$ and $[\![A]\!]^o$ is a member or subset of $[\![B]\!]^f$.

If we assume that principles of discourse congruence require each given utterance to be contrasted with some other "available" utterance, then a question-answering or

---

[5]  Schwarzschild actually favors a formulation more like the following, where the italicized part is meant to capture the "minimize focused material" constraint discussed in 17.5 above. Schwarzschild leaves out the $[\![A]\!]^o \neq [\![B]\!]^o$ requirement, presumably because it is supposed to follow from the minimality requirement.

(i)  **Constraint on Contrast in Discourse**
An utterance B is felicitously contrasted with another utterance A iff *B is minimally focused such that* $[\![A]\!]^o$ is a member or subset of $[\![B]\!]^f$.

statement-denial dialog should be judged felicitous only if (76) allows the response (ignoring *Oh no*) to contrast with the first utterance. The reader can easily verify that this correctly predicts, for instance, the following data.

(67)  A:  John introduced Steve to Sue.
      B:  Oh no, John introduced [Bill]$_F$ to Sue.    FELICITOUS
(68)  A:  John introduced Steve to Sue.
      B:  Oh no, John introduced Bill to [Sue]$_F$.    INFELICITOUS
(77)  A:  Who did John introduce to Sue?
      B:  John introduced [Bill]$_F$ to Sue.    FELICITOUS
(78)  A:  Who did John introduce to Sue?
      B:  John introduced Bill to [Sue]$_F$.    INFELICITOUS

Under the same assumption, the following constraint on the use of focus follows.

(79)  **Contrast Constraint on Focus**
      A constituent may be focused only if it is contained in an utterance B s.t. there is some utterance A in the discourse s.t.
      $[\![A]\!]^o \neq [\![B]\!]^o$ and $[\![A]\!]^o$ is a member or subset of $[\![B]\!]^f$

Obviously, Schwarzschild draws on Rooth's work; like Rooth 1992, he assumes that the focus in a given clause involves a comparison/contrast between the ordinary semantic value of that clause and at least one distinct proposition which is a member of its focus semantic value.

However, Schwarzschild does not allow the relevant comparison/contrast to be chosen as freely as Rooth 1992 allows it to be. For one thing, according to Schwarzschild, it must be an "utterance" containing the focus that is being contrasted with something. Schwarzschild doesn't specify what exactly is to count as an "utterance." But it is clear from his discussion, as well as crucial for his entire enterprise, that it cannot be just any clause. Another major difference is that for Schwarzschild, the distinct proposition(s) with which the comparison/contrast is being drawn is/are always (the members of) the ordinary semantic value of another utterance in the same discourse. That is why focus is now, invariably, a discourse-regulating device.

Schwarzschild says that "in the simplest cases, a speaker contrasts her utterance with a close, usually preceding utterance" (Schwarzschild 1994, section 2.1). At the same time, he allows the contrast target to be an utterance which is not immediately preceding, as in (80) below (from Schwarzschild 1994, section 1.2).

(80)  A:  (a) John ordered roast beef and (b) Bill ordered pasta.
      B:  Oh, so John is eating meat again.
      A:  Oh no, sorry, (c) [John]$_F$ ordered pasta and (d) [Bill]$_F$ ordered roast beef.

(c) is contrasted with (b) and (d) with (a), even though (b) and (a) are not in the immediately preceding (i.e. B's) utterance.

Further, Schwarzschild allows for the possibility that in some cases the contrast target is not an actual utterance at all, but is rather "understood" – something like an "implicit utterance" in the same discourse.

Note that Schwarzschild's contrast constraint does not force an utterance to necessarily contrast with the question that it answers. Schwarzschild argues that that is as it
should be, based on examples such as the following (Schwarzschild 1994, section 2.1).

(81)   A:   <u>Mary visited France</u> and Bill visited Belgium.
       B:   Oh, really, where did John go?
       A:   Oh, sorry, [John]$_F$ <u>visited France</u>, Mary visited Germany.

The underlined portion of the last utterance, says Schwarzschild, while it answers B's
question, does not contrast with it – it rather contrasts with the underlined portion of
the first utterance.

Having presented the contrast constraint, Schwarzschild 1994, 1997 argues that
based on such a constraint plus some plausible further assumptions, it is possible to
answer both questions presented at the end of the last section.

Consider example (82). We assume that the denotation of (82A) is as in (83) (à la
Hamblin), and that the focus semantic value of (82B) is as in (84).[6]

(82)   A:   Who did John invite for dinner?
       B:   John only invited [Bill]$_F$ for dinner.      FELICITOUS
(83)   $[\![(82A)]\!]^o$ = the set of propositions of the 'form'
                'John invited d for dinner,' for some individual d $\in$ D
(84)   $[\![(82B)]\!]^f$ =
       the set of propositions of the 'form'
       'Out of the set C of relevant propositions, only the proposition that John invited
       d for dinner is true,' for some individual d $\in$ D.

Starting with the second of our two questions, why can the utterance containing *only*
felicitously follow the *only*-less question? Schwarzschild 1994, 1997 argues that given
that *only* in (82B) associates with the focus (although we haven't seen yet why it does
or why that is obligatory), this can be explained.

It is important to note here that Schwarzschild's position is that the entire answer,
including *only*, is what has to be contrasted with the question. An alternative that
quickly comes to mind is that *only* is not involved in the contrast at all, and it is its argument clause that gets contrasted with the question. Then the felicity of (82) would be
immediately explained. However, Schwarzschild takes the contrast constraint to apply
to an "utterance," and the argument clause is clearly not intended to count as one. The
assumption that it is the whole of (82B) that has to be involved in the contrast is crucial
for Schwarzschild's account of the obligatory association with focus in (82), as will
become evident below.

Consider, then, the interpretation of (82B) where *only* is associated with the focus
(= where the domain of quantification C for *only* is a subset of the set given in (85)).
On that interpretation, the focus semantic value of (82B) boils down to the set given in
(86).

---

[6]   By the locution "only $\alpha$ has this property" I mean "$\alpha$ has this property **and** none other than $\alpha$
has this property." See the note ending section 17.6.

(85)  '*only* is associated with the focus' means that C is a subset of this set:
      [[John invited [Bill]$_F$ for dinner]]$^f$=
      the set of propositions of the 'form'
      'John invited d for dinner,' for some individual d ∈ D
(86)  [[(82B)]]$^f$ when *only* is associated with the focus:
      the set of propositions of the 'form'
      'John invited for dinner only d,' for some d ∈ A ⊆ D
          where A is the set of relevant potential invitees – i.e., roughly, those individ-
          uals that serve as the 'd's involved in the contextually given set C.

Our problem is as follows. The contrast constraint is taken to require [[(82A)]]$^o$ to be a subset of [[(82B)]]$^f$. But in fact, [[(82A)]]$^o$ is not a subset of [[(82B)]]$^f$.[7] (Not even if we decide to add the reasonable assumption that [[(82A)]]$^o$, just like [[(82B)]]$^f$, concerns only the restricted set A of potential invitees.) To see this, suppose that the relevant potential invitees are Bill and Sue, and consider (87) below. The proposition in (87) is a member of [[(82A)]]$^o$, but not a member of [[(82B)]]$^f$.

(87)  'John invited Bill for dinner'

Schwarzschild 1994, 1997 suggests that to resolve this problem, what we need to do is (i) to assume that the domain of individuals D contains not just the atomic individuals but also all the corresponding sums of individuals (i.e., roughly, "to let D be closed under conjunction"); and (ii) to make sure that focus semantic values are defined in such a way that they are closed under disjunction.
    To take a concrete example, suppose that there are exactly two relevant potential invitees: Bill and Sue. If D contained only atoms, then [[(82B)]]$^f$ would contain the propositions in (88), but nothing like (87).

(88)  'John invited for dinner only Bill,'
      'John invited for dinner only Sue'

However, let us see what happens if we adopt (i) and (ii) above. If D contains sums as well, [[(82B)]]$^f$ will contain, besides the propositions in (88), the proposition in (89) as well.

(89)  'John invited for dinner only Bill and Sue'

Further, if focus semantic values are closed under disjunction, [[(82B)]]$^f$ will contain (90), too.

(90)  '[John invited for dinner only Bill] or [John invited for dinner only Bill and Sue]'

But (90) is equivalent to (87) above. Given that the only relevant individuals that could be invited are Bill and Sue, "John invited either Bill and no-one else or else Bill and Sue and no-one else" is equivalent to "John invited Bill" (which doesn't specify whether Sue was invited or not). So (87), a member of [[(82A)]]$^o$, turns out to also be a member of [[(82B)]]$^f$, after all.

---

[7]  At least, not if there is more than one relevant potential invitee.

In a similar manner, all members of $[[(82A)]]^o$ can be shown to also be members of $[[(82B)]]^f$, for any number of relevant potential invitees. So we get the happy result that $[[(82A)]]^o$ is a subset of $[[(82B)]]^f$, hence the contrast constraint is satisfied, hence (82) is correctly predicted to be felicitous.

Let us now move on to deriving association of *only* with focus from the contrast constraint. So far, we saw that **if** *only* in (82) is associated with the focus, then the contrast constraint gets satisfied. But why is it that *only* in (82) associates with the focus in the first place, and why is this association obligatory? Schwarzschild 1994, 1997 argues that the reason is that **only if** *only* in (82) is associated with the focus does the contrast constraint get satisfied.

Let us look at a very concrete and simple example to see what happens when *only* is **not** associated with the focus. Let us suppose that the context independently determines that the only relevant potential invitees for any meal are Bill and Sue. The question-denotation $[[(82A)]]^o$ would contain the propositions in (91).

(91)   $[[(82A)]]^o$ contains:
    'John invited Bill for dinner,'
    'John invited Sue for dinner,'
    'John invited Bill and Sue for dinner'

Now we want to set the domain of quantification C for *only* in (82B) to a set which is **not** a subset of $[[$John invited $[Bill]_F$ for dinner$]]^f$. Let us try to see if C in (82B) could be set to (92).

(92)   {'John invited Bill for breakfast,'
    'John invited Bill for lunch,'
    'John invited Bill for dinner,'
    'John invited Sue for breakfast,'
    'John invited Sue for lunch,'
    'John invited Sue for dinner,'
    'John invited Bill and Sue for breakfast,'
    'John invited Bill and Sue for lunch,'
    'John invited Bill and Sue for dinner'}

Using (92) in our dialog (82), we get that $[[(82B)]]^f$ boils down to (93), which includes the propositions in (94).

(93)   $[[(82B)]]^f$ when C is set to (92):
    the set of propositions of the 'form'
    'Out of all the acts in (92), the only thing John did was invite d for dinner,' for some $d \in D$,
    closed under disjunction

(94)   'Of the acts in (92), the only thing John did was invite Bill for dinner,'
    'Of the acts in (92), the only thing John did was invite Sue for dinner,'
    'Of the acts in (92), the only thing John did was invite Bill and Sue for dinner,'
    'Either [of the acts in (92), the only thing John did was invite Bill for dinner] or else [of the acts in (92), the only thing John did was invite Bill and Sue for dinner]'

But $[\![(82A)]\!]^o$ is not a subset of (93). For instance, (87), repeated below, is a member of $[\![(82A)]\!]^o$ but not a member of (93). Note that the last proposition in (94) is not equivalent to (87): it entails (87), but is not entailed by it.

(87)   'John invited Bill for dinner'

It seems that indeed, when there is no association of *only* with focus, the contrast constraint is violated. (For a more general demonstration of this, I refer the reader to Schwarzschild's papers.) Obviously, this conclusion relies on the assumption, emphasized above, that it is the whole of (82B) – and not the argument of *only* – that must contrast with (82A).

## 17.9   Questions and Information Structure in Discourse (Roberts 1996b)

Roberts 1996b adopts the view, which goes back to Lauri Carlson 1983, that information is organized in the discourse in relation to questions being addressed. Roberts 1996b develops a detailed formal theory of this organization, which (to the best of my knowledge) constitutes the first rigorously formulated model-theoretic theory of how information is structured in discourse. The theory of focus proposed in Roberts 1996b is couched within this new framework, and relies crucially on the notions of **relevance** and the **last question under discussion**, defined therein. In this section, I will outline what I take to be the central features of Roberts' theory of information-structure, without filling in all the formal details. This I think should be sufficient for the purpose of presenting her theory of focus, which I will proceed to do in the following section.

Roberts assumes a version of Hamblin's theory of questions (where a question denotes the set of possible answers to it). For simplicity, let me assume that the logical translation of questions is as illustrated in (95).

(95)   *Who arrived?*   translates as   ?[arrived(who$_1$)]
        *Who invited who*   translates as   ?[invited(who$_1$,who$_2$)]
        *Is Sue pretty*   translates as   ?[Pretty(s)]

Roberts assumes that a question denotes the set of propositions obtained by substitution of all values of the right type for the wh-words in the logical translation. This might be represented by the informal semantic rule in (96).

(96)   Let M,g be an arbitrary model and assignment function, and let $\phi$ be an arbitrary formula.
        $[\![?[\phi]]\!]^{M,g}$ is the set of all ordinary semantic values obtained by replacing the wh-words in $\phi$ with (distinct, new) variables, and then interpreting the result relative to every assignment g′ which is identical to g except perhaps for the values of those variables.

For example, if we assume that *who* is of type e, we get the following denotations. ("Human/animate" content of *who* ignored.)

(97) $[\![$*Who arrived?*$]\!]^\circ = \{[\![arrived(x)]\!]^g : g \text{ assignment}\}$
$[\![$*Who invited who?*$]\!]^\circ = \{[\![invited(x,y)]\!]^g : g \text{ assignment}\}$
$[\![$*Is Sue pretty?*$]\!]^\circ = \{[\![Pretty(s)]\!]\}$

Further, Roberts makes the following assumptions regarding what constitutes an answer to a given question.

(98)   A proposition p is a **partial answer** to a question Q iff
p contextually entails the truth value of at least one element of the denotation of Q.
A proposition p is a **complete answer** to a question Q iff
p contextually entails the truth value of each element of the denotation of Q.

Roberts 1996b expands the model-theoretic representation of the context of utterance to include not just the propositional information assumed so far in the discourse (the "common ground"), but also the collection of those questions that are assumed to be under discussion in the discourse, and have not yet been answered. These questions are called the **questions under discussion** (QUDs, for short). (Both propositions and question-denotations which are contained in the context are called "moves," reminiscent of the view of discourse as a game in which propositions and questions are constantly being offered and responded to.)

Just as we customarily assume that when an assertion is accepted by the interlocutors it gets added to the common ground (à la Stalnaker 1978), we now assume in addition that when a question which has been (explicitly or implicitly) raised is accepted by the interlocutors it gets added to the set of questions under discussion. Once a question has been answered, it is removed from this set (it is no longer under discussion). Roberts adds that a question may also be removed from this set if it is deemed practically unanswerable.

Now it is widely accepted that general principles of cooperation à la Grice regulate the flow of discourse, and direct the interlocutors to make their utterances relevant to preceding discourse. Roberts holds that the basic notion of relevance that operates in discourse can and should be defined in terms of the contribution of each given utterance – or "move" – to the goal of answering the questions under discussion. Therefore, the basic notion of relevance is that of relevance **to a question**.

What does relevance to a question consist of? Well, a move that actually answers the question is certainly relevant to it. For instance, (99B) is relevant to (99A) – it provides (at least) a partial answer. But a question can also be relevant to another question. Consider for instance the piece of discourse in (100). Surely, (100B) is relevant to (100A) and (100C) is relevant to (100B).

(99)   A:   Who arrived?
       B:   Mary arrived.
(100)  A:   Who invited who?
       B:   (Well,) who did Mary invite?
       C:   (Let's see,) did she invite Nathan?

To capture this, Roberts defines the **subquestion** relation in (101) below (see Roberts 1996b, last clause in the definition of information structure).

(101)   A question $Q_2$ is a **subquestion** of a question $Q_1$ iff
        the complete answer to $Q_2$ contextually entails a partial answer to $Q_1$.

This relation is then used to define Roberts' basic notion of relevance. To simplify things a little, I choose to define a notion that I call **direct relevance**, as in (102) below, based on Roberts' definition of "Relevance" and her preceding discussion of strategies of inquiry.

(102)   A move $\alpha$ is **directly relevant** to a question Q iff
        (i)   if $\alpha$ is a proposition, then $\alpha$ is a partial answer to Q;
and     (ii)  if $\alpha$ is a question, then $\alpha$ is a subquestion of Q.

Returning to (99) and (100) above, the reader can easily verify the following. $[\![(99B)]\!]^o$ is directly relevant to $[\![(99A)]\!]^o$, because it constitutes a partial answer to it. $[\![(100B)]\!]^o$ is directly relevant to $[\![(100A)]\!]^o$, because it is a subquestion of it. (If we know the complete list of individuals that Mary invited, then we have the truth value of all those elements of $[\![(100A)]\!]^o$ in which the invitor is Mary.) $[\![(100C)]\!]^o$ is directly relevant to $[\![(100B)]\!]^o$, because it is a subquestion of it. (To supply the truth value of "Mary invited Nathan" is to supply a partial answer to $[\![(100B)]\!]^o$.)

Roberts further proposes that as a general rule, the interlocutors aim to answer the most recently accepted question under discussion first. Thus, Roberts regards the collection of questions under discussion as a "push down" store: the questions get "stacked" one on top of the other, and the top question (the last one to have been accepted) must be the first one to be popped off the stack (i.e. to be answered and therefore removed).

Accordingly, Roberts' context of utterance keeps track of the order in which moves have entered the discourse (the set of questions under discussion is defined as an ordered set). The latest question in the set of questions under discussion is called **the last question under discussion** (or last QUD), and we let the notation *last(QUD($\alpha$))* represent, for any move $\alpha$, the last question under discussion at the time that $\alpha$ is made (i.e. in the context of utterance immediately preceding $\alpha$). Now Roberts can formulate the idea that the last question is to get answered first, by requiring each move in the discourse to be directly relevant **to the last question under discussion**. It is assumed then that as a general rule, the following holds.

(103)   Each move $\alpha$ in the discourse is required to be **directly relevant** to last(QUD($\alpha$)).

For some illustration, consider again discourse (100), repeated below.

(100)   A:   Who invited who?
        B:   (Well,) who did Mary invite?
        C:   (Let's see,) did she invite Nathan?

Suppose first that (100) is continued with the following assertion.

(100D)#1   Kim invited Sue.

Continuation (100D)#1 is intuitively lacking in relevance. That is captured by the fact that the proposition expressed by (100D)#1 is not (by definition) directly relevant to the last QUD, i.e. to the question expressed by (100C): it does not provide an answer to it (not even a partial answer). I don't mean to claim that it would be completely out-rageous for someone to utter (100D)#1; you **could** utter it, of course. But what you would be doing then is ignoring B's and C's utterances, preferring to "attack" A's ques-tion "from a different direction" instead. Which may offend C or B and should be pre-ceded by some pause or exclamation to signal the change in turn of conversation.

A somewhat more cohesive discourse would result if (100) is continued with (100D)#2 instead.

(100D)#2   Mary invited Lyn.

Again, the question expressed by the continuation is (by definition) not directly rele-vant to the last QUD. This captures the intuition that (100D)#2 still fails to be an entirely direct continuation. $[\![(100D)\#2]\!]^\circ$ **is** directly relevant to the immediately pre-ceding question though (to $[\![(100B)]\!]^\circ$), so if you choose to utter (100D)#2, you are ignoring only C's utterance; hence the increased cohesiveness.

Finally, the most direct and natural continuation of (100) would be to provide an answer to $[\![(100C)]\!]^\circ$ – as in (100D)#3, for instance.

(100D)#3   Yes, she did.

In that case the continuation is (by definition) directly relevant to the last QUD, as required by (103) above.

Once $[\![(100C)]\!]^\circ$ is answered (note that any answer to it is a complete one), it is popped off the QUD stack, and the last QUD becomes $[\![(100B)]\!]^\circ$. Therefore, at that point, the most natural continuation should be a move directly relevant to $[\![(100B)]\!]^\circ$. As the reader can verify for herself, this correctly predicts the following: it would be perfectly natural to continue (100) as in (104) or in (105); in contrast, assuming that Mary may have invited more than one individual, it would be less natural to continue (100) as in (106).

(104)   D:   Yes, she did.
           E:   She invited Lyn, as well.
(105)   D:   Yes, she did.
           E:   Did she invite Lyn, too?
(106)   D:   Yes, she did.
           E:   (and) Kim invited Sue.

If it happens to be assumed in the context that Mary cannot have invited more than one person, then (106) becomes a perfectly natural continuation as well. That too is correctly predicted. In that case, the proposition expressed by D's utterance – that Mary invited Nathan – contextually entails a complete answer to $[\![(100B)]\!]^\circ$. But that means that $[\![(100B)]\!]^o$ now gets popped off the QUD stack, leaving $[\![(100A)]\!]^o$ as the last QUD. $[\![(106E)]\!]^o$ gives a partial answer to $[\![(100A)]\!]^o$, so it is directly relevant to the current last QUD.

Note, incidentally, that the following continuation is also very natural. Is this correctly predicted?

(107)   D:  Yes, she did.
        E:  Did she invite anybody else?

Well, formally, $[\![(107E)]\!]^o$ is directly relevant to the last QUD, viz. $[\![(100B)]\!]^o$, only if the answer to it is negative. Only then does the (true) complete answer to $[\![(107E)]\!]^o$ provide a partial answer to $[\![(100B)]\!]^o$ (it contextually entails that all members of $[\![(100B)]\!]^o$ apart from "Mary invited Nathan" are false). In fact, it then contextually entails a complete answer to $[\![(100B)]\!]^o$. If, on the other hand, the answer to $[\![(107E)]\!]^o$ is positive, then it is not directly relevant to $[\![(100B)]\!]^o$, since it doesn't actually determine the truth value of any particular member of $[\![(100B)]\!]^o$. This may suggest that some refinement of (103) may be in order. Alternatively, we can simply say that while (107E) does not satisfy (103), it sounds like a natural continuation because it almost satisfies it. If the answer to $[\![(107E)]\!]^o$ is negative, it would satisfy (103), and moreover save us the trouble of considering further subquestions of $[\![(100B)]\!]^o$. If the answer to $[\![(107E)]\!]^o$ is positive, at least it tells us that we can't get the complete answer to $[\![(100B)]\!]^o$ that easily, and have to go on with its subquestions.

## 17.10   Focus as a Discourse-Regulating Device: The Question-Under-Discussion Constraint (Roberts 1996b)

Roberts 1996b's theory of focus consists of (i) a modification of the definition of focus semantic values to cover foci in questions, and (ii) a new constraint on the use of focus, which is to replace any older constraint.

In chapter 14 (see 14.4 and 14.5.4), I introduced the assumption that focus semantic values are derived, quite simply, by substitution of all values of the right type for the focused subformula(s) in the ordinary logical translation. Both Schwarzschild and Roberts assume this sort of procedure. However, Roberts 1996b proposes a revision, whereby values are substituted not only for foci, but also for wh-words. The revised semantic rule for focus semantic values may be informally stated as in (108) (adapted from the final definition of focus alternative sets in Roberts 1996b).[8]

(108)   $[\![\phi]\!]^{f\text{-}M,g}$, the **focus semantic value** of a formula $\phi$ relative to an arbitrary model M and an arbitrary assignment function g, is the set of all ordinary semantic values obtained by replacing the F-marked subformulas and the wh-words in $\phi$ with (distinct, new) variables, and then interpreting the result relative to every assignment $g'$ which is identical to g except perhaps for the values of those variables.

---

[8]   The formal definition could be along the lines of 14.5.4.

Like Schwarzschild 1994, 1997, Roberts 1996b too proposes a constraint on the use of focus which is formulated in terms of the relationship to some preceding move in the same discourse. However, while Schwarzschild requires each utterance to be appropriately related to some utterance/move or other, Roberts 1996b requires an appropriate relationship to a very specific utterance/move, namely, to the **last question under discussion**.

Roberts' constraint on the use of focus might be stated as follows. (The constraint in (109) is based on Roberts 1996b, section 2.1, definitions of congruence and of the ps of prosodic focus in an utterance.)

(109)   **The Question-Under-Discussion constraint on Focus**
An utterance B whose logical translation is of the form $\beta$ or ?[$\beta$], where $\beta$ is a formula, is felicitous only if $[\![\beta]\!]^f = \mathrm{last}(\mathrm{QUD}[\![B]\!]^o))$.

Roberts explicitly states that this constraint imposes a presupposition. In doing so, Roberts offers her own theory of what the focal presupposition consists of: any utterance B presupposes that the last question under discussion (in the context immediately preceding B) denotes precisely that set of propositions which constitutes the focus semantic value of B.

Let us take some examples. We may assume that in each of the following two-utterance dialogs, the last QUD at the time of B's utterance is the question expressed by A's utterance. (After all, there is no other candidate for this role.) Now let us see if the QUD constraint on focus yields the correct predictions.

(110)   A:   Who did Mary invite?
         B:   Mary invited [Sue]$_F$.                    FELICITOUS
(111)   A:   Who did Mary invite?
         B:   [Mary]$_F$ invited Sue.                    INFELICITOUS
(112)   A:   Who invited who?
         B:   Well, who did [Mary]$_F$ invite?           FELICITOUS
(113)   A:   Who invited who?
         B:   Well, who did Mary [invite]$_F$?           INFELICITOUS

Obviously, we get the right predictions for (110) and (111): $[\![(110A)]\!]^o = [\![(110B)]\!]^f$, but $[\![(111A)]\!]^o \neq [\![(111B)]\!]^f$. The revised definition of focus semantic values, as in (108), allows Roberts to get the correct predictions for (112) and (113) as well. Note that Roberts does not claim that wh-words are foci (cf. Rochemont 1986); at the same time, she does let them play a role in determining the focus semantic value. We get the right predictions for (112) and (113) because the relevant semantic values are as in (114) and (115).

(114)   For (112B), the focus semantic value of the scope of ? is $[\![\mathrm{invited}(m_F, who_1)]\!]^f = \{[\![\mathrm{invited}(x,y)]\!]^g : g$ assignment$\}$, which is identical to $[\![(112A)]\!]^o$, as required.

(115)   For (113B), the focus semantic value of the scope of ? is $[\![\mathrm{invited}_F(m, who_1)]\!]^f = \{[\![v_{1,\langle e,\langle e,t\rangle\rangle}(m,y)]\!]^g : g$ assignment$\}$, which fails to be identical to $[\![(113A)]\!]^o = \{[\![\mathrm{invited}(x,y)]\!]^g : g$ assignment$\}$.

This is a very nice result, since the new theory encompasses the role of focus both in assertions and in questions. As we just saw, this theory is able to yield the desired felicity predictions. Moreover, I think it elegantly captures the most basic intuition about the role of focus.

Looking at the assertions, recall the good old intuition that the focus of a declarative sentence is "the answer to the question being addressed." Indeed, given Roberts' QUD constraint, the focus of a declarative sentence turns out to provide an answer to the question currently addressed in the discourse. The declarative presupposes that the last QUD is identical to its focus semantic value, and the proposition expressed by the declarative necessarily constitutes a (partial or complete) answer to that question, in the sense of definition (98), section 17.9.

As for the focus of a question, it is perhaps harder to pin-point in this case what our basic intuition is. And yet, we certainly do feel that the focus of a question in a way parallels the focus of a declarative. We might say that in (110A) the invitee is missing, and the focus of assertion (110B) fills in the missing invitee. Similarly, the focus of question (112B) too fills in a missing element: in (112A), both the invitor and invitee are missing; in (112B), the focus fills in one of these missing elements, viz. the invitor.

The "filling in of an element" accomplished by the focus of (112B) does not provide an answer to (112A). What it does do, intuitively, is to "narrow down" the quest for information. We might even say that (112B) is, intuitively, a subquestion of (112A). This intuition is nicely captured by Roberts' QUD constraint, because the requirement that the focus semantic value of the scope of ? in (112B) be identical to the denotation of (112A) forces $[\![(112B)]\!]^o$ to constitute a subquestion of $[\![(112A)]\!]^o$, in the sense of definition (101), section 17.9 above. Note, incidentally, that the word *who* in (112B) does not fill in any element, in accordance with its non-focus status on Roberts' theory.

It should be clear at this point that on Roberts' theory, focus invariably plays an essentially discourse-regulating role (as already stressed in 17.6 above). Now recall that, as discussed in 17.9, we assume that discourse is regulated by a requirement of relevance-to-the-last-QUD, quite independently of the phenomenon of focusing. Roberts 1996b (end of section 1.2) notes that what that means is that the discourse-regulating role of focus is at least to some extent redundant. Take dialog (110), for instance. We assume that (110B) is expected to address the question expressed by (110A) anyway (even in a written text that contains no clues to the prosody or focal structure), just because it is expected to be a cooperative (relevant) response. The focal structure of (110B), in imposing the ps that $[\![(110A)]\!]^o$ $(=[\![(110B)]\!]^f)$ is the question being addressed, provides redundant confirmation that such is indeed the case.

However, as Roberts immediately proceeds to explain, the role of focus goes beyond mere confirmation or accentuation of the organization of discourse. The focal ps – like other pss – is often satisfied by accommodation. For instance, upon hearing (111B) (*[Mary]$_F$ invited Sue*) out of context, we readily accommodate the information that the last QUD – the question currently being addressed – is "who invited Sue?" But that means that focusing may play the crucial role of assisting the hearer in figuring out what the last QUD actually is. Indeed, in this manner, focusing often saves us the trouble of expressing questions explicitly.

To illustrate this, I would like to consider the following two exchanges.

(116)  A:  John came to the party.
       B:  [Mary]$_F$ invited him.
(117)  A:  Who invited who?
       B:  (Hmm, let's see . . .) [Mary]$_F$ invited people.

The QUD constraint requires that the QUDs obtaining at the time of B's utterance be as indicated in (118).

(118)  last(QUD($[\![(116B)]\!]^\circ$)) = 'Who invited John?'
       last(QUD($[\![(117B)]\!]^\circ$)) = 'Who invited people?'

I think it is perfectly reasonable to assume that these questions do indeed serve as the QUDs obtaining at the time of B's utterance, even though they are never expressed explicitly. This in turn explains the felicity of B's utterance, which on this assumption satisfies both the QUD constraint and the requirement of direct relevance to its last QUD (given in (103), section 17.9 above). Examples (116) and (117) illustrate the role of focusing in clarifying what the last QUD is, since it is clearly the focal structure of B's utterance that directs the hearer to the hypothesis that the question being addressed is as indicated in (118).

   Of course, it is also crucial for the felicity of (116) or (117) as a whole that the hypothesized implicit question seem cooperative (relevant) in the context of A's utterance. This point is captured by Roberts' theory of information structure via the requirement that the last QUD at the time of B's utterance be directly relevant to **its** last QUD.

   Well, does B's utterance really satisfy this requirement? Take the case of (117) first. What could the last QUD of the hypothesized last(QUD($[\![(117B)]\!]^\circ$)) be? An obvious candidate is the question expressed by A's utterance. And if $[\![(117A)]\!]^\circ$ is indeed the last QUD of the hypothesized last(QUD($[\![(117B)]\!]^\circ$)), then the relevance requirement is satisfied – at least, it is satisfied in any model where some individuals were non-invitors. In any model containing non-invitors, the hypothesized last(QUD($[\![(117B)]\!]^\circ$)) is (by definition) a subquestion of $[\![(117A)]\!]^\circ$.[9] In the case of (116), the last QUD of the hypothesized last(QUD($[\![(116B)]\!]^\circ$)) is not explicitly expressed in the given piece of discourse. But a reasonable candidate would be "what happened regarding the party guests?" or some such question, of which both "Did John come to the party?" (completely answered by (116A)) and our hypothesized "who invited John?" (answered by (116B)) are subquestions.

   Having presented the QUD constraint on focus, Roberts goes on (Roberts 1996b, section 2.2.1) to provide her answers to the two questions presented at the end of section 17.7.

   Consider example (119). We assume that the denotation of (119A) is as in (120). The QUD constraint is to apply to an "utterance," and that is taken to mean that it applies to the whole of (119B), *only* included. So we need to look at the focus semantic value of (119B), which is as in (121).[10]

---

[9]   In a model with non-invitors, a complete answer to "who invited people?" entails a partial answer to "who invited who?" For instance, once we know that "Lee invited people" is false, we also know of all members of $[\![(117A)]\!]^\circ$ where Lee is the invitor that they are false.

[10]   By the locution "only $\alpha$ has this property" I mean "$\alpha$ has this property **and** none other than $\alpha$ has this property." See the note ending section 17.6.

(119)   A:   Who did Mary invite for dinner?
       B:   Mary only invited [Sue]$_F$ for dinner.      FELICITOUS
(120)   $[\![(119A)]\!]^o =$
      the set of propositions of the 'form'
      'Mary invited d for dinner,' for some individual d $\in$ D
(121)   $[\![(119B)]\!]^f =$
      the set of propositions of the 'form'
      'Out of the set C of relevant propositions, only the proposition that Mary
      invited d for dinner is true,' for some individual d $\in$ D.

The structure of Roberts' account is roughly parallel to that of Schwarzschild's. Roberts shows that **if** we assume that *only* in (119B) associates with the focus – as we know it does, empirically – then the constraint on the use of focus together with the general requirement of relevance in discourse are satisfied, and we can explain why the utterance containing *only* can felicitously follow the *only*-less question. She suggests, roughly, that the reason that *only* is forced to associate with the focus is that **only if** *only* in (119) is associated with the focus do the constraint on the use of focus and the general requirement of relevance in discourse get simultaneously satisfied.

Consider the interpretation of (119B) where *only* associates with the focus (= where the domain of quantification C for *only* is a subset of the set given in (122)).[11] On that interpretation, the focus semantic value of (119B) boils down to the set given in (123).

(122)   '*only* is associated with the focus' means that C is a subset of this set:
      $[\![Mary\ invited\ [Sue]_F\ for\ dinner]\!]^f =$
      the set of propositions of the 'form'
      'Mary invited d for dinner,' for some individual d $\in$ D
(123)   $[\![(119B)]\!]^f$ when *only* is associated with the focus:
      the set of propositions of the 'form'
      'Mary invited for dinner only d,' for some d $\in$ A $\subseteq$ D
          where A is the set of relevant potential invitees – i.e., roughly, those indi-
          viduals that serve as the 'd's involved in the contextually given set C.

Faced with (119), we encounter the following problem. The QUD constraint on focus requires the last QUD at the time that (119B) is uttered to be identical to $[\![(119B)]\!]^f$ – that is, it should be the question given in (124).[12]

(124)   'What individual d $\in$ A is s.t. Mary invited for dinner only d?'

But there is no utterance in (119) that expresses this question. The question expressed by (119A) is distinct from it: for instance, (125) below is a member of $[\![(119A)]\!]^o$, but not a member of $[\![(119B)]\!]^f$ (=the question in (124)). (Unless Sue is the one and only relevant potential invitee, I guess.)

---

[11]   Roberts provides the following example where C would clearly be a **proper** subset of the set in (122). Suppose the interlocutors already know that Mary invited a visiting colleague for dinner and wanted to get someone else in her department to accompany them. Then the set C should involve all the other people in her department, including Sue, but not the visitor.
[12]   I take it that given Roberts' theory too we should actually assume that d can be a sum (plural individual).

(125)   'Mary invited Sue for dinner'

How then does (119B) satisfy the QUD constraint?

Having allowed QUDs to be implicit, the solution is clear: the question in (124) is indeed the last QUD obtaining when (119B) is uttered, even though it is never explicitly expressed in the discourse. Of course, this solution can only be maintained if we can assume that (124) is a cooperative (relevant) new QUD in the context of the earlier QUD expressed by (119A); otherwise, we would be unable to explain the felicity of (119) as a whole.

But certainly (124) is relevant in the context of (119A). Roberts notes that while the question expressed by (119A) and question (124) are not identical, they are very similar indeed: in any given model, any complete answer to (124) (= $[\![(119B)]\!]^f)^{13}$ entails a complete answer to $[\![(119A)]\!]^o$, and any complete answer to $[\![(119A)]\!]^o$ entails a complete answer to (124) (=$[\![(119B)]\!]^f$). Needless to say, this relationship makes (124) a subquestion of $[\![(119A)]\!]^o$, satisfying the requirement of direct-relevance-to-the-last-QUD. But more than that, I think that intuitively, (119B) seems like a truly direct answer to (119A).[14] The great similarity between (124) and $[\![(119A)]\!]^o$ could account for that intuition.

Let us now move on to deriving association of *only* with focus. Roberts' proposal is, roughly, that **only if** *only* in (119B) is associated with the focus do the QUD constraint and general requirement of relevance in discourse get simultaneously satisfied. Actually, Roberts is careful to state, more precisely, that while there are other ways of fixing the domain of quantification C that would still satisfy the QUD constraint and relevance requirement, those ways are quite restricted.

Clearly, the precise requirement on the interpretation of (119B) is as follows. For the QUD constraint on focus and the direct-relevance-to-the-last-QUD requirement to both be satisfied, C must be fixed in such a way that (121) above (i.e. $[\![(119B)]\!]^f$) would turn out to constitute a subquestion of $[\![(119A)]\!]^o$. In other words, the complete answer to (126) below must contextually entail a partial answer to $[\![(119A)]\!]^o$ = "who did Mary invite for dinner?"

(126)   'What d ∈ D is s.t. out of the set C of relevant propositions, only the proposition that Mary invited d for dinner is true?'

As we saw above, such is indeed the case when C is fixed as a subset of the set in (122), to which we refer as the case of "association of *only* with focus." Moreover, no further contextual assumptions are needed to guarantee that. As I understand it, Roberts' idea is that there might be other possible choices for C as well, but it is hard to think of any that come easily to mind and do not require unusual contextual assumptions.

Let us see, for example, what happens if C for (119B) is fixed as (127) below. In that case, (121) = (126) = $[\![(119B)]\!]^f$ becomes the question in (128). Could question (128) play the role of the necessary implicit move in between (119A) and (119B)?

---

[13]   Any answer to (124) is a complete answer to it.
[14]   The notion of a truly direct answer was introduced in 13.3.

(127)　The set of things that Mary promised Mother would happen this morning =
　　　　{'Mary invited Sue for dinner,'
　　　　'Mary brushed her teeth'}
(128)　'What d ∈ D is s.t. out of the two things Mary promised Mother to do this
　　　　morning, the only thing she did was invite d for dinner?'

Well, there are only two complete answers to (128) that could possibly be true, viz. the
following.

(129)　a.　Sue is such an individual and nobody else is.
　　　　b.　Nobody is such an individual.

Note that if the true complete answer to (128) happens to be (129a), then (128) becomes
a subquestion of $[\![(119A)]\!]^\circ$. (Since (129a) entails a partial answer to $[\![(119)]\!]^\circ$.) Note,
moreover, that (119B) interpreted with C set to (127) explicitly claims that (129a) is in
fact the true complete answer to (128). So the interlocutors may assume that (128) is
indeed a subquestion of $[\![(119A)]\!]^\circ$. But if so, then the answer to our question seems to
be positive: question (128) should indeed be able to serve as the necessary implicit move
in between (119A) and (119B); if (128) is the implicit move, both the QUD constraint
on focus and the requirement of direct-relevance-to-the-last-QUD get satisfied. Hence,
it should be possible to set C for (119B) to (127).

　　As far as I can tell, the empirical fact is that in dialog (119), association of *only* with
focus is obligatory – that is, C **cannot** be set to (127). This seems at odds with the conclusion drawn in the last paragraph. However, I think it can be explained. I think that
the reason (119B) cannot be interpreted with C set to (127) is that (119B) would then
be providing too much information. Recall the two submaxims of Grice's maxim of
Quantity: don't give too little information, and don't give too much information. The
requirement of direct-relevance-to-the-last-QUD is a formulation of the first of these
submaxims, and (119B) interpreted with C set to (127) does indeed obey this first submaxim. However, (119B) interpreted with C set to (127) violates the second submaxim,
which is not treated in Roberts 1996b.

　　I do think that if it is made clear in the discourse why question (128) is suddenly
being addressed, then (119B) **can** be interpreted with C set to (127) and still remain
(indirectly) relevant to (119A). For instance, I think that (130) below seems felicitous
and cohesive.

(130)　A:　Who did Mary invite for dinner?
　　　　B:　Well, let's see. I remember Father saying that of the two things Mary
　　　　　　promised Mother to do, she only invited a friend for dinner – I believe that
　　　　　　was Sue. Yes, he said that she only invited [Sue]$_F$ for dinner.

　　Summing up, association of *only* with focus is forced in dialog (119) because that is
the only way of fixing the domain of quantification C for *only* that, if we posit (126) =
(121) as an implicit move in between (119A) and (119B), would satisfy both the QUD
constraint on focus and the two submaxims of Quantity.

　　One of the virtues of Roberts' account is that it covers association with focus in questions, as well. For instance, consider (131).

(131)   A:   Who did Mary invite for dinner?
        B:   Did she only invite [Sue]$_F$?

The QUD constraint on focus determines that the focal ps of (131B) is identical to the focal ps of (119B): both presuppose that the last QUD is $[\![$only[invited(m,s$_F$)]$]\!]^f$. Also, (131A) = (119A). Therefore, the choice of value for the domain of quantification C for *only* in (131B) is restricted in exactly the same way that it was restricted in (119).

## 17.11   Conclusion

Rooth 1992; Schwarzschild 1994, 1997 and Roberts 1996b, agree that the complete theory of the semantics/pragmatics of focus can and should consist of the definition of focus-induced interpretations plus a single general constraint on the use of focus. They all agree that ideally, no semantic/pragmatic rules governing specific constructions or lexical items should ever have to refer directly to the notion of focus.

The constraints proposed by these three researchers are not far removed from each other: the focus semantic value of given utterances/clauses is required to be identical to or a superset of some set of propositions present in the context of utterance. Rooth and Schwarzschild, but not Roberts, specify further that within this set, it must be possible to draw a contrast/comparison between the ordinary semantic value of the clause in question and some other proposition(s). I am not sure that it really matters whether this is specified or not, since the focus semantic value of a clause usually contains both the ordinary semantic value of that clause and some other proposition(s) anyway.

A major difference between Rooth's theory on the one hand, and Schwarzschild's and Roberts' theories on the other hand is the following. Rooth's constraint directly covers a variety of focusing effects not all of which have to do with discourse congruence. Schwarzschild and Roberts, in contrast, treat focus uniformly as a discourse-regulating device.

On the following two examples, the three researchers largely agree. Clearly, in both examples, the role of focus in John's utterance is a discourse-regulating role: it relates John's utterance to a question or clause previously uttered by Father. (In example (8), for Roberts, the relation is mediated by an implicit question, viz. "who is the individual d s.t. of all that Mother asked John to do at her ball, the only thing he did was introduce d to Sue?")

(132)   Father:   Who arrived?
        John:   [Sue]$_F$ arrived.
(8)   Father:   Is it true that of all the things Mother asked you to do at her ball you only managed to introduce Steve to Sue?
        John:   Not exactly . . . [grin] I only introduced [Bill]$_F$ to Sue.

On the following example, however, opinions diverge. According to Rooth, focus fulfills its role via the fact that the focus semantic value of S$_2$ is identical to or a superset of the domain of quantification for *only*, and has nothing to do with Father's question. According to Schwarzschild and Roberts, the role of focus is and must be fulfilled via the fact that the focus semantic value of $S_1$ is identical to or a superset of either Father's question itself or (for Roberts) a closely related implicit question.

(133)   Father:   Who did John introduce to Sue?
        Mary:    He only introduced [Bill]$_F$ to Sue.
        LF of Mary's utterance:   [$_{S_1}$ only [$_{S_2}$ John introduced [Bill]$_F$ to Sue]]

It seems that the empirical facts support Schwarzschild's and Roberts' approach. All three researchers can explain the facts that "association of *only* with focus" exists and that it is **optional**, in the sense that given the sentence *John only introduced [Bill]$_F$ to Sue*, *only* does not always associate with the focus in that sentence. However, only Schwarzschild and Roberts, but not Rooth, can explain the extent to which focusing effects are **obligatory**.

Rooth cannot explain the fact that associated foci affect discourse congruence in the same way that other foci do, as illustrated by the contrast between (133) above and (134) below. Association with focus in Mary's utterance is sufficient to satisfy Rooth's constraint on focus (his FIP), and there is nothing in Rooth's theory that can force the focus on *Bill* to also be related to Father's question.

(134)   Father:   Who did John introduce Bill to?
        Mary:    He only introduced [Bill]$_F$ to Sue.      INFELICITOUS

Further, Rooth cannot explain the fact that **in context**, association with focus becomes obligatory. In (133) above, it should be quite possible for the focus on *Bill* to satisfy Rooth's FIP via the fact that the focus semantic value of $S_2$ is identical to Father's question. Therefore, there is nothing to force that focus to also associate with *only*.

By positing a constraint on the use of focus that makes focus a uniformly discourse-regulating device, Schwarzschild and Roberts automatically explain why any foci, including associated ones, affect discourse congruence. At the same time, they thereby lose Rooth's account of the existence of association with focus. Instead of that account, Schwarzschild and Roberts derive association with focus indirectly, based on the discourse-regulating role of focus. Further, they show that the account they propose simultaneously explains the extent to which association with focus is obligatory. (Recall that they argue that in examples like (133), association of *only* with focus is forced because without it, the focus would not be able to fulfill its discourse-regulating role.)

We see then that as far as the empirical facts about examples like (133) go, Schwarzschild's and Roberts' approach enjoys a clear advantage. Note, however, that Rooth's approach to focus effects has the important advantage that it has been shown to enjoy some **generality**. As illustrated in 17.3, Rooth's FIP can account for a variety of different focus effects.

So far, Schwarzschild's and Roberts' approach has not been shown to be applicable to other focus effects besides the association of *only* with focus. Nor is it immediately obvious how it would be. I think that it would be perfectly legitimate if under their general approach (focus effects being derived from the discourse-regulating role of focus), the accounts of different focus effects do not quite parallel each other. But the accounts would have to be provided.

Let me comment on one more feature which distinguishes Schwarzschild's and Roberts' theories from Rooth's. Recall that Rooth's theory leaves open the question of what "the scope of the focus" or "the level at which the focus gets interpreted" is going to be. For example, Rooth's FIP allows the focus in (135) below to get interpreted either at the level of $S_1$ or at the level of $S_2$. For Rooth, it is precisely this choice which determines whether the focus is going to be associated with *only* or not.

(135)  John only introduced [Bill]$_F$ to Sue.

LF of (135):  [$_{S_1}$ only [$_{S_2}$ John introduced [Bill]$_F$ to Sue]]

Schwarzschild and Roberts both assume, in contrast, that the focus in (135) must get interpreted at the level of $S_1$. In other words, they both assume that it is $[\![S_1]\!]^f$ which must be identical to (or a superset of) a preceding move in the same discourse. They both talk about the "utterance" containing the focus as the entity which should be appropriately related to a previous move, and assume that the relevant "utterance" is the whole of (135), and not just the embedded clause $S_2$.

Schwarzschild's and Roberts' assumption that focus must get interpreted at the level of the "utterance" is a crucial one, though they don't emphasize it much. (Schwarzschild 1994 includes some relevant remarks.) Their account of the existence and obligatory nature of association of *only* with focus in examples like (133) relies on that assumption. At the same time, they do not state in general terms what is to count as a relevant "utterance."

This would have to be investigated further. Certainly, (actual) complex utterances have to be carved up into relevant "utterances" or "sub-utterances" that each get related via focusing to a preceding move in the discourse. But what are the principles governing this division? What would constitute independent evidence for the right identification of relevant sub-utterances, besides its utility in accounting for focus effects? And how is each sub-utterance to take its place among moves in a discourse?[15]

Let us now compare the ways in which Schwarzschild and Roberts indirectly derive (obligatory) association with focus. Schwarzschild relies on the assumption that focus semantic values are closed under disjunction. This, combined with taking into account sums (plural individuals), allows Schwarzschild to claim that the focus semantic value of an answer containing *only* may be identical to the denotation of an *only*-less question. A short reminder of how this works: take the case of (136) below, with the "association of *only* with focus" interpretation of (136B). $[\![(136B)]\!]^f$ becomes identical to (or a superset of) $[\![(136A)]\!]^o$, because each member of $[\![(136A)]\!]^o$, of the "form" "John invited $d_1$", becomes a member of $[\![(136B)]\!]^f$ as well, due to its equivalence with the disjunction

---

[15]  Are the relevant sub-utterances sentences? clauses? formulas? intonation phrases? A separate sentence would surely count as a relevant sub-utterance. And what about embedded clauses? Does a modified embedded clause never count, or would it be a mistake to conclude that from (133), given that in actual fact *only* is a VP modifier (see 18.1.1)? How does sentential *it's only (true) that . . .* behave, then? How do other focus-sensitive S and VP modifiers behave? A clause/formula which is a conjunct, a disjunct, an antecedent or consequent of a conditional, a restriction or nuclear scope in a quantificational structure – these would presumably count as relevant distinct sub-utterances, since they can separately constitute an answer to a question or participate in explicit binary contrast. (Some brief remarks on focus in a nuclear scope can be found in 21.1.2.) And what about adverbial clauses? sentential complements? etc.

"either John invited only $d_1$, or else he invited only $d_1$ and $d_2$, or else he invited only $d_1$, $d_2$ and $d_3$ . . ." and so on for all $d_i \in D$ – a disjunction which is itself known to be a member of $[\![(136B)]\!]^f$.

(136)　A:　Who did John invite?
　　　　B:　He only invited [Bill]$_F$.　　　　FELICITOUS

Schwarzschild does not suggest any way in which the assumption of closure under disjunction is independently motivated, and I don't see how it could be independently motivated. Now consider what the effect of this assumption is. We would normally assume that while $[\![(136A)]\!]^o$ contains **partial** answers to "who did John invite?", all members of $[\![(136B)]\!]^f$ are of the "form" "John invited only d," for some $d \in D$, and hence a **complete** answer to that same question. The assumption of closure under disjunction simply adds all the partial answers into $[\![(136B)]\!]^f$. It seems that a more direct account of the congruence of dialog (136) would be to directly rely on the very fact that all the members of $[\![(136B)]\!]^f$ are complete answers to $[\![(136A)]\!]^o$, without making the more dubious assumption that focus semantic values are closed under disjunction.

I think it is fair to say that that is precisely what Roberts does in her account. Roberts points out that $[\![(136A)]\!]^o$ and $[\![(136B)]\!]^f$ are two closely related questions, in that all complete answers to the one are also complete answers to the other. Based on that, she is able to claim that her constraint on the use of focus is satisfied via the fact that $[\![(136B)]\!]^f$ is identical to an implicit discourse move in between (136A) and (136B), viz. the question "what individual $d \in A$ is s.t. John invited only d?".

Of course, in order to indirectly derive (obligatory) association with focus, Roberts too relies on certain additional assumptions besides her constraint on the use of focus. In particular, she relies on the notions of relevance and of the last question under discussion, as formulated within her formal theory of information structure in discourse. I think that Roberts' additional assumptions are better motivated than Schwarzschild's. Indeed I think that much of the beauty of Roberts' theory of focus lies precisely in the fact that it is elegantly integrated with her independently motivated theory of information structure in discourse.

Suffice it to go back to section 17.9, to get an idea of the variety of predictions about discourse congruence that Roberts' theory of information structure can make, completely independently of the phenomenon of focus. To take an example, consider once more move E in the following discourse.

(137)　A:　Who invited who?
　　　　B:　(Well,) who did Mary invite?
　　　　C:　(Let's see,) did she invite Nathan?
　　　　D:　Yes, she did.
　　　　E:　(OK, and) Kim invited Sue.

As discussed in 17.9, in a context where Mary may have invited many individuals, move E seems out of place, whereas in a context where Mary could only have invited one individual, move E seems quite natural. The account sketched in 17.9 crucially relies on the conception of the set of questions under discussion as a "push down" store, where the topmost question must be answered first: it is only when D contextually entails a complete answer not only to question C but also to question B that question B gets "popped off" the QUD stack and it is time again to address question A, and hence appropriate to utter E. Note in this connection that if we are willing to imagine that *Kim* and *Sue* are focused, then Schwarzschild's theory of focus would predict that utterance E **could** be felicitous in (137) (being appropriately contrasted with utterance A), but would not be able to explain why E is in fact a felicitous continuation only in a context where Mary could only have invited one individual.

Roberts 1996b further suggests (in section 3) that there are many more areas of investigation that can be fruitfully studied within her general framework of information structure.

I end with some comments regarding the use and status of implicit utterances/moves in Schwarzschild's and Roberts' theories. Given an utterance within a certain piece of discourse, it is often the case that Schwarzschild is able to directly relate that utterance to an explicit utterance in the same discourse, whereas Roberts must assume one or more implicit moves. For example, in (81).

(81)  A:  <u>Mary visited France</u> and Bill visited Belgium.
      B:  Oh, really, where did John go?
      A:  Oh, sorry, <u>[John]$_F$ visited France</u>, Mary visited Germany.

According to Schwarzschild, the underlined portion of the last utterance contrasts with the underlined portion of the first utterance. **The** function of the focus on *John* is to bring out the contrast. According to Roberts, the essential function of focus, invariably, is to indicate "the answer to the question being addressed." Her theory determines that *[John]$_F$ visited France* answers the question "who visited France?", and hence that that question is implicit in discourse (81), and is relevant within it.

I think the intuition is clear that *[John]$_F$ visited France* is not a truly direct answer to B's question.[16] Obviously, both researchers account for that intuition. And what about the intuition that there is a link between the two underlined portions? Schwarzschild's theory obviously accounts for that, which seems like an advantage over Roberts'. Given Roberts' theory, it seems reasonable to say that the link is that the implicit question "who visited France" becomes relevant in (81) because A is correcting her previous utterance. And yet this sort of situation is not covered by the formal definition of direct relevance. But then again, perhaps more types of "relevance" would have to be recognized anyway, when the theory of information structure is extended to further types of discourse.

At any rate, Schwarzschild's accounts are often, as in the case of (81), less abstract, and simpler. Is that a general advantage of his theory as compared with Roberts'? Perhaps. But here are three points to consider. (i) There is no doubt that the existence of implicit moves in the discourse would have to be recognized in any case. (Schwarzschild too would sometimes have to rely on an implicit utterance/move as his contrast target.) (ii) To say that *[John]$_F$ visited France* contrasts with *Mary visited France* and to say that it answers "who visited France?" as a way of correcting *Mary visited France*

[16] Cf. 13.3 above.

both seem to me to be intuitively reasonable. (iii) At least, Roberts' abstract moves are embedded within a general theory of how discourse is organized in relation to questions, which is motivated independently of focus, and are extrapolated from the structure of pieces of discourse in which all moves are fully explicit.

# 18

# *Focus-Induced Interpretations: Some Theoretical Choices to be Made*

In this chapter, I will address a couple of issues that have to do with the theory of focus-induced interpretations. I see these as general issues pertaining to any theory of focus-induced interpretations, and not ones that could or should distinguish between the structured meanings approach and the alternative semantics approach. (Discussion will be given in terms of alternative semantics, as is the usual practice in this book.)

## 18.1  Focus-Induced Interpretations of Constituents Other Than a Clause?

In the preceding chapters, I spoke exclusively of focus-induced interpretations of complete clauses. However, it is usually assumed in the literature that other syntactic constituents have their own focus-induced interpretations as well. (See Rooth 1985, 1992; von Stechow 1989, 1991, among others.) It would be interesting if there were convincing empirical evidence that this assumption is necessary. So I thought it worthwhile to point out that as far as I can tell at present, no such empirical support exists – I explain why below. As far as I can tell, including focus-induced interpretation of non-clauses is neither beneficial nor harmful. This may also serve as some justification for my decision to refer only to clausal focus-induced interpretations elsewhere in this book. Of course I have been cheating a bit in one respect, viz. in pretending that *only* is a sentential adverb. This section will also be an opportunity to set that right.

### 18.1.1  *Only as an NP or VP Modifier*

As discussed in Rooth 1985, ch. III, there are reasons to believe that the focusing adverb *only* sometimes functions as an NP modifier and sometimes functions as a VP modifier. Indeed, there is reason to believe that it never functions as a sentential adverb, contrary to what I have been assuming (for convenience) in the preceding chapters. Consider the following examples.

(1)  Only <u>John</u> smiled.
(2)  Only <u>John's father</u> smiled.

(3)   John loves only <u>Sue</u>.
(4)   Only <u>two cats</u> smiled.
(5)   John only <u>smiled</u>.
(6)   John only <u>loves Sue</u>.

Constituency tests suggest that syntactically, *only* in (1)–(6) modifies the underlined NP or VP. Restrictions on association with focus suggest that semantically/pragmatically too, *only* interacts with the underlined NP or VP: the fact is that *only* can associate with a focus that occurs inside the specified NP or VP, but not with a focus that occurs elsewhere. To see that, just examine the possible interpretations of the above examples with various choices of focus: in (1), *only* can associate with a focus on *John* but not with a focus on *smiled*, in (5), *only* can associate with a focus on *smiled* but not with a focus on *John*; in (6), *only* can associate with either *loves* or *Sue* (or *loves Sue*), in (3), *only* can associate with *Sue* but not with *loves*; *only* in (2) can associate with either *John* or *father*, but not with *smiled*; etc. The fact that auxiliary *only* cannot associate with a focus in subject position was noted in Jackendoff 1972, who pointed out that *only* contrasts with *even* in that respect:

(7)    [John]$_F$ even won the lottery.
(7′)   'Even John won the lottery' is a possible interpretation of (7).
(8)    [John]$_F$ only won the lottery.
(8′)   'Only John won the lottery' is not a possible interpretation of (8).

The contrast can presumably be explained based on the assumption that *even* can be a sentential operator, whereas *only* cannot.

Does the above mean that focus semantic values of NPs and VPs must be defined in the grammar? Let us agree that syntactically, *only* is an NP or VP modifier, and let us consider our semantic/pragmatic desiderata and options. Since the NP and VP cases are parallel, I will content myself with discussing the VP case alone.

First of all, we want the semantic interpretation of our sentences. We no longer want the rules in (9). Instead, we might add to our logic the rules in (10) (cf. Rooth 1985, ch. II). (Again I officially specify the assertion only, omitting the ps part.)

(9)   **S-adverb quantifying over propositions**                    (cannot be right)
      Syntax: if $\phi$ is of type t, so is only[$\phi$]
      Semantics: $[\![only[\phi]]\!]^g = \{w \in W : \text{for all } p \in C \subseteq D_t, \text{ if } w \in p \text{ then } p = [\![\phi]\!]^g\}$,
      where C is a contextually given set of propositions.

(10)  **VP-adverb quantifying over properties**                    (a possible analysis)
      Syntax: if $\alpha$ is of type $\langle e,t \rangle$, so is only[$\alpha$].
      Semantics: $[\![only[\alpha]]\!]^g =$ that function from D to $D_t$ s.t. for all $d \in D$,
                  $[\![only[\alpha]]\!]^g(d) = \{w \in W : \text{for all } P \in C \subseteq D_{\langle e,t \rangle}, \text{ if } w \in$
                  $P(d) \text{ then } P = [\![\alpha]\!]^g\}$,
      where C is a contextually given set of properties.

Take for instance example (11) below, with the LF in (12) and the logical translation in (13). According to (10), (11) is interpreted as in (14).

(11)   John only loves [Sue]$_F$.
(12)   John [$_{VP}$only [$_{VP}$loves [Sue]$_F$]]

(13)  only[love(s$_F$)](j)
(14)  'Of all the properties in C, the only one John has is "loves Sue".'

Secondly, we want to describe and explain the observed association with focus effect. Given the interpretation in (14), the reading of (11) that we are interested in (its most prominent reading) will have to be described as follows: C is identified with the set in (15).

(15)  The set of properties of the 'form' 'loves d,' for some d ∈ D
      = {$[\![love(x)]\!]^g$ : g assignment}

It seems convenient now to assume that subformulas of type $\langle e,t \rangle$ too have focus semantic values, and say that the set in (15) is $[\![love(s_F)]\!]^f$, i.e. that the set with which C is identified is the focus semantic value of the VP argument of *only*.

It is not theoretically costly to define focus semantic values for expressions of all types, instead of just for formulas. Informally:

(16)  $[\![\alpha]\!]^{f\text{-}M,g}$, the **focus semantic value** of an expression $\alpha$ relative to an arbitrary model M and an arbitrary assignment function g, is the set of all ordinary semantic values obtained by replacing the F-marked expressions and wh-words in $\alpha$ with (distinct, new) variables, and then interpreting the result relative to every assignment g′ which is identical to g except perhaps for the values of those variables.

It is also easy enough to let the FIP of Rooth 1992 apply at the level of non-clauses (which is, indeed, precisely what Rooth 1992 does):

(17)  **Rooth's Focus Interpretation Principle**
      A constituent may be focused
          iff
      it is contained in a constituent A of which the following holds:
      somewhere in the environment there is an (independently) salient set of denotations of the right type – call it Γ – s.t.
        (i)   $\Gamma \subseteq [\![A]\!]^f$, and
        (ii)  $[\![A]\!]^o \in \Gamma$, and
        (iii) there is some a s.t. a ≠ $[\![A]\!]^o$ and a ∈ Γ.

The association with focus effect can now be explained as a consequence of the need to satisfy the FIP via the domain of quantification C for *only* (C serving as the required set Γ), in which case it is the VP argument of *only* that must serve as the required focus-containing constituent A.

Thirdly, we want to explain why it is that *only* cannot associate with a focus outside its argument. Given (10), (16) and (17), this fact follows automatically, since such a focus cannot affect the focus semantic value of the VP argument of *only*.

We may conclude at this point that it is possible to have an elegant account of the behavior of *only* based on focus semantic values of non-clauses. However, we may still ask: would it be possible to have an equally successful (or better) account which utilizes only focus semantic values of complete clauses?

Let us try out an alternative account. Instead of the rules in (10), we could use the rules in (18) (cf. Rooth 1985, ch. III). In that way, despite the fact that *only* takes a property as its argument, it would induce quantification over propositions. So, if C is to get identified with a focus semantic value, that would have to be a focus semantic value of a complete formula.

(18) **VP-adverb quantifying over propositions** (also a possible analysis)
    Syntax: if $\alpha$ is of type $\langle e,t \rangle$, so is only$[\alpha]$.
    Semantics: $[\![ \text{only}[\alpha] ]\!]^g =$ that function from D to $D_t$ s.t. for all $d \in D$,
               $[\![ \text{only}[\alpha] ]\!]^g(d) = \{ w \in W : \text{for all } p \in C \subseteq D_t, \text{ if } w \in p$
               then $p = [\![ \alpha ]\!]^g(d) \}$,
    where C is a contextually given set of propositions.

However, there is a problem: C would get identified with the focus semantic value of **what** formula? In the case of (11), we would want C to end up identified with $\{ [\![ \text{love}(x)(j) ]\!]^g : g \text{ assignment} \}$; however, the translation of (11) given in (13) above does not contain the formula love($s_F$)(j), whose focus semantic value that is. Rooth 1985, pp. 124–5, argues (though in a somewhat different framework) that this kind of problem can be solved. I think it is fair to say that the essence of his proposal is that C gets identified with the focus semantic value of the formula $\alpha(x)$ – in the case of (11), the focus semantic value of love($s_F$)(x).

Certainly, love($s_F$)(x) is not a subformula of (13) either. However, $\alpha(x)$ does seem to play a role in the semantics given in (18), and perhaps that is why its focus semantic value can be accessed. After all, $\alpha(x)$ corresponds to $[\![ \alpha ]\!]^g(d)$ in (18). Indeed, according to (18), (19) holds.

(19) $[\![ \text{only}[\alpha] ]\!]^g = [\![ \lambda x [\forall v_{1,t}[[C'(v_{1,t}) \wedge v_{1,t}] \rightarrow v_{1,t} = \alpha(x)]]] ]\!]^g$,
    where $[\![ C' ]\!]$ is the characteristic function of (= the property of being a member of) a contextually given set of propositions C

Applying (18) to our example (11), we get (20). Assuming that C can be identified with the focus semantic value of love($s_F$)(x), given in (21), relative to an assignment g s.t. g(x) = d (and assuming further that the FIP is somehow changed so that it can get satisfied via this identification), our problem is solved. (20) turns into (22). Applied to j, (22) yields the desired interpretation, given in (23).

(20) $[\![ \text{only}[\text{love}(s_F)] ]\!]^g =$ that function from D to $D_t$ s.t. for all $d \in D$,
         $[\![ \text{only}[\text{love}(s_F)] ]\!]^g(d) = \{ w \in W : \text{for all } p \in C \subseteq D_t, \text{ if } w \in p$
         then $p = [\![ \text{love}(s_F) ]\!]^g(d) \}$,
    where C is a contextually given set of propositions.
(21) $[\![ \text{love}(s_F)(x) ]\!]^{f-g} = \{ [\![ \text{love}(y)(x) ]\!]^{g'} : g' \text{ is identical to g except that it may assign a different value to y} \}$
        $= \{ [\![ \text{love}(y)(x) ]\!]^{g'} : g'(x) = g(x) \}$
(22) $[\![ \text{only}[\text{love}(s_F)] ]\!] =$ that function from D to $D_t$ s.t. for all $d \in D$, $[\![ \text{only}[\text{love}(s_F)] ]\!](d)$
        $= \{ w \in W : \text{for all } p \in \{ [\![ \text{love}(y)(x) ]\!]^g : g(x) = d \}, \text{ if } w \in p \text{ then } p$
        $= [\![ \text{love}(s_F) ]\!](d) \}$
(23) $\{ w \in W : \text{for all } p \in \{ [\![ \text{love}(y)(x) ]\!]^g : g(x) = \text{John} \}, \text{ if } w \in p \text{ then } p = [\![ \text{love}(s_F) ]\!]$
    (John) $\} = \{ w \in W : \text{for all } p \in \{ [\![ \text{love}(y)(j) ]\!]^g : g \text{ assignment} \}, \text{ if } w \in p \text{ then } p = [\![ \text{love}(s_F)(j) ]\!] \}$

And what about ensuring that *only* would not associate with foci outside its argument? Rooth (1985, pp. 125–7) shows that that is achieved too, if we stipulate that C must indeed be fixed at the level of the VP, as in (22). In that case, no foci in the expression which is going to semantically combine with $[\![only[\alpha]]\!]^g$ (i.e. the name or generalized quantifier corresponding to the subject NP) would be able to affect the choice of C.

The conclusion seems to be that we can do without focus semantic values of non-formulas, if we are willing to adopt a version of the FIP which takes into account focus semantic values of formulas which don't correspond to any syntactic constituent.

Let us also see what happens if we replace the FIP with Roberts' constraint in (24).

(24) **The Question-Under-Discussion Constraint on Focus**
An utterance B whose logical translation is of the form $\beta$ or $?[\beta]$, where $\beta$ is a formula, is felicitous only if $[\![\beta]\!]^f = last(QUD([\![B]\!]^o))$.

Roberts' account of the association of focus effect in (11) works equally well whether *only* is treated as a sentential operator (as per (9) above) or as a VP operator (as per (10) or (18)). (Indeed, Roberts 1996b herself assumes the latter.) Consider the short dialog consisting of (25) followed by (11):

(25)  Who does John love?
(11)  John only loves [Sue]$_F$.

If either (9) or (18) is used, then $[\![(11)]\!]^f$, and hence the last question under discussion presupposed by (11), is the set in (26). If (10) is used, then $[\![(11)]\!]^f$, and hence the last QUD, is the set in (27).

(26)  the set of propositions of the 'form'
'Of all the relevant propositions in C, the only true one is the proposition that John loves d,' for some individual d ∈ D.
(27)  the set of propositions of the 'form'
'Of all the relevant properties in C, the only one John has is the property of loving d,' for some individual d ∈ D.

Either way, Roberts' account applies: the presupposed last QUD, be it (26) or (27), is very closely related to (25) (in that any complete answer to the one is a complete answer to the other), but only if the value of C is chosen appropriately. So the dialog as a whole is felicitous only if the value of C is chosen appropriately. In the case of (26), C will be fixed as (a subset of) the set in (28), and in the case of (27), it will be fixed as (a subset of) the set in (29).

(28)  the set of propositions of the 'form' 'John loves d,' for some d ∈ D
(29)  the set of properties of the 'form' 'loves d,' for some d ∈ D

Note, further, that there is nothing in Roberts' grammar which identifies the set in (28) or (29) as the focus semantic value of any constituent or subformula. (Indeed, there is nothing in Roberts' grammar that even sets the value of C to (28) or (29), in the first place.) The thing is, Roberts' account of association of *only* with focus only ever refers to the focus semantic value of the entire *only*-containing clause. It never refers to the focus semantic value of the argument of *only*. So it makes no difference whether the argument of *only* is a clause or a VP, and no use need ever be made of focus semantic values of non-clauses.

But what about ensuring that *only* would not associate with foci outside its VP argument? Can we do that under Roberts' theory? Let us consider example (30). Recall that what we need to explain is why (30) cannot be interpreted as in (30′).[1]

(30)  [John]$_F$ only loves Sue.
(30′)  'Only John loves Sue' is not a possible interpretation of (30).

Since association of *only* with focus is usually forced by the presence of a corresponding *only*-less question, let us examine the dialog consisting of (31) followed by (30):

(31)  Who loves Sue?
(30)  [John]$_F$ only loves Sue.

If we let *only* be a sentential operator and use (9), then (30) is interpreted as in (31), and its focus semantic value, and hence its presupposed last QUD, is as in (32). In that case, fixing C as a set of propositions of the "form" "d loves Sue" makes (32) correspond very closely to the denotation of (31) (any complete answer to the one is a complete answer to the other). So we get the wrong prediction that our dialog should be felicitous, as long as *only* associates with the focus.

(31)  'Of all the relevant propositions in C, the only true one is "John loves Sue".'
(32)  the set of propositions of the 'form'
      'Of all the relevant propositions in C, the only true one is the proposition that d loves Sue,' for some individual d ∈ D.

However, if we insist that *only* is a VP operator and use (10), we get the correct prediction. In that case, (30) is interpreted as in (14), and its focus semantic value, and hence its presupposed last QUD, is as in (33). But now there is no value that could be assigned to C which would make (33) correspond very closely to the denotation of (31). So we predict, correctly, that our dialog as a whole is infelicitous.[2]

(14)  'Of all the relevant properties in C, the only one John has is "loves Sue".'
(33)  the set of propositions of the 'form'
      'Of all the relevant properties in C, the only one d has is the property of loving Sue,' for some individual d ∈ D.

---

[1]  Note that, contrary to what is sometimes assumed in the literature, (30) is not infelicitous – it can answer a question such as *who is the guy that only loves Sue?*
[2]  Actually, Roberts' theory as it stands does predict felicity, because (33) is a subquestion of the denotation of (31), and hence directly relevant to it. But as discussed at the end of 17.10 above, it makes good sense to assume that direct relevance is not a sufficient condition for felicity.

I conclude that it is possible to have an elegant and successful account of the behavior of *only* without making any reference to focus semantic values of non-clauses. Indeed, combining Roberts' theory of focus with a VP-operator semantics for *only* as in (10) above provides just such an account.

### 18.1.2   Sentence-Internal Contrasting Phrases

The one case that I (as well as Roth, p.c., 1996) could think of where focus semantic values of constituents other than a clause might prove crucial is the case of sentence-internal contrasting phrases, as in (34) below (to be thought of as the beginning of a joke).

(34)   An AMERICAN farmer was talking to a CANADIAN farmer . . .

(Rooth 1992, p. 80)

The emphasized words in such examples are commonly taken to be foci; perhaps foci of a particular type (cf. Rochemont 1986, ch. 2). But these foci do not seem to relate the example to a preceding "move" in the discourse. Rather, they seem to indicate contrast – symmetric contrast – between two (or more) phrases within the sentence.

Assuming that the focal structure is as indicated in (35), our example can easily be covered by the FIP of Rooth 1992, with each focus interpreted at the level of its NP or N' (it doesn't matter which).

(35)   An [$_{N'_1}$ [American]$_F$ farmer] was talking to a [$_{N'_2}$ [Canadian]$_F$ farmer] . . .

The focus on *American* satisfies the FIP with $[\![N'_2]\!]^f$ serving as the required comparison class $\Gamma$, since $[\![N'_1]\!]^o$ and $[\![N'_2]\!]^o$ are two distinct members of $[\![N'_2]\!]^f = \{[\![\lambda x[X(x) \wedge farmer(x)]]\!]^g$ : g assignment}. In exactly the same way, the focus on *Canadian* satisfies the FIP with $[\![N'_1]\!]^f$ as the set $\Gamma$.

Clearly, it is crucial for the above account that there exist focus semantic values of nominal constituents. However, there are problems with this simple account. Indeed, it may be best not to try and subsume sentence-internal contrasts under the theory of focus.

It is argued in Roberts 1996b (section 2.2.2.2) that (35) is not the correct analysis of the example impressionistically transcribed in (34). Roberts notes that, examining the prosody in more detail, it seems that when the sentence in (34) is uttered out of the blue (as the beginning of a joke), it has to be pronounced as indicated in (36). (Note that (36) contains two intonation phrases (double-underlined), each containing two intermediate phrases (single-underlined).)

(36)

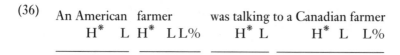

Given the assumption that all pitch accents must occur within a focus (see section 13.4), the analysis in (35) cannot be correct. Roberts 1996b suggests instead that the focal structure of the example intended by (34) (uttered as a beginning of a joke) is as indicated in (37). (That is, each intermediate phrase has a maximally broad focus.)[3]

(37)   [An American]$_F$ [farmer]$_F$ [was talking]$_F$ [to a Canadian farmer]$_F$

On Roberts' theory, the focal structure in (37) means that our example presupposes a very general question (such as "what happened" or "who was doing what"), thereby explaining why it is felicitous out of the blue. But the sentence-internal contrast still remains to be explained. That is, we need to explain the fact that the two adjectives *American* and *Canadian* are the most prosodically prominent words in the entire utterance, and the clear intuition that that is motivated by the contrast between them. Note in this connection that the phonological principles discussed in chapters 12 and 13 do not say anything about the relative prosodic weight of multiple intermediate phrases. Roberts suggests that a contrast is being "superimposed" here on an "otherwise broadly focused prosodic structure," probably metalinguistically, by means of the prosodic phrasing and the speaker's decision to give more prominence to the first and last of the four intermediate phrases.

I conclude that it may be best to give sentence-internal contrasts an account that is not based on focus semantic values of non-clauses.


## 18.2   Recursive Definition of Focus-Induced Interpretations?

In this book, I have been assuming a definition of focus-induced interpretations based on substitution into, or $\lambda$-abstraction on, the focus position(s). But what Rooth 1985 originally proposed, which is also often adopted in subsequent literature, is a **recursive** definition of focus-induced interpretations. In this section, I will very briefly present and consider this option. I will concentrate, as usual, on focus semantic values.[4]

Focus semantic values are defined recursively by adding to each semantic rule in the recursive definition of ordinary semantic values a parallel new rule which defines a focus semantic value. Let us use our language L of 14.5.2 above, with F-marked expressions added, as in 14.5.3. The parallel recursion of focus semantic values will start, of course, with the values of basic expressions. These may be defined as in (38). Our new rule for F-marked expressions will be as in (39).[5]

(38)   **focus semantic values of basic expressions**
       For any constant or variable $\alpha$, $[\![\alpha]\!]^{f\text{-}M,g} = \{[\![\alpha]\!]^{M,g}\}$
(39)   **focus semantic values of F-marked expressions**
       If $\alpha$ is an expression of type $\tau$, then $[\![[\alpha]_F]\!]^{f\text{-}M,g} = D_\tau$.

---

[3]   In the last focus, the word *farmer*, being "old," does not carry a pitch accent – see discussion in 13.4.
[4]   A recursive definition of structured meanings can be found in Krifka 1991.
[5]   We can adopt Roberts 1996b's treatment of foci in questions by adding a rule for wh-words analogous to (39).

For all the other semantic rules, we want parallel new rules with the effect described in (40). I will give just two examples, the ones in (41) and (42); the reader can fill in the rest (or consult Rooth 1985).

(40)   **informal schema for focus semantic values of complex expressions**

Given a semantic rule that computes the ordinary semantic value of a complex expression $\alpha$ with the component expressions $\alpha_1, \ldots, \alpha_k$, we want the focus semantic value of $\alpha$ to be the set of things obtainable by applying that semantic rule to members of $[\![\alpha_1]\!]^f, \ldots, [\![\alpha_k]\!]^f$.

(41)   For any types $\sigma, \tau$, if $\alpha$ is of type $\langle\sigma,\tau\rangle$ and $\beta$ is of type $\sigma$, then
$[\![\alpha(\beta)]\!]^{f\text{-}M,g} = \{a(b) : a \in [\![\alpha]\!]^{f\text{-}M,g} \text{ and } b \in [\![\beta]\!]^{f\text{-}M,g}\}$

(42)   If $\alpha$ is of type $\tau$ and u is a variable of type $\sigma$, then
$[\![\lambda u[\alpha]]\!]^{f\text{-}M,g} = $ the set of functions $f \in D_{\langle\sigma,\tau\rangle,M}$ s.t.
for any $h \in D_{\sigma,M}$, $f(h) = a$, for some $a \in [\![\alpha]\!]^{f\text{-}M,g[u\to h]}$,
where $g[u \to h]$ is a function identical to g except (perhaps) that it assigns to u the value h.

Is there any good reason to prefer the recursion method of defining focus semantic values to the substitution-based definition?

The recursion method offers more leeway in manipulating focus semantic values, because the recursive definition could include all sorts of rules that compute focus semantic values of complex expressions in a variety of different ways (instead of just rules that fit the schema in (40)). Consider for example the idea that foci associated with *only* should be "neutralized," so that they will not affect the focus semantic value of the sentence containing *only* (cf. Rooth 1992, pp. 94–5). It is hard to see how this idea might be reconciled with the substitution-based definition of focus semantic values. Given the recursion method, on the other hand, it might be implemented by positing some rule along the lines of (43).

(43)   For any expression $\alpha$, $[\![\text{only}[\alpha]]\!]^{f\text{-}M,g} = \{[\![\text{only}[\alpha]]\!]^{M,g}\}$

What this means is that if we find empirical evidence that focus semantic values must be manipulated in a variety of different ways, that would support adopting the recursion method. I do not know of any convincing evidence of this sort. (Needless to say, I do not think that (43) or any similar rule should be posited, since I think Schwarzschild and Roberts have shown convincingly that foci do not get "neutralized".)

One idea that may lie behind the recursive definition of focus semantic values is that it is desirable to obey in this manner an extended version of a compositionality hypothesis. This may seem convincing especially if one regards focus semantic values as part of the semantic component of the grammar, and wants the semantics to be uniformly compositional. I do not find this line of thought very convincing. As is well known, the rationale behind observing a strong version of compositionality regarding the semantics (i.e. requiring that a semantic value be assigned to each syntactic constituent) is that it is to serve as a strong hypothesis, which restricts the range of possible semantic rules and possible semantic interpretations. However, we just saw that of the recursion method and substitution method of defining focus semantic values, it is actually the latter and not the former which is more restrictive.[6]

Kratzer's work reported in the next section provides some evidence that in fact, the substitution method should be preferred to the recursion method.

## 18.3    Co-Variation in Focus Positions?

Kratzer 1991 points out a problem with focus semantic values. She presents the following example (Kratzer 1991, p. 830).

(44)    A:    What a copy cat you are! You went to Block Island because I did. You went to Elk Lake Lodge because I did. You went to Tanglewood because I did.
        B:    You exaggerate. I only went to [Tanglewood]$_F$ because you did.

We assume that *only* is a VP modifier. We also assume that VP deletion involves a reconstruction process copying the missing VP from an appropriate antecedent VP at LF. So the LF of the last sentence in (44) is as in (45).

(45)    I [$_I$past [$_{VP}$only [$_{VP}$ [$_{VP}$go to [Tanglewood]$_F$]
        because you did [$_{VP}$go to [Tanglewood]$_F$] ] ]]

According to alternative semantics as we know it — and it doesn't matter whether we use a recursive definition of focus semantic values or define them based on substitution – the two focus positions in (45) will each get manipulated separately. Therefore, the focus semantic value of the argument of *only* (= the VP enclosed in the large brackets) is as in (46).

(46)    the set of properties of the 'form'
        'went to $d_1$ because you went to $d_2$,' for some $d_1,d_2 \in D$

Kratzer argues that this yields the wrong prediction, because if the domain of quantification for *only* is identified with the set in (46), we get that (45) is interpreted as in (47), whereas in reality it is clearly interpreted as in (48).

(47)    'Of all the properties of the "form" "went to $d_1$ because you went to $d_2$," the only property I have is the property of having gone to Tanglewood because you went to Tanglewood.'

---

[6]   That, of course, is **not** to say that recursive/compositional semantics in general is irrelevant to focus. Note, in particular, that when studying foci in complex sentences, we will need to identify clauses/sub-utterances/subformulas that will serve as the "scope" of those foci, and when considering the focal ps there, we will presumably need to identify the local contexts of those clauses/sub-utterances/subformulas (cf. 17.11, fn.15; end of 21.1.2); to do that, we will presumably rely on recursively defined context change potentials. But I don't see that that should require a recursive definition of the focus semantic values themselves. I think that the focus semantic values of the relevant clauses/sub-utterances/subformulas can be defined by substitution.

(48)  'Of all the properties of the "form" "went to d because you went to d," the only
property I have is the property of having gone to Tanglewood because you went
to Tanglewood.'

Kratzer concludes that the theory of focus-induced interpretations has to be revised,
so that it would be possible to force co-variation of two (or more) focus positions when
necessary.

Kratzer proposes a specific revision. One crucial feature of her proposal is that all
F features present at surface structure receive distinct indexes. For instance, we have
the indexing in (49a). Another crucial feature of her proposal is that focus semantic
values are defined by substitution into focus positions (as I have been assuming in this
book). Kratzer defines her substitution in such a way that F-marked constituents with
distinct indexes are replaced with distinct variables, while F-marked constituents with
identical indexes are replaced with occurrences of the same variable. The first case is
illustrated in (49b).

(49)  a.  $[Sue]_{F1}$ kissed $[Kim]_{F2}$.
      b.  $[\![(49a)]\!]^f = \{[\![kissed(y)(x)]\!]^g : g \text{ assignment}\}$

Now at surface structure, our Tanglewood example (the last sentence in (44)) only
contains one F-feature. In the process of reconstruction, this F-feature gets
copied together with its index. So the resulting VP contains two **coindexed** foci, as in
(50).

(50)  I $[_{I'}$past $[_{VP}$only $[_{VP} [_{VP}$go to $[Tanglewood]_{F1}]$
      because you did $[_{VP}$go to $[Tanglewood]_{F1}]$ $]$ $]]$

The focus semantic value of the VP argument of *only* is based on substitution into two
coindexed focus positions, and it therefore becomes the set in (51). If this set becomes
the domain of quantification for *only*, we get the interpretation in (48) above, as desired.

(51)  the set of properties of the 'form'
      'went to d because you went to d,' for some $d \in D$

Kratzer's proposal is based on defining focus semantic values by substitution and is
not compatible with a recursive definition of focus semantic values. Therefore, it suggests that the VP deletion examples provide evidence for choosing the substitution
method over the recursion method.

# 19

# *Focus and Scope*

---

## 19.1   The "Pure Scope" Theory of Focus

As already mentioned in 18.1.1 above, there is good reason to treat *only* in sentences like (1) and (2) as an NP modifier. A natural analysis would have *only* take a name as its argument, to yield a generalized quantifier; we would add to our logic the rules in (3).

(1)   Only John smiled.
(2)   John loves only Sue.
(3)   Syntax: if $\alpha$ is of type e, then only$[\alpha]$ is of type $\langle\langle e,t\rangle,t\rangle$.
   Semantics: $[\![\text{only}[\alpha]]\!]^g$ = that function from $D_{\langle e,t\rangle}$ to $D_t$ s.t. for all $P \in D_{\langle e,t\rangle}$,
   $$[\![\text{only}[\alpha]]\!]^g(P) = \{w \in W : \text{for all } d \in C \subseteq D, \text{ if } w \in P(d)$$
   $$\text{then } d = [\![\alpha]\!]^g\}$$

Now consider again the association of *only* or *even* with focus.

(4)   John only loves [Sue]$_F$.
(5)   John even loves [Sue]$_F$.

There is a simple way of dealing with this phenomenon without positing special focus-induced interpretations: we can say that the focused constituent serves as the (semantic) argument of the focusing adverb. For example, in (4), *only* would take the focused *Sue* as its argument. This could create the generalized quantifier "only Sue", which would in turn be the object of *love*. In these respects, (4) would be treated as analogous to sentence (2) above.

How do we make the focus an argument of *only*? We could assign to (4) the logical translation in (6). Which could be done via a semantically relevant level of representation at which (4) has the same syntactic structure as sentence (2), following Fischer 1968. (This might be called a "reconstruction theory of association of *only* with focus".)

(6)   LOVE(only(s))(j)     where *LOVE* is a type-shifted version of *love*, of type $\langle\langle\langle e,t\rangle,t\rangle, \langle e,t\rangle\rangle$, and equivalent to $\lambda v_{1,\langle\langle e,t\rangle,t\rangle}[\lambda y[v_{1,\langle\langle e,t\rangle,t\rangle}(\lambda x [\text{love}(x)(y)])]]$

Alternatively, we could say that a syntactic rule analogous or similar to QR (Quantifier Raising) moves the focused constituent up and attaches it at a semantically relevant level of syntactic representation as sister to *only*, following Anderson 1972. To make this concrete, we could say that the LF of (4) is something like (7).[1]

(7)  [s[NPonly Sue_i] [s John loves __i]]

One standard procedure for interpreting NPs raised out of and adjoined to their clause is to "quantify them into" the clause. (As is well known, the procedure of "quantifying in" an NP is specifically designed to give that NP wide scope.) The same procedure could be applied here as well, for instance by translating (7) into the logical formula in (8). (The raising-to-*only* + quantifying-in analysis might be called a "scope theory of association of *only* with focus".)

(8)  only(s) ($\lambda$x[love(x)(j)])

Given the treatment of *only* in (3), formulas (6) and (8) both denote the proposition in (9), or – more informally – the proposition in (10), yielding the correct truth conditions for sentence (4).

(9)  {w ∈ W : for all d ∈ D, if w ∈ $[\![\lambda x[love(x)(j)]]\!]$(d) then d = Sue}
(10)  'Nobody other than Sue is loved by John.'

Now, it is proposed in Chomsky 1976 that **all** focused phrases are "scoped" out of their clauses – that is, they are all raised out of their base position and placed (at a semantically relevant level of representation) outside their clause. Following this proposal, the LF of (11), for example, might be as in (12).

(11)  John loves [Sue]_F.
(12)  [s[NPSue]_i [s John loves __i]]

A theory where focused phrases are uniformly "scoped" out of their clauses might be called a "scope theory of focus."

Chomsky 1976 argues for his scope theory of focus on the basis of the so-called "weak crossover effects" observed with sentences like (13).

(13)  The woman he loved betrayed [John]_F.
(14)  unavailable for (13): 'the x s.t. the woman x loved betrayed x is John.'

The relevant effect is that (13) does not have the "bound variable" reading paraphrased in (14), in contrast with the sentence *[John]_F was betrayed by the woman he loved*, which does have this very reading. The point is that in this respect, the behavior of (13) is parallel to that of (15) and (17) below. (15) and (17) too do not have a "bound variable" reading, in contrast with *Who was betrayed by the woman he*

---

[1]  For the sake of simplicity, I once more assume that at LF auxiliary *only* is adjoined to S, rather than to VP.

*loved?* and *Every man was betrayed by the woman he loved*, which do have such a reading.

(15) Who did the woman he loved betray?
(16) unavailable for (15): 'which x is s.t. the woman x loved betrayed x?'
(17) The woman he loved betrayed every man.
(18) unavailable for (17): 'Every man x is s.t. the woman x loved betrayed x.'

If the focus in (13) is scoped out of its clause, then (13), (15) and (17)-with-*every man*-taking-wide-scope share the same structural configuration:

(13') [John]$_i$  [$_S$ the woman he$_i$ loved betrayed $\_\_$$_i$]
(15') [who]$_i$  [$_S$ the woman he$_i$ loved betrayed $\_\_$$_i$]
(17') [every man]$_i$  [$_S$ the woman he$_i$ loved betrayed $\_\_$$_i$]

This allows us to attribute the impossibility of coindexing the pronoun with *John* in (13) to the same constraint (the "weak crossover condition" or whatever it is) which prohibits coindexing the pronoun with the wh-phrase or quantified phrase in (15) and (17).

The above suggests that a scope theory of focus might be quite successful: the hypothesis that focused phrases are uniformly scoped out of their clause accounts for the "weak crossover effect" and at the same time almost automatically makes the focus an argument of *only*, whereby association of *only* with focus is accounted for (using the independently motivated treatment of *only* given in (3)) without positing special focus-induced interpretations.

## 19.2    The "Focus-Induced Interpretations + Scope" Theory

### 19.2.1    From "Pure Scope" to "Focus-Induced Interpretations + Scope"

However, certain arguments have been raised against treating association of *only* with focus by making the focus an argument of *only* and without utilizing focus-induced interpretations.

One problem shows up when we turn to association of *only* with multiple foci, as in (19).[2]

(19) John only introduced [Bill]$_F$ to [Sue]$_F$.

Assuming "reconstruction," we would presumably need to "double" our *only*, since we would need one *only* for each focused phrase. This is not as elegant as we might wish. And what about a "scope" version of the theory? The beauty of the scope theory was that the NP adjoined to S at LF was a normal NP, and the rules used (see (3) above) were a close variant of the usual procedure for forming and interpreting generalized

---

[2]  I am here talking about two foci with equal status. For discussion of two foci each having a different status, see chapter 20.

quantifiers, and were independently motivated by sentences like (1) and (2). But, as noted in Rooth 1985, p. 34 and in von Stechow 1991, p. 809, this beauty seems to be blemished somewhat when we turn to association with multiple foci. The LF of (19) would be as in (20).

(20)   [s[NPonly + Bill_i + Sue_j] [s John introduced _i to _j]]

The NP adjoined to S in (20) is weird, and we need something like the rules in (21), which do not involve an ordinary generalized quantifier and are not independently motivated, to allow us to translate (20) as (22).

(21)   Syntax: If $\alpha,\beta$ are expressions of type e, then only[$\alpha,\beta$] is an expression of type $\langle\langle e,\langle e,t\rangle\rangle,t\rangle$.
       Semantics: $[\![only[\alpha,\beta]]\!]^g$ = that function from $D_{\langle e,\langle e,t\rangle\rangle}$ to $D_t$ s.t. for all $\underline{P} \in D_{\langle e,\langle e,t\rangle\rangle}$, $[\![only(\alpha,\beta)]\!]^g(\underline{P}) = \{w \in W : \text{for all } d_1,d_2 \in D, \text{ if } w \in \underline{P}(d_1)(d_2) \text{ then } d_1 = [\![\alpha]\!]^g \text{ and } d_2 = [\![\beta]\!]^g\}$

(22)   only[b,s] ($\lambda x[\lambda y[introduce(x)(y)(j)]]$)

So if we thought that the scope theory of association of *only* with focus seemed simpler and less ad hoc than the theory utilizing focus-induced interpretations, we might have to revise that opinion. (To be fair, though, note that we are **not** talking here about complicating the scope theory much – after all, (21) follows from a simple generalization of the rules in (3).)

A more serious problem with the focus-as-argument-of-*only* theory is that it has not been generalized to account for other effects of focusing, and it is not clear how it might be so generalized. (cf. Rooth 1985, pp. 39–41, 62–4.)

Take for instance question-answer congruence. How would the theory under consideration help us to explicate the role of focusing in (24) and relate (24) to the corresponding question in (23)?

(23)   Who did John introduce to Sue?
(24)   John introduced [Bill]_F to Sue.

It doesn't seem to help to see *Bill* as scoped out: raising *Bill* does not in itself explain the semantic/pragmatic role of focusing. Note also that an NP can easily be scoped out without functioning as a focus. For instance in (25), on the reading paraphrased in (26), *every candidate* is presumably scoped out, but need not be focus (*two examiners* can easily be the focus).

(25)   Two examiners questioned every candidate.
(26)   'For every candidate x, two examiners questioned x'

Are we going to try and uniformly characterize a focus as a constituent that is marked as the intended argument of some (non-adjacent) operator? Well, what would the relevant operator be in (24)? And what would that have to do with question-answering?

In contrast, the most attractive feature of theories based on focus-induced interpretations is precisely the fact that such theories enable us to simultaneously account for various effects of focusing, utilizing one and the same focus-induced interpretation.

There remains the possibility of some sort of a combination theory. One thing we could do is take the theory where *only* does **not** take non-adjacent foci as its argument(s) but is rather a sentential (or VP-) adverb that gets affected by focus-induced interpretations – and combine that theory with the hypothesis that foci are raised out of their clause at LF. The result might be called a "focus-induced interpretations + scope" theory of focus.

As noted in Rooth 1996 (section 3), it is easy enough to derive focus-induced interpretations on the basis of representations where foci are raised out of and "quantified into" their clauses. For instance, suppose (11) is translated into (27), or – type-shifting the generalized quantifier denoting expression back to an individual denoting expression – into (28).

(11)   John loves [Sue]$_F$.
(27)   $[\lambda X[X(s)]]_F \, (\lambda x[love(x)(j)])$
(28)   $\lambda x[love(x)(j)] \, (s_F)$

The rule assigning a structured meaning to this translation would be very simple: form the pair consisting of the property denoted by the F-less $\lambda$-abstract and the individual corresponding to the F-marked subformula. The rule assigning a focus semantic value to this translation would instruct one to form the set of propositions obtainable by semantically combining the denotation of the F-less $\lambda$-abstract with a semantic object matching the type of the F-marked subformula. (Here "semantically combining" means "performing function application".) Either way, the rule is, crucially, a special rule needed specifically for foci; we are no longer satisfied with merely applying the independently needed "quantifying in" rule as in the "pure scope" theory.

Do we want a "focus-induced interpretations + scope" theory of focus then? Some relevant considerations are briefly discussed in the following subsections.

### 19.2.2   Crossover Effects

The decision taken in Rooth 1985 was to interpret foci in situ, rather than scope them out. Rooth 1985, pp. 70–80, argued that the "weak crossover" effects described in section 19.1 above (as well as "strong crossover" effects) can be explained without the assumption that foci are assigned scope at LF.

Let us first consider (13) and (29). The "bound variable" reading in (30) is available for (29) but not for (13).[3] This fact can be explained assuming that the NP *John* must get scoped out of its clause. (29′) is a possible LF, yielding the desired reading. (13′), in contrast, is not a possible LF, because it displays the banned "crossover configuration."

(29)   [John]$_F$ was betrayed by the woman he loved.
(13)   The woman he loved betrayed [John]$_F$.

---

[3]   In fact, it is probably not entirely impossible, in context, to interpret *he* in (13) as "John," but that can be considered a case of accidental coreference rather than real anaphora (variable binding).

(30) 'the x s.t. the woman x loved betrayed x is John.'
(29') [John]ᵢ [s _ᵢ was betrayed by the woman heᵢ loved]
(13') [John]ᵢ [s the woman heᵢ loved betrayed _ᵢ]

However, note that this state of affairs does not force the conclusion that foci must get scoped out of their clauses. One can argue instead that the NP *John* has to be scoped out not because of the fact that it is focused, but rather because scoping it out is the only possible way of getting the "bound variable" reading. Indeed, Rooth 1985 argues that the most straightforward combination of his (in situ) theory of focus interpretation with standard semantics for variable binding entails that a true "bound variable" reading requires scoping out.[4]

Rooth 1985 notes that the "weak crossover" effect can be replicated in examples where *only* associates with focus. For instance, (31), but not (32) has the "bound variable" reading in (33).

(31) We only expect [John]_F to be betrayed by the woman he loves.
(32) We only expect the woman he loves to betray [John]_F.
(33) 'The only x s.t. we expect the woman x loves to betray x is John.'

The scope theory of focus could attribute this fact to the prohibited "crossover configuration" which results when the focus becomes the argument of *only* at LF, as shown in (32').

(32') We only [John]_Fi expect [s the woman heᵢ loves to betray _ᵢ]

However, Rooth shows that such an explanation is not necessary. He shows that the same fact could be explained by the assumption that *John* would have to be scoped

---

[4] Let us take (i) as a simple example. Suppose *him* in (i) is **not** scoped out. Assuming that we may coindex the two pronouns and hence translate them as occurrences of the same variable, we can get a logical translation along the lines of (ii). This does give us an anaphoric reading. However, note that the focus semantic value of the sentence is now as in (iii), which means that the sentence addresses the question "who is a y s.t. the woman x loved betrayed y?".

(i) The woman he loved betrayed [him]_F.
(ii) (the woman x loved) (betrayed (x_F))
$\langle\langle e,t\rangle,t\rangle$ $\langle e,\langle e,t\rangle\rangle$ e
(iii) $[\![$(the woman x loved)(betrayed(x_F))$]\!]^{f\text{-}g}$ = {$[\![$(the woman x loved)(betrayed(y))$]\!]^{g'}$ : g' is identical to g except that it may assign a different value to y}

Suppose, in contrast, that *him* in (i) **is** scoped out. Then, assuming again that we may coindex the two pronouns and hence translate them as occurrences of the same variable, we can get, by standard "quantifying-in," a logical translation along the lines of (iv), which reduces to (v). In this case, the focus semantic value of our sentence is as in (vi), which means that the sentence addresses the question "who is a y s.t. y was betrayed by the woman y loved?".

(iv) $[\lambda X[X(x)]]_F$ $(\lambda x[$(the woman x loved)(betrayed(x))$])$
(v) $\lambda x[$(the woman x loved)(betrayed(x))$]$ $(x_F)$
(vi) $[\]\!]^f$ = {$[\]\!]^g$ : g assignment}

out of its clause in order to produce the "bound variable" reading. In the case of (32), such scoping out is prohibited due to the "crossover configuration" shown in (32″).

(32″)  We only expect [John]ᵢ [ₛthe woman heᵢ loves to betray __ᵢ]

We may conclude that "crossover" effects do not provide valid evidence that foci must be raised out of their clause at LF.

### 19.2.3  Absence of Island Effects

It seems that in general, foci do not exhibit sensitivity to islands. For instance, consider the following examples, from Rooth 1996. The underlined quantifiers in (34)–(36) cannot take scope outside the NP in which they are embedded. In contrast, the focused NP in (37) or (38) is perfectly capable of associating with the adverb *only* occurring outside its containing NP. Similarly, (39)–(40) contrast with (41)–(42).

(34)  Dr. Svenson rejected [ₙₚthe proposal that <u>no student</u> submitted]
(35)  Dr. Svenson rejected [ₙₚthe proposal that <u>exactly one student</u> submitted]
(36)  Dr. Svenson rejected [ₙₚthe proposal that <u>almost every student</u> submitted]
(37)  Dr. Svenson only rejected [ₙₚthe proposal that [John]_F submitted]
(38)  Dr. Svenson rejected only [ₙₚthe proposal that [John]_F submitted]
(39)  Dr. Svenson will complain if <u>exactly one lab assistant</u> doesn't finish his job.
(40)  Dr. Svenson complains when <u>almost every lab assistant</u> leaves the lights on.
(41)  Dr. Svenson will only complain if [Bill]_F doesn't finish his job.
(42)  Dr. Svenson only complains when [Bill]_F leaves the lights on.

Rooth 1985 sees the island insensitivity of foci as evidence for a theory where foci are interpreted in situ, and against a theory where foci are assigned scope at LF. Rooth 1996, however, notes a number of considerations that suggest that this evidence is inconclusive.

One consideration is that there seem to be various scope-bearing operators that do exhibit insensitivity to islands – in particular, indefinites and in-situ wh-words. For instance, Rooth 1996 notes that the underlined NP in (43) can take scope outside the containing NP, and the underlined *who* in (44) is semantically interpreted at the level of the wh-complement of *tell*.

(43)  Dr. Svenson usually rejects [ₙₚthe first three proposals that <u>a student</u> submits]
(44)  Tell me who rejected [ₙₚthe proposal that <u>who</u> submitted]

Rooth suggests that we should aim at a theory that uniformly explains insensitivity to islands, for all island-insensitive operators.

Another consideration is that even if foci do get scoped out, it may be possible to analyze sentences like (37), (38), (41) and (42) above in such a way that island constraints would turn out not to be violated after all. Rooth notes in particular the analysis of Steedman 1991, which succeeds in "bridging" the scope island.

I will not get into details of Steedman's analysis here. Note, however, that Steedman's analysis relies on a "nested foci" configuration as in (45).

(45)   Dr. Svenson only rejected [$_{NP}$ the proposal [that [John]$_F$ submitted]$_F$]

I would like to suggest that one way of looking at this "nesting" is as follows. Why not say that the ordinary focal structure of this sentence, as it is presumably meant to be pronounced, i.e. with a single pitch accent on *John*, is with focus not on *John* but rather on the entire relative clause. The word *submitted* does not carry a pitch accent because it is relatively "expected" – it is much as if the sentence said *John's proposal*. This analysis fits with the intuition that (45) seems to constitute a felicitous answer to the question "Which proposal did Dr. Svenson reject?" The "nested" focus is in fact unnecessary (and the inner F-feature should be eliminated). Besides that, is narrow focus on *John* also a possibility? I am not sure there is anything that forces us to accept that. Even given an explicit contrast as in (46), it could be claimed that the island configuration forces our speakers to focus the whole relative clause. How could such a claim be refuted?

(46)   A:   Dr. Svenson only rejected the proposal that John submitted

                                                                   pa

       B:   No, Dr. Svenson only rejected the proposal that Bill submitted

                                                                   pa

If we do want to insist that narrow focus on *John* **is** possible in our example, I agree with Rooth that that should have to be linked to the distribution of in-situ wh-words. One may wonder if that in turn should not be linked to the notion of an "echo" question, and hence to some sort of metalinguistic questioning or focusing.

I would conclude, with Rooth 1996, that it is not clear that a theory that scopes foci out can be refuted on the basis of island insensitivity.

## 19.3   Do Foci Take Wide Scope? (Part 1)

If we were to observe that focused NPs invariably take scope over all other operators in their sentence, that would of course strongly support a theory on which focused NPs are invariably raised (to the matrix sentence level) and quantified in. The empirical fact, however, is, most definitely, that foci need not take wide scope. I believe that that is at present quite widely acknowledged.

Nonetheless, it seems to me that some discussion might be in order here. For one thing, suggestions have been made in the literature (be they more or less in earnest) to the effect that constituents which are "the focus" or "the answer to the question" do, empirically, take wide scope.[5] Secondly, it might be worthwhile to clarify a few points concerning the relation between prosody, focal structure, scope, and context. Finally, prosodic or focal structure may sometimes **bias** scope relations, and in special cases even disambiguate them entirely; when and why this happens is a worthwhile area of investigation.

---

[5]   Most notably, in Jackendoff 1972's discussion of his "dependent" and "independent" foci (his section 8.6). See also Groenendijk and Stokhof 1984, where the (short) answer gets quantified into the question, receiving wide scope; see rule p. 290 and footnote 26, pp. 402–3.

Jackendoff 1972 suggests that prosody, via the information that it carries regarding focal structure, disambiguates scope relations. He offers some intriguing examples and interesting discussion. And yet, as a general rule, prosody alone does not disambiguate scope relations. I see the relation between prosody, focus and scope as sketched in the following paragraph. (This or a similar view can be found in Gussenhoven 1983; Lauri Carlson 1984; Ward and Hirschberg 1985; Kadmon and Roberts 1986.)

As with any other kind of ambiguity, context plays a crucial rule in resolving scope ambiguities. Now, prosody does carry information about the context of utterance. (This includes important clues to the choice of focus (as discussed in chapter 13), and hence to what the current QUD (question under discussion) might be, plus various other clues to the organization of the discourse.) Via this information, prosody may indeed help us effect disambiguation of scope relations. Whenever we are not actually presented with sufficient preceding context to disambiguate a given example, we may use prosodic clues to figure out what the context might be like, and in that way to guess at what the intended reading might be. At the same time, prosody generally only gives us partial information about the context, and so it generally only gives us partial information about what the intended reading might be.

In this section, I will mainly consider the scope interactions between focus and negation. I will concentrate on examples with a single intonation phrase, ending in a declarative fall, and containing a single focus.

According to Jackendoff 1972, section 8.6, the prosody of the following examples determines not only that the focus is as marked, but also that this focus takes wide scope over the negation.

(47)  [All]$_F$ the men didn't go.
　　　H*　　　　　L　　L%　　　　　　　(adapted from Jackendoff's (8.160), p. 352)
(48)  He doesn't hate [most]$_F$ of the songs.
　　　　　　　　　　　H*　　　　L　L%　　(Kadmon & Roberts 1986; cf. Jackendoff's
　　　　　　　　　　　　　　　　　　　　　　　　　　　　　　(8.182), p. 357)

Of course, our "hard facts" include the intonation contours but not the F-markings, so consider the example in (49).

(49)  He doesn't hate most of the songs.
　　　　　　　　　　H*　　　L　L%

In Kadmon and Roberts 1986, we show that this example is in fact ambiguous: we note that while in dialog (50) the determiner does take wide scope over the negation, in dialog (51) the determiner takes narrow scope under the negation.[6] (Capitals indicate major prosodic prominence.)

---

[6]　If there are exactly 100 songs involved, and of those "he" hates exactly 50, then (49) in (50) is false (only half are not hated by him), while (49) in (51) is true (only half are hated by him).

(50) Nirit: Well, he hates the last three songs I played. What songs DOESN'T he hate?

Craige: He doesn't hate MOST of the songs.              MOST¬
              H*          L   L%

(51) Nirit: He likes 'Smooth Operator,' but MOST of the 'Top 40' things he HATES, right?

Craige: No.

Nirit: What do you mean 'no'? He always has some disparaging remarks to make about them.

Craige: OK, so he hates MANY of the songs. All I said was he doesn't hate MOST of the songs.              ¬MOST
         H*         L   L%

(52) is another example. Its ambiguity is illustrated in (53) and (54).

(52) It didn't start three times
            H* H*L L%

(53) A: This car is in terrible shape. I can't start it now.

B: Do you have this problem often?

A: In the last week or so, it didn't start three times            3¬
                H* H*L L%

(54) A: You must get a new car. How often did you manage to even start this one this winter?

B: To be honest? This whole winter, it didn't start three times       ¬3
                H* H*L L%

The immediate conclusion is that prosody doesn't disambiguate scope relations. Now it seems that in the given dialogs, the focus of (49) is unambiguously on *most* and the focus of (52) is unambiguously on *three times*. Therefore, we may also conclude that the choice of focus does not disambiguate scope relations.

This last conclusion should come as no surprise. Certainly, a sentence can have two readings which share the same choice of focus. Consider, for instance, example (48), where the focus is fixed. Surely, (48) has two possible translations along the lines of (55a) and (55b).[7] Indeed, to get the correct predictions, we must assume that in dialog (50) it has the reading indicated by (55a), whereas in dialog (51) it has the reading indicated by (55b).

(55) a. $[most]_F(song) (\lambda x[\neg hate(x)(he)])$

b. $\neg (HATE([most]_F(song)) (he))$

The two corresponding focus semantic values are given in (56). (I abbreviate $v_{1,\langle\langle e,t\rangle,\langle\langle e,t\rangle,t\rangle\rangle}$ as $v_{Det}$.)

---

[7] *he* is treated here as a constant of type e, for simplicity. *HATE* is a type-shifted version of *hate*, of type $\langle\langle\langle e,t\rangle,t\rangle, \langle e,t\rangle\rangle$, and equivalent to $\lambda v_{1,\langle\langle e,t\rangle,t\rangle}[\lambda y[v_{1,\langle\langle e,t\rangle,t\rangle}(\lambda x[hate(x)(y)])]]$.
*most(song)* is a generalized quantifier equivalent to
    $\lambda X[|\{x : song(x) \wedge X(x)\}| > |\{x : song(x) \wedge \neg X(x)\}|]$.

(56)  a.  {[[v_{Det}(song)(λx[¬hate(x)(he)])]]^g : g assignment}
     b.  {[[¬(HATE(v_{Det}(song))(he))]]^g : g assignment}

Obviously, the disambiguation of scope relations must rely on the context, as already suggested above. In Kadmon and Roberts 1986, we consider dialogs (50) and (51) in some detail, in order to argue that in each of the two dialogs, the desired reading of (49) is genuinely recoverable from the context of utterance. Let us take a look at this contextual disambiguation.

The prosody of (49) merely tells us that *most* is the focus, so that one of the readings in (55) must be intended (but without telling us which one), and therefore that the last QUD (à la Roberts 1996b) must be either (56a) or (56b) (again without telling us which one).[8] To figure out the intended reading, one must use further clues from the preceding discourse.

In dialog (50), Nirit's utterance makes it clear that Nirit is concerned with sets of songs that "he" does hate vs. sets of songs that "he" doesn't hate. Therefore, Nirit's explicit question is taken to concern the property of "not being hated by him," viz. [[λx[¬hate(x)(he)]]]. Thus, Nirit's question is determined to be the one in (56a). This question then is taken to be the question addressed by Craige when she utters (49). Which means that (56a) is taken to be the focus semantic value of (49). Therefore, (49) is determined to have the reading indicated in (55a).

In dialog (51), the context of (49) is somewhat more complex. No question which (49) could address has actually been uttered, so the last QUD of (49) is implicit, and one must figure it out.

In her first utterance, Nirit asks for confirmation of the proposition that "he" hates most of the "Top 40" songs, the proposition denoted by (57). Craige denies this proposition, i.e. her "No" means (58).

(57)  HATE(most(song)) (he)
(58)  ¬ (HATE(most(song)) (he))

Later, Craige says *he hates MANY of the songs*. The prosody alone strongly suggests that the focus semantic value of this sentence is as in (59) below. This hypothesized focus semantic value is supported by its evident relevance to preceding discourse: Nirit's previous utterance made it clear that she understood Craige to be taking issue with "hating" rather than with "most," and Craige is now correcting this impression by addressing the question of the correct determiner.

(59)  {[[HATE(v_{Det}(song))(he)]]^g : g assignment}

Now the hearer is in a position to recover the question addressed by (49). Two relevant things are now salient in the discourse. First, there is the question in (59), which

---

[8]  In other words, the last QUD is "how many songs doesn't he hate?", but that's ambiguous between (i) and (ii).

    (i)  'For what quantity/proportion is it the case that that many songs are not hated by him?'
    (ii)  'For what quantity/proportion is it not the case that that many songs are hated by him?'

has just been addressed, which concerns the value of the determiner. Secondly, the opening *All I said was* refers back to Craige's denial of a positive assertion, the proposition indicated in (58). The hearer can construct an appropriate implicit QUD on the basis of the denial in (58), by questioning the value of the determiner (in that denial), as suggested by (59). The question constructed in this way is the one in (60).

(60)  $\{[\![\neg(\text{HATE}(v_{\text{Det}}(\text{song}))(\text{he}))]\!]^g : g \text{ assignment}\}$

And that in turn means that (49) is interpreted as indicated in (55b).

A remaining question is, why does prosody often create a bias in favor of one of the possible readings, in the sense that it makes that reading more prominent "out of the blue"?

Note, first, that surely various elements in the prosody, syntax, semantics and pragmatics of various utterances contribute to creating a bias of this kind, and hence it may be difficult at times to isolate the effect of prosody. Secondly, I should think that various elements in the prosody itself contribute to creating such a bias, and that they make their contributions in various ways. But I also have a specific hypothesis to mention.

As already noted above, I take it that when we lack sufficient actual context to disambiguate a given utterance – which is certainly the case when the example is presented completely out of the blue – we use prosodic clues to figure out what the context might be like, and in that way to guess at what the intended reading might be. And yet, as illustrated above, a certain prosodic pattern may well be consistent with contexts of various forms and structures. In Kadmon and Roberts 1986, we propose that given an utterance presented out of context, the hearer is more likely to imagine a simpler rather than a more complex context of utterance, and therefore the reading associated with the simpler context becomes the prominent one.

I believe that our proposal does indeed point to a central factor at work in making some readings more prominent than others. We haven't defined what it takes for a context to count as "simpler." But I think you will agree, intuitively, that the context in (50) is simpler than the context in (51). That, we claim, is what favors the MOST¬ reading of example (49).

To get the MOST¬ reading of (49), the hearer has to imagine a context such as (50), in which a question about "not hating" has been posed. To get the ¬MOST reading, the hearer has to imagine a context such as (51), in which two different things have happened: posing a question about "hating," and denying a proposition which constitutes a possible answer to such a question. If you like – even though that is not reflected in the logical formula (56b) – the question addressed by Craige when uttering (49) in (51) might be described as in (61), from Kadmon and Roberts 1986, and that is a relatively complicated question to address.

(61)   'What was the determiner that I denied was the proper answer to the question of how many songs he hates?'

I would add that besides the matter of "simplicity," hearers are also more likely to imagine contexts that – in the world as they know it – are relatively common or pragmatically plausible. Take for instance the case of example (52). I think that one factor that favors the 3¬ reading here is that one is more likely to count occasions where a car fails to start than occasions where a car does start. This factor is I think independent of prosody.

Let me end this section with an example which shows that a focused NP does not necessarily take scope over an unfocused NP. (Intended prosody: single intonation phrase ending in a declarative fall, all pitch accents marked.)

(62) Two Israelis won [three tennis contests]$_F$.

    pa   pa     pa

I believe that (62) has all of the following three readings.

(63)  a.  cumulative reading
          'two Israelis won three tennis contests between them'
      b.  distributive reading with *two Israelis* taking wide scope
          'two Israelis each won three tennis contests'
      c.  distributive reading with *three tennis contests* taking wide scope
          'three tennis contests were each won by two Israelis'

Of course, (62) is only felicitous in contexts appropriate to its focal structure. For instance, in (64). I think that in (64) the two pieces of news are both completely ambiguous in the way indicated in (63).

(64)  Nirit [impressed, holding a newspaper]:
          I see that two Palestinian writers got the three most important literary
          prizes.
      Ali:   Yes, I noticed. There was also something about two Israelis being victo-
             rious lately, wasn't there?
      Nirit: Yes, two Israelis won [three tennis contests]$_F$.

# 20

# *Complex Focal Structures with "Contrastive Topics"*

## 20.1  TOPIC-Focus and FOCUS-Focus

Jackendoff 1972, section 6.7, identifies and discusses a systematic pattern in the way intonation contours are used in dialogs like the following.

(1)  A:  I know who Bill kissed, but what about Larry? Who did Larry kiss?
B:       Larry      kissed     Nina.
     (L+)H* L H%      (L+)H* L L%

(2)  A:  I know who kissed Mary, but what about Nina? Who kissed Nina?
B:       Larry      kissed     Nina.
     (L+)H* L (L%)     (L+)H* L H%

(3)  A:  I know who Larry hugged, but what about kissing? Who did Larry kiss?
B:  He     kissed         Nina.
    (L+)H* L H%   (L+)H* L L%

(4)  A:  I know how Larry greeted Mary – he hugged her. But what about Nina? What
     did Larry do with Nina?
B:  He     kissed         Nina.
    (L+)H* L (L%)   (L+)H* L H%

Needless to say, Jackendoff does not offer the above transcriptions of intonation. It seems clear from his discussion though that pitch accents are placed as marked (I think these can be either H* or L + H*), and that B's utterance is divided into two prosodic phrases (two intonation phrases, or at least two intermediate phrases), of which one ends in a fall in pitch and the other ends in a rise.[1]

Note that in (1B) and (3B) we have the rising melody followed by the falling melody, whereas in (2B) and (4B) we have the falling melody followed by the rising melody. Further, this must be so: switching answers around (to form the sequences (2A) + (1B), (1A) + (2B), (3A) + (4B) and (4A) + (3B)) results in infelicity.

---

[1]  Jackendoff identifies the falling and rising melodies involved with the "A accent" and "B accent" of Bolinger 1965, respectively.

Jackendoff 1972 provides the following account. First of all, the accented words in (1B)–(4B) are all foci. Each B utterance, then, contains two foci. Which in turn means that its ps skeleton contains two variables. For instance, the ps skeleton of both (1B) and (2B) is as in (5).

(5)    x kissed y

Jackendoff assumes that the focus-induced interpretations are derived in the usual way, i.e. by substituting into or $\lambda$-abstracting over the positions of the two variables simultaneously. Hence (1B) and (2B), for instance, are both taken to make the assertion in (6).

(6)    $\langle$Larry, Nina$\rangle \in \{\langle d_1, d_2\rangle : d_1$ kissed $d_2\}$

Secondly, Jackendoff holds that in the examples under consideration, the two foci differ in their status, and that the intonation unambiguously indicates the status of each focus. Take for instance (1B). Assuming the ps skeleton in (5), Jackendoff notes that the value of x is "chosen first," while the value of y is "chosen second," to match it: the first focus indicates a choice to address a question concerning Larry (rather than someone else), the second focus indicates that "Mary" is intended to be a true answer to that chosen question. The value of y is thus dependent on the previously picked value of x. So Jackendoff calls the focus on *Larry* the "independent variable" and the focus on *Nina* the "dependent variable." The situation in (2B) is obviously reversed: the focus on *Nina* is the "independent" one, while the focus on *Larry* is "dependent." Jackendoff states that the rising melody is unambiguously associated with the "independent" focus, while the falling melody is unambiguously associated with the "dependent" focus. This generalization covers the pattern observed in (1)–(4).

The element which Jackendoff calls the "independent" focus is often referred to elsewhere as a "(sentence) topic" or "contrastive topic." Jackendoff himself notes (p. 262) the connection to the traditional notions of "topic" and "comment." Consider example (7B) below. The "independent" focus is the subject NP *Larry* and the "dependent" focus is the VP *kissed Mary*. Thus, (7B) is exhaustively divided into its "independent" and "dependent" parts.

(7)    A:    I know what Bill did, but what about Larry? What did Larry do?
       B:        Larry              kissed       Nina.
           (L+)H* L H%  (L+)H*    (L+)H*L L%

What Jackendoff notes is that in examples that are exhaustively divided in this manner, the "independent" focus corresponds to the "topic" and the "dependent" focus corresponds to the "comment."

I agree with Jackendoff that prosodically-marked topics can sensibly be considered foci, and adopt the following terminology. I will call the "independent" (question-picking) focus the **TOPIC-focus**, and I will call the "dependent" (question-answering) focus the **FOCUS-focus**.[2] (Each term is to be pronounced as a compound, with main stress on the left hand word.)

---

[2]    Inspired by: *You bring the FRUIT salad, and I'll bring the SALAD salad.* (I am not sure who I got this example from – Larry Horn, perhaps.)

## 20.2   Recent Accounts

### 20.2.1   Roberts 1996b

Roberts 1996b (section 2.2.2.1) suggests that an account of the TOPIC-focus + FOCUS-focus configuration can be given within her theory of information structure and focus.

The pieces of discourse in (8)–(11) below can serve to illustrate what Roberts sees as the data to be accounted for. For ease of exposition, I will be marking the foci rather than the prosody; I assume that these foci are prosodically marked as outlined above. I mark the boundary between the two prosodic phrases with |. (8)–(11) are all felicitous; on the other hand, the focal structures under consideration cannot be switched around between the examples on the left and the examples on the right.

(8)   A:   I know who Bill kissed,
      but what about Larry?
      Who did Larry kiss?
   B:   $[Larry]_{TF}$ | kissed $[Nina]_{FF}$.

(9)   A:   I know who kissed Mary,
      but what about Nina?
      Who kissed Nina?
   B:   $[Larry]_{FF}$ | kissed $[Nina]_{TF}$.

(10)   A:   Who kissed who?
    B:   Well, who did Larry kiss?
    C:   $[Larry]_{TF}$ | kissed $[Nina]_{FF}$.
          (adapted from Roberts 1996b)

(11)   A:   Who kissed who?
    B:   Well, who kissed Nina?
    C:   $[Larry]_{FF}$ | kissed $[Nina]_{TF}$.

(12)   $[Larry]_{TF}$ | kissed $[Nina]_{FF}$.   (= (1B) above.)
(13)   Who did Larry kiss?
(14)   $[Larry]_{FF}$ | kissed $[Nina]_{TF}$.   (= (2B) above.)
(15)   Who kissed Nina?
(16)   Who kissed who?

Let us concentrate on (12) for a moment. It is intuitively clear that (12) can answer (13) but not (15). So Roberts aims to predict that (12) presupposes (13). But it also seems clear that (12) is closely linked to question (16). (I would say that the intuition is that (12) implies that (13) is being considered as a subquestion of (16).) Indeed, including (16) as part of (10) makes for a natural piece of discourse. Also, note that while (16) is not explicitly mentioned in (8), (8) does mention two different answers to (16) (that Bill kissed his kissee, and that Larry kissed Nina). Roberts therefore aims to also predict that (12) presupposes (16). (In fact, Roberts indicates that she would like to predict that (12) presupposes the fact that (13) is part of a "strategy of inquiry" aimed at answering (16).)

Roberts easily predicts that both (12) and (14) presuppose (16). Like Jackendoff 1972, Roberts assumes simultaneous substitution into the two focus positions. This makes the focus semantic value of both (12) and (14) as in (17) below. But that in turn automatically predicts, via the QUD constraint on focus, that the last QUD of both (12) and (14) is identical to (17), i.e. to the question expressed by (16).

(17)   $\{ [\![ kissed(x,y) ]\!]^{g} : g \text{ assignment} \}$   'Who kissed who?'

Predicting that (12) presupposes (13) – and similarly, that (14) presupposes (15) – is not quite as easy. Also like Jackendoff 1972, Roberts assumes that the rising and falling melodies determine the order in which the two values are filled in; the value corresponding to the TOPIC-focus is filled in first. Once the TOPIC-focus is filled in, we get two distinct subquestions of (17): in the case of (12), we get (18) (= the question expressed by (13)), and in the case of (14), we get (19) (= the question expressed by (15)).

(18)  $\{[\![kissed(l,y)]\!]^g : g \text{ assignment}\}$   'Who did Larry kiss?'
(19)  $\{[\![kissed(x,n)]\!]^g : g \text{ assignment}\}$   'Who kissed Nina?'

This is taken to explain the intuition that (12) presupposes (13) while (14) presupposes (15).

And yet, the official theory of Roberts 1996b (see 17.9 and 17.10 above) does not actually predict this intuition. Roberts suggests that a separate constraint on TOPIC-focus would have to be posited (in addition to the QUD constraint on focus) in order to make the desired prediction. (In fact, according to Roberts, the prediction that (12) presupposes a "strategy of inquiry" involving (13) while (14) presupposes a "strategy of inquiry" involving (15), but I won't get into that here.)

Roberts does not formulate the constraint she has in mind. Presumably, the only way of deriving the question to be presupposed is via making a substitution into the position of the FOCUS-focus only. So the constraint would have to be (or to include) more or less what is stated in (20).

(20)   Given an utterance B whose logical translation is the formula $\beta$, the QUD stack obtaining when B is uttered must contain the question identical to
the set of all ordinary semantic values obtained by replacing that subformula in $\beta$ which is marked as FOCUS-focus with a variable, and then interpreting the result relative to every assignment g.

Note, for a start, that (20) is actually a constraint on FOCUS-focus and not on TOPIC-focus. It seems quite strange to me that a constraint on FOCUS-focus should be imposed solely for the purpose of treating sentences that contain a TOPIC-focus.

Anyway, I think there is a problem. To force a question to be presupposed, we must presumably force it to be contained in the QUD stack, as I have done in (20). However, there is nowhere in the QUD stack where our question might be placed. Concentrating again on (12), (20) requires (18) (= $[\![(13)]\!]^o$) to be in the QUD stack obtaining when (12) is uttered. But (18) cannot be the last QUD of (12), since Roberts' theory determines that the last QUD of (12) is (17) (= $[\![(16)]\!]^o$). Nor can (18) precede (= be lower on the stack than) the last QUD of (12), viz. (17), due to the following reason. Given the general requirement that each move $\alpha$ in the discourse must be **directly relevant** to last(QUD($\alpha$)), we have that any question preceding (17) in the QUD stack must be a superquestion of (17). But (18) is **not** a superquestion of (17).

This seems to me to be a real problem. So long as we hold that the focus semantic value of (12) is obtained by simultaneous substitution into the two focus positions, and therefore that the last QUD of (12) is (17) (= $[\![(16)]\!]^o$), I don't see how (12) could be made to presuppose (18) (= $[\![(13)]\!]^o$). I therefore conclude that as far as I can see, Roberts has not really provided an account of the TOPIC-focus + FOCUS-focus configuration within her theory of information structure and focus.

Let me add that it seems strange to me to take (17) to be the last QUD of (12). I think the intuition is clear that the question which (12) addresses most directly is (18) (= [[(13)]]°) and not (17) (= [[(16)]]°).[3] I would therefore prefer to consider (18) the last QUD of (12).

To elaborate on this point a little, consider the dialogs in (21) and (22) below. I believe that while the prosody in (21) suggests the focal structure in (12), the prosody in (22) suggests the focal structure in (23), where the two foci are of the same status.

(21) A: Who kissed who?
    B:       Larry      kissed    Nina.
          (L+)H* L H%        (L+)H* L L%
(12) [Larry]$_{TF}$ | kissed [Nina]$_{FF}$.

(22) A: Who kissed who?
    B:       Larry      kissed     Nina.
          (L+)H*   (L)        (L+)H* L L%
(23) [Larry]$_{FF}$ ( | ) kissed [Nina]$_{FF}$.

Now the intuitions seem to me to be as follows. In (21), the question directly addressed by B is question (18) (= [[(13)]]°). I would say that B is not a truly direct answer to A's question, but rather offers a strategy of inquiry that aims to (eventually) answer A's question via answering question (18) first. In (22), on the other hand, it seems clear that B is a truly direct answer to A's question. Some evidence for the intuitions just reported comes from the following facts. (21B) fits well in dialogs (8) and (10) above, but would not fit in (24) below. On the other hand, (22B) does fit well in (24) below.

(24) A: I know that some boy kissed some girl, but I forget who the kids involved actually were. Who kissed who?
    B:       Larry    kissed   Nina.
       (L+)H*   (L)      (L+)H* L L%

## 20.2.2 Büring 1999

Büring 1999 develops a novel account of the TOPIC-focus + FOCUS-focus configuration. Büring presents a number of different types of dialogs which exhibit this configuration. He gives the examples in (25)–(27) below. I supply parallel examples in (28)–(30).

(25) A: Do you think Fritz would buy this suit?
    B: Well, [I]$_{TF}$ | certainly [wouldn't]$_{FF}$
(26) A: What did the popstars wear?
    B: The [female]$_{TF}$ popstars | wore [caftans]$_{FF}$.

---

[3] Cf. discussion of truly direct answers in 13.3 above.

(27)  A:  Did your wife kiss other men?
      B:  [My]$_{TF}$ wife | [didn't]$_{FF}$ kiss other men.

(28)  A:  Who did Bill kiss?
      B:  (I don't know.) [Larry]$_{TF}$ | kissed [Nina]$_{FF}$.
(29)  A:  Who did the boys kiss?
      B:  [Larry]$_{TF}$ | kissed [Nina]$_{FF}$.
(30)  A:  Who did Larry kiss?
      B:  [Larry]$_{TF}$ | kissed [Nina]$_{FF}$.

Büring notes the different uses B makes of the TOPIC-focus here. In (25) and (28), B turns the conversation from the person A was talking about to somebody else. In (26) and (29), B "narrows down" the topic of conversation. In (27) and (30), while B does answer A's question, he also indicates that he would like to address a different matter (in the case of (27), probably the matter of A's wife).

Büring also notes that in examples like (25) and (28), as well as examples like (26) and (29), the presence of a TOPIC-focus is crucial for the coherence of the discourse. For instance, dialogs (31) and (32) below, with no TOPIC-focus, are infelicitous. Note also that in (33) below, there is no implication that B wishes to discuss a different matter.

(31)  A:  Who did Bill kiss?
      B:  (I don't know.) #Larry kissed [Nina]$_{FF}$.
(32)  A:   Who did the boys kiss?
      B:  #Larry kissed [Nina]$_{FF}$.
(33)  A:  Who did Larry kiss?
      B:  Larry kissed [Nina]$_{FF}$.

We may now move on to Büring's theory. Büring does not consider what I call a TOPIC-focus a focus. That means that in (12), for instance, there is only one focus (that which I call the FOCUS-focus). Hence, the focus semantic value of (12) is something like the set in (34).

(12)  [Larry]$_{TF}$ | kissed [Nina]$_{FF}$.
(34)  {'Larry kissed Sue,' 'Larry kissed Mary,' 'Larry kissed Lisa,' . . .}

Büring posits a third type of semantic value in addition to the ordinary semantic value and focus semantic value: a topic semantic value. Büring specifies that a topic semantic value is a set of sets of propositions (= a set of questions). These sets of propositions are all just like the focus semantic value, except (perhaps) for the value filled in for the position of the TOPIC-focus. So the topic semantic value of (12) is something like (35). Which is equivalent to (36).

(35)  {{'Larry kissed Sue,' 'Larry kissed Mary,' 'Larry kissed Lisa,' . . .},
      {'Bill kissed Sue,' 'Bill kissed Mary,' 'Bill kissed Lisa,' . . .},
      {'John kissed Sue,' 'John kissed Mary,' 'John kissed Lisa,' . . .}, . . .}
(36)  {'Who did Larry kiss?', 'Who did Bill kiss?', 'Who did John kiss?', . . .}

Büring specifies that the topic semantic value of a sentence that does not contain a TOPIC-focus is the singleton set containing its focus semantic value.

I suggest that Büring's values for (12) may be specified more precisely as follows.

(37)   $[\![(12)]\!]^f = \{[\![kiss(l,y)]\!]^g : g \text{ assignment}\}$

(38)   $[\![(12)]\!]^t = \{\{[\![kiss(x,y)]\!]^{g'} : g' \text{ is identical to } g \text{ except that it may assign a different value to } y\} : g \text{ assignment}\}$

In order to account for the facts of discourse congruence illustrated earlier in this subsection, Büring proposes the following principle.

(39)   **Büring's Principle of Question-Answer Congruence**
Statement A is a felicitous answer to question Q iff $[\![Q]\!]^\circ \in [\![A]\!]^t$.

(39) renders (28)–(30) and (33) felicitous and renders (31) and (32) infelicitous, as desired. That (28) and (30), repeated below, are predicted to be felicitous is obvious.

(28)   A:   Who did Bill kiss?
       B:   (I don't know.) [Larry]$_{\text{TF}}$ | kissed [Nina]$_{\text{FF}}$.
(30)   A:   Who did Larry kiss?
       B:   [Larry]$_{\text{TF}}$ | kissed [Nina]$_{\text{FF}}$.

(29) too is predicted to felicitous, assuming that possible values for the TOPIC-focus can be sums (plural individuals).

(29)   A:   Who did the boys kiss?
       B:   [Larry]$_{\text{TF}}$ | kissed [Nina]$_{\text{FF}}$.

(33) is felicitous because the topic semantic value of (33B) is a singleton set containing just the question expressed by (33A).

(33)   A:   Who did Larry kiss?
       B:   Larry kissed [Nina]$_{\text{FF}}$.

Finally, the reader can easily verify that (31) and (32), repeated below, are predicted to be infelicitous.

(31)   A:   Who did Bill kiss?
       B:   (I don't know.) #Larry kissed [Nina]$_{\text{FF}}$.
(32)   A:    Who did the boys kiss?
       B:   #Larry kissed [Nina]$_{\text{FF}}$.

One fact which so far remains unexplained is the intuition that (30) and (27) – but not (33) – imply that B would like to discuss another matter. To account for this fact, Büring stipulates the following.

(40)   A sentence S containing a TOPIC-focus carries the implicature that there is an element Q in $[\![S]\!]^t$ which is still disputable after S is uttered.

(30B) is now predicted to implicate that one of the questions in $[\![(30B)]\!]^t$, i.e. one of the questions of the "form" "who did d kiss?", for some $d \in D$, is still disputable after (30B) is uttered.

I think that the implicature observed in examples like (30) and (27) is weaker than what's stated in (40), heavily context dependent, and worthy of a Gricean explanation. I think that what (27) and (30) really implicate is that some element (i.e. question) in the topic semantic value of B's utterance is still to be considered after that utterance has been made – not necessarily because the answer to it is still disputable, but quite possibly because B wishes to remind A of that answer. I also think that the implicature that some element in $[\![S]\!]^t$ is still to be considered after S is uttered is not always present. Suppose that the only potential relevant kissers are Larry and Bill, and that we know that each of them kissed just one girl. In that case, (41) below is still felicitous, without (41C) implying that any member of $[\![(41C)]\!]^t$ is still to be considered. Two more examples where the implicature is not present are (42) and (43).

(41)  A:  Who kissed who?
      B:  (Let's see . . .) $[Larry]_{TF} | kissed [Nina]_{FF}$.
      C:  (Right, and) $[Bill]_{TF} | kissed [Sue]_{FF}$.
(42)  A:  Finally, who did $[Larry]_{FF}$ kiss?
      B:  $[Larry]_{TF} | kissed [Nina]_{FF}$.
(43)  A:  $[The majority]_{TF}$ of the men $| [didn't]_{FF}$ go.
      B:  Right, but $[a minority]_{TF} | [did]_{FF}$ go.

But this suggests that our implicature is a conversational implicature, in which case I think a Gricean argument should be demonstrated.

Let us now check how Büring's theory fares with the intuition, discussed by Roberts, that (12) presupposes both (13) and (16).

(12)  $[Larry]_{TF} | kissed [Nina]_{FF}$.
(13)  Who did Larry kiss?
(16)  Who kissed who?

Büring's principle (39) predicts that (12) should be a felicitous answer to (13). But not only to (13). (12) is also predicted to be a felicitous answer to (28A) and to (29A), for instance.

(28A)  Who did Bill kiss?
(29A)  Who did the boys kiss?

So on Büring's theory, (12) does not presuppose that it is answering (13). What it does presuppose is that it is answering one of the questions in $[\![(12)]\!]^t$, i.e. one of the questions of the "form" "who did d kiss?", for some $d \in D$. I am not quite happy with this prediction. My intuition is that (12) is much more closely related to (13) than to (28A) or (29A) – I think the only one of these three questions that (12) truly answers directly is (13). This intuition is not explained by Büring's theory.

As for (16), principle (39) certainly does not predict that (12) should presuppose it. $[\![(16)]\!]^o$ is not a member of $[\![(12)]\!]^t$, so (12) is not predicted to be a felicitous answer to (16).

That seems to me to be a problem. It means that Büring's theory fails to predict that (44) below is felicitous. But (44) certainly is felicitous, and no less so than (28)–(30) are.

(44)   A:   Who kissed who?
        B:   (Well, let's see . . .) [Larry]$_{TF}$ | kissed [Nina]$_{FF}$.

## 20.3   My Account

As indicated above, I feel that there are problems with each of the two accounts discussed in section 20.2. In this section, I would like to propose a new account of the TOPIC-focus + FOCUS-focus configuration, which will also involve a new analysis of focal structure in questions.

I adopt the general framework of Roberts 1996b, in the slightly simplified form presented in section 17.9. (Though I will somewhat enrich the representation of moves in the discourse.) I believe that focal structure should indeed be treated in terms of the relation between an utterance and its last QUD, as proposed by Roberts. In fact, I adopt Roberts' QUD constraint on focus, although I use it as a constraint on FOCUS-focus only. Departing from Roberts' theory, I believe that the TOPIC-focus + FOCUS-focus configuration should be formally linked to a set of sets of propositions (= a set of questions), as proposed in Büring 1999. In fact, I adopt Büring's characterization of topic semantic values.

I will propose a new constraint on TOPIC-focus. Adding my constraint will yield a theory on which just as an utterance presupposes that its focus semantic values is identical to its last QUD, an utterance also presupposes that its topic semantic value is identical to the focus semantic value of its last QUD. In addition, I will define focus semantic values of questions (rather than only of the scope of ?[$\phi$], as in Roberts 1996b), and argue that substitution into the positions of wh-words should not be part of the process of deriving focus semantic values.

My current theory of focal structure consists of (A)–(E) below. Examples and discussion will follow.

(A)   At LF and in the logic, a TOPIC-focus is marked with the feature TF, and a FOCUS-focus is marked with the feature FF.

(B)   Phonologically, both the TOPIC-focus constituent and the FOCUS-focus constituent are identified as discussed in chapter 13. In addition, TOPIC-focus is indicated by phonological phrasing and a rising melody, as illustrated in 20.1 above.

(C)   I assume that in addition to ordinary variables, the syntax of our logic contains FF-marked variables and TF-marked variables, and that each assignment function separately assigns values to the plain, FF-marked and TF-marked variables. (Cf. 14.5.4 above.)

(D)   Focus semantic values and topic semantic values are derived as follows. Let $\beta$ be an arbitrary expression of the form $\phi$ or ?[$\phi$], where $\phi$ is a formula. Let M be an arbitrary model, and g an arbitrary assignment function.

(D-1)   $[\![\beta]\!]^{f\text{-}M,g}$, the **focus semantic value** of $\beta$ relative to M and g, is the set of all ordinary semantic values that are obtainable by steps (1) and (2).

1. Replace each FF-marked subformula in $\beta$ with a distinct FF-marked variable matching that subformula in type.
2. Interpret the result of (1) relative to some assignment g′ which is identical to g except that it may assign different values to the FF-marked variables.

(D-2) $[\![\beta]\!]^{t\text{-}M,g}$, the **topic semantic value** of $\beta$ relative to M and g, is the set of all those sets of ordinary semantic values that are obtainable by steps (1), (3) and (4).

3. In the result of step (1), replace the TF-marked subformula with a TF-marked variable matching it in type.
4. For each assignment g′ which is identical to g except that it may assign a different value to the TF-marked variable, form the set of ordinary semantic values obtainable by interpreting the result of step (3) relative to all assignments g″ s.t. g″ is identical to g′ except that it may assign different values to the FF-marked variables.

(E) Alterations of the theory of discourse moves and direct relevance:

(E-1) A **move** in the discourse is an ordered pair whose first member is an ordinary semantic value (a proposition or a question) and whose second member is a focus semantic value (a set of propositions or a set of questions). The move corresponding to a logical expression $\beta$ is $\langle[\![\beta]\!]^\circ, [\![\beta]\!]^f\rangle$.

Default principle: In the absence of other information, the second member of the move corresponding to a logical expression $\beta$ will be assumed to be the entire set of ordinary semantic values of the type of $\beta$.

(E-2) Given two moves in the discourse A and B, A counts as a **subquestion** of B only if the second member of A is a subset of the second member of B.

(F) The focal structure of an utterance imposes the following constraints.

(F-1) **The Question-Under-Discussion constraint on FOCUS-focus**
An utterance B whose logical translation is $\beta$ – where $\beta$ is of the form $\phi$ or ?[$\phi$], where $\phi$ is a formula – is felicitous only if
$[\![\beta]\!]^f$ = the first member of last(QUD($\langle[\![\beta]\!]^\circ,[\![\beta]\!]^f\rangle$)).

(F-2) **The Question-Under-Discussion constraint on TOPIC-focus**
An utterance B whose logical translation is $\beta$ – where $\beta$ is of the form $\phi$ or ?[$\phi$], where $\phi$ is a formula, and $\beta$ contains a TF-marked subformula – is felicitous only if
$[\![\beta]\!]^t$ = the second member of last(QUD($\langle[\![\beta]\!]^\circ,[\![\beta]\!]^f\rangle$)).

Consider the definition of focus semantic values in (D-1) above. Note first that according to (D-1), there is no simultaneous substitution into the TOPIC-focus and FOCUS-focus positions. Instead, focus semantic values are derived by substitution into the FOCUS-focus position(s) only. For example, the focus semantic value of both (45) and (12) is the set in (46). (Here I am in agreement with Büring.)

(45) Larry kissed [Nina]$_{FF}$.
(12) [Larry]$_{TF}$ | kissed [Nina]$_{FF}$.
(46) $\{[\![\text{kiss}(l,y)]\!]^g : g \text{ assignment}\}$

This position immediately succeeds in making a prediction that was problematic on Roberts' theory, viz. that (12) presupposes (13).

(13)   Who did Larry kiss?

Given that $[\![(12)]\!]^f = (46)$, Roberts' QUD constraint on focus, which I adopt, determines that the last QUD of (12) is (46).[4] But (46) is the ordinary denotation of (13). Hence, we predict that (12) presupposes (13), as desired. Indeed, we predict that (12) is a truly direct answer to (13), which nicely matches my own intuition about the facts. Further, we capture the similarity between (45) and (12), both of which supply the answer "Nina" to question (13).

Next, note the application of (D-1) to questions. (D-1) defines focus semantic values not only for formulas, but also for questions. It dictates substitution into the FOCUS-focus positions only, and not into the wh-word positions. Consequently, on my theory, a question has its own focus semantic value, and that value is a set of questions derived by substitution into the focus position(s). For example, the focus semantic value of (47) is defined as the set in (48). (48) is a set of sets of propositions of the sort indicated by (35), i.e. a set of questions of the sort indicated by (36).

(47)   Who did [Larry]$_{FF}$ kiss?
(48)   $\{\{[\![kiss(x,y)]\!]^{g'} : g'$ is identical to g except that it may assign a different value to y$\}$ : g assignment$\}$
(35)   $\{\{$'Larry kissed Sue,' 'Larry kissed Mary,' 'Larry kissed Lisa,' . . .$\}$,
       $\{$'Bill kissed Sue,' 'Bill kissed Mary,' 'Bill kissed Lisa,' . . .$\}$,
       $\{$'John kissed Sue,' 'John kissed Mary,' 'John kissed Lisa,' . . .$\}$, . . .$\}$
(36)   $\{$'Who did Larry kiss?', 'Who did Bill kiss?', 'Who did John kiss?', . . .$\}$

I believe that this treatment of foci in questions yields an insightful overall view of focus, as it captures the intuitive use of foci in questions and makes for a uniform conception of the role of focus in declarative and interrogative utterances.

I think that intuitively, the focus on *Larry* in (47) signals that the speaker is choosing the question "who did Larry kiss?" out of a set of alternative questions. Further, I think that the relevant alternative questions are understood to be precisely the questions of the "form" "who did d kiss?" (for some d ∈ D), viz. the members of (48).

Given my treatment of foci in questions, FOCUS-focus in general can be characterized as "the last element to be filled in." In the case of a declarative utterance, filling in the FOCUS-focus determines a choice of **proposition** from among all members of the focus semantic value, which are in this case propositions. (These members are identical to the possible answers to the last QUD, and that is why the FOCUS-focus of a declarative can be described as "the answer to the question being addressed".) In the case of an interrogative utterance, filling in the FOCUS-focus determines a choice of **question** from among all members of the focus semantic value, which are in this case questions.

---

[4]   Or, using my formulation of Roberts' constraint in (F-1) above, that the "ordinary" member of the last QUD of (12) is (46).

Let us now move on to the analysis of TOPIC-focus. Consider the definition of topic semantic values in (D-2). (D-2) is intended to derive precisely the topic semantic value characterized by Büring. For example, it determines that the topic semantic value of (12) is the set in (48). As already noted above, (48) is a set of sets of propositions (= a set of questions), of the kind indicated by (35) and (36).

(12)   [Larry]$_{TF}$ | kissed [Nina]$_{FF}$.
(48)   {{[[kiss(x,y)]]$^{g'}$ : g' is identical to g except that it may assign a different value to y} : g assignment}
(35)   {{'Larry kissed Sue,' 'Larry kissed Mary,' 'Larry kissed Lisa,' ...},
        {'Bill kissed Sue,' 'Bill kissed Mary,' 'Bill kissed Lisa,' ...},
        {'John kissed Sue,' 'John kissed Mary,' 'John kissed Lisa,' ...}, ...}
(36)   {'Who did Larry kiss?', 'Who did Bill kiss?', 'Who did John kiss?', ...}

Adopting Büring's position regarding topic semantic values immediately accounts for the fact that (12) draws attention to alternative questions like "Who did Larry kiss?", "who did Bill kiss?", "Who did John kiss?", etc., a fact that Roberts' theory does not explain.

Next, consider the QUD constraint on TOPIC-focus in (F-2) above. (F-2) formulates the central idea that I wish to bring into the theory of TOPIC-focus. The idea is that just as an utterance presupposes that its focus semantic value is identical to (the ordinary denotation of) its last QUD, an utterance also presupposes that its topic semantic value is identical to the focus semantic value of its last QUD.

This idea requires, of course, the assumption that a discourse move doesn't merely consist of a denotation, but also has a focal structure. Hence the definition of moves as ordered pairs given in (E-1).

My QUD constraint on TOPIC-focus predicts that (12) does not simply presuppose (13), but rather presupposes (13) with focus on *Larry*. In other words, I predict that (12) presupposes (47).

(12)   [Larry]$_{TF}$ | kissed [Nina]$_{FF}$.
(13)   Who did Larry kiss?
(47)   Who did [Larry]$_{FF}$ kiss?

To see how this prediction is made, note that the QUD constraint on FOCUS-focus in (F-1) determines that the "ordinary" member of the last QUD of (12) is [[(12)]]$^f$, i.e. (46), and that the QUD constraint on TOPIC-focus in (F-2) determines that the "focus" member of the last QUD of (12) is [[(12)]]$^t$, i.e. (48).

(46)   {[[kiss(l,y)]]$^g$ : g assignment}
(48)   {{[[kiss(x,y)]]$^{g'}$ : g' is identical to g except that it may assign a different value to y} : g assignment}

Hence, the last QUD of (12) is ⟨(46), (48)⟩. But ⟨(46), (48)⟩ is none other than the move corresponding to (47): (46) – obviously – is the denotation of (47), and (48) – as already discussed above – is the focus semantic value of (47) as derived by definition (D-1).

The prediction that (12) presupposes (47) is, I believe, a desirable consequence of my theory. It matches my intuition about (12), and enables me to make some additional predictions.

I feel that intuitively, (12) does indeed presuppose (47). To see that this feeling is based on empirical fact and not just on my intuition as a theoretician, consider examples (8) and (10).

(8)   A:  I know who Bill kissed, but what about Larry? Who did Larry kiss?
      B:  [Larry]$_{TF}$ | kissed [Nina]$_{FF}$.
(10)  A:  Who kissed who?
      B:  Well, who did Larry kiss?
      C:  [Larry]$_{TF}$ | kissed [Nina]$_{FF}$.

(adapted from Roberts 1996b)

Clearly, in both examples, *Who did Larry kiss?* must have narrow focus on *Larry*. And these examples are no idiosyncratic curiosities; they illustrate typical contexts in which (12) may occur. Indeed, dialogs like (8) are often used in the literature to bring out the intended prosody of utterances containing TOPIC-focus.

Of course, (12) does not have to actually follow (47). But that's always the case with the question being addressed, since that question can be implicit in the discourse.

Next, I would like to point out that my theory predicts the fact that of the dialogs below, (49) is felicitous, while (50)–(52) are not. (The reader can verify this for herself.) Note that this prediction cannot be made on either Roberts' or Büring's theory.

(49)  A:  Who did [Larry]$_{FF}$ kiss?
      B:  [Larry]$_{TF}$ | kissed [Nina]$_{FF}$.
(50)  A:  Who did Larry [kiss]$_{FF}$?
      B:  #[Larry]$_{TF}$ | kissed [Nina]$_{FF}$.
(51)  A:  Who [did]$_{FF}$ Larry kiss?
      B:  #[Larry]$_{TF}$ | kissed [Nina]$_{FF}$.
(52)  A:  [Who]$_{FF}$ did Larry kiss?
      B:  #[Larry]$_{TF}$ | kissed [Nina]$_{FF}$.

In addition, I can account for the following contrast between (53) below and (49) above. As noted by Büring, (53B) implies that speaker B wishes to draw attention to one or more additional alternatives to A's question, viz. alternatives such as "Who did Bill kiss?". But (49B), in contrast, does not have such an implication (cf. 20.2.2 above). This contrast between (53) and (49) is not predicted by either Roberts' or Büring's theory.

(53)  A:  [Who did Larry kiss]$_{FF}$?
      B:  [Larry]$_{TF}$ | kissed [Nina]$_{FF}$.

Before I show how I propose to account for the contrast between (53) and (49), I had better explain first how I account for the very fact that (53) is felicitous. The problem is that my theory does not allow (53A) to be the last QUD of (53B), because $[\![(53A)]\!]^f$ $\neq [\![(53B)]\!]^f$. My explanation is that the last QUD of (53B) is not the explicitly mentioned question (53A), but rather question (47). That in turn means that in discourse (53), the implicit (47) must be directly relevant to its last QUD. What is the last QUD of (47)? An obvious candidate is (53A). Is (47) directly relevant to (53A)? Yes it is, since $[\![(47)]\!]^o$ is a subquestion of $[\![(53A)]\!]^o$.

So far so good, but there is still a problem. If (47) can be the last QUD of B's utterance in (53), why can't it be the last QUD of B's utterance in (50)–(52)? It is in order to solve this problem that I stipulated the restriction on the subquestion relation in (E-2) above. Given (E-2), move (47) still counts as a subquestion of move (53A), since $[\![(47)]\!]^f = (48)$ is a subset of $[\![(53A)]\!]^f =$ the set of all questions. But (47) does not count as a subquestion of A's utterance in the infelicitous (50)–(52). For instance, $[\![(47)]\!]^f = (48) = \{\{[\![kiss(x,y)]\!]^{g'} : g'$ is identical to g except that it may assign a different value to y\} : g assignment\} is not a subset of $[\![(50A)]\!]^f = \{\{[\![v_{1,\langle e,\langle e,t\rangle\rangle}(l,y)]\!]^{g'} : g'$ is identical to g except that it may assign a different value to y\} : g assignment\}.

I can now return to the contrast between (53) and (49). My account is as follows. In (49), B directly answers A's question. Hence, no particular implication is created. In (53), B does not directly answer A's question, but rather directly answers (47). The hearer must wonder why; after all, B could have directly answered A's question by uttering (45).

(45)  Larry kissed [Nina]_FF.

Well, as far as the ordinary denotation is concerned, (47) and (53A) are equivalent. So B's decision to address (47) rather than (53A) must have to do with the focal structure of (47). The hearer concludes then that B wanted to draw attention to members of the focus semantic value of (47). But there is no need to draw attention to the member "Who did Larry kiss?", since that member has been explicitly mentioned by A. Therefore, B's goal must be to draw attention to alternatives to A's question such as "Who did Bill kiss?" (Note that the present account of (53) amounts to deriving Büring's implicature as a conversational implicature.)

Finally, let us consider the relation between (12) and (16).

(12)  [Larry]_TF | kissed [Nina]_FF.
(16)  Who kissed who?

Certainly, (12) can (intuitively) form part of a strategy aimed at answering (16), as suggested by Roberts' work. Note, in this connection, that Büring's theory does not link (12) to (16) at all; recall, in particular, that it fails to predict that (44) below is felicitous. I think that we can account for the connection between (12) and (16) without officially defining a "strategy of inquiry," by showing that pieces of discourse such as (54) and (44) below are felicitous because they are each the explicit manifestation of a sequence of (explicit and implicit) moves which obeys the two QUD constraints as well as the requirement of direct relevance.

(54)  A:  Who kissed who?
      B:  Well, who did [Larry]_F kiss?
      C:  [Larry]_TF | kissed [Nina]_FF.

(cf. (10) above; adapted from Roberts 1996b)

(44)  A:  Who kissed who?
      B:  (Well, let's see . . .) [Larry]$_{TF}$ | kissed [Nina]$_{FF}$.

Consider (54). What is the last QUD of (54C) (= (12))? It is B's question, of course, which means that (54C) obeys both QUD constraints.

And what about the last QUD of (54B) (= (47))? The QUD constraint on FOCUS-focus determines that the "ordinary" member of the last QUD of (54B) must be $[\![(47)]\!]^f$ = (48), that is, a set of questions of the kind indicated by (36).

(48)  {{$[\![kiss(x,y)]\!]^{g'}$ : g′ is identical to g except that it may assign a different value to y}
      : g assignment}
(36)  {'Who did Larry kiss?', 'Who did Bill kiss?', 'Who did John kiss?', . . .}

But wait a minute, that is interesting. For the first time, we run into a discourse move whose "ordinary" member is neither a proposition nor a question, but rather a set of questions. What we see here is that it is a consequence of my theory that sets of questions must be recognized as possible ordinary denotations. I think that recognizing such denotations is independently motivated by the existence of questions like (55) and (56). After all, what do these questions denote?

(55)  Who did each individual kiss?
(56)  For each individual, who did that individual kiss?

I think it must be recognized that a question of this kind is not just a question, but actually a collection of questions. I think (55) and (56) both denote (48). (This would of course require a suitable revision of the definition of possible question–denotations and QUDs, though I won't include the revision here.)

Returning to the last QUD of (54B) (= (47)), what we saw so far is that its "ordinary" member is (48). The QUD constraint on TOPIC-focus does not apply to (54B) and therefore does not provide information regarding the "focus" member of the last QUD of (54B). So the "focus" member is determined by the default principle given under (E-1) – it is the set of all questions. We get then that the last QUD of (54B) is ⟨(48), the set of all questions⟩. Which, I would say, is just the move corresponding to (56) below. Hence the last QUD of (54B) is (56).

(56)  [For each individual, who did that individual kiss]$_F$?

I am satisfied with this result. It seems to me that intuitively, (47) does indeed pick "Who did Larry kiss?" out of a set of questions of the sort indicated by (36), and, further, that this choice does not simply correspond to a way of answering (16), but rather corresponds more specifically to a way of answering (55)/(56).

(Note the difference between (16) and (55)/(56): given (16), it is legitimate to list in reply kisser-kissee pairs arranged in any order – you can use the order of kissings in time, the order in which they come to mind, or whatever; but given (55)/(56), the kisser-kissee pairs must be ordered by the kissers: all the kissings of kisser 1, all the kissings of kisser 2, and so on.)

It is only left to verify that (56) is licensed as a move in the context of dialog (54). Since (56) itself is not an utterance in (54), the QUD constraints do not apply to it. But the requirement of direct relevance does apply to it – (56) must be directly relevant to its last QUD. What is the last QUD of (56)? An obvious candidate is (54A) = (16). And indeed, (56) is a subquestion of (16), and therefore directly relevant to it.

Now consider (44).

(44)   A:   Who kissed who?
       B:   (Well, let's see . . .) [Larry]_{TF} | kissed [Nina]_{FF}.

As usual, the last QUD of (12) (= (44B)) must be (47). Since (47) is not an utterance in this dialog, the QUD constraints do not apply to it. We only need to verify then that (47) is directly relevant to its last QUD. This time, we are free to assume that the last QUD of (47) is simply A's utterance, i.e. (16), since (47) is a subquestion of (16). Alternatively, we could assume that the last QUD of (47) is (56), just as in the more explicit dialog (54). Either way, (44) comes out felicitous.

I believe that the above account of the connection between (12) and (16) is superior to Roberts'. Recall that Roberts' theory links (12) to (16) directly, because on her theory $[\![(12)]\!]^f = [\![(16)]\!]^o$. But this link is too direct, given the intuition that (12) more directly addresses (13), or, actually, (47).

The link that Roberts makes between (12) and (16) is also too uniform. I think that the kinds of examples that Büring brings up show quite clearly that this kind of connection is not always present, and that an example with a TOPIC-focus and a FOCUS-focus may in fact be used in situations where the corresponding double-wh question is not relevant. I repeat the examples:

(25)   A:   Do you think Fritz would buy this suit?
       B:   Well, [I]_{TF} | certainly [wouldn't]_{FF}                    (Büring 1999)
(26)   A:   What did the popstars wear?
       B:   The [female]_{TF} popstars | wore [caftans]_{FF}.            (Büring 1999)
(27)   A:   Did your wife kiss other men?
       B:   [My]_{TF} wife | [didn't]_{FF} kiss other men.              (Büring 1999)

(28)   A:   Who did Bill kiss?
       B:   (I don't know.) [Larry]_{TF} | kissed [Nina]_{FF}.
(29)   A:   Who did the boys kiss?
       B:   [Larry]_{TF} | kissed [Nina]_{FF}.
(30)   A:   Who did Larry kiss?
       B:   [Larry]_{TF} | kissed [Nina]_{FF}.

Let us briefly go through (28)–(30), to see why they are felicitous and why they need not involve (16). Take (29) first. As usual, (12) (= (29B)) addresses (47). (47) in turn is directly relevant to (29A), as long as Larry is one of the boys. There is no reason to assume that (16) is relevant in the context.

Next, look at (30). With maximally broad focus in A's utterance, (30) is the same as (53).

(53)   A:   [Who did Larry kiss]$_{FF}$?
      B:   [Larry]$_{TF}$ | kissed [Nina]$_{FF}$.

Again (12) (= (30B)) addresses (47). (47) in turn is certainly a subquestion of (53A), hence directly relevant to it. As already discussed above, (53) implies that B is interested in some alternative to question (47) ("Who did Bill kiss?," for instance). But it is enough for B to be interested in one specific alternative to (47), and there is no further implication that the more general question (16) is relevant in this context.

Finally, take (28). As usual, (12) (= (28B)) addresses (47). In (28), (47) is in fact **not** directly relevant to A's utterance. I think that this is as it should be, since it is intuitively clear that B is changing the topic of conversation in this dialog. Certainly, there is a connection between (47) and (28A), which allows B to move from one to the other: their ordinary denotations are both members of $[\![(47)]\!]^f$. But that is perfectly compatible with (16) being completely irrelevant in the context.

Some concluding remarks: In this section, I have proposed that TOPIC-focus creates a ps regarding the focal structure of the last QUD. For instance, the TOPIC-focus in (12) indicates that the focal structure of the last QUD of (12) is as indicated in (47).

(12)   [Larry]$_{TF}$ | kissed [Nina]$_{FF}$.
(47)   Who did [Larry]$_{FF}$ kiss?

I have argued that this proposal enables us to solve problems encountered by previous theories, and to make a variety of desirable new predictions. We get correct predictions regarding the intuitive ps of (12), regarding an extended range of facts involving discourse congruence, and regarding the use of TOPIC-focus to imply that the speaker wishes to discuss another matter.

I believe, in addition, that my proposal yields a coherent conception of FOCUS-focus and TOPIC-focus as two closely-related components of the same system of focal structure. TOPIC-focus is in fact very much like a FOCUS-focus, except that it operates on a "deeper" level of a two-layered focal structure. I will try to explain what I mean by that.

The simplest thing to note is that just as a FOCUS-focus is "the last element to be filled in," a TOPIC-focus is "the penultimate element to be filled in," as is already clear in Jackendoff 1972. But let us note also that on my theory, a TOPIC-focus is "the **last** element to be filled in **in the last QUD**." Indeed, I would say that the TOPIC-focus is the "penultimate element" in the current utterance precisely because it represents the "last element" in the preceding move in the same discourse.

We might say that the two kinds of focus operate as follows. A FOCUS-focus alone reflects a little bit of the history of our utterance, since it tells us what the last move is. A TOPIC-focus + FOCUS-focus configuration reflects a bit more of the history of our utterance, since it tells us what the last two moves are. Let me illustrate this with our familiar examples.

We can have a coherent piece of discourse composed of the following two moves (viewed in terms of ordinary denotations only).

    (b)   'Who did Larry kiss?'
    (c)   'Larry kissed Nina'

I think the focal structure of (45) can be viewed as a means of recording the discourse history of (c), by indicating that the preceding move is (b).

(45)   Larry kissed [Nina]$_{FF}$.

We can also have a coherent piece of discourse composed of the following three "moves."

    (a)   'For each individual, who did that individual kiss?'
    (b)   'Who did Larry kiss?'
    (c)   'Larry kissed Nina'

I think the focal structure of (12) can be viewed as a means of recording the discourse history that (c) has here, by indicating that the preceding move is (b) and that the move before that is (a).

(12)   [Larry]$_{TF}$ | kissed [Nina]$_{FF}$.

A last note: It should have become clear by now why I agree with Jackendoff that TOPIC-foci can sensibly be considered foci.

## 20.4   Do Foci Take Wide Scope? (Part 2)

Jackendoff 1972 holds that a single focus too can be marked as either FOCUS-focus or TOPIC-focus. For instance, he holds that the declarative fall in (57) determines the focal structure in (59), while the continuation rise in (58) determines the focal structure in (60).

(57)   All the men didn't go.            (See Jackendoff 1972, p. 352, ex.(8.160).)
      H*       L      L%
(58)   All the men didn't go.            (See Jackendoff 1972, p. 352, ex.(8.159).)
      H*       L      H%
      or
      L*
      or
      L*+H
(59)   [All]$_{FF}$ the men didn't go.
(60)   [All]$_{TF}$ the men didn't go.

Jackendoff claims that (57) and (58) do not exhibit the scope ambiguity present in sentence (61).

(61)   All the men didn't go.

As is well known, (61) can mean "all the men are s.t. they didn't go" (the $\forall\neg$ reading), and it can mean "it is not the case that all the men went" (the $\neg\forall$ reading). According to Jackendoff, (57) only has the $\forall\neg$ reading, and (58) only has the $\neg\forall$ reading.

His account of this is as follows. In (57), things are perfectly simple, with *all* being "the last element to be filled in." So the assertion made by (57) is (62) (where Q is a determiner). Hence, says Jackendoff, we have the $\forall\neg$ reading.

(62)   all $\in$ {Q : Q of the men didn't go}

In (58), *all* is marked as "the penultimate element to be filled in." But that means that some other thing must play the role of the last thing to be filled in. That other thing is the negation. The negation "associates with the focus," thereby dissociating itself from the ps skeleton, which now becomes *Q of the men went*. The assertion made by (58) is (63). Hence, we have the $\neg\forall$ reading.

(63)   all $\notin$ {Q : Q of the men went}

This account seems quite elegant, but it cannot be right.

For one thing, Jackendoff's account of (57) relies on the incorrect assumption that if the negation is part of the ps skeleton (or, in current terms, part of the question being addressed), it necessarily takes narrow scope relative to the focus. The groundlessness of this assumption was already demonstrated in detail in 19.3 above. The expression *Q of the men didn't go* is itself ambiguous between a $Q\neg$ reading and a $\neg Q$ reading. Hence, Jackendoff's assertion in (62) is in fact ambiguous. (In current terms: to hypothesize that the last QUD is "how many of the men didn't go?" is still ambiguous.)

Further, the assumed empirical facts are wrong. Contrary to Jackendoff's claim, the prosody of examples such as (57) and (58) does not disambiguate the scope relations. Both (57) and (58) are in fact ambiguous between the $\forall\neg$ and $\neg\forall$ readings. In the case of (57), the $\forall\neg$ reading is prominent. But the $\neg\forall$ reading is also possible, as in (64) below.

(64)   A:   Despite our efforts to prevent them, some of the men went to the opponent's lecture.
       B:   Be glad that all the men didn't go.
                H*        L        L%

In the case of (58), the $\neg\forall$ reading is prominent, but the $\forall\neg$ reading is also possible, as in (65).

(65)   A:   I am glad to say that in the end, I managed to convince most of the men not to go to the opponent's lecture.
       B:   Hey, all the men didn't go. You don't consider Bill a man, do you?
              H*        L       H%

Similarly for examples (66) and (67) below. Jackendoff claims that (66) only has the $\forall\neg$ reading, while (67) only has the $\neg\forall$ reading. But in fact (66) and (67) are both ambiguous.[5]

---

[5]   The relative oddness of (66) is probably due to the available – and unambiguous – alternative of using *any*. See section 19.3 above for a detailed discussion of a similar example with *most*.

(66)  I didn't see all of the men.        (See Jackendoff 1972, p. 357, ex.(8.182).)
        H*   L   L%

(67)  I didn't see all of the men.        (See Jackendoff 1972, p. 357, ex.(8.181).)
        H*   L   H%
        or
        L*

I conclude that pairs like (57) and (58) or (66) and (67) do **not** show that FOCUS-focus takes wide scope while TOPIC-focus takes narrow scope.

Indeed, I don't believe examples like (58) or (67) contain a TOPIC-focus at all. Given that the negation does not necessarily take wide scope, I see no reason to assume that it dissociates itself from the ps skeleton and functions as the FOCUS-focus (= "the last element to be filled in"). Further, its being unaccented is a good reason to assume that it is not a focus. So I would prefer to maintain that the negation in (58) and (67) is unambiguously part of the question being addressed, and that the prosodically marked focus in (58) and (67) is a FOCUS-focus.[6]

Let us move on to examples exhibiting a TOPIC-focus + FOCUS-focus configuration. Such examples are studied in Büring 1997.[7] Consider first example (69). (Büring attributes the German version to Jacobs 1984.)

(68)  All politicians are not corrupt.
(69)  [All]$_{TF}$ politicians | are [not]$_{FF}$ corrupt.

Sentence (68) is clearly ambiguous between a $\forall\neg$ and a $\neg\forall$ reading. But (69) is unambiguous: it only has the $\neg\forall$ reading. The question is, what brings about the disambiguation in (69)?

Given (69), one might be tempted to take a position akin to Jackendoff's, viz. that given a TOPIC-focus + FOCUS-focus configuration, the FOCUS-focus must take wide scope over the TOPIC-focus. That, however, cannot be correct. As shown in Büring 1997, the disambiguation effect is not present with all quantifiers.

Büring argues, for instance, that example (70) below is ambiguous between the $\neg$ 2/3 and 2/3 $\neg$ readings, a fact which he brings out by placing (70) in the contexts in (71) and (72).

---

[6]   And what about the bias? Why is it that out of the blue, the prosody in (57) and (66) favors an $\forall\neg$ reading, while the prosody in (58) and (67) favors a $\neg\forall$ reading? As discussed in 19.3, I believe that one crucial factor is that readings are disambiguated by contexts, and that out of the blue, a context in which the $\forall\neg$ reading would arise (viz. a context in which a "negative predicate" is relevant) more easily comes to mind. This should favor the $\forall\neg$ reading all around. Another crucial factor must be the continuation rise in (58) and (67), which suggests that there is something more to be said. Out of the blue, one must imagine a role for the continuation rise. One possible role would be to signal that the correct answer is yet to be mentioned, given a $\neg\forall$ reading (i.e. given a situation where (58) or (67) serves to rule out a possible answer to a negation-less question). This last factor can apparently be decisive.

[7]   Büring discusses German examples, but since I think the behavior he observes is the same in English, I will use parallel English examples here.

(70)   [Two thirds]$_{TF}$ of the politicians | are [not]$_{FF}$ corrupt.
(71)   A:    And so it seems to me that two thirds of the politicians are corrupt.
    B:    That's an exaggeration. Half of them might be, but [two thirds]$_{TF}$ of the politicians | are [not]$_{FF}$ corrupt.

$$\neg\,2/3$$

(72)   A:    You can't deny the moral decline of politics. Just look at the statistics: 45 cases of corruption within one year.
    B:    Take a positive look at that: [two thirds]$_{TF}$ of the politicians | are [not]$_{FF}$ corrupt.

$$2/3\,\neg$$

We see then that example (69) is a special case. So the question is why there is disambiguation in this special case (while normally there isn't). Let us compare (70) and (69) in more detail.

We may assume that (70) can be translated into the logic as either (73) or (74), and (69) can be translated as either (75) or (76).

(70)   [Two thirds]$_{TF}$ of the politicians | are [not]$_{FF}$ corrupt.
(73)   $\neg_{FF}$ [[2/3]$_{TF}$(politicians) (corrupt)]                                    $\neg\,2/3$
(74)   [2/3]$_{TF}$(politicians) ($\lambda$x[$\neg_{FF}$ corrupt(x)])                      $2/3\,\neg$

(69)   [All]$_{TF}$ politicians | are [not]$_{FF}$ corrupt.
(75)   $\neg_{FF}$ [[all]$_{TF}$(politicians) (corrupt)]                                   $\neg\,\forall$
(76)   [all]$_{TF}$(politicians) ($\lambda$x[$\neg_{FF}$ corrupt(x)])                      $\forall\,\neg$

But that means that (70) and (69) share the same two topic semantic values, the ones given in (77) and (78). The set in (77) contains questions such as in (79), and the set in (78) contains questions such as in (80).

(77)   (For the wide–scope negation reading:)
    $[\![(73)]\!]^t = [\![(75)]\!]^t =$
    $\{\{[\![v_{yes/no}[v_{Det}(politicians)(corrupt)]]\!]^{g'} : g'$ is identical to g except that it may assign a different value to $v_{yes/no}\} : g$ assignment$\}$
(78)   (For the narrow–scope negation reading:)
    $[\![(74)]\!]^t = [\![(76)]\!]^t =$
    $\{\{[\![v_{Det}(politicians)(\lambda x[v_{yes/no}\ corrupt(x)])]\!]^{g'} : g'$ is identical to g except that it may assign a different value to $v_{yes/no}\} : g$ assignment$\}$
(79)   (For the wide–scope negation reading:)
    {'Is it true or not that all politicians are corrupt?,'
    'Is it true or not that most politicians are corrupt?,'
    'Is it true or not that two thirds of the politicians are corrupt?,'
    'Is it true or not that no politicians are corrupt?,' . . .}
(80)   (For the narrow–scope negation reading:)
    {'Are all of the politicians corrupt or non-corrupt?,'
    'Are most of the politicians corrupt or non-corrupt?,'
    'Are two thirds of the politicians corrupt or non-corrupt?,'
    'Are none of the politicians corrupt or non-corrupt?,' . . .}

We now need to see where the two examples differ. Büring's proposal is that the difference involves the following felicity condition (cf. the "implicature" of Büring 1999, discussed in 20.2.2).

(81)   Given a sentence S containing a TOPIC-focus, there must be at least one disputable element in $[\![S]\!]^t$ after S is uttered.

Büring's account is as follows. If (70) is uttered on the $\neg\, 2/3$ reading, the possibility remains that some member of (77) is still disputable afterwards. For instance, one can continue by uttering (82). Similarly, if (69) is uttered on the $\neg\forall$ reading – in that case too, one can continue with (82). Hence, both examples can have the wide-scope negation reading.

(82)   . . . and it might or might not be the case that there are in fact no corrupt politicians.

If (70) is uttered on the $2/3\, \neg$ reading, the possibility remains that some member of (78) is still disputable afterwards. For instance, one can continue by uttering (83).

(83)   . . . and it may or may not be the case that some politicians are corrupt.

However, if (69) is uttered on the $\forall\neg$ reading, it is **not** possible that some member of (78) is still disputable afterwards. If it has been stated that all the politicians are non-corrupt, that covers the entire group of politicians. It is no longer disputable afterwards, for any determiner Q, whether Q-many politicians are corrupt or non-corrupt – certainly, Q-many politicians are non-corrupt. Hence, (70) can have the narrow-scope negation reading, but (69) cannot.

Büring has thus shown that (i) in general, the FOCUS-focus does not necessarily take wide scope relative to the TOPIC-focus, and (ii) the fact that in cases like (69), the FOCUS-focus does have to take scope over the TOPIC-focus can be explained on the basis of special properties of this type of example.[8]

---

[8]   It was actually argued above that (81) is not quite right as it stands, and that drawing attention to some other member of $[\![S]\!]^t$ (besides $[\![S]\!]^f$) should be derived as a conversational implicature. But it should not be a problem, I think, to reformulate Büring's account of the disambiguation of (69) accordingly.

# 21

# *Focus and Presupposition: The Focal Presupposition and its Interaction with Other Presuppositions*

It is essential, I feel, to reach a more comprehensive integration of the study of focus and the study of ps than is available today. This remark is obviously related to our growing understanding of the focal ps. In addition, I have long been intrigued by what seem to be interactions between the focal ps and pss of other triggers, and I think that these are well worth exploring. I will take a brief look at such matters in the present chapter.

## 21.1   The Focal Presupposition

### *21.1.1   Summary of the View Presented Above*

In 13.2.2, the question was briefly discussed of whether or not the focal ps is an existential ps. While (1), for instance, would usually be judged to presuppose (2), examples like (3) and (4) suggest that focus does not necessarily carry an existential ps.[1] Accordingly, Jackendoff 1972 takes the focal ps of (1) to be something like (5).

(1)   [Mary]$_F$ likes Bill.
(2)   Someone likes Bill.
(3)   [Nobody]$_F$ likes Bill. (due to Jackendoff 1972, p. 246)
(4)   I doubt that anyone won the departmental lottery this week, because it's unlikely that [Mary]$_F$ won it, and I know that nobody else did. (due to Rooth 1994, 1996)
(5)   The set of individuals who like Bill is under discussion.

As was also suggested in 13.2.2, there is a close relation between the focal ps and discourse congruence effects. For instance, saying that (1) presupposes (5) above and saying that (1) is a felicitous answer to (6) below seem to be much the same thing.

(6)   Who likes Bill?

---

[1]   Even more so when compared with their cleft counterparts – see 13.2.2.

According to all three theories discussed in chapter 17 (Rooth 1992; Schwarzschild 1994, 1997; Roberts 1996b), the ps that the grammar associates with focus is not an existential ps. Schwarzschild and Roberts assume, in addition, that the focal ps and the discourse congruence effects of focus do indeed boil down to the same thing. On their theories, the focal ps is identified with a formal requirement on discourse congruence, and it is assumed that the sole function of focus is precisely to impose this formally defined focal ps.

I have been assuming throughout that the most central or crucial intuition about focus is that it is "the answer to the question being addressed." For instance, the intuition that what the focal structure of (1) indicates is that (1) addresses question (6), offering the answer "Mary." Roberts' theory of focus directly reflects that intuition, and relates it to the focal ps. On Roberts' theory, the focal ps is this: each utterance presupposes that its last QUD (= the question currently under discussion) is identical to its focus semantic value.[2]

### 21.1.2   Further Considerations

There may be reasons, however, to consider the question of an existential focal ps further. For one thing, it still remains to explain the judgment that focus does (often) carry an existential ps. Further, it is suggested in Rooth 1994 that assuming an existential focal ps might allow for a better account of the effects of focusing observed with adverbs of quantification and in Dretske's conditional examples.

In (7)–(10) below (from Rooth 1985 and Dretske 1972), the choice of focus seems to govern an implicit restriction on the quantification, as shown by the interpretations given in (7')–(10').[3,4]

(7)    [Mary]$_F$ always takes John to the movies.
(8)    Mary always takes [John]$_F$ to the movies.
(9)    If Clyde doesn't [marry]$_F$ Bertha, he won't be eligible for the inheritance.
(10)   If Clyde doesn't marry [Bertha]$_F$, he won't be eligible for the inheritance.

(7')   All events of <u>someone taking John to the movies</u> are events of [Mary]$_F$ taking John to the movies.
(8')   All events of <u>Mary taking someone to the movies</u> are events of Mary taking [John]$_F$ to the movies.
(9')   All possible worlds where Clyde <u>continues to have a relationship with Bertha but</u> doesn't [marry]$_F$ Bertha are worlds where he won't be eligible for the inheritance.
(10')  All possible worlds where Clyde <u>marries someone but</u> doesn't marry [Bertha]$_F$ are worlds where he won't be eligible for the inheritance.

Interestingly, the added restriction (underlined) is an existential statement corresponding to the focal structure of the clause in (11) or (12).

---

[2]   In chapter 20, I suggested that in the presence of a TOPIC-focus, the focal ps also concerns the focal structure of the last QUD.
[3]   As usual, the focus effect is optional (cf. (17) and (21) below).
[4]   For work on the focus effect with adverbs of quantification, see e.g. Rooth 1985, 1995; Krifka 1992; von Fintel 1994.

(11)   Mary takes John to the movies.
(12)   Clyde marries Bertha.

It is easy enough to derive an existential statement based on focal structure: just take the union of the focus semantic value – or, equivalently, take the existential closure of the ps skeleton. In this manner, based on (13), for instance, you get the existential statement in (14) – that is, (15).

(13)   [Mary]$_F$ takes John to the movies.
(14)   $\cup[\![(13)]\!]^f = \cup\{[\![\text{take-to-movies}(x,j)]\!]^g : g \text{ assignment}\}$
          $= [\![\exists x[\text{take-to-movies}(x,j)]]\!]^\circ$
(15)   'Someone takes John to the movies'

The question is, what is it that causes the relevant existential statements to become part of the restriction in (7)–(10)? Rooth 1994 argues that a theory on which the grammar imposes an existential focal ps is better equipped to answer this question.

Rooth points out that given an existential focal ps, the present kind of focusing effect can be reduced to a special case of an independently observed phenomenon, viz. that of an implicit restriction being set in such a way that the ps of some element in the utterance would get satisfied.[5] For instance, if we assume that (13) presupposes (15), then the interpretation in (7') above amounts to setting the restriction in such a way that that ps would be satisfied. That, says Rooth, would be exactly analogous to interpreting (16) as in (16') so as to satisfy the ps of *answers the phone*.

(16)   When he's in his office, Hans always answers the phone.
(16')   When he's in his office <u>and the phone rings</u>, Hans always answers the phone.

At the same time, Rooth 1994 presents as a conflicting consideration the undeniable empirical fact that focus is not always judged to carry an existential ps. To show this, he gives examples like (4) above, as well as examples like (17) below. (17) does not seem contradictory, in contrast with its cleft counterpart in (18).

(17)   If Clyde doesn't marry [Bertha]$_F$, he won't qualify, because he won't marry anyone. (adapted from Rooth 1994, his (29))
(18)   # If it isn't Bertha that he marries, he won't qualify, because he won't marry anyone. (adapted from Rooth 1994, his (31))

Rooth 1994 briefly mentions the idea that the conflict he presents might be resolved as follows. We assume that the grammar determines that the union of the focus semantic value is invariably presupposed. However, we let the focus semantic value be calculated, in some cases, by substitution of generalized quantifiers. When this happens, the corresponding existential statement becomes trivial – tautological – as illustrated in (19).

---

[5]   Cf. Roberts 1989, 1995, 1996a (see 9.3 above); van der Sandt 1989.

(19)   $\cup[\![(13)]\!]^f = \cup\{[\![v_{1,\langle\langle e,t\rangle,t\rangle}(\text{take-to-movies}(j))]\!]^g : g \text{ assignment}\}$
i.e. 'someone takes John to the movies
    or everyone takes John to the movies
    or nobody takes John to the movies, etc., etc.'

Of course, one would like to know in **what** cases this happens. I suppose one could say that substitution of individuals (cf. (14) above) is the default option. Another question is, how are we now going to account for those focus effects – like the ones discussed in section 17.3 – which involve a set of propositions rather than a corresponding existential closure (i.e. a focus semantic value rather than its union). Are we going to say that the grammar imposes two focal pss, one involving the focus semantic value (the ps imposed by the FIP, say), and another involving its union (the existential ps)?

I would like to suggest a different approach. Let us assume, following Roberts 1996b, that the grammar imposes the focal ps concerning the last QUD, and no other ps. I would suggest that the existential ps which often accompanies focus arises on the basis of considerations of relevance in discourse.

When (13), repeated below, is presented out of context, as a factual statement, it is judged to presuppose (15). I think the reason is as follows. The hearer automatically seeks to figure out what in its context might make it a relevant thing to say. The focal structure of (13) directly indicates that the question being addressed is (20).

(13)   [Mary]$_F$ takes John to the movies.
(15)   'Someone takes John to the movies'
(20)   Who takes John to the movies?

But when would (20) be a relevant question to address? Typically, (20) would be relevantly addressed in a context where it is believed that someone takes John to the movies, but the identity of the individual(s) who take(s) him to the movies is not known. So that is what the hearer assumes about the context. (In contexts where it is not known whether someone takes John to the movies or not, a more likely question to address would be "does anybody take John to the movies?")

Note that on this view, focus is taken to (sometimes) involve both a conventionally triggered ps and a conversationally triggered ps (cf. chapter 11). On Roberts' theory, focus is invariably accompanied by the focal ps concerning the last QUD, because that ps is conventionally triggered. At the same time, I have just suggested that an existential ps may arise conversationally. The existential ps is context-dependent, and that is why it is not always present.

And what about (7)–(10)? Here we are dealing with the focal ps of a non-factual clause, contained in a quantificational structure. If we can make the assumption that our non-factual clause ((11) or (12) above) has a conversationally triggered existential ps, then all is well: in (7')–(10'), an implicit restriction has been added so as to satisfy that ps, just as Rooth suggested.

I think that we can indeed make that assumption. I have already had occasion to indicate, in 11.3 above, that it seems perfectly reasonable to me to assume that pss of non-factual clauses can arise conversationally and be subject to "filtering." But let us try out an example.

Suppose (7) is interpreted along the lines of (7'').

(7″)   All events of type __ are events of [Mary]$_F$ taking John to the movies.

Although Roberts 1996b does not deal with foci in non-factual clauses, it makes sense, I think, to assume that here too (13) conventionally presupposes question (20), and that this ps has to be satisfied by its local context. The hearer is aware, independently, that she has to figure out some implicit restriction or other. So the hearer will aim to set the restriction in such a way that the ps regarding (20) would get satisfied. In connection with what type of event then would question (20) arise? A natural candidate is an event of someone taking John to the movies. It is difficult, without further context, to think of another type of event. So we get the impression that here too (13) has an existential ps, and we get the interpretation in (7′) above.

   Note that if there is enough contextual information to suggest another type of event that might give rise to (20), the existential ps of (13) – and with it the existential state-ment in the restriction – may well disappear. For instance, in (21). The last sentence in (21) does not quantify just over Saturdays on which Grandma is busy and someone takes John to the movies, but rather over all Saturdays on which Grandma is busy; after all, this sentence is intended to provide evidence for the preceding sentence, by entail-ing that on all Saturdays when Grandma is busy, there will indeed be someone to take John to the movies.

(21)   Don't worry, there will always be someone to take John to the movies on Satur-day. When Grandma is busy, [Mary]$_F$ will take him.


## 21.2   Focus and the "Disappearance" of Presuppositions

Strawson 1964 offers an interesting discussion of certain cases of ps "disappearance," linking the presence/absence of a ps to "what the sentence is about."

   Strawson contrasts our usual intuitive reaction to (22) (presented out of context) with our judgments regarding (23) and (24).

(22)   The king of France is bald.
(23)   The Exhibition was visited by the king of France.

(Strawson 1964, p. 95[6])

(24)   A:   What examples, if any, are there of famous contemporary figures who are bald?
       B:   The king of France is bald.                    (Strawson 1964, p. 96)

We usually agree that (22) carries the ps that there is a king of France. Given that there is no king of France, we readily agree that (22) is infelicitous, and is neither true nor false. Sentence (23), on the other hand, does **not** seem to carry the same ps. Suppose there is an exhibition in town. We readily judge then – despite the nonexistence of a king of France – that (23) is felicitous, and is simply false. Finally, the existential ps of (22) seems to disappear in dialog (24) – it is quite natural to judge that (24B) is simply false.[7]

---

[6]   Page numbers for Strawson 1964 refer to the reprinted version in Steinberg and Jakobovits 1971.
[7]   Objections to Strawson's intuitions are raised in Fodor 1979 (and other articles in the same volume).

Strawson suggests, roughly, that the following generalization holds.

(25)    A definite NP will carry its existential ps just in case it is part of the 'topic' or 'what the sentence is about.'

When presented with (22) out of context, we usually assume that it is supposed to be "about" (the properties of) the king of France.[8] Hence, the existence of the king of France is presupposed. In (23) and (24), on the other hand, we usually take the "topic" not to involve the king of France: (23) is naturally taken to be "about" (what happened concerning) the exhibition, and (24) is obviously "about" baldness or the question of who is bald. Hence, the existence of the king of France is not presupposed.

But what exactly does Strawson mean by "topic" or "what the sentence is about"? Gundel 1974 (see pp. 37–8); Reinhart 1982 (see pp. 5–7, 14–16) and Horn 1986 (see pp. 169–71) all believe that Strawson's "topic" or "what the sentence is about" corresponds to the concept of "topic" or "sentence topic," in the sense of Gundel 1974 or Reinhart 1982.[9] So their version of Strawson's generalization might be stated as follows.

(26)    A definite NP carries an existential ps iff it is part of the sentence-topic.

I disagree with these authors. In my opinion, Strawson's "topic" or "what the sentence is about" corresponds to "the question being addressed" and hence to "the material not included in the focus."[10] So I would choose to state Strawson's generalization as follows.

(27)    A definite NP carries an existential ps iff it is not part of the focus. (Or, more precisely, iff it is not part of a FOCUS-focus.)

I believe that of (26) and (27), (27) is the one that better corresponds both to Strawson's intentions and to the empirical facts.[11]

Regarding Strawson's intentions, I would note Strawson's use of (direct and indirect) questions as his means of describing what sentences are "about." For instance, the "topic" of (23) is not described as "the Exhibition" but as a question such as "what notable visitors the Exhibition has had" or "how the Exhibition is getting on" (p. 96).

As for empirical coverage, consider examples (28)–(30) below. I confess that I have never been able to determine with certainty what the sentence-topics of various sentences are supposed to be (not even in context). But I think that given the indicated focal structure, it would normally be assumed that in (28)–(30), the sentence-topic coincides with the grammatical subject.

---

[8]    That's because what the sentence is about generally tends to occur early in the utterance.

[9]    Corresponding also to the concept of "theme" of Mathesius 1928 and followers in the Prague tradition, and to the concept of "topic" (as the complement of "comment") of Hockett 1958.

[10]    And hence also to the notion of "psychological subject" of Paul 1880 and to the notion of "topic" (though **not** "topic proper") of Sgall et al. 1986.

[11]    Note, in this connection, McNally 1998, who suggests that including a notion of "(sentence) topic" corresponding to that of Gundel 1974 or Reinhart 1982 in our semantic/pragmatic theory might in fact prove unnecessary.

(28)   The king of France introduced her to [Bill]$_F$
(29)   She introduced him to [the king of France]$_F$
(30)   She introduced the king of France to [Bill]$_F$

If so, we have that while (26) and (27) both predict – correctly, I think – that *the king of France* carries an existential ps in (28) but not in (29), they disagree on (30). *The king of France* in (30) is (presumably) not part of the sentence-topic. Hence (26) predicts that (30) does not presuppose the existence of the king of France. *The king of France* in (30) is not part of the focus. Hence (27) predicts that (30) does presuppose the existence of the king of France. It seems to me that the prediction of (27) – that the ps is present – is the correct one.

It should be noted that Strawson does not claim that the generalization that I stated in (25) or (27) strictly holds. He rather talks of "what the sentence is about" as just one relevant factor, which creates some tendency for the facts to pattern along the lines of (25)/(27). Strawson gives the following rationale for this pattern. (Here "topic" means topic in Strawson's sense.)

The topic affects the way in which a statement is assessed as being true or false. Usually – though not always – "the statement is assessed **as** putative information **about its topic**" (p. 97, emphasis in the original). And that in turn is what's responsible for the pattern observed. In an example such as (29) above, the nonexistence of the king of France does not affect the topic, so we may still regard the example as putative information about its topic, and say that the ps failure determines that it is incorrect information. But in the case of examples like (30), the ps failure means that the example "cannot really have the topic it is intended to have" so that the example "can be seen neither as correct, nor as incorrect, information **about its topic**" (p. 98).

There is not much work developing Strawson's ideas or applying them to other pss besides the existential ps of definite NPs. (Some work that I would like to note though is the work in Lappin and Reinhart 1988 and Reinhart 1995.[12]) I would be very interested to see further research pursuing Strawson's ideas. There are a lot of open questions. Is Strawson's pattern really only a tendency, or is it more of a strict generalization? Which of the other pss exhibit the same pattern and which do not? (And why?) Am I right in suggesting that Strawson's pattern involves not sentence-topics, but rather focal structure? How are we going to integrate our theories of the existential ps of definites and of focus so as to provide a formal account of Strawson's pattern? This last question may eventually prove to be a rather crucial one – it may, perhaps, lead to new insights and theoretical developments concerning the very nature of focus and of ps.

## 21.3   Focus and "Altered" Presuppositions

Focal structure affects not only the presence or absence of pss, but also the form that pss take. Examples (31)–(35) tend to presuppose (36)–(40) respectively. These pss can easily be canceled, of course, if the negation is metalinguistic, as in (41)–(45).

[12]   Lappin and Reinhart 1988 develop further the idea that assessment strategies are relevant to the presence or absence of pss. Reinhart 1995 argues that Strawson's ideas relating assessment to topichood, as well as the approach of Lappin and Reinhart 1988, are best suited to the treatment of presuppositional effects of NPs with weak determiners (e.g. NPs of the forms *a CN* and *no CN*).

(31)   My cat didn't do it.
(32)   The exhibition wasn't visited by the king of Slobovia.
(33)   She didn't stop drinking coffee.
(34)   I don't regret that the goldfish died.
(35)   I didn't forget to introduce Bill to Sue.

(36)   I have a (unique) cat.
(37)   Slobovia has a (unique) king.
(38)   She used to drink coffee.
(39)   The goldfish died.
(40)   I knew that I was supposed to introduce Bill to Sue.

(41)   [My cat]$_F$ didn't do it – I don't have a cat.
(42)   The exhibition wasn't visited by [the king of Slobovia]$_F$ – Slobovia doesn't have a king.
(43)   She didn't stop [drinking coffee]$_F$ – she never used to drink coffee.
(44)   I don't regret that [the goldfish died]$_F$ – the goldfish didn't die.
(45)   I didn't forget [to introduce Bill to Sue]$_F$ – I wasn't supposed to introduce Bill to Sue.

Now, (41)–(45) do not retain any trace of the pss in (36)–(40). Consider, however, examples (46)–(50) below. While these examples lose the pss in (36)–(40), they do retain some altered form of these pss: they presuppose (or at least tend to presuppose) (51)–(56), respectively.

(46)   [My]$_F$ cat didn't do it – I don't have a cat.
(47)   The exhibition wasn't visited by the [king]$_F$ of Slobovia – Slobovia doesn't have a king.
(48)   She didn't stop drinking [coffee]$_F$ – she never used to drink coffee.
(49)   I don't regret that the [goldfish]$_F$ died – the goldfish didn't die.
(50)   I didn't forget to introduce [Bill]$_F$ to Sue – I wasn't supposed to introduce Bill to Sue.

(51)   Somebody has a (unique) cat.
(52)   Slobovia has some (unique) head of state.
(53)   She used to drink something.
(54)   Some animal died.
(55)   I knew that I was supposed to introduce someone to Sue.

The relevant generalization would seem to be roughly as follows. In the case of ps-triggers like definite NPs, *stop*, *regret*, *forget*, we observe the following. When the ps that they would normally trigger cannot be presupposed, the ps becomes instead an existential statement derivable from their usual ps by existentially binding the focus position.

The sort of ps "alteration" illustrated above is observed in Kempson 1975 regarding the existential ps associated with *even*. We usually judge that (56) carries the ps in (57).

(56)   Even Max tried on a fancy tie.
(57)   Someone other than Max tried on a fancy tie.

Kempson notes, however, that in (58), (56) is judged to presuppose not (57) but rather (59).

(58)   All the kids tried on something. Mary tried on a pair of trousers, Sue a long shawl. Even Max tried on a fancy tie. (Kempson 1975)

(59)   Someone other than Max tried on something.

I do not know of any published work that relates the alteration of pss to focal structure, with the notable exception of Wilkinson 1996. Wilkinson suggests both that the existential ps of *even* systematically gets altered in the manner just illustrated, and that such alteration is due to the presence of a focus (a focus not associated with *even*). She would point out, for instance, that in (56), *a fancy tie* is "new information," suggesting that it is in fact focused. (I think that the focal structure of (56) as it occurs in (58) is as in (60).)

(60)   Even [Max]$_{TF}$ | tried on [a fancy tie]$_{FF}$.

The "altered" ps in (59) differs from the "ordinary" ps in (57) in that the position of the focused *a fancy tie* is existentially bound.

Wilkinson's work nicely demonstrates the importance of recognizing that a focus may cause ps alteration, since she makes good use of this phenomenon in her analysis of the readings exhibited by examples with *even*. Let me give a quick account of how she deals with two problems regarding the existential ps of *even*.

Let us assume, for simplicity, that *even* is always a sentential operator. Following Rooth 1985, the following rule may be formulated (based on Horn 1969's semantics of *even*).

(61)   The sentence evenS asserts that $[\![S]\!]^o$ is true.
       The sentence evenS presupposes that
       (i)    there is some proposition $p \in C$ s.t. $p \neq [\![S]\!]^o$ and p is true; and
       (ii)   for all $p \in C$ s.t. $p \neq [\![S]\!]^o$, p is more likely than $[\![S]\!]^o$.
              where C is a contextually given set of propositions.

Rooth 1985, 1992 analyzes the association of *even* with focus, illustrated in (62)–(63), just as he analyzes the association of *only* with focus. That is, a focus in S may have the effect of setting the value of C in rule (61) to a subset of $[\![S]\!]^f$.

(62)   I even introduced [Bill]$_F$ to Sue.
       Presupposes:
       (i)    There is someone other than Bill that I introduced to Sue.
       (ii)   Bill is the least likely individual for me to introduce to Sue.

(63)   I even introduced Bill to [Sue]$_F$.
       Presupposes:
       (i)    There is someone other than Sue that I introduced Bill to.
       (ii)   Sue is the least likely individual for me to introduce Bill to.

Von Stechow 1991 argues that for examples such as (65) below, the existential ps determined by the above theory would be too strong. (64) is a context, provided by

Krifka 1991, in which (65) is to be considered. Clearly, *water* is focused, and both *even* and *only* associate with *water*.

(64)   At yesterday's party, people stayed with their first choice of drink. Bill only drank wine. Sue only drank beer.

(65)   John even only drank water.

The theory sketched above determines that (65) presupposes (66).

(66)   There is some x other than water s.t. John drank only x.

But empirically, (65) does not presuppose (66); indeed, as von Stechow points out, (66) is incompatible with (65) (since (66) entails that John did not drink water). Von Stechow 1991 and Krifka 1991 therefore suggest that the existential ps of *even* should be weakened.

Wilkinson argues convincingly that such weakening is undesirable. She shows that it is also unnecessary, since the problem pointed out by von Stechow can be easily resolved once ps alteration is recognized. Wilkinson points out that in the context in (64), *John* in (65) would have to be focused. (I think it would be a TOPIC-focus.) The focus on *John* effects "ps alteration," so the ps is as in (67) rather than as in (66). (67) seems like the correct ps, and is satisfied by the context in (64).

(67)   There is some x other than water s.t. someone drank only x.

On to the second problem. K&P 1979 note that example (68) is ambiguous between the readings indicated in (69) and (70).

(68)   It is hard for me to believe that Bill understands even *Syntactic Structures*.

(69)   'That Bill understands even *Syntactic Structures* is something that I find hard to believe.'
(presupposing that *Syntactic Structures* is particularly difficult)

(70)   'It is even hard for me to believe that Bill understands *Syntactic Structures*.'
(presupposing that *Syntactic Structures* is particularly easy)

According to K&P, this ambiguity is a scope ambiguity. For our purposes, suffice it to describe the essence of their analysis by saying that the ambiguity is a matter of which of the clauses in (68) serves as the argument of *even*. When the argument of *even* is the embedded clause (complement of *believe*), applying rule (61) yields reading (69), i.e. the reading which carries the pss in (71).

(71)   (i)   There is something other than *Syntactic Structures* that Bill understands.
       (ii)  *Syntactic Structures* is the least likely thing for Bill to understand.

When the argument of *even* is the matrix clause, applying rule (61) yields reading (70), i.e. the reading which carries the pss in (72).

(72)  (i)  There is something other than *Syntactic Structures* that it is hard for me to believe that Bill understands.

  (ii)  *Syntactic Structures* is the least likely thing for me to have difficulty believing that Bill understands.

Rooth 1985 offers a counterexample to K&P's analysis. His example (Rooth 1985, pp. 157–8) is (74) below in the context of (73).

(73)  Because they had been stolen from the library, John couldn't read *The Logical Structure of Linguistic Theory* or *Cartesian Linguistics*. Because it was always checked out, he didn't read *Current Issues in Linguistic Theory*.

(74)  The censorship committee kept John from reading even *Syntactic Structures*.

Empirically, (74) has, in this context, only the reading indicated in (75).

(75)  Even *Syntactic Structures* is something John was kept from reading. (The censorship committee kept him from reading it.)

But rule (61) cannot produce this reading. Clearly, to derive this reading K&P's way, the argument of *even* would have be the matrix clause. Try to apply rule (61), and you get the wrong existential ps. Rule (61) predicts the ps in (76), but (74) clearly does not have that ps in the context of (73).

(76)  There is something other than *Syntactic Structures* that the censorship committee kept John from reading.

Rooth 1985 proposes a different analysis of the ambiguity of (68) (and of the reading in (75)), which need not concern us here.[13]

Wilkinson argues convincingly that Rooth's alternative analysis is not satisfactory. She shows that Rooth's counterexample can be easily accounted for once ps alteration is recognized. Wilkinson points out that in the context in (73), *the censorship committee* in (74) would have to be focused. This focus effects ps alteration, so the ps is as in (77) rather than as in (76). (77) seems correct, and is satisfied by the context in (73).

(77)  There is something other than *Syntactic Structures* that something kept John from reading.

Having acknowledged the ps altering effect of focus (as well as the importance of recognizing it), we face the challenge of coming up with a good analysis of this effect.

Wilkinson suggests that the analysis of the ps altering effect of focus should be based on the assumption that focus carries an existential ps. I would agree with that. Wilkinson suggests that the focus which is not associated with *even* carries an existential ps

[13]  On Rooth's analysis, both readings of (68) are derived with the embedded clause serving as the argument of *even*, one with the meaning represented by rule (61), and one with an additional ("negative polarity") meaning which imposes the existential ps that there is some proposition $p \in C$ other than $[S]^0$ which is **false**.

which gets "introduced into" the pss of *even*. (p. 202) She also offers a way of formalizing precisely that, rewriting the semantic rule for *even* to directly refer to the union of a focus semantic value. This is ad hoc, and understandably so, since the analysis of the ps altering effect of focus is not what Wilkinson 1996 is concerned with. The challenge still lies ahead of us of formulating a general and explanatory theory of the interaction between the focal ps and pss of other triggers.

I will end with a little bit of discussion concerning the theory we are looking for. Compare example (33), which presupposes (or tends to presuppose) (38), and example (48), which presupposes (or tends to presuppose) (53).

(33) She didn't stop drinking coffee.
(38) She used to drink coffee.
(48) She didn't stop drinking [coffee]$_F$ – she never used to drink coffee.
(53) She used to drink something.

It seems obvious that we should use (78) or (79) in order to associate with (48) the ps in (53) instead of the one in (38).

(78) Ps skeleton of (33) as it occurs in (48):
     She didn't stop drinking x
(79) Existential ps associated with the focal structure of (33) in (48):
     $\exists$x[she didn't stop drinking x]

However, it is not obvious to me how that should be done.
    I find it tempting to try and develop the rough hypothesis in (80).

(80) An utterance presupposes whatever its focal ps presupposes.

The idea is that computing the focal ps of an utterance/clause is the most basic step in determining what pss it might have. Other pss are determined based on the focal ps. You might regard (80) as expressing ps transitivity: utterance A presupposes its focal ps B, which in turn presupposes C; hence, A presupposes C. The nice thing about (80) is that it would seem to cover Strawson's focus-driven ps "disappearance" (see 21.2 above) as well as the focus-driven ps "alteration" considered here.

    Let us be very rough for a moment and identify the focal ps with the ps skeleton. We might say then that the focal ps of (81) is as in (82), and that of (83) is as in (84).

(81) The king of France is [bald]$_F$.
(82) The king of France is X.
(83) The exhibition was visited by [the king of France]$_F$.
(84) The exhibition was visited by x.

Presumably, (82) presupposes that there is a king of France whereas (84) does not. So according to (80), (81) inherits such a ps whereas (83) does not. Returning to ps alteration, consider again example (33) as it occurs in (48). We compute for it the focal ps in (85), and (85) in turn presumably presupposes (86).

(48)  She didn't stop drinking [coffee]$_F$ – she never used to drink coffee.
(85)  She didn't stop drinking x.
(86)  She used to drink x.

Of course, it might not be easy to figure out the details. After all, neither (85) nor (86) are really presupposed (since they are both open formulas). Should we use the ps skeleton, or its existentially closed counterpart, or the last QUD of our example, or what? Suppose we use the existential closure – wouldn't its ps still be (86)? Does it make sense to derive pss that are open formulas? Do they automatically get existentially closed?

In addition, the generalization in (80) does not actually seem to systematically hold. I think that (87) may well inherit the ps of *stop* as long as that ps is not denied, and that (88) may well retain the "normal" form of the ps of *stop*, as long as that is not denied.

(87)  She didn't stop [drinking coffee]$_F$.
(88)  She didn't stop drinking [coffee]$_F$.

I must stop here and leave further thoughts on the matter to further research. I would love to see the empirical and theoretical work being developed which would be necessary for explicating the pattern of ps alteration discussed here and relating it to Strawson's pattern discussed in the preceding section.

# References

Anderson, S. 1972: "How to get *even*." *Language* 48, 893–906.

Ariel, Mira 1990: *Accessing Noun-Phrase Antecedents*, Routledge.

Atlas, J. D. and S. Levinson 1981: "*It*-clefts, informativeness and logical form: radical pragmatics (revised standard version)." In P. Cole (ed.), *Radical Pragmatics*, Academic Press, 1–61.

Barker, Chris 1996: "Presuppositions for proportional quantifiers." *Natural Language Semantics* 4.3, 237–59.

Bartch, Renate 1973: "The semantics and syntax of number and numbers." In J. P. Kimball (ed.), *Syntax and Semantics*, vol. 2, Seminar Press.

Beaver, David 1993a: "Two birds and one stone." In Hans Kamp (ed.), *Presupposition*, DYANA-2, Deliverable R2.2.A, Part II, August 1993.

Beaver, David 1993b: "The kinematics of presupposition." In Hans Kamp (ed.), *Presupposition*, DYANA-2, Deliverable R2.2.A, Part II, August 1993. Also appeared in *Proceedings of the 8ths Amsterdam Colloquium*, ILLC, 1992.

Beckman, Mary and Janet Pierrehumbert 1986: "Intonational structure in English and Japanese." *Phonology Yearbook* 3, 255–310.

Bittner, Maria 1994: "Cross-linguistic semantics." In *Linguistics and Philosophy* 17.1, 53–108.

Boër, Steven E. 1979: "Meaning and contrastive stress." *The Philosophical Review* 88.2.

Boër, Steven E. and William G. Lycan 1976: "The myth of semantic presupposition." Indiana University Linguistics Club publication.

Bolinger, Dwight 1958: "A theory of pitch accent in English." *Word* 14, 109–49.

Bolinger, Dwight 1965: "Pitch accents and sentence rhythm." In I. Abe and T. Kanekiyo (eds.), *Forms of English: Accent, Morpheme, Order*, Harvard University Press.

Bolinger, Dwight 1972: "Accent is predictable (if you are a mind-reader)." *Language* 48.3, 633–44.

Bolinger, Dwight 1981: "Two kinds of vowels, two kinds of rhythm." Indiana University Linguistics Club publication.

Bolinger, Dwight 1986: *Intonation and Its Parts*, Stanford University Press.

Bolinger, Dwight and Louis J. Gerstman 1957: "Disjuncture as a cue to constructs." *Word* 13, 246–55.

Bonomi, Andrea and Paolo Casalegno 1993: "*Only:* association with focus in event semantics." *Natural Language Semantics* 2.1, 1–45.

Bowers, John S. 1969: "Surface structure interpretation in English superlatives." ms., MIT.

Bresnan, Joan 1971: "Sentence stress and syntactic transformations." *Language* 47.2, 257–81.

Büring, Daniel 1997: "The great scope inversion conspiracy." *Linguistics and Philosophy* 20.2, 174–95.

Büring, Daniel 1999: "Topic." In P. Bosch and R. van der Sandt (eds.), *Focus – Linguistic, Cognitive, and Computational Perspectives*, Cambridge University Press, 142–65.

Carlson, Gregory N. 1977: *Reference to Kinds in English*, Ph.D. dissertation, University of Massachusetts, Amherst. Reproduced by the GLSA, Linguistics Dept., University of Massachusetts, Amherst.

Carlson, Lauri 1983: *Dialogue Games: An Approach to Discourse Analysis*, Synthese Library, Reidel.

Carlson, Lauri 1984: "Focus and dialogue games." In L. Vina and J. Hintikka (eds.), *Cognitive Constraints on Communication*, Reidel, 295–333.

Chierchia, Gennaro 1992: "Anaphora and dynamic binding." *Linguistics and Philosophy* 15.2.

Chierchia, Gennaro and Sally McConnell-Ginet 1990: *Meaning and Grammar: An Introduction to Semantics*, MIT Press.

Chierchia, Gennaro and Mats Rooth 1984: "Configurational notions in Discourse Representation Theory." In C. Jones and P. Sells (eds.), *Proceedings of NELS 14*, GLSA, Linguistics Dept., University of Massachusetts, Amherst, 49–63.

Chomsky, Noam 1971: "Deep structure, surface structure and semantics interpretation." In D. Steinberg and L. Jakobovits (eds.), *Semantics*, Cambridge University Press, 183–216.

Chomsky, Noam 1976: "Conditions on rules of grammar." *Linguistic Analysis* 2, 303–51.

Chomsky, Noam and Morris Halle 1968: *The Sound Pattern of English*, Harper and Row.

Clark, H. 1977: "Bridging." In P. Johnson-Laird and P. Wason (eds.), *Thinking*, Cambridge University Press, 10–63.

Clark, H. and S. Haviland 1977: "Comprehension and the given-new contrast." In R. Freedle (ed.), *Discourse Production and Comprehension*, Ablex, 1–40.

Cooper, Robin 1979: "The interpretation of pronouns." In Frank Heny and Helmut S. Schnelle (eds.), *Syntax and Semantics 10: Selections from the Third Groningen Round Table*, Academic Press, 61–92.

Cooper, Robin 1983: *Quantification and Syntactic Theory*, Reidel.

Cresswell, Maxwell J. 1973: *Logic and Languages*, Methuen.

Cresswell, Maxwell J. and Arnim von Stechow 1982: "De re belief generalized." *Linguistics and Philosophy* 5.4, 503–35.

Dekker, Paul 1992: "An update semantics for DPL." In P. Dekker and M. Stokhof (eds.), *Proceedings of the 8th Amsterdam Colloquium*, University of Amsterdam.

Dekker, Paul 1993: *Transsentential Meditations: Ups and Downs in Dynamic Semantics*, Ph.D. dissertation, University of Amsterdam.

Donnellan, Keith 1971: "Reference and definite descriptions." In D. D. Steinberg and L. A. Jakobovits (eds.), *Semantics*, Cambridge University Press.

Dretske, Fred I. 1972: "Contrastive statements." *Philosophical Review*, 411–37.

Dretske, Fred I. 1977: "Referring to events." *Midwest Studies in Philosophy* 2, 90–9.

Egli, Urs 1974: "Zur Interogation der Semantik in die Grammatik." Kronberg/Tr, Scriptor.

Erteschik-Shir, Nomi 1986: "Wh-questions and focus." *Linguistics and Philosophy* 9.2, 117–49.

Erteschik-Shir, Nomi 1998: *The Dynamics of Focus Structure*, Cambridge Studies in Linguistics, Cambridge University Press.

Evans, Gareth 1977: "Pronouns, quantifiers and relative clauses." *Canadian Journal of Philosophy* 7, 467–536.

Evans, Gareth 1980: "Pronouns." *Linguistic Inquiry* 11, 337–62.

von Fintel, Kai 1994: *Restrictions on Quantifier Domains*, Ph.D. dissertation, University of Massachusetts, Amherst.

von Fintel, Kai 1995: "A minimal theory of adverbial quantification." ms., MIT.

Fischer, Susan D. 1968: "Cleft Sentences and Constrastive Stress." ms., MIT.

Fodor, Janet Dean 1979: "In Defence of the Truth Gap." In Ch. Oh and D. Dinneen (eds.), *Syntax and Semantics 11: Presupposition*, Academic Press.

Frege, Gottlob 1892: "Über Sinn und Bedeutung." *Zeitschrift für Philosophie und Philosophische Kritik* 100, 25–50. Translation: "On Sense and Reference." In Peter Geach and Max Black (eds.), *Translations from the Philosophical Writings of Gottlob Frege*, Basil Blackwell, 1960.

Gazdar, Gerald 1979a: *Pragmatics: Implicature, Presuppositions, and Logical Form*, Academic Press.

Gazdar, Gerald 1979b: "A solution to the projection problem." In Ch. Oh and D. Dinneen (eds.), *Syntax and Semantics 11: Presupposition*, Academic Press, 57–89.

Geach, Peter 1962: *Reference and Generality*, Cornell University Press.

Giora, Rachel 1983: "Segmentation and segment cohesion: on the thematic organization of the text." *Text* 3.2, 155–81.

Grice, H. Paul 1967: The William James Lectures, Harvard University (unpublished). Eventually published in H. P. Grice, *Studies in the Way of Words*, Harvard University Press, 1989.

Grice, H. Paul 1975: "Logic and conversation." In Peter Cole and Jerry L. Morgan (eds.), *Syntax and Semantics 3: Speech Acts*, Academic Press, 41–58.

Groenendijk, Jeroen and Martin Stokhof, 1982: "Semantic analysis of wh-complements." *Linguistics and Philosophy* 5.2. Reprinted in Groenendijk and Stokhof, *Studies on the Semantics of Questions and the Pragmatics of Answers*, Ph.D. dissertation, University of Amsterdam, 1984.

Groenendijk, Jeroen and Martin Stokhof, 1984: "Questions and linguistic answers." In Groenendijk and Stokhof, *Studies on the Semantics of Questions and the Pragmatics of Answers*, Ph.D. dissertation, University of Amsterdam, 1984.

Groenendijk, Jeroen and Martin Stokhof 1990: "Dynamic Montague Grammar." In L. Kálman and L. Pólos (eds.), *Papers from the Second Symposium on Logic and Language*, Adakémiai Kiadó, Budapest, 3–48.

Grosz, Barbara J., Arvind K. Joshi, and Scott Weinstein 1983: "Providing a unified account of definite NPs in discourse." SRI International Technical Note 292, Menlo Park, California.

Gundel, Jeannette K. 1974: *The Role of Topic and Comment in Linguistic Theory*, Ph.D. dissertation, University of Texas. Reproduced by the Indiana University Linguistics Club.

Gussenhoven, Carlos 1983: *The Semantic Analysis of the Nuclear Tones of English*, Indiana University Linguistics Club.

Gussenhoven, Carlos 1984: "Testing the reality of focus domain." *Language and Speech* 26, 61–80.

Gussenhoven, Carlos 1991: "The English rhythm rule as an accent deletion rule." *Phonology* 8, 1–35.

Halliday, M. A. K. 1967: "Notes on transitivity and theme in English, part 2." *Journal of Linguistics* 3.2, 199–244.

Hamblin, C. L. 1973: "Questions in Montague Grammar." *Foundations of Language*, 41–53. Reprinted in B. Partee (ed.), *Montague Grammar*, Academic Press, 1976.

Hausser, Roland 1976: "The logic of questions and answers." ms., München.

Hayes, Bruce 1995: *Metrical Stress Theory: Principles and Case Studies*, University of Chicago Press.

Heim, Irene 1982: *The Semantics of Definite and Indefinite Noun Phrases*, Ph.D. dissertation, University of Massachusetts, Amherst. Reproduced by the GLSA, Linguistics Department, University of Massachusetts, Amherst.

Heim, Irene 1983a: "File change semantics and the familiarity theory of definiteness." In R. Bäuerle, R., Schwarze, and A. von Stechow (eds.), *Meaning, Use and Interpretation of Language*, de Gruyer.

Heim, Irene 1983b: "On the projection problem for presuppositions." In M. Barlow, D. Flickinger, and M. Wescoat (eds.), *Proceedings of WCCFL 2*, Stanford University, 114–25.

Heim, Irene 1992: "Presupposition projection and the semantics of attitude verbs." *Journal of Semantics* 9, 183–221.

Hirschberg, Julia 1985: *A Theory of Scalar Implicature*, Ph.D. dissertation, University of Pennsylvania.

Hockett, Charles 1958: *A Course in Modern Linguistics*, Macmillan.

Horn, Laurence R. 1969: "A presuppositional analysis of *only* and *even*." In *CLS 5*, Chicago Linguistic Society, University of Chicago, 98–107.

Horn, Laurence 1972: *On The Semantic Properties of Logical Operators in English*, Ph.D. dissertation, UCLA. Reproduced by the Indiana University Linguistics Club, 1976.

Horn, Laurence R. 1985: "Metalinguistic negation and pragmatic ambiguity." *Language* 61.1, 121–74.

Horn, Laurence R. 1986: "Presupposition, theme and variation." In A. M. Farley, P. T. Farley, and K.-E. McCullough (eds.), *CLS 22, Part 2: Papers from the Parasession on Pragmatics and Grammatical Theory*, Chicago Linguistic Society, University of Chicago, 168–92.

Horn, Laurence R. 1989: *A Natural History of Negation*, University of Chicago Press.

Horn, Laurence R. 1992: "The said and the unsaid." In C. Barker and D. Dowty (eds.), *Proceedings of SALT 2*, Working Papers in Linguistics No. 40, The Ohio State University, 163–92.

Householder, Fred 1957: "Accent, juncture, intonation, and my grandfather's reader." *Word* 13, 234–45.

Jackendoff, Ray S. 1972: *Semantic Interpretation in Generative Grammar*, MIT Press.

Jacobs, Joachim 1983: *Fokus und Skalen: Zur Syntax und Semantik von Gradpartikeln im Deutschen*, Niemeyer.

Jacobs, Joachim 1984: "Funktionale Satzperspektive und Illokutionssemantik." *Linguistische Berichte* 91, 25–58.

Jacobs, Joachim 1988: "Fukus-hintergrund-gliederung und grammatik." In H. Altman (ed.), *Intonationsforschungen*, Tübingen, 183–216.

Kadmon, Nirit 1985: "The discourse representation of NPs with numeral determiners." In S. Berman, J. Choe, and J. McDonough (eds.), *Proceedings of NELS 15*, GLSA, Linguistics Dept., University of Massachusetts, Amherst, 207–19.

Kadmon, Nirit 1987: *On Unique and Non-Unique Reference and Asymmetric Quantification*, Ph.D. dissertation, University of Massachusetts, Amherst. Reproduced by the GLSA, Linguistics Dept., University of Massachusetts, Amherst. Also published by Garland Press, 1992.

Kadmon, Nirit 1990: "Uniqueness." *Linguistics and Philosophy* 13.3, 273–324.

Kadmon, Nirit and Craige Roberts 1986: "Prosody and scope: the role of discourse structure." In A. M. Farley, P. T. Farley, and K.-E. McCullough (eds.), *CLS 22, Part 2: Papers from the Parasession on Pragmatics and Grammatical Theory*, Chicago Linguistic Society, University of Chicago, 16–28.

Kamp, Hans 1981: "A theory of truth and semantic representation." In J. Groenendijk, T. Janssen, and M. Stokhof (eds.), *Formal Methods in the Study of Language: Proceedings of the Third Amsterdam Colloquium, Part I*, Amsterdam: Mathematical Center, 277–321. Reprinted in J. Groenendijk, T. Janssen, and M. Stokhof (eds.), *Truth, Interpretation and Information*, GRASS 2, Foris, 1984, 1–41.

Kamp, Hans and Uwe Reyle 1993: *From Discourse to Logic*, Kluwer.

Karttunen, Lauri 1973: "Presuppositions of compound sentences." *Linguistic Inquiry* 4.2, 169–93.

Karttunen, Lauri 1974: "Presuppositions and linguistic context." *Theoretical Linguistics* 1, 181–94.

Karttunen, Lauri 1976: "Discourse referents." In J. McCawley (ed.), *Syntax and Semantics 7: Notes From the Linguistic Underground*, Academic Press, 363–85.

Karttunen, Lauri and Stanley Peters 1979: "Conventional implicature." In Ch. Oh and D. Dinneen (eds.), *Syntax and Semantics 11: Presupposition*, Academic Press, 1–56.

Kempson, Ruth M. 1975: *Presupposition and the Delimitation of Semantics*, Cambridge University Press.

Kempson, Ruth M. 1982: "Negation, ambiguity and the semantics-pragmatics distinction." ms., presented at the Winter LSA meeting.

Kiss, Katalin É. 1998: "Identification focus versus information focus." *Language* 74.2, 245–73.

Kratzer, Angelika 1977: "What 'must' and 'can' must and can mean." *Linguistics and Philosophy* 1, 337–55.

Kratzer, Angelika 1989: "An investigation of the lumps of thought." *Linguistics and Philosophy* 12, 607–53.

Kratzer, Angelika 1991: "The representation of focus." In Arnim von Stechow and Dieter Wunderlich (eds.), *Semantik/Semantics: An International Handbook of Contemporary Research*, de Gruyter.

Krifka, Manfred 1989: "Nominal reference, temporal constitution and quantification in event semantics." In R. Bartsch, J. van Benthem, and P. von Emde Boas (eds.), *Semantics and Contextual Expression*, Foris, 75–116.

Krifka, Manfred 1991: "A compositional semantics for multiple focus constructions." In S. Moore and A. Z. Wyner (eds.), *Proceedings of SALT 1*, Cornell University Working Papers in Linguistics No. 10, 127–58.

Krifka, Manfred 1992: "A framework for focus-sensitive quantification." In C. Barker and D. Dowty (eds.), *Proceedings of SALT 2*, Working Papers in Linguistics No. 40, The Ohio State University, 215–36.

Krifka, Manfred 1993: "Focus and presupposition in dynamic interpretation." *Journal of Semantics* 10.4, 269–300.

Krifka, Manfred 1995: "Focus and the interpretation of generic sentences." In G. N. Carlson and F. J. Pelletier (eds.), *The Generic Book*, University of Chicago Press, 398–411.

Kripke, Saul 1990: Talk presented at a workshop on anaphora, Princeton University.

Kuno, Susumu 1980: "The scope of the question and negation in some verb-final languages." *CLS 16*, Chicago Linguistic Society, University of Chicago, 155–69.

Ladd, D. Robert 1980: *The Structure of Intonational Meaning: Evidence from English*, Indiana University Press.

Ladd, D. Robert 1990: "Intonation: emotion vs. grammar" (review of Bolinger 1989: *Intonation and its uses*, Stanford University Press), *Language* 66.4, 806–16.

Lakoff, George 1972: "Linguistics and natural logic." In Donald Davidson and Gilbert harman (eds.), *Semantics of Natural Language*, Reidel, 545–665.

Landman, Fred 1986: "Conflicting presuppositions and modal subordination." In A. M. Farley, P. T. Farley, and K.-E. McCullough (eds.), *CLS 22, Part 2: Papers from the Parasession on Pragmatics and Grammatical Theory*, Chicago Linguistic Society, University of Chicago, 195–207.

Landman, Fred 1987: "A handful of versions of Discourse Representation Theory." ms., University of Massachusetts, Amherst.

Landman, Fred 1998: "Plurals and maximalization." In Susan Rothstein (ed.), *Events and Grammar*, Kluwer.

Landman, Fred 1999: *Events and Plurality*, Studies in Linguistics and Philosophy, Kluwer.

Lappin, Shalom and Tanya Reinhart 1988: "Presuppositional effects of strong determiners: a processing account." *Linguistics* 26, 1021–37.

Lerner, J. and T. Zimmermann 1981: "Mehrdimensionale Semantik: Die Präsupposition und die Kontextabhängigkeit von 'nur'." Working Paper no. 50, SFB 99, Konstanz.

Levinson, Stephen 1983: *Pragmatics*, Cambridge Textbooks in Linguistics, Cambridge University Press.

Lewis, David 1973: *Counterfactuals*, Harvard University Press.

Lewis, David 1975: "Adverbs of quantification." In E. L. Keenan (ed.), *Formal Semantics of Natural Language*, Cambridge University Press, 3–15.

Lewis, David 1979: "Scorekeeping in a language game." In R. Bäuerle, U. Egli, and A. von Stechow (eds.), *Semantics from Different Points of View*, Springer, 172–87.

Liberman, Mark 1975: *The Intonational System of English*, Ph.D. Dissertation, MIT.

Liberman, Mark and Alan Prince 1977: "On stress and linguistic rhythm." *Linguistic Inquiry* 8.2, 249–336.

Link, Godehard 1987: "Algebraic semantics of event structures." In J. Groenendijk, M. Stokhof, and F. Veltman (eds.), *Proceedings of the 6th Amsterdam Colloquium*, ITLI publication, University of Amsterdam, 243–62.

Mathesius, Vilem 1928: "On linguistic characterology with illustrations from modern English." In *Actes du Premier Congrès International de Linguistes à La Haye (1928)*, 56–63. Reprinted in J. Vachek, *A Prague School Reader in Linguistics*, Indiana University Press, 1964, 59–67.

McCawley, James D. 1981: *Everything that Linguists have Always Wanted to Know about Logic*, University of Chicago Press, Chicago.

McNally, Louise 1998: "On recent formal analyses of 'topic'." In J. Ginzburg, Z. Khasidashvili, C. Vogel, J. J. Levy, and E. Vallduví (eds.), *The Tbilisi Symposium on Logic, Language and Computation: Selected Papers*, Studies in Logic, Language and Information, CSLI Publications, 147–60.

Montague, Richard 1970: "Universal grammar." *Theoria* 36, 373–98. Reprinted in R. Thomason (ed.), *Formal Philosophy*, Yale University Press, 1974.

Partee, Barbara H. 1987: "Noun phrase interpretation and type-shifting principles." In Jeroen Groenendijk, Dick de Jongh, and Martin Stokhof (eds.), *Studies on Discourse Representation Theory and the Theory of Generalized Quantifiers*, GRASS 8, Foris.

Partee, Barbara H. 1991: "Topic, focus and quantification." In S. Moore and A. Wyner (eds.), *Proceedings of SALT 1*, Cornell University Working Papers in Linguistics, 159–87.

Paul, Hermann 1880: *Prinzipien der Sprachgeschichte*, Niemeyer.

Pierrehumbert, Janet 1980: *The Phonology and Phonetics of English Intonation*, Ph.D. dissertation, MIT.

Pierrehumber, Janet and Julia Hirschberg 1990: "The meaning of intonation contours in the interpretation of discourse." In P. R. Cohen, J. Morgan, and M. E. Pollack (eds.), *Intentions in Communication*, MIT Press, 271–311.

Prince, Alan S. 1983: "Relating to the grid." *Linguistic Inquiry* 14.1.

Prince, Ellen F. 1992: "The ZPG letter: subjects, definiteness and information status." In S. Thompson and W. Mann (eds.), *Discourse Description: Diverse Analyses of a Fund Raising Text*, John Benjamins, 295–325.

Reinhart, Tanya 1982: "Pragmatics and linguistics: an analysis of sentence topic." Indiana University Linguistics Club publication.

Reinhart, Tanya 1995: "Topics and the conceptual interface," ms.

Roberts, Craige 1987: *Modal Subordination, Anaphora, and Distributivity*, Ph.D. dissertation, University of Massachusetts, Amherst. Reproduced by the GLSA, Linguistics Dept., University of Massachusetts, Amherst.

Roberts, Craige 1989: "Modal subordination and pronominal anaphora in discourse." *Linguistics and Philosophy* 12, 683–721.

Roberts, Craige 1993: "Uniqueness presuppositions in definite NPs." ms., the Ohio State University.

Roberts, Craige, 1995: "Domain restriction in dynamic semantics." In E. Bach, E. Jelinek, A. Kratzer, and B. H. Partee (eds.), *Quantification in Natural Language*, Kluwer, 661–700.

Roberts, Craige 1996a: "Anaphora in intensional contexts." In Shalom Lappin (ed.), *Handbook of Contemporary Semantics*, Blackwell, 215–46.

Roberts, Craige 1996b: "Information structure in discourse: towards an integrated formal theory of pragmatics." In J. Hak Yoon and A. Kathol (eds.), *Ohio State Univsersity Working Papers in Linguistics, volume 49*.

Roberts, Craige 1998: "The place of centering in a general theory of anaphora resolution." In M. A. Walker, A. K. Joshi, and E. Prince (eds.), *Centering Theory in Discourse*, Clarendon Press.

Rochemont, Michael S. 1986: *Focus in Generative Grammar*, John Benjamins.

Rooth, Mats 1985: *Association with Focus*, Ph.D. dissertation, University of Massachusetts, Amherst. Reproduced by the GLSA, Linguistics Department, University of Massachusetts, Amherst.

Rooth, Mats 1992: "A theory of focus interpretation." *Natural Language Semantics* 1.1, 75–116.

Rooth, Mats 1994: "Association with focus or association with presupposition?" In P. Bosch and R. van der Sandt (eds.), *Focus and Natural Language Processing*, vol. 2, IBM, Heidelberg.

Rooth, Mats 1995: "Indefinites, adverbs of quantification and focus semantics." In G. N. Carlson and F. J. Pelletier (eds.), *The Generic Book*, University of Chicago Press.

Rooth, Mats 1996: "Focus." In Shalom Lappin (ed.), *Handbook of Contemporary Semantics*, Blackwell, 271–97.

Russell, Bertrand 1905: "On Denoting." *Mind* 14, 479–93.

Russell, Bertrand 1919: *Introduction to Mathematical Philosophy*, Allen and Unwin.

van der Sandt, Rob 1989: "Anaphora and accommodation." In Bartsch et al. (ed.), *Semantics and Contextual Expression*, Foris.

Scha, Remko 1983: *Logical Foundations for Question Answering*, Ph.D. Dissertation, Groningen.

Schmerling, Susan F. 1976: *Aspects of English Sentence Stress*, University of Texas Press.

Schwarzschild, Roger 1994: "The contrastiveness of associated foci." ms., Hebrew University of Jerusalem.

Schwarzschild, Roger 1997: "Why some foci must associate." ms., Rutgers University.

Schwarzschild, Roger 1999: "GIVENness, AvoidF and other constraints on the placement of accent." *Natural Language Semantics*, 7.2, 141–77.

Searle, John R. 1965: "What it a Speech Act?" In Max Black (ed.), *Philosophy in America*, Cornell University Press, 221–39.

Selkirk, Elisabeth O. 1984: *Phonology and Syntax: The Relation between Sound and Structure*, MIT Press.

Selkirk, Elisabeth O. 1996: "Sentence prosody: intonation, stress, and phrasing." In J. Goldsmith (ed.), *The Handbook of Phonological Theory*, Blackwell, 550–69.

Selkirk, Elisabeth O. 1999: "The interaction of constraints on prosodic phrasing." In M. Horne (ed.), *Prosody: Theory and Experiment*, Kluwer.

Sells, Peter 1985: "Restrictive and non-restrictive modification." Report #CSLI-85–28, CSLI, Stanford University.

Sgall, Petr, Eva Hajicová, and J. Panevová 1986: *The Meaning of the Sentence in its Semantic and Pragmatic aspects*, Academia, Prague and Reidel, dordrecht.

Shimojima, Atsushi 1993: "Definite descriptions revisited by situations." ms., talk presented at the *Fourth Conference on Logic and Linguistics*, Ohio State University, 1993.

Soames, Scott 1979: "A projection problem for speaker presuppositions." *Linguistic Inquiry* 10, 623–66.

Soames, Scott 1982: "How presuppositions are inherited: a solution to the projection problem." *Linguistic Inquiry* 13, 482–545.

Soames, Scott 1989: "Presupposition." In D. Gabbay and F. Guenthner (eds.), *Handbook of Philosophical Logic* vol. 4, Kluwer.

Stalnaker, Robert 1974: "Pragmatic presuppositions." In M. K. Munitz and D. K. Unger (eds.), *Semantics and Philosophy*, New York University Press, 197–213.

Stalnaker, Robert 1978: "Assertion." In Peter Cole (ed.), *Syntax and Semantics 9: Pragmatics*, Academic Press, 315–32.

von Stechow, Arnim 1981: "Topic, focus and local relevance." In W. Klein and W. Levelt (eds.), *Crossing the Boundaries in Linguistics*, Reidel.

von Stechow, Arnim 1989: "Focusing and backgrounding operators." Technical Report 6, Fachgruppe Sprachwissenschaft, Universität Konstanz.

von Stechow, Arnim 1991: "Current issues in the theory of focus." In A. von Stechow and D. Wunderlich (eds.), *Semantik/Semantics: An International Handbook of Contemporary Research*, de Gruyter, 804–25.

Steedman, Mark 1991: "Syntax, intonation and 'focus'." In E. Klein and F. Veltman (eds.), *Natural Language and Speech: Proceedings of the Symposium, ESPRIT Conference*, Brussels, Stringer Verlag, 515–40.

Steinberg, D. and Jakobovits, L. (eds.) 1971: *Sĕmantics*, Cambridge University Press.

Strawson, Peter F. 1950: "On Referring." *Mind* 59, 320–44.

Strawson, Peter F. 1964: "Identifying reference and truth-values." *Theoria* 30, 96–118. Reprinted in D. D. Steinberg and L. A. Jakobovits (eds.), *Semantics*, Cambridge University Press, 1971, 86–99.

Taglicht, Josef 1984: *Message and Emphasis: on Focus and Scope in English*, Longman.

Tichy, P. 1978: "Questions, answers and logic." *American Philosophical Quarterly* 15.

Thomason, Richmond H. 1981: "Deontic logic as founded on tense logic." In R. Hilpinen (ed.), *New Studies in Deontic Logic*, Reidel.

Thomason, Richmond H. 1990: "Accommodation, meaning and implicature: interdisciplinary foundations for pragmatics." In P. R. Cohen, J. Morgan, and M. E. Pollack (eds.), *Intentions in Communication*, MIT Press, 325–63.

Vallduví, Enric 1990: *The Informational Component*, Ph.D. dissertation, University of Pennsylvania. Published by Garland Press, 1992.

Vallduví, Enric and M. Vilkuna 1998: "On Rheme and Kontrast." In Peter Cullicover and Louise McNally (eds.), *Syntax and Semantics 29: The Limits of Syntax*, Academic Press, 79–108.

Ward, Gregory and Julia Hirschberg 1985: "Implicating uncertainly: the pragmatics of fall–rise intonation." *Language* 61, 747–76.

Welker, Katherine 1994: *Plans in the Common Ground: Towards a Generative Account of Conversational Implicature*, Ph.D. dissertation, the Ohio State University.

Wilkinson, Karina 1996: "The scope of *even*." *Natural Language Semantics* 4.3, 193–215.

Wilson, Deirdre 1975: *Presuppositions and Non-Truth-Conditional Semantics*, Academic Press.

# Index

Page numbers in bold type indicate main or detailed references. Subheadings use abbreviated forms of some terms.